The Middle East
and the United States

SECOND EDITION

The Middle East and the United States

A Historical and Political Reassessment

edited by

David W. Lesch
Trinity University

Westview Press
A Member of the Perseus Books Group

Copyright © 1996, 1999 by Westview Press, A Member of the Perseus Books Group

Published in 1999 in the United States of America by Westview Press, 5500 Central Avenue, Boulder, Colorado 80301-2877, and in the United Kingdom by Westview Press, 12 Hid's Copse Road, Cumnor Hill, Oxford OX2 9JJ

Library of Congress Cataloging-in-Publication Data
The Middle East and the United States : a historical and political
  reassessment / edited by David W. Lesch. — 2nd ed.
    p.   cm.
  Includes bibliographical references (p.   ) and index.
  ISBN 0-8133-3559-0 (pbk.)
    1. Middle East—Foreign relations—United States.   2. United
States—Foreign relations—Middle East.   I. Lesch, David W.
DS63.2.U5M43   1999
327.56073—dc21   98-40724
                                                                            CIP

The paper used in this publication meets the requirements of the American National Standard for Permanence of Paper for Printed Library Materials Z39.48-1984.

10   9   8   7   6   5   4   3   2   1

To my parents,
Warren and Margaret Lesch

Contents

Part Three
War and Peace, War and Peace

Part Four
The Gulf Crisis and War

Preface to
the Second Edition

Typically, a lot happens in the Middle East in the span of a few years. This has definitely been the case since the first edition of this book was published in 1996; indeed, the first edition was barely able to mention the assassination of Israeli Prime Minister Yitzhak Rabin in November 1995 before the final draft went off to the publisher. As such, we could only minimally speculate about the repercussions of this tragic event, expressing a certain amount of foreboding for the future of the Arab-Israeli peace process that dampened what had generally been cautious optimism.

Since then we have observed, inter alia, the following: the Hamas bombings in Israel in early 1996; the shutdown of the Israeli-Syrian negotiations; Israel's Operation Grapes of Wrath in Lebanon in April 1996 to root out and punish Hizbullah for lobbing rockets into northern Israel; Likud Party's Benjamin Netanyahu becoming prime minister in the May 1996 election in Israel; the interminable delays and mutual recriminations in the Palestinian-Israeli negotiations over implementation of the Oslo accords, with the subsequent question of what the U.S. role should be to break the deadlock; Saddam Hussein's continued tussles with the United States over the accessibility (or lack thereof) of sites in Iraq to United Nations inspections teams, particularly that which occurred in October 1997 through February 1998, when the Clinton administration seemed perched to militarily intervene in Iraq to enforce compliance with the UN amid growing estrangement from Washington by its erstwhile Gulf war allies in the Middle East and in Europe (and the realization, albeit belated, in Washington of the inextricable link between the Gulf and Arab-Israeli arenas); intensified butchery in Algeria between extremist Islamist groups and what they believe to be an illegitimate government; and continuing economic problems in most countries in the region facing the dilemma of the generally accepted necessity to shake off legacies of public sector domination, an approach, however, that also generates a host of religio- or sociopolitical reactions that could threaten the ruling regimes.

Those contributors who in the first edition wrote on current and/or recent issues have updated their chapters by commenting on what has transpired over the last three years in relation to their topics. The more historically oriented chapters are essentially the same, with a few minor alterations here and there. Of particular note, I invited two scholars to each contribute a new chapter to the book, enhancing the comprehensiveness that was a primary objective in the first edition. Gary Sick, a renowned specialist on American policy in the Gulf and a member of the National Security Council staff during the Carter administration, leads off Part 4 with a chapter that critically analyzes the development of U.S. policy in the Gulf region since the days of the Nixon Doctrine and, especially, the 1979 Iranian revolution. With the question of U.S. commitment to security in the Gulf coming under increasing scrutiny as we move further away in time from the Gulf war and, more recently, as Iraq's confrontation with the United Nations and the United States has intensified, I felt the book could benefit from an overall exposition of U.S. policy toward the Gulf that would provide additional context to this section.

I also asked Robert Allison to contribute a piece. I first became aware of Bob's work when I reviewed his excellent book *The Crescent Obscured: The United States and the Muslim World, 1776–1815,*[1] which outlines, among other things, the development of the distorted American image of the Islamic world in the early days of the republic, vividly displaying the fact that the American public's generally negative image of Islam in recent decades is anything but a new phenomenon. After reading his book, I thought that an essay derived from it would fit nicely as a kind of postscript following Yvonne Haddad's concluding chapter on Islamist perception of U.S. foreign policy. Chronologically, Allison's chapter belongs at the beginning of the book, but it is less an examination of an event or series of events, as the other chapters tend to be, than an interpretive essay on how much perception and politics influenced (and were influenced by) American foreign policy and the position of the United States in the Middle East at a formative stage in the republic—a dynamic, of course, that continues to this day. In this regard, I think the juxtaposition with Haddad's piece is illuminating.

I would like to thank those who updated and revised their chapters; in most cases, this was not just simply a task of adding a few lines but, in fact, required additional primary research and serious contemplation of recent developments in the region. For example, Robert Freedman is adding to his original chapter a timely and important section that examines the post-Soviet position of Russia in the Middle East, particularly in the Gulf; as Georgiy Mirsky so aptly stated in his chapter in the first edition, the Middle East is about the only region left where Moscow can play a significant role. The continued commitment to quality maintenance by all the contributors is noteworthy. Again, I extend my sincere gratitude to Eunice Herrington in the Department of History at Trinity University, for her time, effort, and devotion to this project; she was instrumental in helping me put together the first edition, and she was no less so this time around—the computer, translation, and organizational problems with this type of volume are seemingly infinite, and I could not have completed the task without her. I also would like to thank Karl Yambert at Westview Press, whose support and efforts on behalf of this volume helped pave the way for the second edition. As I mentioned in the first edition, (still) not every topic is covered, as there are always constraints of a variety of shapes and sizes on exactly what can be included. For example, I think U.S.-Turkish relations is a topic more than worthy of inclusion (particularly in relation to the developing Israeli-Turkish-Syrian triangle), but this, and possibly some others, will have to wait, *insha'allah,* for a third edition.[2]

David W. Lesch
San Antonio, Texas

Notes

1. Robert J. Allison, *The Crescent Obscured: The United States and the Muslim World, 1776–1815* (New York: Oxford University Press, 1995). My review of this book is in *Middle East Journal* 50(4) (Autumn 1996), pp. 623–624.

2. In the meantime, on the subject of the Israeli-Turkish-Syrian triangle, see Alain Gresh, "Turkish-Israeli-Syrian Relations and Their Impact on the Middle East," *Middle East Journal* 52(3) (Spring 1998), pp. 188–203. Also see Henri J. Barkey, ed., *Reluctant Neighbor: Turkey's Role in the Middle East* (Washington, D.C.: United States Institute of Peace Press, 1996).

Preface to
the First Edition

Surveys of the history of U.S. foreign policy toward the Middle East have, for the most part, been one-dimensional and have done little to enhance our understanding of the complexities of the role the United States has historically played in the area and the way in which Washington has been viewed by those in the region itself. This book, which offers a variety of interpretations of U.S. policies in the Middle East in the twentieth century, contains a significant amount of original research and revisionist interpretation. It reveals the complex nature of the region and illustrates the different perceptions of U.S. roles in the area. It is set in a chronological framework in order to provide reference points to discuss the ebb and flow of U.S. foreign policy toward the Middle East; however, there is inevitably some overlap, particularly with regard to the circumstances and events surrounding the Arab-Israeli peace process and the 1990–1991 Gulf crisis and war.

An analysis that is at once cross-cultural and multidimensional provides the best context in which to examine U.S. actions in the Middle East. Scholars have too often viewed U.S. involvement through a narrow prism usually anchored in Washington, which invariably results in a skewed perspective. A final evaluation of the success or failure of U.S. policies may not always be determined within the context of U.S. objectives or perceptions, since oftentimes they are contrary to the goals and aspirations of those in the region affected by that policy. Thus, for both scholarly research and governmental policymaking, an analysis that is cross-cultural and multidimensional—examining a particular episode or issue at the international, regional, bilateral, and domestic levels from a variety of perspectives—offers the most comprehensive method for constructing a cogent explanation or judging an effective policy.

In this book, distinguished scholars, diplomats, and commentators from across North America, Europe, and the Middle East offer objective and sobering analyses of past, present, and future U.S. policies toward the Middle East. The result is a more balanced examination of U.S.–Middle East relations than has yet been available for students, scholars, and the general reader. Because many of the contributors write about the U.S. role from the vantage point of Washington, the congruencies and incongruencies among the diverse viewpoints clearly emerge, creating illuminated avenues of comment and conjecture on the efficacy of U.S. foreign policy toward the Middle East.

Several authors were intimately involved in the events about which they have written. Their perspectives are important because scholars can only examine a particular historical episode in retrospect, whereas contemporaries formed outlooks based upon actual participation, with the ideologies of the period shaping their points of view. As Kierkegaard stated, "It is perfectly true, as philosophers say, that life must be understood backwards. But they forget the other proposition, that it must be lived forwards."[1]

Not every event is covered in this book, not every perspective conveyed, since there are limits to what can be accomplished in one volume. There are also limits to the historical lessons we can draw from the various episodes and themes discussed, since the dynamics of the region have changed over time. At the least, however, the book will confirm that a work of art can be interpreted in utterly different fashions by different people. It is important to note, too, that it makes clear that there are elements and forces in the Middle East that have been largely independent of great power competition—whether we were consciously aware of them or not. When we begin to understand that U.S. policies and actions do not exist solely within the framework of international politics, we can begin to construct a sagacious foreign policy toward the Middle East—and other regions as well.

D. W. L.

Notes

1. I employ this quote in much the same fashion as James G. Blight and David A. Welch do in their book *On the Brink: Americans and Soviets Reexamine the Cuban Missile Crisis* (New York: Noonday Press, 1990), where I first saw the passage. I believe this book to be a seminal work on the 1962 Cuban missile crisis; as I attempt to do in this volume, Blight and Welch bring together scholars and contemporary policymakers who offer many perspectives to examine U.S. foreign policy.

Acknowledgments

As with so many things, the whole is equal to the sum of its parts. The multifarious task of organizing, collecting, and generating a book of this size and assemblage required the support and assistance of many individuals. First and foremost, without the interest and generosity of Flora Atherton Crichton, through the Flora Atherton Lectures Fund in Politics and Public Affairs, this book would not have been possible. The president of Trinity University, Dr. Ronald Calgaard, has been an avid supporter of this project and in many ways provided the wherewithal for its completion. My colleagues in the Department of History at Trinity have been very supportive of my efforts, which often complicated their own tasks; the staff in the department has been equally helpful, particularly Eunice Herrington, whose assistance has been indispensable. Robert O. Freedman and Louis Cantori have been my "eyes in the sky" during this whole process—I could receive no better advice. I would also like to thank Barbara Ellington, senior editor at Westview Press, who believed in this project from the very beginning—she is an outstanding editor. Others who have been extremely helpful in a variety of ways are the following: Ambassador Alfred Leroy Atherton Jr., John McCusker, Ann Van Pelt, Alan Kownslar, Terry Smart, Donald Clark, Gary Kates, Char Miller, Edward Roy, and Bill Walker. I would also like to commend the contributors for their commitment to the profession and their flexibility and willingness to work with me in putting this volume together. Finally, I could not complete a project of any significance without the support, understanding, and advice of my wife, Suzanne, and the exuberance of my son, Michael. Thank you one and all.

D. W. L.

Note on the Text

One of the challenges of compiling an edited volume written by different individuals is ensuring stylistic consistency among chapters. In particular, many authors have used their own system of transliteration. I generally retained each author's style except for names and terms that appear throughout the text. In these cases, I selected one variation of spelling, which is often the more recognizable version rather than a strict transliteration: for example, "Hussein" rather than "Husayn" or "Hussain"; "Faisal" rather than "Faysal" or "Feisal"; "Nasser" rather than "Nasir"; and "Mussadiq" rather than "Mossadeq," "Mossadegh," or "Musaddiq." Many of the chapters include a diacritic mark (') for the important Arabic consonant 'ayn; however, I have eliminated the diacritic mark for the Arabic hamza. One hopes few exceptions have slipped through.

In addition, the body of water bounded by Iran, Iraq, and the Arab Gulf states is known either as the Arabian or Persian Gulf; this book has no particular preference and allows the individual authors to choose for themselves which appellation to utilize. The war in the Middle East in 1990–1991 is generally known in the United States as the Persian Gulf crisis and Persian Gulf war, a conflict that was precipitated by the surprise Iraqi invasion of Kuwait. In the Gulf itself, this event is generally referred to as the Second Gulf war (the first being the Iran-Iraq war of 1980–1988), the Kuwaiti crisis, the War to Liberate Kuwait, the Iraqi crisis, or simply the Gulf crisis and war, the latter being employed by most contributors in this book. Some references to other conflicts have also been standardized. For instance, two major conflicts involving Israel are generally referred to as the 1967 Arab-Israeli war and the 1973 Arab-Israeli war; however, the first is also known as the June War or Six Day War, the second as the October War, the Yom Kippur War, or the Ramadan War. In certain instances, individual contributors employ these terms.

D. W. L.

Introduction

David W. Lesch

U.S. involvement in the Middle East has spanned the breadth of this country's existence, beginning most dramatically with the administration of President Thomas Jefferson, which tried to stop pirating by the North African or "Barbary" provinces of the Ottoman Empire in the early 1800s. This was a war to ensure freedom of navigation on the high seas, which impacted U.S. trade issues especially because the new republic no longer enjoyed the benefits of British naval protection. For the most part, however, U.S. interaction with and interest in the Middle East during the nineteenth century was quite limited, and that which did exist was limited primarily to the private activities of missionaries and merchants. However, World War I propelled the United States onto the world stage—and into European politics—in a way it had neither experienced nor wanted. Given this turn of events the United States quickly developed an interest in the disposition of the Middle East provinces of the defeated Ottoman Empire. The result was the first significant official foray by Washington into the region this century: the sending of the King-Crane Commission to Syria. But other than showing a passing interest in the growing involvement of multinational oil companies in the Middle East, no U.S. administration gave the region high priority during the interwar years (1918–1939).

The strategic value of the region was demonstrated by events in World War II, when, in 1942 and 1943, Anglo-American forces attacked and defeated German-Italian forces during the North African campaign. Soon, the realization that reconstruction of Europe and Japan—as well as the postwar economic boom in the United States—would become more and more dependent upon Middle East oil (which makes up two-thirds of the world's known oil reserves) boosted the policy significance of the region in the eyes of Washington's policymakers. Thus, the value of the Middle East became contemporaneously linked to the emerging cold war between the United States and the Soviet Union. Washington dutifully grasped a global foreign policy and came to believe it was the only nation that could successfully prevent Moscow from extending its influence in the region in the wake of the weakened British and French imperial positions; the Middle East, therefore, became a policy priority for post–World War II administrations. The emergence of the state of Israel in 1948 reinforced U.S. interest in the Middle East, but this event also com-

1

plicated Washington's relations with and objectives toward the Arab world as Arabs increasingly perceived U.S. and Israeli interests as being one and the same. But complication and complexity defined the U.S.–Middle East relationship during the forty or so years of the cold war, intertwined as it was with the decolonization process, Arab nationalism and state building, the Arab-Israeli conflict, the "Arab cold war," the growing strength of OPEC (the Organization of Petroleum Exporting Countries), and Islamist movements. The end of the U.S.-Soviet cold war in 1989 removed some tensions and mitigated others in the Middle East; at the same time, however, the new regional environment produced by the termination of the cold war and then shaped by the 1990–1991 Gulf war created new sets of questions to be answered, tensions to be addressed, and problems to be resolved. It is within this atmosphere that old and new problems meet, where history and politics meld together, and where conflict and peace exist side by side.

This volume endeavors to cover these issues. Part 1, entitled "From Idealism to Realism: Wilsonian Intent to Cold War Practice," begins with an examination of the King-Crane Commission, which emanated from the idealistic intentions of President Woodrow Wilson's Fourteen Points enunciated near the end of World War I—especially that of self-determination for subject peoples—and which was ostensibly created to assess the wishes of the native population in Syria regarding postwar independence. The commission did not quite fit the reality of European politics or, for that matter, American politics, and, as James Gelvin points out, it was not quite so idealistic, as it seemed just to reflect and transfer democratic elitism. Indeed, by examining the King-Crane Commission from the Syrian perspective, Gelvin concludes that the commission actually established a pattern for subsequent U.S. encounters with nationalism and state building in the Middle East that had unforeseen and often deleterious results for both the United States and the region.

The incipient nature of U.S. policy in the Middle East evident in the immediate post–World War I period became more pronounced following what has been called the great divide of World War II, which awakened policymakers to the necessity of a more active and goal-oriented foreign policy commensurate with the onset of the cold war and related regional issues.[1] Yet, there was still the strong desire rooted in the American heritage to portray the United States as anything but a second-generation imperialist merely trading places with the Europeans. This schizophrenia made itself apparent in U.S. development diplomacy toward the Third World in the immediate post–World War II period, symbolized by President Harry S. Truman's Point Four program, which was intended to be something like a Marshall Plan for the Third World. The inherent difficulties of this policy framework in light of the new global and regional realities in the Middle East were exemplified by the short but dramatic mission of Truman's special assistant to the Middle East, Edwin Locke Jr., whose story is examined by Paul Kingston in Chapter 2.

The manifest great divide in the Middle East, where a cold war–based, realpolitik foreign policy supplanted any pretense of a developmentally based one, can arguably be the Muhammad Mussadiq crisis of 1953, when covert efforts primarily engineered by the United States succeeded in overthrowing the popularly elected Iranian prime minister; at the time, Washington and London thought he would tilt Iran toward the Soviet Union, which would have been viewed as an unacceptable strategic setback that could also have led to a potentially disastrous superpower confrontation. The Mussadiq crisis reveals how the United States began almost instinctively to follow in the footsteps of British imperialism, demonstrating a preference for the status quo rather than the forces of change. This episode and surrounding events are examined in a triangular fashion: Mark Gasiorowski offers the view from Washington (Chapter 3), Sussan Siavoshi, the Iranian perspective (Chapter 4), and Sir Sam Falle, the on-the-ground viewpoint (Chapter 5). Falle was a high-level official in the British Embassy in Tehran at the time of the crisis and maintains that U.S. and British actions were correct, not only then but also in retrospect.

Part 2, entitled "The Cold War in the Middle East," examines many of the episodes that defined the acceleration of the superpower conflict in the region and how this dynamic affected and was in turn affected by the regional and domestic environments in the Middle East. The perceived success of the Iranian coup reinforced the Dwight D. Eisenhower administration's emphasis on a more interventionist policy, which was characterized by covert activities designed to fight the Soviets in the cold war in the Third World via tactics short of nuclear confrontation. The Mussadiq crisis seemed to be repeated in various fashions in the Middle East throughout the remainder of the decade, some with perceived equally positive results, some with more negative results.

Peter Hahn (Chapter 6) offers a description of this transitional stage in U.S. diplomacy toward the Middle East as strategic necessities of the cold war became the paramount consideration by studying Washington's relationship with Egypt from the last stage of the King Farouk regime to the early Nasserist period ending with the Suez crisis in 1956. Ambassador Richard Parker, Robert Satloff, David Lesch, and Erika Alin (Chapter 7 through Chapter 10, respectively) examine the Jordanian, Syrian, and Lebanese crises of 1957–1958 and the associated complex political environment of the Middle East in the 1950s, when the international cold war in the region was at its height and superimposed on the Arab-Israeli conflict, Arab state building, and the emerging Arab cold war. This section ends with a discussion by Malik Mufti (Chapter 11) on the relationship of the United States with pan-Arabism, specifically that proffered by Egyptian President Gamal 'Abd al-Nasser versus that espoused by the Ba'thists in Iraq and Syria following the 1956 Suez crisis and bridging the Arab cold war to the seminal 1967 Arab-Israeli war. Mufti concludes that U.S. policies under Eisenhower and his secretary of state, John Foster Dulles, as well as those under the John F. Kennedy and Lyndon B. Johnson administrations, which have been "roundly criticized" in the past (as in this volume), have been to a large extent misinterpreted and were actually much more prescient and successful than is popularly perceived, especially as the United States began to see Arab nationalism as an antidote to communism. As others have observed, however, maybe the objectives were achieved *despite* U.S. policy, especially as the dynamics of Malcolm Kerr's "Arab cold war" tended to define the political and diplomatic parameters in the Middle East during this period.[2]

Since the emergence of the state of Israel in 1948 and the subsequent Arab-Israeli conflict, there seems to be a constant cycle of opportunities for peace, followed by missed opportunities for peace or the establishment of something less than a full or comprehensive peace, which in turn creates an environment in which tensions still exist and issues are left unresolved. This, then, leads to the resumption of some form of conflict, which in turn usually creates another opportunity for peace, which, again, goes unfulfilled at least for one party to the conflict—and so forth and so on. The role of the United States in this process has varied considerably, from pacifier to antagonist, from mediator to peacemaker, from belligerent to bystander. Part 3, appropriately entitled "War and Peace, War and Peace," examines the role the United States has played in this seemingly never-ending cycle. Since the end of the cold war, however, there is the popular perception that this cycle can be terminated with a sustainable comprehensive peace in the Arab-Israeli arena. Some believe the September 13, 1993, signing of the Declaration of Principles between Israel and the Palestine Liberation Organization (PLO) on the White House lawn constitutes the beginning of this new peaceful trend in the Middle East; others feel it was just another missed opportunity that will lead to further frustration and potential instability. All agree there are still many obstacles to a complete resolution of the Arab-Israeli dispute.

Fawaz Gerges begins this section (Chapter 12) with a discussion of the 1967 Arab-Israeli war, which initiated the peace process as we know it today and effectively brought the superpower cold war together with the Arab-Israeli issue. In the 1969–1970 War of Attrition and the 1973 Arab-Israeli war the Soviets became intimately involved, the result being a near superpower confrontation during the latter stages of the 1973 hostilities. By examining the impact of the 1967 war on Arab nationalist perceptions of the United States, Gerges argues that it had a "devastating negative impact" on Arab views of the U.S. role in the peace process; yet the "indispensable and preponderant" role of Washington in this process was also made abundantly clear, that is, it was perceived that the United States "held most of the cards."

Janice Stein (Chapter 13) discusses the intricate, tension-filled, and dramatic superpower negotiations during the latter stages of the 1973 Arab-Israeli war, the results of which altered the international and regional configuration in the Middle East and contributed to a "second cold war" between the Soviet Union and the United States that lasted until the early 1980s. Bernard Reich (Chapter 14) then analyzes the "special relationship" that developed between Israel and the United States during the "peace process" of the 1970s and 1980s leading up to and through the Israeli-PLO Declaration of Principles; JoAnn DiGeorgio-Lutz (Chapter 15) discusses the "precarious nature" of the U.S.-PLO relationship during this same period from the Palestinian perspective—the irony of all this being the fact that both Israel and the PLO circumvented U.S. mediation by secretly negotiating the Declaration of Principles in Oslo, Norway. Yet the signing of this historical pact, as well as the signing of the Israeli-Jordanian peace treaty of October 1994 on the White House lawn, reflect the view that the United States must continue to play an important role in the peace process.

Concluding this section, Mohamed Sid-Ahmed (Chapter 16) offers a thoughtful essay on the different perspectives of the meaning of "peace" in the Middle East, contending that the various definitions of the term from (and within) the Arab side and the Israeli side do not always coincide. He believes that unless an acceptable definition emerges that better reflects the desires and needs of the Arabs, specifically the Palestinians, and if the United States continues its impartial attitude toward the Arab-Israeli issue, a lasting peace may be difficult to secure.

Part 4, "The Gulf Crisis and War," focuses on the series of events leading up to and following the Iraqi invasion and occupation of Kuwait in August 1990 and the subsequent liberation of Kuwait by the U.S.-led international coalition in February 1991. Never has the United States been more intimately involved in the Middle East than during this episode. The war climaxed over a half-century of U.S. vital interest in the Persian Gulf area. U.S. policy has been based primarily on maintaining stability in the area so as to ensure easy access to and the safe transport of oil—and, during the cold war, to keep the Soviets from fishing in troubled waters. Balance-of-power politics played an important part in U.S. calculations toward achieving these objectives: The United States initiated at first a relationship with Iran in the Mussadiq coup and enhanced this relationship by supporting the shah of Iran as the U.S. "policeman" of the Gulf as part of the Vietnam-induced 1969 Nixon Doctrine (for U.S. President Richard M. Nixon), which sought to secure U.S. surrogates to represent U.S. global strategic interests (and also envisioned Israel playing a similar role in the heartland of the Middle East). With the fall of the shah in the 1979 Iranian revolution and with the ensuing Iran-Iraq war, Washington began to see Iraq's Saddam Hussein as its new gendarme in the region, keeping back Khomeinism, restoring Gulf stability, and even possibly playing the role that Egyptian President Anwar Sadat never filled, that of leading a moderate Arab consensus toward peace with Israel. U.S. and British support backfired, however, a turn of events that became readily apparent when Iraq invaded Kuwait in 1990, eliciting the decision by the administration of George Bush to intervene militarily. The Gulf war, along with the end of the cold war, contributed to a new regional configuration full of prospects for peace and stability as well as conflict and instability; importantly, this resulted in an enhanced role for the United States in a part of the Middle East that had traditionally been wary of and/or downplayed U.S. influence. Gary Sick, who served on the National Security Council staff during the Carter administration, begins this section with an examination of U.S. policy in the Gulf in the post–World War II era, particularly focusing on the enhanced role of the United States in the region following the 1979 Iranian revolution. In addition to providing context for this section, Sick also critically analyzes the changing role of the United States in the area, as the interests defined and the subsequent policies enacted by Washington have been adjusted and readjusted in reaction to the frequent shifts in the regional balance of power in the Gulf.

Shafeeq Ghabra (Chapter 18) follows with a discussion, from the Kuwaiti point of view, of the development of the relationship between the United States and Kuwait. Stating that Kuwait, with divergent interests, was something of a reluctant ally of the United States out of necessity during the Iran-Iraq war, Ghabra concludes that much work is still needed to solidify relations between the two nations in order to preserve mutual interests and present a unified and stable presence in a potentially unstable area. Amatzia Baram then examines the U.S.-Iraqi relationship that developed out of the Iran-Iraq war and analyzes Saddam Hussein's decision to invade Kuwait (Chapter 19). Baram contends that whereas the Bush administration perceived the relationship to be a positive development worth nurturing in the aftermath of the Iran-Iraq war, the measures it took in an attempt to curb Saddam Hussein's excesses only compelled Baghdad to conclude early on that the United States and Iraq were on a "collision course"; the Iraqis understood that the achievement of their national goals would have to come at the expense of their relationship with the United States.

Examining the Saudi view of its relationship with the United States before, during, and after the Gulf conflict, F. Gregory Gause (Chapter 20) concludes that although the dilemma that has traditionally faced Saudi rulers (keeping the United States as its "over-the-horizon" defense while maintaining its distance from Washington for domestic and regional purposes) was smashed with the open reception of U.S. troops during the Gulf war, a quandary that still exists to some extent because of domestic public opinion weighted against too close an attachment, especially in terms of any sort of formal military cooperation. Yair Evron (Chapter 21) deals with Israeli policy during the Gulf crisis and war, specifically focusing on the important relationship between Israel and the United States amid an international coalition comprised of Arab states, including the traditional leader of the "rejectionist" states, Syria. He also discusses Saddam Hussein's attempts to draw Israel directly into the conflict (primarily by lobbing Iraqi scud missiles into Israel proper) and to elicit a response that would threaten the continued participation of the Arab component of the coalition. Taking a look at the end of the cold war, Evron also analyzes the changing strategic relationship between the United States and Israel, one that might in the future be characterized by mutual interests and cooperation vis-à-vis regional initiatives and potential threats. Robert O. Freedman (Chapter 22) follows with an examination of the Soviet role in the Gulf war, the postwar situation, and the Middle East peace process within the context of broader events occurring at the international level. With the Gulf war as a major turning point in the "erosion" of the Kremlin's position in the Middle East, Freedman concludes that Mikhail Gorbachev's efforts to maintain a Soviet role in the region ultimately proved futile, as his subtle attempts to engineer an independent posture, despite a cooperative stance with the United States on the surface, gave way to U.S. dominance arising out of Soviet domestic necessity and regional realities. Freedman also analyzes the important role that Moscow has played and will continue to play in the region in the aftermath of the breakup of the Soviet Union. Because of its traditional ties with Iraq, Russia's interests and policies in the Gulf have been active but inconsistent, especially as the Russians are torn between domestic politics and economic needs that dictate a more friendly relationship with Baghdad and more distance from the United States; yet at the same time, other economic and strategic realities ordain an improvement in the Russian position with the Gulf Cooperation Council (GCC) states and continuing cooperation with Washington regarding the UN sanctions on Iraq.

Part 5 is entitled "Retrospective and Reassessment" and contains chapters on a variety of historical and current issues of interest in the wake of the cold war, which so dominated and defined U.S. policy toward the Middle East in the post–World War II era. Even though the cold war as we have known it has ended, its legacy and its aftermath are subjects of intense discussion. Indeed, the theme that links all of the chapters in this section is change—from the cold war to the end of the cold war (and its regional effects upon the Arab-Israeli situation) to the changing Soviet role (from that of a superpower to a supplicant). Many Middle East states are experiencing various levels of severe socioeconomic distress, a situation that has led to a concomitant rise in oppositional Islamist movements, something that is unfortunately portrayed by many as the new implacable foe of the United States and the West. There is change in the Arab world in its coming to grips with the roots of this discontent and the problem of regime legitimacy and in defining its role in the international community. And finally, amid all of the change in the Middle East and in the international arena, there is the question of what role the United States should play.

From the vantage point of Moscow, Georgiy Mirsky, in an essay derived from scholarly examination and personal experience (Chapter 23), discusses the motivations, ideological commitment, and interests of Soviet policy toward the Middle East during the cold war era and the transformation of this policy in the post–cold war world. Noting that the Kremlin historically preferred to undermine the West through support of national liberation movements (many of which were thoroughly un-Marxist/Leninist), Mirsky adds that the ideological baggage associated with and created to substantiate such policies quickly disappeared following Gorbachev's glasnost (or what Mirsky calls the "de-ideologization" of Soviet foreign policy), clearing the way for a more cooperative relationship with the United States in the Middle East, the one area of foreign policy where the Kremlin still can play an influential role.

John Duke Anthony (Chapter 24) then looks at the increasingly important relationship between the United States and the GCC nations in the aftermath of the Gulf war and outlines and assesses the negative and positive aspects of the relationship and its potential for the future. This is particularly important considering the fact that the administration of Bill Clinton departed from the traditional balance-of-power approach in the Gulf and adopted a "dual containment" policy designed to contain Iraq and Iran. By default, however, this policy attaches U.S. strategic interests squarely with those of the GCC states, far exceeding the past arm's-length relationship between Washington and the Arab Gulf nations. It does so in a way that necessitates an enhanced U.S. military commitment to the region since the GCC is the weakest link in the triad of regional powers in the Gulf and is unable at present or in the foreseeable future to provide for its own security needs.

William Quandt (Chapter 25) offers a retrospective examination of U.S. foreign policy toward the Middle East and a look at what opportunities and problems in the region lie ahead for policymakers. Although acknowledging that many people, particularly those in the region itself, have had good reason to be highly critical of U.S. actions in the Middle East, he asserts that the objectives as traditionally defined by U.S. policymakers have been for the most part achieved, and with relatively little cost in both human and economic terms, especially when compared to U.S. policy in Southeast Asia. To continue this relative success, U.S. administrations must begin to define these objectives commensurate with the changes that have occurred in the international and regional environment in recent years while remaining sensitive to the fact that many of the problems and issues concerning the region are intrinsic to the area and cannot be solved in Washington.

The rise of Islamist movements in the Middle East has created a good deal of consternation among policymakers in Washington as well as with Westerners in general, as many see this phenomenon as inherently inimical, if not potentially dangerous, to U.S. and Western interests in the region. In an attempt to understand the Islamist perspective toward U.S. foreign policy in the Middle East, Yvonne Haddad (Chapter 26) paints a less optimistic picture than Quandt, examining the root causes of Islamism in general as well as its specific views toward the role that the United States and the West have played in the area. In addition, Haddad offers a glimpse at the potential conflictual future in the Middle East unless certain long-standing grievances held by many groups in the region are addressed in what they perceive to be a satisfactory manner.

Even though they are chronological opposites, the first and last chapters address—by design—the World War I period, where much of the Middle East map was artificially drawn by the victorious entente powers. The divisions and issues that resulted from this period are still very much alive today, and in many ways they are still creating challenges and obstacles for U.S. foreign policy toward the Middle East. Indeed, the perception of the United States held by many in the Middle East has changed dramatically over the course of the twentieth century. This is clearly indicated by the positive view toward the United States observed by a U.S. visitor to the region in 1922 (revealed in the epigraph to Chapter 1), in contrast with the antagonistic, paranoid, cynical, and hateful comments typically made by Islamists today depicted in the numerous quotes employed by Haddad in Chapter 26. And as Robert Allison shows in his postscript on the development of the distorted image of the Middle East and Islam held by Americans during the formative period of the United States, climaxing with the Tripolitan war, these types of negative comments flowing back and forth are anything but a recent phenomenon. As will become apparent throughout this book, involvement in the Middle East has been an adventurous and, at times, tumultuous experience for the United States, one that has not been without its successes. But it is also one that has had numerous failures; even what the United States typically considers successes, however, are not always viewed as such by those in the region itself. The United States is certainly by far the most influential outside power in the Middle East, but it is also far from the most popular; the two do not always, and sometimes should not, go together. Is this the dilemma of a superpower with global interests working through a regional environment, or could U.S. policy have been much more prescient? The answer probably lies somewhere between.

Notes

1. Raymond Hare, "The Great Divide: World War II," *Annals* 401 (May 1972), pp. 23–30.

2. See Malcolm H. Kerr, *The Arab Cold War: Gamal 'Abd al-Nasir and His Rivals, 1958–1970* (New York: Oxford University Press, 1971).

Part One

From Idealism to Realism: Wilsonian Intent to Cold War Practice

1

The Ironic Legacy of
the King-Crane Commission

James Gelvin

In the immediate aftermath of World War I, a U.S. observer in Syria wrote:

> Without visiting the Near East, it is not possible for an American to realize even faintly, the respect, faith and affection with which our Country is regarded throughout that region. Whether it is the world-wide reputation which we enjoy for fair dealing, a tribute perhaps to the crusading spirit which carried us into the Great War, not untinged with the hope that the same spirit may urge us into the solution of great problems growing out of that conflict, or whether due to unselfish or impartial missionary and educational influence exerted for a century, it is the one faith which is held alike by Christian and Moslem, by Jew and Gentile, by prince and peasant in the Near East.[1]

If, during the three-quarters of a century that have passed since these words were written, those who have chronicled the relations between the United States and the nations of the Middle East have had few, if any, opportunities to repeat our observer's findings, they can at least take solace from the fact that the goodwill that may have existed seventy-five years ago has been dissipated precisely because of U.S. intervention in the "great problems" engendered by the destruction of the Ottoman Empire.

The first official U.S. foray into the politics of the post-Ottoman Middle East came about as the result of a suggestion made by President Woodrow Wilson to the Council of Four entente powers (France, Great Britain, the United States, and Italy) assembled in Paris to determine the terms of peace. In an attempt to resolve an acrimonious dispute between Britain and France over the future disposition of the Arab provinces of the Ottoman Empire, Wilson suggested the formation of an interallied commission on Syria. The commission would travel to the Middle East "to elucidate the state of opinion and the soil to be worked on by any mandatory. They should be asked to come back and tell the Conference what they found with regard to these matters. . . . If we were to send a Commission of men with no previous contact with Syria, it would, at any rate, convince the world that the Conference had tried to do all it could to find the most scientific basis possible for a settlement."[2] Although both France and Britain acquiesced to the idea of the commission, neither power appointed delegates to participate in its activities. As a result, the commission became a U.S. commission and thus has been commonly referred to by the names of its two commissioners, Henry Churchill King, president of Oberlin College in Ohio, and Chicago businessman and Democratic Party activist Charles R. Crane. King and Crane traveled to Palestine, Syria, Lebanon, and Anatolia in the summer of 1919 to meet with local representatives. Their findings, filed with the U.S. delegation at Paris, were subsequently ignored by the peace negotiators.

Diplomatic historians have usually cited the King-Crane Commission as either an example of U.S. naïveté in the face of European realpolitik or as a representation of the principles that differentiate the "new diplomacy" from the old. In reality, the legacy of the commission is far more complex. Although the commission's impact on entente policy was doomed from the beginning by a variety of factors—a confusion of secret agreements, historic claims, and postwar realities; the Parti Colonial in France and the Republican Party in the United States; and the British realization that "the friendship of France is worth ten Syrias"[3]—contemporary students of U.S. foreign policy can draw two lessons from the story of the commission. The first lesson is that in diplomacy, like in physics, neutral observers do not exist; rather a world power necessarily influences the object of its interest simply by turning its attention to it, by defining it as a problem to be solved and then framing the possible terms for its solution. Second, a review of the effects of the visit of the King-Crane Commission on the Syrian population[4] underscores the need for U.S. policymakers to reassess the preconceptions and misapprehensions that have guided them, often with disastrous results, when formulating policies that deal with "nation building" and nationalism.

The Doctrine of Self-Determination and Its Application in the Middle East

During World War I and the subsequent peace negotiations, the French, British, and U.S. governments all made declarations that indicated support for self-determination for the peoples of the Ottoman Empire. At the same time, however, all three governments committed themselves to policies that made true self-determination impossible.

For Woodrow Wilson, the liberation of peoples and postwar self-determination were sine qua nons for U.S. participation in the war. From December 1917 through September 1918, Wilson delivered a series of addresses, enunciating U.S. principles in Fourteen Points (8 January 1918), Four Supplementary Points (11 February 1918), Four Additional Points (4 July 1918), and Five Additional Points (27 September 1918). "Self-determination," Wilson warned, "is not a mere phrase. It is an imperative principle of action which statesmen will henceforth ignore at their peril."5 In Point Twelve of the original Fourteen Points, Wilson directly addressed the status of Turks and non-Turks in the Ottoman Empire, promising the latter "an absolutely unmolested opportunity of autonomous development."6

Stung by the revelation of secret agreements reached during the war for a colonial-style division of the Ottoman Empire, and wishing to allay the doubts of Arab nationalists who suspected entente perfidy, France and Britain adopted Wilson's call for self-determination for the inhabitants of the Middle East. On November 9, 1918, they issued the following joint declaration, which they distributed throughout liberated Syria: "The object aimed at by France and Great Britain in prosecuting in the East the War let loose by the ambition of Germany is the complete and definite emancipation of the peoples so long oppressed by the Turks and the establishment of national governments and administrations deriving their authority from the initiative and free choice of the indigenous populations."7

In the same statement, however, the two powers displayed their ambivalence to the principle of self-determination by making their support for the doctrine conditional on the acceptance by the indigenes of guidance from "advanced nations":

> In order to carry out these intentions France and Great Britain are at one in encouraging and assisting the establishment of indigenous Governments and administrations in Syria and Mesopotamia, now liberated by the Allies, and in the territories the liberation of which they are engaged in securing and recognising these as soon as they are actually established.
>
> Far from wishing to impose on the populations of these regions any particular institutions they are only concerned to ensure by their support and by adequate assistance the regular working of Governments and administrations freely chosen by the populations themselves. To secure impartial and equal justice for all, to facilitate the economic development of the country by inspiring and encouraging local initiative, to favour the diffusion of education, to put an end to dissensions that have too long been taken advantage of by Turkish policy, such is the policy which the two Allied Governments uphold in the liberated territories.

For many Arab nationalists, particularly those who had preferred sitting out the war in Egypt to joining the British-inspired Arab Revolt of Sharif Hussein and his sons, the Anglo-French statement appeared to be little more than a rationalization for a thinly veiled colonialism.8 As if to confirm their suspicions, French President Georges Clemenceau visited London in December 1918, where, in the words of British Prime Minister Lloyd George, it was "agreed that Syria should go to France [as a mandate] and Mesopotamia to Great Britain."9 To mollify the French further, the British (as well as the United States) disavowed any interest in Syria in a meeting of the Council of Four held three days before the peace conference authorized the assignment of mandates in the region.

Whereas the French and British attitude toward both self-determination for the inhabitants of the region and the King-Crane Commission was thus clear, U.S. support for both was surprisingly ambiguous. Its European allies might easily have argued that the United States had, on several occasions, already placed its imprimatur on their wartime and postwar arrangements for the region. After all, not only had Woodrow Wilson issued a statement of support for the Balfour Declaration[10] in September 1918 without bothering to ascertain the attitude of the inhabitants of Palestine toward the establishment of a Jewish homeland in their midst, but one month later he approved the official U.S. Department of State commentary on the Fourteen Points, which recognized the preeminent position of France in Syria and affirmed that Britain was "clearly the best mandatory for Palestine, Mesopotamia, and Arabia."[11] Little wonder, then, that Henry King and Charles Crane, in a memorandum written to the U.S. president before their tour of the Middle East, argued that the mandate for Syria should go to France "frankly based, not on the primary desires of the people, but on the international need of preserving friendly relations between France and Great Britain,"[12] or that, within a week of proposing the commission, Wilson had, according to Ray Stannard Baker, a close associate and head of the U.S. press bureau in Paris, "clean forgotten" about it.[13]

Support among the entente powers for the activities of the commission thus ranged from lackluster to dismissive. The commission's recommendations were nonbinding, and even if the commission were to find, as it did, that Syrian public opinion supported a united Syria and (in ranked order) no mandate, a U.S. mandate, and a British mandate,[14] all three options had already been foreclosed. It was in this context that Lloyd George, like the proverbial Western sheriff who remarked, "First we give him a fair trial, then we hang him," urged his French colleague to support the activities of the commission, but "first let us agree [about the disposition of territory] between ourselves."[15]

The U.S. Perspective on Self-Determination and Public Opinion

Not only did decisions made in Paris preclude the possibility that the King-Crane Commission would influence entente policy, but preconceptions held by both the commissioners and their president—preconceptions about democracy, progress, public opinion, and nationalism that both underlay the commission's flawed procedure and circumscribed the range of its possible findings—impeded the commission's ability truly to "elucidate the state of opinion and the soil to be worked on by any mandatory" in Syria.

The extent to which his father's Calvinism shaped Woodrow Wilson's worldview and principles of his foreign policy is a well-worn cliché.[16] But because Wilson was a historian as well as the son of a Presbyterian minister, he tempered his belief in a mankind tainted by original sin with the optimism implicit in the Whiggism common to the academic milieu from which he emerged. History, for Wilson, was the chronicle of liberty—"the enlargement of the sphere of independent action at the expense of dictatorial authority."[17] From the Greek polis and the confrontation at Runnymede through the ratification of the U.S. Constitution, human progress could thus be measured in two ways: by the multiplication of the personal freedoms available to the (Anglo-Saxon) heirs of this tradition, and by the spread of democracy—the political correlate to this tradition—throughout the world.

In his writings, Wilson argued that the expansion of international trade, print media, and, most important, public education during the previous century had created an autonomous realm of public opinion in most nations that facilitated the global diffusion of democratic ideals and structures.[18] Wilson's definition of public opinion thus differed dramatically from the definition used by his German idealist contemporaries: Rather than being the repository of common sense ("all-pervasive fundamental ethical principles disguised as prejudices"),[19] Wilson's public opinion was an *informed* public opinion shaped by the most enlightened strata of society.[20] This was the public opinion upon which the doctrine of self-determination rested, the public opinion that Wilson charged the King-Crane Commission to elucidate.

The members of the King-Crane Commission shared Wilson's understanding about the nature of public opinion. Their fact-finding consisted of holding audiences with, and receiving petitions drafted by, those whom they considered to be the most important and most representative Middle East opinion makers: thirty-four mayors and municipal councils, fifteen administrative councils, sixty-five councils of village chiefs, thirty Arab shaykhs, seventeen professional and trade organizations, and so on. It should not be surprising, therefore, that in its final report the commission advocated strengthening Syrian nationalism through an expansion of education "in clear recognition of the imperative necessity of education for the citizens of a democratic state and the development of a sound national spirit."[21]

Although members of the King-Crane Commission disagreed about the extent to which the Syrian population was prepared for self-determination and how long "the systematic cultivation of national spirit" in Syria would take, all agreed on the liberal and secular foundations on which Syrians had to base their nationalism. In the conclusion to its final report, the commission recommended imposing a mandate on Syria but optimistically predicted that the period during which a mandatory power would have to oversee Syrian affairs might be brief. According to the report, mandatory control could be relinquished as soon as the leaders of the Syrian nationalist movement demonstrated their sincerity in midwifing a modern democratic nation-state that protected the rights of minorities:

> The western world is already committed to the attempt to live in peace and friendship with the Moslem peoples, and to manage governments in such a way as to separate politics from religion. Syria offers an excellent opportunity to establish a state where members of the three great monotheistic religions can live together in harmony; because it is a country of one language, which has long had freedom of movement and of business relations through being unified under the Turkish rule. Since now the majority declare for nationalism, independent of religion, it is necessary only to hold them to this view through mandatory control until they shall have established the method and practice of it. Dangers may readily arise from unwise and unfaithful dealings with this people, but there is great hope of peace and progress if they be handled frankly and loyally.[22]

In contrast to the findings of the commissioners, the reports filed by William Yale, one of two technical advisers attached to the King-Crane Commission, cast doubt on the short-term "possibility of developing among the people of Syria a national spirit upon the community of language which exists, the similarity of race, the sense of economic dependence, and the germ of nationalism." Yale predicted disaster without a long-term and energetic mandatory presence in Syria:

> There is a liberal movement among the Syrian Moslems, a movement which under proper guidance and with proper assistance may be able to awaken a new spirit in the younger generation, might have been able to lessen the fanaticism not only of the effendi class but of the lower classes. At the present time this liberal movement was too feeble, too weak in numbers and conviction . . . to rally to their support the ignorant fanatical masses which are swayed by the Ulemas and the Young Arab Party.[23]

Ironically, the very search by members of the King-Crane Commission for their counterparts in Syrian society directly (and adversely) affected the latter's ability to shape Syrian public opinion. Those whom Yale entrusted to nurture "liberal nationalism" naturally believed, like the commissioners, that educational achievement or professional status entitled them to play a special role in nation building. While actively courting the commissioners, this grouping simultaneously sought to convince the Syrian population that, having achieved the approbation of the commission, it would secure Syrian independence through negotiation and compromise— if not absolute independence, then at least independence under the benevolent guidance of the Americans or British. The refusal by the entente powers to accept the recommendations of the King-Crane Commission destroyed the credibility of this sodality within the nationalist movement and thus assured the emergence a new and very different kind of nationalist leadership.

The "Liberal Movement"

The thin strata of society behind what William Yale (ingenuously) identified as the "liberal movement" had emerged in Syria as the result of two processes that had, over the course of the half-century that preceded the dissolution of the Ottoman Empire, increasingly determined institutions and social relationships in the Arab Middle East. Both the accelerating rate of integration of the region into the world economy and attempts made by the Ottoman government to rationalize and strengthen central control increased the salience of capitalist relations and encouraged their diffusion (albeit unevenly) throughout the empire. These effects, in turn, not only induced the reconstruction and/or enlargement of certain previously existing social classes, but they prompted the emergence of new social classes as well. Members of two of these classes, often intertwined through reciprocal ties of interest and/or consanguinity, formed the core of Yale's "liberal movement": the so-called middle strata, comprising intellectuals, trained military officers, professionals, and so on, who were necessary to implement Ottoman "modernization" and state-building policies, and a reconstituted urban notability whose economic and political status was increasingly based on a combination of land ownership and good relations with Istanbul.[24]

Two types of bonds united these groups with their counterparts in the West. Because both the formation of the middle strata and the post-1860 transformation of the urban notability depended upon the spread of peripheral capitalism and modern institutions of governance in the Middle East, the categories used by these groups to organize the world and their society were coherent with the categories used by analogous groups—both in the metropole and in other peripheral areas—who benefited from, or whose origins can be traced to, the worldwide expansion of capitalism. In addition, elective ties of affinity, nurtured, for example, through education, religious affiliation, and/or wartime experiences, often linked members of these groups to their European counterparts. These natural and emulative bonds not only account for the strategies used by these newly empowered groups to craft state institutions in post-Ottoman Syria, but also explain why, during the same period, an influential bloc readily worked within the parameters set by the Paris Peace Conference in an attempt to win Syrian independence.

The Arab government that was established in Damascus at the close of World War I depended upon individuals from these groups to administer the territory of inland Syria and to mobilize the support of the indigenous population. Working both within the government and through allied political and cultural organizations (the most important of which were al-Fatat, the Arab Club [al-nadi al-'arabi], and the Literary Society [al-muntada al-adabi]),[25] the self-proclaimed elite within the nationalist movement (labeled in their own writings the *mutanawwirun, mustanirun,* or *mufakkirun*) designed governmental and extragovernmental institutions to expand the authority of the state, reorganize traditional structures within civil society, introduce mores and values compatible with or derived from those of Europe, and inculcate new national myths and symbols among the population. In a report written in November 1919, for example, British traveler Gertrude Bell described her visit to one such institution, the "School for the Daughters of Martyrs" *(madrasat banat al-shuhada),* which was established in Damascus to educate orphans whose fathers had died during the Arab Revolt. The school, according to Bell,

> is run on private subscriptions by a committee of ladies presided over by Naziq bint al 'Abid, a girl of 21 belonging to one of the best families of Damascus. She is a niece of 'Izzat Pasha, who was the all-powerful Secretary of Abdul Hamid for a period of years, during which he earned great wealth and the bitter recriminations of the C.U.P. [Committee of Union and Progress] when it came into the saddle. In spite of their threats Izzat managed to escape to Europe, where he had already lodged a respectable part of his fortune. Sitt Naziq was educated in a mission school at Beyrut, speaks English, and is the most advanced lady in Damascus. She and her mother sat unveiled among a company of men, a select company, but none of them related to the 'Abid family. Another Mohammadan lady of the committee was present, and she also was unveiled. . . . The mistresses were mostly Christians educated in Beyrut and speaking fairly good English.

Besides the orphans there were an equal number of girls of good Damascene families who pay for the education they receive. These girls 16 to 18 years old, were not seen by the men of the party. Girls and children were brought out into the large garden which surrounds the house to sing patriotic songs. In one of them a chorus of the elder girls addressed the orphans, reminding each one that her father died in the cause of liberty and bidding her never to forget that she was "bint ul 'Arabi," while the children replied that they would never forget their birth, nor King Husain who fought for their race, nor finally (this stanza was specially prepared for the U.S. Commission) President Wilson who laid down—save the mark—the principles of freedom.[26]

A more comprehensive picture of the attitudes and activities of like-minded *mutanawwirun* during the period preceding the visit of the King-Crane Commission to Damascus is displayed in an unusual parable, entitled "The True Vision," that was published on the front page of the official gazette of the Arab government in May 1919.[27] The fantasy begins with a description of the author at his desk, contemplating the news of demonstrations held in Egypt to show popular support for Egyptian independence: "We hardly see such good order in the demonstrations of the most advanced Western nations. I said to myself, 'By God! They unjustly accuse the East and its people of savagery, immaturity, and an inability to imitate the civilization of the West. What is more indicative of their readiness [for independence] than this admirably ordered and perfect demonstration?'" Troubled by his meditations and by concerns about the upcoming visit of the King-Crane Commission to Damascus, the author falls asleep. His dreams transport him to an unfamiliar Middle East location where the inhabitants speak classical Arabic and dress in traditional attire. In the tent of their chieftain lies a strange mechanism and two mirrors: one mirror reflects the past, the other forecasts the future. The author, having begged the apparition for a glimpse of the future, spends the remainder of the dream watching upcoming events unfold, "like in a movie."

The author's first vision is of the near future. On the eve of the arrival of the King-Crane Commission, "the people of distinction and their intellectuals" (*'ilyat al-qawm wa mufakkiruhum),* assembled in a general congress, make preparations to convince the commission that the Syrian population is mature (the words "*madani,*" "*umrani,*" and "*adabi*" are used throughout the article) and therefore merits independence. To accomplish this, as the parable continues, the delegates plan to use locally based artisan guilds and patriotic clubs to organize demonstrations similar to those of Egypt and to distribute placards among the population calling for complete independence:

In conformity with this plan each citizen placed a sign on his forearm and on his breast on which was printed "We demand complete independence." Shop owners placed signs with this slogan written in English and Arabic on their shops. Hardly had these plans been made when all inhabitants—regardless of religion, sect, and nationality—showed these placards . . . and one could not walk down the street without seeing the signs on every building and wall. As the size of demonstrations swelled, the people daubed this slogan on the tarbooshes of small boys and embroidered it on the frontlets of small girls.

I laughed when I saw a bald man with the slogan written on his head. I saw the owners of carriages and horses who placed this slogan on the faces of their horses and the sweets-sellers put the slogan on the lids of containers of sweets and milk. I was truly amazed when I saw the work of the residents of Salhiyye—they spelled out this slogan with lanterns on Mt. Qasiun by night in letters that could be read for seven miles. The people kept up this sort of activity until the delegation left Damascus.

Impressed by the "intelligence, advancement, and worthiness for independence" of Syrians, the King-Crane Commission returns to Paris and convinces the peace conference to offer the Syrians independence. Under the benevolent leadership of Faisal, now king of Syria, and guided by a new congress, presumably composed of the same notables and intellectuals who had convened in the previous congress, the nation can now enjoy the fruits of its independence:

I saw . . . the people now turning their attention to the founding of schools and colleges until no village remained without an excellent primary school. I saw prosperity spreading throughout the country and railroads connecting populous villages and farms. I saw farmers using the most modern agricultural techniques, extensive trade, and flourishing industry. Damascus appeared to me to be the most advanced of cities in terms of its construction. Its streets and lanes were paved with asphalt and the Barada River was like the Seine, traversing the city from east to west. On its banks was a corniche on which towering buildings stood. I saw Aleppo: its water, brought by canals from the Euphrates, sustained its gardens and parks and anointed its waterless desert. . . . Factories were founded throughout the kingdom so that the country had no need for manufactured goods from the West, but instead exported its products to China, India, and Africa. Its people grew rich, its power increased, and it moved to the forefront of advanced nations.

As is common with prophetic narratives, the accuracy of the dreamer's vision increasingly fades the further it advances into the future. Much of what the author wrote about imminent events did transpire as foretold. The Syrian General Congress, composed primarily of representatives whose backgrounds placed them among the "people of distinction," met in early June 1919 to formulate a consentient list of demands to be presented to the U.S. commission.[28] The Arab government distributed *khutab* (sermons) to be read at Friday prayers and, in conjunction with political and cultural associations and government-sanctioned guilds, sponsored petition campaigns and mobilized demonstrations in support of the "Damascus Program" promulgated by the congress.[29] Local political activists and *makhatir* (government officials assigned to quarters within cities) ensured that shopkeepers throughout Syria placarded their storefronts with the slogan, "We demand complete independence."[30] However, the long-term vision for Syria espoused by the author— a vision suffused with Eurogenic ideals and expressed through an alien discourse— not only failed to materialize but proved to be far removed from the concerns of the vast majority of the Syrian population.

With adequate resources, it might have been possible for the Arab government and its allies gradually to enlist the support of the Syrian population for its "true vision": The *mutanawwirun* not only enjoyed the requisite social prestige to attract the spontaneous consent of nonelites but, because of their access to institutions of governance, they possessed potentially formidable coercive powers as well. However, on September 13, 1919, the British government decided to reduce its substantial subsidy to the Arab government by half and to withdraw its forces from Syria. This decision undercut both the economic and the political positions of the Arab government and its allies and generated a crisis from which they never recovered.[31] Widely interpreted as portending French rule in Syria ("protection and mandate are synonyms, and are the precursors to annexation"),[32] the action seemed to confirm the bankruptcy of the plan to achieve the complete independence of Syria through negotiation. Almost overnight, the slogan "Complete independence for Syria within its natural boundaries, no protection, tutelage, or mandate *(la himaya, la wisaya, wa la intidab)*" replaced its shorter but obviously inadequate predecessor on placards posted throughout Syria.[33]

The Response of Nonelites to the Failure of the Commission

> The enemy have cloaked themselves in hypocrisy, and
> enfolded it in rancor and hatred.
> They took an oath of loyalty and they were disloyal,
> and from among them you have trusted some as
> allies who were treacherous. . . .
> What is amiss with those who have carried the scales of
> guidance on their arms, that they have failed to
> discern the truth?
> If they do not help those who need help and bring
> success to those who deserve it, then let the
> scales be broken.
>
> —Khayr al-Din al-Zirikli[34]

For many in the Arab Middle East, the expansion of capitalist relations and the reorganization of imperial institutions that had taken place during the seventy years preceding the dissolution of the Ottoman Empire induced social changes that ranged from disorienting to calamitous. Not only did the status of those local elites who lacked landed wealth and/or bureaucratic connections decline but rivalry intensified among established and emergent elites for highly coveted posts in the reinvigorated state bureaucracy. The spread of capitalism frequently transformed peasant life: Peasants often found themselves at the mercy of usurers, planted cash crops for export, and supplemented family incomes by participating, sometimes seasonally, sometimes permanently, in the urban labor force. Coastal cities and extramural urban areas expanded, and newcomers to cities frequently settled in neighborhoods (such as the Maydan in Damascus and al-Kallasa in Aleppo) that lacked homogeneity and established social structures. New demands made by the state (such as the universally loathed conscription), agricultural crises, alterations in patterns of land

tenure, conflicts on the periphery of the empire and World War I, and postwar inflation and rural insecurity further disrupted the lives of nonelites.

The social and economic shocks experienced by both nonelites and former elites
had two relevant effects. First, because the expansion of market relations and the intrusion of a uniform apparatus of power into previously unregulated or underregulated
domains increasingly determined the nature and extended the scope of ties among Syrians, the significance of horizontal, associational, and national linkages among the
population grew at the expense of vertical, communal, and parochial bonds—a necessary precondition for "proactive" collective activity and what historian George Mosse
calls the "nationalization of the masses."[35] Second, the social and economic shocks engendered an ideological backlash among the self-described "aggrieved" *(mankubun)*,[36]
who frequently expressed their disaffection through a populist discourse that extolled
the historic ties and common interests that united Syrians into an egalitarian national
community, celebrated the central role played by nonelites in preserving "traditional"
values, and affirmed the integrity of community boundaries.

Starting in September 1919, populist activists—disempowered notables, merchants, *qabadayat* (local toughs), *ulama,* petit-bourgeois merchant/*ulama,* and so
on[37]—took advantage of the opportunities for mobilization that both the prolonged
social transformations and the immediate economic and political crises provided to
create the structures necessary for a sustainable populist movement. Over the course
of the next nine months, these activists founded an array of interconnected organizations (the most important of which were the Higher National Committee *[al-
lajna al-wataniyya al-'ulya],* based in Damascus, and local committees of national
defense *[lijan al-difa' al-watani]*) that challenged the authority of the crippled Arab
government, the discredited *mutanawwirun,* and the representatives of the entente
powers meeting in Paris.

The populist organizations attracted widespread support, particularly among the
Sunni Muslim population of inland Syria, for several reasons. As described earlier,
in anticipation of the arrival of the King-Crane Commission in Syria, the Arab government and its extragovernmental allies applied modern techniques for mass mobilization that had, even before the founding of the populist organizations, accli-
mated much of the population to participation in national politics. But where the
Arab government attempted to reach a settlement with the entente powers through
negotiation and compromise, the populist organizations preached the more popular
doctrine of militant anti-imperialism and marshaled and/or supplied local volunteer
militias and guerrilla bands to resist mandatory authority. The organizations connected individuals to a national political machine through neighborhood and village
branch organizations and supervisory committees *(al-lijan al-far'iyya, al-lijan al-
taftishiyya)* and promoted participation by sponsoring electoral campaigns, demonstrations, military exercises, and charitable activities. Finally, the populist organizations assumed responsibility for services—protecting and provisioning urban
quarters, assessing taxes, licensing monopolies, ensuring a "fair price" for grain, pro-

viding relief for the indigent and families of soldiers—which the local notability and the Arab government could no longer provide.

In contrast to the anonymous dreamer and his colleagues—who were willing to accept a temporary mandate in exchange for technological assistance and the accouterments of civilization—populist spokesmen articulated a vision for Syria that met the concerns of "the great mass of the nation [that] is not confined to the educated, the notables, and the merchants of the cities who read the daily newspapers, follow international and domestic politics, and are concerned with scientific discoveries and technological innovation."[38] Scornful of the aspirations of the Westernized elites ("[The French] only want to possess the sources of wealth and turn the free population into slaves in the name of progress, and only the Syrians [will] feel the effects"),[39] populist spokesmen eschewed the dichotomization of Syrian society inherent in "A True Vision"—a dichotomization that stigmatized and alienated a vast majority of the population by pitting the cultured and educated formulators of public opinion against the passive nonelites—and expounded a vision of Syria that was both comprehensive and inclusive. Populist organizers thus counterposed their own definition of public opinion to the definition used by Woodrow Wilson and his epigones in Syria:

> The people possess a spirit which transcends the inclinations of individuals . . . and the nation possesses an independent personality stronger than the personalities of its members. . . . Those who would penetrate the heart of the Syrian people . . . know that public opinion is made from two sources: the first is its historical traditions in which there is strong faith and fidelity. This is fixed and immutable at its core, and even though it changes form it is imperishable and indestructible. The old illiterate, the religious 'alim, the cultured youth all equally respect historical traditions and aspire to the general goal. . . . [T]he people compel outside influences to be compatible with their traditions, and they desire to harmonize the elements of public opinion by making the second element compatible with the first, that is, with historic tradition.[40]

The aggressive posture assumed by the leaders of the populist movement and the potential empowerment of their constituents alarmed both foreign observers and the *mutanawwirun*. Populist rhetoric, suffused with Islamic and apocalyptic images and embellished with anecdotes that described the treachery of "those who would sell the nation like merchandise," foreign conspiracies, French and Zionist atrocities, the defilement of Muslim innocents, and exculpatory vengeance, aroused their apprehensions as well. "Over 90% of the Moslems of Syria are ignorant and fanatical, and can be swayed by their religious leaders," reported William Yale. "They are profoundly anti-Christian and anti-foreign and can be easily led to excesses by the recognized leaders, the clergy, land owners, and tribal chiefs."[41] Similarly, in a letter addressed to a former finance minister, a physician working in the foreign ministry of the Arab government depicted the populist movement as a form of mass pathology: "Individual dementia is among the greatest afflictions I know, but worse still is the complete dementia of a nation. . . . I am not a prophet, yet I see the end result very clearly if the transgressors do not return to their senses."[42]

The transgressors did not, of course, "come to their senses." To the contrary, worsening economic conditions, widening border warfare, the demands made by an apparently incompetent yet increasingly rapacious Arab government, and the announcement of the decision made by the entente powers at San Remo in April 1920 (to divide Syria and impose mandates) boosted support for the populist movement and the organizations it spawned while further undermining the authority of the Arab government and the counsel of the *mutanawwirun*. When the Arab government finally acquiesced to a French ultimatum that threatened unspecified "acts" unless the government accepted a French mandate, antigovernment rioting—which left scores dead in Damascus and hundreds dead in Aleppo—erupted throughout Syria. In the aftermath of this final display of the "state of opinion and the soil to be worked on by any mandatory," the French army marched on Damascus and France began its quarter-century occupation of inland Syria—one year to the day after the departure of the King-Crane Commission from the Middle East.

The King-Crane Commission and the Construction of Syrian Nationalism

> In truth, the politics which followed in Syria were very strange, inasmuch as the intellectuals—the men of public opinion—and the men of the government themselves stirred up, by all means possible, the excitement of the people and pushed it to the extreme. Then, all of a sudden, they retreated before the slightest obstacle which blocked their way, and they abandoned the people who were perplexed, not knowing how to explain their position. . . . This created a situation of enormous emotional turmoil and squandered the trust which the people had placed in their leaders. They openly accused their leaders of treachery to the point that, gradually, that trust was dissolved, and the leaders to whom the people had entrusted the reins of government were not able to lead and they were scoffed at.
>
> —As'ad Daghir[43]

Following World War I, revolutionary violence convulsed much of the non-Western world, from Turkey through India to China and Korea. The situation in the Arab Middle East was no different, with conflagrations erupting in Egypt (1919), Syria (1919–1920), and Iraq (1920). Despite the fact all the affected areas could sustain complex, programmatic political movements (as opposed to movements that might be characterized as temporary, defensive, and prepolitical)[44] because all had been subjected to analogous processes—the uneven and asymmetric spread of dependent capitalism and the introduction of modern institutions of governance—a unique interplay of local, regional, and international determinants ignited and shaped each uprising.

Although Woodrow Wilson had originally proposed an interallied commission merely to ascertain and convey the wishes of the Syrian population, the King-Crane Commission had the unintended effect of catalyzing and, in many ways, defining the political movement that arose to resist the imposition of a mandate on Syria. Gulled by the promise implicit in the commission's tour of Syria, the *mutanawwirun* constructed structures that expedited the mobilization of the population. Because these elites were oriented toward Europe and the peace conference, however, they designed institutions, demonstrations, and propaganda campaigns for the purpose of presenting to an outside audience an image of a sophisticated nation eager and prepared for independence. They thus deferred the task of integrating the majority of the population into their framework of legitimacy. As a result, during the period that preceded the French mandate, the *mutanawwirun* never truly involved nonelites in their nationalist project: They never dickered with the population over questions of ideology and program, they never synthesized a political discourse that was compelling to nonelites, and they never established connections with the population comparable to those that the Wafdist leadership had established with the population of Egypt, for example. In short, the announcement of the formation of the King-Crane Commission and its subsequent visit to Syria initiated an unintended chain of events that culminated in the strengthening of a populist nationalism dissociated from the guidance of the more Westernized nationalist elites.

Notes

1. *Editor and Publisher*, 2 December 1922, iii.

2. Notes by Sir Maurice Pascal Alers from the 20 March 1919 meeting of the Council of Four, in Arthur S. Link, ed., *The Papers of Woodrow Wilson*, vol. 56 (Princeton, 1987), p. 116.

3. British Prime Minister David Lloyd George to French President Georges Clemenceau, 25 April 1919, in ibid., 58:134.

4. Unless otherwise indicated, the term "Syria" is meant to designate the territory of the Middle East that comprises present-day Syria, Lebanon, Jordan, Israel and the Occupied Territories, and western Iraq.

5. Ray Stannard Baker and William E. Dodd, eds., *Public Papers of Woodrow Wilson*, vols. 5–6: *War and Peace: Presidential Messages, Addresses, and Public Papers (1917–1925)* (New York, 1927), 5:180.

6. Ibid., 5:160–161.

7. J. C. Hurewitz, ed., *The Middle East and North Africa in World Politics: A Documentary Record*, vol. 2: *British-French Supremacy, 1914–1945* (New Haven, 1979), 112.

8. For the position of the Syrian nationalists in the Egyptian exile community, see James L. Gelvin, "Popular Mobilization and the Origins of Mass Politics in Syria, 1918–1920," Ph.D. diss., Harvard University, 1992, 209–211. See also Muhibb al-Din al-Khatib, autobiographical manuscript stored in the Dar al-Watha'iq al-Tarikhiyya, Damascus.

9. Link, *The Papers of Woodrow Wilson*, 58:328.

10. The Balfour Declaration (named after British Foreign Secretary Arthur Balfour and issued on November 2, 1917) was in the form of a letter from Balfour to a leading British Zionist, Lord Walter Rothschild; it promised British support for the creation of "a national home for the Jewish people" in Palestine. The declaration provided a much-needed boost to the Zionist movement by providing the legal framework for continued Jewish immigration and land purchases in Palestine, the twin pillar of the Zionists' policy to make Palestine their na-

tional home. The British issued the declaration for a number of reasons: to preempt what was expected to be a similar announcement by Germany; to win the support of worldwide Jewry, especially in the United States and USSR, that would aid the war effort; and to have a group beholden to British interests in Palestine in order to protect the right flank of the Suez Canal, act as a buffer between the anticipated French position in Syria and the British position in Egypt, and provide a land bridge from the Mediterranean Sea to the Persian Gulf (from Palestine across Transjordan and Iraq to the Gulf).

11. Charles Seymour, ed., *The Intimate Papers of Colonel House: The Ending of the War* (Boston, 1928), 153, 199.

12. Link, *The Papers of Woodrow Wilson,* 58:322–326.

13. Ray Stannard Baker in ibid., 56:442. Baker also wrote the following entry in his diary (21 May 1919; see ibid., 58:368) about the circumstances that led to the commission's departure: "[Wilson] told me with a kind of amused satisfaction—he gets very little fun out of his conferences, but he had it today—of the discussion this morning of the Syrian question and of a red-hot conflict of view between Lloyd George and Clemenceau. It seems that Lloyd George calmly proposed to give to Italy (to induce a settlement of the Fiume question) a slice of Syria which Clemenceau had already decided to gobble down. This perfectly frank scramble for territory, which in a moment of anger was fought with all guards down, seemed to amuse the President very much. It also had the effect of once more reviving the plan for the Syrian Commission (King and Crane). The President told the Four, positively, that *our* commissioners were leaving for Syria on Monday! It has given him his chance."

14. According to the report of the King-Crane Commission, "It is certain from the oral statements that accompanied the petitions that the term, 'Absolute independence,' was seldom used in the sense of an entire freedom from only foreign guidance such as that of a mandatory under the League of Nations, inasmuch as the request was frequently combined with a choice of mandate or a request for foreign 'assistance.' While a few of the Young Arab clubs certainly desired freedom from all foreign control, the great majority asked for independence and defined a mandate to mean only economic and technical assistance." "Report of the American Section of the International Commission on Mandates in Turkey (28 August 1919)," in U.S. Department of State, *Papers Relating to the Foreign Relations of the United States,* vol. 12: *The Paris Peace Conference: 1919* (Washington, D.C., 1947), 767.

15. Link, *The Papers of Woodrow Wilson,* 58:133–134.

16. See Arthur S. Link, *Wilson the Diplomatist: A Look at His Major Foreign Policies* (Baltimore, 1957), 12.

17. Woodrow Wilson, "Political Sovereignty," in *Selected Literary and Political Papers and Addresses of Woodrow Wilson* (New York, n.d.), 91–92.

18. See, for example, Woodrow Wilson, "The Character of Democracy in the United States," in ibid., 89–93.

19. G. W. F. Hegel, *Philosophy of Right,* trans. T. M. Knox (New York, 1952), 204.

20. In an interview with Ida M. Tarbell, Wilson quoted the following lines from "The Princess," by Alfred Lord Tennyson: "A nation yet, the rulers and the ruled— / Some sense of duty, something of a faith, / Some reverence for the laws ourselves have made, / Some patient force to change them when we will, / Some civic manhood firm against the crowd." *Collier's,* 28 October 1916, 37.

21. For the strategy of the King-Crane Commission, a complete listing of the groups it received, and its conclusions, see "Report of the American Section of the International Commission," cited in note 13 above.

22. Ibid., 863.

23. William Yale, "A Report on Syria, Palestine, and Mount Lebanon for the American Commissioners," Yale Papers, Boston University, Box X/Folder 8/22–23.

24. For details about the "middle strata" and its role in nationalist movements, see E. J. Hobsbawm, *Nations and Nationalism Since 1780: Programme, Myth, Reality* (Cambridge, 1990), 90–94, 117–122; Miroslav Hroch, *Social Preconditions of National Revival in Europe: A Comparative Analysis of the Social Composition of Patriotic Groups Among the Smaller European Nations,* trans. Ben Fowkes (Cambridge, 1985), particularly 129–155. For a discussion of the changing nature of the urban notability during the nineteenth century, see Philip Khoury, *Urban Notables and Arab Nationalism: The Politics of Damascus, 1860–1920* (Cambridge, 1983).

25. It is important to note that, contrary to the assumptions of William Yale and other Western observers, neither the Arab government nor any of the allied organizations were monolithic; moreover, the government and the political and cultural clubs included members who espoused a variety of ideologies and practices. For example, as late as the autumn of 1919, al-Fatat included three factions: the "dissenters" (*rafidun*) who refused to support any mandate; a "pro-British/anti-French" faction allied with Emir Faisal; and a faction that still held out hope for a U.S. mandate. See ʿIzzat Darwaza, *Mudhakkirat wa Tasjilat* (Damascus, 1984), 2:76–77, 81–82; Gelvin, "Popular Mobilization," 55–63, 74–85. In this essay, the term "Arab government" refers to the faction of the government that included Emir Faisal, his entourage, and his allies.

26. India Office, London: L/PS/10/802. Gertrude Bell, "Syria in October 1919," 15 November 1919, 11.

27. *al-ʿAsima,* 7 May 1919, 1–2.

28. See Khoury, *Urban Notables,* 86–88; Yusuf al-Hakim, *Dhikrayat,* vol. 3: *Suriya wa al-ʿahd al-Faysali* (Beirut, 1966), 90–97; Safiuddin Joarder, *Syria Under the French Mandate: The Early Phase, 1920–1927* (Dacca, 1977), 209–211.

29. Archives Diplomatiques, Nantes (hereinafter AD): 2430/no no. Cousse to Dame, 18 April 1919; Ministère des Affaires Etrangères, Paris (hereinafter MAE): L:AH vol. 4/237–238; Picot to Pichon, 22 May 1919; MAE L:SL vol. 14/#897; Picot to MAE, 17 June 1919; MAE L:SL vol. 44/3D; Minault (Latakia) to Administrateur du Vilayet de Beyrouth, 18 July 1919; Ministère de la Defense, Vincennes (hereafter MD) 7N4182/Dossier 4/340; Picot to MAE 21 July 1919; MAE L:SL vol. 43/39–41. "Renseignements d'Agent," 10–20 July 1919; AD 2430 Dossier Confidential-Départ/#240, 11 August 1919. For texts of sermons distributed 11 and 18 April 1919, see AD 2343/286, Cousse to Haut Commissionaire, 24 April 1919.

30. MD L:SL vol. 12/32–38. Cousse to Haut Commissionaire, 6 April 1919; Gelvin, "Popular Mobilization," 321–322.

31. See Malcolm Russell, *The First Modern Arab State: Syria Under Faysal, 1918–1920* (Minneapolis, 1985), 93–131.

32. See leaflet entitled, "Independence or Death!" in MAE L:SL vol. 43/72–73, 21 July 1919 (in Arabic with French translation).

33. See Gelvin, "Popular Mobilization," 240.

34. Khayr al-Din al-Zirikli, *Diwan Zirikli: al-aʿmal al-shiʿriyya al-kamila,* (Amman[?], n.d.), 24–25 (translation by author).

35. See Charles Tilly, Louise Tilly, and Richard Tilly, *The Rebellious Century, 1830–1930* (Cambridge, Mass., 1975), 51–53; George L. Mosse, *The Nationalization of the Masses: Po-*

litical Symbolism and Mass Movements in Germany from the Napoleanic Wars Through the Third Reich (New York, 1977).

36. For copies of leaflets signed "mankub," see: MAE L:SL vol. 43/62, 64. n.d.; MD 7N4182/Dossier 4/340. Picot to MAE, 21 July 1920.

37. For a listing of the backgrounds of the primary and secondary leadership of the Higher National Committee of Damascus, see Gelvin, "Popular Mobilization," 125–130, 457–458.

38. Muhibb al-Din al-Khatib, "The Job of Guidance," *al-'Asima,* 16 October 1919, 1–2.

39. Foreign Office, London: FO371/5188/E7808/#42. "Arabic Press Abstracts for Week ending June 14, 1920," 26 May 1920.

40. *al-'Asima,* 23 October 1919, 1–2. It is interesting to contrast this statement with one made by Woodrow Wilson: "When I try to disentangle the ideas of the people and endeavor to express them if at first there is disaccord I am not astonished. I have firm confidence that their ideas will rally to mine." Quoted by Daniel Halevy, *President Wilson,* trans. Hugh Stokes (New York, 1919), 244.

41. Yale, "A Report on Syria," 24.

42. Sudan Archives, University of Durham: SA/493/6/51. Amin M'aluf to Ahmad Shuqayr, 1 June 1920.

43. As'ad Daghir, *Mudhakirrati 'ala hamish al-qadiya al-'arabiyya* (Cairo, 1956), 122.

44. See Tilly, Tilly, and Tilly, *The Rebellious Century,* 50–54; E. J. Hobsbawm, *Primitive Rebels: Studies in Archaic Forms of Social Movement in the 19th and 20th Centuries* (New York, 1959), 1–2, 110.

2

The "Ambassador for the Arabs": The Locke Mission and the Unmaking of U.S. Development Diplomacy in the Near East, 1952–1953

Paul W.T. Kingston

This chapter examines President Harry S. Truman's policy toward the Near East[1] during the last years of his administration.[2] It focuses on the creation, in late 1951, of a regional office based in Beirut. Its mandate was to coordinate U.S. economic policy in the region including capital assistance from the Mutual Security Program (MSP), refugee assistance channeled through the United Nations Relief and Works Administration (UNRWA; the United Nations alone will be referred to as the UN), and technical assistance from the Technical Cooperation Administration (TCA), commonly known as Point Four. Truman appointed Edwin Locke Jr., a young banker, to head the office. His official title was special assistant to the secretary of state, and he was given the rank of ambassador with direct lines of communication to the president.[3]

The "Locke mission" is interesting from several perspectives. First, it has become a forgotten episode in the history of U.S. policy in the Near East that reflects a more general scholarly neglect of U.S. policy in the region in the last years of the Truman administration. The prevailing perception is one of drift and frustration caused both by the failure to reach any political settlement to the Arab-Israeli conflict and by the parallel difficulties in pursuing an economic approach to peacemaking, symbolized by the cautious recommendations of the Economic Survey Mission (ESM) in 1949. This chapter suggests, however, that the Truman administration attempted to reinvigorate the economic approach to peacemaking in the early 1950s. As such, the Locke mission emerges as a link between the initial launching of the ESM in 1949 and the later attempts by Eric Johnston under the Eisenhower administration to resurrect the same kind of approach. Finally, the dispatching of the Locke mission also represents a concerted, if failed, attempt to promote a more regional U.S. approach to the Near East, a break from past U.S. emphases on bilateralism.

The main issue at stake here is whether an economic approach to pursuing U.S. objectives in the region was realistic. Certainly, the creation of the regional economic office and the appointment of Locke was greeted in many circles with much fanfare. The *New York Times* carried the story on its front pages;[4] the British, in part influenced by Locke's appointment, transferred their own regional economic office, the Development Division of the British Middle East Office (BMEO), to Beirut;[5] the Arab states were clearly buoyed by the prospects of a stronger U.S. economic presence in the region; and, as we shall see, the announcement won praise—and indeed had been the result of pressure—from those within the U.S. State Department who had persistently called for the application of a Marshall Plan–type policy to the region.

However, despite the promising beginning, the Locke mission ended in ignominy and, ultimately, oblivion: Locke resigned within a year of his appointment without having effected any appreciable shift in U.S. economic policy in the region, and the Beirut-based regional economic office was disbanded. After briefly examining the origins of U.S. economic diplomacy in the Near East, I set out to examine why Truman's economic approach to the Near East faltered so badly. This entails examining the relationship of the Locke mission to the three pillars of U.S. development policy in the region: technical assistance under the Point Four program, capital assistance under the Mutual Security Program, and refugee assistance channeled through UNRWA. Part of the explanation revolves around the person of Locke himself who, in persistently advocating a more pro-Arab line, emerged as an early if unlikely example of that much maligned group of State Department officials known as the "Arabists."[6] Equally important are the vague terms of reference given to Locke that merely masked fundamental conflicts in objectives among the various bureaucratic parties concerned and that served to sap the "collective will" of the Truman administration. Ultimately, however, the question must be examined not at the level of personalities nor of policy implementation but at the level of philosophical approach. Locke represents that generation of Americans who believed that the injection of U.S. finance and expertise into troubled parts of the underdeveloped world could help to create a more empathetic political environment in the short run while laying the foundations for self-sustained growth and, thus, political stability in the long run. The assumptions behind this optimistic approach have now been openly questioned. Capital and technology by themselves rarely promote development; development does not necessarily promote political stability. Nevertheless, these were the assumptions that governed policy in the early cold war and it is worth reminding ourselves how strong their hold was on policymakers and development planners.

The Origins of Truman's Economic Approach to the Near East

The roots of postwar U.S. economic diplomacy in the Near East are found in the wartime participation of the United States in the Middle East Supply Centre

(MESC). Originally created to regulate the flow of imports and exports in and out of the region so as to conserve shipping space for military purposes, the MESC ultimately became involved in promoting regional economic production. It did such a good job at this latter task that some began to consider the idea of continuing the development functions of the MESC after the war. Despite some initial and favorable consideration, the idea was ultimately rejected by the U.S. government and, at the close of the war, the MESC was immediately disbanded. The reasons were threefold. First, there was a strong desire not to continue to underwrite the British Empire in the region (which, it was felt, a regional economic approach would do). Second, there was an equally strong sense that a bilateral approach to the Near East would better serve U.S. commercial interests by allowing for the unfettered expansion of private trade and investment in the region. Finally, economic orthodoxy in the United States dictated that private investment would best promote economic development in the "undeveloped" parts of the world. Hence, initial U.S. economic policy in the Near East would be based on bilateralism with an emphasis on the private sector.

Three factors forced U.S. Near East policymakers to change these calculations: the Arab-Israeli conflict, the emerging cold war, and the rise of anti-Western Arab nationalism. The Palestine War of 1948 and the subsequent upheavals in the Arab world as a whole, for example, forced U.S. Near East policymakers to think more in regional terms. This led to the initiation of a series of Chief of Mission meetings, the first being held in Istanbul in November 1949. It also resulted in the emergence of a more favorable attitude toward Britain's regional presence, particularly the string of British military bases across the region symbolized by that at Suez and, as W. R. Louis has noted, led U.S. Near East policymakers to defer to, if not underwrite, Britain's regional security system.[7] This ultimately led to the (stillborn) joint Anglo-American proposal to create a Middle East Command (MEC) in October 1951. Finally, this new interest in regionalism was extended to the economic realm, symbolized by the dispatching of the ESM under the auspices of the UN and headed by Gordon Clapp, the former director of the Tennessee Valley Authority (TVA).

Clapp assumed his task enthusiastically and initially considered creating two organizations—one to deal exclusively with refugee relief and the other to deal more directly with economic development. The latter was, in effect, the reemergence of an earlier British proposal to create a Middle East Development Board. He was strongly supported in these views by George C. McGhee, assistant secretary of state for Near Eastern affairs; both believed in the potential of economic development to erase intractable political problems. However, the initial foray into regionalism produced few dividends. The Chief of Mission conferences did not produce a coherent regional approach but merely acted as forums for exchanging information. Moreover, Clapp dramatically scaled down his originally ambitious ideas. Instead of two organizations, the UN amalgamated relief and resettlement functions into one organization, the UNRWA. Such cautiousness was dictated by a number of factors. Clapp himself concluded in his final report that "the region is not ready, the projects are not ready [and] the people and the governments are not ready for large scale development."[8] Moreover, the British changed their tune and raised strong objections to the idea of creating a regional development organization for fear of arousing the indignation of Arab nationalists. Instead, they advocated the creation of a development board in each country.[9] Thus, we witness an interesting shift with Britain, the dying imperial power moving away from a regional policy, and the United States, an emerging imperial power looking at the potential of a regional policy in a more favorable light. The launching of the Point Four program in 1950, however, seemed to offer some consolation and, in its initial years, it became active in the independent states of the Middle East, notably Iran, Lebanon, and Jordan, where the first general agreement under Point Four was signed.

However, in 1951, there was a significant polarization of both the global and regional climate. Driven by the outbreak of the Korean War and sparked by the nationalization of the Anglo-Iranian Oil Company by Iranian Prime Minister Muhammad Mussadiq in March, the assassination of King Abdullah of Jordan in July, and the unilateral abrogation of the 1936 Anglo-Egyptian treaty by the Wafdist government in October, there was a revival of discussions about the utility of economic approaches to diplomacy. Globally, this culminated in the establishment of the MSP, the main task of which was to coordinate all overseas economic, technical, and military assistance programs. Regionally, this led first to an allocation of $160 million for the Near East from the MSP. It then resulted in a U.S.-backed decision by the UN General Assembly to strengthen the ability of UNRWA to promote refugee resettlement as well as relief by giving it an expanded budget of $250 million over three years. Finally, on the strong recommendation of McGhee, President Truman created the regional economic office in Beirut as a mechanism for coordinating all regional economic activity. With the appointment of Locke to head the office on November 13, 1951, it seemed that the regional economic approach to securing peace and stability in the Near East would finally be given a chance to work.[10]

Locke, Point Four, and Lebanon

A youthful forty-one years, Locke seemed an inspired choice to head the new regional economic office, combining both a successful career in the private and public sectors with an interest in the Middle East. His public-sector experience, acquired during and immediately after World War II, was impressive and included such positions as executive assistant to Donald Nelson, head of the War Productions Board (1943–1944), Truman's personal representative to Chang Kai-Shek in China (1945), and Truman's special assistant in the White House (1946). Locke's natural environment, however, was the private sector, where his demonstrated instinct and friendly charm eventually led to his appointment in 1946 as vice president of Chase Manhattan Bank. He used his position to generate various business opportunities in the Middle East, principally Saudi Arabia, where he entered into negotiations to build both a cement plant and, later, a Coca-Cola plant. His growing involvement in the region eventually earned him a seat on the board of governors of the American University of Beirut. Locke, therefore, was seen as exactly the kind of person who could activate an economic approach to achieving peace and security in the Near East.[11]

Locke arrived in Beirut in early December 1951. It seemed an opportune moment. After protracted negotiations over the terms of U.S. involvement in development activities,[12] the Lebanese government agreed to ratify the Point Four General Agreement in November 1951 and, with the subsequent announcement of Locke's appointment, was looking forward to a significant infusion of U.S. aid into the country. Therefore, Locke, upon his arrival, was given a very friendly and high-profile welcome, the kind befitting a potential new patron. Harold Minor, the U.S. minister in Lebanon, was clearly surprised at the receptivity of the Lebanese to the arrival of Locke—or "Saint Locke," as one leftist Lebanese paper sarcastically noted. In reaction to one of the many receptions in Locke's honor, Minor reported, "I have never in my many years in the Foreign Service attended a function more jovial and friendly. The Lebanese were simply bubbling over with enthusiasm. . . . It was something like a football rally." He went on to suggest that the Lebanese government seemed willing to cooperate with Locke to a degree that "we had hardly dared hope for."[13] Certainly, Locke would turn out to be a darling of Beirut society, hosting numerous dinner parties and, on several occasions, being the personal guest of President Faris al-Khuri at his mountain home. This was the kind of access to the top echelons of power in Lebanon that U.S. representatives had hitherto not known.

From the outset, Locke seemed determined to take advantage of this favorable atmosphere. Having arrived in Beirut only the day before, Locke immediately wrote to his contact in the State Department, Arthur Gardiner, suggesting that a significant expansion of the development program for the Arab states would be needed if his mission was to be a success.[14] Within a week, Locke was also transmitting these ideas directly to Truman, bypassing the State Department and TCA. This was to become a feature of the Locke mission and it revealed the degree to which he perceived (and, as it turned out, misperceived) that he could count on Truman's personal support. Nevertheless, this letter is important, for it sets the tone for his entire mission. The main thing, wrote Locke, is that "a lot more life needs to be put into our aid programs here and in the other Middle Eastern countries." Not only were there "too many plans and too little action" (a complaint heard universally among the recipient governments in the region), but those plans that were being made operational under the Point Four program were making no significant impact economically or psychologically. This, above all, was Locke's self-appointed agenda, "to get these people [the Arabs] thinking in positives rather than negatives." In a classic espousal of the economic approach to peacemaking, Locke emphasized that "if we can get them started in an important way on developing the very attractive natural resources that they have, I believe that the political problems will suddenly become much less difficult to solve."[15]

Locke was looking for impact projects to fulfill his Near East mandate and, in Lebanon, there seemed one ready at hand: the Litani River project. Lebanon had been one of the first countries to receive assistance from Point Four even before a general agreement had been signed. It was in the form of a survey mission for the Litani River basin and was initiated by the first director of Point Four, Dr. Henry Bennett, upon his inaugural tour of the Middle East as a way of getting activity off the ground for the newly established TCA. Six months later, however, rumblings were surfacing in the Lebanese press about the lack of immediate, concrete results, and there was further fear that the project would be geared to the interests of private Lebanese citizens and, perhaps, Israel. The result was what one report referred to as "a vigorous campaign" in the Lebanese press against Point Four's association with the Litani River project.[16] Although one of Locke's first public actions was to issue a statement deflecting such criticisms, in fact he looked upon them as valid.[17] According to Locke, U.S. involvement in the Litani River project, based as it was on technical assistance, was ill-designed to obtain quick results. Nor was it likely to solicit anything more than "polite unenthusiastic foot-dragging cooperation from [the] Lebanese."[18] Needed was a more significant infusion of development capital, and this was precisely what Lebanon could not provide. Its public finances were insufficient to keep up with the demands for development projects and, even where capital was available, it was tremendously difficult to achieve any kind of political consensus over its use. Nor did the kind of private investment needed for large projects seem to be forthcoming, as demonstrated by the failure of the Syrian government to raise capital for the development of the port at Latakia through the sale of public bonds. In Locke's opinion, an infusion of U.S. development capital would solve both of these problems; it would provide a "take-off" point for sustained economic growth and improve the climate for private investment. All of this would, in turn, lay the psychological foundations for a more solid political alliance.

However, not all U.S. representatives in Lebanon were delighted with the rather spectacular arrival of Locke in Beirut and his promise of a dramatic expansion of U.S. aid to the Middle East. The bulk of this opposition emanated from Lebanon's Point Four team, whose program Locke was pledging to aggrandize. Part of the problem stemmed from confusion over the exact nature of Locke's mandate. When the regional economic office was first created, the local field offices of Point Four were assured that Locke's mandate would not allow him to interfere in the specific work of country programs or to supersede the authority of local country directors. Whether such a distinction could work in practice was problematic; the British certainly had had their share of administrative problems in launching the regionally based BMEO in 1945.[19] By choosing Beirut as Locke's headquarters and by sending him out at a time when the local Point Four office was without Country Director Hollis Peter, Washington seemed to be asking for problems.[20]

They did not take long to appear. Less than a month after Locke's arrival, one member of Lebanon's Point Four staff, Richard Farnsworth, complained in a personal letter to Peter that their operations in Lebanon had been taken over "Locke, stock, and barrel," so much so that the Lebanese government was beginning to submit project requests to Locke's office directly.[21] Well over a month later, Point Four's staff in Lebanon continued to complain about "the Locke concept": "[He] is still 'Mr. TCA' in Lebanon," wrote U.S. official William Crockett, "and I am afraid will remain so as long as he stays in Lebanon."[22] When Peter finally arrived in Beirut at the end of March, he was forced to spend much of his time clarifying the actual extent of Locke's authority to the rather confused Lebanese—and to Locke himself.[23]

Had the confusion been merely administrative, little harm would have been done to basic U.S. policy in the country. However, the real conflict in Beirut revolved around fundamental policy issues—issues that had never been satisfactorily resolved as a result of the amalgamation of Point Four with the MSP in May 1951. Point Four's approach, epitomized by the views of its founding administrator, Dr. Bennett, and shared by most in the field, was based on the idea that development would only come by building up human capital at the grass-roots level. This required a long range development policy based on the provision of technical assistance in such areas as education, health, and agriculture. Moreover, those results had to be part of a cooperative effort, one in which the local government made significant contributions of both finance and manpower. The concern here, of course, was with the long-term sustainability of projects. Those more politically minded in the State Department, however, had little time for an approach to development policy that ignored short-term political imperatives. George McGhee, who in many ways had masterminded the economic approach to peacemaking between the Arabs and the Israelis by first suggesting the formation of the ESM, was clearly unimpressed with the scope and philosophy of the Point Four program as it emerged in its severely reduced form in 1950;[24] Dean Acheson, secretary of state at the time, referred to Point Four in retrospect as "the Cinderella of the foreign aid family."[25]

The emergence of Locke, ostensibly an ambassador for the Point Four program yet an emissary whose ideas turned out to be much at odds with its philosophy, brought this latent conflict over U.S. development policy to the surface. At a meeting in Washington, D.C., between representatives of Point Four and those from the Near East Division of the State Department to discuss Locke's request for an infusion of financial aid into the Litani River project, the two parties found themselves unable to reach any consensus. Whereas the latter argued strongly for Locke's proposal on the basis that the overriding need was to get some large and visible project under way in one of the Arab states, Point Four staff continued to object on the basis that "the principle of picking up the check on partially completed projects was a basic departure from TCA philosophy and policy."[26] After several conversations with Locke upon his return to Beirut, Peter revealed much the same story: "It is quite clear that Ed Locke and I do not see eye to eye on the points of major importance in the Aid Program to Lebanon. I believe he listened politely at my expounding the Point Four philosophy which we feel must be an integral part of each project . . . while he believes there is a real distinction to be made between pure technical assistance on the one hand and economic or financial grant aid on the other."[27]

Peter was further concerned by Locke's propensity to project his ideas about U.S. development policy in the region in an official manner in meetings with Lebanese

officials. Fouad Ammoun, Lebanese director-general of foreign affairs, even suggested that Locke had virtually promised them increased amounts of aid, $5 million
in fiscal year 1952 and $10 million in fiscal year 1953.[28] This was not only a break
in diplomatic protocol, not to speak of constitutional procedure, but it also threatened the viability of the existing Point Four program in the country. The basic
dilemma, of course, was that if the Lebanese were led to believe that a large infusion
of U.S. capital was imminent, they would be less interested in making the kind of
small-scale commitments of local finance that were so important to all Point Four
projects. Indeed, this seemed to be the case: At one point in the protracted negotiations over the terms of a Point Four agreement for the almost completed fiscal year
1952, Fouad Ammoun admitted that the Lebanese had not acted more quickly because they were waiting to see what Locke could produce.[29] This also explained, in
Peter's opinion, the rather cavalier attitude taken by the Lebanese toward the visit of
the World Bank's regional representative, Dorsey Stephens.[30] The dilemma, as U.S.
official Victor Skiles stated, was that "[if] U.S. aid is to be accepted not as a cooperative endeavor but as a substitute for local financing . . . we will have failed miserably in the total effort."[31]

Not all disagreed with Locke's ideas, notably Afif Tannous, an agriculturalist of
Lebanese origin based with the Point Four team in Beirut. He was understandably
delighted to be part of an expanded development assistance program for his mother
country. This, however, made the matter potentially more dangerous by creating divisions within the U.S. diplomatic community in the country. For the time being,
Minor and Peter worked to maintain a facade of diplomatic unity in order to avoid
unduly embarrassing Locke or damaging the prestige of his newly established position. Peter stressed, however, that this was being done at the cost of giving the impression of Point Four staff support for Locke's ideas, which was not always the
case.[32] Peter, therefore, warned Washington that Locke's presence in Beirut could
jeopardize his own ability to fulfill Point Four's mandate in the country. He wrote:
"I do not believe it is too late to obtain the cooperation and enthusiastic support of
the Lebanese Government officials for a real Point Four program, but it is hard for
them to concentrate on this aspect which requires considerable understanding and
foresightedness with the promise of large sums dangling in front of their noses."[33]

Locke and Regional Development in the Near East

Locke's actions in Lebanon during the early stages of his mission cannot be understood without placing them in the broader context of the Near East as a whole.
Locke's mandate, after all, was a regional one and would require a regional solution.
Here, Locke's diagnosis was similar to that made in Lebanon. What he found was
an economic assistance program badly structured to meet the needs of the Near East.
U.S. assistance under the Point Four program was judged to be slow and insufficient
by Arab governments—a "broken reed" as one Jordanian official remarked. This was
particularly so in contrast to the large sums of capital assistance being provided by

the United States to Israel, a point that Locke was constantly reminded of during travels to various Arab capitals. Moreover, though the United States was providing capital assistance to UNRWA, the funds were going largely unused due to the reluctance of Arab states to accept anything that smacked of the principle of reintegration. Acceptance of UNRWA assistance for refugee resettlement was looked upon as tantamount to abandoning the rights of the refugees to return to their homes. The result was an aid program ill-equipped to solve the kind of political problems in the region for which it was ultimately designed. It was these political problems that underlay all of Locke's thinking on the matter. As he wrote in a memorandum to Truman: "I feel that I must say frankly to you that our entire economic effort to help the Near East achieve a more secure freedom, a lasting peace and a rising standard of living is in danger of being overwhelmed by political turmoil."[34]

Locke's sense of urgency was further accentuated by the tight legislative schedule in Washington. Before Locke scarcely had his feet on the ground in Beirut, the State Department was already drawing up its proposed budget for the MSP for fiscal year 1953. By mid-February, it had released its initial estimates, which showed little change in the size or distribution of aid to the Near East. Having staked the success of his mission on the need for an increased allocation to the region, Locke once again bypassed the State Department and cabled directly to Truman, expressing his utmost concern at what he saw as the continued drift of U.S. policy in the region: "If we do not (rpt [repeat] not) now (rpt now) make it clear to the Arab states that we mean what we have been saying these past three years about wanting to help them develop their countries, I am mortally afraid we will have lost our last chance and that the reaction to this . . . program will be bitter and sharp, and the inclination to look for other friends greatly increased."[35]

Locke's recommendation to Truman was the establishment of a $100 million Arab development fund designed to provide capital assistance to the Arab states, especially the non-oil states of Lebanon, Syria, Jordan, and Egypt. This would, in effect, add a fourth stream to U.S. development policy in the region, separate and distinct from already existing programs to Israel, UNRWA, and Point Four. The purpose of the fund was to finance the completion of several impact projects in the fields of transportation and/or river development, placing special emphasis on the former as a result of Locke's experiences in China.[36] In all, he presented nine possible projects.[37] In an attempt to make his proposal more palatable to Congress, Locke presented it up as a "one-shot" deal that would pave the way for the greater involvement of the World Bank and private capital.

There had been numerous criticisms made of U.S. development policy in the region, but never had a call for change come so explicitly and forcefully and never from such high levels of government. In effect, Locke was calling for not only a break with the traditional approach to development as advocated by Point Four, but also a significant shift in U.S. policy toward the Arab world. Aid was to be raised to a level on par with that given to Israel, and it was to be given on an unconditional basis, free from linkages with the Arab refugee issue. On this last point, Locke was especially insistent:

"If we try bargain for pol[itical] and military advantages as direct quid pro quo, believe results w[ou]ld be nil and our whole position considerably weakened. . . . Realize this entails certain risks but consider it infinitely less than contains as at present."[38] In short, Locke's proposal was a genuine attempt at instituting an economic approach to peacemaking in the Arab world. It advocated a separation of the economic from the political in a way that U.S. contributions to UNRWA could not.

Locke faced serious obstacles in effecting such a significant shift in U.S. policy in the region. The dissenting views of many Point Four officials have already been mentioned; no doubt, these were joined by opposition from those wary of undermining U.S. support for Israel. However, the most immediate obstacle was time—a problem not helped by Locke's sudden illness in Beirut in mid-February, which forced him to delay a trip to Washington designed to allow him to make his case before the State Department and, if necessary, Congress. By the time Locke returned to Washington at the end of March, the bill to extend the MSP, which made no provision for the kind of program advocated by Locke, had reached an advanced stage in its presentation to Congress.[39]

To compensate for his absence, Locke tried several methods to build support for his proposal. In mid-March, Donald Bergus, then second secretary in the Lebanese legation, was sent to Washington to lobby the State Department. This was accompanied by a flurry of supportive telegrams from U.S. officials in Lebanon and Syria, the latter seeing in Locke's plan an opportunity to break the impasse over the introduction of Point Four into the country.[40] As was mentioned earlier, Locke also took the unorthodox step of building up an Arab constituency for his ideas by officially informing the president and prime minister of Lebanon of his proposal to increase U.S. assistance to the Arab world, much to the horror of Peter.[41] It seems apparent, however, that Locke was really counting on the personal support of Truman. "I beg of you," wrote Locke after falling ill in Beirut, "to give this every consideration. I stake on this proposal such reputation as I may have and feel that it is the only way to get the results I know you want me to get out here."[42]

Truman did not provide the kind of hands-on support Locke was looking for. Although he expressed appreciation for Locke's imaginative approach, Truman passed the buck, so to speak, by referring Locke's request back to the State Department, where it ran aground over conflicting policy interests.[43] In Bergus's initial meeting with officials from the MSP, for example, objections were raised on the grounds that unconditional aid would set dangerous precedents and would probably militate against promoting the kinds of reforms that the United States felt were needed.[44] Averell Harriman, the director for mutual security under the auspices of the MSP, later raised these same issues in a memo to Secretary of State Acheson.[45] In short, the kinds of objections raised by the Point Four team in Beirut seem to have carried much weight in Washington.

Neither did there seem to be a great deal of respect for Locke's political analysis. Crucial to Locke's argument was his oft-repeated view that the political situation in the Near East was "precarious" and "threatening," requiring immediate action. But, to paraphrase Harriman's query, was it so serious as to require amendments to the mutual security bill in such a way that might jeopardize the entire program put forward?[46] There were similar questions raised about whether increased aid to the Arab states would, in fact, improve matters. One memo described Locke's aim of winning the friendship of the Arab world as "an endless task" that did not provide a basis for formulating programs of an extraordinary character.[47] There was particularly strong objection to his idea of divorcing development from the Palestinian refugee issue. In response to one compromise suggestion that Locke's program of capital assistance be confined to Syria as a way of breaking the impasse in relations with that country, Reeseman Fryer, a Point Four official, responded that: "To offer Syria an unconditional development program much greater in magnitude, different in organizational structure and purpose from the programs now getting underway in Lebanon, Jordan, Egypt and Iraq would tend to undermine Point 4 programs in the latter countries by appearing to pay a premium for non-cooperation—'It pays to hold out.'"[48] The only way a program of expanded assistance could be justified, wrote Fryer, was if it was paralleled by an appropriate concession on the part of the Syrian government—one that would have to revolve around the issue of refugee settlement.[49] In short, unconditional economic assistance to the Arab world was out of the question.

Thus, Locke's proposal never did see the light of day. Ostensibly it was rejected on the grounds that its passage through Congress would prove an impossibility;[50] in reality, the Truman administration was not inclined to consider any dramatic changes in its policy toward the Near East. Truman may have wanted "action" in the Near East, but he was not willing to become actively involved himself in promoting such changes. With Locke's proposal also threatening the viability of Point Four's operations in the Near East—it had already shown signs of doing just that in Lebanon—without offering any immediate solution to the Palestinian refugee issue, he was also unable to muster much support within the appropriate bureaucratic circles in Washington. Locke, in short, must have been a rather isolated figure upon his return to Washington, a far cry from his more heady days as Truman's special representative to China and, subsequently, the White House itself. It is this sense of isolation and inertia in Washington policy circles that would eventually lead to Locke's unmaking as a representative of U.S. policy in the Near East.

Locke, the Arab Refugees, and UNRWA

After the proposal to create an Arab Development Fund was shelved, Locke was kept in Washington for an additional month. Part of the reason for Locke's delayed return was to ensure that he did not go back to Beirut completely empty-handed. Due to his own indiscretions, there was a high sense of expectation in such Arab states as Syria and Lebanon of a possible shift in U.S. development policy. This led to the creation of a smaller $25 million fund aimed at financing more moderately demanding projects, which Locke was to draw up in cooperation with the local Point Four country directors. However, the principle reason for delaying Locke in Washington was to brief him more thoroughly on the goals and procedures of both the State Department and his mission. This meant clarifying Locke's role within the Point Four program, a task that met with some success, if Peter's subsequent comments are any guide.[51] Even more fundamental to U.S. interests in the region, however, was the need to make UNRWA more effective. Locke had been appointed as the U.S. representative on the Advisory Commission of UNRWA in late February but had been unable to take up his duties with any seriousness due to his illness and subsequent return to Washington. Since State Department policy now held that a capital aid program for the Arab states only be considered if and when the considerable resources of UNRWA, of which 70 percent came from the United States, were fully utilized, Locke was now instructed to help make that U.S. contribution an effective one.[52] Thus, upon returning to Beirut, Locke's mandate had been clarified: much reduced involvement in the Point Four program and much enhanced involvement in UNRWA.

Locke's appointment to the Advisory Commission of UNRWA came at a propitious moment in its history. In January, the UN General Assembly, including its Arab members, had approved a three-year, $250 million reintegration program designed to remove the refugees from their dependence on international relief. The agreement of the Arab states to this program had been obtained on the theory that settlement and integration would not interfere with the legal rights of the refugees to repatriation and compensation. In the Arab world, it became known as the "Blandford Plan," after John Blandford, the U.S. director of UNRWA, who was a former manager of the TVA. Following the vote, Blandford became involved in a series of bilateral negotiations on specific refugee settlement projects with the Arab states.

Despite Locke's fundamental objection to using UNRWA as a channel for U.S. development (as opposed to relief assistance to the Arab world), he did take an active part in its affairs. Upon his return from Washington, Locke began a series of visits to refugee camps in order to get a firsthand view of actual camp conditions. He would often visit the camps unannounced, meet with refugee leaders, listen to their grievances, and receive their petitions. What he found appalled him: inadequate health and educational facilities, a lack of employment opportunities, complaints about reductions in rations, and particularly vitriolic rhetoric reserved for the West in general and for the "dictator" of UNRWA, Blandford.[53] What was interesting about these trips was Locke's tendency to distance himself from past U.S. policy in the region and to set himself up more as a spokesman for the refugees. After a meeting with refugee leaders in Beirut during early autumn, for example, Locke held a news conference and declared the refugee situation "more serious now than it has ever been" and intimated that he would push for a change in U.S. policy toward these "forgotten people."[54] So delighted were the refugees with this newfound and high-level U.S. advocate that one refugee leader described him as the "Ambassador for the Arabs."[55] It was this image—the public champion of the refugees—that Locke brought to the meetings of the Advisory Commission of UNRWA.

One of the most immediate and acute problems facing UNRWA upon Locke's return was the widening disparity between the growing number of refugees, on the one hand, and the shrinking resources available for relief on the other. Although the Blandford Plan had pledged $50 million for relief, much of that had been earmarked for the first year of the program with the hope that the reintegration program, for which there was $200 million, would increasingly be able to pay the bills in subsequent years. In the absence of any concrete agreements on reintegration projects, however, UNRWA very quickly began to face a financial crisis. Less than eight months after the passage of the program, the estimates for the relief budget for fiscal year 1953 had already been raised from $18 million to $23 million, a figure even Locke felt was optimistic.[56]

In Locke's opinion, one of the reasons for this budgetary crisis was the undisciplined and profligate manner in which UNRWA spent money. To correct the situation, Locke launched within the Advisory Commission a campaign for greater fiscal austerity. Initially, Locke raised the idea of cutting refugee rations, though he avoided making any personal or governmental commitments and eventually backed away from the suggestion for political reasons.[57] A more concerted effort was made to improve the administrative efficiency of the agency. Locke was astounded, for example, that at a time when UNRWA was trying to reduce the financial allocations for relief, the number of staff on its payroll was increasing out of all proportions.[58] There were similar problems with the procurement operations, which Locke described as amateurish and amazingly soft, particularly when it came to the negotiation of prices for wheat purchases from local governments.[59] There was also talk of corruption within UNRWA itself—of supplies like wheat and medicine being sold privately on the open market.[60] To investigate these problems, Locke successfully put pressure on Blandford to hire an outside auditing firm to examine UNRWA's supply division. Although no corruption was actually uncovered, the report revealed, in Locke's words, a situation "even less satisfactory than I had imagined."[61]

The real issue facing UNRWA, however, was how to push forward with the reintegration program, so crucial in solving UNRWA's budgetary problems let alone in improving the plight of the growing number of refugees. Here, the signals were mixed. Jordan had proved reasonably cooperative over plans to finance dam construction and irrigation development on the Yarmuk River. Originally drawn up by a Point Four engineer, Miles Bunger, the Yarmuk–Jordan River scheme was subsequently adopted by UNRWA, which allocated an initial $10 million from the reintegration fund. Negotiations with the Syrian government were slower, but, in the beginning of October they, too, had resulted in a $30 million reintegration agreement.

However, the difficulty of implementing these agreements was quickly apparent, the Syrian agreement being a case in point. Despite his numerous trips to Damascus to meet with Syrian President Adib al-Shishakli—a "stalky little guy" with whom he professed to get on "beautifully"[62]—Locke was never very optimistic about the prospect of significant progress in refugee settlement there. Even after the initial talks between the Syrian chief of state, Colonel Fawzi Selu, and Blandford in February 1952—which some thought was an encouraging start—Locke's summary of the discussions led him to a much different conclusion: "1. [Selu] didn't think the amount of aid in Blandford's Plan was sufficient and moreover felt the Agency should pay for any land it wanted; 2. He was more interested in industrial than agricultural development—he feels the West is turning the Middle East into a great farm; 3. He is worried about competition for jobs between Syrian nationals and Palestinian refugees . . . If that's progress, I'm the son of a donkey."[63] The substance of the $30 million agreement with Syria in October bore out this initial skepticism. By the end of November, only one project was actually underway—the conversion of a rundown army barracks southwest of Homs into an orphanage; it was expected, at a cost of $100,000, to remove, at most, 200 refugees from the relief rolls. All of the additional agricultural projects under consideration were hampered by the marginality of the land being offered.[64] Debates over the technical and political feasibility of the proposed Yarmouk scheme were causing similar delays in Jordan.

The frustrations over this halting progress spilled over into meetings of the Advisory Commission and were symbolized by the deteriorating relations between Locke and Blandford, the two most prominent Americans involved in UNRWA. There were a variety of issues over which the two locked horns. The conflict over budgetary practices within UNRWA has already been mentioned. This was accompanied by a series of backstabbing exchanges over Blandford's decision to replace UNRWA's U.S. representative in Amman with a former British military officer. Locke, who was somewhat suspicious of British policy in the region, wanted to see Americans in key positions in UNRWA, both to improve its efficiency and to take advantage of any good press, particularly in Jordan, where the most promising program existed.[65] Locke and Blandford also squared off over whether Arab members should be accepted on the Advisory Commission; Blandford eventually succumbed to Locke's strong advocacy of this issue when it received the support of the State Department.[66]

The most substantial dispute between the two concerned UNRWA's approach to the resettlement issue. Locke was critical of Blandford's desire for political agreement before planning the specifics of any resettlement program, an approach that had led to delays in building up the technical arm of UNRWA. In Locke's opinion, this had left UNRWA an "empty shell" and unable to draw up, let alone execute, the kind of reintegration projects that would ultimately attract the cooperation of Arab governments. The result was "a lot of talk and a lot of running around," but no action.[67] Locke felt that by strengthening UNRWA's technical side Blandford would be able to negotiate on a much more compelling, project-by-project basis. It was a position often forwarded by Syrian officials in their negotiations with UNRWA.[68] Thus, he pushed Blandford repeatedly in meetings of the Advisory Commission to hire more technicians who could proceed with the immediate job at hand. Faced with Blandford's persistent opposition, however, Locke reverted to his initial lack of optimism about the prospects for UNRWA's success. The extent of his disillusionment was revealed by comments made in a letter to Truman at the end of September:

UNRWA . . . is doing a pretty awful job and getting practically nowhere. What meat it would be for a new Truman committee—inefficiency on a broad scale, overstaffing and complete lack of results. The frame of mind of the refugees, now in their fifth year of homelessness, is becoming increasingly desperate. I have come to the firm conclusion that UNRWA is not the answer. No one believes in it anymore, especially in the Near East and least of all the refugees themselves.[69]

"Locke Hits Out at U.S. Aid Policy"

Where was Locke to go from here? (The headline that serves as the title for this section portends his fate.) Although he had been sent to the Near East to activate policy, he had no confidence in the tools at his disposal. He had discarded UNRWA as a viable mechanism for U.S. development policy in the Near East. Neither was he impressed with the potential of the Point Four program to make a noticeable political impact. It was true that the State Department had agreed to the establishment of a $25 million capital investment program for the Near East. However, when Locke convened a meeting of regional TCA country directors in late August to draw up a plan of action, he was extremely unimpressed with the nature and quality of the project proposals, especially those from the Lebanese group, whom Locke described as less than cooperative.[70] Moreover, as the following remarks to Truman indicate, Locke had become increasingly impatient with the "indecisive" State Department: "That organization, as I found out by personal experience last spring, has fallen into the way of doing things by committee and by unanimous vote which means that new ideas are under severe and sometimes almost insuperable handicap."[71] No doubt, this growing antagonism was fueled by rumors that the State Department's recall of Locke was imminent.[72]

These growing frustrations coincided with the marked deterioration of the Near East political climate in the autumn of 1952. Revolution in Egypt, a change of government in Lebanon, continued drift in Jordan, and the uncertainty of the political situation in Syria: All were factors pushing local Arab leaders into championing a more radical anti-Western stance, particularly in regard to the Arab-Israeli conflict and the refugee problem. The opening of the UN General Assembly in the autumn of 1952 provided the Arab states with a diplomatic forum where they could voice their criticisms. The net result was, in Locke's words, an "explosive situation," with the Arab states "feeling their oats," the Israelis becoming more "restive," and the Russians making continuous and discreet advances.[73]

Locke's response to this growing sense of crisis was to revive his old proposal for the creation of an Arab development fund. It was his hope that the deteriorating political situation might now induce Truman to give it personal endorsement.[74] However, with Eisenhower's victory in November and the emergence of a new sense of expectancy in the Arab world about an impending realignment of U.S. policy in the region, Locke changed his tactics. Eisenhower was looked upon as having fewer ties with Israel and as being more conscious of the benefits of closer ties to the Arab states. In order to create some bureaucratic momentum for a policy shift, some diplomats began to advocate a formal reevaluation of U.S. policy in the region.[75]

Locke approved of this campaign but saw little hope of its success using normal diplomatic channels. Having first come out to the Near East with the hope of making a psychological impact on Arab public opinion, Locke now reversed his target and sought to make an impact on U.S. public opinion. At the beginning of December, he gave three interviews with a U.S. reporter, all of which appeared in the Beirut newspaper, the *Daily Star,* the second under the byline, "Locke Hits Out at U.S. Aid Policy."[76] He then gave a talk at the influential Lebanese policy institute, le Cenacle Libanais, on December 6, calling for the formulation of a "new and hard-hitting policy" in the Near East based on the creation of a U.S.-financed Arab development fund that could push ahead with such vital projects as the development of the Euphrates River and the Yarmuk Plan. In effect, it was a rehashed version of the proposal that he had presented to Truman six months earlier.[77]

The reactions to Locke's outbursts were swift and predictable. In Amman, Green, who on the whole was supportive of the kind of approach being suggested by Locke, was taken aback by his public attacks on U.S. policy;[78] in Beirut, Minor was equally shocked at Locke's public policymaking and warned that "I can only see harm in this";[79] and in Washington, those who had become increasingly concerned about the adverse effects that Locke's appointment was having on U.S. policy in the region finally had their excuse for action. One day after his talk at le Cenacle Libanais, Locke was called back, "for consultations" in Washington; one week later he resigned. Thus, less than one year after his high-profile return to public service, Locke was on his way back to the private sector.

What is interesting about "the Locke affair," as it was called for a short time in Beirut, was the reaction it received in parts of the Arab world. When Locke took his criticisms of U.S. development policy public, the Lebanese press responded with support and praise: "The Arab world can only be grateful for such men as Locke who have . . . seen the flow of American policy and have spoken out," read one editorial in the *Daily Star;*[80] "wise and righteous," read another, containing an added hope that Locke would now be free to continue his campaign unshackled by diplomatic protocol.[81] Moreover, when Locke returned to Beirut at the end of December to finalize his affairs, he was given a hero's welcome. The Syrian government hosted a dinner in his honor in Damascus, and the Lebanese government awarded him the Order of the Cedars, the highest honor of state. Clearly, by publicly championing the Arab cause within the Truman administration, Locke had won himself a secure if fleeting spot in Arab history texts. As Peter summed it up, "There can be no question now . . . that he is the man of the hour—the white hope of the Arabs who is assumed to have spoken out on the basis of his convictions."[82]

The affair has since become a forgotten episode in the history of U.S. policy in the region. This may seem somewhat surprising, given Locke's penchant for publicity even after his return to the United States.[83] Moreover, Locke's recommendations were not without support in U.S. policy circles; their roots went back to George McGhee, Gordon Clapp, and the ESM. Nevertheless, history has probably been an accurate judge of the significance of the Locke mission. To start with, even if Locke's ideas did strike a sensitive vein within the State Department, his tactics left much to be desired and lost him the respect of all those who might have lent him support. Moreover, his call for unconditional aid to the Arab states, friend or foe, would never have carried much weight, especially in the context of an intensifying cold war that stressed the importance of helping one's allies. Perhaps the most important reason for the disappearance of the Locke mission from history was its complete overshadowing by the incoming Eisenhower administration, rumored to be interested in pursuing a more evenhanded regional policy. In that sense, Locke found himself all of a sudden swimming with the tide rather than against it.

However, though the Eisenhower administration did make efforts to improve relations between the United States and the Arab world, it never considered the kind of changes to U.S. development policy in the Near East that Locke had hoped to see. The United States did continue to channel its assistance through UNRWA, though with the resignation of Blandford in early 1953 the grandiose settlement plans gradually gave way to the reality of day-to-day relief operations. Moreover, though Point Four did begin to consolidate its presence in the region, it never did receive the kind of capital resources that Locke felt were needed. Finally, by insisting on regional linkages and prior political agreements, the Eisenhower administration, despite the diplomatic efforts of Eric Johnston, was never able to activate the kind of "impact project" approach to development advocated by Locke. In short, what was labeled as "an economic approach" to peacemaking in the Near East has always been burdened with explicit political baggage.

This raises a more general question, one that is ultimately relevant to an evaluation of the Locke mission. Would the kind of more strictly economic approach advocated by Locke have been any more effective? Certainly, the Arab states were calling for it and, in that sense, Locke was really acting as a conduit for Arab views. However, whereas what was called the "ECA approach" may have worked in the context of the developed states of Europe (a debatable point at best), its application in the developing world has proven more problematic. It has taken theorists and practitioners of development many years to realize that modernization was not simply a linear process dependent on the infusion of technology and capital. The development process has been complicated by a whole series of structural and cultural factors, ones that are consistently ignored in the context of aid policies such as those suggested by Locke. These complicating factors have been particularly salient in the Middle East, plagued as it has been by the Arab-Israeli conflict, the extraordinarily high degree of regional interaction, and the superimposition upon them of the cold war. Locke, by so exclusively placing his hopes for an improved relationship between the Arab world and the United States on the provision of more U.S. finance and technology, essentially ignored all of these factors. Thus, although more pro-Arab on the surface, his proposal can in fact be criticized for its insensitivity to the details of Arab politics—a common criticism of U.S. policy in general in the Middle East in the 1950s. Whether linked or unconditional, greater amounts of capital assistance would not have been the decisive factor in winning Arab friendship, nor would they have effected any dramatic and broad-based economic take-off. It might have improved the lives of a few peasants, provided work for a few Arab bureaucrats and technicians, and even settled a few Palestinian refugees—all very laudable on human grounds. However, it could not have effected the kind of broad structural changes in the region that were at the root of its instability. These were simply beyond the scope of U.S. power.

Notes

I would like to thank Myriam Noisette and David Wesl for commenting on earlier drafts of this chapter. Needless to say, all errors of judgment and interpretation are my responsibility. I would also like to thank the Connaught Fund at the University of Toronto for generously funding this research and the National Archives in Washington, D.C., and the Truman Library in Independence, Missouri, for facilitating it.

1. For definition's sake, the term "Near East" is used to refer to the Levant states of Syria, Lebanon, Jordan, Israel, and also Egypt.

2. Truman succeeded the presidency upon Franklin D. Roosevelt's death in April 1945. Elected outright in 1948, Truman served out one full one term; Republican Dwight D. Eisenhower took office in 1953 by defeating Adlai Stevenson in the 1952 presidential election.

3. For background on Truman's policy toward the Middle East in the last years of his administration, see H. Fields, "Pawns of Empire: A Study of United States Middle East Policy, 1945–53," Ph.D. diss., Rutgers University, 1975; J. Hurewitz, *Middle East Dilemmas* (New York: 1953); M. Kolinsky, "The Efforts of the Truman Administration to Resolve the Arab-Israeli Conflict," *Middle East Studies* 20(1) (January 1984); and I. Pappe, *Britain and the Arab-Israeli Conflict, 1948–51* (Basingstoke: 1988).

4. *New York Times,* 14 November 1951.

5. Cf. Parker to Hare, "Transfer of the British Middle East Office from Cairo," 29 December 1951, Lot 57D/298, Near East (hereinafter NE) Files, National Archives (hereinafter NA). In fact, Bill Crawford, the head of the Development Division, responded enthusiastically to Locke's appointment, describing him as "one of the brightest guys to hit this part of the world." Crawford to Evans, 23 January, 1952, Foreign Office (hereinafter FO) 371/98276/E11345/5.

6. Cf. R. Kaplan, *The Arabists: The Romance of an American Elite* (New York: 1993), for a recent journalistic account.

7. Cf. W.R.L. Louis, *The British Empire in the Middle East: Arab Nationalism, the United States, and Postwar Imperialism* (Oxford: 1984).

8. Cf. United Nations Conciliation Commission for Palestine, *Final Report of the United Nations Economic Survey Mission for the Middle East* (Lake Success, N.Y.: 1949).

9. Cf. Laborne to Clapp, 6 October 1949, Morton to Clapp, 8 November 1949, Clapp to Morton, 11 November 1949, Morton to Clapp, 2 December 1949, and Keeley to Clapp, 17 March 1950, all contained in Papers of Gordon Clapp, Box 3, United Nations Economic Survey Mission (hereinafter UNESM), Harry S. Truman Library (hereinafter HSTL).

10. For details on the events leading up to Locke's appointment, see "Oral History Interview with Edwin Locke Jr." and "Oral History Interview with George McGhee," HSTL.

11. Edwin Locke Jr., interview by author, 7 February 1994.

12. In 1951, Syria and Yemen had still not signed Point Four agreements. Cf. Pinkerton to U.S. Department of State, "Point IV Agreement with Lebanon," 883A.00-TA/2-2851, and

Geren to U.S. Department of State, "Why a Point IV Agreement has not been concluded with Syria," NA 883.00TA/5/28/51.

13. Minor memo, 9 January 1952, Papers of Edwin Locke Jr., Box 4, HSTL.

14. Locke to Gardiner, 21 December 1951, ibid.

15. Locke to Truman, 26 December 1951, ibid.

16. Cf. "Campaign Against Point IV Litani River Project," Beirut to U.S. Department of State, 883A.00-TA/1-752.

17. Cf. "Statement by Ambassador Edwin Locke Jr.," 23 December 1951, Papers of Edwin Locke Jr., Box 4, HSTL.

18. Locke to U.S. Secretary of State, 883A.00-TA/1-3152.

19. Cf. P. Kingston, "Pioneers in Development: The British Middle East Development Division and the Politics of Technical Assistance, 1945–1960," D.Phil. diss., Oxford University, 1991.

20. Cf. Staff Memorandum, U.S. Department of State, "Responsibilities of Ambassador Locke in the Near East," 12 May 1952, Lot 57D/298, NE Files, for details on the policy discussions surrounding the creation of the regional office.

21. Farnsworth to Peter, 16 January 1952, Record Group (hereinafter RG) 84, Lebanon, Classified General Records, Box 28, NA Records Administration (NARA).

22. Crockett to Skiles, 29 February 1952, RG 84, Lebanon, Classified General Records, Box 28, NARA.

23. Peter to Reeseman Fryer, 1 April 1952, RG 84, Lebanon, Classified General Records, Box 28, NARA.

24. Cf. Oral History Interview with George McGhee, p. 44, HSTL.

25. Cf. D. Acheson, *Present at the Creation: My Years in the State Department* (New York: 1969).

26. Cf. Memo of Conversation, "Telegrams from Amb. Locke Proposing the U.S. Complete the Markabi, Kasmie, and Taibe Projects for Lebanon," 883A.00-TA/2-1352.

27. Peter to Reeseman Fryer, 1 April 1952, RG 84 Lebanon, Classified General Records, Box 28, NARA.

28. Cf. "Negotiation of Point 4 Program Agreement in Lebanon," 883A.00-TA/4-2452.

29. Cf. ibid.

30. Peter to Reeseman Fryer, 7 June 1952, RG 84 Lebanon, Classified General Records, Box 28, NARA.

31. Skiles to Tannous, 28 February 1952, ibid.

32. Peter to Reeseman Fryer, 1 April 1952, ibid.

33. Ibid.

34. Locke to Truman, "Action Program for the Near East," 25 April 1952, Presidential Secretary's Files, Papers of Harry S. Truman, HSTL.

35. Locke to Truman, 19 February 1952, Papers of Edwin Locke Jr., Box 5, HSTL.

36. Locke, for example, justified these priorities by citing the "remarkable success" of the Japanese in developing Manchuria during World War II based on the modernization of infrastructure in the areas of transportation, fuel, and power. Cf. Locke to U.S. Secretary of State, 880.00-TA/3/24/52.

37. These were: improvement to the port of Beirut, improvement to the port of Tripoli, the construction of a port at Latakia, the construction of a natural gas pipeline from Kirkuk to the Levant region, the development of the Litani River, the development of the Tigris and

Euphrates Rivers in Syria, the development of the Orontes River, the development of the Yarmouk-Jordan area, and the implementation of the equatorial Nile plan.

38. Locke to U.S. Secretary of State, 880.00-TA/3/24/52.

39. Cf. Harriman to Acheson, 880.00-TA/4/9/52 for background on the legislative obstacles concerning Locke's proposal.

40. Cf. Cannon to U.S. Secretary of State, 880.00-TA/3/15/52, Tannous to U.S. Secretary of State, 883A.00-TA/3/5/52, and Tannous to U.S. Secretary of State, 883A.00-TA/3/17/52.

41. Peter to Reeseman Fryer, 1 April 1952, RG 84, Lebanon, Classified General Records, Box 28, NARA.

42. Locke to Truman, 19 February 1952, Presidential Secretary's Files, HSTL.

43. Cf. Berry memo, "Grant Aid for Arab States for Fiscal Year 1953," 880.00-TA/2/29/52.

44. Cf. Memo of Conversation, "Arab States Development Programs" 880.00-TA/3/17/52.

45. Harriman to Acheson, 880.00-TA/4/9/52.

46. Ibid.

47. Cf. Thorp to Acheson, "Near East Aid Program," 880.00-TA/2/25/52.

48. Reesemen Fryer to Andrews, 9 May 1952, Lot 57D/298, NA.

49. Ibid.

50. Memorandum of Conversation with the President, "The Locke Proposal," 1 May 1952, Dean Acheson Papers, Box 67, HSTL.

51. Cf. U.S. Department of State, Staff Memorandum, "Responsibilities of Ambassador Locke in the Near East," 12 May 1952, and Gardiner to Locke, 15 May 1952, Lot 57D/298, NE Files, NA. See also Peter to Reeseman Fryer, 7 June 1952, RG 84, Lebanon, Classified General Records, Box 28, NARA; and Gardiner to Locke, 15 May 1952, Lot 57 D/298, Records of the Office of Near Eastern Affairs, NA.

52. Cf. Thorp to Secretary of State, "Near East Aid Program," 880.00-TA/5/2/52.

53. Cf. Locke to Gardiner, 4 September 1952, Papers of Edwin Locke Jr, Box 5, HSTL, and Fidler to Locke, "Discussion with Palestine Arab Refugee Leaders," 15 September 1952, Papers of Edwin Locke Jr., Box 5, HSTL.

54. Cf. *Le Soir* (Beirut), 15 September 1952.

55. Cf. "Notes on Locke's Visits to Refugee Camps," Notebooks 1 and 2, Papers of Edwin Locke Jr., Box 4, HSTL.

56. Locke to Gardiner, 4 September 1952, Papers of Edwin Locke Jr., Box 5, HSTL.

57. Ibid.

58. Ibid.

59. Ibid.

60. Cf. Amawi to Locke, 3 October 1952, Papers of Edwin Locke Jr., Box 5, HSTL, for a discussion of possible corruption within the United Nations Relief and Works Administration.

61. Locke to Gardiner, 30 July 1952, and Locke to Gardiner, 24 September 1952, Papers of Edwin Locke Jr., Box 5, HSTL.

62. Edwin Locke Jr., interview by author, 7 February 1994.

63. Locke to Gardiner, 23 February 1952, Papers of Edwin Locke Jr., Box 5, HSTL.

64. Cf. Locke to Gardiner, 29 November 1952, ibid.

65. Cf. Green to U.S. Secretary of State, 320.2AA/9-2752, and Lobenstine to Byroade, 320.2AA/10/4/52.

66. Cf. Funkhouser to Hart, "Arab Membership on ADCOM," 320.2AA/9/12/52, Memorandum of Conversation, "UNRWA Relief Budget and Syrian Membership on the Advisory Commission," 320.2AA/9/17/52, and Lobenstine to Byroade, 320.2AA/10/4/52.

67. Locke to Gardiner, 23 February 1952. Papers of Edwin Locke Jr., Box 5, HSTL.

68. Cf. Geren to U.S. Department of State, "Selo Gives Opinion on U.S. Aid," 883.00/10/16/52.

69. Locke to Truman, 24 September 1952, Papers of Edwin Locke Jr., Box 5, HSTL.

70. Cf. Locke and Peter to TCA Country Directors, Near East, 880.00-TA/8/4/52,and Locke to Gardiner, 6 September 1952, Papers of Edwin Locke Jr., Box 5, HSTL.

71. Locke to Truman, 24 September 1952, Papers of Edwin Locke Jr., Box 5, HSTL.

72. Fidler memo, 9 October 1952, ibid.

73. Locke to Truman, 24 September 1952, ibid.

74. Ibid.

75. Minor to U.S. Secretary of State, 880.00-TA/11/24/52.

76. Cf. *Daily Star* (Beirut), 28 November, 30 November, and 2 December 1952, all found in the papers of Edwin Locke Jr., Box 4, HSTL.

77. Edwin Locke, "The Arab Economy: The Truth and the Challenge," 5 December 1952, Papers of Edwin Locke Jr., Box 4, HSTL.

78. Green to Minor, 3 December 1952, RG 84, Lebanon, Box 28, NARA.

79. Minor to Green, 9 December, 1952, ibid.

80. Cf. *Daily Star* (Beirut), 13 December 1952.

81. *Daily Star* (Beirut), 27 December 1952.

82. Peter to Young, 19 December 1952, RG 84 Lebanon, Classified General Records, Box 28, NARA.

83. At the end of January, Locke spoke at a meeting of the American Friends of the Middle East in which he repeated his criticisms of U.S. development policy in the Near East, this time directing some added invective at officials of the State Department, whom he described as "scrubs." Cf. *Daily Star* (Beirut), 10 February and 21 March 1953. For a rather unabashedly vicious response from one of the "scrubs," see Bruins to Hart, 320.2-AA/3/23/53.

3

U.S. Foreign Policy Toward Iran During the Mussadiq Era

Mark Gasiorowski

Muhammad Mussadiq, who served as the Iranian prime minister from April 1951 until August 1953, is revered by almost all secular democratic Iranians and admired even by many supporters of the regimes of the shah and Ayatollah Khomeini. He ended a long period of British hegemony in Iran by nationalizing the British-controlled oil industry, instilling a strong sense of national pride in most Iranians, and setting the stage for several decades of rapid economic growth fueled by oil revenues. He also tried to democratize Iran's political system by reducing the powers of the shah and the traditional upper class and by mobilizing the urban middle and lower classes. Although he ultimately failed in this latter endeavor, his efforts made him a hero in the eyes of those Iranians who have dreamed of establishing a democratic regime in their country.

At the start of the Mussadiq era the United States had a very positive image in Iran, created by the small group of U.S. teachers, missionaries, archaeologists, and administrators who had ventured there and by the commitment to freedom, democracy, and independence espoused by the U.S. government and most Americans. The United States initially supported Mussadiq, upholding Iran's right to nationalize the oil industry, trying to mediate an agreement with the British, giving Iran a small amount of economic aid, and generally praising Mussadiq and his democratic aspirations. However, U.S. support for Mussadiq gradually declined, and under the administration of President Dwight D. Eisenhower the United States engineered a coup d'état that drove Mussadiq from office and ended the movement toward democracy he had been leading. The United States thereafter strongly backed the shah, greatly facilitating his efforts to create an authoritarian regime in the decade after the coup. Consequently, the Mussadiq era also marked a period in which the popular image of the United States in Iran began to change from that of benevolent outsider to malevolent supporter of the shah's despotic regime.

This chapter examines U.S. policy toward Iran during the Mussadiq era. It focuses particularly on the strategic considerations that led U.S. officials to change from a policy of supporting Mussadiq to one of opposing and eventually overthrowing him, thus engendering the malevolent image many Iranians still have of the United States. The chapter does not provide a detailed account of the August 1953 coup or the events leading up to it, which are examined at length elsewhere.

Prologue: U.S. Policy Toward Iran Before the Mussadiq Era

Before World War II the United States had little strategic or economic interest in Iran, and relations between the two countries were cordial but distant. The United States had established diplomatic relations with Iran in 1856 but did not send a diplomat of ambassadorial rank there until 1944. During the late 1800s and early 1900s contact between the two countries was very limited, consisting mainly of missionary activity with a handful of U.S. missionaries, teachers, and archaeologists; these Americans created a very positive image of the United States in Iran. Nevertheless, relations between the two countries were evidently of such little importance by the late 1930s that Iran's monarch, Reza Shah Pahlavi, recalled his ambassador to Washington for several years after derogatory comments about him appeared in the U.S. press.[1]

With World War II raging in Europe, Britain and the Soviet Union jointly invaded Iran in September 1941 to establish a supply route to the Soviet army. The invading forces quickly overpowered the hapless Iranian army and forced Reza Shah, who was seen as a German sympathizer, to abdicate in favor of his twenty-one-year-old son, Muhammad Reza Pahlavi, the late shah. Following U.S. entry into the war the United States sent troops to Iran in conjunction with the supply operation, initiating a period in which U.S.-Iranian relations grew rapidly. By early 1944 some 30,000 U.S. soldiers were stationed in Iran, guarding the supply route against bandits and German agents, expanding and improving Iran's transportation system and oil production facilities, and building plants to assemble aircraft, trucks, and oil drums. The United States sent military missions to Iran to reorganize and train the Iranian army and Gendarmerie and gave Iran some $8.5 million in lend-lease aid during the war. Unlike Britain and the Soviet Union, the United States did not meddle in Iran's domestic affairs during the war, reinforcing its image as a champion of freedom and independence.[2]

As the German threat eased in 1944, the Soviet Union began to expand its influence and demand oil concessions in the northwestern Iranian provinces of Azerbaijan and Kurdistan, which it had been occupying since 1941. Constrained by its need to maintain the wartime alliance, the United States initially made no effort to block these activities. However, as World War II drew to a close in 1945, the Soviet posture toward Iran grew more menacing and was paralleled by similar activities elsewhere in the world. As U.S. officials grew increasingly concerned about Soviet expansionism, and after Harry S. Truman replaced the more diplomatic Franklin D. Roosevelt as president, the United States began to pressure the Soviet Union to withdraw its forces from Iran. Soviet officials demurred, and in December 1945 and January 1946 Soviet-backed rebels established the Autonomous Republic of Azerbaijan and the Kurdish People's Republic in northwestern Iran. Powerless to stop these activities, the Iranian government sought backing from the United States and Britain and petitioned the United Nations (UN) to demand a Soviet withdrawal. U.S. officials issued protests to the Soviet government and strongly supported Iran's position at the UN. Backed by the United States, Iranian prime minister Ahmad Qavam traveled to Moscow in March 1946 and negotiated an agreement under which Soviet troops would be withdrawn from Iran. The Iranian army reoccupied Azerbaijan and Kurdistan in December 1946, crushing the autonomy movements and ending one of the first chapters in the cold war.[3]

As the crisis in Azerbaijan and Kurdistan was drawing to a close, the U.S. Department of State and other U.S. government agencies conducted a thorough review of U.S. interests in Iran. Reflecting the considerable effort U.S. officials had made earlier to eject Soviet forces from northwestern Iran, U.S. officials concluded that Iran was "of vital strategic interest" because Persian Gulf oil would be critical in the event of a war with the Soviet Union.[4] However, despite this finding, no major changes occurred in U.S. policy toward Iran during the late 1940s. U.S. policymakers at this time were pursuing a strategy of "strongpoint defense" in their efforts to contain Soviet expansionism. This strategy called for a concentration of U.S. defense efforts in Western Europe and Japan—on the western and eastern borders of the Soviet Union—and accorded a much lower priority to other regions, including the area south of the Soviet Union where Iran lay. Consequently, though the shah and the various Iranian prime ministers of this period made repeated requests for U.S. military and economic aid, Iran was not given a large aid package under the Truman Doctrine, as were Greece and Turkey, and it received less U.S. aid in the late 1940s than countries like Ireland, Portugal, and Sweden, despite its larger size and poorer economic conditions.[5]

The United States did slowly increase its involvement in Iran in other ways during this period, however. The military training missions begun during World War II were renegotiated and extended in 1947 and 1948. The U.S. embassy staff grew considerably in size, enhancing diplomatic, commercial, and cultural interactions between the two countries. More important, the Office of Strategic Services, the predecessor to the Central Intelligence Agency (CIA) established a station in the Tehran embassy in early 1947 to take over covert operations then being conducted by U.S. military attachés and embassy political officers. These covert operations included intelligence-gathering and propaganda operations aimed at the Soviet Union and its allies in Iran, cross-border espionage and subversion raids into Soviet territory, and efforts to map out escape and evasion routes and organize "stay-behind" guerrilla networks for use in the event of a Soviet invasion. Although these operations were all aimed ultimately at the Soviet Union, they did have the effect of strengthening or weakening various Iranian political actors in minor ways during this period.[6]

In the late 1940s unrest grew steadily among politically active Iranians, due mainly to the absence of meaningful opportunities for political participation and to growing resentment toward the Anglo-Iranian Oil Company (AIOC), a British-owned firm that was earning large profits from its monopoly over Iran's oil industry. Much of this unrest was mobilized and articulated by the Tudeh (Masses) Party, a pro-Soviet Communist Party established in 1941 that had become Iran's largest political party before falling into disfavor after the Azerbaijani crisis. In October 1949 a group of prominent political figures established an organization known as the National Front to press for political reforms and nationalization of the AIOC's assets in Iran. The National Front quickly became extremely popular and managed to elect eight of its members to the Majlis (the Iranian parliament) in late 1949. It was led by Muhammad Mussadiq, a charismatic Majlis deputy from a wealthy landowning family who had established a reputation as an ardent nationalist and democrat and one of Iran's few honest politicians.[7]

By early 1950 U.S. officials had become alarmed about political conditions in Iran, with one describing Iran as "dangerous and explosive" and another warning that it might become a "second China."[8] Simultaneously, the National Security Council was undertaking a major reevaluation of U.S. global strategy, which was codified in the April 1950 document known as NSC-68. The new strategy called for a "renewed initiative in the cold war" involving large increases in military and economic aid to countries located all along the Sino-Soviet periphery—not just those on the western and eastern borders of the Soviet Union.[9] The growing unrest in Iran and this new global strategy together led U.S. officials to undertake a thorough review of U.S. policy toward Iran, which concluded that a major effort had to be made to prevent the Tudeh Party from coming to power and delivering Iran into Soviet hands. As a result, during the following year U.S. officials agreed to provide Iran with $23 million per year in military aid and a modest amount of economic aid; they approved a $25 million Export-Import Bank loan to Iran (which was never actually provided); and they supported Iran's request for a $10 million World Bank loan. They also sharply increased the number of U.S. Foreign Service and CIA officers working in the Tehran embassy and named Henry Grady, a highly respected diplomat, to be the new U.S. ambassador.[10] By early 1951 the United States had positioned itself to play a major role in Iranian politics.

The Truman Administration and the First Mussadiq Government

Throughout 1950 unrest continued to grow in Iran, with political reform and oil nationalization remaining the most contentious issues. Prime Minister Ali Razmara initiated a program of political and socioeconomic reforms but also attempted to implement an agreement with the AIOC negotiated under his predecessors that fell far short of popular demands. In response, Mussadiq and the National Front began to call for outright nationalization of the oil industry, and a member of the Islamist group Fedayan-e Islam (Devotees of Islam) assassinated Razmara in March 1951.

The shah then appointed Hussein Ala, a loyal ally, to replace Razmara. The country was swept with a new wave of unrest, leading the Majlis to nominate Mussadiq for the premiership and pass a bill nationalizing the oil industry. Bowing to popular sentiment, the shah appointed Mussadiq prime minister on April 29 and signed the oil nationalization bill into law on May 2.[11]

Nationalization of the AIOC posed a serious threat to Britain's weak economy and dwindling prestige, so the nationalization decree initiated a period of growing confrontation between Britain and Iran. In the following months British officials adopted a three-track strategy aimed at reestablishing Britain's control over Iran's oil industry either by pressuring Mussadiq into a favorable settlement or removing him from office. The first track was a halfhearted effort to negotiate a new oil agreement that would recognize the principle of nationalization but retain de facto British control over Iran's oil. This effort collapsed in August 1951, and the British thereafter refused to negotiate directly with Mussadiq. The second track consisted of a series of hostile measures aimed at undermining popular support for Mussadiq. The most important of these was a successful effort to persuade the major world oil companies to boycott Iranian oil exports. The British also imposed a series of bilateral economic sanctions on Iran and began an ominous military buildup in the region. The third element of the British strategy was a series of covert efforts to overthrow Mussadiq. These efforts continued throughout Mussadiq's tenure as prime minister and were carried out primarily through a network of politicians, businessmen, military officers, and clerical leaders that had been cultivated by British intelligence officers during their long years of intrigue in Iran.[12]

After Mussadiq assumed office the Truman administration publicly expressed strong support for him, recognizing that he was very popular and therefore could serve as an effective alternative to the Tudeh Party. Officials in Washington again undertook a review of U.S. policy toward Iran, concluding that Iran must be kept in the Western camp at all costs because of its strategic location and that a protracted oil crisis might weaken the U.S. economy and threaten U.S. and Western security. Accordingly, for the remainder of Truman's term in office the administration pursued a policy of supporting Mussadiq, opposing British efforts to overthrow him, and attempting to mediate an agreement that would satisfy both parties to the oil dispute and minimize disruption of the world oil market.[13]

Soon after the oil nationalization law was enacted, U.S. officials began to implement a plan to ease the effect of the British oil blockade on the world oil market. Under this plan U.S. oil companies were asked to provide oil to U.S. allies that had been adversely affected by the blockade. Some 46 million barrels of oil were delivered under this plan in the first year of the blockade, amounting to roughly 20 percent of Iran's 1950 production. Although this effort was intended to help stabilize the world oil market, it also reinforced the oil blockade and therefore inadvertently helped to weaken the Iranian economy and undermine Mussadiq's popular support.[14]

At the same time, U.S. officials began a concerted effort to facilitate a negotiated settlement of the oil dispute. They privately advised the British to accept nationalization of the AIOC and agree to a 50-50 division of profits with Iran—an arrangement that had become common throughout the industry by that time. In July 1951 Secretary of State Dean Acheson asked special envoy Averell Harriman to lead a mission to Tehran and London to mediate the dispute. Harriman worked assiduously to bring the British and Iranian positions closer together, inducing the British to send a negotiating team to Iran under the leadership of Sir Richard Stokes. The Stokes mission made little headway, and negotiations between Britain and Iran collapsed in August.[15]

Throughout this period the British had been working strenuously to replace Mussadiq with their close ally, Sayyid Zia al-Din Tabatabai. This had involved direct pressures on the shah to dismiss Mussadiq and appoint Sayyid Zia as prime minister as well as efforts to build support in the Majlis through the British intelligence network for Sayyid Zia's candidacy. British officials even went so far as to work out a set of guidelines for settling the oil dispute with Sayyid Zia. U.S. officials were generally aware of these activities and neither supported nor opposed them. The British effort to install Sayyid Zia had not made much headway by the time the Stokes mission collapsed. Accordingly, in September 1951 British officials began to implement a plan to invade southwestern Iran and seize the oil fields. When U.S. officials were told about this plan, President Truman notified British Prime Minister Clement Attlee that the United States would not support an invasion and urged him to resume negotiations. As a result, Attlee was forced to abandon the invasion plan, telling his cabinet that "in view of the attitude of the United States Government, [he did not] think it would be expedient to use force" in Iran.[16]

Mussadiq traveled to New York in October to address the UN Security Council about the oil dispute. U.S. officials invited him to Washington, hosting him warmly and making another concerted effort to mediate the dispute. These efforts again failed to bring about a settlement. During the following year U.S. officials made a series of additional proposals that called for Iranian oil to be marketed by a consortium of U.S. and other oil companies. When antitrust concerns led the major U.S. oil companies to reject this plan, U.S. officials first tried to persuade U.S. independents to accept it and then, in the fall of 1952, decided to waive antitrust laws to persuade the majors to participate. Despite these efforts, U.S. officials were unable to settle the oil dispute.[17]

Having failed to reverse the nationalization law, to install Sayyid Zia as prime minister, or to seize the oil fields forcibly, the British began to search for other options in their efforts to regain control over Iran's oil. Another option soon materialized. Ahmad Qavam, who had been prime minister during the 1945–1946 Azerbaijani crisis, approached the British seeking support in his bid to replace Mussadiq as prime minister. British officials sent an emissary to meet with Qavam in Paris in March 1952. Qavam told the emissary that he would settle the oil dispute on terms acceptable to the British, and he produced a list of potential cabinet ministers for their approval. The British supported Qavam by accepting his plan to end the oil dispute and having their network of Iranian allies help him. Qavam spent the next several months trying to build support in Iran for his candidacy.[18]

Mussadiq evidently learned about Qavam's activities and suddenly resigned on July 16. The shah then appointed Qavam prime minister. During the next several days the National Front organized a series of massive demonstrations calling for Mussadiq's return to office. Army and police units attacked the demonstrators, killing at least sixty-nine and injuring over 750. Since Qavam had no popular backing, Mussadiq's supporters dominated the streets of Tehran. On July 21 the shah bowed to the popular will and appointed Mussadiq to a second term as prime minister. Qavam slipped quietly into exile.[19]

The Truman Administration and the Second Mussadiq Government

The Qavam episode initiated a period of growing political instability in Iran. Morale in the armed forces dropped sharply. The Tudeh Party became much more active. Mussadiq filled his new cabinet with close supporters and persuaded the Majlis to grant him emergency powers, angering National Front leaders such as Ayatollah Abul Qassem Kashani, Hussein Makki, and Muzaffar Baqai. More ominously, a group of military officers led by General Fazlollah Zahedi began to plot against Mussadiq with the Rashidian brothers, who were the central figures in the British intelligence network. Zahedi had briefly served as interior minister in Mussadiq's first government and had supported the National Front until the July 1952 uprisings, when the resurgence of Tudeh activity and plummeting morale in the armed forces apparently drove him into the opposition.[20]

Kashani, Makki, and Baqai soon approached Zahedi, expressing their dissatisfaction with Mussadiq and thereafter collaborating loosely with him in his plot. Zahedi also obtained the support of Abul Qassem Bakhtiari, a leader of the Bakhtiari tribe who had worked with him in collaboration with German agents during World War II. He then met with the British chargé d'affaires, asking for assurance that the British would not oppose him, would agree to a settlement of the oil dispute on terms similar to those worked out with Qavam, and would obtain U.S. acquiescence in his activities. The chargé reported this to London and was told to help Zahedi. British intelligence officers then provided arms to the Bakhtiari. The chargé described Zahedi's activities to U.S. Ambassador Loy Henderson. Either Zahedi or a close lieutenant also met with Henderson in early September, telling him that a government would soon come to power that would halt the growth of Tudeh influence. Henderson reported these conversations back to Washington but remained noncommittal.[21]

U.S. policy toward Iran during this period was ambiguous. Ambassador Henderson was alarmed about the resurgence of the Tudeh Party and the generally chaotic situation in Iran in the aftermath of the Qavam episode, and he recommended that Washington prop up the Mussadiq government with a large aid package. Although this did not occur, U.S. officials renewed their efforts to resolve the oil dispute and continued to support Mussadiq, both publicly and in private conversations with the British. However, at the same time, CIA officers in Tehran began to turn some of their anti-Soviet covert operations in directions that undermined Mussadiq's base of support. Under a propaganda operation code-named BEDAMN, they distributed newspaper articles and cartoons that depicted Mussadiq as corrupt and immoral and portrayed him as exploiting Kashani. They provided financial assistance to certain clergymen to drive them away from Mussadiq and create a clerical alternative to Kashani. CIA officers with long-standing ties to the Pan-Iranist Party and the Toilers' Party—both had strongly supported Mussadiq—made efforts to turn these organizations against Mussadiq. In a particularly noteworthy case, two CIA officers in the fall of 1952 approached Baqai, who had headed the Toilers' Party, encouraging him to break with Mussadiq and giving him money. Similar approaches may have been made to Kashani, Makki, and other prominent figures.[22]

By November 1952 both the Pan-Iranists and the Toilers' Party had split into pro- and anti-Mussadiq factions; Kashani, Makki, Baqai, and other National Front leaders had openly turned against Mussadiq, seriously weakening him. These three men, like most other Iranian politicians at the time, were extremely opportunistic and may well have had other reasons for breaking with Mussadiq. Moreover, the British were carrying out very similar—and probably much more extensive—covert activities against Mussadiq at this time. Therefore, although these CIA activities may well have helped to undermine Mussadiq's base of support, they were not the only forces operating against him in this period, and it is impossible to say with any certainty how much of a role they actually played in weakening him.

Mussadiq evidently learned about Zahedi's plot and moved to stop him before it could be implemented. As a member of the Iranian senate, Zahedi enjoyed parliamentary immunity and therefore could not be arrested. However, Mussadiq issued arrest warrants on October 13 for the Rashidians and for General Abdul Hussein Hejazi, a close ally of Zahedi. A General Aryana was dismissed from the army in connection with the plot. More important, on October 16 Mussadiq broke diplomatic relations with Britain, claiming British officials had supported Zahedi. This act alarmed U.S. officials and persuaded some of them that the situation in Iran had gotten out of hand.[23]

No longer able to operate from the safety of their Tehran embassy, the British decided to seek U.S. help in their efforts to oust Mussadiq. Christopher Montague Woodhouse, who had been heading British intelligence operations in Iran, was sent to Washington in November to present U.S. officials with a plan to oust Mussadiq. The plan called for a coordinated uprising to be engineered by the Rashidians and certain Bakhtiari tribal elements, with or without the shah's approval. Although the British believed Zahedi was well suited to lead the coup, they proposed several possible coup leaders. Woodhouse met with CIA and State Department officials. Most high-ranking CIA officials favored a coup by this time, although some lower-ranking Iran specialists and the CIA station chief in Tehran were opposed to the idea. State Department officials told Woodhouse that Truman would not support a coup but that president-elect Dwight Eisenhower and his foreign policy advisers probably would.[24]

The Eisenhower Administration and Mussadiq

Dwight Eisenhower entered office in January 1953, and the administration harbored bold plans to restructure U.S. foreign policy in ways that would more effectively contain the Soviet Union. Its new global strategy, which was eventually set out in the October 1953 National Security Council study NSC-162, called for a broad effort to enhance containment while reducing U.S. defense expenditures. An important element of this effort was a decision to strengthen pro-Western countries located along the Sino-Soviet periphery—a project that the Truman administration had begun but set aside as the Korean War and European reconstruction distracted its attention. These countries were to be strengthened with large military and economic aid programs, defense alliances, and, where necessary, covert political operations conducted by the CIA.[25] As a result of this new global strategy, the Eisenhower administration redirected the U.S. military and economic aid programs away from Europe toward the Third World; it constructed a ring of defense alliances around the Soviet Union and China; and it greatly increased the CIA's use of covert operations. With its proximity to the Soviet Union, and Mussadiq's failure to resolve the oil crisis, Iran was a crucial pawn in this new strategy and quickly became a major preoccupation for the Eisenhower administration.

Secretary of State designate John Foster Dulles and his brother, Allen Dulles, who was deputy head of the CIA's covert operations division under Truman and was to become CIA director under Eisenhower, had been following the situation in Iran with growing alarm. Although they did not regard Mussadiq as a Communist, they believed conditions in Iran would probably continue to deteriorate as long as he remained in office, strengthening the Tudeh Party and perhaps enabling it to seize power. In light of Iran's crucial role in the U.S. strategy for containing the Soviet Union, they viewed this possibility with grave concern. The Dulles brothers therefore concluded that Mussadiq had to be removed from office—a conclusion that was not shared at this time by Assistant Secretary of State for Near Eastern and South Asian Affairs Henry Byroade, Ambassador Henderson, the CIA station chief in Tehran, or several lower-ranking State Department and CIA officials. Allen Dulles had met with Woodhouse in November 1952 and expressed his support for a coup to overthrow Mussadiq. The Dulles brothers were ready to begin preparations for a coup by the time Eisenhower was inaugurated.[26]

On February 3, 1953, two weeks after the inauguration, top U.S. and British officials met in Washington to discuss the situation in Iran. At this meeting a decision was made to develop and carry out a plan to overthrow Mussadiq and install Zahedi as prime minister. The operation was to be led by Kermit Roosevelt, who headed the CIA's Middle East operations division. Roosevelt traveled to Iran several times during the following months to prepare for the coup, meeting with Zahedi, the Rashidians, members of the Tehran CIA station, and two Iranians code-named Nerren and Cilley, who were the main operatives in the BEDAMN propaganda operation. A U.S. specialist on Iran working under contract for the CIA was assigned to develop an operation plan for the coup with a British intelligence officer. Roosevelt presented the coup plan to the Dulles brothers and other top U.S. officials in a June 25 State Department meeting. He was directed to implement it immediately.[27]

Zahedi had continued to intrigue against Mussadiq after the exposure of his plot in October 1952. He remained in contact with Bakhtiari tribal leaders, who were given arms and money by the British during this period. His allies in the Majlis undertook a series of parliamentary maneuvers to try to oust Mussadiq. In February 1953 a group of retired military officers loyal to Zahedi and Bakhtiari tribesmen led by Abul Qassem attacked an army column, apparently trying to spark a coup. Mussadiq responded by issuing an arrest warrant for Zahedi, who had lost his parliamentary immunity. Zahedi's allies then organized a series of violent disturbances in Tehran that nearly toppled the Mussadiq government. A similar incident occurred in late April, when several Zahedi associates apparently kidnapped and murdered the commander of the national police, a staunch Mussadiq supporter. Rumors of coup plots circulated throughout the winter and spring of 1953.[28]

Following the June 25 State Department meeting, Roosevelt and his CIA team began to work in loose coordination with Zahedi. They used the BEDAMN network to launch an extensive propaganda barrage against Mussadiq and organize antigovernment and anti-Tudeh demonstrations, adding considerably to the turmoil that was engulfing Tehran. They sought the support of top military officers, arranging to have certain army units participate in the coup. In late July and early August they sent two emissaries to see the shah and obtain his support. When these approaches proved unsuccessful, Roosevelt arranged through the Rashidians to meet personally with the shah. After direct U.S. and British involvement were confirmed through special radio broadcasts, the shah agreed to support the plot.[29]

Having obtained the shah's backing, Roosevelt was ready to proceed with the coup. The shah signed decrees dismissing Mussadiq and appointing Zahedi prime minister. The commander of the shah's Imperial Guard delivered the first of these decrees to Mussadiq on the night of August 15 and was promptly arrested. Army and police units loyal to Mussadiq then set up roadblocks throughout the city, began a massive search for Zahedi, and arrested several of his associates. An armored column that had been assigned to move into Tehran in conjunction with Mussadiq's dismissal failed to arrive. As the coup plot unraveled the shah fled the country in panic, first to Baghdad and then to Rome. Zahedi was brought to a CIA safe house, where he remained for the next several days. Roosevelt made contingency plans to evacuate himself, Zahedi, and a few other participants.[30]

Despite these setbacks, Roosevelt and his colleagues began to improvise a new plan. They distributed copies of the decrees dismissing Mussadiq and appointing Zahedi throughout Tehran in order to publicize the shah's actions. They brought two U.S. newspaper reporters to meet with Ardeshir Zahedi, who told them about the shah's decrees and characterized Mussadiq's rejection of them as a coup, since the decrees were in accord with the constitution. This information was quickly published in the *New York Times*. Ardeshir Zahedi and one of the CIA officers were sent to Kermanshah and Isfahan to persuade the garrison commanders in those cities to send troops to Tehran. The U.S. military advisory group distributed military supplies to pro-Zahedi forces to encourage them to support the plot.[31]

On August 17 Nerren and Cilley used $50,000 given to them by Roosevelt's team to hire a large crowd that marched into central Tehran shouting Tudeh slogans, carrying signs denouncing the shah, tearing down statues of the shah and his father, and attacking Reza Shah's mausoleum. This crowd played the role of an agent provocateur: It generated fear of a Tudeh takeover among Tehran residents and was even joined by many real Tudeh members, who assumed it had been organized by the party's leadership. These disturbances continued on the following day. Mussadiq therefore ordered the police to disperse the crowds, even though the Tudeh was tacitly supporting him against Zahedi and the shah. The Tudeh responded by ordering its members off the streets, removing an important obstacle to Mussadiq's opponents.[32]

By the evening of August 18 the police were closing in on the CIA safe house where Zahedi was hiding. Roosevelt therefore began to look for a new way to spark a coup. Knowing that Ayatollah Kashani was strongly opposed to Mussadiq and had considerable influence over lower- and middle-class Iranians, he decided to seek Kashani's help in organizing another crowd to agitate against Mussadiq. Following the Rashidians' advice, he had two CIA officers meet with Ahmad Aramesh, an influence peddler who apparently had connections with Kashani. They asked Aramesh to ask Kashani to organize an anti-Mussadiq crowd and gave him $10,000 to finance the effort. At the same time, the Rashidians and Nerren and Cilley probably made independent efforts to organize such a crowd.[33]

Although it is not clear whether Kashani or these figures were involved, a large crowd suddenly emerged near the Tehran bazaar in the late morning of August 19. The crowd attacked government office buildings and the offices of newspapers and political parties that supported Mussadiq. It was joined by army and police units and by onlookers who had become alarmed by the "Tudeh" demonstrations of the previous days. Realizing that events had turned decisively against him, Mussadiq refused to order his security forces to disperse the crowd. At the same time, an army unit seized the Tehran radio station and began to broadcast bulletins condemning Mussadiq and supporting Zahedi. An air force general led a column of tanks to the safe house where Zahedi was hiding and rescued him from the police units closing in around him. Military units and large groups of demonstrators then seized the army headquarters and marched on Mussadiq's home, where a nine-hour tank battle ensued. The walls around Mussadiq's house were destroyed and the house itself was stormed; some 300 people were killed. Mussadiq escaped into a neighbor's yard but surrendered to Zahedi's forces the next day. Several days later the shah returned to Iran and personally thanked Roosevelt, telling him, "I owe my throne to God, my people, my army—and to you."[34]

The shah's comment to Roosevelt seems to have been appropriate, for the United States did indeed play a key role in overthrowing Mussadiq and ending the threat he had posed to Iran's autocratic monarchical system. Roosevelt and his colleagues had

planned, financed, and led the coup, taking decisive action after the attempt to arrest Mussadiq had failed that later made the coup successful. Zahedi, its nominal
leader, hid in a CIA safe house almost until the coup had been completed. The shah
was not consulted about the decision to undertake the coup, the manner of its execution, or the candidate chosen to replace Mussadiq, and he had been reluctant to
support the coup and had fled the country at the first sign of failure. The British had
played only a minor role in the coup, helping develop the initial plan for it—which
failed—and directing the Rashidians to work with Roosevelt. Although the AIOC's
oil boycott had weakened Iran's economy and thus helped undermine popular support for Mussadiq, many other outcomes could have resulted from Mussadiq's declining popularity. Zahedi and his allies had failed repeatedly to overthrow Mussadiq
during the previous year. Although they might possibly have engineered a coup
without U.S. help, outstanding arrest warrants greatly hindered Zahedi's activities,
and he had no real popular support. No other Iranian appears to have had the popularity of military connections necessary to carry out a coup without external backing. It therefore seems safe to conclude that the United States played a decisive role
in overthrowing Mussadiq and severely weakening the political movement he led.

Conclusion

This chapter has emphasized that U.S. security interests—as conceived by the Truman
and Eisenhower administrations—required that Iran be kept in the Western camp
during the cold war, and therefore it has implied that domestic political conditions in
Iran could not be permitted to move beyond certain boundaries in the eyes of U.S.
policymakers. Under the Truman administration these boundaries initially were drawn
rather broadly: Mussadiq did not seem to pose a threat to U.S. interests, and U.S. policymakers believed he could serve as an effective counterbalance to the Tudeh Party.
However, these perceptions slowly changed as Mussadiq remained in power and unrest grew in Iran. When Eisenhower entered office, the more stridently anti-Communist views of his foreign policy advisers and the changing perceptions of Mussadiq
among some holdovers from the Truman administration together led the United States
to drop its support for Mussadiq and take steps to overthrow him. Consequently, U.S.
security interests associated with the cold war and changing views in Washington
about how Mussadiq's regime affected these interests were responsible for the fateful
U.S. decision to undertake the August 1953 coup.

   During the following decade these same considerations led U.S. policymakers to
provide extensive support to the shah, building up his autocratic regime as a bulwark
against Soviet expansionism. Immediately after the coup they provided him with
$68 million in emergency aid, amounting to roughly one third of the total revenue
Iran had lost as a result of the British oil embargo. Over $300 million in additional
U.S. economic aid was given to Iran during the next ten years. After the coup U.S.
officials renewed their efforts to settle the oil dispute, fostering an agreement that
permitted Iran to begin exporting oil again in late 1954. Iran's oil income grew

quickly as a result of this agreement, exceeding total U.S. aid receipts by 1958 and thereafter serving as the shah's main source of revenue. The United States also began a major effort to strengthen the shah's security forces soon after the coup, reorganizing and training his domestic intelligence apparatus and giving him almost $600 million in military assistance during the next decade.[35]

With the threat from Mussadiq and the National Front effectively contained, the economy growing rapidly, and an increasingly effective security apparatus in place, the shah consolidated his grip on power in the late 1950s and early 1960s. By late 1963 this process had been completed: The shah presided over an authoritarian regime under which organized opposition to his authority was not tolerated, and there seemed little chance that he would fall from power. However, many politicians were aware that Iranians deeply resented the shah's regime; they increasingly blamed the United States for restoring him to power in 1953 and then helping him to consolidate the new regime. This resentment generated a new challenge to the shah in the 1970s that differs from the one posed by Mussadiq: nondemocratic, violent, and deeply anti-American. This new challenge brought the shah's regime crashing down in the late 1970s and created a series of crises for the United States during the following decade that only recently have begun to subside.

The strategic considerations that led U.S. policymakers to undertake the 1953 coup and then build up the shah's regime therefore helped set in motion a chain of events that later destroyed his regime and created severe problems for U.S. interests. One can only hope that the end of the cold war will make it possible for the United States and other major powers to think more clearly about domestic political effects of their actions and thus avoid the kind of outcome that resulted from U.S. policy toward Iran during this era.

Notes

1. Abraham Yeselson, *United States–Persian Diplomatic Relations, 1883–1921* (New Brunswick, N.J.: Rutgers University Press, 1956); John A. Denovo, *American Interests and Policies in the Middle East, 1900–1939* (Minneapolis: University of Minnesota Press, 1963), ch. 9.

2. T. Vail Motter, *United States Army in World War II: The Middle East Theater, the Persian Corridor, and Aid to Russia* (Washington, D.C.: Department of the Army, Office of the Chief of Military History, 1952); Mark Hamilton Lytle, *The Origins of the Iranian-American Alliance, 1941–1953* (New York: Holmes and Meier, 1987), chs. 2–4.

3. Bruce Robellet Kuniholm, *The Origins of the Cold War in the Near East* (Princeton: Princeton University Press, 1980), chs. 5–6.

4. U.S. Joint Chiefs of Staff (hereinafter JCS), *United States Strategic Interests in Iran* (Washington, D.C.), JCS 1714/1, October 4, 1946, p. 6.

5. John Lewis Gaddis, *Strategies of Containment* (New York: Oxford University Press, 1982), chs. 2–3; U.S. Department of State, *Foreign Relations of the United States, 1947,* vol. 5 (Washington, D.C.: U.S. Government Printing Office, 1970), pp. 905ff.; ibid., 1948, vol. 5, pp. 170ff.; ibid., 1949, vol. 6, pp. 528ff.; U.S. Agency for International Development, *U.S.*

Overseas Loans and Grants: Series of Yearly Data, vols. 1–5 (Washington, D.C.: U.S. Agency for International Development, 1984).

6. Rouhollah K. Ramazani, *Iran's Foreign Policy, 1941–1973: A Study of Foreign Policy in Modernizing Nations* (Charlottesville: University Press of Virginia, 1975), pp. 159–162; confidential interviews conducted by the author with several CIA officers stationed in Iran during this period.

7. Ervand Abrahamian, *Iran Between Two Revolutions* (Princeton: Princeton University Press, 1982), ch. 5. On Mussadiq's background and beliefs, see Farhad Diba, *Mohammad Mossadegh: A Political Biography* (London: Croom Helm, 1986); James A. Bill and Wm. Roger Louis, eds., *Mussadiq, Iranian Nationalism, and Oil* (Austin: University of Texas Press, 1988); and Homa Katouzian, ed., *Musaddiq's Memoirs* (London: JEBHE, National Movement of Iran, 1988).

8. U.S. Department of State, *Foreign Relations of the United States, 1950,* vol. 5 (Washington, D.C.: U.S. Government Printing Office, 1976), pp. 510, 523.

9. U.S. National Security Council (hereinafter NSC), *United States Objectives and Programs for National Security,* NSC-68, April, 14 1950, reprinted in Thomas H. Etzold and John Lewis Gaddis, eds., *Containment: Documents on American Policy and Strategy* (New York: Columbia University Press, 1980), p. 434; Gaddis, *Strategies of Containment,* ch. 4.

10. U.S. Department of State, *Foreign Relations of the United States, 1950,* vol. 5, pp. 509–529, 551, 604; confidential interviews conducted by the author with several retired CIA officers.

11. Mostafa Elm, *Oil, Power, and Principle: Iran's Oil Nationalization and Its Aftermath* (Syracuse, N.Y.: Syracuse University Press, 1992), chs. 4–5.

12. For a fuller examination of these activities, see Mark J. Gasiorowski, *U.S. Foreign Policy and the Shah: Building a Client State in Iran* (Ithaca: Cornell University Press, 1991), pp. 62–67.

13. NSC, *The Position of the United States with Respect to Iran,* NSC 107/2, June 27, 1951.

14. NSC, *National Security Problems Concerning Free World Petroleum Demand and Potential Supplies,* NSC 138, December 8, 1952, pp. 9–10.

15. Elm, *Oil, Power, and Principle,* ch. 8.

16. Henry Byroade, interview by author, Potomac, Maryland, August 7, 1984; "Record of Interdepartmental Meeting," March 20, 1951, Foreign Office (hereinafter FO) 371/91525; "View that HMG Should Refrain from Any Statement," August 26, 1951, FO/371/91582; "Approach to a New Persian Government," September 8, 1951, FO/371/91590; "Text of Reply from President Truman," September 26, 1951, FO/371/91591; CAB 128/20, pp. 231–234. All of these documents are from the British Public Records Office, London (hereinafter cited as PRO).

17. Elm, *Oil, Power, and Principle,* chs. 11–12; "American Proposal that the Royal Dutch/Shell Group Should Take Over and Operate the Abadan Refinery Considered Impractical," November 6, 1951, FO/371/91610 (PRO); Paul Nitze, interview by author, Washington, D.C., July 5, 1984.

18. "Qavam's Proposals," January 7, 1952, FO/371/98683 (PRO); "Intervention of Mr. Julian Amery," February 7, 1952, FO/371/98683 (PRO); "Qavam's Proposals," March 25, 1952, FO/371/98683 (PRO); "Internal Situation," n.d., FO/248/1531 (PRO); Sir George Middleton, interview by author, London, January 16, 1985.

19. Elm, *Oil, Power, and Principle,* ch. 16.

20. "Annual Report on Persian Army for 1952," September 12, 1952, FO/371/98638 (PRO); "Internal Situation," cited in note 18; *New York Times,* August 15, 1952, p. 2, and August 20, 1952, p. 1; Fitzroy Maclean, *Eastern Approaches* (London: Cape, 1950), p. 266; Henderson to Acheson, July 7 and 21, August 3, 4, and 15, and October 17, 1952, Record Group 84, Box 29. The latter documents are from the U.S. National Archives, Washington (hereinafter cited as USNA).

21. "Internal Situation," cited in note 18; "Tribal Affairs and Tribal Policy," n.d., FO/248/1521 (PRO); "Intrigues Among the Bakhtiari Tribes," November 28, 1952, Record Group 84, Box 28 (USNA); Middleton interview by author; Henderson to Acheson, September 9, 1952, Record Group 84, Box 29 (USNA).

22. Elm, *Oil, Power, and Principle,* pp. 244–246; confidential interviews conducted by the author with several retired CIA officers.

23. *New York Times,* October 13, 1952, p. 4, and October 16, 1952, p. 6; "Annual Report on Persian Army for 1952," December 9, 1952, FO/371/98638 (PRO).

24. Christopher Montague Woodhouse, *Something Ventured* (London: Granada, 1982), pp. 116–119; Kermit Roosevelt, interview by author, Washington, D.C., June 5, 1985, Henry Byroade, interview by author, Potomac, Md., August 7, 1984, and CIA officer who was working in Iran at the time, interview by author.

25. Gaddis, *Strategies of Containment,* ch. 5.

26. Interviews conducted by author with Henry Byroade and Gordon Mattison, Bethesda, Md., June 30, 1984, Roy Melbourne, Chapel Hill, N.C., February 1, 1984, and several CIA officers who worked in Iran at this time.

27. Kermit Roosevelt, *Countercoup: The Struggle for the Control of Iran* (New York: McGraw-Hill, 1979), pp. 120–124; Roosevelt interview; confidential interview with the Iran specialist, August 5, 1984.

28. Henderson to Acheson, January 19, 1953, Record Group 59, Box 4117; "Internal Affairs," February 18, 1953, FO/371/104562 (PRO); "Internal Affairs," February 24, 1953, FO/371/104562 (PRO); "Internal Affairs," February 28, 1953, FO/371/104563 (PRO); "Dr. Musaddiq's Quarrel with the Shah," February 23, 1953, FO/371/104563 (PRO); "The Murder of Chief of Police Afshartus," May 8, 1953, FO/371/104566 (PRO); "Internal Situation," n.d., FO/371/104563 (PRO).

29. Confidential interviews with several retired CIA officers; Princess Ashraf Pahlavi, *Faces in a Mirror* (Englewood Cliffs, N.J.: Prentice Hall, 1980), pp. 134–140; Roosevelt, *Countercoup,* pp. 147–157.

30. Confidential interviews with several retired CIA officers.

31. Confidential interviews with several retired CIA officers. See also articles published in the *New York Times* during this period.

32. Ibid.

33. Ibid.

34. *New York Times,* August 20, 1953, p. 1, and August 21, 1953, p. 1; Roosevelt, *Countercoup,* p. 199.

35. Gasiorowski, *U.S. Foreign Policy and the Shah,* ch. 4.

4

Iranian Perceptions of the United States and the Mussadiq Period

Sussan Siavoshi

The 1979 Iranian revolution had some harsh messages for the West in general and the United States in particular. The anger and hatred toward the United States, particularly during the hostage crisis, were expressed through slogans such as "death to America," "the World devouring, imperialist America," and "America, the world arrogance." The U.S. self-image, however, was far from that portrayed by the Iranians. For the most part, Americans, holding to their own memories of their struggle against imperial Britain in the eighteenth century, preferred to see themselves as anti-imperialist and benevolent and as supporters of the right to self-determination. So when confronted with Iranian rage, something that was unexpected and incomprehensible to most Americans, they labeled it as an irrational display of hostility caused by fanaticism—a tantrum thrown by an immature and ungrateful nation against its protector.

The difference in the conception of both "the self" and "the other" held by Iranians and Americans has kept tension between the two countries at a high level. Understanding the reasons for such confrontation requires careful, extensive, and complex historical analysis that is not within the confines of this study.[1] However, it has been suggested that U.S. involvement in the 1953 coup against Prime Minister Muhammad Mussadiq, whom most of the participants in the revolution of 1977 considered as a true democrat and a sincere nationalist, was a turning point in the Iranian view of the United States. Until 1953, the United States had enjoyed a tremendously positive reputation among most of the politically attentive Iranians. To most Iranians that reputation was severely damaged as the result of the coup. The following two and a half decades of concentrated U.S. involvement in Iran solidified the view of the United States as imperial, arrogant, and contemptuous.

No one would dispute the fact that both the United Kingdom and the United States were actively involved in the toppling of Mussadiq's administration. What has been a matter of contention is whether the coup was a benevolent or a malevolent occurrence, the answer to which is directly related to the issue of the legitimacy of Mussadiq's government and the meaning of sovereignty in the Third World. This study attempts to take the 1953 coup, one of the most important moments of U.S. intervention in Iran, and analyze perceptions engendered by that intervention within politically attentive Iranian groups. Iranian perceptions, however, were affected not only by Western behavior but also by Western rhetoric toward Iran. The perception of Iran held by the British and the Americans influenced the formation or transformation of Iranian perceptions of both countries in return. In other words, there was a symbiotic relationship between the Western and Iranian views of the "other." One fed on the other. For this reason I will also address, briefly, the British and the U.S. images of both the Iranians and the political developments in the era of Mussadiq's leadership.

Between 1949 and 1953 Iran experienced the emergence, ascendance, and failure of a movement that had a profound impact on the future course of its history. The oil nationalization movement started as a protest against British control over the oil industry but soon developed into an expression of popular desire for Iran's dignity as an independent nation-state. The leader of the movement was the charismatic and democratically oriented Muhammad Mussadiq. The organizational expression of the movement was the National Front, which was originally founded by Mussadiq and eighteen other prominent individuals in November 1949 to achieve two interrelated goals: abolition of the internal dictatorship and elimination of foreign control and influence over Iranian affairs. The broad goals of the National Front made it a kind of umbrella organization consisting of different groups and personalities with diverse ideologies. It included economic liberals as well as social democrats; religious as well as secular individuals; sociocultural liberals as well as sociocultural conservatives. However, the leadership of the movement was clearly in the hands of the secular liberals headed by Mussadiq himself. Mussadiq was elected prime minister by the Iranian parliament in April 1951 after he asserted himself as the champion of the oil nationalization movement and soon after passage of the bill authorizing nationalization of the Anglo-Iranian Oil Company. Mussadiq's ascendance to power was short-lived, however. Too many problems and too many forces (both internal and external) challenged Mussadiq and his administration. There was soon a rift in his own National Front, and many of his initial supporters, due to disagreements either on policy and style or because of sheer opportunism, left the movement. The breakup of the National Front provided the impetus for Mussadiq's opponents, who until then were afraid of Mussadiq's popularity, to publicly attack him. In the midst of this stormy period, there was a virtual whirlwind of foreign (read: British and U.S.) intrigue. It should come as no surprise that Mussadiq's government did not survive the storm.

Western Perceptions

Was the coup a benevolent act? To some it definitely was. Not surprisingly, U.S. and British policymakers were among those who believed in the coup. Western judgment, particularly in Britain and, by 1953, the United States, about Mussadiq and his role as the leader of a Third World country was mostly negative. The British perception of Iran, the oil nationalization, and Mussadiq was influenced by two factors: The first was the British imperial, inegalitarian view of the world, which divided it into two categories—the mature and civilized West and the childlike and exotic East; the second factor was the material loss (both economic and political) resulting from oil nationalization in Iran. British parliamentary debates and, with very few exceptions, British press reports on Iran throughout this period were quite revealing. The British self-understanding included the image of a British oil company that was generously compensating Iran for exploitation of its oil[2] and a group of British policymakers who were rational, fair-minded, and cautious.[3] Contrast this with the British image of Iranians as generally irrational and emotional, only a half-civilized lot with a national character described as self-doubting and strange.[4] The entire nationalization movement was reduced to the malicious intention of xenophobic rabble-rousing leaders consisting of both atheistic Communists and fanatical religious leaders who used an "obscure sense of popular discontent" and directed it against the generous and civilizing mission of the British oil company, making the company a scapegoat.[5] The British portrayal of Mussadiq as "the anxious vulture of the oil industry"[6] demonstrated contempt and disgust for both the man and the movement he represented.

Some of these views, particularly during the coup d'état, were later supported by the Americans as well.[7] *Time* magazine referred to Mussadiq as a fanatical nationalist whose obsession with martyrdom would ruin Iran.[8] *Newsweek* characterized him as inconsistent, unreasonable, and irrational[9] and warned against the "red threat."[10] In the few turbulent days before the success of the coup—when events appeared to be favoring Mussadiq over the shah and his supporters—an editorial in the *Washington Post* predicted that Mussadiq's success had no other beneficiary but the Communist Tudeh Party and its benefactor, the Soviet Union.[11] After the success of the coup, the reaction of the U.S. press, manifested in editorials in major newspapers, was one of "relief" and "rejoice."[12] Throughout the era of 1949–1953, U.S. newspaper reports and analyses basically reflected the gradually changing, official U.S. government view of Mussadiq and his role in Iranian politics. It seems that the essential factor in changing the attitude of the Americans (they initially supported the nationalist movement of Mussadiq) was the advent of the cold war.[13] In 1953 Dwight Eisenhower became president of the United States. His administration actively subscribed to the ideology of the cold war, including the U.S. "mission" to defend the world against the Soviet Communist menace. The proximity of Iran to the Soviet Union and U.S. exaggeration of the strength of the Iranian Communist Party were instrumental in changing the view of Mussadiq and his ability to contain communism in Iran. However, one should not underestimate the British power of persuasion in altering the minds of U.S. policymakers. The British succeeded in portraying Iranian nationalism as a force incapable or unwilling to resist Communist domination in Iran.

Overall, a review of the dominant perceptions in the West, particularly among the policymaking elite, reveals that the issue of legitimacy of Mussadiq as the prime minister and Iranian national sovereignty were overshadowed by the issue of perceived U.S. and British national interests. The memoirs of Kermit Roosevelt, a U.S. official with a large hand in the coup d'état, point to the irrelevancy of sovereignty in Iran—let alone the legitimacy of a particular government—from the point of view of the policymakers in the United States. The ideologically determined belief in Iranian inability to determine their destiny, as well as the realpolitik concern about the possible advances of the "diabolical" U.S. archrival, the Soviet Union, were the two predispositions that set parameters for U.S. debate over the wisdom of the coup. It should come as no surprise that the coup was considered by the U.S. policymakers as not only beneficial to the United States but also to the unruly, "childlike" Iranians.

Iranian Perceptions

On the domestic scene there were three general forces, each with a particular view of Mussadiq and his role in shaping Iran: first, the conservatives (consisting of the court, many of the powerful army officers, rich merchants, landlords, and pro-British politicians); second, the leftist Tudeh Party, with ties with the Soviet Union; and third, a coalition of different groups within the National Front.

The Conservative View

The conservative Iranian analysis of the movement can be found in two interpretations of Mussadiq and the oil nationalization era: a book by Muhammad Reza Pahlavi, *Answer to History,* and another by his sister, Ashraf Pahlavi, entitled *Taslimnapazir* (Undefeatable). Ashraf portrayed the king as a "rational" proponent of oil nationalization who, unlike the opportunistic and irrational Mussadiq, was waiting for a more favorable moment to nationalize the precious resource.[14] Both she and her brother depict Mussadiq as a power-hungry, irrational leader who directed Iran along a disastrous path.[15] Neither of the siblings had anything positive to say about Mussadiq's crucial role in leading the nationalist movement. They considered Mussadiq's overthrow, therefore, not as the defeat of a nationalist movement seeking independence for Iran but rather as the triumph of rational and positive nationalism led by the shah over the fanaticism and negativism of Mussadiq and his supporters.[16]

This view was echoed by the newspapers associated with the anti-Mussadiq and antinationalist groups. In fact the coup d'état was celebrated as a "national uprising" conducted by a god-fearing and king- and country-loving populace against a megalomaniac usurper and his Communist Tudeh supporters.[17] According to the conservative viewpoint, Mussadiq had lost his legitimacy because of his contempt for the shah and his insistence on restricting the latter's prerogative as the supreme leader of the country. United States and British involvement therefore were either minimized[18] or considered as a benevolent gesture on the part of the "free world" to help Iran to save itself from the menace of communism. There were, however, many politically attentive Iranians who interpreted very differently the nature of the oil nationalization movement, Mussadiq's government, and the events between 1949–1953, including the coup. They considered the coup as a malevolent act.

The Tudeh Party's Position

As a group of Marxist-Leninist intellectuals, the leaders of the Tudeh Party argued that a revolutionary potential existed in the exploited classes of workers and peasants.[19] The realization of this potential, the argument went, would be found in the model provided by the Soviet Union, a country that had completely eliminated the czarist imperialist institutions in Russia and had created a new foundation for relations among countries around the world.[20] The Tudeh theoreticians maintained that because of the economic situation created by the end of World War II, Iran was ripe for a socialist revolution. They argued that in the beginning of the oil nationalization movement in Iran there were three political tendencies. The first consisted of the true anti-imperialist forces. The second encompassed all those who were dependent upon British imperialism, such as the commanders of the military, state officials, the feudal landlords, and the comprador capitalists. The third tendency was one engendered by U.S. imperialism, which tried to replace the older imperial powers such as Great Britain.[21] The oil nationalization period provided the perfect opportunity for the first tendency to surface. The problem, the Tudeh leaders argued, lay with the bourgeois leadership that took over the budding movement. By its very nature the bourgeoisie was ultimately less frightened of imperialism than of a true national movement that was struggling against not only foreign domination but also internal exploitation.[22] The Tudeh Party adhered to the view that the fundamental contradiction of the era was between the socialist camp, headed by the Soviet Union, and the imperialist capitalist camp, headed by the United States; any attempt to seek cooperation from the United States was a betrayal of the cause of liberation movements.[23] Based on this view the activities of the National Front and the Mussadiq administration, which initially included gestures of cooperation with the United States in fighting British domination, were harshly criticized.[24] To Tudeh members, tension or rivalry between the United States and Britain was nonexistent or irrelevant as far as the interests of the Iranian people were concerned.

The Tudeh Party's view of Mussadiq and his administration changed, particularly after tension arose between the U.S. administration and Mussadiq's government in mid-1952. By late 1952 the Tudeh leaders came to the conclusion that despite certain inherent problems associated with national bourgeois movements, such as their *ideological* naïveté about the nature of imperialism (and thus the tendency to compromise with forces of reaction), there was another aspect to the nature of these movements: their *substantive* anti-imperialist character. At a certain junction, when imperialism is the principal enemy, this substantive character could make the national bourgeoisie an ally to the progressive forces within society. The true interpretation of the nature and activities of the national bourgeoisie, represented by the National Front, revealed that between 1949 and 1953 this organization played an important role in leading the anticolonial struggle of the Iranian people.[25]

In general the leftist intellectuals, both Tudeh and non-Tudeh, considered the oil nationalization era as potentially revolutionary. It so happened that the liberal national bourgeoisie were able to assume the leadership positions in the budding movement and to make a valuable contribution by attacking British imperialism. But for the movement to succeed the leadership had to aggressively confront enemies, including U.S. imperialism and domestic reactionary allies. The National Front, due to its lack of resolve, itself due to class interest, failed to push the struggle to its logical conclusion and therefore lost in the end.[26] In fact, according to Kianouri, the head of the Tudeh Party, after the coup it became evident that some of the members of the National Front who had defected, such as Muzaffar Baqai, Hussein Makki, and Amidi-Nouri, were closely associated with U.S. imperialism.[27] Mussadiq himself was afraid to take assertive and confrontational postures vis-à-vis the enemies of the movement and therefore was unable to take advantage of crucial opportunities (both in mid-1952 and in the early 1953) when the progressive forces were ready to eradicate the roots of imperial and reactionary forces.[28] The August 28, 1953, coup was a turning point through which the "progressive" side of the "contradiction," that is, the masses, gave up its position of strength to its "reactionary" enemy.[29] The active involvement of the United States in the coup was proof of the nature of capitalist imperialism and its inevitable aggressive and violent behavior. The question of how to deal with the United States, therefore, was informed by the perception about the nature of the United States. Accordingly, since it is in the nature of the U.S. politico-economic system to be uncompromising, aggressive, and arrogant, Iran, like any other country that aspired for dignity and independence, felt it necessary to take a strong and defiant stand and must not be deceived by any apparent benevolent statement of intent by U.S. leaders. Because when it came down to matching deeds with words the United States would betray Iran as it had in 1953.

The Mussadiqist Perception

The 1953 coup effectively put an end to the activities of the National Front. However, many of its members, both religious and secular, remained active and tried to push for the ideals set down by the leader of the movement. The first Mussadiqist organization founded after the coup was the National Resistance Movement of Iran (NRMI). Its views on the nature of the coup d'état were shared by many Mussadiqists.[30] To counter the views of the conservatives, who supported the shah and considered Mussadiq a usurper, the NRMI leaders asserted that based on the Iranian constitution the monarch must reign but not rule. Therefore, Mussadiq's insistence on restricting the power of the shah was only to uphold the constitution. They argued that Mussadiq was the elected prime minister of Iran and had acquired a mandate from the people and, as such, his removal from power was illegal and criminal. As far as the foreign powers and their involvement in Iranian affairs were concerned, the Mussadiqists argued there was no doubt that the U.S. government was heavily involved in the coup. But, interestingly, they left the door open for future cooperation with the United States. To understand this attitude we should concentrate on the nationalists' interpretation of global politics and Iran's position in it. Many of the leaders and supporters of the National Front considered the biggest factor shaping the political destiny of Iran to be the influence of foreign powers.[31] The 1953 coup confirmed their belief about the inevitability and necessity of Iran's dependent stature. A legitimate and democratically elected administration in Iran, due to its overall global weakness, was easily crushed by foreign powers. Russia and Great Britain were the two old colonizing powers that were historically meddling in Iranian affairs in ways that were detrimental to Iranian interests as a sovereign and prosperous nation. The United States was considered a third power with interests at odds with those of both Britain and Russia.[32] U.S. cooperation with the British in carrying out the coup stemmed from a combination of British conniving and manipulating tactics and U.S. naïveté,[33] which led to the latter's involvement in an endeavor that would ultimately be deleterious to U.S. interests in the region. In the Middle East the Mussadiqists argued that U.S. interests, unlike those of Britain, were strategic and not economic. The paramount goal of the United States in the area was to create a buffer zone to contain what Washington policymakers perceived to be an expansionist Soviet Union.[34] The Iranian nationalists, the Mussadiqists asserted, shared this goal and would like to contain Communist influence in Iran. But the best way the United States could achieve its goal and persuade the countries of the region to see the real danger of communism was to allow nationalist and democratic governments to come to power. Only genuinely democratic and nationalist regimes would be able to address the fundamental problem of the Third World and rescue it from the seduction of Communist movements. This commonality of interest between the United States and liberal nationalists, the argument went, was bound to be understood by the policymakers in Washington. Despite their grievances regarding the role of the United States in the coup of 1953, in general the views of the liberal nationalists toward the United States remained one of relative optimism.

The Clerics' Perception

Was there a clerics' perception of the Mussadiq period and of the coup d'état? The short answer to this question is no, there was no monolithic religious perception on these issues. However, there is a prevalent contemporary Western interpretation of the clerics' political positions and behavior, which must be addressed. The revolution of 1979 and its ensuing power struggle for the most part has been erroneously and simplistically described as the war between the secular forces, on the one hand, and the religious forces led by the Ayatollah Khomeini, on the other. It is true that ultimately the postrevolutionary regime, both in terms of its laws and its power holders, acquired a clear religious character and that the secular forces were ousted. But the polarization of the polity was not set a priori and it was the specific dynamic of the revolutionary process and particularly its aftermath that created a dichotomy between secular and religious forces in the political arena. In fact throughout modern Iranian history, opposing political forces were not defined by their secularity or religiosity but by their acceptance of or struggle against the status quo. This trait was present during the constitutional revolution of 1905–1911, in which some of the *ulama* fought very hard alongside the secular intellectuals to limit the power of the despotic Qajar monarchy and to create a democratic polity. They accepted the general secular tone of the constitution and the ideological leadership of the secular intellectuals. However, there were certain members of the religious community who fought against the constitutionalists because of their close connection to the monarchy or because they were suspicious of the secular implication of the constitutional revolution. The character and behavior of the religious community during the oil nationalization period was in many ways similar to the constitutional era. During 1949 to 1953, there were religious personalities who supported Mussadiq and there were those who opposed him. There were some who supported the coupmakers and there were those who continued, at great risk, to identify themselves with the aspirations of the generally secular Mussadiq.

Among the royalist clergy was the influential Tehran cleric Ayatollah Bihbahani who, unlike his famous constitutionalist grandfather, was proestablishment and status quo–oriented. He was closely associated with the coupmakers. Ayatollah Burujirdi, one of the most influential *marja'i taqlid* (source of emulation), remained publicly neutral and urged the clergy to stay out of politics. Many of his followers, including Ayatollah Khomeini, did not participate in the events between 1949 and 1953. There were, however, members of the clergy who sided with Mussadiq and became actively involved in the oil nationalization movement. The most prominent and politically active religious figure of the 1949–1953 era was the Ayatollah Abul Qassem Kashani. His personal experience with British imperialism made Kashani an anti-British activist who was attracted to the idea of nonalignment. Therefore, he readily joined Mussadiq and his movement in 1950. But, as a result of both ideological reasons and personal and policy differences, tension arose between the two men. Kashani was particularly alarmed when the Tudeh Party stopped its attack on Mussadiq and when it seemed that a working coalition between the Communist forces and Mussadiq had been established. By mid-1953 Kashani openly broke ranks with Mussadiq and, in collaboration with some of the secular former members of the National Front such as Muzaffar Baqai and Hussein Makki, both of whom were secular politicians, tried to undermine and ultimately topple Mussadiq's government. With this action he sided with the shah and the foreign coupmakers. His statements immediately before the coup portrayed Mussadiq as a demagogue who had hidden his true dictatorial nature behind the mask of a democrat.[35] Kashani separated the movement from Mussadiq and considered the latter as a man whose active role in the movement was to fulfill his political ambition. Ever since Mussadiq achieved his goal and became prime minister, Kashani stated, he did not take one step to improve Iran's condition.[36] After the coup Kashani continued his attack on Mussadiq, praised the shah, and, therefore, publicly sanctioned the coup.[37] But he remained firmly against the British and opposed the resumption of diplomatic relations between Iran and Britain, which had been broken during Mussadiq's administration.[38] Kashani did not have much to say about the United States. But the little he did say was an indication that Kashani, despite his ambivalence toward the West, considered the United States as a global force fighting against the real enemy, that is, the godless ideology of communism.[39]

There were other religious figures who remained loyal to Mussadiq and his ideal to the bitter end. Some of them participated in founding the NRMI. Although the NRMI had a little more religious coloring than the original National Front, its loyalty to Mussadiq's aspirations was prominent. Among this group of religious liberal nationalists were Ayatollah Zanjani, Ayatollah Talegani, and Ayatollah Angaji. In tune with other Mussadiqists, these men considered the coup a criminal act and Mussadiq to be a national hero. Their points of view have already been discussed in the section on the Mussadiqist opposition to the coup.

Conclusion

The perception of the conservatives and the Tudeh Party was somewhat predictable. The conservatives considered Mussadiq's reformist policies detrimental to their interests (political or economic or both). Many of them had close ties with the British and owed their power to the British oil company's meddling in Iranian affairs. Even those who did not mind nationalization of the oil industry still found accommodation with the foreign powers as a more suitable course of action for preservation of their interests. But the Tudeh Party was a socialist organization with a strong anti-capitalist ideology, and, despite its inactivity during the coup, its ideological and political positions dictated a negative reaction toward the coupmakers. Its perception was generally based on its abstract and methodical structuralist Marxist discourse.

The more politically sophisticated reaction was that of the primary victims of the coup, the liberal nationalist leaders. They saw policymaking not just in terms of structural determinants but as a combination of both structural and volunteeristic factors. They also had a more complex view of the decisionmaking processes and institutions in the United States. They perceived, rightly, that in general within the U.S. foreign policy apparatus there were different groups arguing for different policy options[40] and that the liberal nationalists, even after the hostile coup, would have a chance to count on and strengthen the argument of those in the U.S. administration who saw Iran and the region in terms similar to those of the Iranian nationalists. What they failed to realize was that by 1953 the cold war vision, with all its implications, had become by far the most dominant vision among the higher echelons of the foreign policy makers in the United States. The advent of the cold war mentality and the insecurity created by the image of the Soviet Union as the diabolical enemy had led the United States to abandon both the complex view of the world and those who advocated the complex view. In Washington, John Foster Dulles replaced Dean Acheson as secretary of state; some time before that, in Iran, U.S. Ambassador Henry Grady was replaced by Loy Henderson. These changes were accompanied by a perceptual transformation with regard to the Soviet threat and the position of different forces within Third World countries, including Iran. The cold war perception demanded images of highly polarized polities in which lines between friendly and unfriendly forces were unambiguously drawn. Based on this perception there existed only pro- and anti-Communist forces in a life-and-death struggle. There was no room for gray areas, no room for accommodation. Therefore, allowing the Tudeh Party to function within the Iranian polity, a policy pursued by the Mussadiq administration, was considered not an act to help a budding democracy to operate honestly but rather as Mussadiq aligning against the West and with the Soviet Union. Whatever the rationale, the decision to topple the democratically elected Mussadiq administration and the subsequent support for the increasingly dictatorial regime of Muhammad Reza Pahlavi was interpreted by Iranians, liberal and nonliberal alike, as a highly hypocritical act committed by a country that professed to be the leader and protector of the free world.

But the success of the coup and the apparent subsequent tranquillity, mostly caused by repression of democratic practices and institutions in Iran by the U.S.-backed Pahlavi regime, convinced U.S. policymakers of the wisdom of the coup and the correctness of their own stereotypical cold war views. Very soon the U.S. intelligence "success story" in Iran became the model for similar plans and covert actions both in the Middle East and Latin America. But the long-term wisdom of such an approach to foreign policy became a matter of serious debate as time passed. In Iran the intensity and the nature of U.S. involvement in Iran between 1953 and 1979, support for the unpopular, increasingly repressive, and, in the eyes of most politically attentive Iranians, illegitimate regime of Muhammad Reza Pahlavi undermined the viability of the sophisticated perception of the liberal nationalists. As such one of the most promising opportunities for liberal and moderate politics in Iran was lost to a large extent as the result of the more or less continuously contemptuous judgment by the United States of Iranian liberal forces. Along with it went U.S. moral clout in Iran. The political severity of the U.S.-backed regime of Muhammad Reza Shah changed the power configuration of oppositional ideologies and outlooks. As a result, the view that used to be held only by the left in 1953, the organic, structuralist, and somewhat rigid view of the United States as arrogant, imperial, and contemptuous, became much more tangible and believable for most politically attentive Iranians, whether on the left or right. The dominant tone of the 1977–1979 revolution bore witness to this perceptual development.

Notes

1. For the best analytical work in the area of perception regarding post–World War II U.S.-Iranian relations, see Richard Cottam, *Iran and the United States: A Cold War Case Study*, Pittsburgh, University of Pittsburgh Press, 1988.

2. Norman Kemp, *Abadan,* London, Wingate, 1953, p. 19.

3. Peter Avery, *Modern Iran,* London, E. Benn, 1964, p. 418.

4. C. M. Woodhouse, *Something Ventured,* London, Granada, 1982, p. 106. Woodhouse was a member of British intelligence service stationed in Iran for part of the oil nationalization era. His book is full of mocking and contemptuous remarks about Iranians in general and Musaddiq in particular.

5. Kemp, *Abadan,* p. 19.

6. Ibid., p. 26.

7. See articles in different issues of *Newsweek,* such as July 28 and August 4, 11, and 18, 1952. See also *Time,* especially January 7, 1952, pp. 18–21. For an example of U.S. media reports on Iran during the oil nationalization period, see William A. Dorman and Mansour Farhang, *The U.S. Press and Iran: Foreign Policy and the Journalism of Deference,* Berkeley, University of California Press, 1987, pp. 31–62.

8. *Time,* July 18, 1952, p. 6.

9. *Newsweek,* August 11, 1952, p. 36.

10. *Newsweek,* July 28, 1952, pp. 38–39, and August 18, 1952, p. 34.

11. See Dorman and Farhang, *The U.S. Press and Iran,* p. 42.

12. Ibid., pp. 48–49.

13. Kermit Roosevelt, *Countercoup,* New York, McGraw-Hill, 1979, ch. 1.

14. Ashraf Pahlavi, *Taslimnapazir,* Paris, n.p., 1983, pp. 93 and 194.

15. Muhammed Reza Pahlavi, *Answer to History,* New York, Stein, 1980, pp. 79–92, and Ashraf Pahlavi, *Taslimnapazir,* pp. 93–94.

16. Pahlavi, *Taslimnapazir,* pp. 93–94.

17. See Ashraf Pahlavi, *Faces in the Mirror,* New York, Prentice-Hall, 1980, pp. 168–169.

18. Pahlavi, *Taslimnapazir,* p. 95.

19. Abdul Samad Kambakhsh, *Nazari bih junbish-i Kargari va Kummunisti dar Iran* [A Look at the Workers' and Communist Movement in Iran], part 2 (Stockholm: Tudeh Party, 1975), pp. 6, 32.

20. Nouredin Kianouri, *Hizb-i Tudeh-i Iran va Doctor Musaddiq* [Iran's Tudeh Party and Doctor Musaddiq], Tehran, 1980, p. 6.

21. Ibid., p. 15.

22. *Asnad-i Tarikhi-yi Junbish-i Kargari, Sosial dimukrasi va kummuniti-yi Iran* [Historical Documents of the Workers', Social Democratic, and Communist Movement of Iran], vol. 1, Tehran, Padzahr, n.d., p. 352.

23. For a later admission of this theoretical weakness, see Iraj Iskandari, "What Do We Mean by the National Bourgeoisie," *World Marxist Review* 2(9) (September 1959), p. 72.

24. *Asnad-i Tarikhi,* pp. 350–356.

25. "Report of the Executive Board of the Tudeh Party Central Committee on the Central Committee Last Plenum," in *Asnad-i Tarikhi,* pp. 361–364.

26. See Kambakhsh, *Nazari,* pp. 97–115; and for a leftist but non-Tudeh interpretation, see Bizhan Jazani, *Capitalism and Revolution in Iran,* London, n.p., 1980, pp. 25–33.

27. *Hizb-i Tudeh,* p. 15.

28. Bijan Jazani, *Vaqaye-e Si Saleh dar Iran,* [Tehran?], n.p., 1976, p. 41.

29. Ibid.

30. *Tariq-i Moasir-i Iran: Asnad-i Nihzat-i Muqavimat-i Milli-i Iran* [The Contemporary History of Iran: The Document of the Milli Resistance Movement of Iran], vol. 5, Tehran, 1984, pp. 51–52.

31. See, for example, the transcript of the March 1, 1985, interview with Ali Asghar Hajj-Sayyed Javadi, one of the leading liberal nationalists, Oral History Project, Center for Middle Eastern Studies, Harvard University, tape 2, p. 2.

32. *Nashriyat-i Rah-i Musaddiq va Zama-im An: Salha-yi 1332–36* [The Publication of the Musaddiq's Path and its Supplements], Tehran, n.p., 1985, p. 211.

33. See Karim Sanjabi, *Hopes and Despairs: The Political Memoirs of Doctor Karim Sanjabi,* London, Jebhe, 1989, p. 192.

34. Ibid., p. 216.

35. See *Majmoo'a-yi az Mokatebat va Payamha-ye Ayatollah Kashani* [A Collection of Ayatollah Kashani's Correspondence and Messages], ed. M. Dehnavy, Tehran, Chapakhsh, 1983, vol. 3, p. 396.

36. Ibid., p. 407.

37. *Majmoo'a-yi,* vol. 4, 1983, p. 28.

38. Ibid.

39. Ibid., pp. 35 and 147–148.

40. See Javadi interview, tape 2, p. 2.

5

The Mussadiq Era in Iran, 1951–1953: A Contemporary Diplomat's View

Sir Sam Falle

In the 1950s, I served Great Britain in Iran, Lebanon, and Iraq and at the Foreign Office in London on the Middle East oil desk. These postings gave me a worm's-eye view of a period of unprecedented change in the Middle East. There were revolutions in three countries: Iran, Iraq, and Egypt; I was present at the first two. The causes were intrinsically the same: resurgent nationalism against the British, who were, in any event, beginning to dismantle their empire and to dissociate themselves from their so-called stooges or puppets. In the midst of this change, the British and Americans shared the fundamental policy of denying the region to the Soviet Union while preserving oil supplies for the West, though sometimes they differed on the details. Both countries eventually came to agree on policy and methodology during the Muhammad Mussadiq crisis in Iran, a seminal event not only in Iran but also in the entire Middle East, especially in terms of the development of U.S. foreign policy. In now turning to this episode, I take a different perspective than most who have commented on and written about the Mussadiq period.

When I arrived in Iran in 1949, the cold war was gathering impetus. The British had left India, and Prime Minister Clement Attlee's Labour government hoped for a steady and orderly transfer of power throughout the old empire. The United States had already become, by far, the most powerful country in the free world. The Middle East was disproportionately important, considering its relatively small population, because of its vast oil reserves and strategic position between the cold war adversaries. Arab nationalism, suppressed for many centuries by the Ottoman Empire and briefly by the British and French, was awakening. The Arabs, angry, wounded, and humiliated by the creation of Israel, still felt that they were not yet free from "imperialism." Iran had just emerged from World War II, during which it had in practice been partitioned between Britain and the Soviet Union. The British oil company, then known as the Anglo-Persian Oil Company (later Anglo-Iranian Oil Company, or AIOC, and then British Petroleum), continued to take the major share of the profits of Iran's oil for itself and the British government.

Thus, the Iran to which I came in 1949 was uneasy. The Soviet threat remained in the north, and the British and their oil company in the south were regarded as imperialist oppressors, even though Anglo-Iranian official relations were correct. The British and also the Russians had deposed Iran's ruthless modernizing ruler, Reza Shah Pahlavi in 1941 for his pro-Nazi sympathies. His thirty-year-old son, Muhammad Reza Pahlavi, sat uneasily on the peacock throne. He had little of his father's courage or ruthlessness, and I suspect he was a reluctant tyrant in his later years. In 1952 he was summed up by one of my Iranian acquaintances: "His Majesty is very, very, weak."[1] At that time he was certainly vacillating and indecisive. Furthermore, he disliked the British for deposing his father; I wrote in an official minute, "The Shah hates our guts." However, on the positive side, it is worth noting that he reacted courageously and not vindictively to an attempt on his life by the Tudeh Party in February 1949. He neither lost his nerve nor ordered reprisals.

The AIOC had been exploiting Iranian oil since the beginning of the century. This cheap oil was of immense importance to the Royal Navy, which had converted from coal just before World War I. "Anglo-Persian" built a great refinery at Abadan on the Gulf and dominated the economic life of Iran. To be fair, it was a remarkable commercial enterprise, providing a living as well as tolerable working conditions for its Iranian employees and investing huge sums of money in Iran. Sadly, however, the leadership of the AIOC failed to understand the nationalist spirit of postwar Iran. More foresight on their part could have saved the United States, Britain, and Iran from a sea of troubles, certainly from Mussadiq and perhaps even from Ayatollah Khomeini. Here I pay tribute to the United States for the famous "golden gimmick," the ARAMCO (Arab-American Oil Company) 50-50 profit-sharing agreement with Saudi Arabia in December 1950, which recognized the fact that the host country would want at least an equal share of the profits; in Iran, the AIOC had actually been paying more taxes to the British government off its profits than it did royalties to the Iranian government. If only AIOC had been equally wise. In international terms it might have made sense for ARAMCO and the U.S. government to have warned the AIOC and the British government in advance of the imminent deal with the Saudis, but this does not excuse us. It should have been obvious which way the wind was blowing. The AIOC had already signed the "supplemental agreement" with the Iranian government in July 1949 (supplemental because it affirmed and augmented the concession of 1933). Although this was an improvement over previous terms, it lacked the apparent clear-cut simplicity and fairness of 50-50 profit-sharing. The fact that the U.S. tax system ensured that ARAMCO did better than AIOC would have under a similar agreement does not affect the main issue. Sir William Fraser, AIOC's boss, saw the danger and tried to dress up the supplemental agreement, but it was too late.

Ali Razmara, chief of staff of the army, was appointed prime minister by the shah in June 1950. He tried to get the supplemental agreement through the Majlis, the

Iranian parliament, but the Majlis forced its withdrawal in December 1950. Nationalism and strong feelings against the company were too strong, even for Razmara to combat, and in any event the ARAMCO 50-50 agreement finally scuppered the supplemental agreement. Razmara had been the best hope, indeed the last hope, for a settlement of the oil crisis anywhere near the AIOC's terms—or perhaps for any settlement at all. He was strong and capable, fully supported by the shah. He was a practical liberal nationalist, to use the jargon of the time. He was prepared to work with the British toward a solution, for which he has, of course, been condemned as an imperialist stooge. On the surface this was a time of relative calm in which a reasonably competent cabinet tried to move forward with a seven-year development plan. The cabinet ministers raised expectations of far-reaching reforms at all levels of Iranian society, and this was, of course, the moment for the AIOC to make an unequivocal 50-50 offer, although Razmara seemed to accept the supplemental agreement.

Razmara was assassinated in March 1951, presumably because of his efforts on behalf of the supplemental agreement. Dr. Muhammad Mussadiq became prime minister in April 1951 with tremendous popular support. His appeal was simple and straightforward: unequivocal nationalism, the nationalization of the oil industry, and the elimination of the AIOC's influence, indeed of all British influence, from Iran. His first act was oil nationalization, on May 2, 1951. This was a heady moment for Iran, and the rejoicing crowds cried, "Oil has been nationalized: Long Live Dr. Muhammad Mussadiq, Iran's beloved prime minister!" And they really meant it, because, at last, they could walk tall, the imperialists had been defeated, and the streets of Tehran would soon be paved with the gold that the AIOC had been stealing from them.

The AIOC was badly shaken but still hoped that the crisis could be solved by negotiation. They sent a representative, Basil Jackson, with a 50-50 offer, which was not accepted, perhaps partly because of its presentation but more so because of Mussadiq's aversion to the British and the company. His position, power, and popularity were based on his nationalization of the AIOC, and it was probably politically impossible for him to allow them to return, certainly not openly, perhaps not even in disguise. This is one of the most important factors in this story.

The United States viewed the crisis with alarm, not out of sympathy for the AIOC but out of fear that chaos and economic collapse in Iran could lead to a Tudeh takeover. This was a dominant theme. In July President Harry S. Truman sent a most distinguished and able diplomat, Averell Harriman, as his special envoy to mediate. Mussadiq was better disposed toward the Americans than the British, and Harriman persuaded him to accept a British ministerial mission led by Cabinet Minister Sir Richard Stokes. This again failed; not so much because of its substance but partly on account of its presentation, and mostly because it was British. Indeed, the distinguished historian, Professor Wm. Roger Louis, writes: "It is debatable whether any Englishman, even of the stature of Mountbatten, could have successfully negotiated with Mussadiq."[2] Yet it was not as straightforward as that; the next offer after Stokes was from the World Bank, and it was also turned down on the grounds that it would infringe upon Iranian sovereignty. If we assume that Mussadiq, in his own very theatrical way, had the interests of Iran at heart, this was his first serious mistake. He had been entirely consistent in his opposition to the British for reasons that are easy to understand. But it was foolish to antagonize the Americans, who were fundamentally most sympathetic to him personally and to his ideas. But his rejection of the World Bank offer gave the Americans food for thought and made them understand how intensely different (and difficult) it was to negotiate with him.

On September 25, 1951, the British staff in Abadan were given notice to quit the country. The British government had considered the use of force to protect their great asset, but Prime Minister Attlee was opposed to this. The arguments against intervention were powerful and, if there were any doubt, certainly clinched by U.S. opposition. The next occurrence was an international boycott of Iranian oil, which caused a shutdown of the Abadan refinery and the cessation of the flow of oil. I visited the refinery while it was shut down; nobody bothered me but it was an uncanny experience, seeing that vast complex, all silent and dead.

Early in 1952 I left Shiraz, from where I had followed the above events with increasing disquiet, to take up the post of Oriental Secretary in the British Embassy in Tehran. Things looked bleak but not completely hopeless. We were fortunate in having a brilliant chargé d'affaires, George Middleton, and a first-class, very wise, and experienced U.S. ambassador, Loy Henderson. They worked well together. My job was political adviser and, when necessary, interpreter for Middleton. We were all three in sympathy with Iranian nationalism and recognized that, at that period in time, its personification was Mussadiq, although more and more rational and responsible Iranians were increasingly beginning to doubt his competence and to fear that he was leading the country to economic ruin. Middleton, like Mussadiq, was bilingual in French, and the personal relations between the two were excellent. They had many meetings, often exasperating for Middleton but personally agreeable. Middleton really liked "Mossy" and tried with immense perseverance to reach a settlement with him. I vividly recall one occasion when he returned from a marathon session almost elated: "I think we have done it at last, Sam." He sent his telegram to London describing the proposed settlement. I expressed some skepticism, to his annoyance, but two days later Mussadiq turned the whole idea on its head. This was typical and happened time and time again, but Middleton persisted until even he realized that Mussadiq was not prepared to make any deal. Even though Middleton was British, Mossy liked him back, for he was modern-minded and saw the Iranian point of view. Mussadiq would have been wise to use this able and sympathetic interlocutor in order to move toward agreement, but he always balked at the last moment.

The next significant episode during this period was the Ahmad Qavam interlude in July 1952, when this elder statesman briefly took Mussadiq's place as prime minister. This tends to be represented as a last, desperate attempt by the British to replace Mussadiq with their own man. I was in the thick of all this and can attest that the facts were very different. We were in no position either to depose Mussadiq or impose Qavam, although it was clearly in our interest that he should take over. He was as much of a nationalist as Mussadiq but more restrained, and he regarded the Soviet Union rather than Britain as the principal threat to Iran. Mussadiq's resignation on July 16 was precipitated by the shah's refusal to agree to his prime minister's request for control of the armed forces, which constituted the shah's principal source of influence. Qavam's five-day stay as prime minister is a story in itself. Briefly, however, he fell because the shah lost his nerve, failed to support him, and succumbed to a Tudeh-controlled mob. Both Henderson and Middleton believed Qavam could have held if the shah had backed him. He had considerable support among thinking Iranians. Middleton wrote: "The Shah was in the grip of fear: fear of taking a decision that might expose him to the fury of the populace, should Qavam not, in the event, remain in control. This attitude of the Shah is one of the central features of this crisis; we had long known that he was indecisive and timid, but we had not thought that his fear would so overcome his reason as to make him blind to the consequences of *not* supporting Qavam" (emphasis added). There is more in the same vein and I do not want to belabor the point, but it is important because popular mythology holds that Qavam was doomed from the beginning and his prime ministership was one more example of British stupidity and failure to move with the times. Middleton also wrote:

> The Shah defended his prerogatives against Mussadiq to the point of the latter's resignation and then he began to get cold feet at once and very nearly discouraged the Opposition from voting for Qavam. When the Opposition [in the Majlis] proved encouragingly firm and voted for Qavam, he refused him the support he required to stabilize the situation. When, despite his hesitancy, his troops remained loyal and effective, in the face of physical attacks and powerful propaganda, [contrary to the mythology] he withdrew his backing from them and exposed their commanders to the risks of savage reprisals. He hates taking decisions and cannot be relied upon to stick to them when taken; he has no moral courage and easily succumbs to fear; he is pre-occupied with his personal position on the Throne and thinks to retain it by a policy of appeasement; and, I am now convinced, we must see in him a deep-rooted dislike and distrust of the British. He has constantly ignored all sound advice given to him by responsible Persian statesman and by the United States Ambassador and myself, and is swayed by the advice of his Minister of Court who, I suspect, echoes His Majesty's doubts and fears.

Even Middleton, who had been prepared to give Mussadiq the benefit of every possible doubt, had reached the end of the road, although he was always prepared to go on talking. He wrote:

> If we look beyond this crisis and take a wider view it is clear that the responsibility for Persia's present ills lies principally with Mussadiq and his entourage. His strength lies in his power of demagogy, and he has so flattered the mob as the source of his power that he has, [I fear,] made it impossible for a successor to oust him by normal constitutional methods. His followers, and principally Ayatollah Kashani, have probable gone further than he intended on enlisting the support of the Tudeh for Monday's trial of strength. The chief question now facing us is whether Mussadiq's government or any other (short

of a military dictatorship) can avoid the "kiss of death" which is the well-known consequence of flirting with communists.

So Mussadiq returned in triumph on the shoulders of the mob and with the backing of the Tudeh Party. The shah acceded to all of Mussadiq's demands, which he had previously refused, and he became steadily more helpless and terrified. Although Middleton had more or less given up hope for Mussadiq, this was not yet the U.S. position, although Loy Henderson and George Middleton were generally pretty close in their assessments.

When I came to Tehran at the beginning of that year (1952), support for Mussadiq was by no means monolithic. He had, of course, touched the nationalist chord, which was full of resentment against imperialism and the desire of a once great nation to be respected again. But he had delivered nothing positive; he had destroyed but he had not built up, and he had cut off almost all of Iran's revenues. He had not known when to close a deal and had constantly asked for more. He must have understood that, although the U.S. government was sympathetic to him personally and to his nationalist aspirations, there were limits to even its generosity. It could not afford to conclude an agreement that would start a vast series of renegotiations with the world's oil producers. At the same time, he was well aware of U.S. concern that Iran might turn to communism. So he decided to go on bargaining and came with an unacceptable counterbid to the Truman-Churchill proposal of September 1952. This proposal stated that the amount of compensation should be subject to arbitration, that the Iranian government and the AIOC should negotiate on the resumption of oil production, and that the United States would grant $10 million in budgetary aid. Mussadiq demanded £50 million as an advance against oil. The proposal ultimately failed and certainly reinforced a negative view of Mussadiq.

Another major player in all this was General Fazlollah Zahedi. He seemed like a possible focus of opposition to Mussadiq and possibly even a successor. He had been imprisoned by the British during World War II for pro-Nazi activities, a strong point in his favor, from the point of view of most Iranians, for having been on record as opposing the British. Both Middleton and I met him and were favorably impressed. He was tough, clearheaded, and rational. October 1952 was a tense time and ended in the severance of diplomatic relations between Iran and Britain. (It is worth mentioning that, throughout this difficult time for Anglo-Iranian relations, we were never personally harassed and I did not feel any danger or threat.)

I next went to Washington, D.C., as a member of a small delegation to discuss Iran. Many in Washington still thought that Mussadiq was the last, best hope; we disagreed, believing that his remaining in power would lead to a Communist takeover.

What happened in 1953 is now well known: the overthrow of Mussadiq; the restoration of the shah, who had fled for a brief period; and the establishment of a pro-Western government in Tehran under General Zahedi. This was followed by the remarkable consortium oil agreement, which reflects the greatest credit on all concerned and even enabled AIOC to obtain 40 percent of the consortium with handsome compensation.

It is a widely held view among those interested in the history of the Middle East that it was a grave mistake to depose Mussadiq. It is interesting to speculate what would have happened if the Democrats had won in the United States in 1952. Democrat Adlai Stevenson, as president, would presumably have retained Dean Acheson as secretary of state and George C. McGhee as assistant secretary of state for Near East and South Asian affairs and continued to negotiate with Mussadiq. It is impossible to predict whether they would have succeeded, bearing in mind that there were limits to what the United States could concede. Mussadiq did indeed reject the "final offer" by the Republicans on March 10, 1953. With hindsight it could conceivably have been better to continue until some sort of agreement was reached with Mussadiq, but we shall never know. I very much doubt it, even today.

Let us go back forty years. The Korean War had just ended; World War III had been avoided. It was thought at the time that a Communist takeover of Iran would have been a disaster of appalling magnitude and might indeed have led to global conflict. It is questionable whether the United States could have tolerated the Soviet Union on the Gulf. One cannot in any way compare this scenario with what actually happened: a pro-Western government until 1979 and, thereafter, the irritant of Khomeini, who was impartial in his hatred of the superpowers. It was impossible to predict in 1953 that the shah, who was in a relatively strong position at the time of his restoration, could have developed into such a disagreeable tyrant, nor could we have foreseen Khomeini. We saw the immediate danger, and I remain completely convinced that it was right and, indeed, vital, *given the circumstances of the time,* to topple Mussadiq.

While we are considering "what ifs," there is another, intriguing possibility. Let us imagine that the AIOC and the British government had listened to their wisest advisers. A 50-50 oil agreement would have been concluded between the AIOC and the Iranian government no later than 1950. It seems highly probable that Mussadiq would never have come to power. Iran would have become prosperous some five years earlier, and the poverty, misery, and political instability of the Mussadiq years would have been avoided. The shah's throne would not have been threatened, and there would have been far less reason for a passionate, xenophobic nationalist movement. In spite of Iran's endemic corruption, some of the oil wealth would have gone toward development and even filtered down to the people years earlier. It is possible that the weak shah, not having been threatened and terrified to the extent he was during the Mussadiq period, might have developed into a capable and benevolent ruler. He seemed genuinely to want to help his people, and his tyranny was probably motivated by fear as much as anything. So perhaps there would have been less opposition to him, and perhaps he would have survived. Nevertheless, he would still have tried to Westernize too fast, angering the *mullahs,* and his family would have been no less corrupt. Then we can ask whether tough U.S. support could have saved him at the end of the 1970s.

Many scholars have criticized U.S. and British policy vis-à-vis Mussadiq. Their arguments, in summary, are as follows: Mussadiq was a rare phenomenon in Iran in that he was both honest and a democrat. He represented resurgent Iranian nationalism and was both beloved and respected by the Iranian people. He was not a Communist—far from it—and he came from the landed ruling class, although he differed in his humanity and caring approach. Consequently, he was exactly the sort of leader whom the West should have supported, since he stood for nonviolent, progressive change. This was precisely what was needed to combat communism and lead Iran to true freedom and prosperity. Such an Iran would have been friendly to the United States. For the wrong reasons, however, the U.S. government deposed Mussadiq, supported the increasingly tyrannical shah, and thereby helped to bring about the Khomeini revolution, with all its unfortunate consequences for U.S.-Iranian relations. The corollary to this argument is that an oil deal should have been made with Mussadiq, whatever the cost; or, even if this had proved impossible in the medium term, he should have been supported as our last, best hope in Iran and a bulwark against communism.

This chapter spells out the case that favored the deposing of Mussadiq. Clearly it would have been more desirable and in the interests of the United States, Iran, and, indeed, Britain if we could have made a reasonably satisfactory deal with Mussadiq. It might even, with the benefit of hindsight, have been better to make a poor deal than no deal at all. There were, however, limits beyond which it would have been impossible to go without upsetting the global oil business. Maybe it would have been worth it, and the cost to the United States might have been less than that of the Khomeini revolution. It is difficult to say, but, in my opinion, Mussadiq turned down some good offers that might have prevented the crisis.

In 1952 we were very worried about the Soviet, Chinese, and world Communist threats, with extremely good reason: Tensions were high and real. There was the Korean War and Stalin was still alive in all his psychopathic and dangerous malevolence. At the time, the prospect of a communist Iran was alarming and, we thought, could have led to World War III.

The U.S. government was anxious to see, at least up to our visit to Washington in November 1952, that Mussadiq remain in office. It was with reluctance, and after the rejection of its final offer in March 1953, that it decided to support the coup. As for Mussadiq himself, he was probably an honest, sincere Iranian nationalist. He was certainly a brilliant demagogue. It is questionable, to say the least, whether he was capable of running Iran. Many Iranians—by no means all "lackeys of the imperialists"—to whom we spoke at the time were convinced of the contrary. There was a sort of mob rule. To this day, I remain utterly convinced that the Communist danger was too great to ignore and would have produced knee-jerk reactions that could have led to global catastrophe. Not only our intelligence services but an enlightened liberal of the caliber of George Middleton, who tried desperately to reach agreement with Mussadiq, were in no doubt that the lovable old man had to go.

To conclude on a personal note: In the British Foreign Service I was known as "Red Sam." This was because I believed in liberal causes, resurgent nationalism, and the like. Later I was a fervent supporter of both Egyptian President Gamal 'Abd al-Nasser and the Iraqi nationalists. Thus, Dr. Mussadiq was initially a man after my own heart, and I am on record as a remorseless critic of the AIOC. The fact that even I eventually became convinced that he had to be replaced says something; all my beliefs, or, if you like, prejudices, were in the other direction—on his side. Sadly, he could not control the Communists, and they would have removed him from power and replaced him with one of their own.

The Mussadiq crisis of 1951–1953, and, as I see it, the first Iranian revolution, led to two contradictory and consequently misleading conclusions. First, the strength of nationalism and the need for foreign governments and commercial enterprises to come to terms with it were clearly demonstrated. The second point, however, is that foreign powers were nevertheless able to depose at will uncooperative governments in Third World countries. The latter was highly dangerous and led to grievous miscalculation in the 1956 Suez crisis when, as in Iraq in 1958, the former was ignored.

Notes

1. These and other quotes contained in this chapter are gleaned from the personal records of the author.

2. Wm. Roger Louis, *The British Empire in the Middle East, 1945–1951* (Oxford: Clarendon Press, 1984), p. 652.

Part Two

The Cold War in
the Middle East

6

National Security Concerns in U.S. Policy Toward Egypt, 1949–1956

Peter Hahn

From the late 1940s through the Suez crisis of 1956, U.S. officials faced a bewildering variety of security problems with regard to Egypt. In the late 1940s, a bitter dispute raged between Great Britain, a cold war partner that wished to remain in possession of its military base facilities in the Suez Canal Zone, and Egypt, a nationalistic state that sought to escape British military occupation. Each side sought U.S. endorsement of its position in this dispute, which remained unsolved into the early 1950s. After the Egyptian revolution of 1952, President Gamal 'Abd al-Nasser negotiated the departure of British forces from his country and challenged the remnants of Western imperialism elsewhere in the region. U.S. officials found it impossible to reconcile Nasser's nationalism to their security interests in the Middle East and therefore sought to undermine his prestige and influence in the region. When Britain decided to wage war on Egypt in late 1956, however, U.S. officials took steps to halt the attack on the grounds of U.S. national security. From the late 1940s to 1956, Washington consistently made policy toward Egypt on the basis of its security interests.

During the decades preceding World War II, Egypt emerged as a region of strategic importance to the British Empire. Britain militarily occupied Egypt in 1882 in order to protect the Suez Canal and lines of communications to India, and it gained enormous advantages during World War I by closing the canal to the Central Powers and by staging troops in Egypt for the Gallipoli and Jerusalem campaigns. Having legally secured the right to occupy Egypt through the 1936 Anglo-Egyptian

Adapted from *The United States, Great Britain, and Egypt, 1945–1956: Strategy and Diplomacy in the Early Cold War*, by Peter L. Hahn. Copyright © 1991 by The University of North Carolina Press. Reprinted by permission.

treaty, the British used the Suez Canal Zone during World War II to deny Axis forces in North Africa easy access to oil fields in the Middle East, to ensure vital communications and transit between the Indian Ocean and the Mediterranean, and to develop a major base that boasted airfields, supply dumps, repair shops, and personnel facilities. At war's end, nearly 200,000 British troops were stationed in the Canal Zone base.[1]

U.S. officials who examined the security situation in the Middle East during the early years of the cold war recognized the immense potential strategic importance of Egypt. As international tensions escalated during 1945 and 1946, defense officials identified the British base in the Suez Canal Zone as a facility of vital importance. In the event of war against the Soviet Union, they reasoned, Western access to the base would prove essential to victory. To promote national security, in other words, U.S. officials would support London's quest to maintain its base in Egypt.

The U.S.-Soviet confrontation over Turkey in 1946 first attracted the attention of Pentagon officials to Egypt. "Any action which threatens Britain's control of the Suez Canal and deprives her of a sizable portion of the Middle East oil fields," the Joint War Plans Committee (JWPC) observed, "threatens her position as a world power." Soviet conquest of the Suez Canal "would have serious adverse effects upon British capabilities in a major war."[2]

Contingency war plans devised in the Pentagon in 1946 also stressed the importance of maintaining access to British air bases in Egypt. In the event of hostilities, according to a war plan code-named PINCHER, U.S. bombers would attack the Soviet Union's oil industry in order to cripple its war-making capability. Bombers would need air bases in Egypt in order to reach a sufficient number of vulnerable targets in the southern Soviet Union. Bombers dispatched from England, Pakistan, or Japan would lack the range to strike such targets. From airfields in the Suez Canal Zone, Western bombers could reach Moscow, the "nerve center" of Soviet power, and a host of other valuable targets. "Early availability of secure V[ery] H[eavy] B[omber] operating bases in the Cairo area," the war plan MAKEFAST added in late 1946, "is essential to the attainment of the strategic air offensive objectives."[3]

Military bases in Egypt also possessed other attractive features. Pentagon planners were confident that bases in the Canal Zone could be defended against the southward Soviet thrust anticipated in the opening stages of war. Egypt's proximity to the Soviet Union qualified it as a staging area for offensive operations into south-central Russia. The Suez Canal corridor enabled provision of the country from the Indian Ocean should the enemy close the Mediterranean. Egypt would likely emerge as a base for psychological warfare measures targeted especially at secessionists in southern Russia. As the JWPC stressed, the importance of possessing bases in Egypt "can hardly be over-emphasized."[4]

Pentagon planners confirmed the importance of British bases in Egypt as the cold war escalated in 1948 and 1949. In June 1948, during the Berlin crisis, the Joint Strategic Planning Group (JSPG) observed that facilities in Egypt needed to defeat the Soviet Union in war "far exceed[ed] those envisaged" in earlier plans. In July, the

Joint Chiefs of Staff (JCS) stressed that Egypt remained essential "as a base from which to initiate an air offensive against vital elements of the Soviet warmaking capacity." In December, army officers recognized Egypt's "important role" in any military engagement in the Middle East. In March 1949, U.S. Secretary of Defense James Forrestal confirmed Egypt's abiding importance to U.S. national security. "In the event of global war," the National Security Council (NSC) resolved in late 1949, after the Chinese Communist revolution and the Soviet detonation of an atomic bomb, "the United States would probably wish to use facilities in the Cairo-Suez area in conjunction with the British." Indeed, army planners presumed, "should emergency dictate, the U.S. will avail itself of any facilities held by the British."[5]

From 1950 to 1953, the strategic value of British facilities in Egypt diminished slightly but remained significant. The development of long-range aircraft reduced the importance of Egypt as a launching point for any strategic air offensive against Soviet targets, but the country remained vital as a poststrike landing-and-refueling point for heavy bombers launched from Britain and as a defensive barrier, supply depot, and staging area. Renovations at Abu Sueir, Canal Zone (started in 1949 and completed in 1952) made it the only air base in the Middle East capable of handling heavy bombers. U.S. military officials secretly stockpiled supplies at Abu Sueir and Cairo International Airport. In the eyes of U.S. strategists, national security dictated that British military facilities in Egypt remain accessible to Western powers in the event of war.[6]

U.S. interest in maintaining British military facilities in Egypt for national security reasons conflicted with U.S. interest in mollifying Egyptian nationalism for political reasons. In the late 1940s, Egyptian nationalists began to challenge Britain's presence in their country. Specifically, they demanded revision or abrogation of the 1936 Anglo-Egyptian treaty that authorized the British base in the Canal Zone. Extensive Anglo-Egyptian negotiations in the late 1940s failed to reach a settlement, and nationalists turned to other tactics, including work stoppages, boycotts, and terrorist attacks, to compel the British to leave. Until the early 1950s, Britain resisted the Egyptian demands, and a deadlock ensued.[7]

The Anglo-Egyptian conflict confronted the United States with a thorny dilemma. Some officials of the U.S. Department of State wanted to recognize Egyptian national aspirations in order to ensure the loyalty of the Egyptian people and other Third World nations in the cold war as well as to honor the U.S. ideal of self-determination. To Pentagon officials, however, a British departure from Egypt, in the absence of satisfactory promises by Egypt to allow access to its bases, would imperil national security.[8]

U.S. officials considered access to military bases in Egypt so vital that they repeatedly subsumed their conflicting political interests in Egypt. In May 1946, for example, U.S. officials interceded on London's behalf in Anglo-Egyptian negotiations that had stalemated over the question of Britain's right to return to bases in Egypt after it departed the country. U.S. Secretary of State James Byrnes told King Farouk that he hoped Egypt would avoid "running the risk of undermining the security of the Middle East" in its quest for "full sovereignty." Egypt's hostile reaction to that message made U.S. officials reluctant to intercede again, but they quietly encouraged the British to remain firm in negotiations with Cairo.[9]

In preparation for the Anglo-American "Pentagon talks" of October 1947, U.S. Department of Defense officials insisted that the United States endorse Britain's position in Egypt for reasons of national security. Despite their fears that angering Egyptian nationalists might undermine the very Western interests that the Pentagon wished to preserve, officials at Foggy Bottom agreed. At the talks, State Department officials suggested that Britain appease Egyptian nationalism by agreeing in principle to withdraw eventually from Egypt, but they relented easily when British officials protested that this step would signal weakness. U.S. and British officials agreed that "the British should have the right to maintain [in Egypt] . . . certain strategic facilities . . . during peacetime in such a condition that they could be effectively and speedily used in case of an immediate threat to the security of the Middle East." It would be "dangerous in the present world situation for the British Government to abandon such strategic facilities to which it is entitled by treaty in Egypt." In these Anglo-American talks—conducted as the cold war was intensifying—U.S. officials sacrificed their interest in appeasing nationalism to national security considerations.[10]

U.S. officials showed slightly more concern for Egyptian nationalism in 1949. Because Egypt blamed the United States for the creation of Israel, the war in Palestine had embittered Cairo against Washington. To avoid further alienation, U.S. officials refused a British request to participate in talks between British and Egyptian military officers about the future of the British bases in the Canal Zone. By early 1950, however, State Department officials again interceded in Anglo-Egyptian negotiations to urge the government of Egyptian Prime Minister Mustapha Nahas to recognize that Western defense rights in Egypt were consonant with Egyptian sovereignty. "If Egypt insists that Britain withdraw her troops from the Suez zone," Assistant Secretary of State George C. McGhee told the Egyptian ambassador, "it would result in a weakening of Egypt's military strength at precisely a time when Egypt desires to increase her powers of resistance." In July, following the eruption of the Korean War, McGhee refused an Egyptian appeal for support in negotiations with London, instead warning that "Russian aggression in the Near Eastern area" loomed possible, in which case "it would be essential to our common strategic plans to have the British on the spot."[11]

In late 1950 and early 1951, however, U.S. officials came to fear that unmollified Egyptian nationalism might abet the rise of neutralism in that state and throughout the Middle East. "The Near Eastern nations are at a point of decision," Samuel K.C. Kopper, deputy director of the Division of Near Eastern Affairs, noted in December 1950, "as to whether to cast their lot irrevocably with the West, to remain neutral, or to drift into the Soviet orbit." Pressuring Egyptian leaders to align with the West, McGhee concluded in early 1951, was bound to fail. A compromise solution to the base dispute, McGhee realized, "would outweigh the present advantages of the British position."[12]

In 1951, therefore, U.S. officials devised the Middle East Command (MEC) concept to bridge the gap between strategic and political interests in Egypt. The MEC idea envisioned a multilateral, anti-Soviet defense arrangement that would include Egyptian military officers with headquarters in Cairo. Unfortunately, the chance that Egypt would approve MEC diminished in the summer of 1951, when the United Nations (UN) Security Council, at the behest of Britain and France, passed a resolution censuring Egyptian restrictions on canal shipping destined for Israel. Before Western powers found the time to propose MEC to the government in Cairo, Prime Minister Nahas had commenced parliamentary procedures to nullify the 1936 Anglo-Egyptian treaty. Egypt summarily rejected MEC.[13]

State Department officials were deeply troubled by Egypt's rejection of MEC, by its abrogation of the treaty, and by a wave of violence between British troops and Egyptian guerrillas in late 1951 and early 1952. The turmoil helped trigger the revolution of July 1952, in which a clique of military officers led by Gamal 'Abd al-Nasser ousted King Farouk. Alarmed by the parallel rise of revolutionary nationalism in Egypt and Iran, Secretary of State Dean G. Acheson feared that the entire Middle East might turn hostile to the West unless Britain made concessions to end its impasse with Egypt. Pentagon officials, on the other hand, favored fully endorsing Britain's stubborn position. The NSC reconciled these positions by resolving in April 1952 "to induce the U.K. to modify its position in ways which, while maintaining basic Western interests, might make possible an early negotiated settlement." But Britain would not be induced to make any concessions, and the Anglo-Egyptian impasse persisted into 1953. In light of national security requirements, U.S. officials refrained from strongly pressuring the British to make those concessions that might have served the U.S. political interest of mollifying Egyptian nationalism.[14]

In 1952 and 1953, changing circumstances in the Middle East and elsewhere rendered the Canal Zone military base less essential to U.S. and British security. British officials concluded in late 1952 that Soviet development of atomic weapons made it dangerous to concentrate 80,000 soldiers in a single base site within Soviet bomber range. Attacks by Egyptian guerrilla fighters, moreover, inflicted severe human, psychological, and financial costs. The Canal Zone base, though still important, seemed to the British no longer indispensable. They decided to move their headquarters to Cyprus, relocate troops to the home isles, and rely on rapid air transit in the event of an emergency.[15]

Similar ideas developed on the western shore of the Atlantic. When Turkey joined the North Atlantic Treaty Organization (NATO) in 1952, the Pentagon began thinking about shifting its Middle East security focus from Egypt to the northern tier of the region. After Pakistan joined the Southeast Asia Treaty Organization (SEATO) in 1954, a northern tier pact offered to complete a chain of anti-Soviet pacts from East Asia to northern Europe. The governments of the northern tier seemed more ready than Arab states such as Egypt to cooperate with Western defense plans. More secure than the lone, gigantic base at Suez, a series of smaller facilities scattered along the Soviet perimeter also provided advantages in intelligence collection and offensive capabilities. For example, Thor and Jupiter missiles, developed in the mid-1950s, could carry nuclear payloads but for only short distances.[16]

In 1953, President Dwight D. Eisenhower and Secretary of State John Foster Dulles approved a shift in U.S. strategic focus from Egypt to the northern tier. Conversations during a tour of the Middle East in the spring of 1953 convinced Dulles that Egypt, beset by rampant forces of nationalism, would not serve as a reliable security partner but that northern tier states would. Turkey and Pakistan, he observed, would serve as cornerstones of a defense pact of states that "are most conscious of the Soviet threat and most disposed to cooperate with western powers." Dulles declared the original MEC idea to be "on the shelf." In 1954, U.S. Air Force officials canceled planned improvements at the Abu Sueir airfield. The northern tier idea came to fruition with the signing of a Turkish-Iraqi pact in Baghdad on February 24, 1955. Britain joined the Baghdad Pact in April 1955; Pakistan joined in September and Iran in October.[17]

In light of Egypt's diminished strategic importance, U.S. officials pressed the British to make concessions needed to break their deadlock with Egypt. With strong U.S. urging, a reluctant Churchill government approved a base treaty in July 1954 (signed in October 1954). The accord terminated the 1936 treaty, provided for withdrawal of British forces over twenty months, permitted British civilian technicians to maintain the base, and authorized the British military to return in the event of Soviet attack on Turkey or any Arab state. British forces completed their departure in June 1956.[18]

U.S. officials hoped that Nasser, with his independence secured, would cooperate with Western security plans, endorse the northern tier pact, and eventually join it. "We are counting on Egypt," Deputy Assistant Secretary of State John D. Jernegan noted on August 16, 1954, "to play an important leadership role . . . in the achievement of United States policy objectives in the Middle East." Nasser talked about forming an Arab League collective security pact and Dulles suggested linking this pact to the northern tier arrangement via an Egyptian-Turkish mutual defense treaty. Nasser's initial reaction and his acceptance of $40 million in U.S. economic aid in late 1954 encouraged U.S. hopes that Nasser would become a security partner.[19]

By early 1955, however, such U.S. optimism seemed unfounded. Nasser refused to accept U.S. military aid because of the standard condition that a U.S. military mission would administer it, a condition that to him smacked of colonialism. He also rejected a secret U.S. plan, which would have violated congressional rules for administering aid, to divert $5 million of the $40 million in economic aid to military hardware purchases.[20]

As negotiations on military aid stalemated, Nasser emerged as a thorn in America's side in the Middle East. He reversed himself on the northern tier idea and became a chief critic of the Baghdad Pact. He claimed as Egypt's mission the riddance of Western imperialism from the Middle East. He reacted strongly to Israeli provocations and responded coolly to the Anglo-American "Alpha" peace plan. In the absence of U.S. military aid grants, Nasser purchased a massive quantity of arms from the Soviet Union in September 1955.[21]

Eisenhower and Dulles at first tried to appeal to Nasser by offering to finance construction of the Aswan dam, and they tried to pacify the Egyptian-Israeli situation by sending special emissary Robert Anderson to broker a deal in early 1956. But Nasser would neither accept the conditions of the dam aid offer nor cooperate fully with the Anderson mission. Worse, in early 1956, he encouraged anti-British rioters in Jordan and Bahrain, continued to criticize the Baghdad Pact, bought weapons from Poland, and recognized the People's Republic of China. NSC officials concluded that Nasser's "positive neutralism actually works in favor of the Soviet bloc since it is directed against established western positions."[22]

U.S. officials had concluded by March 1956 that, despite their efforts to woo Nasser, he had emerged as a threat to their national security interests in the Middle East. With the British, therefore, they concocted the Omega policy, a series of steps designed to undercut Nasser's prestige among Arab peoples and possibly to remove him from power. Omega would "let Colonel Nasser realize," Dulles noted, "that he cannot cooperate as he is doing with the Soviet Union and at the same time enjoy most-favored-nation treatment from the United States." Omega planned for the gradual withdrawal of the Aswan aid offer, but in July, under strong congressional pressure, Dulles canceled the deal abruptly. Nasser retaliated against the Aswan renege by nationalizing the Suez Canal Company and announcing that its revenues would finance the dam.[23]

Nasser's seizure of the canal company provoked the Suez Crisis of late 1956. The British at once resolved to use force to recover control of the waterway and knock Nasser from power, and they eventually conspired with the French and the Israelis to launch a tripartite attack against Egypt that began October 29. President Eisenhower, by contrast, decided early in the crisis that force would threaten U.S. national security interests. A British attack on Egypt would foment Anglophobia around the world, inflame Arab nationalism (and thus imperil oil supplies to the West), and result in a long and costly British occupation of the Suez Canal Zone. For the United States to allow London to wage war on Egypt, Eisenhower told the NSC on July 31, "might well array the world from Dakar to the Philippine Islands against us." A breach with London would "be extremely serious, but not as serious as letting a war start and not trying to stop it."[24]

Accordingly, Eisenhower sought to use diplomacy to delay a British attack, on the calculation that time would cool British tempers and avert war. In late July he dispatched Deputy Under Secretary of State for Political Affairs Robert Murphy and Dulles to London to soothe British anger. In August, Eisenhower and Dulles arranged the London Conference to devise a diplomatic solution to the question of control of the canal, in September they proposed establishment of a Suez Canal Users Association to govern the waterway, and in October they encouraged Britain and Egypt to resolve their differences through negotiations sponsored by the United Nations. Eisenhower also publicly and privately appealed to British Prime Minister Anthony Eden to practice restraint. "The use of force," he cabled Eden on September 3, "would . . . vastly increase the area of jeopardy." The developing world "would be consolidated against the West to a degree which, I fear, could not be overcome in a generation and, perhaps, not even in a century."[25]

Once hostilities began on October 29, Eisenhower moved to end the fighting promptly for three national security reasons. First, he regretted that the attack on Egypt diverted global attention from Moscow's brutal crushing of the rebellion in Hungary. Second, he feared that the Soviets would politically support Egypt and thereby win favor among developing nations. Unless the United States ended the fighting, Dulles observed, "all of these newly independent countries will turn from us to the USSR. We will be looked upon as forever tied to British and French colonialist policies." "How can we possibly support Britain and France," Eisenhower added, "if in so doing we lose the entire Arab world." U.S. inaction would enable the Soviet Union to seize "a mantle of world leadership through a false but convincing exhibition of concern for smaller nations."[26]

Third, Eisenhower gravely worried about Soviet threats to intervene militarily to defend Egypt. On November 5, one day after crushing the rebellion in Budapest, Moscow threatened to send troops to Egypt and to fire rockets on London and Paris. The JCS interpreted this statement as "serious intent on the part of the Soviets." Eisenhower observed that Soviet leaders were "scared and furious" over Hungary, "and there is nothing more dangerous than a dictatorship in this frame of mind." The president warned Moscow that the United States would defend its allies, but he also tightened his diplomatic and financial squeezes to convince Britain and France to halt the fighting. Both powers accepted a UN cease-fire on November 6.[27]

From the mid-1940s to the mid-1950s, U.S. officials consistently made policy toward Egypt on grounds of national security. From 1946 to 1953, the overriding strategic importance of British military facilities in Egypt compelled them actively and passively to endorse Britain's determination to remain in the Suez Canal Zone over Egypt's strong opposition. Such security concerns, in light of the cold war and the Korean War, convinced officials in Washington to subsume their conflicting political interest in befriending Egyptian nationalism. Only when the move to the northern tier diminished the strategic importance of Egypt did U.S. officials find it safe to pressure Britain to reach a settlement providing for withdrawal of British forces from the Suez Canal Zone.

After the 1954 Anglo-Egyptian treaty, U.S. officials hoped to win Nasser's cooperation with their plans for securing the Middle East against Soviet expansion. But Nasser refused U.S. overtures and emerged as a leading critic of Western influence in the region. Therefore, again for reasons of national security, U.S. officials together with the British initiated the Omega policy to undermine Nasser's prestige in the Middle East and, perhaps, even his power in Cairo.

National security concerns also determined U.S. behavior during the Suez crisis of late 1956. Fear that the Soviet Union would gain politically or intervene militarily compelled Eisenhower to oppose British plans for war against Nasser and then to use his power to halt the attack once it began. Contrary to its political concerns, the United States censured its British ally and rescued Nasser from aggression during the

Suez conflict. Such actions were entirely consistent with Washington's national security imperatives, which prevailed, as before, over its competing political interests.

Notes

1. D. A. Farnie, *East and West of Suez: The Suez Canal in History* (Oxford: Clarendon, 1969), pp. 32–93; and Peter Mansfield, *The British in Egypt* (London: Weidenfeld and Nicolson, 1971), pp. 201–219, 265–275.

2. JWPC 450/3, 10 March 1946, Record Group (RG) 218, Records of the Joint Chiefs of Staff, CCS 092 USSR (3-27-45), section 6 (hereinafter RG 218 with appropriate filing designations), National Archives, Washington, D.C. (hereinafter National Archives).

3. "PINCHER," JPS 789, 2 March 1946, U.S. Department of Defense, Joint Chiefs of Staff, Records of the Joint Chiefs of Staff: Soviet Union (Washington, D.C.: University Publications Microfilm, 1978), reel 1; and "Air Plan for MAKEFAST," n.d. [autumn 1946], RG 165, Records of the Army Staff, ABC 381 USSR (2 March 1946), section 3, National Archives.

4. JWPC 450/3, 10 March 1946, RG 218, CCS 092 USSR (3-27-45), section 7. See also JIS 226/3, 4 March 1946, RG 218, CCS 092 USSR (3-27-45), section 5.

5. JSPC 684/40, 2 June 1948, RG 319, Records of the Army Staff, P&O 686 TS, case 1, National Archives (hereafter RG 319 with appropriate filing designations); JCS 1887/1, 28 July 1948, RG 218, CCS 381 EMMEA (11-19-47); unsigned report on Egyptian airfields, 1 December 1948, RG 319, P&O 686, case 273; NSC 47/2, 17 October 1949, Harry S. Truman Papers, President's Secretary's Files, Subject File: NSC Series, box 193, Harry S. Truman Library, Independence, Missouri (hereinafter Truman Library); and memorandum by Maddocks, 4 February 1949, RG 319, P&O 686 TS, case 9. See also NSC 45, 17 March 1949, RG 273, Records of the National Security Council, National Archives (hereafter RG 273 with appropriate filing designations).

6. NSC 68, 14 April 1950, U.S. Department of State, Foreign Relations of the United States, 1950 (Washington, D.C.: U.S. Government Printing Office, 1959–1990), 1:261–262 (hereinafter FRUS with volume and page citations); Walter S. Poole, The History of the Joint Chiefs of Staff, vol. 4: The Joint Chiefs of Staff and National Policy, 1950–1952 (Wilmington, Del.: Glazier, 1980), pp. 161–172; Bradley to Lovett, 25 June 1952, RG 330, Records of the Office of the Secretary of Defense, CD 092 (Egypt) 1952, National Archives (hereafter RG 330 with appropriate filing designations); NSC 129/1, 24 April 1952, RG 273; and JSPC 684/130, 1 November 1952, U.S. Department of Defense, Joint Chiefs of Staff, Records of the Joint Chiefs of Staff: The Middle East (Washington, D.C.: University Publications Microfilm, 1978), reel 1.

7. Peter L. Hahn, *The United States, Great Britain, and Egypt, 1945–1956: Strategy and Diplomacy in the Early Cold War* (Chapel Hill: University of North Carolina Press, 1991), pp. 94–109, 132–139.

8. See, for example, memorandum of conversation by Battle, 27 January 1952, RG 59, General Records of the U.S. Department of State, 774.00, National Archives (hereafter RG 59 with appropriate filing designations); report by Hendershot, 4 April 1952, RG 59, 611.80; Summary of Discussion, 23 April 1952, and NSC 129/1, 24 April 1952, RG 273; and Bradley to Lovett, 25 June 1952, RG 330, CD 092 (Egypt) 1952.

9. Byrnes to Tuck, 24 May 1946, RG 59, 741.83. See also Tuck to Byrnes, 27 May and 11 June 1946, and Clark to Byrnes, 27 June 1946, ibid.

10. U.S.-U.K. Agreed Minute, n.d. [16 October 1947], Foreign Office (hereinafter FO) 800/476, Records of the Foreign Secretary's Office, ME/47/17, Public Record Office (hereinafter PRO), Kew Gardens, London. See also Memorandum of Conversation by Hare, 9 October 1947, FRUS 5 (1947):561–562; State Department Policy Memoranda, n.d. [c. early October 1947], ibid., pp. 521–522, 543–544; and Royall to Marshall, 29 September 1947, and Unsigned Memorandum for the Record, 23 September 1947, RG 319, P&O 091.7 (section 2), case 50.

11. Memorandum of Conversation by Acheson, 13 April 1950, Dean G. Acheson Papers, U.S. Secretary of State Series, box 64, Truman Library; and Memorandum of Conversation by Stabler, 17 July 1950, RG 59, 641.74. See also Acheson to Holmes, 17 February 1949, FRUS 6 (1949):194–195.

12. Paper by Kopper, 27 December 1950, FRUS 5 (1950):11–14; and Minutes of Meeting, 2 May 1951, FRUS 5 (1951):113–120.

13. Peter L. Hahn, "Containment and Egyptian Nationalism: The Unsuccessful Effort to Establish the Middle East Command, 1950–1953," *Diplomatic History* 11(1) (Winter 1987):23–40.

14. NSC 129/1, 24 April 1952, RG 273.

15. Memorandum by Eden, 27 October 1952, Records of the Cabinet Office, CAB 129/56, C(52)369, PRO; Minutes of Meeting, 29 October 1952, Cabinet Meetings Minutes, CAB 128/25, CC 91(52)7, PRO; and Minutes of Meeting, 11 December 1952, Records of the British Defence Committee, CAB 131/12, D(52)12/4, PRO.

16. JCS to Lovett, 17 October 1952, RG 330, CD 092 (Middle East 1952); NSC 155/1, 14 July 1953, NSC 5428, 23 July 1954, and progress report on NSC 5428, 7 April 1955, RG 273; and unsigned Memorandum by State Department, 17 May 1954, RG 59, 611.41.

17. Circular Telegram by Dulles, 30 July 1953, RG 59, 780.5. See also Washbourne to Division of Operations, 28 September 1954, and Memorandum for the Record by Logan, 8 December 1954, RG 341, Records of the Headquarters of the U.S. Air Force, National Archives.

18. Shuckburgh diary, 27 July 1954, Evelyn Shuckburgh, *Descent to Suez: Diaries, 1951–1956* (New York: Norton, 1987), p. 233; and Murray to Eden, 3 November 1954, PREM 11/702, Records of the Prime Minister's Office, PRO (hereinafter PREM with appropriate filing designations).

19. Jernegan to Murphy, 16 August 1954, RG 59, 774.13. See also Hart to Byroade, 26 October 1954, and Caffery to Dulles, 6 November 1954, RG 59, 774.5MSP.

20. Caffery to Dulles, 16 September and 27 November 1954, RG 59, 774.5MSP; Memorandum by Operations Coordinating Board (hereinafter OCB) working group, 21 December 1954, OCB.091, Egypt folder, OCB Central File Series, NSC Staff Papers, Dwight D. Eisenhower Library, Abilene, Kansas (hereinafter Eisenhower Library); and Stevenson to Eden, 17 January 1955, Political Correspondence of the Foreign Office, FO 371/113608, JE1057/1, PRO.

21. Byroade to Dulles, 20 May and 9 June 1955, FRUS 14 (1955–1957):192, 234; Powers to Radford, 18 August 1955, RG 218, CJCS (Radford) 091 Egypt; State Department Report, 12 September 1955, IR 7042, Records of the Research and Analysis Branch, RG 59; and progress report on NSC 5428, 2 November 1955, RG 273.

22. Progress Report on NSC 5428, 17 May 1956, RG 273. See also Progress Report on NSC 5428, 2 November 1955, RG 273; Dulles to Macmillan, 5 December 1955, FRUS 14

(1955):820–821; Memorandum of Conversation, [30 January 1956], Dwight D. Eisenhower Papers (Ann Whitman File): International Series, box 20, Eisenhower Library (hereafter Whitman File with appropriate filing designations); Hoover to Dulles, 16 March 1956, John Foster Dulles Papers, White House Memoranda Series, box 4, Princeton University, Princeton, N.J. (hereinafter Dulles Papers with appropriate filing designations); and Eisenhower diary entry, 8 March 1956, Whitman File: Diary Series, box 9.

23. Dulles to Eisenhower, 28 March 1956, Whitman File: Diary Series, box 13. See also memorandum of conversation, 19 July 1956, and Byroade to Dulles, 26 July 1956, FRUS 15 (1955–1957):867–873, 906–908.

24. Memorandum of Conversation by Goodpaster, 31 July 1956, Whitman File: Diary Series, box 16. See also Eden to Eisenhower, 27 July 1956, PREM 11/1098; Minutes of Meeting, 27 July 1956, Whitman File: Cabinet Series, box 7; Memorandum of Conversation by Goodpaster, 28 July 1956, Whitman File: Diary Series, box 16; and Memorandum of Conversation by Dulles, 30 July 1956, Dulles Papers, Telephone Conversation Series, box 5.

25. Eisenhower to Eden, 3 September 1956, PREM 11/1100. See also Dulles to Murphy, 30 July 1956, and Dulles to Eisenhower, 2 August 1956, Whitman File: Dulles-Herter Series, box 5; Minutes of Meeting with Dulles, 1 August 1956, PREM 11/1098; Memorandum for the Record, 12 August 1956, Whitman File: Diary Series, box 17; Position Paper, 11 September 1956, Dulles Papers, Subject Series, box 7; and Lloyd to Eden, 8–12 October 1956, PREM 11/1102.

26. Summary of Discussion, 1 November 1956, Whitman File: NSC Series, box 8; and Eisenhower to Dulles, 1 November 1956, Whitman File: International Series, box 19.

27. Circular Telegrams by JCS, 6 November 1956, RG 218, CCS 381 EMMEA (11-19-47), section 47; Memorandum of Conversation by Goodpaster, 6 November 1956, FRUS 16 (1955–1957):1014; and Memorandum of Conversation by Goodpaster, 7 November 1956, Dulles Papers, White House Memoranda Series, box 4.

7

The United States and King Hussein

Richard B. Parker

In 1955 the eastern Arab world seemed to be in a state of incipient disorder, with strong anti-Western overtones—a reaction to the establishment of the Israeli state of 1948, among other things.[1] Some states appeared less secure than others. Syria was headed in directions the United States did not like, a turn of events that had been apparent since before the elections of 1954 as leftists, though a minority, increasingly dominated politics. The American perspective on this was well presented in a gloomy telegram of October 14, 1955, from Damascus.[2] The course of events reflected the rather conservative, not to say apocalyptic, views of James Moose, the laconic Arkansan who was then U.S. ambassador to Syria. Moose, one of the early so-called Arabists in the U.S. diplomatic corps, said the principal cause of the anti-Western mood in Syria was Israel, the creation of which the United States was primarily responsible for, in Syrian eyes. Moose warned that the leftists would take over unless the United States took countermeasures and suggested a more balanced policy toward Israel, in addition to the following:

1. Prompt and sympathetic consideration of Syrian requests for military vehicles.
2. Further efforts to restrain Saudi and French intrigues.
3. Cautioning the Iraqis against adventures in Syria.
4. Encouraging Lebanon and Jordan to join the Baghdad Pact.
5. U.S. adherence to the Baghdad Pact.
6. Concertation with the United Kingdom, Turkey, Iraq, and, when appropriate, Lebanon and Jordan.

Moose evidently believed that there were important elements in Syria fundamentally well disposed toward the United States and that a sufficiently vigorous policy of support might enable them to resist the leftists, but his suggestions were a rather thin gruel. In particular, and in retrospect, it is hard to envisage Lebanese and Jordanian adherence to the Baghdad Pact as something that would counter anti-Western sentiment in Syria. Rather, one would have expected it to increase Syrian feelings of isolation and resentment, particularly since the pact was widely regarded as an attempt to divert attention from the real problem in Syria's (and Moose's) eyes—Israel.

It is noteworthy that Moose does not mention the negative attraction that Egyptian President Gamal 'Abd al-Nasser, who was bitterly opposed to the Baghdad Pact, was beginning to exert, which led to creation of the United Arab Republic (UAR) in 1958. Was Nasser not an important factor in Syrian politics in 1955? That would be surprising, given the following he had in Jordan and Lebanon at the time. Moose also seemed to have some confidence in the ability of the Iraqis to take over Syria if given free rein to do so. He suggested that as one possible course of action, if his other recommendations were not accepted. Moose also commented that a U.S. policy favoring Israel over the Arab states could not be concealed by propaganda nor made more palatable by aid operations. He added that "neither can its unfortunate effects be offset by intelligence operations."[3] This latter warning was not heeded, and we subsequently had the fiasco of 1957 described by Wilbur Crane Eveland and David Lesch, among others.[4]

In his telegram of October 22, 1955,[5] U.S. Ambassador Lester Mallory in Amman called Moose's analysis "penetrating" and said his overall conclusions were generally applicable to Jordan: There was "universal popular enthusiasm for the flame of Arab political liberation ignited by Nasser's arms deal with the Soviets," the government was weak and afraid to take unpopular measures, British influence (heretofore a principal element of stability) was steadily declining, and the Palestinians were supplanting the East Bankers. He went on to say that "bitterness towards and distrust of the United States following Palestine war receded substantially in the face of [President Dwight D.] Eisenhower and [Secretary of State John Foster] Dulles policies of impartiality. Due to events of the past year, much of this gain has been lost. It appears unlikely unfavorable trends can be reversed during continuation of the policies recently followed by US in this era."

Mallory does not say what recent events and policies he had in mind, but I believe the events included Israel's Gaza raid of February 28, 1955, and U.S. reaction thereto, the breakdown of U.S.-Egyptian talks on arms supply and the subsequent Egyptian-Czech/Soviet arms deal, the Bandung Conference, and Nasser's increasing popularity throughout the Arab world. All pointed to a sharpening polarization between the United States and militant Arabs.

As for policy, the most significant recent expressions of U.S. views on the Middle East had been John Foster Dulles's speech of August 26, 1955, which was not well received by either the Arabs or the Israelis and which marked, in effect, the end of project Alpha (an attempt to start negotiations on an Arab-Israel settlement). Mallory may have had that in mind or he may have been putting the U.S. Department of State on notice of some lesser policy development affecting Jordan, an unfavorable decision by the people who ran the aid program, perhaps, but there is no further clarification.

Mallory went on to suggest several courses of action to stem the anti-Western tide. He pointed out that money would not do the trick, nor would guarantees against Israel; he also contended that arms aid, which by implication might help, was unthinkable. (We must remember that during this period the United States was still resolutely opposed to becoming a major arms supplier to the area.) Outright pressures, such as withdrawing the U.S. aid program and U.S. support for the United Nations Relief and Works Administration (UNRWA; the United Nations itself will simply be referred to as the UN), would not work either because the Soviets would be glad to fill any vacuum the United States created in withdrawing its aid (which in any event was modest, then running about $7 million per year in development aid and technical assistance, with $25 million going to UNRWA for refugees in all Arab states). He suggested, however, that expansion of the Baghdad Pact to include the United States and Jordan would be useful and noted that Jordan was "economically nonviable" (a recurring phrase in those days), and that the only way to overcome its weakness was for Jordan to join with a more viable unit, such as Iraq. He concluded, however, that in the end one had to return to the "hard and overriding fact that to have Jordanians [and presumably other Arabs] on our side requires restraint in our relations with Israel."

The fact that both Moose and Mallory suggested Jordanian accession to the Baghdad Pact was, perhaps, a reflection of what they were hearing from their British colleagues and others about the Jordanian interest in taking such a step. Jordan's interest was so evident, particularly on King Hussein's part, that the British sent Sir Gerald Templer, hero of the postwar antiguerrilla effort in Malaya and chief of the Imperial General Staff, to Amman on December 9, 1955, to discuss Jordanian accession.

As inducement, the British were offering revision of the 1936 Anglo-Jordanian treaty and, more important to King Hussein, equipment for an armored brigade (or one infantry division and one armored division, depending on the source). Hussein wanted to accept the offer, but he was foiled by the resignation of four government officials who represented the West Bank. It was clear to the diplomatic corps in Amman that Egyptian opposition had played an important role in stirring up Jordanian public opinion against the Baghdad Pact, and Hussein later complained that he had been betrayed by Nasser. In his book *Uneasy Lies the Head,* Hussein claims that Nasser had given his blessing to his joining the pact, saying, "Any strength to Jordan is a strength for the Arab world. Therefore I can see no objection." But then, Hussein notes, everything changed. "Without warning the Egyptians launched a heavy barrage of propaganda against Jordan. Within a matter of hours Jordan was torn by riots."[6]

The Templer visit was a serious miscalculation by both the British and King Hussein. Both had misjudged the national temperament and the impact of Egyptian propaganda against the pact, particularly among Palestinians, who constituted two-thirds of the population.[7] On December 14, 1955, the Sa'id al-Mufti government resigned because al-Mufti, an amiable elder statesman from the Circassian community who was, perhaps, personally agreeable to joining the pact, would not go against popular sentiment, fearing that in so doing he would endanger his community, among other things.

The following day Hazza' al-Majali, considered a hard-liner, was charged with forming a new government. He was understood to support the pact, as well as to be recruiting a cabinet that would approve adherence to it. If that was indeed his intent, he, too, was foiled because widespread demonstrations and rioting against the pact broke out on December 16. After several days of violence, Hussein dissolved the parliament, asked Majali to resign, and made Ibrahim al-Hashim, even older than al-Mufti, prime minister of a caretaker government that lasted until a second, and more serious, round of rioting broke out on January 7, 1956. Hashim was succeeded by Samir Rifa'i, a respected politician originally from Safad, on January 8.

The two series of riots and demonstrations three weeks apart were an eye-opener in more ways than one. They showed the limited ability of the British-led Jordanian army, then known as the Arab Legion, to maintain order in the face of determined opposition. They also showed the strength of popular animosity toward the established order and its ties with the West, as well as the incapacity of traditional political leaders to control that animosity. Less important, perhaps, but a serious matter for those on the scene, it also revealed the precarious situation of the official U.S. community in Amman and Jerusalem. The Americans were spread over three of Amman's seven hills, or jabals—Luweibdeh, Amman, and Hussein. There was no circumferential road between Jabal Amman, where the residence of the ambassador as well as the homes of many other embassy officers were, and Jabal Luweibdeh, where the chancery, or U.S. embassy office building, was located. The transit from one jabal to the other had to be made through the wadi, or valley, of central Amman, where the violence was most serious: Hence the reference from the U.S. embassy in Amman to the halting of traffic "from Jebel to Jebel," which the U.S. State Department Historian's office apparently did not understand.[8]

The problem was acute enough that after the first round of riots, the U.S. aid mission bulldozed a track from Jabal Amman to Jabal Luweibdeh with the approval and support of the Arab Legion. A related problem was the embassy's communication with the scattered U.S. community, which was some 100 to 125 strong. To deal with that, a system of block wardens was established, staffed largely by the members of the aid mission, who were at home and unable to go to work because of the disturbances. This rather simple system later became standard throughout the U.S. Foreign Service.

Communication with Washington was difficult because the embassy had no radio facilities or secure telephone link for communication with Washington and had to rely on the local PTT (the Jordan government's post, telephone, and telegraph service) for sending messages internationally via either cable or radio. There was not even a telex connection with the post office. Rather, messages were encoded in the embassy and then hand-carried to the telegraph office in the main post office, which happened to be downtown—and dangerous for non-Arabs to reach during riots. Our consular officer, John Panos, an Alexandrian Greek by origin who could pass for an Arab, was pressed into messenger service. He was also instrumental in the even more dangerous task of rescuing Americans trapped in the Philadelphia Hotel during the second round of rioting.

The second round was more dangerous than the first because Lt. General John B. Glubb, or Glubb Pasha, commander of the Arab Legion, refused to intervene until given the order to do so by the king, who did not do so until late in the day. Early on January 7, Glubb privately informed us that the authorities were going to let the "schoolboys" demonstrate peacefully, and it started off quietly enough, with a crowd marching down the main street of Jabal Amman toward downtown in the early afternoon. En route they passed the aid mission's car park, full of the brightly colored Ford station wagons used by the technicians, most of whom were at home. Someone threw a rock and there was the sound of breaking glass. Immediately there was a general stoning of the compound and great damage was done. (Rock throwing was a popular means of protest in Amman long before the *intifada* and it was facilitated by close-at-hand debris from construction sites in the expanding town.)

Inspired by the successful stoning, the demonstrators became a mob and headed down the hill to attack, first of all, the Philadelphia Hotel, perhaps because foreigners stayed there. The mob was held at bay, however, by the proprietor, Mr. Nazzal, who was armed with a shotgun in the best tradition of the Old American West. The mob then moved into the center of town and began attacking government offices in the Salt Road, several of which were sacked and partially burned. At one point part of the mob moved up Jabal Luweibdeh and headed for the studio of Radio Sharq al-Awsat (Middle East Radio), a British information operation based on Cyprus. They were dissuaded from attacking it by the landlord's daughters, who confronted the demonstrators with bared breasts and cries of distress. The British correspondent then in the studio, Richard Beeston, fully expected to be incinerated and was very grateful to the women who saved him when Glubb did not. Meanwhile, as darkness approached, another part of the crowd began prying open the rolling shutters of storefronts in the center of town, and the looting was about to begin. Amman teetered on the brink of chaos. Only at this point did the Arab Legion finally intervene, sending in troops and imposing a curfew that was maintained for days until calm was restored.[9]

As people realized just how serious the events had been, recriminations began to fly. Glubb was blamed for not intervening sooner, and there were the usual conspiratorial explanations for his failure to save the Jordanians from themselves. Glubb had been honest and correct in insisting that he be given orders to intervene, and any failure to issue them lay at the king's door. We in the embassy thought the king did not want to issue those orders for fear it would be an unpopular act.

In any event, Hussein sacked Glubb on March 1.[10] The Arab Legion's performance on January 7 was undoubtedly one factor in the king's decision, but he was also reacting to the criticisms by younger Arab officers of the legion and those by local politicians and intellectuals chafing at the subordinate role Jordanians had in running their own country. One of the officers in particular, 'Ali Abu Nuwwar, who had been the military attaché in Paris and had been brought back as the king's aide-de-camp, was generally thought to have been critically influential in getting him to remove Glubb and put the legion under Arab command. The rest of the British officers left within about six months.

It was time for Glubb to go, but the British assumed that Nasser was behind his dismissal, and this was one reason for British Prime Minister Eden's increasingly hard line toward Egypt, which eventually led to the Suez crisis some months later.[11] The Egyptians, however, claimed to be as surprised as the British, and in the absence of hard evidence to the contrary, I suspect they were. They immediately jumped in to crow about it in their propaganda, however, and I can still hear the fulsome praise for Hussein by broadcaster 'Abd al-Hakim 'Amr blasting out of a neighbor's radio.

The riots and Glubb's dismissal appeared to put the seal on Britain's decline in Jordan. But the loss of British influence had been apparent for some time. Its durability had been regarded by most as instrumental in keeping Hussein on his throne. Jordanians told jokes about Hussein's dependence on Glubb, and the monarchy was not a popular institution. All wondered how long it would last without a British-officered army to support it, and Deputy Chief of Mission Richard Sanger remarked that Hussein had figuratively packed his crown jewels with Glubb's baggage. No one disagreed with him.

That would have been all that Glubb would have taken with him of any value, except for a silver-framed picture of Hussein given him by Bahjat Talhouni, the royal chamberlain, at the foot of the steps leading to the departing aircraft. (We thought this was an ironic gesture on Hussein's part, after what he had just done to his faithful servant, but Glubb seemed sincerely to appreciate it.) The man who packed his effects, Mr. Garabedian from Jerusalem, told me that there was nothing in Glubb's house worth shipping and that one thing was clear: Glubb had not used his position to make money. We also saw Hussein's actions as meaning that he had decided to throw in his lot with the Nasserites and their version of Arab nationalism, which was sweeping through the Arab world—not that Hussein had ever not been a nationalist at heart, but his ultimate reliance on the British to command his army made him a status quo figure in a revolutionary region.

The British reacted calmly to Glubb's departure but expressed doubts that Jordan would survive the departure of the British officers. The most important single question was whether Britain would continue its annual subsidy, which at that point amounted to a little over £10 million sterling ($28 million) per year, without which the Jordan government would have been unable to pay the army.[12] The British said they were studying the matter. The Americans, who had not previously put a high priority on Jordan and were opposed in principle to budgetary support to foreign governments except in extremis, had no interest in picking up the check and urged the British to continue their support. For his part, the king spoke of his continued desire for close ties with Great Britain and the West.[13]

There was talk of a contractual arrangement under which some British officers would remain, and there was initial optimism that the subsidy would continue, but all this came to naught as Jordan moved steadily closer to Egypt, Syria, and Saudi

Arabia (the so-called ESS powers) and took an increasingly cool stance toward the United Kingdom and the United States. The last British officer left late in the summer and the British subsidy was terminated at about the same time. The ESS combine announced that they would pick up the burden, but only the Saudis came through with their share.

The U.S. embassy in Amman had noted on March 16 that Glubb's dismissal was "not an unmitigated evil" because it had gone far to remove Jordan's inferiority complex vis-à-vis the other Arab states and the king had become a hero instead of a puppet[14] (although he was young and inexperienced, "providing he does nothing foolish [he] may remain in the saddle for some time"). That optimistic vision was not widely shared, and two weeks later the embassy gloomily commented that the movement of Jordan toward neutralism was continuing:

> It is not a passive movement but . . . is stimulated. Foreign governments and domestic groups are working on Jordan and are prying her loose from West. Internal political situation has deteriorated to point where lack of any real national loyalties, differences between King and Prime Minister, cupidity and ambition among Legion officers now without British restraint, destructive opposition by political outs, and continuing activities of Communists and allied groups makes easier conquest by Egyptian propaganda machine and subversive elements.[15]

It was during this critical period that Secretary of State Dulles was moving toward the fateful decision to withdraw the offer to help finance the High Aswan dam. Egyptian subversive activities in Jordan, Libya, and Iraq were increasingly irritating to Washington, but U.S. officials were nevertheless surprised to learn from a visitor, Donald Bergus, then officer-in-charge of Israel-Jordan affairs in the Near East, in June or early July, that the offer was going to be withdrawn. I recall being told by Bergus that nuclear energy was going to reduce dependence on Arab oil, which explained in part our willingness to risk Arab anger over this turnabout.[16]

As the summer of 1956 wore on and the Suez crisis deepened, the atmosphere in Amman was increasingly tense. Feelings were running high and there was fear of hostile demonstrations against Westerners. One of our Palestinian servants, a young man from Beit Iksa, decided on his own to carry some large stones up to the roof to be dropped on the mob when it attacked, and people began bringing in supplies in anticipation of an extended curfew. Old friends and contacts were courteous, but there was an uneasy feeling in the air that the British and Americans were in for a hard time and were going to get their comeuppance for their failure to deal with the Palestine problem and for their opposition to the rightful aspirations of Arabs. In the midst of this I came down with a severe case of infectious hepatitis and was evacuated to Beirut in August and then home in late September, hors de combat until January 1957, when I reported for duty as the Israel-Jordan desk officer in the State Department, working for Bergus.

A recurring topic in our conversations and reporting during this period was the possibility of a coup against Hussein, to be carried out by a shadowy group in the army known as the Free Officers in alliance with various nationalist/leftist groups. The language of the cables generally lumps them all together as Nasserists-Communists. The king had heretofore relied on older politicians without political party affiliation or support—people who were members of the establishment, like Saʿid al-Mufti and Samir Rifaʿi. On October 27, 1956, however, following the first multiparty parliamentary elections (and, as it turned out, the last for thirty-seven years), the king named Sulayman al-Nabulsi as prime minister. The latter formed a cabinet that included a prominent Baʿthi, ʿAbdallah Rimawi, as foreign minister and six members of Nabulsi's National Socialist Party. That party was an essentially centrist group that had more substance on paper than it did in popular following; it was no match for the Baʿth in terms of organizational capabilities. Long regarded as the principal figure in what might be termed the semiloyal opposition, Nabulsi had often been touted as the sort of man the king should choose to demonstrate his nationalist credentials and to lead the country into the modern era.

Once in office Nabulsi did not prove to be an effective leader, and his loyalties soon became suspect. Although he made private protestations of his support for the king, his public utterances raised doubts. Mallory commented on March 29, 1957, that there was no doubt he was "intent on destroying Jordan in favor of a still undefined federation with Syria and Egypt."[17] Whatever his intentions, Nabulsi was unable to control Rimawi and his fellow Baʿthists, referred to by someone as "Rimawi's fleas," who were evidently intent on overthrowing the monarchy and establishing a republican form of government.

For his part, Hussein was clearly having doubts about the wisdom of alignment with Egypt and Syria. Given the recent historical record, he had good reason to distrust their ultimate intentions toward Jordan and himself and I doubt that he ever had illusions about them. He seemed to feel, however, that after dismissing Glubb he had no alternative but to ride the tiger of Arab nationalism, and he may have thought he could manage to avoid being eaten. As time wore on, however, his doubts must have been augmented by Egyptian and Syrian failure to make good on the promise to replace the British subsidy, which put him in a difficult financial situation. He had commented favorably on the Eisenhower Doctrine (a policy designed to halt Communist expansion in the Middle East and to isolate and reduce the power of Egyptian President Gamal ʿAbd al-Nasser) as early as February 1957, and in the embassy's view he had "publicly shown himself to be on our side."[18] Whether this would do him much good in terms of help from the United States was far from certain at that point. The record indicates that the U.S. government continued to hope that someone else would take responsibility for Jordan, and there was no inclination in Washington to pick up the tab.

At about this time, however, an analyst in the State Department's Bureau of Intelligence and Research (INR), Charlotte Moorehouse, wrote a memorandum on Jordan's precarious political situation that was widely read within the government. She described the position in which the king found himself and warned that Israel would not stand idly by if the Kingdom of Jordan disappeared and some Arab army

moved into its territory. Rather, Israel would choose to occupy the West Bank, leading to another Arab-Israeli war more dangerous for world peace than its 1956 predecessor. Her argument caught the attention of upper-level officials in the State Department, and concern over Jordan's fate suddenly became serious.

The embassy's telegram of March 29, 1957 (mentioned earlier), reported various
portents of the king's intention to do something drastic, and on April 11, he dismissed Nabulsi. Washington viewed the situation as being extremely critical and
U.S. CIA Director Allen Dulles told the National Security Council (NSC) that
power rested largely with the army, whose loyalty to the king was uncertain.[19] The
State Department's response was to send a message to Hussein saying it was following developments closely and admired his courage in moving to safeguard the best
interests of Jordan.[20]

On April 13, there occurred the famous confrontation between Hussein and 'Ali
Abu Nuwwar, by now the chief of staff of the Jordanian military, on the road to
Zerqa, the army encampment north of Amman.[21] Abu Nuwwar was dismissed and
Ali Hiyari was appointed in his place. A new cabinet was formed under Hussein
Fakhri al-Khalidi, a respected Jerusalem notable, on April 15 and, by April 17, Allen
Dulles could report to the NSC that the situation was "somewhat better." Hussein
had seized the initiative and the army was behind him.[22]

Two days later General Hiyari fled to Damascus. On the following day he held a
press conference, attended by Abu Nuwwar, in which he said there had been no plot
against King Hussein and that the Zerqa confrontation had been staged by the king,
who had conspired with foreign military attachés and diplomats, meaning the British
and Americans, against the independence of Jordan and its Arab ties. A propaganda
battle now began in earnest between Amman and Damascus, and the U.S. embassy
in Amman described a complicated situation, in which army morale was weakened
as leftist forces organized resistance to the king and large amounts of money were
being funneled into the country for subversive purposes.[23] Secretary of State Dulles's
reaction was to suggest that "if there was any way we could get any offer of assistance
to strengthen the hand of the King we should do so." He would have liked to do so
through the Saudis but assumed such a plan would leak to the Egyptians.

Then, on April 24, in an action that began a relationship between Jordan and the
United States that was to last for many years, Hussein turned to the Americans. In
a message passed through the second-ranking CIA man in Amman, he said that he
was prepared to impose martial law, suspend the constitution, and speak out forcefully against the Syrians and Egyptians; he wanted to know if he could count on the
United States if either Israel or the Soviet Union intervened. Dulles proposed to respond affirmatively, and Eisenhower, vacationing in Georgia, agreed.[24] This decision
did not come as a total surprise, because we administration officials had been in contact with Hussein and had sent him an encouraging message, as noted above, which
he probably interpreted as meaning we would be receptive if he asked for help. As
far as I know, however, there was no inducement offered to him and there was no
promise of support prior to his request.

Briefly, on April 24, Dulles urged Israeli Ambassador to the United States Abba Eban and the Israelis to exercise restraint and sent a message to the king telling him this was being done and that the United States would regard Soviet intervention as warranting a response under the Eisenhower Doctrine. Orders were issued to the U.S. Navy Sixth Fleet to head for the eastern Mediterranean, and Press Secretary James Hagerty held a press conference in Augusta in which he said both Eisenhower and Dulles regarded the independence and integrity of Jordan as vital. Suddenly, the "open sesame" had been uttered and the administration began scrambling to see what could be done to aid Jordan. The pinchpenny phase was over, as indicated by the Eisenhower-Dulles conversation of April 25.[25] Eisenhower is reported as effectively authorizing "anything he [Hussein] needs in the way of encouragement." Dulles now possessed what amounted to carte blanche, within reason.

The response was twofold. The first response, and in many ways the most remarkable, was an open-ended offer of support and aid, which led to a long-term economic aid program that became something of a sacred cow for the U.S. government very quickly. The second response was an offer to help with specific operational problems, the most pressing of which were seen to be surface communications and propaganda capabilities.

The aid offer on April 25 began with instructions to Ambassador Mallory to tell the king of U.S. concern and U.S. desire to support him and to ask him whether military and economic assistance would be useful.[26] Not surprisingly, his response was affirmative. Four days later an agreement to give Jordan $10 million in mutual security funds (and thus not Eisenhower Doctrine monies) was signed. The International Cooperation Administration (ICA), the aid agency, reluctantly agreed to this "political" use of funds, which were supposed to be for economic development, but Dulles rode roughshod over the agency thanks to presidential backing.[27]

There was a conviction in Washington that to avoid overidentification with and reliance on the West it would be better if Jordan's Arab brethren were also contributing to the support. Iraqis and Saudis were the obvious candidates to do this. Nuri al-Sa'id was then prime minister of Iraq. His refusal to help was particularly shortsighted and may have reflected an aspect of his character that made him unloved at home—he sounded *bakhil,* or stingy. King Sa'ud's unresponsiveness was more understandable. Saudi Arabia was already committed to contribute $14 million per year to Jordan under the ESS subsidy. Sa'ud could say fairly that his country was already doing its part. In addition, control of Saudi foreign policy was increasingly in the hands of Prince Faisal, and he was at that point sympathetic to Nasser rather than Hussein. In the end, the Saudis paid their first installment to Jordan and that was the end of the ESS aid.

The initial U.S. grant of $10 million was followed in June by another $10 million for the army and another $10 million in budgetary support. With this, the United States had assumed the British subsidy. In 1958, budgetary aid was increased to about $40 million and continued at that level through 1963 despite repeated efforts by various U.S. bureaucrats to chip away at it. It was progressively reduced thereafter and terminated in 1967, to be resumed in 1971. Military assistance, much of it in the form of arms sales, continued (with a brief interruption in 1968) until Jordan's unfortunate alignment with Iraq in the Gulf crisis of 1990–1991.

There were, however, many operational considerations and problems that under-lay the various economic and military aid programs the United States initiated in subsequent years in Jordan. It was understood that an agreement had been signed to give Jordan "X" million dollars for this purpose or that, and one tended to assume that was all there was to it. Each such agreement, however, entailed a welter of ad-ministrative and operational actions by a wide variety of people on both sides. The success or failure of the agreement rested on their performance, and that was often determined by the most elemental considerations of personal competence and imag-ination. No amount of money will help if people do not know how to spend it.

A great deal of thought and effort, for instance, went into providing Jordan with radio capability to respond to on-air attacks from Cairo and Damascus. There were two basic problems: power and content. As to the first, the Egyptians had powerful broadcasting facilities and their "Voice of the Arabs" program could be heard, and was listened to, across the Arab world. The Jordanians had a puny transmitter, which could hardly be heard beyond Jordan. Secondly, Cairo was the artistic and intellec-tual capital of the Arab world and had a large pool of talented performers on which to draw both for entertainment and for effective commentary. In particular, the Egyptians had a commentator named Ahmad Sa'id, who was widely listened to be-cause of his witty and sarcastic comments about King Hussein and other enemies of Nasser. The Jordanians had nobody of similar stature and no entertainers who might attract a foreign audience. No one would tune in to Jordan radio except maybe to find out what was going on in Amman.

We helped the Jordanians acquire a more powerful radio station, although it took a long time to do so, and we could not supply them their own Ahmad Sa'id. By 1967, the Jordanians had developed sufficient skill in the propaganda war that their broadcasts helped push Nasser into the miscalculation that set off the June War.

The U.S. commitment to Jordan was critical to the regime's survival in 1957. It was also extremely important in the summer of 1958, after the July 14 revolution in Baghdad. Jordan was then cut off from Iraq; Saudi Arabia, under Prince Faisal's di-rection, would not help with oil supplies. It was the British, however, and not the Americans, who flew in troops, but that is another story.

In hindsight, whether U.S. support for Jordan was the right policy to follow de-pends largely on one's point of view. On the one hand, for the pragmatic policy-maker in Washington, it was certainly a success. It helped preserve a leader and a government, both friendly to the West at a time when Washington and Moscow were battling one another for influence in the region. It further contributed to the economic development and prosperity of Jordan. (Today, people are beginning to talk again about Jordan being unviable, but that seems to be wrapped up in the question of who will succeed Hussein.) People in the area no longer look down on King Hussein as they once did. He has outlived his rivals and has shown what courage and a bit of luck can do. With pitifully few assets and against all odds, he has become a respected elder statesman, and the United States helped him do it.

On the other hand, the Arab nationalist appearing in the Malcolm Kerr book *Arab Cold War* would likely see the episode as a travesty, the sole purpose of U.S. policy being to protect Israel, with Jordan being merely a pawn in that game. Under this view, Jordan never should have been created: Uniting it with Syria and Egypt was the course to follow. Had that occurred, and had the imperialist powers not intervened, the Arabs today would be closer to their goal of unity, the disaster of 1967 would not have occurred, and Israel's day of reckoning would be looming.

However we evaluate it, there is one aspect of the policy process that stands out clearly: the importance of the personality factor on both sides. Eisenhower's avuncular response to Hussein's courage assured favorable replies to the king's request for help. It is difficult to envisage a similar response to the unfortunate King Faisal of Iraq, who had no chance to show his courage. There is a quality about Hussein that strikes a responsive chord in Washington. Whatever his personal weaknesses, he impresses people as being a gentleman—honest, decent, and reasonable. Those qualities are rare enough in today's world to earn him respect, and that is about all he has had in the way of assets in the power game.[28]

Notes

1. The author served in the U.S. Foreign Service from 1951 to 1979. He was assigned to the U.S. embassy in Jordan in the mid-1950s and also served as ambassador to Algeria, Lebanon, and Morocco. Many of the insights appearing in this chapter were drawn from his personal experiences with the people, places, and events during this period of the U.S.-Jordanian relationship.

2. Document 312 in *Foreign Relations of the United States, 1955–1957,* vol. 13, hereinafter *FRUS* with volume, year, and page or document numbers.

3. Ibid.

4. See Wilbur Crane Eveland, *Ropes of Sand: America's Failure in the Middle East* (New York: W. W. Norton, 1980); and David W. Lesch, *Syria and the United States: Eisenhower's Cold War in the Middle East* (Boulder: Westview Press, 1992).

5. *FRUS* 13 (1955–1957), doc. 5.

6. King Hussein, *Uneasy Lies the Head: The Autobiography of His Majesty King Hussein I of the Hashemite Kingdom of Jordan* (New York: Bernard Geis Associates, 1962).

7. Regarding the Templer mission, Donald Bergus, then officer in charge of Israel-Jordan affairs in the U.S. Department of State, recalls Nasser saying to someone, "The British tried to move Hussein from one pocket to the other and almost lost him in the process" (personal communication of November 17, 1993).

8. *FRUS* 13 (1955–1957), doc. 8.

9. In Jerusalem there was also excitement. A mob made a determined effort to storm the branch office of the American Consulate General on the Nablus Road near the Mandelbaum Gate. They were dissuaded from entering by tear-gas grenades thrown through the transom by two marine guards and by a shotgun blast from Slator Blackiston, who lived with his family in an apartment above the office. One person was wounded and Blackiston was transferred

for his own safety soon thereafter. A mob also attacked the Turkish consulate but was held off by the consul general, Mr. Bayramoglu, with a pistol.

Three other U.S. concerns were attacked by mobs on the same day, all of them well out in the country, two of them far removed from the Palestinians. One crowd sacked the Baptist hospital at Ajloun, north of Amman. Serious material damage was done. Another attacked a Quaker village development project at Dibbin in the hills of Gilead, also north of Amman. In both cases there were suspicions that local notables who saw these eleemosynary efforts as a threat to their positions had used the pretext of the Baghdad Pact issue to incite the attacks. There were no such suspicions regarding the attack, presumably by refugees, on the Mennonite relief operation near Jericho. That was evidently the work of political agitators. There were no human casualties among the Americans, but a discouraging amount of damage was done. The Dibbin operation, which had been widely praised as a model self-help project for village development, was abandoned as a result, but the other two continued to function.

10. There is a good description of Glubb's sacking in U.S. embassy in Amman, Telegram no. 458 of March 2. *FRUS* 13 (1955–1957):26. For a thoroughly researched account of these and other events in this chapter, see Robert Satloff's *From Abdullah to Hussein* (New York: Oxford University Press, 1994).

11. For more on the British reaction, see Keith Kyle, *Suez* (New York: St. Martin's Press, 1991).

12. The figures for 1956 announced earlier by the British were £7.5 million in military subsidy payments and £3.35 million in economic assistance.

13. *FRUS* 13 (1955–1957):32.

14. Ibid.: doc. 25.

15. Ibid.

16. Bergus recalls that he made the statement about nuclear energy replacing oil but says that he can only plead that he was reflecting what he had been told by ARAMCO personnel, who had predicted that by 1970 Arab oil would only be used as a raw material for various chemicals; its role as a source of energy would be taken over by nuclear power. Ibid.

17. *FRUS* 13 (1955–1957): doc. 59.

18. Amman's 928 of February 13, in ibid.: doc. 57.

19. *FRUS* 13 (1955–1957): doc. 60.

20. Hussein's courage became something of a byword during this period. In one telephone conversation between Eisenhower and Dulles, perhaps that of April 25 (*FRUS* 13 [1955–1957]: doc. 74), Dulles referred to him as "the brave young king." Bergus, who was in Dulles's office during the conversation, reported this back to the Near East division of the State Department, and after that Hussein was referred to as the "BYK." *FRUS* 13 (1955–1957): doc. 60.

21. Ambassador Mallory maintains that there was no conversation between Hussein and Abu Nuwwar. Rather, when Hussein learned late at night that the roads leading into Amman were blocked by military vehicles: "He took a car, summoned Abu Nuwwar and went to Zerqa. It was reported that Abu Nuwwar was shaking in his boots. Arriving at the army base, a crowd gathered and Hussein climbed atop a tank and addressed the troops, saying an insurrection was planned. He was effective and the troops demanded to know those responsible [in order] to take them apart. Despite Abu Nuwwar's efforts to replace Bedouin troops with Palestinians, the corps was faithful. What followed was the end of Abu Nuwwar, who, I gathered at the time, had ties to the Egyptians" (personal communication of November 25,

1993). This account squares with the more detailed version given by King Hussein as reported by J. B. Slade-Baker in *Sunday Times* (London), May 5, 1957.

22. *FRUS* 13 (1955–1957): doc. 65.

23. Amman's 1343 of April 21, *FRUS* 13 (1955–1957): doc. 67.

24. Commenting on this episode, Bergus writes: "April 24 was quite a day. I got the message from CIA, took it straight to Bill Rountree [assistant secretary for Near East Affairs] and we both walked straight into Dulles's office. Dulles picked up the phone and said, 'Get me the President.' After a minute or two he said that the folks in Augusta, Georgia said DDE had just teed off from the first hole. Did the Secretary, they said, think his business was important enough to call the president off the course, or could it wait until he got to his message center, some holes down the course? Dulles said to us, 'I think this is important enough to call the President back, don't you?' Rountree and I solemnly agreed." Ibid.

25. *FRUS* 13 (1955–1957): doc. 74.

26. Ibid.: doc. 77.

27. Bergus comments that we got the money to King Hussein in record time. "Wade Lathram [director of regional affairs in NEA] found some language in the foreign aid legislation which gave us almost carte blanche to preserve stability, or something like that. ICA were furious at being one-upped, but they went along." Ibid.

28. We continued to support King Hussein, even though a document such as NSC 5820/1 of November 4, 1958, apparently calls for and/or is an acquiescence to an end to the Hashemite Kingdom of Jordan (a subject discussed elsewhere in this book). I and former diplomats I contacted, who were intimately connected with U.S.-Jordanian relations at the time, recall that there was never any question of the unswerving support of the United States for King Hussein and the viability of Jordan. They commented that there were people who talked about the policy advocated in NSC 5820/1, but it was never seriously promoted as policy, even though Eisenhower signed off on it. This may say something about the relevance of NSC discussions to the policy followed on the ground.

8

The Jekyll-and-Hyde Origins of the U.S.-Jordanian Strategic Relationship

Robert B. Satloff

In June 1994, King Hussein bin Talal of the Hashemite Kingdom of Jordan was welcomed at the White House by President Bill Clinton for the third time in a presidential term not yet half over. That gave the king—leader of a small, weak, refugee-filled, resource-poor state—more White House visits than any other chief of state in the world. The following month, the president hosted King Hussein and the prime minister of Israel in a historic signing ceremony marking the end of a forty-six-year state of war. The process climaxed in October of that year with the signing of a formal Israeli-Jordanian peace treaty at a border location connecting the two countries, an event personally attended by President Clinton. Earlier in 1994, Jordan joined a select group of just five countries in the world to receive direct U.S. military assistance.[1] Within hours of the July signing ceremony, the U.S. Congress supported the president in voting for hundreds of millions of dollars in relief of Jordan's financial debt to the United States. Taken together, these events capped the restoration of a relatively warm bilateral relationship four years after the two countries found themselves on opposite sides of a war, a conflict that produced cleavages that still divide the Arab world and define U.S. Middle East policy. Clearly, there is something special about the U.S.-Jordanian relationship that deserves examination and assessment.

This chapter explores the strange and contradictory sources—the Jekyll-and-Hyde origins, if you will—of the U.S.-Jordanian strategic relationship in the mid- to late 1950s, when the United States succeeded Britain as Jordan's great power patron. The thesis put forward here is that the creation of that strategic relationship was far from assured; that America was reluctant to assume Britain's responsibility for propping up an enterprise that was viewed as unviable; and that even after the Jordanian Hashemites believed they had received a firm commitment of support from the United States, Washington was angling to find firmer partners among popular nationalists in the Arab world and was willing to sacrifice the Hashemites to sweeten the deal. In the end, the relationship endured because each side chose to see in it what each wanted to see in it, because a little money goes a long way in Jordan, and because the tenacious Hashemite leadership in Amman refused, in the end, to succumb to coups and revolutions like the Hashemites of Iraq and other Arab monarchies in Egypt, Libya, and Yemen. To Washington, nothing succeeds like success, and—if nothing else—the Hashemites succeeded in surviving.

From the establishment of the Emirate of Transjordan in 1921 to the creation of the Hashemite Kingdom in 1946 to the "union" of the East and West Banks of the Jordan River in 1950, the existence and survival of the state was linked to Britain.[2] British ministers first created the emirate; British officers commanded its armed forces; British experts provided professional guidance to its bureaucracy; British ambassadors served as virtual proconsuls, weighing in on virtually all important policy decisions; and the British exchequer ensured the kingdom's solvency (just barely) through an annual subsidy to sustain the Arab Legion, Jordan's celebrated army. Indeed, Jordan and Britain were so closely linked that the United States balked at extending de jure recognition to the former in 1946 because the extensive treaty rights assigned to the latter in the 1936 Anglo-Jordanian treaty gave it virtual imperial authority.[3]

Whereas the Jordanian elite generally recognized the umbilical link that connected the British and Hashemite monarchies, a popular trend began to emerge in Jordan in the early 1950s that was strongly critical of the Amman-London connection. This theme resonated with particular strength among Jordan's Palestinians, many of whom (like many Israelis) believed the British were responsible for their travails and, in the end, their tragedy in Palestine. When Jordan took its first tentative steps toward more liberal governance in the mid-1950s, anti-Britishism normally crystallized into two demands: the "Arabization" of the Jordanian army (i.e., replacement of British officers—especially Sir John Bagot Glubb—with Arab officers) and the imposition of rent on Britain for its use of bases in Jordan, instead of reliance on a British subsidy to support the Arab Legion. Among the more radical elements in Jordan, especially the Ba'thists, there were vocal demands for the outright abrogation of the Anglo-Jordanian treaty. At the very least, most Palestinians and many East Bankers opposed any expansion of the strategic partnership with London, especially at a time when the coals of Arab nationalism were being stoked by Egyptian President Gamal 'Abd al-Nasser. Rioting against the possible Jordanian accession to the Baghdad Pact in December 1955 and January 1956 was the most visible indication of this opposition. Partly to respond to this popular sentiment, partly to prove his credentials as an Arab nationalist, and partly to mark his own political coming-of-age, King Hussein fulfilled one of these demands and dismissed Glubb Pasha on March 1, 1956.[4]

Glubb's dismissal marked a turning point in Anglo-Jordanian relations and, indeed, in Britain's position in the Arab world. Some, including many in Whitehall, believed that Glubb's dismissal merely corrected an anachronistic leftover from a bygone era, thereby opening the way for the evolution of a healthier, more mature partnership between the two allies and, indeed, between Britain and the larger Arab world. However, many others—in the London and Arab capitals—saw Glubb's dismissal as a dishonorable swipe at Britain by an impoverished mendicant and, as such, the beginning of the end of Britain's "moment" in the Middle East. Would Arab nationalists find succor in Glubb's dismissal and press for more? Would Britain, under Prime Minister Anthony Eden, stem the tide and prevent any further loss of British prestige in the region? For sober Jordanians, the question of the future of the British connection was particularly acute. After all, despite the bluster, Jordan's national existence relied upon the munificence of Her Majesty's government, in the form of Britain's £6 million subsidy to the Jordanian army.

With Egypt's nationalization of the Suez Canal in July 1956—and the British-led tripartite campaign to wrest it back from Nasser's control three months later—the question of Jordan's British connection came to a head. On Hussein's express orders, the parliamentary elections of October 21, 1956—held less than ten days before Britain's planned invasion, known as Operation Musketeer—were the freest the kingdom had ever witnessed (before or since); those elections returned a parliament with a large number of individual royalists, but there was no unified group among them able to match the ideological ferocity of the small but well organized parties of the radical left.

The largest grouping in parliament was the National Socialist Party (NSP), a collection of aristocrats-cum-populists led by a onetime schoolteacher from Salt, Sulayman al-Nabulsi, who himself had failed in his bid for parliament. During the election campaign, the NSP had formed an alignment with the radicals; in the new age of "street politics" in Jordan, the NSP's landed leaders were swept up in the maelstrom of mass rallies and general strikes. They had popular appeal, but only as individuals with little real popular base, so they linked up with the better organized Ba'th and pro-Communist National Front to maximize their electoral attraction. In return, the NSP offered the radical parties a sort of legitimacy that they would not muster for themselves. In the end, the NSP's electoral gambit worked in its favor, but its decision to retain that alliance after the elections tilted the scales in the other direction, rewarding its coalition partners with political power in excess of their own electoral strength.

For nearly a week after the election, King Hussein hesitated before naming a prime minister who could command a vote of confidence from parliament; all previous prime ministers had been "king's men" who understood, valued, and identified with the Hashemite monarchy and its existential connection to Britain and the West. In the meantime, the new parliament convened and, with the Egyptian and Syrian army chiefs of staff in attendance, unanimously approved resolutions in support of the Arab struggle against "imperialism" and the severance of diplomatic relations with France, then already engaged in the bloody struggle for Algeria. Even the nominally royalist party declared its support for a resolution calling for the unilateral abrogation (as opposed to the more moderate position of negotiated termination) of the Anglo-Jordanian treaty. With parliament so arrayed on the nationalist side, Hussein chose Nabulsi as his prime minister, hoping that he was the most moderate of the radical options. Nabulsi's coalition cabinet included a Ba'thist, a National Front leader, and, most important, not a single representative of the Hashemite loyalists, the "king's men."[5]

Three days after Nabulsi took office, Israeli forces moved against Egypt in collusion with Britain and France. Popular opinion in Jordan was overwhelmingly supportive of Nasser, and even the king wanted Jordan to intervene militarily on the side of Egypt. Nabulsi, together with the upwardly mobile nationalist who now headed the post-Glubb army, Abu Nuwwar, was well aware of Jordan's military weakness, and together they took steps that maintained the image of engagement but kept the kingdom out of war. The political fallout from Suez, however, proved more difficult to handle. On November 1, parliament ordered a cut in diplomatic relations with France; the only reason it did not also break ties with Britain was because a unilateral abrogation of the treaty would have pushed Jordan into bankruptcy. Nabulsi, however, did accept in principle demands from his more radical cabinet colleagues to press for the replacement of the British subsidy with Arab aid, for the negotiated end of the Anglo-Jordanian treaty, for the eviction from Jordan of "reactionary" Iraqi troops that had arrived as reinforcements during the Suez crisis, and for the establishment of diplomatic relations with Moscow and Beijing. Collectively, these steps would amount to a severing of Jordan's historic connection with the West.

But many of the key actors in the Jordanian drama were not at all ready for such a bold and rapid change. Nabulsi and his NSP colleagues wanted reform but were fearful of its consequences; they had high regard for the ideal of Arab unity but less so for the sincerity of Arab leaders. In practice, therefore, they adopted a policy of trying to hold on to the British connection until a firm agreement had been signed with the Arab alliance of Egypt, Syria, and Saudi Arabia (the so-called ESS states) to provide adequate aid in place of the British subsidy. For his part, Abu Nuwwar was not interested in ceding to Cairo the control he had only recently acquired over Jordan's armed forces. What he wanted was a platform from which to realize his own mercenary political ambitions, not the political aspiration of Arab unity, so he was eager to hold out for the patron with the highest bid. And after his emotional outburst in support of Nasser, King Hussein began to recognize the existential threat to the Hashemite monarchy that would follow upon the severing of Jordan's links to the West. Whereas Nabulsi adopted tactics that sought to postpone the termination of the treaty, Hussein (and Abu Nuwwar) followed a different path—they undertook a secret initiative to solicit U.S. patronage in place of British.

November 1956 witnessed the beginning of a race to see whether the palace's feverish efforts to secure U.S. support would bear fruit before the radicals could demolish Jordan's remaining links with the West. On November 9, Abu Nuwwar told the U.S. military attaché in Amman that in exchange for military and economic aid of "sufficient volume," he would "guarantee" a crackdown on Jordan's Communists, the dissolution of parliament, and the imposition of martial law. "I and the people of Jordan will follow U.S. policies," he modestly offered, adding his own willingness to fly to Washington to seal the deal personally with President Dwight D. Eisenhower. At the same time, he warned that without U.S. support, Jordan would be forced to accept Soviet offers of aid that had been made via the Soviet Embassy in Cairo.[6] About a week later, King Hussein made a personal appeal for U.S. assistance, adding that despite his preference for Western support, Jordan would turn to Cairo and Moscow if necessary.[7]

Amman's search for U.S. support was complemented by London's own efforts. Even though radicals in Jordan's government wanted to goad Britain into a speedy abrogation of the treaty, cooler heads prevailed. Instead of lashing out at the Jordanian ingrates, British officials took advantage of the Nabulsi interlude to try to arrange for the United States to assume Britain's commitment to Jordan and succeed Britain as Jordan's strategic patron. London's rationale, however, had little to do with altruism or with an enduring, romantic attachment to the Hashemites of Amman; rather, finding strategic support for Jordan was the best way to secure the position of the pro-British Hashemite regime in Baghdad, the real objective of British policy at the time. For different reasons, therefore, the strategies of Britain, Hussein, and Abu Nuwwar converged on the need to secure a U.S. commitment to Jordan.

Washington, however, was not interested in taking over London's burden. When King Hussein approached U.S. officials in November, their immediate response was cool and noncommittal, merely urging the king against "jumping from [the] frying pan into [the] fire."[8] When British Foreign Minister Selwyn Lloyd himself lobbied for U.S. support for Jordan, the answer was a definitive "no." On December 10, Lloyd told U.S. Secretary of State John Foster Dulles quite candidly that he believed Jordan was doomed as an independent country. "What is its future?" Dulles asked. "I don't think it's got one," Lloyd replied. Surprisingly, the prospect of losing Jordan to the Soviets did not alarm the U.S. cold warrior at all. Dulles told Lloyd that satellites not contiguous to the Soviet Union's own territory could easily be "pinched off"; moreover, he observed that because Moscow knew this too, it was unlikely to "make a big investment in areas which they could not hold." Dulles's message to Britain was clear: Pouring too much money into Jordan would be wasteful. The "brutal fact," Dulles later explained, was that "Jordan had no justification as a State." For him it was far better to target U.S. largesse where it could make a real difference in the contest between East and West.[9]

When Washington refused to step in for Britain, Round One of the Jordanian infight was won by the radicals. In December 1956, Hussein was officially informed that the United States turned down his request for aid. At the time, the U.S. ambassador suggested that Jordan would be better served by patching up its tattered relations with Britain.[10] But as London itself had recognized, it was too late for that sort of reconciliation. With no other option and with time running out, Hussein was forced to acquiesce in an arrangement negotiated by Nabulsi to secure aid (at least on paper) from Egypt, Syria, and Saudi Arabia in place of the British subsidy. In public, Hussein extended his "utmost gratitude and appreciation" to his Arab patrons; in private, he admitted that he had "no choice." Three days after the signing in Cairo of what was called the Arab Solidarity Agreement, Britain officially requested the convening of negotiations to terminate the Anglo-Jordanian treaty.[11]

During November and December 1956, King Hussein was essentially a passive actor in the Jordanian drama, waiting to see whether outside patrons would come to Jordan's aid before he accepted the offer from the Arab nationalist alliance. This led to a period, the first weeks of 1957, that signaled the nadir of his young reign, when all the elements that had kept the kingdom intact for three decades—a loyalist government, a strong and cohesive army, and a dependable and faithful patron—began to slip away. Emboldened by the king's submission, the radicals inside the cabinet began to press for more; sensing the king's weakness, conspirators inside the army, nebulously led by Abu Nuwwar,[12] began to plot for their takeover of the regime; fearful of the king's imminent demise, the British focused on tidying up their affairs in Jordan and shoring up Nuri al-Sa'id in Iraq. Before all was lost, however, Hussein summoned up the courage and resources to arrest what looked like an inexorable slide toward extinction. This time, the key to Hussein's strategy was in taking actions that would shape a U.S. decision in favor of lending strategic support to Jordan, not just waiting passively for a decision in Washington that would determine his fate and that of his kingdom.

The period from February to April 1957 witnessed a series of confrontations between Hussein, on the one hand, and, respectively, the Nabulsi government and the Abu Nuwwar–led army on the other hand, that clearly defined the options for the future of the regime. Sometimes Hussein won and sometimes he lost, but throughout his actions underscored his willingness to stitch together the fragments of his regime in such a manner that would make him deserving of U.S. support.

The issue on which Hussein first built his case against Nabulsi's government was its allegedly soft attitude toward communism and, specifically, its apparently blunt dismissal of the Eisenhower Doctrine. In a stunning message to Nabulsi on February 2, Hussein bluntly declared: "We want this country to be inaccessible to Communist propaganda and Bolshevik theories, and we should resist anyone who objects to our tendencies and beliefs. . . . We believe in the right of this country to live a free life."[13] For the first time since Glubb's ouster, the king had taken a political gamble that ran against the nationalist tide. He followed up his attack on communism with a series of direct interventions in government decisionmaking, including orders that the national media should not attack the Eisenhower Doctrine and that no action should be taken regarding the establishment of diplomatic ties with Communist states. As the U.S. ambassador in Amman noted, despite the surface civility that defined relations between king and government, "the battle was now joined."[14]

The showdown came in early spring. At the end of March, Hussein appeared to usurp the cabinet's authority by dispatching a personal envoy to Damascus, Cairo, and Jeddah with a message not previously vetted by the government. In response, the Nabulsi cabinet decided to present the king with formal requests to retire several senior public servants and to establish relations with Moscow; if Hussein refused, the cabinet would resign and take to the streets. At first, Hussein acquiesced and it looked as though Nabulsi had carried the day. However, when Nabulsi proposed a fresh list of forced retirements that included some of the king's own men, the king struck back; he sent Nabulsi letters giving him the option of resignation or dismissal. Confident of popular sympathy, the cabinet resigned. With Ba'thists and other radical nationalists rallying the crowds against him, and with the added incendiary invective of Egypt's notorious radio propagandist, Ahmad al-Sa'id, Hussein was unable to cobble together a cabinet that could succeed Nabulsi's and survive.

Political clashes were exacerbated by military challenges. For a dangerously long time, Hussein retained confidence in the loyalty of the army's commanders, especially in Abu Nuwwar, even when it was apparent that Abu Nuwwar and his cohorts atop the "liberated" Jordan Arab Army posed as much a danger to the regime as did the perfidy of elected politicians. In planning to dismiss Glubb in 1956, Hussein found common cause with a group of junior officers who fashioned themselves the Jordanian Free Officers; it took nearly a year before the king realized that the Glubb operation was a marriage of convenience between the king and his colleagues, the latter of which had grander designs on the kingdom itself.[15] Indeed, it was not until the enigmatic Operation Hashim of April 8, when troops deployed at four key intersections controlling Amman's main roads, effectively encircling and choking off the capital, that doubts did emerge in Hussein's mind about the loyalty of Abu Nuwwar and some of his senior lieutenants. By that time, Abu Nuwwar and his colleagues had already begun to collude with radical cabinet members, Ba'th Party loyalists, and Syrian army officers. Operation Hashim—most likely a rehearsal for future action that was intended as a show of strength by the amateurish Free Officers—was only defused through the personal intercession of the king with the regimental commander, who lost his nerve and withdrew. It set the stage, however, for the obscure events of Zerqa on April 13, when the king preempted a sloppy conspiracy with the support of Bedouin troops and a visible display of his own personal courage that heartened loyalists and broke the spirit of the rebels.[16]

Zerqa proved to be the knockout blow to the military conspiracy[17] against the king, but it did not end the political confrontation with the nationalists and their more radical supporters that proved to be an even more onerous problem. On April 15, Hussein eventually succeeded in forming a cabinet headed by Palestinian Hussein Fakhri al-Khalidi; the king was forced to accept Nabulsi as foreign minister. In less than a week, though, it was clear to the Palace that the new government would not last, that Nabulsi and his NSP colleagues preferred an alliance with the extremist opposition, and that a final showdown was inevitable. On April 22, opponents of the king convened a "National Congress" in Nablus, attended by representatives of all secular parties and opposition movements in Jordan, including the NSP. The congress approved resolutions calling for the dissolution of Khalidi's government, rejection of the Eisenhower Doctrine, expulsion of the U.S. ambassador and military attaché (allegedly for their roles in Hussein's Zerqa success), and the establishment of a federal union with Syria and Egypt—resolutions that, if implemented, would end Jordan's independent national existence. Two days later, Nabulsi resigned, provoking protest strikes throughout the West Bank and in Amman. Later that day, Khalidi resigned too.

With the decisive rematch imminent, Hussein opted to strike first and declare military rule. To do so, he believed he needed some assurance of outside support. By this time, the negotiations to terminate the Anglo-Jordanian treaty had concluded; for the first time since the founding of the emirate under Abdullah (Hussein's grandfather), Jordan was without a superpower.[18] At that crucial moment, the twenty-one-year-old king turned again to Washington. This time, despite its earlier coolness toward the idea of supporting Hussein, the United States ultimately decided to weigh in on the king's behalf.

Early on the evening of April 24, the king passed a message to Washington, reportedly via his Amman contact in the U.S. Central Intelligence Agency. In that message, he outlined his plans to impose martial law and asked for a commitment of U.S. support should either Israel or the Soviet Union intervene to take advantage of the uncertain situation. About three hours later, the king received his answer via an announcement from the White House press secretary, then with Eisenhower at the presidential retreat in Georgia: The president and the secretary of state regarded "the independence and integrity of Jordan as vital." In the meantime, Dulles had already spoken with Israeli Ambassador to Jordan Abba Eban and, as a warning to the Soviets, ships from the U.S. Navy Sixth Fleet had already begun to steam to the Lebanese coast, technically at the request of Lebanese President Camille Chamoun. In addition, plans were set in motion for the deployment of ground and air units from Europe to Turkey or Lebanon, and the United States asked Iraq and Saudi Arabia to stand ready to support Jordan militarily if so requested by King Hussein. In the end, U.S. military planners also gave urgent consideration to the airlift of paratroopers into air bases in Mafraq and Amman, but the king's own declaration on April 24—"I think we can handle the situation ourselves"—made that move unnecessary.[19]

That night, Hussein summoned a handful of his grandfather's old supporters and courtiers to the palace and, with their (albeit hesitant) support, declared martial law, imposed a curfew throughout much of the country, and branded "international communism" as the root of Jordan's troubles. Five days later, the new U.S.-Jordanian alliance was cemented with the approval of a $10 million aid program, the most quickly negotiated in history, the stated goal of which was to ensure Jordan's "freedom" and maintain its "economic and political stability."

Thus was born the strategic relationship between the United States and Jordan, the latter of which is one of the few non-European countries whose "independence and integrity" has been declared "vital" to U.S. national interests. Indeed, that declaration is especially significant since Jordan was not actually facing a serious external threat of invasion by Communist or pro-Communist forces, as envisioned by the Eisenhower Doctrine, but rather the danger of internal collapse. Two years after that declaration, the embryonic strategic relationship was apparently confirmed with

Hussein's first visit to the United States. At the time, he was hosted at the White house by President Eisenhower, who had admired the young monarch's "spunk" in fighting for his throne, thereby inaugurating a tradition maintained through peace and war with every U.S. president ever since.[20]

On the surface, the United States had come full circle, from rejecting Hussein's entreaties in autumn 1956 to swiftly and substantively supporting the king's initiatives in spring 1957 in the form of tangible and public commitments of U.S. assistance. Surely this meant that Dulles's disparagement of Jordan's ability and will to exist had given way to a recognition of the king's tenacity and the willpower of the Hashemites to survive against all odds. To use Dulles's own language, surely the investment of U.S. political and financial capital in Jordan in 1957 and subsequent years meant that Jordan had become "viable." But that was not the case.

For official Washington, post-April 1957 Jordan stood little better chance of survival than pre-1957 Jordan. Even after Hussein's courageous moves on his own behalf, Dulles still did not alter his view that Jordan was not a "viable state," as he told the visiting Pakistani prime minister on July 12, 1957.[21] This view was evidently shared by U.S. diplomats serving in Amman, who—in contrast to their British counterparts—apparently believed that the "situation [was] pretty well hopeless." In one biting report, the British ambassador in Amman complained that "[Britain] and the Jordanians are faced with a situation in which our holding operation may be brought to an end not by Nasser but by the U.S. government." The U.S. chargé d'affaires, he noted, "did not see how the United States or the [United Nations] could underwrite a monarchy which depended simply on bedouin bayonets."[22]

Even Hussein's staying power in the face of adversity did not alter this fundamentally pessimistic U.S. view of Jordan's fortunes. Following the Iraqi revolution of July 1958 and the rebels' assassination of the young Faisal, Crown Prince 'Abd al-Ilah, and Prime Minister Nuri al-Sa'id, the United States twice prepared for King Hussein's evacuation and relocation from Jordan. The first occasion was on July 17, 1958, when a pro-Ba'thist revolution in Jordan appeared imminent. At the time, the Sixth Fleet was ordered to prepare two airplanes with appropriate air cover to evacuate King Hussein.[23] Then, in mid-August, when the king's position again appeared perilous, he made arrangements with U.S. and British diplomats to fly him, his family, and his retainers to Europe.[24]

In the end, neither the coup nor the revolution ever materialized, the king endured, and the regime survived. Yet despite Hussein's instinct for and record of survival, the United States actually decided to *base* its Middle East policy on the assumption—indeed, the wisdom—of the demise of the Hashemite kingdom. In fact, the actual government policy of the Eisenhower administration during the second half of the president's second term—drafted, endorsed, and implemented but never publicly confirmed—was to offer the "independence and integrity" of Hashemite Jordan as a sacrifice to win an accommodation with the insurgent forces of Arab nationalism.

This policy was most clearly articulated in November 1958. By this time—eighteen months after the king broke the back of his domestic opponents and three months after the Iraqi revolution—it was clear that no complementary military putsch was to occur in Jordan and that, despite his enduring financial woes and continual jeremiads of near-insolvency, Hussein and his regime would most likely survive. However, two years after the Suez crisis, many in Washington believed that the key to locking the Soviets out of the Middle East was to recognize the difference between Arab nationalists of Nasser's stripe and outright Communists, finding some common ground with the former so as to seek their help in the global battle against the latter. Though he had won his own battle against Nasserism, Hussein was thought still to be vulnerable and therefore a small sacrifice to satisfy the appetite of Arab nationalism.

This policy was baldly and coldly outlined in the top-secret National Security Council policy directive 5820/1 of November 4, 1958, on "U.S. Policy Toward the Near East," approved by Eisenhower with an order that it be implemented "by all appropriate Executive departments and agencies of the U.S. governments."[25] The underlying rationale of U.S. Middle East policy is derived from the introductory statement contained in NSC directive 5820/1:

> The most dangerous challenge to Western interests arises not from Arab nationalism *per se* but from the coincidence of many of its objectives with many of those of the USSR. . . . It has become increasingly apparent that the prevention of further Soviet penetration of the Near East and progress in solving Near Eastern problems depends on the degree to which the United States is able to work more closely with Arab nationalism and associate itself more closely with such aims and aspirations of the Arab people as are not contrary to the basic interests of the United States.

Therefore, topping the list of operational items enumerated as "major policy guidance" was the following:

> Endeavor to establish a effective working relationship with Arab nationalism while at the same time seeking constructively to influence and stabilize the movement and to contain its outward thrust, and recognizing that a policy of U.S. accommodation to radical pan-Arab nationalism as symbolized by Nasser would include many elements contrary to U.S. interests. . . . Support the idea of Arab unity.

Nowhere did this policy of "accommodating" Arab nationalism imply a greater reversal of existing policy than regarding Jordan. Following is the full excerpt of U.S. "policy guidance" concerning Jordan from NSC 5280/1 (emphasis added):

A. *Recognizing that the indefinite continuance of Jordan's present political status has been rendered unrealistic* by recent developments and that attempts on our part to support its continuance may also represent an obstacle to our establishing a working relationship with Arab nationalism, *seek*, in the context of constructive efforts by the [United Nations] and individual states, *to bring about [the] peaceful evolution of Jordan's political status* and to reduce the U.S. commitment in Jordan.

B. Bearing in mind that an abrupt change in Jordan's status would be viewed generally as a political defeat for the West, be prepared in the interim, for essentially political reasons, to provide necessary assistance which might be used for economic development, budgetary support, and military assistance. *Seek to transfer to Jordan's Arab neighbors major responsibility for economic support of Jordan if at all possible.*[26]

C. Make every effort to avoid conflict between the Arabs and Israel as a result of an abrupt change in Jordan's status.

D. *Encourage such peaceful political adjustment by Jordan, including partition, absorption, or internal political re-alignment, as appears desirable to the people of Jordan and as will permit improved relations with Jordan's Arab neighbors.* Seek to insure the peaceful acquiescence of Israel and of Jordan's Arab neighbors in any such adjustment.

Officially approved by the president, NSC directive 5280/1 was as clear as it was remarkable: U.S. policy was to seek the termination of the Hashemite Kingdom of Jordan, the independence of which was deemed "vital" to U.S. interests only eighteen months earlier. Jordan was either to become a Palestinian republic or have its territory incorporated into neighboring Arab states as a way to remove a thorn in the side of the Arab nationalist movement and to cement a working relationship between the movement and Washington. The directive contained no specific reference to King Hussein, but it was unlikely that its authors envisioned a role for him or his family in what was coldly and euphemistically termed the kingdom's "internal political re-alignment."

NSC directive 5280/1 was just one of the more egregious examples of a U.S. policy of accommodating Arab nationalism that was born under Eisenhower and survived well into the 1960s. But its vision of Jordan's future never materialized. Instead, as symbolized by the White House visits and allotment of military assistance noted in the opening paragraph of this chapter, Jordan retains the sort of special relationship with the United States as envisioned in the Eisenhower/Dulles statement of April 24, 1957. How, then, does one explain the Janus-like origins of this relationship? Which U.S. policy—the one exemplified by the Georgia retreat declaration or the one epitomized by 5280/1—was the real U.S. policy? And why did the latter not come to pass?

The answer, if one exists, is that both policies were, in fact, part and parcel of overall U.S. policy. First, as long as Hussein was willing to fight, the United States would offer modest help. Both elements of that equation were important. On the one hand, the Americans were clearly impressed with Hussein's efforts on his own behalf, as evidenced by Eisenhower's compliment of Hussein's "spunk." That sort of self-help was at the core of what the Eisenhower Doctrine was trying to encourage. On the other hand, U.S. policymakers recognized the relatively small cost of keeping Jordan afloat. In retrospect, when Dulles told Lloyd that "big investments" in areas not contiguous to the Soviet Union did not make sense for either Washington or Moscow, he was thinking of numbers far larger than the paltry subsidies in the single-digit or low double-digit millions that Jordan required to stave off bankruptcy. Second, and here 5280/1 came in, the United States would have welcomed a new regime in Amman in accordance with the terms of 5280/1 if one came about; however, it was too busy elsewhere in the region (especially in Egypt) and the rest of the world to actually manufacture one.[27] And in the absence of a substantial provocation or a strong rationale to force a change, U.S. policy toward Jordan was, in an operational sense, defined by what has been a constant ever since the shaky moments following the Iraqi revolution: King Hussein's indefatigable and indomitable will to survive. That, more than any other factor, explains both the unfulfilled vision of 5280/1 and the remarkable events more than three decades later.

Notes

1. The others are Israel, Egypt, Turkey, and Greece. Though Jordan's allotment ($9 million for fiscal year 1993, with a similar amount proposed for 1994) was relatively insignificant, both in absolute and relative terms, it is remarkable that it received an allotment at all.

2. A number of works take this as their major theme, including Nasser H. Aruri, *Jordan: A Study in Political Development (1921–1965)* (The Hague: Nijhoff, 1972); Mary C. Wilson, *King Abdullah, Britain, and the Making of Jordan* (Cambridge: Cambridge University Press, 1987); and P. J. Vatikiotis, *Politics and Military in Jordan: A Study of the Arab Legion, 1921–1957* (London: Cass, 1967).

3. See Uriel Dann, "The United States and the Recognition of Transjordan, 1946–1949," in his *Studies in the History of Transjordan, 1920–1949: The Making of a State* (Boulder: Westview Press, 1984), 93–116.

4. For details of Glubb's dismissal, see Robert B. Satloff, *From Abdullah to Hussein* (London: Oxford University Press), ch. 8. For Glubb's own account, see his autobiography, *A Soldier with the Arabs* (London: Hodder and Stoughton, 1957).

5. Traditionally, Jordanian monarchs relied on transplanted Palestinians and Syrians, Hijazi loyalists, or Circassian refugees to fill the highest and most sensitive positions in government and army. Transjordanians—the native population of the East Bank of the Jordan and especially the *hadari* (city and town dwellers) among them—were the most suspect and least likely to hold positions of authority. This point is well made in Philip Robins's doctoral dissertation, "The Consolidation of Hashemite Power in Jordan, 1921–1946," University of Exeter, 1988.

6. British Ambassador Charles Johnston to Foreign Office (FO), November 21, 1956, Public Records Office, London, FO 371-121731/VR 1073/289 [secret]; U.S. Ambassador Lester Mallory to U.S. Department of State (DOS), November 9, 1956, National Archives and Records Administration, Washington, D.C., DOS 684a.86/11-956 [top secret], in *Foreign Relations of the United States* (hereinafter *FRUS*), vol. 13 (1955–1957):59.

7. Mallory to DOS, November 17, 1956, and DOS to Amman, November 18, 1956, DOS 684a/11-1756 [top secret] in *FRUS* 13 (1955–1957):61–62; Johnston to FO, November 20, 1956, FO 371.121555/VJ 1203/60.

8. Ibid.

9. On the Lloyd-Dulles meeting, see FO 371.121501/VJ 1051/262 [top secret] and Lot 62 D 181, CF 814 [secret]; in *FRUS* 13 (1955–1957):73–74; also, FO 371.121482/VJ 10345/2 [secret]; FO 371.121525/VJ 11345/7 [secret], and the Memorandum of Dulles's meeting with British Ambassador to Washington Sir Roger Makins, January 17, 1957, DOS 785.5/1-1757 [secret] in *FRUS* 13 (1955–1957):81–84.

10. DOS to Amman, December 24, 1956, DOS 685.00/12-2456 [top secret]; Mallory to DOS, December 27, 1956, DOS 685.00/12-2756 [top secret] in *FRUS* 13 (1955–1957):77–79; Johnston to FO, January 1, 1957, FO 371.121525/VJ 11345/10a [secret].

11. See Hussein's speech praising the Arab Solidarity Agreement, January 23, 1957, in Ministry of Information, *al-Majmu'a al-kamila khutub jalalat al-malak al-Hussein bin Talal al-mu'athm 1952–85* [Complete Collection of the Speeches of His Majesty King Hussein bin Talal the Great, 1952–1985], 3 vols. (Amman: Directorate of Press and Publications, n.d. [1986?]), 1:123–124; Johnson to FO, January 22, 1957, FO 371.127901/VJ 1051/28-29 [secret].

12. The actual relationships inside the Jordanian army between Abu Nuwwar and other conspirators remains clouded in myth and rumor.

13. Text of the royal message in FO 371.127989/VJ 1941/4.

14. Mallory to DOS, February 13, 1957, DOS 685.00/2-1357 [secret] in *FRUS* 13 (1955–1957):84–86.

15. For a description of the formation and activities of this clandestine organization by one of its leading members, see Shahir Yusuf Abu Shahut, *al-Jaysh wa al-siyasa fi al-urdunn: dhikriyatan harakat al-dhubat al-urduniyeen al-ahrar* [Army and Politics in Jordan: Memoirs of the Jordanians Free Officers Movement] (al-Qabas: [n.p.] 1985).

16. For the events of Zerqa, see Satloff, *From Abdullah to Hussein*, 166–167; for Hussein's own version, see his memoir, *Uneasy Lies the Head* (New York: Bernard Geis Associates, 1982).

17. Not *all* military conspiracies, but this one. Keeping an eye on the loyalty of the army was an important royal pastime throughout the 1950s. By the mid-1960s, the main challenge had shifted from the loyalty of the kingdom's own armed forces to the threat of Palestinian paramilitary forces and the external threat from Syria.

18. Negotiations ended on a friendly note March 13. See "Exchange of Notes Terminating the Treaty of Alliance of March 15, 1948, Amman, March 13, 1957," Treaty Series no. 39 (1957).

19. See correspondence in *FRUS* 13 (1955–1957):103–109; Joint Chiefs of Staff to Commander in Chief, U.S. Forces/Europe, April 24, 1957, National Records and Archives Administration (hereinafter NA/RA) JCS 381 EMMEA (11-19-47), sec. 57 [top secret]; Wilbur Crane Eveland, *Ropes of Sand: America's Failure in the Middle East* (London: Norton, 1980), 183; *New York Times,* April 25 and May 8, 1957.

20. See *FRUS* 13 (1955–1957):109.

21. For a memorandum of that conversation, see ibid.:152–154.

22. Johnston to FO, August 12, 1958, FO 371.134009/VJ 1015/74 [secret guard].

23. Chief of Naval Operations to Commander in Chief, Sixth Fleet, July 17, 1958, no. 29527 [top secret], NA/RA JCS 381 EMMEA (8-23-57) Section 6/Lebanon/Red File.

24. See reference in New York (Britain's United Nations mission) to FO, August 20, 1958, PREM (Prime Minister's papers) 11/2381 [secret].

25. "Note by the Executive Secretary to the National Security Council on U.S. Policy Toward the Near East," National Security Council (NSC) 5820/1, November 4, 1958 [top secret], in NA/RA 381 (8-23-57) S.11 R.B., submitted by James S. Lay Jr., executive secretary.

26. In November 1958, "Jordan's Arab neighbors" consisted of revolutionary Iraq, the United Arab Republic, and Saudi Arabia.

27. This is, in some ways, a corollary to the central theme of Uriel Dann's book on Hussein's brush with Arab nationalism, namely that Abdul Nasser had more important things to worry about than subverting Jordan and that he (Nasser) feared the burden of responsibility that might come with actually succeeding should he have tried. See Uriel Dann, *King Hussein and the Challenge of Arab Radicalism, 1957–1967* (New York: Oxford University Press, 1989).

9

The 1957 American–Syrian Crisis: Globalist Policy in a Regional Reality

David W. Lesch

The Syrian crisis of 1957 (I will refer to it as the American-Syrian crisis) is one of those occasions where the flaws of applying a globalist analytical methodology to the Middle East—in lieu of a serious appreciation of the regional dynamics in the area—are, in retrospect, dramatically revealed. Indeed, the parameters of the crisis itself were determined as much by regional forces as they were by international actors. It was a telling irony, an indication of the policy misconceptions and misapplications surrounding the approach to the Middle East taken by the administration of President Dwight D. Eisenhower in 1957. What started out as a policy designed to isolate and reduce the power of Egyptian President Gamal 'Abd al-Nasser, that is, the Eisenhower Doctrine, was effectively abandoned during the U.S.-Syrian crisis; thus, a modus vivendi was reached with Egypt, whose help Washington sought during the latter stages of the crisis in order to salvage the situation in Syria. Because of this rather embarrassing experience, the Eisenhower administration began to thoroughly realize that the Middle East was much more complex, not simply an area of East-West ingress.

The New U.S. Ally in the Middle East

The American-Syrian crisis officially began on August 12, 1957, when the Syrian government announced the discovery of a U.S.-engineered attempt to overthrow the regime, which the Eisenhower administration believed was close to becoming a Soviet "outpost" in the region.[1] The next day the Syrian government expelled three U.S. diplomats; the United States responded in kind on August 14, declaring the Syrian ambassador to Washington and his second secretary personas non gratas.

The Eisenhower administration, during the height of the cold war, steadfastly held this incident out as a sign of unacceptable growth in Soviet influence in Syria (especially since the leadership in Syria was generally pro-Ba'thist, the new army chief of staff, 'Afif al-Bizri, was thought to be a Communist, and Syria and the Soviet Union had agreed to sign a wide-ranging economic accord a week earlier), with possible calamitous repercussions for the U.S. position in the entire Middle East. With the Suez debacle so fresh in their minds, Eisenhower and his secretary of state, John Foster Dulles, were careful not to appear to be second-generation imperialists and therefore preferred an Arab-led response to "correct" the situation in Syria, either through diplomatic or military pressure. None would be forthcoming.

The administration was confident that it could count on the support of Saudi Arabia to arrange the Arab response, since King Sa'ud, upon his visit to Washington earlier in year, had been officially touted as an ally of the United States in the Middle East as a counterpoise to Nasser. Winning over Sa'ud had been an unofficial corollary to the Eisenhower Doctrine (announced in January 1957 and passed in March), a rather hastily formulated policy intended to fill the perceived vacuum of power in the Middle East following British and French humiliations at Suez.[2] One of the objectives of the Eisenhower Doctrine was to subvert the alliance Nasser had built to isolate Iraq, then the only pro-Western and Arab Baghdad Pact member. To do this, Washington sought to isolate Nasser—then at his zenith of popularity in the Arab world due to his successes in the Suez crisis—and to halt any further increase in Soviet influence in the Middle East. Thus, Washington had to find an Arab leader who could rival Nasser in prestige and convince other Arab states to turn pro-Western, if not join the Baghdad Pact outright. Because of Saudi Arabia's growing oil wealth and its central position in the Islamic world, Eisenhower and Dulles chose Sa'ud, despite his putative limitations, to rival Nasser and they systematically set about augmenting his stature in the region.

Sa'ud, however, had his own set of objectives that he wanted to achieve through this anointment.[3] The Saudi monarch (or those within the Saudi ruling circles who were guiding him) saw U.S. support as his stepladder to a leadership position in the Arab world. But by choosing this route, he (or they) also invited an inherent contradiction, one that left the king vulnerable and ultimately led to his failure: In order to challenge and possibly assume Nasser's mantle, Sa'ud had to distance himself from Washington's policies. However, this was a given, for Nasser had long set the standard for Arab nationalist leadership, and any pretender to this position had to sufficiently detach himself from the West. Thus, there ensued a schizophrenic Saudi foreign policy, supporting Washington's interests vis-à-vis a four-power conference meeting (between Saudi Arabia, Egypt, Syria, and Iraq) in Cairo in February 1957 and the Jordanian crisis in April 1957 (among other things), yet opposing the Eisenhower administration's policies related to the right of Israeli shipping through the Gulf of Aqaba (Sa'ud was against it, Washington for it) and the Buraimi Oasis dispute (which actually caught the United States between two allies since the dispute pitted Great Britain against Saudi Arabia).

King Sa'ud became the Arab spokesman for the Israeli shipping question following Nasser's convenient abdication of that role in the wake of the Suez crisis and the establishment of United Nations (UN) emergency forces in the Sinai Peninsula. That was a brilliant move by Nasser because he took advantage of Saʿud's strong desire to build up his own Arab nationalist credentials and simultaneously hid his own inability to prevent Israeli ships from passing through the gulf by shifting the blame onto Saʿud, thereby promoting a rift in U.S.-Saudi relations in the process.

There were those, however, who had serious doubts about Saʿud's usefulness to the United States in the inter-Arab arena. In Cairo, following the four-power conference, a U.S. diplomat remarked, "If after this meeting [the] United States doesn't fulfill what Saud thinks are its promises, the King could react very dangerously. He has staked his reputation and honor on [the] United States and could switch completely if he feels betrayed."4 The king, as stated earlier, had his own reasons for cooperating with Washington: He wanted U.S. pressure on Israel to withdraw from the Sinai Peninsula (portions of which it occupied during the Suez crisis), as well as solutions to the Suez Canal sovereignty question, the shipping dispute, and the Palestinian refugee problem. Success on any one of these issues would have significantly heightened Saʿud's standing in the Arab world. Although the United States managed to arrange an Israeli withdrawal from the Sinai (and only after Eisenhower personally intervened with a nationally televised speech designed to pressure Israel), it came through on little else.

Events at the conference also demonstrated that Saʿud remained ultimately subordinate to Nasser or, more to the point, to Nasser's popular slogans of Arab nationalism and his ability to cause problems for the king within Saudi Arabia. The communiqué emerging from the four-power meeting, despite Saʿud's attempts to revise it, said nothing about the threat of communism in the Middle East but instead reflected Nasser's stand on foreign policy and inter-Arab issues. This fact was not lost upon U.S. embassy officials in Jeddah, who began to see the chinks in the armor of the U.S.-Saudi partnership and warned the U.S. Department of State in April 1957 that "it was clear [that the] Palestine question, Aqaba, Buraimi and in general, old issues of Zionism and imperialism loom large in Saudi thinking and could easily affect our relations quite seriously."5 The British, for their part, had been very skeptical of the U.S. plan to build up Saʿud as a rival to Nasser. As one British official noted, "The Americans may have been deceived both about the area of real agreement between Saudi and American policy and the degree of influence which Saud exercises over his Arab colleagues. Saud must know that Egypt is able to make serious trouble for him in his own country."6 In retrospect, this observation seems to have been correct on all counts. As a result, by the time the American-Syrian crisis developed, Saudi Arabia and the United States were essentially on different wavelengths regarding Middle East policy. Saudi Arabia as well as other presumed pro-West Arab states, particularly Iraq, were unwilling to take the leadership role in response to the situation in Syria in August-September 1957. This compelled the Eisenhower administration to adopt an alternative and, as it turned out, much more dangerous path toward "correcting" the situation in Syria.

Washington's Response to the Crisis

Both Eisenhower and Dulles felt that the course of events in Syria in August 1957 was "unacceptable." Both believed the United States "could not afford to have exist a Soviet satellite not contiguous to the Soviet border and in the midst of the already delicate Middle East situation."[7] And both were also anxious to take advantage of the initial trepidation expressed by Syria's neighbors, which would subside, it was thought, if the United States did nothing. The administration also knew their friends in the Middle East were looking to it to lead the way, but Eisenhower and Dulles were looking in the opposite direction for a regional response to the crisis, hamstrung as they were by the specter of Suez and Soviet actions in Hungary.

It is clear that the United States was seriously contemplating direct military action against Syria. In a telephone conversation with Chief of Staff General Nathan Twining on August 21, Dulles stated that "we are thinking of the possibility of fairly drastic action."[8] Also on August 21, Dulles wrote to British Foreign Minister Selwyn Lloyd that "it seems to us that there is now little hope of correction from within and that we must think in terms of the external assets reflected by the deep concern of the Moslem states. . . . We must perhaps be prepared to take some serious risks to avoid even greater risks and dangers later on."[9] British Prime Minister Harold Macmillan commented on August 27 that "this question is going to be of tremendous importance. The Americans are taking it very seriously, and talking about the most drastic measures—Suez in reverse. If it were not serious . . . it would be rather comic."[10]

The desire for a regional response supported by Saudi Arabia, however, was most clearly demonstrated in a letter from Eisenhower to Sa'ud dated August 21, 1957: "We believe that it is highly preferable that Syria's neighbors should be able to deal with this problem without the necessity for any outside intervention. In view of the special position of Your Majesty as Keeper of the Holy Places of Islam, I trust that you will exert your great influence to the end that the atheistic creed of Communism will not become entrenched at a key position in the Moslem world."[11]

The constraints upon the willingness and ability of Sa'ud to play this role and the misperception by the administration that the king had significant influence in the Middle East eliminated any hope for a regional response. Macmillan wrote Dulles on August 23 that the "essential point is that the other Arabs should expose the pretensions of the present Syrian regime to be good Arab nationalists and should denounce them for what they are, namely Communists and Communist stooges."[12] The problem was that Syria's neighbors did not agree with Macmillan's assessment. Instead, the White House received two notes from Sa'ud on August 25, one that dealt with the shipping question and the other with Syria. Although their contents are unknown, they were described as being "couched in extremely tough language," suggesting that Sa'ud was placing the blame for the events in Syria squarely on the United States and/or was presenting the administration with a quid pro quo of his own connected with the shipping dispute.[13] In response, the State Department wrote to its embassy in Jeddah: "We find it very disappointing indications you have received of King's attitude toward developments in Syria. . . . In interests [of] Saudi Arabia and in those of all NE [Near East] states we are anxious that [the] King use his political and moral authority to rally opposition in area to present Syrian regime and to facilitate generating of pressures designed to isolate Syria and to work toward an improvement of situation in that country."[14] The U.S. ambassador in Jeddah also emphasized to the king the danger of communism and Soviet influence in the Middle East while trying to play down the relationship with Israel. He was unable to persuade Sa'ud.

Policy Transformation in Washington

Eisenhower faced two major problems with military intervention in Syria. First, during the Suez crisis and the Soviet invasion of Hungary, he had supported the principle that "military force was not a justifiable means for settling disputes."[15] But he was also convinced that Syria was on the road to becoming a Soviet satellite, and he was determined not to let this happen; he was not going to be accused of "losing" any country to communism, much as the Republicans had rhetorically bashed the Truman administration for "losing" China. Thus, the president had to find a way to rationalize this dilemma, first to himself, then to the outside world. He did this by viewing the Syrian situation as inherently different from the Suez crisis. The Arabs, he postulated, were "convinced" that Syria had been clandestinely invaded through infiltration and subversion, whereas during Suez they believed Nasser had acted well within his rights in nationalizing the Suez Canal Company. Eisenhower decided that Arab action against Syria "would be *basically* defensive in nature, particularly because they intended to react to *anticipated aggression,* rather than to commit a naked aggression" (emphasis added).[16] The sticky question of how to deal with subversion, one that critics of the Eisenhower Doctrine had asked when it was announced, had again come to the forefront; the administration was forced to answer it. Now, however, instead of the pretext being an open attack of one country against another, the administration was preparing the way for possible military intervention on the grounds of *anticipated aggression.* All the United States needed was an arbitrary finding that Syria was controlled by international communism.

The second problem facing Eisenhower revolved around the fact that no Arab state was willing to assume a leadership role in response to the crisis. This was apparent when the White House sent an experienced and respected diplomat, Loy Henderson, who was then deputy undersecretary for administration, to the Middle East to sound out Washington's allies in the region regarding the Syrian situation. Unexpectedly, he did not have a solid proposal to put forth to the conferees when he arrived in Istanbul on August 24. In fact, the British ambassador to Turkey described Henderson as having been "inadequately briefed and rather devoid of ideas."[17] The conferees had obviously expected Henderson to arrive with a proposal, but none was forthcoming, and all they could agree upon was that something had to be done soon. Crown Prince 'Abd al-Ilah of Iraq admitted there was no trust between Jordan's King Hussein and himself;

the United States had counted on Iraqi-Jordanian cooperation against Syria.[18] The Jordanians insisted that Saudi support was the key to the whole situation; without it Hussein could only leave Turkey to vacation in Italy and Spain, a move that led Eisenhower to conclude that "contrary to what we had been led to believe . . . [Jordan] did not want to join in any move against Syria."[19]

Within the ruling circles in the Arab world, differences of opinion could also be found as to the seriousness of the Syrian situation. They had to be wary of the sentiments of the populace, who were largely sympathetic with the Syrian regime. Henderson was reported to have been "shocked" by the negative reaction of the Lebanese press to his visit to Beirut, a reaction that was typical below the government level in most Arab states at the time. Nowhere was this more evident than in Iraq; the Iraqi government's refusal to lead an all-Arab response against Syria was as important to the disruption of the Eisenhower administration's plans vis-à-vis Syria as Saudi Arabia's decision not to follow the U.S. lead, for if the administration was depending on Saudi political and economic support, it was also depending on Iraq to provide the muscle needed to intimidate or take direct action against Syria.

Henderson's findings left the White House confused. Referring to Henderson's trip to the Middle East, the president would write in his memoirs that "whereas early information had indicated the possibility of prompt Iraqi military action with the Turks abstaining, there were now hints of a reversal of this arrangement."[20] The United States at first wanted Turkey to play a secondary role, conscious of the fact that many Arabs still had a strong distaste for the Turks rooted in the days of Ottoman rule in addition to the fact that action by a North Atlantic Treaty Organization member might enlarge the dispute to the international level with possible Soviet involvement. However, the Turkish government, already bordering the Soviet Union to the north, was very concerned about a possible Soviet satellite coming into being to the south.

With the failure of the Henderson mission, the administration, especially John Foster Dulles, reverted to standard cold war thinking. From this point on, it viewed the U.S.-Syrian crisis as it related to the Soviet Union, with all the trappings befitting the "Munich mentality," something that would have a particularly telling impact on the Turks. In a letter to Harold Macmillan discussing Henderson's findings, Dulles wrote the following:

> There is nothing that looks particularly attractive and the choice of policy will be hard. We are not completely satisfied with any of the alternatives which have thus far been suggested. There are risks involved in and objection found to all of them. We are continuing to explore other possibilities. . . . I do not suggest that we have reached any conclusion in favor of encouraging positive action. However, Loy Henderson has the impression that the Turks are desperately serious about this situation, and I do not think either of our governments wants to try to impose what could be another Munich.[21]

How Dulles concluded that the Turks should be given the green light to proceed militarily against Syria if they chose to do so, thereby contradicting the rationale of an all-Arab response, is not the question that should be addressed at this time.[22] Suffice it to say that, having failed to acquire the support of Saudi Arabia and Iraq, the administration looked elsewhere to "correct" the situation in Syria. However, this move transformed the crisis, already elevated from the bilateral level to the regional level, then from the regional level to the international level, as the Soviet Union felt compelled to intervene in order to protect its potential client state and enhance its standing in the Third World. The Kremlin directly warned Turkey, and by implication the United States, to stay out of Syria. And, contrary to many previous studies of this incident that conclude the Soviet Union purposefully exaggerated the crisis after the climax had already passed in order to gain propaganda points, Moscow quite probably saved Syria from external intervention. Outside Turkey, the players in the region itself were more than ready to end the crisis, but Dulles insisted on some kind of "victory" over Syria, and thus the Soviet Union, and this raised the level of international tension.

Sa'ud Takes the Initiative

As the United States and the Soviet Union were indulging in their superpower standoff, diplomacy shifted back to the regional level as Saudi Arabia entered the scene. Sa'ud saw the incident as an opportune moment to assert himself in the inter-Arab arena by mediating a percolating crisis. On the more practical side, he also wanted to salvage his assets in Syria and pull it again toward the Saudi orbit and away from Nasser's influence. Iraq was unable to do this because its government was unredeemably regarded as a lackey of imperialism—in addition to the fact that it had lost most of its "assets" in Syria as a result of the exiles and trial verdicts following the exposure of the failed British-Iraqi plot (Operation Straggle) to overthrow the Syrian regime in late 1956; but Sa'ud had distanced himself from Washington sufficiently to act the part of an Arab nationalist leader, and he was totally at odds with the British.[23] It was important that he also maintained valuable leverage over other Arab states, namely the knowledge that Saudi Arabia was one of the linchpins to the Arab coalition the Eisenhower administration had hoped to form (i.e., if Syria and Egypt did not support his mediatory efforts he would throw his weight behind the U.S. initiative). As expected, the Syrian regime, which had repeatedly branded Sa'ud an imperialist tool and a U.S. lackey earlier in the year, started praising the Saudi monarch for his farsightedness, compassion, and commitment to Arab causes. The government began to vociferously support Saudi Arabia's position on the shipping and Buraimi questions and initiated a back-and-forth stream of diplomatic visits between Damascus and Riyadh.

En route to receive "medical treatment" in West Germany, Sa'ud made a twenty-four-hour stopover in Beirut on September 7 to consult with various Lebanese officials and, almost assuredly, with Syrian officials as well (an especially likely event in light of the somewhat coordinated sequence of events that transpired soon thereafter). The Syrians, who earlier in the year would have viewed Sa'ud's mediatory efforts as unwarranted interference in Syrian affairs, now publicly welcomed this visit. Almost overnight, the Lebanese, Jordanian, and Iraqi governments started to back away from their earlier condemnation of Syria and began to make noises in support of the Syrian regime. The Saudi ambassador to Syria stated on September 10 that his country would "spare no effort to support, back, and aid" Syria should it be the object of outside aggression.[24] On September 12, a Saudi official was quoted as saying that "Saudi Arabia will not stand with hands folded in the event of any aggression against Syria."[25] Also on September 12, Sa'ud reportedly sent a note to Eisenhower urging patience and forbearance in dealing with the Syrian situation, and he claimed that reports of the Syrian threat had been exaggerated.[26] As the climax to his diplomatic efforts, Sa'ud appeared at the airport in Damascus in September 25, 1957, to "consult" with Syrian officials (Iraqi Premier 'Ali Jawdat arrived the following day). Arab newspapers across the Middle East, including Egyptian ones, hailed Sa'ud's efforts.

Nasser's Riposte

This course of events was something Nasser was unwilling to accept, for he had worked extremely hard to keep Syria out of the West's sphere of influence (as well as that of Iraq) and to place pro-Nasserist Ba'thist and army elements in the Syrian hierarchy. Now he was in danger of "losing" Syria to Saudi Arabia or even the Soviet Union.[27] As early as September 11, 1957, Nasser was scheming with Syrian officials to counter Sa'ud. Nasser, along with his commander in chief, 'Abd al-Hakim 'Amr, and the chief of staff of the joint Egyptian-Syrian command, Hafiz Isma'il, met in Cairo with the Syrian chief of staff, 'Afif al-Bizri, and Colonel 'Abd al-Hamid Sarraj, who was the head of Syrian intelligence and the real power in Syria. In retrospect it is clear that at this meeting plans were drawn up for a dramatic move to reestablish Nasser's preeminence in the Arab world. He also intended to build up the pro-Nasser army/Ba'thist faction in Syria (through Bizri and Sarraj) in order to check Saudi advances through President Shukri al-Quwatli and Prime Minister Sabri al-'Asali, as well as Soviet influence through Khalid al-'Azm and Communist Deputy Khalid Baqdash. Nasser thus began a diplomatic offensive that was at first subtle so as not to appear to be in conflict with Sa'ud's popular mediation efforts. In addition, Nasser was well aware of the Saudi monarch's relationship with the Americans and probably realized that he too would benefit from Sa'ud's mediation, for the Egyptian president did not want to be in a position where he would be forced to come to Syria's aid against fellow Arab states, least of all Turkey or the United States, or play second fiddle to the only country really capable of protecting Syria—the Soviet Union. Nasser would cleverly allow Sa'ud to commit himself to a peaceful resolution before he made his move.

That move was to send troops to the Syrian coastal city of Latakia on October 13, ostensibly to defend Syria against Turkish "aggression" (the Turks, with encouragement from Washington, had been steadily massing forces along the border). This was done while Saʻud was in Beirut attending a soccer match. The contrast of Saʻud at a sports event and Nasser sending Egyptian troops to the aid of a sister state threatened by outside forces did not go unnoticed, as was, most certainly, Nasser's intent. Helped by a massive propaganda campaign, Egypt became the Arab state that matched words with deeds and honored its defense commitments. *Al-Ahram* (Egypt's government-controlled newspaper) printed on October 14 that the action showed that the defense agreement between Egypt and Syria (entered November 1955) was not "merely ink on paper . . . it is a reality." The Syrian press hailed the arrival of Egyptian troops, and Damascus Radio simultaneously intensified its charges against Turkey for its "provocations" and "aggressions" on the border. On October 17, Syria placed the army on alert and arms were distributed to civilian groups (the Popular Resistance Organization); it would have seemed even more awkward than it already was to have Syrian troops in a state of unreadiness at the exact moment that Egyptian troops were supposedly helping Syria face the imminent threat from Turkey. Had the threat been real, of course, Nasser would not have sent his troops. The Soviet Union had already explicitly warned Turkey and the United States against any action vis-à-vis Syria, so in a sense Nasser was operating under a Soviet defense umbrella. That it was more of a political than a military move is borne out by the fact that only about 2,000 Egyptian troops landed at Latakia, which was a woefully inadequate number for the supposed task. Nasser had effectively turned the tables on Saʻud and won a tremendous propaganda victory.

In addition to upstaging Saʻud and regaining the diplomatic initiative in the Arab world, Nasser had other reasons for sending Egyptian troops to Syria at this particular moment. With Egyptian troops on the ground in Syria, Nasser was in a position to regain his influence in the country, manipulate the political process, and protect his Baʻthist/army assets. It also prevented Bizri's advancement in the Syrian power structure through the vehicle of the joint command (Nasser reportedly did not trust Bizri and shared the U.S. view that he was a Communist).[28] The move was also designed to solidify support for Akram al-Hawrani, who was up for election on October 14, 1957, as speaker of the Chamber of Deputies against incumbent Nazim al-Qudsi, a leading member of the traditionally pro-Iraqi Populist Party. Nasser preferred to see Hawrani win election, and the timing of the Egyptian troop landing was intended to help his chances. In view of the fact that Hawrani won by only a slim margin, Nasser's timely assistance could have been a decisive factor in the outcome. It was important to Nasser to have Hawrani in the position of the speaker of the chamber, for it was, ex officio, the vice presidency of the Syrian Republic, and if the president became ill or was away, the speaker would undertake his functions.[29] With Quwatli in his seventies and often ill (in a real or diplomatic sense), this position assumed added significance. Hawrani, as a leader of the Baʻth Party and the key to its link with the military, had essentially become the number-two figure in Syria, and he was therefore in the catbird seat for the next presidential election. In this way, Nasser and his Syrian supporters could continue to keep the "Russian millionaire," Khalid al-ʻAzm, from his longtime ambition.

As mentioned, Nasser was intent on securing the Ba'th Party's position in Syria. In this fashion, he could enhance the ability of the Ba'thists to withstand and reverse growing Soviet influence in Syria and solidify the country's attachment to Egypt. The fact that the Egyptian troops immediately moved inland toward Aleppo only supports this assertion. Nasser and his Ba'thist allies believed that they could help their cause in elections scheduled to be held soon in Aleppo by staging a dramatic "rescue," with the possibility of changing the view of most Aleppans toward Egypt and thus providing more votes for Ba'thist candidates. It is not surprising that the Egyptians and Ba'thists exaggerated the Turkish threat, giving plenty of air time to the purported Turkish battle cry "On to Aleppo!" Nasser and the Ba'thists, as well as the conservatives, were clearly concerned about Communist advances in Syria (particularly prevalent in northern Syria, including Aleppo) and the concomitant increase in Soviet influence.[30] The Ba'th Party had allied itself with the Communists to combat imperialism and the old guard Syrian politicians; when they succeeded, with proportionately more power accruing to the Communists as Syria's relationship with the Soviet Union tightened during the crisis, the Ba'thists decided to unofficially split from the Communists and utilize Nasser's own willingness to prevent Syria from falling under the influence of the Kremlin. All of this maneuvering proved unnecessary, however, as al-'Asali, bowing to pressure from all sides, indefinitely postponed the elections, thus buying more time for the Ba'thists to figure out a way to prevent their onetime allies from leapfrogging them. The landing of Egyptian troops returned Nasser to prominence in Syria, which made Ba'thist control and union with Egypt more palatable to many and inevitable to all.

The Egyptian troop landing at Latakia took Sa'ud totally by surprise. At a loss, he could only offer to put his armed forces at Syria's disposal, but this was hopelessly outshone by Nasser's initiative, and it was clear to all that the latter was now dictating the pace and direction of the regional diplomatic game. Evidence of this came on October 16, 1957, when King Hussein informed the ambassadors of Turkey, the United States, and Britain that Jordan would fully support Syria in the event of an attack and that Syria's independence should be maintained. Iraq publicly restated its support for Syria; even the Lebanese government reportedly gave Syrian officials assurances that they would offer assistance in case of an attack.[31]

The information disseminated from Cairo also focused at this time on linking Israel and Turkey (with U.S. support) to an alleged plot against Syria, with reports that Israeli Chief of Staff Moshe Dayan of the Israeli Defense Forces had paid a visit to Turkey to discuss such plans. Not only did Nasser effectively portray Egypt as the savior of Syria and Arabism against Turkey and the "imperialists," but also against Public Enemy No. 1, Israel, which compelled other Arab states to follow his lead. In addition, a Turkish delegation visited Saudi Arabia on October 24 as part of Turkey's support for Sa'ud's mediation; however, it cast the king in a negative light in the Arab world since he was personally negotiating with the country that Egypt had effectively portrayed as an aggressor and imperialist tool. Sa'ud had various constraints upon his diplomatic maneuvering; namely, he did not and could not detach himself completely from the

United States, and his efforts therefore seemed to be slow and plodding, especially in comparison to Nasser's actions from October 13 on. The king had to walk a tightrope to maintain a balance between Arab nationalist forces, on the one hand, and the West and pro-West elements in the Arab world on the other. Nasser, however, did not have this constraint, which allowed him to take the bold and decisive step of sending his forces into Syria. Nasser also had the military wherewithal to do so; Sa'ud did not, and the only role the king could play was that of mediator. Sa'ud's fatal mistake was that he could only accomplish his objectives at Nasser's expense. This compelled Nasser to respond to the challenge in a way that Sa'ud could not, and, for all intents and purposes, the "Arab cold war" had already begun.

U.S.-Egyptian Modus Vivendi?

The American-Syrian crisis showed on several occasions how similar objectives can sometimes make strange bedfellows. Both Egypt and the United States were very interested in keeping Syria from becoming Communist and from falling too deeply into the Soviet orbit. In fact, a confidant of Nasser informed U.S. officials on December 11, 1957, that the Egyptian president

> had investigated recent information we [United States] had given him relative to the communist connections of [Syrian Chief of Staff Afif al-] Bizri and is now convinced Bizri [is] a communist and that something must be done about it. . . . He [Nasser] asks of us only that we keep hands off Syria for a maximum period of three months and particularly that we do nothing which could have unintentional effect of making heroes out of Bizri, [Communist Deputy] Bakdash and [pro-Soviet] Khalid Al Azm.[32]

The Egyptian official suggested that there were "several ways of attacking the Syrian problem," but the "only country with capability [to] succeed, and which can do so with minimal repercussions is Egypt. Of [the] countries primarily concerned with [the] Syrian situation, US and Egypt have greatest interest in ensuring that country [has] stable, anti-communist government."[33] On December 10, the U.S. ambassador to Egypt, Raymond Hare, had a conversation with a member of the inner circle of the Revolutionary Command Council (the ruling group within Egypt), 'Ali Sabri, in which the latter stated that Egypt had more reason to worry than the United States regarding the prospect of Arab nationalism taking too much of a left-hand turn, since Egypt "had to live in the area and could not escape the consequences."[34] The State Department reacted by stating that "we wish [to] avoid impeding any Egyptian efforts to bring about change and in particular appreciate considerations re[garding] Bizri, Bakdash and Azm."[35]

The three months Nasser had asked for was one more than he actually needed. The long courtship over union between Egypt and Syria was finally consummated on February 1, 1958, producing the United Arab Republic. The regional solution to the Syrian problem that Eisenhower and Dulles so desperately wanted had occurred, albeit from an unexpected source. The Eisenhower administration calculated that if it could not keep the Soviets out of Syria, it might as well trust the job to someone who could. The United States had tried just about everything short of committing U.S. forces to keep Syria from becoming a Soviet base in the Middle East. Dulles turned to a policy of "containment-plus," keeping the "virus" from spreading out from Syria. Nasser had successfully kept the Soviets at arm's length in Egypt; maybe his stature and power in the Arab world was enough to do the same in Syria.

The U.S.-Egyptian rapprochement did not occur overnight and, at least from the U.S. perspective, was by default bred more out of necessity than prescience. There had been signs during the crisis that their coinciding interests vis-à-vis Syria might produce some sort of a working relationship. In early October, the State Department publicly expressed its desire for closer relations with Egypt. Egyptian press and radio comment reacted favorably to this and generally welcomed U.S. friendship. A piece in *Al-Sha'b* stated on October 12 that Egypt "is anxious to have good relations with the United States and other states." The next day, *al-Jumhuriya* printed that "we antagonize those who antagonize us and pacify those who pacify us."

This budding cooperation was clearly evident early on at the UN debate over the Syrian situation. The Egyptian representative to the UN, Mahmoud Fawzi, apparently told UN Secretary-General Dag Hammarskjold that the Egyptians were doing their best to keep the Syrians from proceeding with their complaint in the UN General Assembly, including trying to dissuade them from insisting that an investigatory commission be sent to the Turkish border.[36] They felt the debate would not be confined to the relatively narrow Syrian-Turkish item but would expand to cover broader issues in the Middle East that could place Nasser in some rather uncomfortable diplomatic positions, especially on the Arab-Israeli front. Fawzi also told the secretary-general that he was "bitter" over how the Soviets were forcing the hand of the Syrians in the UN.[37] Indeed, Soviet guidance of Syrian actions at the UN seemed to have awakened the U.S. and Egyptian delegations to the possibility of limited cooperation.

From the point of view of the Eisenhower administration, cooperation with Egypt became more desirable after Sa'ud's mediation had failed and Nasser had regained his paramount position in the Arab world after the landing of Egyptian troops at Latakia on October 13. Evidence of this is found in a summary record of conversations U.S. officials had had with Fawzi. One of these stated:

> We told Fawzi in our opinion his statement . . . was restrained and we appreciated [the] tone he had struck in it. We said we believed objectives which had outlined to us for handling this item [Syrian complaint in the UN] . . . were shared by U.S. Fawzi said Egypt and U.S. share desire to see in Middle East peaceful, constructive, independent states, free from outside interference of any kind. . . . Fawzi said he appreciated our initiative and our approach which, as far as he was concerned, represented a clean slate from which to start.[38]

The Eisenhower administration began to realize what the Egyptians already knew, that is, the latter were the only ones capable of preventing an increase of Soviet influence in Syria. Fawzi's actions at the UN (and other indications from Cairo) convinced Dulles that Nasser was sincere in his desire to "save" Syria. Having exhausted all other reasonable avenues, Dulles had no choice.

Recognizing the new political balance in the Middle East, *al-Ahram* stated on November 6, 1957, that the Soviet Union "may be on its way to the conquest of space but America can certainly conquer people's hearts." For Nasser, however, he had just traded in one headache for another with his reluctant acquiescence to the union with Syria. Most Syrians saw union with Egypt as a necessary step to avoid more internal turmoil and external interference. But for Egypt and Nasser, it was a political disaster that directly contributed to the heightening tension of the Arab cold war and the environment for the outbreak of the 1967 Arab-Israeli war. Nasser's diplomatic acumen in this particular episode certainly enabled him to achieve his immediate objectives, and it had short-term positive results. But the long-term implications were ultimately negative, as it contributed to a level of responsibility and popularity that Nasser spent the rest of his tenure in power trying to live up to—and never quite reaching.

Conclusion

With Nasser's fait accompli, and lacking any alternative, Sa'ud continued to pursue his mediation policy, but its effects were much more keenly felt in the UN than in the Middle East. Blocked at the domestic level by the disclosure of the coup attempt in Syria, at the regional level by the actions of Sa'ud and Nasser, among other persons, and at the international level by the threats emanating from the Kremlin, the Eisenhower administration opted to pursue "victory" in the UN. In doing this, however, the United States had unwittingly reignited at the international level what was a diminishing crisis by early to mid-October. Sa'ud's official offer to mediate the Syrian-Turkish crisis (as it was termed at the time) actually had the effect of lessening tensions at the UN, as other Arab delegates began to support his efforts. On October 22, 1957, the UN General Assembly officially suspended debate on the Syrian-Turkish dispute pending the outcome of Sa'ud's mediation. It would come to absolutely nothing, as Syria politely rejected his intervention, but it did provide a respite in the UN that allowed the United States and Soviet Union to reassess their positions and separately agree to just let the crisis peter out.[39] Soviet General Secretary Nikita Khrushchev realized the untenable situation in the UN in the wake of Sa'ud's efforts. His objective of deterring the Turks and the Americans from intervening in Syria had been successful, with the concomitant rise in Soviet prestige in the Arab world and influence in Syria. It was time to end the crisis before the Soviets lost at the UN much of what they had won in the Middle East. With this in mind, Khrushchev unexpectedly appeared at a reception at the Turkish Embassy in Moscow on October 29, unofficially ending the American-Syrian crisis.

Regional players had largely dictated the pace and scope of the crisis, whereas the global superpowers, especially the United States, initiated policies in a reactionary fashion that only escalated tensions to higher and more dangerous levels. The Eisenhower Doctrine signified a globalist application of foreign policy to the Middle East, focusing on the Soviet threat, something that most Arabs thought was absolutely incongruous considering the fact that Egypt had just been attacked by Britain, France, and Israel and not by the Soviet bloc or Communist forces. By remaining at, and constantly retreating to, this analytical level, U.S. policymakers failed to appreciate the agendas of regional actors that, in many cases, had nothing to do with the East-West conflict yet set the parameters of the political dynamics of the Middle East.

In Iran, the Eisenhower administration was successful in blunting a nationalist movement that was deemed susceptible to Communist takeover; however, this did not prevent Iranian disillusionment of, and ultimately anger toward, the United States for betraying its stated principles of democracy and self-determination, a hostility that poured forth in 1979 with the added venom of twenty-six years of repression. In Syria, the United States was unable to curb the rise of leftist Arab nationalist forces and ironically found itself ultimately, and indirectly, through Nasser's sangfroid, relying on a nationalist movement to prevent the Soviet Union from expanding its position in the Middle East; the hostility engendered by a feeling of imperialist victimization nonetheless was created, severely hampering U.S.-Syrian relations for more than a generation. The circumstances surrounding Syria during this turbulent period compelled its leaders to think in terms of national survival rather than national development, preordaining choices and options that invariably sent it down a path trodden by many other Third World nations caught in the vice of the cold war: stunted economic growth, regional conflict and hostility, and superpower confrontation.

Notes

1. For a detailed examination of this subject and the events that led up to it, see David W. Lesch, *Syria and the United States: Eisenhower's Cold War in the Middle East* (Boulder: Westview Press, 1992).

2. The Eisenhower Doctrine essentially offered American military and economic aid to those nations in the Middle East that requested it in order to resist the advances of other states who were, in the official opinion of the administration, dominated by "international communism."

3. On Sa'ud's relationship with the United States and his role in the American-Syrian crisis, see David W. Lesch, "The Role of Saudi Arabia in the 1957 American-Syrian Crisis," *Middle East Policy* 1, no. 3, 1992.

4. Foreign Reports, letter to John Foster Dulles from Harry Kern, February 28, 1957, John Foster Dulles Papers, Box 118, John Foster Dulles Collection, Seeley G. Mudd Library, Princeton University, Princeton, N.J.

5. Telegram from the Embassy in Saudi Arabia to the Department of State, April 11, 1957, Foreign Relations of the United States, vol. 8 (1955–1957) (hereinafter *FRUS*), at 492.

6. British Foreign Office (FO) Report, "Middle East: The Nature of the Threat and Means of Countering It" (in preparation for the Bermuda Conference with the United States in

March 1957), March 8, 1957, FO 371/127755, Public Record Office, Kew Gardens, London (hereinafter PRO); Foreign Office Reports in preparation for Anglo-American talks on June 12–14, 1957, "Measures to Ensure Continued Access to Middle East Petroleum Resources," FO 371/127756, PRO; and, "Saudi Arabia and Buraimi and Their Relations to Kuwait," FO 371/127756, PRO.

7. Memorandum of a Conversation, Department of State, Washington, D.C., August 19, 1957, 3:45 p.m., *FRUS* 8 (1955–1957):340–341.

8. Dulles telephone call to General Twining, August 21, 1957, John Foster Dulles Papers, Telephone Calls Series, Box 7, Dwight D. Eisenhower Library, Abilene, Kans. (hereinafter DDEL).

9. Dulles to Selwyn Lloyd, August 21, 1957, Ann Whitman File, Dulles-Herter Series, Box 7, DDEL.

10. Harold Macmillan, *Riding the Storm, 1956–1959* (New York: Harper and Row, 1971), pp. 279–280.

11. Eisenhower to King Saud, August 21, 1957, Ann Whitman File, International Series, Box 42, DDEL.

12. British Foreign Office, August 23, 1957, FO 371/128224, PRO; also, Macmillan, *Riding the Storm,* 279.

13. Memorandum of a Conversation with the President, White House, Washington, D.C., August 28, 1957, *FRUS* 8 (1955–1957):659–660.

14. Telegram from the Department of State to the Embassy in Saudi Arabia, August 27, 1957, *FRUS* 8 (1955–1957):500–502.

15. Dwight D. Eisenhower, *Waging Peace, 1956–1961* (Garden City, N.Y.: Doubleday, 1965), p. 198.

16. Ibid.

17. British Consulate-Istanbul, August 25, 1957, FO 371/128224, PRO.

18. As a U.S. official pointed out, Iraqi troops would have a much easier time penetrating Syria through Jordan than to traverse the vast desert and roadless space directly across the Syrian-Iraqi border. Memorandum of a Conversation Between the President and the Secretary of State, White House, Washington, D.C., September 2, 1957, *FRUS* 8 (1955–1957): 669–670.

19. British Embassy-Amman, August 28, 1957, FO 371/128225, PRO, and Eisenhower, *Waging Peace,* 200–201.

20. Eisenhower, *Waging Peace,* 200.

21. Letter from Secretary of State Dulles to Prime Minister Macmillan, September 5, 1957, *FRUS* 8 (1955–1957):681–682.

22. For a detailed analysis of this policy transformation, see Lesch, *Syria and the United States.* There are no "smoking-gun" documents to prove that the United States gave or was prepared to give the Turks the "green light," but there is enough circumstantial evidence as well as confirmations acquired from players who were intimately involved in the process at the time (who wish to remain anonymous), that I am convinced that the Eisenhower administration did so and that it was only Soviet threats against Turkey that prevented what could have been a very dangerous situation from developing. For a particularly revealing document on the subject, see Telegram from the Department of State to the embassy in Turkey, September 10, 1957, *FRUS* 8 (1955–1957):691–693.

23. On October 6, 1957, the Saudi government officially denied its acceptance of the Eisenhower Doctrine, countering what had been taken for granted in diplomatic circles since

Sa'ud's visit to Washington in February, even though the king never publicly announced his country's adherence to it.

24. Foreign Broadcast Information Service (FBIS), September 11, 1957, A2.

25. FBIS, September 16, 1957, A1.

26. *New York Times,* September 15, 1957.

27. If Syria was "lost" to Saudi Arabia, it is likely that pro-West elements would have gained in strength and possibly even assumed power (with the issues of union with Iraq and membership in the Baghdad Pact resurfacing), but there is nothing to suggest that Saudi Arabia and the United States were working together toward this goal, that is, Washington was not supportive of Sa'ud's mediation until it became useful to do so to escape from a United Nations dilemma later during the U.S.-Syrian crisis; indeed, there exists much evidence that Riyadh and Washington were at odds with each other during most of the crisis period. See Lesch, Syria and the United States, 190–209.

28. Telegram from the Embassy in Egypt to the Department of State, December 11, 1957, *FRUS* 8 (1955–1957):744–746.

29. "Syria's Egyptian Visitors," *Economist,* October 19, 1957, 230–231.

30. Elias Murqus, a former Syrian Communist, offers an interesting criticism of the Communist Party's activities at this time. He felt its overaggressiveness vis-à-vis the Ba'th seriously damaged its chances to gain power. *Tarikh al-ahzab al-shuyu'iyya fi al-watan al-'arabi* (History of the Communist Parties in the Arab World) (Beirut: al-Jam'a al-Lubaniya, 1964), 91–92.

31. FBIS, October 17, 1957, A2.

32. Telegram from the Embassy in Egypt to the Department of State, December 11, 1957, *FRUS* 8 (1955–1957):744–746.

33. Ibid.

34. Ibid.

35. Telegram from the Department of State to the Embassy in Egypt, December 12, 1957, *FRUS* 8 (1955–1957): 746–747.

36. British United Nations (U.N.) Delegation-New York, October 16, 1957, FO 371/128242, PRO.

37. British U.N. Delegation-New York, October 18, 1957, FO 371/128242, PRO. The U.S. delegate at the UN, Henry Cabot Lodge, told Dulles that "Bitar is here and is lonely and overwhelmed by Soviet overtures and would like to talk with someone from the West." Telephone Call from Lodge to Dulles, October 2, 1957, 5:40 p.m., John Foster Dulles Papers, Telephone Calls Series, Box 7, DDEL.

38. Telegram from the Mission at the United Nations to the Department of State, October 24, 1957, *FRUS* 8 (1955–1957):728–729.

39. British U.N. Delegation-New York, October 28, 1957, FO 371/128244, PRO.

10

U.S. Policy and Military Intervention in the 1958 Lebanon Crisis

Erika Alin

The administration of President Dwight D. Eisenhower regarded the 1958 civil crisis in Lebanon as a microcosm of the threat to Western influence emanating from the spread of Soviet communism and Arab nationalism in the Middle East during the 1950s. In analyzing Lebanon's disturbances, it focused on the regional and international contexts and repercussions of the crisis, attributing the crisis to external interference in Lebanese affairs by Egyptian and Syrian Arab nationalists. It feared that a major consequence of the crisis would be a reduction of Western influence in Lebanon and the coming to power of an Arab nationalist leadership in Beirut that would reorient Lebanon's foreign policy away from the West and in the direction of nonalignment and closer relations with Moscow. At a time when U.S. officials believed that Western interests were being challenged not only in Lebanon but throughout the Middle East, the administration feared that a change in the Lebanese government could prove deleterious to the U.S. position in the region.

Concerned with the potentially negative regional and international repercussions of the Lebanon crisis, the United States adopted a public posture of firm support for the pro-Western Lebanese government. It publicly declared that it was ready to use military force to secure Lebanon's political integrity and, following the July 14 overthrow of the pro-Western government of Iraq, dispatched military forces to Beirut to prevent a violent and/or radical change in the country's government and to deter further challenges to Western interests in the Middle East.

Yet even as the Eisenhower administration publicly responded resolutely to the crisis, privately it had reservations regarding both the nature of the challenge to Western interests presented by developments in Lebanon as well as the need for and effectiveness of U.S. military action to resolve the crisis. Despite its emphasis on the external Communist and Arab nationalist challenges to Lebanon, it recognized that

Lebanese tensions were partly rooted in domestic conditions and events particular to that country. And, though it was convinced that the U.S. standing in the cold war required a firm demonstration of commitment to Lebanon's pro-Western government—including the potential use of force—it also realized that Lebanese developments were only indirectly related to the U.S.-Soviet struggle. It also generally believed that the crisis could be resolved without the use of U.S. force. Consequently, U.S. policy toward Lebanese developments in 1958 was marked by ambiguity. As the crisis evolved during the spring and early summer, the Eisenhower administration adopted a wait-and-see posture, publicly announcing its support for Lebanon's pro-Western government yet remaining reluctant to act militarily. This posture, however, came to an abrupt end with the July 14 coup in Iraq, which dramatically raised U.S. fears concerning the stability of pro-Western governments in the region, including that of Lebanon.

U.S.-Lebanese Relations, 1953–1957

The Eisenhower administration regarded Lebanon as an important political asset to its Middle East policy. Lebanon, a former French mandate, had a history of friendly relations with the West. U.S.-Lebanese ties had grown following World War II with the expansion of U.S. business and political interests in the Middle East and the emergence of Beirut as a financial and commercial center in the area. During the mid-1950s, Lebanon's president, Camille Chamoun, grew increasingly supportive of U.S. regional initiatives despite the growing popular appeal of Arab nationalism both in and outside of Lebanon. Furthermore, whereas many Arab countries in the late 1940s and early 1950s experienced domestic crises and upheavals, Lebanon's political system—dominated by the Christian community—seemed to augur well for continued Western influence and relative political stability. Lebanon's significance for U.S. Middle East policy was premised on its role as a stable counterpoint to the growing, nationalist inspired, anti-Western orientation of most Arab states at the time and as a center for U.S. political and commercial operations in the region.

    U.S. officials believed that many Lebanese government officials during Chamoun's initial year in the presidency were "extremely friendly" to the United States. Yet they were not unaware of the potential for growing domestic challenges to Lebanon's "pro-Western neutrality." A spring 1953 Middle East mission headed by Secretary of State John Foster Dulles had concluded that even pro-Western Lebanese officials were reluctant to pursue closer relations with the United States until regional issues that contributed to anti-Western sentiments among Lebanese and other Arabs, such as the Palestine problem and the British presence in the Suez Canal Zone, had been addressed.[1] Over the next several years, regional developments, especially Nasser's assumption of power in Egypt, the emergence of the pro-Western Baghdad Pact defense alliance, and the growing appeal of the Arab nationalist movement following the 1956 Suez crisis, increased popular criticism of the

West in Lebanon. Such developments also contributed to a growing sectarian-based polarization on foreign policy issues among Lebanese.

At the center of the political controversy in Lebanon was the conviction held by many Lebanese that their influence within the country's political system was being challenged by the activities and allegiances of the country's other sectarian communities. The 1943 so-called National Pact, which provided the basis for Lebanon's political system, had aimed to balance political influence among the country's major sects—especially the politically dominant Maronite Christians and Sunni Muslims—and to prevent these communities from entering into external alliances that could upset the domestic political balance.[2] During the mid- and late 1950s, many Lebanese Muslims believed that the political balance mandated by the pact was being violated, directly or indirectly, by President Chamoun. At the domestic level, Chamoun attempted to diminish the influence of politicians opposed to his policies—especially traditional communal leaders—and to increase the authority of the country's Christian presidency; at the foreign policy level, he sought to move Lebanon closer to the West.[3] Lebanese Christians, in turn, especially Maronites, feared that Muslims, increasingly influenced by Arab nationalist sentiments, wanted to incorporate Lebanon into a pan-Arab Muslim political union.

Sectarian political, social, and economic differences among Lebanese had predated Chamoun's presidency. They were, however, exacerbated by Chamoun's policies and by regional developments during the 1950s. Following the 1956 Suez crisis, the Lebanese government's increasingly pro-Western orientation found support primarily among Christians, whereas pan-Arab allegiances were to be found primarily, but by no means exclusively, among the country's Muslim population.[4]

During the mid-1950s, as Arab nationalist allegiances increased among Lebanese Muslims, U.S. officials began to grow "concern[ed] over political developments in Lebanon and [the] possible consolidation [of] opposition to Chamoun."[5] Partly in order to reduce domestic criticism of his policies and gain time to consolidate his political position, Chamoun altered the composition of the Lebanese cabinet to better correspond to growing Arab nationalist sentiments in the country. In September 1955, he replaced the pro-Western prime minister, Sami Solh, with Rashid Karami, a supporter of closer relations with Egypt and especially Syria. Officials at the U.S. embassy in Beirut feared that Karami's policies would "not be favorable to United States interests" and that the new cabinet would align Lebanon with the Egyptian, Syrian, and Saudi Arabian axis that had emerged as a counteralliance to the pro-Western Baghdad Pact.[6] In March 1956, yet another Lebanese cabinet, this time under the leadership of Abdullah Yafi, announced that Lebanon would remain neutral in the cold war and would improve its relations with Syria.[7]

Although U.S. embassy officials recognized that these cabinet changes represented tactical political moves by Chamoun, they were also aware that Chamoun himself was not entirely satisfied with U.S. policies toward Lebanon or the Arab world as a whole. Even as the Lebanese leader credited the Eisenhower administration with demonstrating a greater interest in Arab affairs than had previous U.S. governments, he criticized it for not having "arrived at a correct solution to Arab problems," such as the Palestine issue. He also believed that the administration's emphasis, in its bilateral relations as well as overall regional policy, on the positions of Arab states in the cold war was not effectively supported by a "firm [and] planned policy" to counter Communist challenges and especially to assist pro-Western leaders in the region, the absence of which, he claimed, was evident in the U.S. refusal to provide Lebanon with arms for even a "minimum posture of defense."[8]

During the mid-1950s, the Eisenhower administration expressed concern not only with the growing criticism of Chamoun's government from Arab nationalist Lebanese, and with Chamoun's decision to counter such pressure by according prominent government posts to Arab nationalists, but also with what it perceived as an expansion of Communist activities in Lebanon. By the early 1950s, according to the U.S. Department of State, Beirut had become "a center for the propagation and dissemination of communist propaganda in the Near East."[9] The U.S. embassy, during the administration's early years, reported extensively on Communist recruitment efforts among Lebanese students, women, and Palestinian refugees. It believed that the "inaction, indifference, and even appeasement" of the Chamoun government had contributed to an escalation of Communist activities in the country. Chamoun had permitted Communists to assume a greater public role, refused—embassy and State Department officials complained—to try suspected Communists "in a more energetic manner," and rejected U.S. requests for firmer measures against Communist meetings and street demonstrations.[10]

Although U.S. officials were concerned with Communist involvement in Lebanon, they generally recognized that most Lebanese did not support communism as an ideology but rather used it as a practical means of expressing dissent. They also subsequently recognized that Communists were not a major factor in Lebanon's escalating troubles during 1957 and early 1958.[11] Although Communists shared the anti-Chamoun sentiments of Lebanese Arab nationalists, according to State Department and embassy officials, the Lebanese "Communist Party has not sought to subvert or overturn the Lebanese government" and "none of the [anti-Chamoun] opposition parties or religious groups in Lebanon have seriously entertained offers of communist collaboration."[12]

The appointment of Arab nationalists to prominent cabinet posts in late 1955 and early 1956 provided Chamoun with a political respite that enabled him to begin, in late 1956, to reassert his control over Lebanon's domestic and foreign policies. Following the British-French-Israeli attack on Egypt in the Suez crisis, Chamoun refused to suspend relations with Britain or France, a position that was opposed by many Lebanese Muslims and provoked the resignation of Prime Minister Yafi. Chamoun subsequently reinstated the pro-Western Sami Solh as prime minister and appointed the pro-U.S. Charles Malik as foreign minister. Embassy officials regarded these cabinet changes as a "pronounced defeat for Syria and for Nasser" in Lebanon.[13]

The expansion of pan-Arab popular sentiments among Lebanese Muslims as well as other Arabs following the Suez crisis convinced Chamoun to strengthen

Lebanon's relations with the West, the historical protector of the country's Christian community. The Lebanese government accepted the January 1957 Eisenhower Doctrine, under which the United States committed itself to defending Middle East countries against Communist aggression, becoming the only Arab state to officially do so.[14] Most Lebanese Christians supported the government's position toward the Eisenhower Doctrine; Muslims generally opposed it. Chamoun's acceptance of the U.S. initiative, therefore, increased sectarian-based polarization on foreign policy issues among Lebanese.

In April 1957, largely in anticipation of parliamentary elections scheduled to be held in Lebanon in June, anti-Chamoun politicians established a United National Front, which subsequently became the principal vehicle for coordinating opposition to the government during the period leading up to the 1958 crisis. The National Front was led by prominent Muslim politicians but also included several of Chamoun's Christian opponents and competitors for the presidency. As the June parliamentary elections approached, U.S. concerns regarding Lebanon's future orientation increased. Since Chamoun's six-year presidential term would expire in September 1958, the parliament elected in 1957 would select a successor president the following year. U.S. officials feared that anti-Chamoun and pro-Arab nationalist politicians, if elected to the parliament, would choose an anti-Western president. They believed, in the embassy's words, that electoral "defeat of the political grouping now in power would severely damage U.S. interests and could swing Lebanon into [the] Syrian-Egyptian fold."[15]

As the Eisenhower administration became concerned with the potential impact of the 1957 parliamentary elections on Lebanon's future foreign policy orientation, as the U.S. Central Intelligence Agency (CIA) recognized, the anti-Chamoun opposition formed an "uneasy coalition" that, even if elected to the parliament, would probably "not be effective unless it is able to construct a binding control over its various factions . . . [and] it is doubtful that such control will be achieved."[16] U.S. intelligence reports indicated that it was uncertain whether anti-Chamoun candidates, even if elected, could sustain the political cohesion required to significantly change Lebanon's foreign policies, especially since "the opposition . . . has no common objective other than forcing Chamoun from office."[17] Nevertheless, the Eisenhower administration remained concerned about the potential election outcome. It provided covert financial support to the campaigns of pro-Chamoun candidates, in part to counteract the impact of Egyptian, Syrian, and Saudi support for opposition candidates.[18]

The magnitude of the victory enjoyed by Chamoun supporters in the parliamentary elections caused even U.S. intelligence officials to express surprise.[19] The election outcome was viewed in Washington as a victory over Nasserism in Lebanon. Yet within Lebanon the elections were accompanied by reports of government fraud and U.S. interference, which added to the conviction of opposition politicians that Chamoun was attempting, with U.S. support, to perpetuate his political position at their expense. The cabinet that was formed following the elections consisted almost exclusively of Chamoun supporters and was headed by the pro-Western Solh. The new parliament, devoid of several prominent Muslim politicians who had been defeated in the elections, did not accurately reflect the political sentiments of a large segment of the Lebanese population. The National Front refused to recognize the election outcome and sporadic violence erupted in the country.

U.S. Policy and the Escalating Crisis

During the spring and early summer of 1958, tensions in Lebanon escalated in response to both regional and domestic political developments. These developments included the February 1 unification of Egypt and Syria into the United Arab Republic (UAR)—welcomed by many Lebanese Muslims as the beginning of a pan-Arab political union but feared by many Christians—as well as, at the domestic level, heightened speculations that Chamoun intended to remain in the presidency beyond the expiration of his constitutional term in 1958. During the second week of May, the Lebanese opposition began an armed insurrection against the government, prompting President Chamoun to make the first of three inquiries to the Eisenhower administration, between mid-May and the July 15 U.S. intervention, aimed at determining whether the United States was prepared to militarily intervene in Lebanon.

By late spring 1958, the possibility of Chamoun seeking a second presidential term, in contravention of the one-consecutive-term limit of the Lebanese constitution, had become a key political grievance among Lebanese opposition leaders. Such leaders feared that, if he was reelected Chamoun would deprive them of political influence for another six years and continue strengthening the country's pro-Western posture. Although Chamoun never publicly stated his intention to seek reelection, he implied on several occasions in conversations with U.S. officials that he was considering doing so.[20] The Eisenhower administration doubted that any presidential successor to Chamoun would continue Lebanon's open support for Western policies in the region. During the early spring of 1958, it believed, as indicated by the State Department, that "the only hope for preserving Lebanon's international posture" lay with supporting possible efforts by Chamoun to seek election to a second presidential term.[21] As Ambassador Robert McClintock later recalled, "at one time we had indicated our full support for his re-election," yet "of course we could not say this publicly and our official line would be one of assiduous refusal to meddle in Lebanese politics."[22]

Prior to the initial May 13 White House meeting on the Lebanon crisis, the Eisenhower administration therefore leaned in the direction of supporting a second presidential term for Chamoun. However, when the opposition initiated an armed revolt against the Lebanese government in mid-May, a growing recognition developed among U.S. officials as to the extent of anti-Chamoun sentiments held by many Lebanese. U.S. officials increasingly realized that a reelection campaign by Chamoun could escalate the civil disturbances and, given the Lebanese leader's close alignment with the United States, increase anti-Western sentiments in Lebanon. Following the real onset of the crisis, consequently, they generally preferred that Chamoun step down at the expiration of his term. By mid-May, Eisenhower had become convinced that "the thing for him [Chamoun] to do is announce that he is not going to do any running" for a second term.[23] U.S. officials now preferred that a presidential candidate be found who would only marginally compromise Lebanon's relations with the West while gaining the support of Muslim and Arab nationalist Lebanese.

The Eisenhower administration, however, was reluctant to hurt its relations with the pro-Western Chamoun, especially given its uncertainty regarding the eventual outcome of the crisis. It therefore left open in its communications with Chamoun the possibility that, under certain conditions, it might tacitly support him or, more likely, look the other way should he attempt to extend his presidential tenure. The United States, as Dulles noted in mid-June, "[wa]s not concerned with [Lebanese] constitutional factors and would not object if, after this crisis is solved, he [Chamoun] wished to stay on as President."[24] Given indications that Chamoun perceived U.S. support as important in deciding whether or not to seek a second presidential term, Washington's reluctance to clearly communicate its concerns over the reelection issue undoubtedly contributed to the Lebanese leader's failure, throughout the spring and early summer, to definitively state publicly that he would not seek reelection. This failure in turn contributed to the continuation of the civil crisis.

During the second week of May, antigovernment riots erupted in the Lebanese coastal town of Tripoli, triggered by the murder of an anti-Chamoun newspaper editor. The Eisenhower administration publicly blamed the riots on external Arab nationalist and local Communist instigation. It pointed to "indirect aggression" against Lebanon by the UAR and stated that it had "no doubt" that Communists had "fann[ed] the flames" of the riots and, as Eisenhower notes in his memoirs, "that Chamoun's uneasiness was the result of one more communist provocation."[25] Privately, however, as earlier indicated, many administration officials recognized that Communists were not directly involved in Lebanon's civil disturbances.

Moreover, they were aware that the crisis was partly rooted in Lebanon's unique sectarian political structure and in Chamoun's controversial policies. According to the CIA, Chamoun's policies had alienated a diverse array of Lebanese, including many who were not anti-Western.[26] State Department and intelligence officials noted that Lebanon's sectarian political balance would remain vulnerable to disruption by regional developments, particularly Arab nationalism, and—in the CIA's words—did "not believe that the present political-religious balance, with its slight edge in favor of the Christians, can long be maintained in Lebanon."[27] The domestic sources of the Lebanon crisis were also emphasized in numerous dispatches by Ambassador McClintock.[28] Yet even as U.S. officials were aware that the internal Lebanese political situation was "extraordinarily complex," they tended to underestimate the extent to which domestic factors contributed to opposition to Chamoun's government. They also tended to subordinate a serious consideration of ways to encourage Chamoun to address such factors to the primary objective of ensuring that the crisis did not diminish Western influence in Lebanon or the Arab world. In accordance with the latter objective, the administration emphasized public support for Chamoun and the need to halt external, particularly Egyptian and Arab nationalist, involvement in Lebanon's affairs.

In response to the opposition insurrection against the Lebanese government, President Chamoun requested, on May 13, that the United States—as well as Britain and France—inform him how it would respond to a Lebanese request for external assistance, possibly in the form of military intervention. On May 13, Eisenhower convened the first White House meeting on the Lebanon crisis. During this and subsequent discussions U.S. officials weighed the implications of using force in Lebanon. They recognized that military action could have considerable negative repercussions for U.S. relations with Arab, Muslim, and Third World countries and that it could enable Moscow to score a propaganda victory in the cold war. They feared that, in order to protest an intervention Arab states would close the Suez Canal and suspend oil shipments to the West, threatening "a new and major oil crisis" for the Western alliance. Finally, they doubted that military action would either resolve the Lebanon crisis or guarantee Lebanon's pro-Western orientation.

Although the administration harbored reservations regarding the implications of the use of military force in Lebanon, it was also concerned that, unless it demonstrated a firm commitment to defending Lebanon's pro-Western orientation, U.S. credibility would be questioned around the world. According to Eisenhower, although it was necessary to consider the liabilities of military action, the United States "had to take into account the apparently much larger problems which would arise if the Lebanese needed our intervention and we did not respond."[29] Both Eisenhower and Dulles were concerned that mounting challenges to pro-Western governments worldwide in the mid-1950s were creating the perception that closer relations with the Soviet Union were the wave of the future for Third World countries. Accordingly, Dulles, at the May 13 meeting, "reviewed current Communist methods of warfare throughout the world."[30] Given this global context within which the administration analyzed Lebanese developments, military action was viewed as an important means of sending a deterrent signal to anti-Western forces in the Middle East and elsewhere. Following the May 13 meeting, the Eisenhower administration informed Chamoun and made a public announcement indicating that it was prepared to consider dispatching military forces to Lebanon. U.S. combat forces were placed in a state of readiness.

Despite its determined public posture, the administration's actual response to Lebanese developments during the late spring and early summer continued to reflect a certain ambivalence regarding both the nature and appropriate resolution of the crisis. On the one hand, the administration was convinced that the U.S. position in the cold war required firm action in support of Chamoun's pro-Western government. On the other, it recognized that military pressure and/or action could have negative consequences for U.S. interests—as it had experienced in the previous year's crisis with Syria—and, further, might not be needed to resolve the situation. Since it believed that "almost any course that the United States could pursue would impose a heavy cost,"[31] it basically preferred to avoid taking definitive action and, instead, let the crisis run its course in the hope that Chamoun would assert his control over the situation and/or that the contending Lebanese factions would work out a political compromise of their own accord.

According to Dulles, the United States, following the May 13 meeting, made no commitment to Chamoun beyond "the possibility of moving in troops to protect U.S. life and property if that should prove necessary" as well as aiding Lebanon in developing its military assistance program.[32] Washington had indicated that it would consider intervention if and when it determined that the situation warranted such action but not automatically in response to a Lebanese request. Key officials from the Department of State, the Department of Defense, and the CIA believed that it was important to "de-emphasize the prospect of military action" and attempt to "induce Chamoun to find a solution to the internal political problem."[33] Dulles noted, in mid-June, that there could be "no satisfactory solution to the Lebanese problem except through the lawful government's working one out with all possible assistance except armed intervention."[34]

In accordance with its belief that the Lebanon crisis could and should be resolved domestically, the Eisenhower administration, in mid-May, outlined conditions that had to be met by Lebanon before it would sanction military action. Such conditions could preclude, or at least delay, the need for military action; yet they could also establish a political framework for such action should it eventually be required. The administration made clear that it would not intervene to maintain Chamoun in power for a second presidential term (though privately U.S. officials continued not to object to Chamoun's remaining in the presidency once the crisis had been resolved); that, concurrent with a request for U.S. intervention, Lebanon would have to file an official complaint of its grievances regarding external Arab nationalist/ UAR interference in its affairs with the United Nations (UN) Security Council; and that, prior to an intervention, it would have to secure support for such action from at least two other Arab states. Chamoun was also informed that, should he ultimately request U.S. intervention, such a request would have to be premised on the need for U.S. action to protect U.S. citizens in Lebanon and to preserve the country's independence and integrity.

Specifically, any request for U.S. military action was to avoid references to the 1957 Eisenhower Doctrine. Although the administration feared that growing Nasserist influence could move Lebanon away from the West and toward the Soviet bloc, it recognized that "there has not occurred 'armed aggression from a country controlled by international communism'" against Lebanon.[35] The Eisenhower Doctrine was ambiguous on the circumstances justifying U.S. military action—it failed, among other things, to clearly distinguish Communist from nationalist activities, the latter of which were not legally subject to U.S. action under the doctrine—and the UAR was neither "controlled by international communism" nor engaged in "armed aggression" against Lebanon.[36] In legally justifying the intervention, the administration subsequently emphasized Lebanon's right to collective self-defense under Article 51 of the UN Charter, arguing that although Lebanon had not been subject to a direct foreign armed attack as required for action under the charter, UAR subversion and "indirect aggression" could be viewed as tantamount to such an attack. It also emphasized that the Lebanese government had explicitly requested U.S. military action and that the United States had a right to protect its citizens in Lebanon.

During mid- and late May, various Lebanese groups and personalities attempted to mediate the crisis, proposing, among other things, that a caretaker government headed by the commander of the Lebanese army, General Fuad Shihab, be formed until elections for a successor president were held. General Shihab was widely respected among opposition leaders and Lebanese Muslims, partly because he regarded the crisis as a domestic dispute over Chamoun's reelection and rejected requests by Chamoun to order the armed forces to quell the civil disturbances. Efforts by Lebanese parties to mediate the crisis, however, stalemated. The opposition demanded Chamoun's early resignation and continued to incite civil disturbances. Chamoun, meanwhile, continued to refuse to clarify his position on the reelection issue. On May 22, furthermore, the Lebanese government submitted a complaint of UAR interference in Lebanon's affairs to the UN Security Council, thereby heightening opposition fears that Chamoun was seeking external support, especially from the United States, to remain in the presidency.

On June 15, in response to reports that opposition forces planned to take over the Lebanese presidential palace, Chamoun again asked the Eisenhower administration how it would respond to a request for U.S. intervention. Both Eisenhower and Dulles believed that Chamoun was now "closer than ever" to requesting external assistance.[37] Eisenhower, in response, convened the second top level policy meeting on the Lebanon crisis, following which the United States reiterated its readiness to consider intervention. By mid-June, the Lebanese government had satisfied U.S. conditions for an intervention, having submitted a complaint to the UN Security Council, received support for military action from Jordan and Iraq, and, through the Solh cabinet, announced that an amendment of the constitution's reelection clause would not be introduced to the parliament.

U.S. officials remained convinced that U.S. credibility in the cold war could be jeopardized by a failure to support the pro-Western Lebanese government; yet they continued to prefer a nonmilitary resolution to the crisis. Eisenhower, at the time, had "little, if any, enthusiasm" for military intervention. The potential liabilities of intervention led administration officials to speculate, at the June 15 meeting, on alternative ways of providing military support to strengthen the Lebanese government's position short of direct military action, including the formation of a multinational UN force. None of these suggestions, however, were seriously pursued. By mid-June, with the Lebanese government having fulfilled U.S. conditions for an intervention, the administration recognized that, even though it believed that the crisis should be resolved without U.S. involvement, it would be hard-pressed to justify a failure to respond to a "properly worded" Lebanese request for military action.

Moreover, it feared that Chamoun in fact preferred external military action to domestic initiatives, whether military or political, to resolve the crisis. Dulles believed that Chamoun had to be "disabuse[d] . . . of any thought that he has a blank check from us with regard to military intervention."[38] The administration was convinced that, militarily, "the regular Lebanese army can and will deal with" the crisis by suppressing opposition activities.[39] U.S. officials expressed confusion as to why Chamoun neither effectively used the Lebanese armed forces to quell the disturbances nor replaced General Shihab with a commander prepared to do so. They recognized some of the reasons for Shihab's opposition to involving the army in the disturbances, as well as for Chamoun's reluctance to order the former to do so, including that such involvement could cause a sectarian split in the army and, according to Dulles, that any move by Chamoun to dismiss Shihab could trigger a military coup.[40] Yet the administration nevertheless tended to regard Chamoun's failure to secure army involvement as evidence that the Lebanese leader was reluctant to take the necessary domestic measures to resolve the crisis.

It also questioned why Chamoun was not trying harder to put an end to the controversial reelection issue and, specifically, why he continued to refuse to make a public statement indicating that he would not seek a second term (which he would not do until June 30). Eisenhower believed that Chamoun had made a "political error" in not publicly foreclosing his reelection at an earlier date. In addition, according to Dulles, Chamoun had not made a "loud and effective" case for his government's position, especially the contention that the crisis was the result of UAR interference, to the Lebanese public. The United States believed that Chamoun's failure to seriously attempt to win support for his government's position within Lebanon and, more generally, to gain control over the crisis—either through political or military means—increased both the potential need for U.S. intervention to resolve the crisis and the political as well as possible military complications of such action should it eventually be required.[41]

Chamoun's preference for close relations with the West, and the perceived threat of Arab nationalism in Lebanon, encouraged the Lebanese president to look outside of Lebanon for assistance. Chamoun appeared confident that the United States would automatically intervene if requested to do so. His confidence can be attributed, in part, to the fact that the Eisenhower administration, despite privately and, at times, publicly encouraging the Lebanese government to find a political solution to the crisis, remained reluctant to communicate to Chamoun its reservations regarding his handling of the crisis and to clearly make U.S. military action contingent on evidence that Chamoun had seriously pursued domestic policies intended to resolve the crisis. Instead, the administration essentially deferred to Chamoun's preferences regarding how Lebanese developments should be handled. Dulles believed, as did many other Washington officials, that the United States "should not destroy Chamoun's heart or courage by pressing him to compromise with the opposition" and "should not offer him specific advice with regard to political moves which he might make within Lebanon."[42]

The Intervention and Its Aftermath

On July 14, the Eisenhower administration ordered 14,000 U.S. troops to Lebanon. The immediate impetus for the intervention came from the overthrow of the pro-Western government of Iraq, which heightened U.S. fears concerning the security of pro-Western governments throughout the Middle East. Eisenhower believed, upon receiving news of the Iraqi coup, that the United States was facing its "last chance to do something" to end challenges to pro-Western governments and Western interests in the region. Within the context of the cold war, the administration feared that a failure to respond decisively to developments in Iraq would send a signal of U.S. weakness that could have repercussions for the West's political and military positions worldwide.

On July 14, Chamoun, fearing that the Iraqi coup would embolden the Lebanese opposition, requested U.S. military intervention, in response to which Eisenhower convened, on the same day, the third and fourth White House meetings on the Lebanon crisis. Even before the morning meeting, Eisenhower's "mind was practically made up" concerning the need for intervention.[43] From having maintained a wait-and-see posture toward the use of force throughout the spring and early summer, the administration, within hours following the Iraqi coup, came to see an intervention as the only means of securing the political stability and integrity of the Lebanese state and, even more important, of deterring further challenges to pro-Western countries in the Middle East. In the minds of U.S. officials, the need to act firmly and quickly in response to the Iraqi coup overrode earlier concerns regarding both the necessity and effectiveness of the use of force to resolve the Lebanon crisis.[44]

Lebanese reaction to the landing of U.S. marines on the beaches of Beirut reflected preexisting political loyalties. Many Christians welcomed the action, even though a significant number opposed Chamoun's appeal for external assistance. Government supporters and the opposition initially believed that U.S. troops had been sent to Lebanon to prolong Chamoun's tenure, and many Christians, including Chamoun and foreign minister Malik, were reportedly disappointed with the failure of U.S. troops to more actively support the Lebanese government's position.[45] According to Dulles, the Lebanese government remained "anxious to drag us into this [crisis] in a bigger way" by securing U.S. troop support for the defeat and/or complete disarming of the opposition.[46] Most Lebanese Muslims condemned the intervention, fearing that the United States intended both to uphold Chamoun's tenure and to use Lebanon as a base for intervening in Jordan and possibly also Iraq. Although opposition leaders protested the intervention, they sought to avoid clashes between their armed supporters and U.S. troops, believing that Chamoun wanted to provoke such clashes in order to prompt direct U.S. troop support for his presidency.[47] Overall, as U.S. embassy officials recognized, few prominent Lebanese politicians, whether Muslim or Christian, expressed public support for the intervention.[48]

One day following the arrival of U.S. forces in Lebanon, the Eisenhower administration dispatched Deputy Undersecretary of State Robert Murphy to Beirut. During the month that he remained in the Middle East, Murphy, despite initial administration denials, played a central role in mediating the political compromise that resulted in General Shihab's election to the Lebanese presidency on July 31. Following his arrival in Beirut, Murphy communicated to Washington his analysis of the domestic context of the Lebanon crisis.

In terms of the overriding objective of deterring further challenges to Western interests in the Middle East, U.S. officials believed that the use of military force had been successful, at least in the short term. The Soviet Union did not respond militarily to the intervention. Indeed, most high-ranking U.S. officials, including Eisenhower, had become convinced during the months prior to the intervention that neither Moscow nor Cairo would respond militarily to U.S. action in Lebanon and that such action consequently would not carry significant military risks for the United States.[49] If, prior to the intervention, the administration had been preoccupied with the regional and international dimensions of the crisis, the absence of further immediate challenges to Western regional interests following the intervention convinced it both to limit its military action to Lebanon and to attempt, through Ambassador Murphy, to address what had earlier been considered a second-order concern, that is, the domestic political sources of the crisis. A compromise settlement, capable of at least partially satisfying the demands of Lebanese nationalists, could now minimize the negative regional political fallout from the intervention.

On July 31, after a period of considerable political uncertainty, General Shihab was elected by the parliament to succeed Chamoun. The Eisenhower administration had not openly supported any particular candidate in the political process leading up to Shihab's election and, in order not to be perceived as attempting to influence the elections, Murphy left Lebanon on July 30. However, Murphy's extensive rounds of mediation had played an important role in generating agreement on a presidential successor.[50] Despite continued concerns regarding Shihab's political leanings, especially his relations with Nasser, Dulles subsequently noted that the general's election "was probably the most favorable result under the complicated circumstances existing in Lebanon, particularly since the opposition had voted for Shihab."[51] On September 24, Shihab was inaugurated as president of Lebanon and, one month later, the last U.S. forces withdrew from the country.[52]

Within Lebanon, an easing of political tensions occurred following the presidential election, which was accompanied by a relaxation of tensions between Lebanon and the UAR—since Nasser had generally supported Shihab's election—as well as between the United States and the UAR. Internationally, in late July and early August, the UN became the arena for a diplomatic contest between the United States and Soviet Union that culminated in the convening of a special session of the UN General Assembly on the Middle East on August 13. Eisenhower's address to the assembly was intended to create the public perception that the United States had used force in Lebanon based on sound political and legal principles and that it was interested in improving its relations with Arab countries.

Within Lebanon, Chamoun's departure from the presidency and the subsequent reintegration of opposition leaders into the political system partially removed a principal grievance that had contributed to the escalation of anti-American sentiments among Lebanese Muslims during the mid-1950s. However, many Lebanese and other Arabs had regarded the intervention as an illegal interference in Lebanon's domestic affairs and had viewed U.S. policy throughout the crisis as favoring Chamoun. The intervention, therefore, contributed to the perception, both within Lebanon and the wider Arab world, that the United States "to some extent bec[a]me identified along with the British and French as 'imperialists'" prepared to intervene militarily to secure its interests in the Middle East.[53] Lebanese attitudes toward the United States following the intervention also continued to be affected by the same factors that offended the nationalist sentiments of Arabs in general, such as U.S. support for Israel. Partly as a result of continued anti-Western and pro-Arab nationalist sentiments among many Lebanese, as well as of Shihab's own preferences for a more neutral Lebanese international posture, the CIA accurately predicted, in October 1958, that Lebanon was likely to depart from its pro-Western orientation and move "in the direction of neutralism and accommodation with pan-Arab nationalism."[54]

Conclusion

By sending U.S. troops to Lebanon, the Eisenhower administration sought to uphold Western interests in the Middle East against the perceived challenge of Arab nationalism and, to a lesser extent, communism. During the mid-1950s, the administration had attempted to curtail the spread of anti-Western political forces in the region by supporting pro-Western Arab governments, such as Chamoun's, and encouraging Arab states, through the Eisenhower Doctrine, to align with the West in the cold war. At the same time, however, it had recognized that its efforts to weaken the Arab nationalist movement and to bind Arab states to the West were alienating Arab public opinion and encouraging Arab leaders to pursue closer ties with the Soviet Union. In the wake of the Suez crisis, it had become more sensitive to the nuanced context of local and regional politics and had attempted to pursue a more conciliatory posture toward Arab nationalism. It had refrained from supporting its Western allies' aggression against Egypt in 1956 and from publicly denouncing the 1957 formation of the UAR. Its experiences in the 1957 Syrian crisis had, in addition, resulted in a greater recognition of the potentially negative consequences of U.S. efforts to intervene too directly in domestic Arab political developments, contributing to its subsequent reluctance to become militarily involved in the Lebanese situation prior to the July 14 Iraqi coup.

The events of the summer of 1958 (the Lebanon crisis, the unexpected overthrow of the pro-Western Iraqi government, and the conviction of U.S. officials that only the resort to military force had prevented a further deterioration in Western influence in the Arab world) increased the Eisenhower administration's recognition that safeguarding long-term U.S. interests in the Middle East would require "winning the minds of the Arab peoples." The administration's concern to avoid alienating Arab nationalist public sentiment had encouraged it, following the arrival of U.S. forces in Lebanon, to support a compromise political settlement capable of partially satisfying the demands of pro-Arab nationalist Lebanese and to propose, through Eisenhower's August address to the UN General Assembly, U.S. contributions to an economic development fund for the Arab world.[55] Yet even though sensitive to the need to improve U.S.-Arab relations, the Eisenhower administration's policy toward the 1958 crisis had remained premised on the perception that Arab nationalist and Western interests stood poised against one another in the Middle East.

Notes

1. U.S. Department of State (hereinafter DOS) Position Paper, May 5, 1953, *Foreign Relations of the United States* (hereinafter *FRUS*) 9 (1953–1955).

2. The pact distributes political offices in accordance with a sectarian formula, premised on demographic information from the 1932 census, under which the country's president must be a Maronite Christian, the prime minister a Sunni Muslim, and the speaker of the parliament a Shi'a Muslim, and states that Christians should refrain from calling on Western countries to defend their interests and that, although Lebanon has an "Arab face," Muslims should not attempt to politically unify the country with other Arab states.

3. Chamoun, who had initially pursued relatively neutral regional and international policies, had attained the presidency in September 1952 during a political crisis revolving around former President Bishara al-Khoury's election to a second presidential term. Once in office, Chamoun attempted to diminish the political influence of Lebanon's traditional communal leaders, many of whom had supported his bid for the presidency, and also instituted economic policies perceived by many such leaders as neglecting the predominantly rural regions of their constituents. See Abdo I. Baaklini, *Legislative and Political Development: Lebanon, 1842–1972* (Durham, N.C.: Duke University Press, 1976), 144; Michael C. Hudson, *The Precarious Republic: Modernization in Lebanon* (New York: Random House, 1968), 105–107 and 275; and Wade R. Goria, *Sovereignty and Leadership in Lebanon, 1943–1976* (London: Ithaca Press, 1985), 29.

4. Differences remained within both the Christian and Muslim communities between the political positions of, for instance, Maronite and Greek Orthodox Christians and Sunni and Shi'a Muslims. Chamoun also had influential rivals among Christian politicians. Attitudes toward the Baghdad Pact were particularly illustrative of the emerging controversy over Lebanon's foreign alignment during the mid-1950s. Muslims generally opposed the pro-Western defense alliance. Chamoun, in contrast, reportedly indicated, in April 1955, that "there would be no delay in the Lebanese decision to adhere to the Turco-Iraqi [later Baghdad] Pact" provided that the United States reaffirmed its support of the defense arrangement. See Daily Intelligence Abstracts, April 8, 1955, Box 11, Operations Coordinating Board (hereinafter OCB) Central File Series, White House Office NSC Staff Papers, Eisenhower Library, and Leila M.T. Meo, *Lebanon: Improbable Nation, A Study in Political Development* (Bloomington: Indiana University Press, 1965), 97. By late 1954, a loose coalition of anti-Chamoun politicians had emerged and, in December 1954, a congress of "Muslim parties,

associations, and organizations" submitted a list of demands to Prime Minister Solh, focusing on a more equitable distribution of government posts among the country's sects; a constitutional amendment balancing the authority of the country's president, prime minister, and parliamentary speaker; the formation of an economic union between Lebanon and Syria; and the preservation of the country's Arab character. Fahim I. Qubain, *Crisis in Lebanon* (Washington, D.C.: Middle East Institute, 1961), 32–36.

5. Undersecretary of State Herbert Hoover Jr., DOS to Embassy in Beirut, October 28, 1955, *FRUS* 13 (1955–1957).

6. Embassy in Beirut to DOS, Telegram 151, October 17, 1955, 783A.21/10-1755, DOS Central Files, National Archives.

7. Embassy in Beirut to DOS, Telegram 409, March 29, 1956, 783A.13/4-456, DOS Central Files, National Archives.

8. Embassy in Beirut to DOS, Telegram 1508, May 28, 1956, 783A.11/5-2356, DOS Central Files, National Archives, and Intelligence Notes, July 9, 1956, Box 11, OCB Central File Series, White House Office NSC Staff Papers, Eisenhower Library.

9. *World Strength of the Communist Party Organizations,* Annual Report 10, DOS Bureau of Intelligence and Research (Washington, D.C.: DOS, 1958). See also M. S. Agwani, *Communism in the Arab East* (New York: Asia Publishing House, 1969), 106.

10. "Sino-Soviet Bloc Activities in Lebanon," Research and Analysis Report 7260, May 24, 1956, DOS Bureau of Intelligence and Research, Lot 58 D 776, DOS INR Files, National Archives; Embassy in Beirut to DOS, Telegram 1, July 1, 1953, 783A.001/7-153; and Telegram 623, April 6, 1954, 783A.00/4-254, DOS Central Files, National Archives.

11. See "Political Trends in Lebanon," Research and Analysis Report 7286, July 5, 1956, DOS Bureau of Intelligence and Research, Lot 58 D 776, DOS INR Files, and Embassy in Beirut to the U.S. Information Agency (hereinafter USIA), TOUSI 326, May 19, 1958, Box 1, Record Group 59, General Records of DOS, National Archives.

12. Embassy in Beirut to DOS, Telegram 623, April 6, 1954, 783A.00/4-254, and "Sino-Soviet Bloc Activities in Lebanon," Research and Analysis Report 7260, May 24, 1956, DOS Office of Intelligence Research, DOS Central Files, National Archives.

13. William Rountree to J. F. Dulles, January 12, 1957, *FRUS* 13 (1955–1957).

14. Under the doctrine, Lebanon also received $10 million and $2.2 million in grant economic and military aid. American officials acknowledged that such aid was difficult to justify on economic grounds but believed that it could "make of Lebanon an example of U.S.-Arab cooperation." Briefing Materials Prepared for the Richards Mission to the Middle East, 1956–1957, Record Group 59, Lot File No. 57D 616, DOS General Records, National Archives, and James P. Richards to J. F. Dulles, March 16, 1957, and "Operation Plan for the Lebanon," OCB Report, June 31, 1957, *FRUS* 13 (1955–1957).

15. Embassy in Beirut to DOS, March 16, 1957, *FRUS* 13 (1955–1957).

16. "Assessment of the Political Situation in Lebanon," July 15, 1957, Central Intelligence Agency Action Copy, DA IN 38166, declassified documents, Central Intelligence Agency.

17. "Consequences of Possible U.S. Courses of Action Respecting Lebanon," June 5, 1958, Special National Intelligence Estimate (hereinafter SNIE) SNIE 36.4-58, declassified documents, Central Intelligence Agency.

18. Memorandum of Conversation, Charles Malik and Dwight D. Eisenhower, February 6, 1957, Box 34, International Series, Ann Whitman File, Eisenhower Library.

19. "Results of the Elections in Northern Lebanon," July 9, 1957, Central Intelligence Agency Action Copy DA IN 36 202, declassified documents, Central Intelligence Agency.

20. In late 1957, he had informed then U.S. Ambassador Charles Heath that, save for himself, no viable presidential aspirant existed who would preserve Lebanon's pro-Western alignment. During the spring of 1958, he attempted, more directly, to ascertain the U.S. position on his possible reelection in conversations with Ambassador McClintock, who had noted already upon arriving in Lebanon in January that "Chamoun would probably prefer for personal reasons to continue in power." Embassy in Beirut to DOS, Telegram 2203, December 30, 1957, 783A.11/12-3057, DOS Central Files, National Archives, and Memorandum from Officer in Charge of Lebanon-Syria Affairs (Waggoner) to Director of the Office of Near Eastern Affairs (Rockwell), January 17, 1958, *FRUS* 11 (1958).

21. DOS to Embassy in Beirut, Telegram 3709, May 7, 1958, 783A.00/5-758, DOS Central Files, National Archives.

22. Embassy in Beirut to DOS, Telegram 654, May 12, 1958, 783A.00/5-1258, DOS Central Files, National Archives, and Embassy in Beirut to DOS, July 10, 1958, *FRUS* 11 (1958). The CIA, in early April, indicated that Chamoun—who "actually enjoys the prospect of a bout with the opposition"—probably could outmaneuver his domestic opponents if he chose to seek reelection as a result of his own "extraordinary qualities of force, energy, and courage" and of serious divisions among opposition leaders regarding an acceptable successor presidential candidate. "Assessment of the Political Situation in Lebanon," April 4, 1958, Central Intelligence Agency Action Copy DA IN 106001, declassified documents, Central Intelligence Agency.

23. Memorandum of Telephone Conversation Between the President and the Secretary, May 14, 1958, *FRUS* 11 (1958).

24. Memorandum of Conversation, DOS, June 18, 1958, *FRUS* 11 (1958).

25. Dulles statement in *Department of State Bulletin* 38 (June 9, 1958), *U.S. News and World Report,* July 25, 1958, and Eisenhower, *Waging Peace,* 266.

26. "The Lebanese Crisis," June 14, 1958, SNIE 36.4-1-58, Central Intelligence Agency.

27. "Political Crisis in Lebanon," Report 7784m, April 15, 1958, DOS Office of Intelligence Research and Analysis, quoted in H. W. Brands Jr., *Cold Warriors: Eisenhower's Generation and American Foreign Policy* (New York: Columbia University Press, 1988), 101, and "Consequences of Possible U.S. Courses of Action Respecting Lebanon," June 5, 1958, SNIE 36.4-58, declassified documents, Central Intelligence Agency.

28. See, for example, Embassy in Beirut to DOS, February 21, 1958, and Embassy in Beirut to DOS, June 2, 1958, *FRUS* 11 (1958).

29. Memorandum of Conversation with the President, May 13, 1958, Box 6, White House Memoranda Series, J. F. Dulles Papers, Eisenhower Library.

30. Ibid.

31. Staff Notes, June 23, 1958, Box 33, Eisenhower Diary Series, Ann Whitman File, Eisenhower Library, and Eisenhower, *Waging Peace,* 274.

32. Memorandum of Telephone Conversation, J. F. Dulles and John Reston, May 19, 1958, Box 8, Telephone Call Series, J. F. Dulles Papers, Eisenhower Library.

33. D. J. Decker (Joint Middle East Planning Committee of the Joint Chiefs of Staff) to Chief of Naval Operations (Burke) Regarding Meeting at DOS, May 19, 1958, *FRUS* 11 (1958).

34. Memorandum of Conversation, DOS, June 18, 1958, *FRUS* 11 (1958).

35. Outgoing Telegram to President Chamoun, May 13, 1958, Drafting Office Copy, Box 16, J. F. Dulles Chronological Series, J. F. Dulles Papers, Eisenhower Library.

36. Yet in order to uphold the relevance of a doctrine it had only a year earlier proclaimed, U.S. officials wanted to bring an intervention "into context of the [Eisenhower] Doctrine at

least to some extent" by making reference to the declaration of the Mansfield amendment to the doctrine that the independence and integrity of Middle East countries was vital to U.S. interests. Memorandum of Conversation with the President, May 13, 1958, Box 6, White House Memoranda Series, J. F. Dulles Papers, Eisenhower Library, and Dulles, as quoted in *New York Times,* May 21, 1958.

37. Memorandum of Telephone Conversation, J. F. Dulles and Dwight D. Eisenhower, June 14, 1958, Box 12, Telephone Calls Series, J. F. Dulles Papers, Eisenhower Library.

38. Memorandum of Conversation, DOS, June 18, 1958, *FRUS* 11 (1958).

39. DOS to Embassy in Beirut, Telegram 4890, June 19, 1958, Box 34 (2), International Series, Ann Whitman File, Eisenhower Library.

40. "The Lebanese Crisis," June 14, 1958, SNIE 36.4-1-58, Central Intelligence Agency, and "Political Crisis in Lebanon," quoted from Brands, *Cold Warriors,* p. 85, and Memorandum of Conversation with the President, June 15, 1958, Box 33, DDE Diary Series, Ann Whitman File, Eisenhower Library.

41. Both John Foster Dulles and CIA Director Allen Dulles feared that, if Lebanon's political tensions remained unaddressed, "by the time Chamoun asks, if he does, for armed intervention the situation would have deteriorated to the point where it will be difficult to do it." Memorandum of Telephone Conversation, J. F. Dulles and Allen Dulles, June 20, 1958, Telephone Call Series, J. F. Dulles Papers, Eisenhower Library.

42. Memorandum of Conversation, DOS, June 18, 1958, *FRUS* 11 (1958), and DOS to Embassy in Beirut, Telegram 4890, June 19, 1958, Lebanon (2), Dulles-Herter Series, Ann Whitman File, Eisenhower Library.

43. Eisenhower, *Waging Peace,* 270. Administration advisers, such as Special Assistant for National Security Council Affairs Robert Cutler, concurred that the "president knew exactly what he meant to do" at the morning meeting. Robert Cutler, *No Time for Rest* (Boston: Little, Brown, 1965), 363.

44. In the initial uncertainty surrounding the Iraqi coup, Dulles believed that there was a strong possibility "that force would be used to preserve access to Middle East oil," an access that Eisenhower had also authorized the use of "all necessary means" to safeguard. Memorandum of Conference with the President, July 20, 1958, Staff Memos-July 1958, Box 35, DDE Diary Series, Ann Whitman File, Eisenhower Library. Yet in the absence of further immediate challenges to Western interests following U.S. troop arrival in Beirut, the administration resisted pressure by Britain that it join in intervening in Jordan on July 17.

45. Robert Murphy, *Diplomat Among Warriors* (Garden City: Doubleday, 1964), 404.

46. Memorandum of Telephone Conversation, J. F. Dulles and Dwight D. Eisenhower, July 19, 1958, Telephone Call Series, J. F. Dulles Papers, Eisenhower Library.

47. Embassy in Beirut to DOS, Telegram 617, July 22, 1958, 783A.00/7-2258, DOS Central Files, National Archives.

48. Embassy in Beirut to DOS, Telegram 533, July 19, 1958, 783A.00/7-1958, DOS Central Files, National Archives.

49. Nevertheless, the Joint Chiefs of Staff—as well as a few administration advisers—were less optimistic regarding the probable Soviet reaction and also feared hostile U.S. troop contact with the Lebanese army. Dulles indicated that "the military are reluctant. . . . They say Lebanon exhausts their possibilities." See Barry M. Blechman and Stephen S. Kaplan, *Force Without War: U.S. Armed Forces as a Political Instrument* (Washington, D.C.: Brookings Institution, 1978), 232, and Memorandum of Telephone Conversation, J. F. Dulles and Richard Nixon, July 15, 1958, Box 8, Telephone Call Series, J. F. Dulles Papers, Eisenhower Library.

50. The United States had made it known that it was committed to resolving the successor issue. Once Shihab had appeared capable of gaining sufficient votes for election, moreover, the United States had been widely rumored to also back the Lebanese general and had
sought to ensure that Lebanese Christians—who generally regarded Shihab as sympathetic to
the opposition—accepted his candidacy. Lebanese Christians, Foreign Minister Malik commented, were convinced that the United States was "pushing" Shihab in the elections. Embassy in Beirut to DOS, July 30, 1958, *FRUS* 11 (1958).

51. 374th Meeting of the NSC, July 31, 1958, Box 10, NSC Series, Ann Whitman File,
Eisenhower Library. Although several administration officials had initially described Shihab
as a pro-Western and apolitical military leader, Shihab's refusal to involve the Lebanese army
in the crisis led them to question his motives; CIA officials in particular regarded him as too
"busy dabbling in politics" and having "ambitions of his own for the presidency." NSC Staff
Notes, June 23, 1958, Box 33, DDE Diary Series, Ann Whitman File, Eisenhower Library,
and 366th Meeting of the NSC, May 22, 1958, Box 10, NSC Series, Ann Whitman File,
Eisenhower Library.

52. Shihab's initial cabinet, headed by former Tripoli opposition leader Rashid Karami,
had been rejected by pro-Chamoun politicians, who supported a public strike to protest its
partisan composition, resulting in a resumption of civil disturbances. Eventually a "National
Salvation Cabinet" was formed that on October 17 received a vote of confidence from the
parliament.

53. Embassy in Cairo to DOS, Telegram 2149, January 23, 1959, 783A.5411/1-2359,
DOS Central Files, National Archives.

54. "Developments in the Aftermath of U.S. and U.K. Troop Withdrawals," October 28,
1958, declassified documents, Central Intelligence Agency.

55. Commenting on the Arab reaction to his development fund proposal, Eisenhower
lamented that U.S. officials had "perhaps presumed too much to assume that we knew what
it was that the Arabs wanted." Although most Arab leaders did not openly criticize his UN
speech, many resented not having been consulted concerning the development fund proposal,
believed that the League of Arab States and not the United Nations should administer the
fund, and, in any case, insisted that the United States and Britain had to withdraw from
Lebanon and Jordan before they would discuss details on how the proposal could be implemented.

11

The United States and Nasserist Pan-Arabism

Malik Mufti

In this chapter I shall argue that U.S. Middle East policy from the mid-1950s to the early 1960s consisted primarily of safeguarding U.S. interests by accommodating the populist pan-Arabism of Egyptian President Gamal 'Abd al-Nasser. After its initial attempt (1955–1956) to bring together all regional actors in a grand pro-U.S. alliance collapsed, Washington watched with dismay as Soviet influence appeared to advance, first in Syria and then in Iraq. Nasser successfully played on these fears to enlist U.S. support for his regional ambitions from 1958 to 1962. Around 1963, however, when Nasser himself became a threat to its interests, the United States started building up his pro-Western rivals in Israel, Jordan, and Saudi Arabia while entrusting the campaign of liquidating the remnants of Arab communism to the Ba'th Party in Syria and Iraq.

Washington's Initial Four-Pronged Policy

U.S. interests in the Middle East can be boiled down to two strategic objectives, both of which emerged after World War II. First, the United States was intent on keeping Saudi Arabia and its smaller oil-rich neighbors securely under the U.S. umbrella; and second, it wanted to prevent the expansion of Soviet influence in the Arab world. Initially—during the period roughly from 1947 to 1955—Washington relied on a four-pronged policy approach to accomplish those objectives. First, it sought to maintain the regional status quo by opposing the pan-Arab ambitions of the Hashemites in Baghdad and Amman—particularly given their Hijazi roots. As a 1950 U.S. Department of State paper on Syrian-Iraqi union put it at the time: "There would thus be no contribution to United States interests in giving encouragement to the movement, and any suggestion of intervention by this Government in favor of [a] union [of Arab states] would undoubtedly incur deep resentment

163

among peoples of the Near East, particularly in Saudi Arabia where U.S. strategic interests are of vital importance."[1]

Second, Washington decided instead to support, wherever possible, leaders whose populist nationalism gave them credibility in their peoples' eyes but whose visions did not extend beyond modern reforms within their countries. In other words, U.S. support went to anti-Communists whose pan-Arab rhetoric remained just that. In Syria, this policy resulted in U.S. support first for Colonel Husni Za'im when he seized power in March 1949, then for Colonel Adib al-Shishakli, who succeeded in his coup in December of the same year. Shishakli turned out to be a relatively competent dictator who seemed to fit the U.S. bill well.

In Egypt, the Americans pinned even greater hopes on Colonel Gamal 'Abd al-Nasser and his fellow officers who overthrew the monarchy in 1952. Contacts between the two sides predated the coup and intensified significantly during the years immediately following it. During this time, Nasser enlisted Washington's support for his fledgling regime and for its struggle to free Egypt from lingering British influence by convincing the Americans that his interests and theirs coincided on most issues. In the fall of 1954, for example, "Colonel Nasser declared that Egypt was basically inclined toward the West and that Russia and communism represented the only conceivable danger to Egypt's security."[2] For its part, Washington forced Israel to suspend its diversion of Jordan River waters, by temporarily suspending aid in October 1953, brokering a final Anglo-Egyptian agreement signed on October 19, 1954, and concluding an economic assistance agreement with Egypt on November 6, 1954. A State Department paper, prepared in 1966, recalled nostalgically: "U.S. economic assistance during the sunny early years of the Nasser regime, 1952–1956, amounted to $86 million."[3]

U.S. support continued even after Nasser—having consolidated his hold on power—delivered his famous speech of July 23, 1954, which outlined Cairo's new foreign policy orientation: Henceforth, his government would abandon its isolationist outlook and strive for Arab solidarity under Egyptian leadership. Thus, Wilbur Crane Eveland, a U.S. intelligence operative in the region at the time, remembers that U.S. Central Intelligence Agency (CIA) propaganda experts were kept busy during late 1954 "dreaming up ways to popularize Nasser's government in Egypt and the Arab world."[4] They apparently went to unusual lengths to maintain Nasser's nationalist credibility. According to another operative involved in those events:

> While the "straights" in Washington were increasingly displeased with the anti-American content of Nasser's public utterances and the anti-American propaganda that poured out of Radio Cairo . . . can you guess who was writing a goodly portion of the material? We were. . . . We took pains to make it subtly counter-productive, of course, and we included a lot of patent nonsense, but we kept virtually in control of its production. We even had Paul Linebarger, perhaps the greatest "black" propagandist who ever lived, come to Egypt to coach the Egyptian-American team that turned out the stuff.[5]

The third element of U.S. policy during this period envisaged bringing all the "progressive" but pro-Western Arab regimes that could be sustained into a regional anti-Soviet alliance modeled on the North Atlantic Treaty Organization (NATO). The fourth and final element was a logical extension of this third objective: Avoid regional conflicts that would weaken the alliance, such as those that would pit members against one another and force Washington to choose sides, thereby creating opportunities for Moscow to gain influence.

Collapse of the Four-Pronged Strategy

Unfortunately for the United States, its four-pronged strategy soon fell victim to the conflicting objectives of other regional actors. Nasser, for one, realized that the optimal strategy for him would be to play the two superpowers off one another and to extend Egyptian influence abroad, even if that brought him into conflict with other U.S. allies. Iraq's Hashemites still harbored dreams of ruling a greater Arab homeland, dreams that of course conflicted with Nasser's hegemonic dream. In this they received limited backing from the British, who viewed Iraq as the linchpin to their own regional ambitions and were therefore willing to support the extension of Hashemite influence—primarily through the Baghdad Pact—so long as it did not result in actual border changes (for example, with Kuwait). The Saudis, who initially welcomed Nasser's foray into Arab politics as a counterweight to their nemeses, the Hashemites, gradually began to fear Egyptian expansionism as well.

Most decisively, Israel's concern about the close relationship between Washington and Cairo led it to pursue an aggressive policy culminating in the Gaza raid of February 28, 1955, its first major engagement with Egypt since 1948 and a humiliating blow to Nasser's prestige. The raid scuttled Washington's attempts to focus regional attention on the Soviet threat, brought the Arab-Israeli conflict to the fore, and initiated an arms race that forced Washington to choose sides among friends in the Middle East. Thus, Israel succeeded in its primary objective of driving a wedge between Cairo and Washington. When Nasser's subsequent request for U.S. weapons received a negative response, he announced six months later that he would be purchasing arms from the Soviet bloc instead. Further setbacks, such as the Aswan Dam financing dispute and the failure (despite private lip service by both sides)[6] of a secret U.S. attempt to mediate the dispute between Egypt and Israel in early 1956, led U.S. Secretary of State John Foster Dulles to conclude:

> In view of the negative outcome of our efforts to bring Colonel Nasser to adopt a policy of conciliation toward Israel, we should, I believe, now adjust certain of our Near Eastern policies, as indicated below. The primary purpose would be to let Colonel Nasser realize that he cannot cooperate as he is doing with the Soviet Union and at the same time enjoy most-favored-nation treatment from the United States. We would want for the time being to avoid any open break which would throw Nasser irrevocably into a Soviet satellite status and we would want to leave Nasser a bridge back to good relations with the West if he so desires.[7]

Estrangement, 1956–1958

The adjustments that Secretary of State Dulles eventually specified for President Dwight D. Eisenhower established a pattern that would be repeated whenever the United States sought to discipline Nasser: freeze economic aid to Egypt, extend support to Nasser's Arab rivals, and draw closer to Israel. Thus, in addition to withdrawing its offer to finance the Aswan High dam, Washington halted PL-480 food shipments and other assistance in 1956. It also expressed greater public support for the Baghdad Pact (without actually joining it), as well as the pro-Western governments of Sudan, Libya, Lebanon, and Jordan. Finally, although the United States continued to refrain from providing arms to Israel directly, it now encouraged other Western governments to do so.[8] As Dulles indicated, however, U.S. officials did not want to back Nasser too far into a corner, as they still held hope that he would become a cooperative ally, Hence they rejected repeated British invitations to join the Baghdad Pact, but more significant, of course, was their refusal to back Britain and France in their ill-conceived collusion with Israel during the 1956 Suez crisis.

Eisenhower had begun musing about the need for an Arab counterweight to Nasser even before Suez. Now—with Nasserist radicalism developing into an irresistible force that destabilized the governments of Syria, Lebanon, Jordan, and Iraq itself—he referred to him as "an evil influence" and argued the need "to build up an Arab rival . . . to capture the imagination of the Arab world."[9] After an early candidate, Saudi Arabia's King Sa'ud, proved deficient in the personal and ideological attributes necessary for such a role, however, U.S. officials decided to take things into their own hands. In accordance with the Eisenhower Doctrine (enunciated in January 1957, the doctrine was a policy generally designed to halt Communist expansion in the Middle East, specifically to isolate and reduce Nasser's power), the new approach envisaged a series of bilateral security arrangements with individual states rather than relying on one key ally to act as regional policeman. Saudi Arabia, Jordan, and Iraq responded positively, and U.S. officials concluded the next (and last) step was to bring Syria into line, thereby isolating Nasser and dashing his hopes of parlaying his influence into a negotiating chip with which to play Moscow and Washington off one another. Then, or so the rosy scenario continued, the ensuing network of moderate Arab states would make peace with Israel and come together in an anti-Communist alliance under U.S. leadership.

But bringing Syria into line turned out to be problematic. A power struggle that pitted the pro-Egyptian Ba'th Party against an increasingly pro-Soviet faction headed by Khalid al-'Azm caused the U.S. National Security Council (NSC) to place Syria "in the dangerous category"[10] and to initiate a series of covert operations aimed at reversing Syria's leftward lurch. As is well known, the failure of those plots only strengthened pro-Communist elements in the Syrian military, led by new Chief of Staff 'Afif al-Bizri. The mood in Washington now shifted from concern to panic. Dulles in particular became convinced that a Communist takeover of Syria was imminent. Four days after Bizri's appointment, he concluded that "there is now little hope of correction from within and . . . we must think in terms of . . . external assets."[11]

Accordingly, Dulles sent his deputy, Loy Henderson, to Ankara on August 24, 1957, for talks with Turkish, Iraqi, and Jordanian leaders. Henderson expressed his government's support for unspecified Iraqi or Jordanian "action" against Syria and promised that it would block any interference by the Soviet Union, Egypt, or Israel. He did set one condition however: In order to allay the concerns of the Saudis and others, it had to be clear that the proposed action "[did] not aim at the unification of Syria and Iraq" and that the goal was only "the return to power in Syria of a truly independent leadership." Iraq's rulers had to agree to the stipulation.[12] This point is worth underlining: Even though Washington was extremely fearful of a Communist takeover in Syria, it remained unwilling to countenance any Hashemite action that aimed at revising the regional status quo. As Dulles once reiterated to his underlings, "No success achieved in Syria could possibly compensate for the loss of Saudi Arabia."[13]

As described in more detail elsewhere in this book (see especially Chapter 9, by David Lesch), Iraq and Jordan felt unable to mount an unprovoked military attack on a fellow Arab state, so soon after Suez anyway. Turkey therefore took the lead, massing troops on the Syrian border and carrying out threatening maneuvers all through September.[14] This, however, unleashed a storm of indignation in the Arab world, further tarnishing Washington's image and providing Moscow with a new opportunity to portray itself as the champion of Arab nationalism—and the Third World. Soviet Premier Nikolay Bulganin warned Ankara on September 13 that armed conflict in Syria "would not be limited to that area alone."[15] One week later, two Soviet warships arrived at the Syrian port of Latakia amid great popular fanfare, and Turkey was forced to back off. Suddenly, just as the crisis was winding down into a Soviet propaganda coup, Nasser stepped into the breach. Units of the Egyptian army arrived in Latakia on October 13 and took up positions to "defend" Syria in case of an attack. It was a brilliant stroke. On the one hand, his prestige and popularity as the nemesis of imperialism soared to new heights in Syria and throughout the Arab world. On the other hand, the Soviet Union had gained so much sympathy in Syria during the preceding weeks that Nasser could credibly justify his intervention to the United States as the only way of dampening pro-Communist fervor there.[16]

Sure enough, a report prepared by the commander of U.S. naval forces in the Mediterranean welcomed the Egyptian military landing in Latakia, viewing it as likely "to bolster Pan-Arabism and check Syrian drift into Soviet orbit." The report went on: "'If you can't lick them join them' and Nasser probably better than any prospective replacement anyway."[17] There would be many more twists and turns in the U.S.-Egyptian relationship, but the convergence of interests in Latakia set a precedent and strengthened those officials in Washington who wanted to abandon the attempt to find alternatives to Nasser.

The UAR and the Iraqi Coup

Still, not everyone was convinced—certainly not John Foster Dulles. When Syria and Egypt announced their unification under the flag of the United Arab Republic (UAR) in January 1958, for example, he interpreted it as a plot masterminded by

Moscow, telling an emergency session of the Baghdad Pact Council held in Ankara on January 28 and 29 that the "union between Syria and Egypt would be dangerous to all our interests and if we remained passive it would expand and would shortly take in Jordan and the Lebanon and ultimately Saudi Arabia and Iraq leaving us with a single Arab State ostensibly under Nasser but ultimately under Soviet control. It was clear that we ought to oppose such a union."[18]

It is instructive, however, that when Iraq's Hashemites—acutely aware of the mortal peril posed to them by the UAR—agitated for effective countermeasures, neither Britain nor the United States would hear of it. Thus, Iraqi Crown Prince 'Abd al-Ilah insisted to the British ambassador in late February that to save the monarchy it would be necessary to incorporate Kuwait into the hastily arranged "Arab Federation" of Iraq and Jordan—"both on economic grounds and because of the moral effect"—and "to bring over Syria, by the use of force if there was no other way."[19] Later, Iraqi Prime Minister Nuri Sa'id caused considerable alarm in London by drawing up a memorandum threatening to annex half of Kuwait's territory unless it joined the Arab Federation at once,[20] but to no avail. Britain's ambassador assured his government that he was doing all he could to prevent the Iraqis "from taking any rash step over Syria or Kuwait,"[21] and John Foster Dulles fretted about "Nuri's recent intemperate statements."[22] The matter became moot on July 14, 1958, when Iraqi military leaders overthrew the Iraqi government in a coup and slaughtered its Hashemite leadership.

In the final analysis, both Britain and the United States continued to view Hashemite pan-Arabism as a threat to their interests in the oil-producing shaykhdoms of the Arabian Peninsula. Even John Foster Dulles, paranoid as he was about the Communist "threat" in Syria and elsewhere, never allowed this concern to overshadow the greater strategic objective of maintaining U.S. hegemony over the oil lanes. He put it to the National Security Council this way, in response to an earlier proposal that the United States might discretely encourage the "ultimate union of Arab countries in the Arabian peninsula": "If the policy on the supply of oil from the Arab states to Western Europe were made uniform as a result of the unification of the Arab states, [the intervening portion of the quote is censored] the threat to the vital oil supply of Western Europe from the Near East would become critical."[23] Dulles added that he "was not saying that the State Department opposed moves in the direction of Arab unity; but the State Department wanted to be very careful that we did not end up by uniting the Arab states against the United States and the West."[24] Although Washington might have liked to see the Hashemites in Iraq and Jordan thwart Nasser's newly formed UAR, in short, it would not allow them to do so at the cost of creating a new political entity that could potentially threaten the U.S. protectorates in the Arabian Peninsula.

Nevertheless, 'Abd al-Karim Qasim's sudden Iraqi coup took Washington aback. CIA Director Allen Dulles (the secretary's brother) told Eisenhower that "the hand of Nasser in these developments is very evident" and added that if the coup "succeeds, it seems almost inevitable that a chain reaction will set in which will doom the governments of Iraq, Jordan, Saudi Arabia, Turkey and Iran."[25] Accordingly,

U.S. troops were landed in Lebanon to prop up the Christian Maronite government already besieged by pro-UAR rebels, and British forces arrived in Jordan to stabilize the situation there. Ten days after the Iraqi coup, John Foster Dulles was still arguing that "the real authority behind the Government of Iraq was being exercised by Nasser, and behind Nasser by the USSR."[26]

In fact Qasim initially went out of his way to project a moderate stance: refusing to join the UAR; adopting a hostile stance toward Nasser; dropping all claims on Kuwait (whose emir was one of the first to congratulate him); and abiding by the 50-50 profit-sharing arrangement with foreign oil companies that the Hashemites had long been trying to overturn. As a result, when the new dictator managed to foil two Egyptian-backed plots to overthrow him in late 1958, he apparently did so with some assistance from Britain, which continued to view Nasser as the greater threat to its regional interests.[27] Qasim certainly appreciated the helping hand. According to Britain's ambassador: "He said he wanted to assure me that he wished friendship with Britain to stand fast and continued, with some emphasis, 'I will even say that not even friendship with any Arab country shall interfere with it.'"[28]

But the Americans reached a different conclusion than the British: Qasim's growing reliance on the Iraqi Communist Party (ICP) in his struggle against his domestic opponents induced Washington to replace its hostility toward Nasser with a new phase of close cooperation.

Anti-Communist Cooperation and NSC 5820/1, 1958–1963

Evidence of Washington's renewed tilt toward Nasser could be found even before the Iraqi coup. Egypt's union with Syria and the ensuing wave of pan-Arab enthusiasm that swept the region greatly impressed U.S. officials, prompting them to conclude that "Western interests will be served by placing US-UAR relations on a more normal basis" and to resume limited economic assistance to Egypt.[29] After Qasim's coup and his growing association with the ICP, however, the pro-Nasser chorus became deafening. U.S. Information Agency Director George Allen, for example, argued for a renewed alliance with Nasser even if it meant abandoning allies such as King Hussein: "We must adjust to the tide of Arab nationalism, and must do so before the hotheads get control in every country."[30] Eisenhower balked at Allen's more extreme suggestions, but even he could be heard musing, "Since we are about to get thrown out of the area, we might as well believe in Arab nationalism."[31]

A split developed within the Eisenhower administration regarding the extent to which it should accommodate Nasser. The Department of Defense and Department of Treasury argued that Washington should merely "accept pan-Arab nationalism, of which Nasser is the symbol" and seek to normalize relations with him only as head of the UAR. But the State Department and CIA—representing the majority opinion—wanted to go further, suggesting that the United States actively "accept and seek to work with radical pan-Arab nationalism," even to the extent of cooperating with Nasser on "certain area-wide problems."[32]

In the end their arguments prevailed, and the result was NSC 5820/1, a watershed National Security Council report dated November 4, 1958, that formed the basis of U.S. Middle East policy for the next three years. It began by acknowledging that "the prevention of further Soviet penetration of the Near East and progress in solving Near Eastern problems depends on the degree to which the United States is able to work more closely with Arab nationalism."[33] Securing Washington's "primary objectives" in the region—foremost the "denial of the area to Soviet domination" and secondarily the "continued availability of sufficient Near Eastern oil to meet vital Western European requirements on reasonable terms"[34]—required the United States to "deal with Nasser as head of the UAR on specific problems and issues, area-wide as well as local, affecting the UAR's legitimate interests."[35] And though NSC 5820/1 warned against accepting Nasser's hegemony over the entire Arab world, it also recognized that "too direct efforts on our part to stimulate developments lessening the predominant position of Nasser might be counter-productive."[36]

Nasser's regional rivals received short shrift in NSC 5820/1. U.S. support for Saudi Arabia would remain intact, of course, but even there the report acknowledged the "reduced influence of King Saud" and called for strengthening "United States influence and understanding among groups in Saudi Arabia from which elements of leadership may emerge, particularly in the armed forces and the middle level Saudi Arabian Government officials."[37] As to Jordan, NSC 5820/1 had more drastic recommendations: "Recognizing that the indefinite continuance of Jordan's present political status has been rendered unrealistic by recent developments [seek] to bring about peaceful evolution of Jordan's political status . . . including partition, absorption, or internal political realignment."[38] And though Washington continued to support the preservation of Israel "in its essentials, we believe that Israel's continued existence as a sovereign state depends on its willingness to become a finite and accepted part of the Near East nation-state system."[39]

NSC 5820/1 remained a controversial document, and both Defense and Treasury felt obliged to put their dissenting opinions on record. John Foster Dulles also continued to argue—against his own department—that it went too far in appeasing Nasser at the expense of more important allies such as Britain. But the secretary of state was dying of cancer and would soon leave office. As Qasim increasingly tied his fate to that of the Communists, fewer and fewer voices would be heard opposing the tilt toward the UAR.

Egyptian Opportunism

Nasser's case was greatly helped by the reception accorded in Baghdad to William Rountree, the U.S. assistant secretary of state who visited the region in December 1958. Rountree endured volleys of rotten vegetables and trash thrown at his motorcade by angry Iraqi crowds only to receive a cool and perfunctory reception from Qasim himself. The shrewd Egyptians gave him a warmer welcome, and when he returned to Washington, Rountree reported that they were "showing a real concern over Communist penetration of the Middle East" and that "we can work with Nasser on the Iraqi situation."[40] The desk officer for Iraq at the State Department told Britain's ambassador after Rountree's trip that the "only hope for retrieving the situation now [seems?] to lie in the army acting under the inspiration of Arab nationalism of a pro-United Arab Republic and anti-Communist kind. This need not mean a takeover by the United Arab Republic."[41]

In fact, Nasser had been preparing the ground for a rapprochement with the United States for some time. He had already purged Bizri and his pro-Communist officers within weeks of the UAR's creation in an effort to earn the Syrian business community's trust as well as to defuse the ideological challenge posed by communism to his brand of radicalism—a challenge that grew particularly acute after the coup in Iraq and the subsequent rise of ICP influence there. It was partly in order to nip this threat in the bud and partly to curry U.S. favor that Nasser launched his anti-Communist campaign in earnest with a vitriolic speech in Port Sa'id on December 23, 1958. Many party members lost their lives during the days that followed, and hundreds more were thrown into prison. A second wave of arrests in March liquidated the Communists as a political force in the UAR altogether.

In Iraq, by contrast, the Communist advance seemed inexorable. The crushing of an Egyptian-backed revolt in Mosul in March 1959, followed by extensive purges of Arab nationalists, strengthened the ICP still further. As the party gained control of one professional association after another, as its armed militia grew to 25,000 members by May 1959, and as it began to infiltrate the army itself, even Qasim started to worry. Every time he tried to rein in the Communists, however, a resurgence of Nasserist and Ba'thist opposition would force him to turn to them once again. Thus, a crackdown on the ICP after a particularly grisly outbreak of class warfare in Kirkuk in July 1959 ended in October after a Ba'thist attempt on the president's life.

British officials continued to insist that Qasim represented the best hope of preventing an all-out Communist takeover in Iraq and pointed to the strongly anti-Communist sentiments of senior military officers,[42] but the Americans remained far less sanguine. Mosul and the ICP's subsequent gains dispelled any remaining doubts about the reorientation outlined in NSC 5820/1 and led CIA Director Allen Dulles to describe the Iraqi situation as "the most dangerous in the world today."[43] Another U.S. official captured the mood of helpless frustration that gripped Washington during this period by observing that "we sit and watch unfolding events which seem to point inevitably to Soviet domination of Iraq, acknowledging, I am afraid, an inability to do anything about it. It is almost like watching a movie whose end we will not like but which we are committed to see."[44]

Nasser astutely fueled Washington's anxiety. He told reporters, for example, that he had "reliable information" of a Soviet master plot to create a "red fertile crescent"—a Communist federation encompassing Iraq, Syria, Jordan, Lebanon, and Kuwait. Only Egypt, he implied, blocked the path of this fiendish plan. Not surprisingly, relations with Moscow deteriorated. Three days after the collapse of the Mosul revolt, Soviet General Secretary Nikita Khrushchev declared, "Nasser wants to annex Iraq. As I see it he is a hot-headed young man who has taken on more than he can manage." Nasser retaliated on March 20 by denouncing communism and accusing Khrushchev of "intervention in our affairs."[45]

Nasser's strategy paid off: The loss of Soviet support was more than offset by the advantages of a renewed alliance with Washington, where the initial trepidation concerning Nasser's role in Iraq gave way—much as it had in Syria in 1957—to a sense of enormous relief. An NSC report listed some of those advantages: $125 million in special assistance and surplus commodity sales in 1959; additional export guarantees and loans; U.S. backing for a $56 million Egyptian loan request to the International Bank for Redevelopment and Development (the IBRD, or World Bank); and in "support of the UAR's anti-communist propaganda offensive . . . grant aid for the purchase of newsprint and . . . basic anti-communist material for use by UAR press and radio." Perhaps most important for Nasser, the report added: "Consistent with our recognition of the lack of any desirable alternatives for Syria's future and our understanding that continuance of the present trend in US-UAR relations will depend, in part, on our willingness to assist Nasser in his Syrian economic objectives, we have given special attention to DLF loan applications for the Syrian region."[46]

Both sides clearly understood the quid pro quo involved: It was spelled out by a State Department paper in mid-April 1959: "While we have not directly linked with Nasser's present campaign against communism the steps we have recently taken to aid Egypt, there is no doubt that Nasser knows that we have taken these steps as a sign of approval of his current campaign and that they have emboldened him in his anti-communist efforts."[47]

U.S. Reservations

Washington's renewed affinity with Nasser alarmed those who resented the spread of his influence. Britain, Turkey, Saudi Arabia, Jordan, and Israel all felt that U.S. support for Nasser's subversive campaign against Iraq was tilting the regional balance of power too far in his favor. Turkey had warned from the beginning that it would take military action if the Egyptians tried to bring Iraq into the UAR and made threatening moves along its southern borders both after the Mosul revolt in March 1959 and following the failed attempt on Qasim's life in October. In December, Foreign Minister Fatin Rustu Zorlu confided his fears to the British ambassador: "He believed that the C.I.A. were dickering with the idea that the situation in Iraq was so precarious that Egypt ought to be ready to do something about it in case things went completely wrong. He even thought it possible that some hint of this thinking might be available to the Egyptians."[48]

Saudi Arabia, already embarrassed by the revelation in March 1958 that King Sa'ud had financed an assassination plot against Nasser, also kept up steady pressure on Washington to do something about Nasser's growing influence in Arab politics. King Hussein of Jordan, for his part, tried to put himself forward as a viable alternative to Nasserism and communism in both Syria and Iraq. A skirmish involving armored vehicles on the Jordanian-Syrian border occurred in late April 1959, and in August the British embassy in Amman got wind of a coup plot in Syria that the Jordanians were at least aware of.[49] On the Iraqi side, Hussein was just as assertive. Asked by an interviewer in October whether he would consider invading Iraq, he responded by saying "we would do everything we could to save Iraq from Communism" and that the "showdown" was now imminent.[50] There were reports of tension on the Jordanian-Iraqi border as well later in the month.

But U.S. officials, believing that King Hussein could not hope to compete with either Nasser or the Communists for the allegiance of the Arab masses, categorically refused to support his initiatives. As a State Department official told one of his British counterparts, "There could be no question of a Hashemite restoration either in Iraq or Syria."[51] Quite the contrary: The British embassy in Amman reported on April 24, 1959, that the U.S. military attaché and his assistant had been "touting pro-Nasser views round the various offices" much to the consternation of the Jordanian government.[52] This at a time of ongoing clashes along the Jordanian-Syrian border—and just five months after UAR jets tried to shoot down Hussein's plane. In a conversation with a Canadian diplomat, Nasser once again evoked the Communist bogeyman: "Nasser said categorically that King Hussein's idea of intervening militarily with Arab Legion in Iraq was profoundly unwise. Quote it could ruin everything unquote. It might have some effect in the short term and locally, but the implication that there might be a Hashemite restoration would inevitably play into the hands of the Communists, who would be quick to exploit it."[53] Washington concurred. Not only did U.S. officials oppose Hussein's revisionist pan-Arab ambitions, they even "cautioned" him against "provocative acts" directed at the UAR.[54] Hussein abandoned his efforts in August 1960 after a bomb placed by UAR operatives killed Prime Minister Hazza' al-Majali and ten other Jordanians in Amman.

U.S. officials tried to allay the concerns of their other allies by assuring them that the UAR had no further expansionist ambitions and by pointing out that "Nasser's recent attacks on Communism had done more to stay the advance of Communism in the Middle East than anything the Western Powers could have achieved in years of work."[55] Still, it became evident even to Washington that the excessive reliance on Nasser was growing increasingly problematic: Freed of almost all restraints, he was antagonizing his neighbors to the point where any one of them—Turkey, Jordan, Israel, Saudi Arabia, or Iraq itself—might lash out in a dangerously unpredictable fashion.

The dilemma confronting Washington was the same one it had faced since 1955: to find a credible anti-Communist movement that was not a mere vehicle for Egyptian expansionism. Some other version of radical pan-Arabism seemed the only answer, reflected in a conclusion suggested by Eisenhower in the aftermath of the Iraqi coup: "If we could somehow bring about a separation of Syria from Egypt and thereafter a union of Syria with Iraq, this might prove very useful."[56] Qasim, with his narrow popular base and his dependence on the ICP, would clearly not do. Neither would Hussein's Hashemite alternative, since Washington doubted it could work and feared the consequences for its hegemony in Saudi Arabia and the Persian Gulf if it did.

The Syrian Secession

Deliverance came on September 28, 1961, when a group of Syrian officers mounted a coup d'état and effected Syria's secession from the UAR. The implications of this devastating blow to Nasser's prestige for U.S.-Egyptian relations were not lost on the foreign policy team of the newly elected president, John F. Kennedy. Robert Komer of the NSC observed just five days after the secession: "I am convinced that recent events may present us with the best opportunity since 1954 for a limited marriage of convenience with the guy who I think is still, and will remain, the Mister Big of the Arab World."[57] Kennedy's special envoy, Chester Bowles, fleshed out Komer's observation in a telegram from Cairo in early 1962:

> I believe the time has come for a change of emphasis in our dealings with the UAR in general and with Nasser in particular. If Nasser were now riding high he might view any effort by us to establish a new relationship as an act of weakness. However, Nasser is deeply conscious of the serious problems which now face him and his regime. . . . Under these circumstances I believe that a skillful, sophisticated, sensitive effort to establish a more affirmative relationship is called for. Furthermore, I believe that Nasser is likely to meet us more than half way.[58]

During the winter of 1961–1962, then, Nasser's stock in Washington rose still further, bolstered largely by his diminished ability to provoke other U.S. allies in the Middle East after Syria's secession, but also in part by the Kennedy administration's generally more tolerant attitude toward Third World radicalism. In practical terms this meant increased assistance for Egypt's now seriously ailing economy, including a three-year PL-480 agreement signed in 1962 for the sale of about $430 million worth of surplus foods. In return, Nasser agreed to maintain his anti-Communist stance and—as he put it in 1961 to the new U.S. ambassador, John S. Badeau—to cooperate with the United States in keeping "the Israeli-Arab question 'in the icebox' while devoting themselves to the development of mutual interests."[59] As a result, Badeau could report at the onset of 1964 that "the United States now wields more influence in the Near East than it has at any time since 1955."[60] Yet even before Badeau penned those words, the U.S.-Egyptian relationship had already begun the inexorable process of disintegration that would culminate when Nasser, in his desperation and folly, took a final, fatal step in 1967, which brought his world crashing down around him.

Breakdown, 1963–1967

Exactly two months after Badeau's rosy assessment, Nasser complained to visiting U.S. Assistant Secretary of State Phillip Talbot that "he could not accept . . . Talbot's presentation that U.S. Middle East policy had not changed since the death of President Kennedy."[61] One year later Nasser's envoy in Washington, Mustafa Kamel, also dated the downturn in bilateral relations to the transition from the Kennedy to the Lyndon B. Johnson administrations: "In late 1963, primarily as result of Yemen problem but possibly also as effect of US-Soviet détente, Kamel said Egyptians had sensed slow-down in US aid."[62]

The Egyptians were not imagining things, although the change in fact predated Kennedy's assassination. Its roots lay in the weakening of Nasser's regional influence following the Syrian secession. Whereas the events of 1958 convinced U.S. officials that even the appearance of opposing Nasser would harm their fundamental interests, by 1962 the picture had changed dramatically. In Saudi Arabia, Crown Prince Faisal—now the effective ruler—coupled domestic reform with a foreign policy that did not shrink as readily from confrontations with Nasser. Syria's secessionist regime, wobbly as it was, enjoyed good relations with the United States while trading bitter public invectives with Egypt. Qasim of Iraq, his economy in ruins, found himself bogged down in a Kurdish revolt that conveniently broke out just weeks after his ill-considered bid for Kuwait in June 1961 (which may have received some U.S. backing). His relations with Nasser were, if anything, worse than those of the Saudis and Syrians. Even King Hussein of Jordan proved more resilient and durable than NSC 5820/1 had predicted, and now he too engaged in a spirited propaganda battle with the Egyptian leader. Nasser's isolation gave Washington leverage to diversify its regional assets by strengthening its ties with countries such as Saudi Arabia, Jordan, and, above all, Israel—all of which began receiving significantly increased levels of U.S. military aid during the early 1960s. As Secretary of State Dean Rusk observed on August 7, 1962: "An extensive and intensive review of our policy toward Israel has been conducted in recent months. . . . The relatively high standing of the United States among the Arabs, while still fragile, provides us with a minor degree of maneuvering room in terms of adjustments in policy with respect to Israel."[63]

Twelve days later a presidential envoy informed Israeli leaders that Kennedy had approved Hawk missile sales to their country, initiating a process that would see U.S. military assistance to Israel soar from $44.2 million in 1963 to $995.3 million by 1968.[64] Domestic political considerations undoubtedly played a role in this shift—both Kennedy and Johnson were far more sensitive to the pro-Israeli feelings of the U.S. Jewish community than Eisenhower had been—but they cannot be understood in isolation from the strategic imperative: "to reinforce Israel as a counterweight to Nasser in case he misused or abused American assistance to him."[65] No wonder Nasser's high expectations in late 1961 regarding his new rapprochement with the United States gave way so quickly to disappointment.

As 1963 rolled by, moreover, Washington's "minor degree of maneuvering room" expanded considerably. Ba'thist coups in Iraq (8 February) and Syria (8 March) at last brought to power regimes that fit the U.S. bill exactly: Although radical and nationalist, they could be counted on to slaughter Communists efficiently while maintaining a hostile stance toward Nasser. There are indications that the United States played a role both in the overthrow of Qasim and in the subsequent hostility between the two Ba'thist regimes and Egypt. Jamal Atasi, one of the new cabinet ministers in Damascus, recalled what happened when the Syrian Ba'thists received reports about clandestine meetings between their Iraqi counterparts and CIA operatives in Kuwait:[66]

> When we discovered this thing we began to argue with them. They would assert that their cooperation with the CIA and the US to overthrow 'Abd al-Karim Qasim and take over power—they would compare this to how Lenin arrived in a German train to carry out his revolution, saying they had arrived in a U.S. train. But in reality—and even in the case of the takeover in Syria—there was a push from the West and in particular from the United States for the Ba'th to seize power and monopolize it and push away all the other elements and forces [i.e., both the Communists and the Nasserists].

By mid-1963, then, Nasser had lost his indispensable status in U.S. eyes. Even as the onset of détente and the development of intercontinental ballistic missiles reduced U.S. fears about Soviet penetration of the Middle East generally, the rise of the Ba'th Party to power in Iraq and Syria liquidated any remaining danger of Communist takeovers in those countries. Nevertheless, Nasser remained leader of the most powerful state in the Arab world—still "Mr. Big," as Komer put it—and had he resigned himself to his diminished status, he might have continued to enjoy a constructive relationship with Washington. But Nasser could not do that. From the beginning his "statesmanship" had consisted of appealing to the vulgar enthusiasms of the mob by pulling off one spectacular public relations coup after another, each time by exploiting the blunders and misperceptions of others: Suez in 1956; Latakia in 1957; the UAR in 1958. Incapable of formulating more serious long-term policies for his country, Nasser now cast about for yet another quick fix to restore him to past glory.

Endgame

The years between 1963 and 1967 witnessed a series of foreign policy gambits by Nasser aimed at showing the United States that it could not take him for granted. All of them failed when U.S. counterpressure forced him to retreat, but not before undermining his standing in Washington still further. Nasser's most fateful adventure was in Yemen, where his intervention in the civil war ultimately sucked in a third of his entire army and occasionally spilled over both into the British-controlled South Arabian Federation to the south and—more dangerously—north into Saudi Arabia in the form of bombing raids on royalist bases. These raids provoked extreme alarm in Riyadh and forced the U.S. Air Force to carry out demonstration flights over Saudi towns in July 1963 as a show of support for the oil-rich kingdom's territorial integrity. Nasser had come perilously close to crossing the reddest of all U.S. redlines in the Middle East. In addition, Nasser responded to Washington's arms sales to Israel by signing a military agreement of his own with Moscow in June 1963;

by exerting pressure on Libya to expel U.S. and British forces from Wheelus Air Base in early 1964; and by indulging in violent tirades against the United States. After a visit to Egypt by Soviet leader Khrushchev in May 1964, the pipeline from Washington shut down as U.S. officials "simply allowed the Egyptian request for aid renewal to get lost in a maze of formalities without ever saying no to it."[67] Nasser's initial response was defiant. In a fiery speech on December 23, 1964, he praised the Soviet Union, announced his intention to continue arming rebels fighting U.S.-Belgian "aggression" in the Congo, and concluded: "Whoever does not like our conduct can go drink up the sea. If the Mediterranean is not sufficient, there is the Red Sea, too."[68]

But as Egypt's deteriorating economy sparked protest demonstrations, illegal strikes, and even coup plots in late 1964 and 1965, Nasser realized he could not do without U.S. aid. He therefore took steps to appease the United States, terminating his support for the Congo rebels, urging moderation in the Arab-Israeli dispute over the Jordan River waters, and toning down his anti-American rhetoric. Most important, he signed an agreement with King Faisal on August 24, 1965, that envisaged a total withdrawal of Egyptian troops from Yemen within thirteen months. PL-480 food shipments were resumed forthwith, albeit in reduced amounts and for shorter periods.

By mid-1966, however, Nasser—convinced now that the Americans were conspiring with the British and Saudis to bring him down—changed tacks yet again, drawing still closer to Moscow, hunkering down in Yemen, and resuming his propaganda offensive against the United States and its regional allies. Was he right? Probably as far as Britain and Saudi Arabia were concerned; the Saudis certainly seemed determined not to permit him an honorable exit from Yemen. But were the Americans also plotting his downfall? One background paper prepared for President Johnson in August 1966 suggests not:

> There are those—certainly the British and probably the Saudis—who think that any successor regime in Egypt would be better than the present one. This is dubious. Egypt's aspirations to lead the entire area go back many decades, if not centuries. They antedate Nasser and will not disappear with him. . . . If the Egyptians should decide to depose him that is their business. But there is no American interest in becoming a party to a plot or in letting the situation in Egypt degenerate into total instability in the hope that something better will turn up.[69]

In other words, Nasser could be contained successfully through a policy of calculated sanctions and rewards. Others were not so sanguine. David Nes of the U.S. embassy in Cairo warned that "we are moving inexorably toward a showdown in the area arising from this current attempt of our 'friends' to bring Nasser down and his largely defensive reactions. I agree with Bob Strong that even if we do no more than stand by and watch we shall be inextricably involved."[70]

In any case, U.S. aid to Egypt dried up once again and Nasser retaliated in characteristic style—lambasting the United States as "leader of the imperialist camp" and vowing to remain in Yemen "until the British-American-Saudi danger is completely re-moved" and threatening to resume bombing of Saudi border towns.[71] Nes in Cairo mused gloomily on May 11, 1967: "We seem to have driven Nasser to a degree of ir-rationality bordering on madness, fed, of course, by the frustrations and fears gener-ated by his failures domestic and foreign. Our debate here revolves around where he will strike next—Libya, Lebanon?"[72] But Nasser, woefully underestimating the feroc-ity of Israel's determination to crush him and deluding himself that Washington still cared enough to rescue him from disaster, chose instead to roll the dice in Sinai.

Conclusion

John Foster Dulles once summarized Washington's attitude toward Arab national-ism by likening it to "an overflowing stream—you cannot stand in front of it and oppose it frontally, but you must try to keep it in bounds. We must try to prevent lasting damage to our interests in the Near East until events deflate the great Nasser hero myth."[73] And that is precisely what the Americans did. Despite some false steps, they ultimately succeeded in keeping Arab nationalism in bounds, and in doing so they achieved their two fundamental strategic objectives: maintaining con-trol over the oil fields and denying the region to the Soviets. When Hashemite pan-Arabism threatened Saudi Arabia or Kuwait, Washington helped build up a coun-terweight in Cairo. When Nasser in turn got too big for his britches, Washington neutralized him by sanctioning the rise of the Ba'thists in Syria and Iraq and by let-ting Israel out of the icebox (where it had moved neither toward resolution of Arab issues nor toward war).

The competence of U.S. Middle East policy during the period in question is often faulted. Eisenhower and Dulles in particular have been roundly criticized (including in this volume) for their clumsy covert operations and for their tendency to see So-viet plots everywhere. Some of this criticism is fair. But in most really crucial respects they were right: They were correct that a "Hashemite solution" in Syria in 1956–1958 would have been—from the standpoint of U.S. hegemonic interests—a cure worse than the disease. Despite a little initial confusion, they did finally rec-ognize that Nasser was a useful ally against the 'Azm-Bizri-Bakdash bloc in Syria; there was a real Communist threat in Iraq after 1958; and given the popular mood of the time, Nasser was in fact the only viable counterweight.

Similarly, there is a long tradition of criticism that blames the breakdown in U.S.-Egyptian relations during the early 1960s on the receptivity of Presidents Kennedy and (especially) Johnson to lobbying by domestic supporters of Israel. But this crit-icism erroneously assumes that the rationale for close U.S. ties to Nasser—which ex-isted under Eisenhower—continued to exist after 1961. This chapter has tried to show that it did not. Kennedy and Johnson were more responsive to their Jewish electorates largely because they could afford to be.

It made sense for the Americans to use Nasser so long as he was useful to them, just as it made sense for them to drop him when he outlived his usefulness. If there is blame to be assigned, it must fall squarely on Nasser's shoulders: It was he who failed to comprehend the magnitude of the change in his strategic relationship with the United States during the early 1960s; it was he who indulged in demagoguery and reckless foreign adventures rather than addressing the pressing problems confronting Egypt's society and economy; and it was he who chose to give the Israelis the excuse they needed to destroy him in 1967.

At the end of the day the Arab world remained divided, Saudi Arabia and the other oil-rich protectorates huddled safely under the U.S. umbrella, and the Soviets were no closer to breaking Washington's regional hegemony. This may not have been the optimum solution for advocates of Arab nationalism, but by the standard of U.S. national interests, it must be reckoned a great foreign policy success.

Notes

1. "The Political Union of Syria and Iraq," 25 April 1960. U.S. Declassified Documents Reference System (Washington, D.C.: Carrollton Press, 1975), microfiche (hereinafter USDD) 1975:26H.

2. George Lenczowski, *The Middle East in World Affairs* (Ithaca: Cornell University Press, 1980), p. 527.

3. Department of State Paper: "U.S.-U.A.R. Relations," 20 [?] February 1966. USDD-1982:000982.

4. Wilbur Crane Eveland, *Ropes of Sand: America's Failure in the Middle East* (London: W. W. Norton, 1980), p. 103.

5. Miles Copeland, *The Game Player: Memoirs of the CIA's Original Political Operative* (London: Aurum Press, 1989), p. 167.

6. Nasser wrote to Eisenhower on 6 February 1956 that "in the interest of peace Egypt recognizes the desirability of seeking to eliminate the tensions between the Arab States and Israel." USDD-1981:192C.

7. Memorandum from Dulles to Eisenhower, 28 March 1956. USDD-1989:001511.

8. Washington allowed France to divert NATO military equipment to Israel in the spring of 1956. Dulles also asked Canada to supply Israel with F-86 aircraft. Dulles Telegram from Paris, 3 May 1956; USDD-1987:000714.

9. Eisenhower Message to Dulles, 12 December 1956. USDD-1989:003548.

10. National Security Council (NSC) Progress Report: "United States Objectives and Policies with Respect to the Near East," 2 November 1955. USDD-1988:001022, p. 3.

11. Dulles Telegram to Selwyn Lloyd, 21 August 1957. USDD-1987:002090.

12. See the notes of Rafiq 'Aref, the Iraqi chief of staff who attended the talks, in Mahkamat al-Sha'b, *Al-Muhadarat al-Rasmiyya li-Jalasat al-Mahkama al-'Askariyya al-'Ulya al-Khassa* (The People's Court: Official Proceedings of the Sessions of the Special Higher Military Court) (Baghdad: Mudiriyyat Matba'at al-Hukuma, 1959–1962), vol. 4, pp. 1516–1519.

13. Quoted in Eveland, *Ropes of Sand,* p. 181.

14. For a detailed analysis of this episode, see Chapter 9 by David Lesch in this volume. See also his *Syria and the United States: Eisenhower's Cold War in the Middle East* (Boulder: Westview Press, 1992).

15. Quoted in Patrick Seale, *The Struggle for Syria: A Study of Post-War Arab Politics, 1945–1958* (New Haven: Yale University Press, 1965), p. 300.

16. For more on Nasser's actions during the American-Syrian crisis, see David W. Lesch, "Gamal 'Abd al-Nasser and an Example of Diplomatic Acumen," *Middle Eastern Studies* 31(2) (April 1995), pp. 384–396.

17. Appendix to a Memorandum by the Chief of Naval Operations for the Joint Chiefs of Staff on "Middle East Policy," dated 7 November 1957. USDD-1984: 000135, pp. 3096–3097.

18. Summary of Dulles's comments reported by Secretary of State Sir J. Bowker in Ankara to the Foreign Office on 28 January 1958. British Foreign Office Documents (hereinafter BFOD) FO371/134386/VY10316/10.

19. Report from Michael Wright in Baghdad on his conversation with Crown Prince 'Abd al-Ilah on 25 February 1958. BFOD:FO371/134198/VQ1015/18.

20. See F. Hoyer Millar's Foreign Office Minute of 25 June 1958 on the talks with Nuri in London. BFOD:FO371/134219/VQ1051/19.

21. Letter from Wright to London, 23 June 1958. BFOD:FO371/134198/VQ1015/49.

22. U.S. Department of State, "Memorandum of Conversation," dated 15 June 1958. USDD-1981:371B.

23. Briefing Note dated 21 January 1958 on the suggestions of the Planning Board of the National Security Council. USDD-1985:000640, p. 2.

24. Summary of the discussion at the 353rd meeting of the NSC, 30 January 1958. USDD-1990:000328, p. 8.

25. "Memorandum of Conference with the President," 14 July 1958. USDD-1993:002371.

26. Memorandum of the discussion at the 373rd meeting of the NSC, 25 July 1958. USDD-1990:000330, p. 3.

27. See, for example, the observation by Britain's ambassador in Ankara in early January 1959 that "we took certain action in favour of Qasim in regard to the recent plot in Iraq." BFOD:FO371/140956/EQ1071/1.

28. Cable from Ambassador Wright in Baghdad to the British Foreign Office, 24 November 1958. BFOD:FO371/133090/EQ1051/69.

29. "Background Paper" dated 9 June 1958 for Eisenhower's meeting with British Prime Minister Harold Macmillan. USDD-1988:001568. Among the steps taken to "normalize" U.S.-UAR relations between January and July 1958: removal of export restrictions on civilian items such as aircraft spare parts; reinstitution of an "Exchange of Persons" program; and release of $400,000 (frozen since 1956) road-building and communications equipment.

30. Summary of the 373rd NSC meeting on 24 July 1958. USDD-1990:000330, p. 6.

31. Summary of the 374th NSC meeting on 31 July 1958. USDD-1990:000331, p. 11.

32. "Briefing Notes" for the NSC meeting of 21 August 1958. USDD-1990:000352, p. 3; and 16 October 1958. USDD-990:000332, p. 2.

33. "NSC 5820/1: U.S. Policy Toward the Near East," 4 November 1958. USDD-1980:386B, p. 2.

34. Ibid., p. 3.

35. Ibid., p. 10.

36. Ibid.

37. Ibid., p. 11. Two years later, Sa'ud would be effectively overthrown by his more reformist brother, Faisal.

38. Ibid., pp. 11–12.

39. Ibid., p. 9.

40. "Memorandum of Conference" dated 23 December 1958. USDD-1983:001435.

41. Cable from Ambassador H. Caccia in Washington to the Foreign Office, 18 December 1958. BFOD:FO371/133086/EQ10345/7.

42. See, for example, Humphrey Trevelyan's report of 19 January 1960 to Selwyn Lloyd on the political situation in Iraq. BFOD:FO371/149841/EQ1015/10.

43. Interview in the *New York Times*, 29 April 1959, quoted in Hanna Batatu, *The Old Social Classes and the Revolutionary Movements of Iraq: A Study of Iraq's Old Landed and Commercial Classes and of Its Communists, Ba'thists, and Free Officers* (Princeton: Princeton University Press, 1978), p. 899.

44. Note by Gordon Gray, special assistant to the president for national security affairs, 1 April 1959. USDD-1984:000586.

45. See Mohamed Hassanein Heikal, *Sphinx and Commissar: The Rise and Fall of Soviet Influence in the Arab World* (New York: Harper and Row, 1978), p. 107.

46. Operations Coordinating Board (OCB) Report on the Near East, 3 February 1960, pp. 6–7. USDD-1984:002567.

47. "The Situation in Iraq: Policy the United States Should Follow to Prevent Communism from Establishing Control of the Country," 15 [?] April 1959. USDD-1992:002638.

48. Cable from Ambassador Burrows in Ankara to the Foreign Office, 12 December 1959. BFOD:FO371/140959/EQ1071/70.

49. See the Cable dated 5 August 1959 from Amman to the Foreign Office (BFOD:FO371/ 141900/VG1017/9), as well as a later dispatch from the Canadian Embassy in Cairo reporting the arrest of fourteen officers in Syria on conspiracy charges. 22 September 1959, BFOD:FO371/141900/VG1017/12.

50. Quoted in a dispatch from the British Embassy in Baghdad on 3 November 1959. BFOD:FO371/140958/EQ1071/52(D).

51. Letter from Burrows to London, 23 May 1959. BFOD:FO371/140957/EQ1071/31.

52. Ibid., BFOD:FO371/140957/EQ1071/28.

53. Report dated 20 October 1959 from Arnold Smith in Cairo to the Canadian Foreign Ministry. BFOD:FO371/141903/VG10110/36.

54. At least that is what Deputy Undersecretary of State Raymond Hare told Nasser in New York on 30 September 1960. USDD-1984:002451.

55. Ambassador Burrows's account of remarks made by a U.S. State Department official to Turkish Foreign Minister Zorlu. Cable from Ankara to the Foreign Office on 23 May 1959. BFOD:FO371/140959/EQ1071/31. Stuart Rockwell, director of the State Department's Office of Near Eastern Affairs, explained his government's position to the British envoy by saying, "He did not think there was any serious danger of overt military intervention by the U.A.R. This being so he thought that it would be unwise to urge moderation on Nasser," since the United States did not wish to be seen as supporting communism against Arab nationalism. Cable from Ambassador Caccia in Washington to the Foreign Office, 19 March 1959. BFOD:FO371/ 140937/EQ10316/96.

56. Memorandum of the discussion at the 383rd meeting of the NSC, dated 17 October 1958. USDD-1990:000332, p. 8.

57. Memorandum from Komer to McGeorge Bundy and Walt Rostow. USDD-1991:001643.

58. Bowles Telegram dated 21 February 1962. USDD-I:454A.

59. Badeau Letter to President Johnson, 3 January 1964. USDD-1976:274C, p. 4.

60. Ibid., p. 3.

61. "Nasir's Comments on His Meeting with Assistant Secretary Talbot," CIA cable, 3 March 1964. USDD-1976:12B.

62. Outgoing State Department telegram dated 12 January 1965 summarizing a meeting between Kamel and Secretary of State Dean Rusk four days before. USDD-1982:002580.

63. "Review of United States Policy Toward Israel," State Department memorandum to the President, 7 August 1962. USDD-1992:003242.

64. Steven L. Spiegel, *The Other Arab-Israeli Conflict: Making America's Middle East Policy, from Truman to Reagan* (Chicago: University of Chicago Press, 1985), p. 135.

65. Nadav Safran, *Israel: The Embattled Ally* (Cambridge: Belknap Press of Harvard University Press, 1981), p. 374.

66. Interviews conducted by author in Damascus, 22 July 1991.

67. Nadav Safran, *From War to War: The Arab-Israeli Confrontation, 1948–1967* (New York: Pegasus, 1969), p. 135.

68. Quoted in Spiegel, *The Other Arab-Israeli Conflict*, p. 122.

69. "Current Status of U.S.-U.A.R. Relations," 12 August 1966. USDD-1980:323B.

70. Letter from Nes to Rodger P. Davies at the State Department, 17 October 1966. USDD-1985:001635.

71. "Nasser's May 2 Speech," State Department memorandum dated 4 May 1967. USDD-1993:001379.

72. Letter from Nes to Rodger P. Davies at the State Department, 11 May 1967. USDD-1985:002605.

73. Memorandum summarizing the discussion at the 374th National Security Council meeting on 31 July 1958. USDD-1990:000331, p. 7.

Part Three

War and Peace,
War and Peace

12

The 1967 Arab–Israeli War: U.S. Actions and Arab Perceptions

Fawaz A. Gerges

On more than one level the June 1967 Arab-Israeli war (also known as the Six Day War) was a watershed in the recent history of the Middle East. In particular, the confrontation radically transformed the nature of regional politics and the relationship between local states and the superpowers. On the one hand, the Arab-Israeli dispute became the most dominant single foreign policy issue in the external relations of the Arab states. The main focus of regional instability shifted from inter-Arab politics to Arab-Israeli interactions. The war also set the stage for the contemporary Arab-Israeli peace process. For the previous ten years, the dispute between Israel and the Arabs had been kept in the "icebox," moving neither toward resolution nor toward war.[1] In this sense, the Six Day War was a catalyst that forced Israel and the Arabs as well as their superpower patrons to participate in the quest for peace. On the other hand, the bloody escalation of the Arab-Israeli conflict made local players much more dependent on their superpower allies. As a result, the Arab-Israeli conflict became increasingly entangled in the U.S.-Soviet cold war rivalry. Thus, bipolarity on the international stage was reflected on the regional level. The increased reliance of the local states on the superpowers restricted their freedom of action and compromised their independence.

This chapter examines the impact of the 1967 Arab-Israeli war on Arab nationalist perceptions regarding the input that the United States had in the crisis, in order to examine how these perceptions influenced Arab attitudes toward the U.S. and Soviet roles in the peace process. I will argue that the Six Day War had a devastating, negative impact on Arab views regarding the U.S. role, as well as on Arab beliefs in the efficacy of the Soviet Union and its reliability as a superpower ally. Although Arab nationalists, particularly in Egypt, were highly critical and suspicious of President Lyndon B. Johnson, they recognized the indispensable and preponderant role of Washington in the post-1967 peace process. They believed the United States wielded much influence over its client—Israel—and held most of the cards in the peace process.

In contrast, Arab rulers, and not just Egyptian President Gamal 'Abd al-Nasser, became conscious of the limited nature of Soviet power and prestige in world politics. Their experiences with the Soviet Union during the 1967 crisis convinced them that Moscow did not have the means or the will to defend the Arabs. This belated realization played a decisive role in the mellowing of Egyptian radicalism during the post-1967 period and, one might venture to claim, in the revolutionary reorientation of Egyptian foreign policy throughout the 1970s.

Thus, this chapter must address several critical questions: How did the Arab confrontational states, particularly Egypt, respond to their crushing defeat at the hands of Israel in June 1967? How did they perceive the role of the superpowers in the war, and did their perceptions of the two contrasting superpower positions influence their behavior toward the peace process? What was the impact of the U.S.-Soviet rivalry on the dynamics of peacemaking? Why did President Johnson abandon previous U.S. support for the 1949 armistice regime, and how did this radical change in U.S. policy complicate the quest for peace? To what extent did the dramatic alteration in the regional balance of power inhibit both Israel and Arab rulers' willingness and ability to compromise? In this sense, did the 1967 war sow the seeds of a bloodier conflagration in the Middle East?

Arab Perceptions of the U.S. Role in the 1967 Arab-Israeli War

The polarization of the Arab-Israeli conflict along East-West lines was directly related to the crushing defeat of the Arab states in 1967 and their perceptions that the United States had colluded with Israel to destroy the "revolutionary Arab regimes which had refused to be a part of the Western sphere of influence."[2] Nasser, the leading Arab nationalist, believed that his regime was the main target of the U.S.-sponsored Israeli attack. He told Mohamed Heikal, a confidant of his, that Johnson succeeded in "trapping us." As for Nasser, this collusion entailed a complex set of political and diplomatic tricks and maneuvers. Moreover, the Egyptian leadership—not just Nasser—believed that the Johnson administration indirectly colluded with Israel by covering its flanks and neutralizing the Soviet Union and by deliberately deceiving Egypt and lulling it into a state of complacency.[3]

The Egyptians pointed to the fact that although the United States had secured from Egypt a commitment not to fire first, it failed to extract a similar pledge from Israel. They said that Egypt was under overwhelming pressure by the United States and the Soviet Union not to fire first. They argued that the Johnson administration impressed on Soviet leaders the urgent need to call upon its Egyptian ally to desist from any military adventure. To show his goodwill, Nasser declared publicly that he would not be the one to initiate hostilities. He said he was given the impression that Israel had also committed itself not to shoot first.[4]

Little wonder, then, that the Arab nationalists were very bitter after Israel's pre-emptive strike on June 5. They felt overwhelming resentment and anger for the Johnson administration, fueled initially by official Egyptian and Jordanian accusations that the United States had participated alongside Israel in the first air attacks against the Arab forces.[5] Although unfounded, these accusations served to confirm a widely held Arab stereotype of U.S. hostility. In particular, the Egyptians felt deceived by the United States; they also believed that the United States had involved the Soviets subconsciously in its strategy to mislead Egypt.

Nasser asserted that the U.S. government helped Israel in several ways by providing it with intelligence and weapons. For example, Israel's attack on the USS *Liberty*—a U.S. intelligence ship stationed off the Sinai coast on June 8—convinced the Egyptian leader of Johnson's complicity: the *Liberty* supplied Israel with critical intelligence about Egyptian military installations. In this context, Nasser claimed that Johnson had known and had approved of Israeli war plans in advance. As Nasser put it, the U.S. role in the war was a continuation of its shutting off of aid to Egypt: Having failed to subdue Egypt through economic warfare, Johnson instigated Israel to use physical force instead.[6] Nasser said the United States "must be made to feel the brunt of its collusion with Israel. We must bring the weight of mobilized Arab anger to bear on her. The severing of relations is imperative."[7] This perception, or rather misperception, was shared by all the confrontation Arab states (most importantly, Egypt, Syria, and Iraq), which promptly broke diplomatic relations with Washington.

To understand the rationale behind Arab perceptions, one has to focus on the nature of the relationship between the Johnson administration and the Arab nationalist forces, particularly on the steady deterioration of U.S.-Egyptian relations since the end of 1964. The gradual suspension of U.S. food aid to Egypt beginning in 1965, coupled with the direct supply of arms to Israel and other conservative states in the area, embittered Egyptian leaders and convinced them that Johnson was not only determined to humiliate and starve their country to death, but also was working closely with their regional enemies to overthrow the revolutionary Arab governments.[8] In September 1965 the Egyptian ambassador to Washington informed a senior U.S. diplomat that the Egyptian leadership believed that the U.S. Central Intelligence Agency (CIA) was seeking to topple the Nasser regime.[9]

By the end of 1966 Nasser seemed to have lost hope for U.S. policy, viewed as irredeemably pro-Israeli and anti-Egyptian.[10] The mood in Washington was equally hostile: "We're not angry [with Nasser]; we're fed up," wrote Harold Saunders, a key National Security Council (NSC) official dealing with the Middle East.[11] The U.S. ambassador to Egypt, Lucius Battle, also said that a good deal of uncertainty and tension and a general sense of discouragement existed in U.S.-Egyptian relations. The two countries, asserted the ambassador, were on a "slippery slope headed toward confrontation of the 1957–58 type." He warned his superiors in Washington to bear in mind that they were approaching a watershed in their relationship with Egypt.[12]

The Arab View of the U.S. Role in the Peace Process

The general Arab view of the U.S. role in the 1967 war and in the subsequent peace process should be studied squarely within this polarized context of suspicion and distrust. The Arab nationalists had no faith in the Johnson administration to act as a neutral mediator in the quest for peace. To them, an identity of interests existed between the White House and Israel, manifesting itself in Johnson's unequivocal support of Israel in the United Nations (UN) General Assembly and Security Council and subsequent actions, which were designed to ensure Israel's military superiority over all its Arab neighbors.[13] Arab rulers had a fixation with the United States that, in their opinion, determined questions of war and peace in the Middle East. They failed to appreciate the complexity of U.S.-Israeli relations and the wide degree of autonomy that Israeli leaders exercised in their ceaseless quest for absolute security.

In both 1956 and 1967, Nasser and his Arab counterparts did not consider seriously the possibility that Israel, by manipulating the polarized international system, was capable of acting on its own in the pursuit of its national interests, with or without superpower collusion. Israel was simply seen as an instrument and agent of the Western powers and imperialism, performing at the behest of its masters; Israel was not working for itself alone but was serving as a U.S. tool to dominate the Arab world. In the words of Algerian President Houari Boumedienne, "Israel played a secondary role in the 1967 war. The battle was American, and only the performance was Israeli." Likewise, Nasser said that the United States—not Israel—was the main party with which to discuss the occupation of Arab territories.[14] Although some of this was merely hyperbole, Arab politicians really believed that the United States held the key to war and peace in the region. Reading the recollections, speeches, and some minutes of the meetings of Arab officials, one gets the impression that Johnson had the power and the means to force Israel to withdraw to the prewar borders but did not want to employ them.[15]

Despite the vehemence of his attack on U.S. policy, Nasser was in no position to confront the United States in the region. When the dust settled over the desert, Nasser found the bulk of his army destroyed, the Sinai occupied, his coffers empty, and his political career in jeopardy. Unlike the war of 1956, Nasser could not turn a military defeat into a political victory. In fact, the Six Day War was markedly different from the Suez crisis. In 1956 Nasser could rightly claim that Egyptian capabilities were no match for the combined forces of Britain, France, and Israel. In spite of his efforts, Nasser could not repeat the same political performance in 1967. The "most powerful state in the Middle East" had been decisively beaten and humiliated by a young, vigorous, and small nation.

As a result, Nasser's status and position in the Arab world were weakened as well. With the totality of defeat, Nasser's long-term goal of constructing a new Arab order disappeared. Undermined were the symbols and ideas of secular Arab nationalism that had served as the building blocks for this order. The revolutionary ideal was discredited in Arab politics. In inter-Arab relations, the overall balance of forces shifted dramatically in favor of the Arab conservatives, who held the power of the purse and who shaped the politics of the inter-Arab state system during the post-1967 period.

Furthermore, the Arab nationalists could no longer rely on the sympathy of world public opinion or on the active intervention of the superpowers. They did not understand the changed international situation in the late 1960s. The United States was bogged down in Vietnam and was not terribly focused on the Middle East. Likewise preoccupied at home and abroad, the Kremlin leadership was building bridges to the West in the hope of gaining economic and political concessions. The Soviets were against a war in the Middle East that might involve them in a direct clash with the United States (and thus endanger their new approach to the West).[16] The Arab radicals were mistaken in their assumption that the Soviets would intervene in a Middle East war. Such thinking was symptomatic of the prevailing, pervasive tendency of the regional actors to inflate their own importance. After the 1967 war, Nasser told his colleagues that he had not weighed carefully the changes in Soviet foreign policy after the death of Soviet leader Nikita Khrushchev.[17]

More significant to the Kremlin leadership were the nuclear stalemate with the United States and the perennial question of international security. In the Six Day War, U.S. and Soviet policymakers communicated at the highest levels to contain the conflict and to prevent its spread and expansion. They exerted considerable pressures on their local allies to accept a cease-fire. Although the war was short, the superpowers used the hotline more than once to clarify any misunderstanding that might force them into an unwanted confrontation. In the aftermath of the war, top U.S. and Soviet officials held talks to try to find a political solution.[18]

Although the Soviets were critical of Israel's actions in June 1967 and were supportive of the Arabs, they did not take concrete measures—except to promise to resupply arms—to help their friends. The Soviets could not even offer their Arab allies much support in the UN Security Council because of U.S. objections to any resolution stipulating that Israel withdraw behind the 1949 armistice lines.[19] It was not until June 10 that the Soviet Union took drastic steps to halt the Israeli advance on the Syrian front. According to Johnson, Soviet Premier Alexei Kosygin used the hotline to inform him that as the result of Israel's ignoring all UN Security Council resolutions for a cease-fire, a very crucial moment had arrived. Kosygin foresaw the risk of a "grave catastrophe" unless Israel unconditionally terminated its military operations within the next few hours. Otherwise, the Soviet premier warned that his government would take all "necessary actions, including military." In addition, the Soviet Union severed diplomatic relations with Israel and threatened to take stronger measures unless the latter ceased hostilities immediately.[20]

Although he recognized that the Soviet Union was sensitive about its special relationship with Syria, Johnson said that he was determined to resist Soviet intrusion in the Middle East. His immediate response was to issue orders to the U.S. Navy Sixth Fleet to move closer to the Syrian coast so as to send a warning signal to the Kremlin: "There are times when the wisdom and rightness of a President's judgment

are critically important. We were at such a moment. The Soviets had made a decision. I had to respond."[21]

But neither the United States nor the Soviet Union had the stomach for a clash.
The Soviets knew that pressure from the U.S. government was the only way to stop
an Israeli advance deep into Syria. Their warning to Johnson was designed to im-
press upon him the need to halt Tel Aviv's march toward Damascus. Soviet calculations proved correct. According to senior Israeli officials, on June 10 the Johnson administration informed its ally that the situation had reached a dangerous point and
that Soviet intervention was no longer inconceivable. Israel agreed to a cease-fire on
the same day, following the occupation of the Syrian Golan Heights.[22]

A crisis between the superpowers was thus averted. Their high-level contacts had
effectively prevented an open clash between them. As the CIA put it, the Soviet
Union had no intention of intervening militarily in the war and so did what it could
to avoid confrontation. Another major concern of the Kremlin leadership, argued a
CIA intelligence assessment, was to forestall a disastrous Arab defeat that would
make the Kremlin the target of Arab criticisms.[23] As a superpower, the Soviet Union
was more concerned about its relationship with the United States than with any abstract obligations to its regional partners. The logic of superpower politics took priority over other interests.

Given the ambivalent position of the Soviet Union, one would have expected
Nasser to swallow his pride and mend fences with the Johnson administration. In
the case of the Suez conflict, Nasser knew that it was the United States rather than
the Soviet Union that ultimately forced the tripartite coalition to cease fire and withdraw. In 1967, however, Nasser believed that Johnson unleashed Israel's military action against Egypt to topple his progressive regime. Unlike Eisenhower, who played
the leading and most effective role in thwarting the tripartite aggression, Nasser asserted that Johnson played a decisive role in Israel's swift victory over the Arabs.[24]

By using the last weapon in his arsenal—severing diplomatic relations with the
U.S. government—and by his accusations against the United States, Nasser embittered Johnson and made him more determined to prevent Nasser from regaining a
position of pan-Arab leadership. The U.S. president made it clear that the United
States "could not afford to repeat the temporary and hasty arrangements" between
Egypt and Israel after Suez. Johnson now had the opportunity to try a different approach, by supporting Israel's hold on the newly occupied territories pending Arab
consent to make peace with Israel.[25]

Indeed, as soon as the fighting started, Johnson, as former Ambassador Richard
Parker puts it, "showed a clear and lasting bias in favor of Israel and a disregard for
the public commitments he and his administration had made to oppose aggression
from any quarter."[26] The United States became more closely allied with Israel in opposition to vital Arab interests. The extremely pro-Israeli stand of U.S. public opinion, coupled with Arab hostility and Johnson's dislike of Nasser, enabled Johnson to
adopt a policy of "unquestioning support for Israel."[27] The extent of the Arab defeat
took U.S. officials by surprise. They had expected Israel to win but were unsure
about the duration or immediate results of an Arab-Israeli contest. On the first day

of the war, the uncertainty and uneasiness of the administration were reflected in its call for all combatants to work for a cease-fire and return to old positions before the start of hostilities.[28]

The U.S. stand changed dramatically, however, as soon as the completeness of Israel's victory became known. In a memorandum to the president on June 7, his special assistant, Walt Rostow, wrote that the Israeli victory created new conditions that the U.S. government quickly should move to exploit. The following day Rostow warned that the greatest risk would be to fail to appreciate the political consequences of Israel's military triumph. He summarized the U.S. official position as being opposed to any UN resolution that would require Israel to concede war gains except in return for an Arab-Israeli final settlement.[29] No doubt Rostow was fully aware that the new bargaining situation created by the war was asymmetrical.

The Johnson administration hoped to use the new asymmetrical situation to extract peace treaties and recognition of Israel's existence from the Arabs. Some U.S. officials argued that the humiliating defeat of Egypt and Syria provided the United States with a golden opportunity to take "big" political measures in the region, since "Soviet policy was in ruins."[30] Even before the war was over the administration had concluded that Nasser's fate was sealed. U.S. diplomats in the field were certain that a general anti-Nasser convulsion would shake Egypt and the Arab world; indeed that the domestic survival of his regime was in doubt, as was the allegiance of other Arab states.[31]

U.S. intelligence agencies also believed that the Egyptian leader's days were numbered, and they began to think seriously about the post-Nasser era. Likewise, the U.S. Department of State thought that the fall of Nasser's regime would lead not only to the reestablishment of U.S. relations with Egypt, but also to the resurrection of U.S. interests in the whole Arab arena.[32] The dominant view in Washington was that no quick palliative solutions or temporizing compromises should be accepted. In the words of the undersecretary of state for political affairs, Averell Harriman, the United States would never have another opportunity as propitious to deal with the underlying problems besetting this turbulent region—"so vital to our own and Western Europe's security."[33] Ironically, Nasser interpreted the U.S. position as motivated by a desire to freeze the present situation, hoping that his regime, along with all revolutionary Arab regimes, "would fall, to be replaced by another more receptive to U.S. interests, or alternatively to instill utter despair in us, driving us to make peace with Israel on its conditions."[34]

The basic outlines of U.S. long-term strategy were defined as follows: (1) cessation of hostilities between Israel and its Arab neighbors; (2) Arab recognition of Israel; (3) support of moderate Arab forces—the leader of which was Saudi Arabia—at the expense of the Arab radicals: Egypt, Syria, and Iraq; (4) a bigger role for Turkey and Iran in the Middle East; (5) regional arms control arrangements; and (6) a new mechanism for social and economic development.[35] In U.S. eyes, the denouement of the war provided a great opportunity to solve the festering Arab-Israeli conflict and to redraw the political map of the region. A central element in this strategy was to cut Nasser's prestige and influence in the Arab world and revise regional political alignments.

Achievement of this objective would require the active involvement of Turkey, Iran, and Israel. For a decade these states had campaigned hard to become integral players in the inter-Arab state subsystem. According to an intelligence assessment by the CIA, before the war Israel had hoped to construct a loose coalition of Iran, Turkey, Iraqi and Syrian Kurds, and moderate Arabs. It follows that the primary Israeli war aim was the destruction of Nasser as the leader of the pan-Arab nationalist movement. If that goal could be achieved, Israeli officials assumed that Israel, Turkey, and Iran would become the dominant regional actors by representing an overwhelming balance of military power.[36]

In the aftermath of the war, both Israel and Iran lobbied the U.S. government to support more substantial roles for them in the area. Israeli officials informed their U.S. counterparts that their victory over the Arabs created new opportunities to build a more viable order in the Middle East. They argued further that the United States and its regional allies would be the main beneficiaries of this order.[37] The shah of Iran also informed the Johnson administration that "Nasser must be eliminated as otherwise he [could] again inflame Arab sentiments." Iran would be more than pleased, he added, to play a more active part and to be a solid pillar in the region, as Japan did in the Far East.[38] (Indeed, some time later, the Nixon Doctrine of 1969 envisaged hegemonic roles for Iran in the Gulf and Israel in the Fertile Crescent. President Richard M. Nixon and his assistant for national security, Henry Kissinger, saw Iran and Israel as the policemen and the protectors of U.S. interests in the region.)[39]

These arguments impressed the Johnson administration, which accepted Tel Aviv's view that no withdrawal should take place except in return for a peace agreement. Johnson placed the major responsibility for the war on Egypt and refused to pressure Israel to concede any territories, as Eisenhower did in 1957. He said Israel must be accepted as a reality in the area and must be recognized by the Arabs.[40] Johnson spelled out five principles that were essential to peace: (1) the recognized right to national life (for all parties to the dispute); (2) justice for the (Palestinian) refugees; (3) innocent maritime passage (through the Suez Canal and the Strait of Tiran); (4) limiting the arms race (in the region between Arabs and Israelis); and (5) political independence and territorial integrity (for all). Both the Israelis and the Arabs saw Johnson's Five Great Principles of Peace as wholly supporting Israel. The convergence of interests between the United States and Israel was almost complete, marking the beginning of a special relationship between the two countries.[41] Thus, the Six Day War brought about a major shift in U.S. policy toward the Middle East.[42] The president and his aides decided not to return to the old, failed policy supporting the 1949 armistice regime. This attitude explained the administration's posture of distant reserve toward the question of Arab-Israeli peace.[43]

The Arab View of the Soviet Role

Given their perceptions of an unholy U.S.-Israeli alliance, the Arab confrontation states—Egypt, Syria, and Iraq, with the exception of Jordan—felt compelled to turn to the Soviet Union for political and military support. They recognized, however, the limited nature of Soviet power and influence.[44] The Soviet failure to provide direct military assistance to the Arabs had important repercussions on Soviet-Arab relations. Egyptian, Iraqi, and Algerian leaders were disappointed with the lack of tangible Soviet assistance. They suspected the Soviets of either being "scared of the Americans" or of having sacrificed their Arab allies on the altar of détente with Washington. Egyptian officials criticized the Soviet Union for actually playing the role demanded of it by Johnson during the crisis in May and June; some senior Egyptian officials were skeptical about the value of Moscow as a friend, whereas others even suspected a collusion between the United States and the Soviet Union. Arab rulers realized that the security requirements of their superpower ally vis-à-vis the United States took priority over Middle East regional concerns.[45]

This realization convinced the Arabs that their alliance with the Soviet Union was tactical rather than strategic. In this context, the Six Day War marked a watershed in Arab-Soviet relations. The Arabs questioned the nature of their alliance with the Kremlin; though Israel enjoyed full protection by the United States, the Arabs did not receive an equal Soviet commitment.[46] It could be argued that one of the main reasons for the decline of Soviet influence in the Arab world in the early 1970s lay in Arab perceptions of Moscow's stand during the war.

Yet despite the feeling of abandonment and indignation, Nasser and the other Arab nationalists could not afford a final divorce from the Communist giant—especially after they cut their political links with the United States and Great Britain. The Soviet Union became their last refuge. Nasser believed that the regional and global configuration of forces were in U.S. and Israeli favor, thus he needed Soviet military and political support to rebuild his military and to counterbalance U.S. and Israeli hegemony. Immediately after the war Nasser moved swiftly to end the ill feeling that was souring Arab-Soviet relations. Nasser publicly praised Kremlin leaders for their political, economic, and military assistance. He informed Soviet officials that he wanted to strengthen and deepen Egyptian-Soviet relations and that he was ready to sign any pact to organize and structure the relationship between their two countries on a more permanent basis.[47] Moscow's deepening involvement with Egypt and Syria took the Arab-Israeli conflict still deeper into the cold war rivalry between the superpowers. The Arab-Israeli dispute became a global-military-strategic problem, not a regional-political problem.[48] The peace process thus became entangled in the web of great power politics.

To the Soviets, the immediate results of the war must have been gratifying. Nasser's crushing defeat humbled him, and he became more receptive to Soviet requests. No longer could he afford to challenge Moscow's influence in the region, as he had in 1959; this reassured the Soviets. By regulating the flow of arms to Egypt and Syria, the Kremlin would have a greater impact on their policies. Nasser was left in no doubt as to Moscow's preference for a peaceful solution to the Arab-Israeli conflict.[49] Time and again, the Soviets would procrastinate and decline to supply their Arab friends with offensive weapons. The war had taught the Soviets the need to exercise more control over their regional allies, and the war's aftermath enabled them to do so. In the next three years the question of arms deliveries became one of the most effective clubs the Soviets wielded over the Arabs.[50]

The Egyptians were frustrated with their treatment by the Kremlin. In fact, Anwar Sadat described the period after the war as a clash between Egypt and the Soviet Union.[51] In the long run, Soviet behavior bred suspicion and bitterness in Arab ranks, especially in Egypt. Sadat claimed that one of the reasons motivating Nasser to accept the 1970 Rogers Initiative—a peace initiative by U.S. Secretary of State William Rogers—was Nasser's belief that the Soviet Union was a "hopeless case."[52] Hence, it was a only matter of time before the Egyptians would rebel against what they perceived to be Soviet heavy-handedness.

In the short term, Soviet political and material influence increased considerably in the Arab world. Soviet leaders kept their promise to restore lost Arab inventories, with the exception of offensive weapons. Soviet military personnel also were sent in increasing numbers to Cairo and Damascus to assist in defense of deep strategic and industrial targets. However, the flourishing Soviet presence in the region was tactical and temporary, the product of a devastating upheaval that left Egypt, the nerve center of the Arab order, with few international options to pursue. The Arabs could not help comparing U.S. support of Israel with the Kremlin's lukewarm commitment to the Arabs. Thus, the seeds of mistrust and suspicion had been sown in Arab-Soviet relations. Although Nasser could not distance himself from his Soviet ally, he eventually reopened his relationship with the United States, and by the time of his death from natural causes in 1970 he had come to recognize the indispensable role of Washington in the peace process. Sadat claimed that Nasser had told him that "whether we like it or not, all the cards of this game [i.e., the Arab-Israeli conflict] are in America's hands. It's high time we talked and allowed the U.S.A. to take part in this."[53]

Although Sadat's account is exaggerated and self-serving it is also important, as it foreshadows the future direction of U.S.-Egyptian relations. More than once Nasser tested the degree of U.S. commitment to a balanced approach to the Middle East crisis. For example, following Richard Nixon's election to the presidency in 1968, Nasser decided to make a fresh start with the United States by initiating a dialogue with the new U.S. leader. In fact, Nasser and Jordan's King Hussein informed Nixon that they were prepared to accept a diplomatic solution with Israel and that they were constrained neither by Syria's opposition nor by opposition from other Arab radicals. Egyptian Prime Minister Mahmoud Fawzi also told Nixon privately that as part of a regional settlement Israel would have freedom of navigation in the Suez Canal. The Egyptians hoped that the Nixon administration would reciprocate by adopting evenhanded policies toward the Arabs and the Israelis. They were disappointed, however, with the lack of a positive U.S. response. According to scholar William Quandt, Kissinger was not persuaded. Thus, the Nixon administration did not change its attitude and maintained close ties with Israel by preserving Israel's military superiority over Arab neighbors without pressing its leaders to withdraw from recently occupied Arab territories.[54]

Nasser still thought that Nixon—unlike Johnson—could play a positive role in the Arab-Israeli conflict. In May 1970, the Egyptian leader personally appealed to Nixon to adopt an evenhanded policy and become actively engaged in the quest for peace. He said Egypt had not given up on the United States, despite U.S. military and political support to Israel: The United States must either order Israel to withdraw from the recently occupied territories or, if it was unable to go that far, refrain from extending any further assistance to Israel as long as the latter occupied Arab lands. Although Egypt and the United States did not have diplomatic relations, Nasser said this did not prevent the two countries from cooperating to achieve peace.[55] According to Sadat, this appeal to Nixon implied a desire on Nasser's part to pursue a political course of action.[56] Although Nixon responded to the appeal, and Rogers in fact outlined a peace initiative, Nasser and the United States could not overcome differences. It would take Nasser's successor (ironically, that turned out to be Sadat) and other new leaders to revive the old connection with the United States—at the sole expense of the Kremlin.

The Khartoum Summit

Nasser accepted the convening of a summit of Arab heads of state in Khartoum, Sudan, at the end of August 1967. As to the Arab militants—Syria, Iraq, Algeria, and the Palestine Liberation Organization (PLO)—it was their feeling that a counteroffensive was urgently needed to stem the tide of U.S. advance in the region. In their view, the termination of diplomatic relations with the United States was not adequate to force it to change its policy. Thus, the Syrians, Algerians, Iraqis, and Palestinians called for a complete boycott of the United States and for a strategic alliance with the Soviet Union. They argued that the peace process would lead to Arab surrender and a U.S.-Israeli dictate. On the regional level, they advanced the idea of a popular war against Israel and of a revolutionary crusade against the conservative Arab regimes. The Syrian rulers, in particular, took an anti-Western posture and poured abuse on reactionary Arab regimes that had remained on the sidelines during the latest round of Arab-Israeli hostilities. Syria boycotted the Khartoum Summit because it refused to accept Arab reaction as a partner.[57]

However, the clarification of the Soviet position played a decisive role in Nasser's decision to accept the convening of the summit. Its purpose was to define a collective Arab strategy toward Israel and the West. In Khartoum, Nasser joined the Arab moderates in supporting a political rather than military solution to the Arab-Israeli conflict. They also agreed to keep the dialogue with the West, and they opposed the militants' proposal to suspend Arab oil production.[58] An oil embargo, Nasser argued, would harm Arab economies more than those of the West and would almost certainly antagonize the West. Nasser's new realism manifested itself in his unwillingness to ask the conservative Arab regimes to sever diplomatic relations with the U.S. government. He also informed Jordan's King Hussein that he was free to pursue a separate negotiated settlement—including signing a defense treaty with the United States—to recover the West Bank and Jerusalem.[59]

Nasser's behavior was designed not only to mend his fences with the Arab conservatives, but also to keep open lines of communication with the United States. He said he wanted to give the United States an opportunity to prove to its few remaining Arab friends that it was serious about reducing its total alignment with Israel. Nasser was not convinced by the arguments of the militants to cut all links with Washington. The war and its aftermath made the Egyptian leader acutely aware of the influential weight of the United States in the region. As Nasser himself put it, "Political positions cannot be built on myths but facts. We do not want and cannot fight America." Thus, the Egyptian leader asked Saudi King Faisal to serve as his channel of communication with the Johnson administration.[60]

Nasser parted company with the Arab radicals on the Arab-Israeli conflict itself: He was not impressed by their call for a total war against the Jewish state. He knew full well that the regional balance of power favored Israel, which had won the sympathy and respect of world public opinion and a decisive edge in international diplomacy. Nasser also took into account the superpower agreement to resolve the problem by political means. Moreover, as mentioned previously, both the Soviet Union and the nonaligned movement informed the Arabs that they would prefer to see a peaceful way out of the Arab-Israeli labyrinth.[61]

For all these reasons, the Egyptian president joined the moderates in Khartoum in support of a political rather than military solution to the conflict. This fact should not be confused by the summit's three declarations on Israel—"no peace, no negotiations, no recognition." The Sudanese premier noted that the three no's were adopted as an instrumental response, a political gesture, to the uncompromising stand of the PLO. Afterward, Nasser, Hussein, and other Arab officials made it clear both publicly and privately that they were prepared to live in peace with Israel in return for Israel's complete withdrawal from Arab territories occupied in 1967 and for a just solution to the Palestine problem. The summit, noted Hussein, empowered Egypt and Jordan to seek a political solution. In particular, Hussein was convinced that a political solution was the only feasible option open to the Arabs. This belief led him to coordinate his efforts with the United States as well as to serve as a link between the United States and Egypt.[62]

It was within this spirit that Egypt and Jordan accepted UN Security Council Resolution 242, which was adopted unanimously by the major powers in November 1967. This resolution called for the withdrawal of Israeli armed forces from territories—not "the" territories—occupied in the recent conflict and the termination of the state belligerency between Israel and its Arab neighbors.[63]

Nasser subsequently accused Johnson of supporting Israel in resisting the implementation of the terms of Resolution 242; instead the Johnson administration applied considerable political pressure in an attempt to force Egypt (and Jordan) into a separate peace settlement with Israel: The basis of any agreement with Egypt centered on total Israeli withdrawal from all occupied Egyptian territories in return for

Egypt terminating the state of war with Israel. Nasser refused to conclude a separate deal with Israel and called for a comprehensive solution: "The issue is not only about withdrawal from Sinai. It is much bigger than that. The issue is to be or not to be." To Nasser, accepting a separate agreement with Israel meant coming to terms with the reality of defeat and abandoning the core of the Arab policy upon which he had built his political career.[64]

The Egyptians were angered when Johnson started to develop intimate ties with Tel Aviv. They believed that Johnson's actions were not only confined to safeguarding Israel, but also assisting it in its occupation of Arab lands. To Nasser and his colleagues, the U.S. president was pushing Egypt to depend further upon the Soviet Union for military, economic, and political support. Egyptian Foreign Minister Mahmoud Riad said that Nasser felt puzzled by the element of self-destruction in U.S. policy that was driving the Arabs into Soviet arms: "The United States leaves us no choice."[65] Egyptian leaders could not understand the radical change in the U.S. position toward the peace process after the 1967 war, especially Johnson's abandonment of previous U.S. support for the 1949 armistice regime. They believed that the U.S.-Israeli drive aimed at "forcing Egypt to accept the fait accompli in the hope that the Arab area would surrender to U.S. and Israeli demands."[66]

This was another attempt by Johnson, asserted Nasser, to humiliate the Arabs, thus adversely affecting U.S.-Arab relations. By the end of 1967, given Nasser's perception of Johnson's hostility, he had concluded that the peace process was dead as long as the balance of power favored Israel; it was only by restoring this imbalance that the United States would be induced to reassess its position. Nasser said that redressing the imbalance, and escalating military pressure, would have a radical impact on the whole Middle East situation, particularly on the positions of the superpowers, and would convince the superpowers of the need to stop maneuvering and to act decisively. Thus, Nasser's subsequent choice of a "war of attrition" can be seen as a result of the lack of progress toward a political settlement in the two years after the 1967 war and of his desire to break the political and military stalemate, something Anwar Sadat would do as well in 1973.[67]

Conclusion

Although the Six Day War set the stage for the Middle East peace process, it did not motivate or force Israel and the Arabs to reach a compromise. Israel's overwhelming victory over the Arabs brought about a radical shift in the regional balance of power in its favor. This shift in the configuration of forces, coupled with the strong pro-Israeli position of the U.S. government, hardened the position of the two antagonists. Although most Arab rulers declared their readiness to live in peace with their Jewish neighbor, none of the Arab confrontational states—except for Jordan—was willing to conclude formal peace treaties with Israel. They were very weak militarily for any risky initiative on the diplomatic front. For Nasser and his Arab counterparts, to give the sort of commitments the United States and Israel were demanding would have meant accepting the reality of defeat, thus endangering the very survival of their regimes. Furthermore, despite their rude awakening in June 1967, Arab leaders were not yet ready to come to terms with Israel; they were still prisoners of their historical fears and prejudices.

Israel, on the other hand, was a satisfied power. As a result of their swift victory over the Arabs, Israeli officials demanded a high price for their withdrawal from some, but not all, of the recently occupied Arab territories. Given the disarray, fragmentation, and impotence of the Arab world and unwavering U.S. support, some Israeli elements believed that they could indefinitely hold on to the occupied Arab territories. By the time UN Resolution 242 was passed, Israel was no longer interested in exchanging land for commitments of any kind from the Arabs. As the then deputy assistant secretary of state for Near Eastern affairs, Rodger Davies, put it: "Israel's appetite had grown with the eating."[68]

The diplomatic stalemate in the Middle East was directly related to the deepening polarization of the Arab-Israeli conflict along East-West lines. As mentioned previously, Arab nationalist perceptions of U.S. involvement in the 1967 war influenced their attitudes toward the U.S. role in the peace process. They believed that the Johnson administration had colluded with Israel against the forces of Arab nationalism. Subsequent U.S. abandonment of its previous support for the 1949 armistice regime reinforced the widely held Arab view of U.S. hostility.

As a result, Arab nationalists did not trust the United States to act as a neutral mediator in the quest for peace; they turned instead to the Soviet Union for political and military succor—despite their recognition of the limited nature of Soviet power—hoping to redress the regional imbalance. Moscow's further involvement with Egypt and Syria took the Middle East crisis still deeper into the cold war rivalry between the superpowers. The entanglement of the Arab-Israeli conflict in the web of great power politics complicated the peace process and made Israel and the Arabs less willing to compromise. Thus, far from being a catalyst for peace, the 1967 war sowed the seeds of yet another bloody conflagration in the region.

Notes

I want to thank former Ambassador Richard Parker, Professor William Quandt, Dr. Avi Shlaim, and Professor Chris Taylor for reading and commenting on an earlier version of this chapter.

1. William B. Quandt, *Peace Process: American Diplomacy and the Arab-Israeli Conflict Since 1967* (Washington, D.C.: Brookings Institution and University of California Press, 1993), p. 1.

2. *Wataiq 'Abdel-Nasser: Khutab, ahadit, tasrihat: Yanayir 1967–Disember 1968* [Abdel-Nasser's Documents: Speeches, Discussions, and Declarations, January 1967–December 1968] (Cairo: Markaz al-dirasat al-siyasiya wa al-istratijiya bi Al-Ahram, 1973), p. 246 (hereinafter this series will be referred to as *Wataiq Nasser, 1967–1968*). Shortly after the war, Nasser told his colleague, Vice-President Zakaria Muhieddin, that Johnson was determined to get rid of Nasser. See Tharwat Akasha, *Mudhakkirati fi al-siyasa wa al-thaqafa* [My Memoirs in Politics and in Culture], vol. 2 (Cairo: Maktaba al-madbuli, 1988), pp. 490, 501–502.

3. *Wataiq Nasser, 1967–1968*, p. 226; Mahmoud Riad, *The Struggle for Peace in the Middle East* (London: Quartet Books, 1981), pp. 36–37; Mohamed Heikal, *1967: Sanawat al-galayan, Harb al-talateen sana* [1967: The Years of Upheaval, the Thirty Years War], vol. 1 (Cairo: Markaz Al-Ahram litarjama wa al-nashr, 1988), p. 846.

4. *Wataiq Nasser, 1967–1968*, p. 226; Riad, *The Struggle for Peace in the Middle East*, pp. 36–37; Heikal, *1967: Sanawat al-galayan*, p. 846; Mohamed Heikal, *Nasser: The Cairo Documents* (London: New English Library, 1972), p. 219.

5. H. M. King Hussein, *Harbuna ma'a Israil* [Our War with Israel] (Beirut: Dar al-nahar lilnashr, 1968), pp. 67–69.

6. Beginning in 1965, Johnson applied economic pressure against Nasser by reducing the flow of foreign aid to Egypt. *Wataiq Nasser, 1967–1968*, pp. 226, 243–248; Lieutenant General Salah al-Din al-Hadidi, *Shahid ila harb sab'a wa sitteen* [Witness to the 1967 War] (Cairo: Maktaba al-madbuli, 1974), p. 180. Diya al-Din Baybars, *Al-asrar al-sakhsiya li 'Abd al-Nasser* [The Personal Secrets of Nasser as Told by Mahmoud al-Jayar] (Cairo: Maktaba al-madbuli, 1976), p. 165; Ahmed Hamroush, *Qissa taura 23 Yulio: Karif 'Abd al-Nasser* [The Story of the 23 July Revolution: The Autumn of 'Abd al-Nasser], vol. 5 (Cairo: Maktaba al-madbuli, 1984), pp. 138–139, 141; Mahmoud Riad, *Mudhakkirat: America wa al-'arab* [Memoirs: America and the Arabs], vol. 3 (Beirut: Dar al-Mustaqbal al-'Arabi, 1986), pp. 40–42; Mohamed Heikal, *1967: Al-infijar, Harb al-talateen sana'* [1967: The Explosion, the Thirty Years War], vol. 3 (Cairo: Markaz Al-Ahram liltarjama wa al-nashr, 1990), pp. 756, 846, 876.

7. Riad, *The Struggle for Peace in the Middle East*, p. 25.

8. *Wataiq Nasser, 1967–1968*, p. 336; Abdel Meguid Farid, *Min muhadarat ijtima'at 'Abd al-Nasser al-'arabiya was duwaliya* [From the Minutes of 'Abd al-Nasser's Arab and International Meetings, 1967–1970] (Beirut: Mu'assasa al-abhat al-'arabiya, 1979), pp. 120–121; Hamroush, *Qissa taura 23 Yulio*, vol. 5, pp. 82–83; Ahmed Youssef Ahmed, *Al-dawr al-Misri fi al-Yaman, 1962–1967* [The Egyptian Role in Yemen, 1962–1967] (Cairo: Al-Hai'a al-Misriya al-amma ilkitab, 1981), p. 319.

9. U.S. Department of State, Memorandum of Conversation, Subject: U.S.-U.A.R. Relations, 17 September 1965, in *The Lyndon B. Johnson National Security Files, the Middle East: National Security Files, 1963–1969* (Frederick, Md.: University Publications of America, 1989), reel 8 of 8 (hereinafter, this series will be referred to as *LBJ Files*).

10. Riad, *The Struggle for Peace in the Middle East*, p. 16; Tom Little, *Modern Egypt* (London: Ernest Benn, 1967), p. 231; Hamroush, *Qissa taura 23 Yulio*, vol. 5, pp. 83–84, 94; Mohamed Heikal, *Sphinx and Commissar: The Rise and Fall of Soviet Influence in the Arab World* (London: Collins, 1978), pp. 161–162, 165–167.

11. Hal Saunders, Recommend Clearing Cable from Hare to Battle with Added Final Sentence, 4 June 1966, in *LBJ Files*, reel 8 of 8.

12. Cairo to Secretary of State, No. 3062, 25 May 1966 [sections one and two of two], in ibid.

13. Mohammed Fawzi, *Harb october am 1973: Dirasa was durus* [The October War of 1973: A Study and Lessons] (Beirut: Dar al-Mustaqbal al-'arabi, 1988), p. 5; Riad, *The Struggle for Peace in the Middle East*, p. 27; Mohamed Hafez Ismael, *Amin Misr al-quami fi asr al-tahadiyat* [Egyptian National Security in the Challenging Age] (Cairo: Markaz Al-Ahram lilnashr, 1987), p. 125.

14. *Wataiq Nasser, 1967–1968*, p. 495; Heikal, *1967: Al-infijar*, pp. 914, 933; Mohamed Heikal, *The Road to Ramadan: The Inside Story of How the Arabs Prepared For and Almost Won*

the October War of 1973 (India: Natraj Publishers, 1981), p. 47; Riad, *The Struggle for Peace in the Middle East,* pp. 76–77.

15. Riad, *The Struggle for Peace in the Middle East,* pp. 25, 37, 39. Riad, *Mudhakkirat,* vol. 3, p. 45.

16. Robert Stephens, *Nasser: A Political Biography* (Middlesex, England: Penguin Books, 1971), p. 521; Richard Parker, "The June War: Whose Conspiracy?" *Journal of Palestine Studies* 21(4) (Summer 1992), pp. 15–17; Abdel-Latif A. Baghdadi, *Mudhakirat* [Memoirs], vol. 2 (Cairo: Al-maktab al-Misri al-hadit, 1977), p. 277.

17. Heikal, *1967: Al-infijar,* pp. 725, 733, 895; Baghdadi, *Mudhakirat* [Memoirs], vol. 2, pp. 275–276.

18. Draft Message to Chairman Kosygin, 8 June 1967, in *LBJ Files,* reel 1 of 8; Lyndon B. Johnson, *The Vantage Point: Perspectives of the Presidency, 1963–1969* (New York: Holt, Rinehart, and Winston, 1971), p. 298.

19. Memorandum for Mr. Rostow: The Security Council Meeting of 6 and 7 June 1967, in *LBJ Files,* reel 1 of 8.

20. The states of Eastern Europe, with the exception of Romania, also broke off diplomatic relations with Tel Aviv. *Pravda,* 10 June 1967; Johnson, *The Vantage Point,* p. 302; Moshe Dayan, *Story of My Life* (London: Weidenfeld and Nicolson, 1976), p. 304; Abba Eban, *An Autobiography* (London: Weidenfeld and Nicolson, 1977), p. 423.

21. Johnson, *The Vantage Point,* p. 302.

22. The weight of evidence indicates that Washington turned a blind eye toward Israel's offensive campaign against Syria. Israel's foreign minister at the time, Abba Eban, noted that some U.S. officials informed him that Syria should not be allowed to escape injury. On June 8 these officials were worried lest the UN Security Council adopt a cease-fire resolution, thus leaving Syria off the hook. During the debate on whether to storm the Golan Heights, Eban told the Israeli cabinet that Washington would be delighted if Syria were beaten. Declassified U.S. documents also show that U.S. officials hoped that Israel would "go fast enough" to create a "de facto" situation on the Syrian front before the UN Security Council passed a cease-fire resolution. The USS *Liberty* incident, however, indicates that the Johnson administration did not sanction Israel's attack on Syria. We still do not know the whole story behind Israel's attack on this U.S.-flagged intelligence-gathering ship in the eastern Mediterranean, killing thirty-four men, although some believe it was a deliberate attempt by Israel to keep Washington in the dark as to its intentions vis-à-vis the Golan Heights rather than an accident, as the Israelis claim. The recently declassified U.S. documents do not provide any critical insights as to Israel's motives. For evidence on the U.S. stand toward the Golan issue, see Walt Rostow to President, 6 June 1967, in *LBJ Files,* reel 1 of 8. See also Eban, *An Autobiography,* pp. 421–422; William B. Quandt, *Decade of Decisions: American Policy Toward the Arab-Israeli Conflict, 1967–1976* (Berkeley: University of California Press, 1977), p. 63; Steven L. Spiegel, *The Other Arab-Israeli Conflict: Making America's Middle East Policy, from Truman to Reagan* (Chicago: University of Chicago Press, 1985), p. 151; Dayan, *Story of My Life,* p. 304.

23. U.S. Central Intelligence Agency (CIA), Memorandum for Walt W. Rostow, Subject: Objectives of the Middle East Combatants and the USSR, 6 June 1967, in *LBJ Files,* reel 1 of 8.

24. *Majmu'at Khutab wa tasrihat wa bayanat al-ra'is Gamal Abdel-Nasser, 23 Yulio 1952–1958* [The Collected Speeches, Declarations, and Statements of President Gamal 'Abd al-Nasser, 23 July 1952–1958], vol. 1 (Cairo: Hai'a al ist'lamat, n.d.), p. 617; *Wataiq Nasser, 1967–1968,* pp. 226, 243–248; Riad, *The Struggle for Peace in the Middle East,* p. 37; Sa'id Mar'iy, *Awraq siyasiya: Min'azma Mars ila al-naksa* [Political Papers: From the March Crisis

to the Disaster] (Cairo: Al-maktab al-Misri al-hadit, 1978), p. 362; Salah Nasr, *Abdel-Nasser wa tajriba al-wahda* [Nasser and the Unity Experience] (Cairo: Al-watan al-'arabi, 1976), vol. 1, p. 281; Heikal, *1967: Al-infijar,* p. 846; Heikal, *Sphinx and Commissar,* p. 72.

25. During his first meeting with King Hussein after the war, President Johnson informed his guest that he was "angry" with Egypt. H. M. King Hussein, *Mahammati kamalik* [My Profession as King] (Jordan: Al-sirka al-'arabiya iltiba'a wa nashr, 1978), p. 221. See also Hussein, *Harbuna ma'a Israil,* p. 95; Johnson, *The Vantage Point,* p. 303; Quandt, *Peace Process,* pp. 51, 54, 62; and Stephens, *Nasser: A Political Biography,* p. 522.

26. Richard B. Parker, *The Politics of Miscalculation in the Middle East* (Bloomington: Indiana University Press, 1993), p. 121.

27. Quandt, *Peace Process,* p. 61; Parker, *The Politics of Miscalculation,* p. 129; Robert Stookey, *America and the Arab States: An Uneasy Encounter* (London: John Wiley, 1975), p. 217.

28. Harriman to the President and Secretary of State, No. 19914, 6 June 1967, in *LBJ Files,* reel 1 of 8.

29. Walt Rostow to the President, No. 299, 7 June 1967; and Department of State to Embassy Paris, No. 209550, 8 June 1967, in ibid.

30. Department of State to Embassy Tehran, Subject: Middle East Crisis, No. 209086, 7 June 1967, in ibid.

31. Cairo to Secretary of State, No. 3292, 7 June 1967, in ibid.

32. Ibid. CIA, Memorandum for Walt W. Rostow, 6 June 1967; and Department of State, Subject: Middle East Crisis, Embassy Tehran, No. 209086, 7 June 1967, in ibid.

33. Harriman to the President, No. 6577, 8 June 1967; and Department of State to Embassy London, No. 208887, 7 June 1967, in ibid.

34. Riad, *The Struggle for Peace in the Middle East,* p. 83; Riad, *Mudhakkirat,* vol. 3, p. 73; *Wataiq Nasser, 1967–1968,* p. 306; Amin Huweidi, *Hurub Abdel-Nasser* ['Abd al-Nasser's Wars] (Cairo: Dar al-mauqif al-'arabi, 1982), p. 149.

35. Walt Rostow to the President, No. 299, 7 June 1967; Department of State to Embassy London, No. 208887, 7 June 1967; and NSC Memorandum for Walt Rostow, Subject: Reactions to Your Paper of 7 June 1967, 8 June 1967, *LBJ Files,* reel 1 of 8.

36. Richard Helms, CIA, to Walt Rostow, Subject: Israeli Objectives in the Current Crisis—Soviet Policy Miscalculation, 6 June 1967, in ibid.

37. Embassy Tel Aviv to Secretary of State, No. 3998, 7 June 1967, in ibid.

38. Department of State to Embassy Tehran, Subject: Middle East Crisis, No. 209086, 7 June 1967; and Harriman to the President, No. 6577, 8 June 1967, in ibid.

39. Henry Kissinger, *White House Years* (Boston: Little, Brown, 1979), p. 1262; George Lenczowski, *American Presidents and the Middle East* (Durham, N.C.: Duke University Press, 1990), pp. 116–140; Quandt, *Decade of Decisions,* p. 9.

40. Johnson, *The Vantage Point,* pp. 303–304, and Quandt, *Peace Process,* p. 55.

41. David Kimche and Dan Bawly, *The Sandstorm, the Arab-Israeli War of June 1967: Prelude and Aftermath* (New York: Stein and Day, 1968), pp. 279, 281; Riad, *The Struggle for Peace in the Middle East,* pp. 39, 55; Quandt, *Decade of Decisions,* p. 64.

42. Strong U.S. support of Israel in the post-Nixon Doctrine and post-Jordanian civil war period was not as big a shift in U.S. foreign policy as popularly thought. All that Nixon did was to carry further the change in U.S. policy toward Israel that was inaugurated by Johnson after the 1967 war.

43. NSC, Memorandum for Walt Rostow, 8 June 1967, *LBJ Files,* reel 1 of 8. Quandt, *Peace Process,* pp. 54, 57.

44. *Wataiq Nasser, 1967–1968,* pp. 221, 226, 242–243; Baghdadi, *Mudhakirat* [Memoirs], pp. 274–275, 298–299.

45. *Wataiq Nasser, 1967–1968,* pp. 221, 226, 242–243; Heikal, *1967: Al-infijar,* p. 754; Cairo to Secretary of State, No. 3292, 7 June 1967; Soviet Objectives in the Middle East, No. 41, 2 January 1968, *LBJ Files,* reels 1 and 7 of 8 respectively; Riad, *The Struggle for Peace in the Middle East,* pp. 29–30, 36–37; Riad, *Mudhakkirat,* vol. 2, p. 46; Hamroush, *Qissa taura 23 Yulio,* vol. 5, pp. 126–163, 188–189; Heikal, *Sphinx and Commissar,* p. 181; Stephens, *Nasser: A Political Biography,* p. 511.

46. Anwar Sadat, *In Search of Identity: An Autobiography* (London: Collins, 1978), pp. 172–173; Munir Hafez, "Al-tarik al-sirri lihukm Gamal Abdel-Nasser," *Rose al-Yusif,* No. 2498, 26 April 1976, pp. 22–23; Baghdadi, *Mudhakirat* [Memoirs], vol. 2, p. 298; Anouar Abdel-Malek, *Egypt: Military Society, the Army Regime, the Left, and Social Change Under Nasser,* trans. Charles Markmann (New York: Random House, 1968), viii; Heikal, *Sphinx,* p. 191; Heikal, *1967: Al-infijar,* pp. 773, 916–918; Hamroush, *Qissa taura 23 Yulio,* vol. 5, p. 186.

47. *Wataiq Nasser, 1967–1968,* pp. 261, 268; Riad, *The Struggle for Peace in the Middle East,* pp. 42–45; Farid, *Min muhadarat,* pp. 29–30, 34, 41; Fawzi, *Harb october am 1973,* pp. 189, 194–195; Heikal, *Sphinx,* p. 193; Hamroush, *Qissa taura 23 Yulio,* vol. 5, p. 186.

48. Stookey, *America and the Arab States,* p. 215.

49. Riad, *The Struggle for Peace in the Middle East,* pp. 49–50, 84; Farid, *Min muhadarat,* pp. 40, 52, 54–61; Fawzi, *Harb october am 1973,* p. 346; Heikal, *1967: Al-infijar,* pp. 788, 914; Heikal, *Sphinx,* pp. 185–188; Huweidi, *Hurub Abdel-Nasser,* p. 150; Hamroush, *Qissa taura 23 Yulio,* p. 288.

50. Heikal, *1967: Al-infijar,* pp. 896, 912–913, 936; Heikal, *Sphinx,* p. 195; Riad, *The Struggle for Peace in the Middle East,* p. 48; Sadat, *In Search of Identity,* pp. 181, 196.

51. Cited in Sadat, *In Search of Identity,* pp. 187, 197; Heikal, *Sphinx,* pp. 193–194.

52. Sadat, *In Search of Identity,* p. 199. The Rogers Initiative was a limited diplomatic initiative designed to convince the Israelis and Egyptians to "stop shooting" and "start talking." The U.S.-proposed cease-fire went into effect in August 1970.

53. Ibid., p. 198.

54. *Wataiq Nasser: Khutab, ahadit, tasrihat: Yanayir 1969-Siptember 1970* [Nasser's Documents: Speeches, Discussions, and Declarations, January 1969-September 1970] (Cairo: Markaz al-dirasat al-siyasiya wa al-istratijiya bi Al-Ahram, 1973), p. 303 (hereinafter, this series will be referred to as *Wataiq Nasser, 1969–1970*); Riad, *The Struggle for Peace in the Middle East,* pp. 94, 96; Heikal, *Sphinx,* p. 198; Quandt, *Peace Process,* p. 77.

55. *Wataiq Nasser, 1969–1970,* pp. 371–372.

56. Sadat, *In Search of Identity,* p. 198.

57. T. Petran, *Syria* (London: Ernest Benn, 1972), p. 201. Syrian rulers were silent, however, about their own procrastination and passivity during the first two days of fighting and about their slow response to Egyptian and Jordanian urgent appeals for help. On June 6, in its report on the military situation on the Israeli-Jordanian front, the U.S. embassy in Jordan made note of Syria's poor response—the "bare minimum to help out since [the] beginning of the conflict." See Amman to Department of State, No. 4098, 6 June 1967, *LBJ Files,* reel 1 of 8. This stand should be measured against the fact that since the early 1960s, Damascus had been pushing the Arab world toward an armed confrontation with Israel. The behavior of the Syrian leaders, writes Patrick Seale, could be explained by the scale and speed of the war that caught them off-balance and mentally unprepared for Israel's all-out, highly mobile blitzkrieg. Patrick Seale, *Asad of Syria* (London: I. B. Tauris, 1988), pp. 138–139, 144; Majid Khadduri, *Republican Iraq: A*

Study of Iraqi Politics Since the Revolution of 1958 (London: Oxford University Press, 1969), p. 291; Marion Farouk-Sluglett and Peter Sluglett, *Iraq Since 1958: From Revolution to Dictatorship* (London: KPI, 1987), p. 100; Hamroush, *Qissa taura 23 Yulio,* p. 202; Riad, *The Struggle for Peace in the Middle East,* p. 55; Stephens, *Nasser: A Political Biography,* p. 521.

58. Farid, *Min muhadarat,* p. 81; Hussein, *Harbuna,* p. 97; Heikal, *1967: Al-infijar,* pp. 932, 935; Stookey, *America and the Arab States,* p. 213.

59. Hussein insisted, however, on a collective Arab strategy toward the question of peace with Israel. Riad, *Mudhakkirat,* vol. 3, pp. 47–48; Hussein, *Mahammati kamalik,* p. 228.

60. A few months earlier Nasser had asked his prime minister to discuss with U.S. officials the possibility of a peaceful solution to the Arab-Israeli conflict. The head of the Egyptian intelligence was also told to maintain contacts with the CIA. In November 1967, Nasser publicly declared that Egypt was talking to the United States because "we could not let anger determine our policy." *Wataiq Nasser, 1967–1968,* pp. 248, 288; Farid, *Min muhadarat,* p. 98; Riad, *Mudhakkirat,* p. 50; Hamroush, *Qissa taura 23 Yulio,* pp. 288–289, 342–343.

61. Mohamed Ahmed Mahgoub, *Democracy on Trial: Reflections on Arab and African Affairs* (London: Andre Deutsch, 1974), p. 145; Riad, *The Struggle for Peace in the Middle East,* p. 54.

62. Mahgoub, *Democracy on Trial,* p. 146; United Arab Republic, No. 41, 2 January 1968, *LBJ Files,* reel 7 of 8; *Wataiq Nasser, 1967–1968,* pp. 289–290; Hussein, *Harbuna,* p. 97; *Majmu'at khutab al-malik Hussein: 25 'ammn min al-tarikh, 1952–1977* [The Collected Speeches of King Hussein: 25 Years of History, 1952–1977], vol. 1 (London: Samir Mutawi's Company for Publication, 1978), p. 662; Wasfi Tal, *Kitabat fi al-qadaya al-'arabiya* [Writings on Arab Issues] (Jordan: Dar al-liwa lisihafa wa nashr, 1980), p. 486; Saad Abu Wardiya, *'Amaliya itiakad al-qarar fi siyasa al-Urdunn al-kharijiya* [The Making of Jordan's Foreign Policy] (Jordan: Daira wa al-taqafa wa al-funun, 1983), p. 251; Peter Snow, *Hussein: A Biography* (London: Barrie and Jenkins, 1972), pp. 198, 251; Riad, *The Struggle for Peace in the Middle East,* pp. 38, 53–56; Farid, *Min muhadarat,* p. 92; Hamroush, *Qissa taura 23 Yulio,* pp. 235, 244; Stephens, *Nasser: A Political Biography,* p. 523.

63. Although the French text included the definite article, its absence from the English text was partly to preserve ambiguity and partly a product of U.S. pressure in the United Nations. The removal of the definite article affected later interpretations of UN Resolution 242, especially by the Israelis.

64. *Wataiq Nasser, 1967–1968,* pp. 429, 481, 590; *Wataiq Nasser, 1969–1970,* p. 301; Riad, *The Struggle for Peace in the Middle East,* pp. 91–92; Riad, *Mudhakkirat,* pp. 76, 80, 94, 103; Mohammed Fawzi, *Mudhakkirat al-Fariq awwal Mohammed Fawzi: Harb al-talat sanawat, 1967–1970* (Damascus: Tlasdar, 1986), p. 202; Huweidi, *Hurub Abdel-Nasser,* p. 152.

65. Riad, *The Struggle for Peace in the Middle East,* pp. 25, 38, 77; Fawzi, *Harb al-talat sanawat,* p. 192; Heikal, *1967: Al-infijar,* p. 887.

66. *Wataiq Nasser, 1967–1968,* p. 498; Riad, *The Struggle for Peace in the Middle East,* p. 39.

67. As a result of the stalemate in the diplomatic arena, the situation deteriorated significantly in the Middle East in spring 1969. Fighting erupted along the Suez Canal, and in April Nasser announced the abrogation of the cease-fire, signaling the onset of the War of Attrition, which lasted until the Rogers Initiative cease-fire in August 1970. *Wataiq Nasser, 1967–1968,* pp. 289–290; Riad, *The Struggle for Peace in the Middle East,* pp. 75, 77–78, 88, 101; Huweidi, *Hurub Abdel-Nasser,* p. 147; Heikal, *1967: Al-infijar,* p. 937; Heikal, *Sphinx,* pp. 191–192; Heikal, *The Road to Ramadan,* p. 56; Stephens, *Nasser: A Political Biography,* p. 518.

68. Cited in Parker, *The Politics of Miscalculation in the Middle East,* p. 128.

13

Flawed Strategies and Missed Signals: Crisis Bargaining Between the Superpowers, October 1973

Janice Gross Stein

On the night of October 24, 1973, the Soviet Union proposed joint military intervention with the United States to end the fighting that had begun when Egypt and Syria attacked Israel eighteen days earlier. After intense fighting, as well as massive Soviet and U.S. airlifts of military supplies to the belligerents (the Soviet Union to Egypt and Syria, the United States to Israel), the Egyptian army was in a perilous position. Israel's forces had crossed the Suez Canal and, despite a cease-fire ordered by the United Nations (UN) Security Council, had advanced to cut off Egypt's Third Army. Moscow warned that if joint U.S.-Soviet action were impossible, it would consider taking unilateral action to halt Israel's military offensive. In response, the United States alerted its nuclear and conventional forces worldwide in an attempt to deter Soviet military intervention. The superpowers found themselves in a dangerous confrontation.

The crisis had developed when least expected, after Soviet General Secretary Leonid Brezhnev and U.S. Secretary of State Henry Kissinger had jointly negotiated the terms of a cease-fire on October 23. Both leaders wanted to stop the fighting and to avoid a crisis between their countries. Moreover, they shared the same tactical objectives: In the wake of Israel's stunning battlefield successes, the United States now fully shared the Soviet Union's interest in ending the war before the Egyptian Third Army was destroyed. Brezhnev and Kissinger were also in constant communication with each other. Under these conditions, no crisis should have occurred. Yet, despite shared objectives and an agreement negotiated between Moscow and Washington, a serious crisis erupted, one that ended in confrontation.

Good bargaining might have averted the crisis and avoided the confrontation, since the zone of agreement between the United States and the Soviet Union was really very wide. At the least, bargaining strategies that read intentions more or less accurately and were signaled clearly could have minimized the damage from a confrontation. Bargaining should certainly not exacerbate the crisis and create the confrontation. Yet both Soviet and U.S. strategies made the crisis more, not less, difficult to manage, contributed heavily to the confrontation, and did long-term damage to the relationship. Bargaining by both superpowers in 1973 was deeply flawed and potentially dangerous. This chapter explores Soviet and U.S. strategies at the end of the 1973 Arab-Israeli war as a textbook case of inappropriate bargaining.

The Context of the Conflict

Egypt and Syria launched a surprise attack against Israel on October 6, 1973. President Anwar Sadat of Egypt decided to go to war because he had lost hope that negotiation could successfully address the issue of Israel's occupation of the Sinai Peninsula. He felt his diplomatic overtures regarding an agreement over the Sinai in the few years preceding the war had been ignored by both Israel and the United States, and therefore he believed that war was his only recourse to reactivate diplomacy and improve his bargaining position. Israel's control of the Sinai, the Golan, the West Bank, and the Gaza Strip emerged from the 1967 Arab-Israeli war, which was precipitated by Egypt's expulsion of a UN peacekeeping force (in place since the end of the 1956 Suez crisis) and a blockade of the Strait of Tiran.

The fighting on both fronts was intense. Israel's army, caught by surprise, took several days to launch a counteroffensive, and it succeeded only after very heavy fighting pushed Syria's army back across the cease-fire lines. The Soviet leadership, anticipating serious Syrian and Egyptian military losses, began a massive airlift and sea lift to its allies, and U.S. President Richard M. Nixon and Secretary of State Kissinger, after an agonizing debate, decided to match the Soviet airlift with a U.S. airlift to Israel. The choice was so difficult because Kissinger was determined to seize the opportunity provided by the war to fracture the Soviet-Egyptian alliance and position the United States as the linchpin of postwar negotiations between Egypt and Israel (and simultaneously not endanger the primary administration foreign policy focus, i.e., détente; however, both superpowers became, through the airlifts, implicated in the war through their respective client-states in the region).

Once assured of resupply, Israel's armies went on the offensive against Egypt and penetrated Egyptian lines on the western bank of the Suez Canal. As the threat to Egypt grew, Brezhnev invited Kissinger to Moscow to negotiate a cease-fire resolution to be put before the UN Security Council. When the cease-fire went into effect, there were no UN observers in the field to determine the positions of both belligerents. A few hours after Egypt and Israel accepted the cease-fire Brezhnev and Kissinger had negotiated, fighting renewed on October 23. Egypt and Israel each accused the other of violating the cease-fire first, but the Israel Defense Forces (IDF) clearly took advantage of the violations to complete the encirclement of the Egyptian Third Army.

In Moscow the crisis developed in two phases. As fighting continued on October 23 and 24, Brezhnev anticipated a catastrophic military defeat of Egypt and a concomitant blow to the reputation of the Soviet Union as ally and arms supplier to the Third World. The road to Cairo was undefended and Egypt was on the verge of military disaster. Brezhnev also felt pressed for time. By October 24, the Soviet Union had only hours to prevent an Egyptian defeat. Here too, his sense of urgency was grounded in reality.

The second phase of the crisis began for Soviet leaders after the United States alerted its forces worldwide. Brezhnev and the Politburo were surprised and angered by the U.S. alert; they met on October 25 for eight hours, in an angry and tense session. In this final phase of the confrontation, Politburo members did not worry about an intentional attack by the United States. Nevertheless, they were intensely angered and greatly disappointed by the U.S. action and seriously concerned about the possibility of inadvertent escalation.

In Washington, the crisis also developed in two distinct but related phases, each following the other in rapid succession. In both phases, U.S. officials perceived a threat, but the nature of the threat changed rapidly under the pressure of events during the course of thirty-six hours. Within hours after his return from Tel Aviv on the morning of October 23, Kissinger learned of the cease-fire violations and received an urgent message from Brezhnev. He worried about the consequences of the destruction of the Egyptian Third Army for U.S. relations with Egypt—and with the Soviet Union. "The Egyptian Third Army on the east bank of the Canal was totally cut off," Kissinger explained. "A crisis was upon us."[1]

Nixon and Kissinger knew that the destruction of the Egyptian Third Army was unacceptable to Moscow. They also shared the Soviet objective of preventing an Egyptian defeat because it would seriously compromise their central objective of creating a postwar political monopoly. Kissinger not only understood Soviet constraints, he shared the estimate regarding the limited time available before the Egyptian Third Army would collapse. From early on October 23 until the evening of October 24, Kissinger identified a threat to U.S. objectives, empathized with Soviet concerns, and considered it urgent to halt Israel's offensive.

Once Brezhnev proposed joint intervention and then warned that he would consider acting alone if necessary to stop the fighting, the nature of the crisis changed dramatically. Kissinger framed the problem as a threat not only to U.S. interests in the Middle East but to U.S. interests worldwide. If the United States backed down, he believed, its bargaining reputation in future encounters with the Soviet Union would be fundamentally compromised.[2] From Washington's perspective, the crisis was now primarily in the U.S.-Soviet relationship. Kissinger, unlike his Soviet counterparts, did not worry about the risk of inadvertent escalation but focused on the threat to the U.S. reputation for resolve.

Although they considered the risk of war to be low, Kissinger and his colleagues in the White House Situation Room nevertheless felt an acute sense of urgency. If the Soviet Union intended to send troops, they would do so in a matter of hours. They had very limited time to find an appropriate way to signal their determination to resist any deployment of Soviet forces in the Middle East. Although leaders in Moscow and Washington felt pressed for different reasons, the sense of urgency was real and shared, though not equally, in both capitals.

U.S. Compellence

I begin with an analysis of U.S. bargaining with Israel. Thirty-six hours elapsed between reports of the first violations of the cease-fire and Kissinger's receipt of Brezhnev's letter on the night of October 24. Initially, Kissinger made a less than vigorous effort to compel Israel to hold its hand. By October 24, however, *before* Brezhnev issued his threat, Washington tried vigorously to compel Israel to stop the fighting. U.S. compellence succeeded, but it was too late. The threat to the Egyptian Third Army had provoked Brezhnev to raise the specter of unilateral intervention. There was also a fundamental ambiguity in U.S. strategy: As the United States repeatedly warned Israel against the "destruction" of the Third Army and urged an immediate end to the fighting, it tacitly acquiesced in its encirclement. And an encircled Third Army was a ticking time bomb.

On October 23, Kissinger learned from Israel that all roads to the Egyptian Third Army had been cut. He immediately tried to arrange a second cease-fire through the United Nations in collaboration with Moscow. Israeli Prime Minister Golda Meir, in a "blistering communication," informed Kissinger that Israel would not comply with or even discuss the proposed resolution.[3] Kissinger did not threaten Israel but persisted, over its objections, in negotiating a second cease-fire. He noted that it called for a return to a line that "we had carefully not specified."[4] In so doing, he signaled Jerusalem that the United States was willing to tolerate, at least for the moment, an IDF encirclement of the Egyptian Third Army.[5]

When Kissinger learned of renewed fighting early on the morning of October 24, he made a vigorous effort to compel Israel to observe the cease-fire. He threatened to leave Israel alone if its actions provoked Soviet intervention.[6] In an effort to underline the seriousness of U.S. intent, Kissinger asked Alexander Haig, the president's chief of staff, to call Israel's ambassador in the United States, Simcha Dinitz, to demand, on behalf of the president, an immediate end to offensive military action by Israel.[7] Israel's response was positive but laced with ambiguity: The IDF was trying to absorb Egyptian fire without responding, it would not try to advance, and Israel would keep the U.S. ambassador in Israel, Kenneth Keating, fully informed "in a further effort to calm the Secretary and demonstrate Israeli good intentions."[8]

Even though U.S. efforts to stop the fighting succeeded, the trapped Egyptian Third Army was still at risk because it had nearly exhausted its food, water, and medical supplies. By the time Ambassador Dinitz assured Kissinger that the fighting had stopped, desperate Egyptian President Anwar Sadat had already made his request for joint action by the United States and the Soviet Union.

Thus, U.S. compellence worked, but it was too little and too late to do any good. Although Israel had promised not to advance any further, Kissinger observed that "this [the Israeli reply] left open the possibility of a war of attrition designed to use up Egyptian supplies and force the surrender of the Third Army."[9] The United States had not yet tried seriously to compel Jerusalem to permit food and medical supplies for the Third Army through their lines. Joseph Sisco, assistant secretary of state for Near Eastern and South Asian affairs, explained why the United States concentrated so heavily on an end to the fighting:

> We put enormous pressure on Israel on October 23 and 24. We pressed first on the ceasefire, then on the siege of Suez City, and finally on the encirclement of the Third Army. We pressed hardest on the ceasefire, because that was the first priority: We wanted to stop the fighting. The distinction among the three issues was not that sharp in our minds. We concentrated on what we had to accomplish urgently. We succeeded in stopping the fighting by the afternoon of October 24.[10]

Shortage of time and fast-moving events on the battlefield led Kissinger to concentrate on the urgent and difficult task at hand.

It is not surprising, then, that it took the extraordinary threat from the United States to abandon Israel to face Soviet intervention alone to compel Jerusalem to halt its military operations. Even then, the United States achieved only the first of several objectives. Kissinger understood that he was asking Israel to exchange a tangible gain on the battlefield for a vague U.S. promise about a peace process in the future and acknowledged how difficult it was for Israel's cabinet to see the logic of this kind of concession.[11] Given his understanding of the forces propelling Israel's behavior, it is surprising that he expected to succeed in compelling Israel to observe the cease-fire before it had consolidated its military victory. Despite its dependence on the United States for military and diplomatic support, Tel Aviv framed the conflict very differently than did Washington. The Israeli leaders used every resource at their disposal to secure the military victory they and their population desperately wanted. Under these conditions, only an extraordinary effort would permit U.S. compellence to succeed.

The Soviet Resort to Compellence

On October 24 at 9:35 P.M. Washington time, Ambassador Anatoliy Dobrynin, the Soviet envoy to Washington, called Kissinger with an urgent letter from Brezhnev. Dobrynin read Kissinger the most important passages:

> Let us together, the USSR and the United States, urgently dispatch to Egypt the Soviet and American military contingents, to insure the implementation of the decision of the Security Council of October 22 and 23 concerning the cessation of fire and of all mil-

itary activities and also of our understanding with you on the guarantee of the implementation of the decisions of the Security Council. . . . It is necessary to adhere without delay. I will say it straight that if you find it impossible to act jointly with us in this matter, we should be faced with the necessity urgently to consider the question of taking appropriate steps unilaterally. We cannot allow arbitrariness on the part of Israel.[12]

When Brezhnev sent his letter to Nixon, there was significant activity by Soviet paratroops and naval forces. On October 23, Moscow ordered two of its amphibious ships, which had been anchored off the coast of Syria, to steam for Egypt.[13] Early the next morning, a Soviet helicopter carrier and two destroyers were moved from their positions off Crete to relieve the Soviet anticarrier group covering the USS *Independence*. Four Soviet airborne divisions were on ready-to-move status and an in-flight command post was also established in the southern Soviet Union.[14] Preparations were made for the imminent departure of several airborne units, and transport aircraft were loaded. Communications nets surged with activity, and flight plans for the next day were changed.[15] The Soviet Union also halted its airlift to Egypt, thereby freeing significant numbers of transport aircraft.[16]

Soviet officials all agree that Brezhnev's proposal of joint U.S.-Soviet military action was a serious signal, for the appeal to the United States was genuine. However, it was based on a misunderstanding that grew directly out of the drafting of the cease-fire agreement, with an attached memorandum of understanding, by Foreign Minister Andrei Gromyko and Kissinger in Moscow. The third clause of the *draft* cease-fire resolution provided for negotiations "under appropriate auspices." To clarify the meaning of the phrase, Gromyko and Kissinger also prepared an additional document that was not made public. The document read:

> It is understood that the phrase "under appropriate auspices" in Point 3 of the resolution shall mean that the negotiations between the parties concerned will take place with the active participation of the United States and the Soviet Union at the beginning, and thereafter, in the course of negotiations when key issues of a settlement are dealt with. Throughout the entire process of negotiation, the United States and the Soviet Union will in any case maintain the closest contact with each other and the negotiating parties.[17]

Brezhnev did not see either the private document, which was initialed by Gromyko and Kissinger, or the final text of the cease-fire resolution, which was drafted hurriedly by Kissinger, Sisco, and Gromyko and quickly cabled from Moscow to the United Nations and to Cairo and Damascus. President Sadat interpreted "appropriate auspices" as a U.S.-Soviet guarantee to enforce the cease-fire if necessary.[18] The Soviet Ambassador to Egypt, Vladimir Vinogradov, reported Sadat's understanding that the United States and the Soviet Union had "guaranteed" the cease-fire to Moscow.

The confusion arose when the Politburo met on October 23 to discuss the appropriate response to the continued violations of the cease-fire. At the meeting, members of the Politburo argued that the agreement reached in Moscow "obligated" the United States and the Soviet Union to take the steps necessary to implement the resolution that had been adopted by the UN Security Council. Victor Israelian, then the head of the Department of International Organization in the Soviet Foreign Ministry, was present at almost all the Politburo meetings and took detailed notes. He explained:

> The formula "under appropriate auspices" was interpreted as joint action by the USA and the USSR to guarantee the ceasefire in the Near East. For instance, [Prime Minister Alexei] Kosygin suggested at the Politburo meeting that a joint Soviet-American team of military officials should be sent to observe the ceasefire. His idea was that this group should include 200 or 250 observers from each of the two states. Kosygin was supported by Ustinov. They thought that this step should be agreed upon with the Americans and that the Americans should be reminded that, when Kissinger visited Moscow, an agreement was reached to "act as guarantors."[19]

The interpretation given the critical clause by Brezhnev and Kosygin did not go unchallenged at the Politburo meeting. Gromyko explained how the term "under appropriate auspices" had been interpreted in the document that he and Kissinger had initialed. He insisted that the dispatch of Soviet and U.S. personnel would require approval by the UN Security Council; most likely, China would veto such a resolution. Besides, Gromyko added, there were already UN personnel in Cairo.[20]

Kosygin irritably dismissed Gromyko's objections: "That's all formalities. They [the UN Truce Supervisory Organization personnel] are dead souls," he insisted. "The fact is that both we and the Americans committed ourselves to carrying out the Security Council decision and we should proceed from that assumption. Action is needed."[21] Brezhnev was adamant that the United States and the Soviet Union should cooperate in sending military personnel as "guarantors" of the cease-fire. At his urging, the Politburo agreed to make this suggestion to the United States.[22]

Thus, Brezhnev was signaling a serious intent to cooperate in enforcing an end to the fighting. He hoped that the United States and the Soviet Union would act together to enforce the cease-fire as the capstone of détente. The first part of his letter to Nixon was not a threat but an offer of collaboration based on what he thought was a joint understanding of their responsibilities. As bizarre as the proposal would sound in Washington, collective enforcement action was considered realistic in Moscow.[23]

The last sentence of Brezhnev's letter to Nixon is more controversial. Brezhnev warned that "if you find it impossible to act jointly with us in this matter, we should be faced with the necessity urgently to consider the question of taking appropriate steps unilaterally."[24] Brezhnev did not explicitly threaten the use of military force, but his tone was menacing. This sentence was not in the original draft of the letter prepared for Brezhnev by Gromyko. Brezhnev added the warning at the last moment before the letter was sent.[25]

There is debate about the course that Brezhnev would have followed if the United States rejected the proposal for joint action. There is good evidence that Brezhnev was bluffing, that he was not prepared to act unilaterally and send Soviet forces to Egypt.

Some Soviet officials considered that the Soviet Union would actually have sent forces if the fighting had not stopped. Vadim Zagladin, who was deputy director of the International Relations Department of the Central Committee, reported that Soviet leaders considered military intervention in the Cairo region.[26] Anatoliy Gromyko, who was in the Soviet Embassy in Washington on October 24, was more cautious: "The Soviet Union seriously considered intervention. The plan was to send troops to the Cairo region. We would have put a cordon around Cairo. On the other hand, we were anxious not to get involved in the fighting. Some of my colleagues might say that this [Brezhnev's letter] was only a form of political pressure."[27] General Yuri Yakovlevich Kirshin of the Red Army confirmed that military leaders were asked to prepare contingency plans for the optimum use of Soviet paratroopers.[28]

Soviet officials with more detailed knowledge of the Politburo meeting deny that the Soviet Union would have sent troops to Cairo. They insist that Brezhnev's threat was a bluff. Ambassador Dobrynin, who was in Washington on October 24 but in close contact with Soviet leaders, doubted that the Soviet Union would have sent troops.[29] Georgi Kornienko, head of the U.S. desk in the Soviet Foreign Ministry and one of the four members of the special working group drafted to work with the Politburo, was adamant: "I am absolutely certain that there were no plans to send Soviet forces to the Middle East. They were put on alert to put pressure on the Americans."[30] Israelian insists that the warning was a bluff, that the Soviet Union had no intention whatsoever of sending troops to Egypt: "Kulikov [the chief of staff of the military] opposed sending any officers there. He opposed sending even observers without a disengagement of Israeli and Egyptian forces. Members of the Politburo had not the slightest desire, on any level, to send forces. There might have been some contingency planning by the military, but there was no intention to send forces."[31]

At the Politburo meeting on October 23, there was no discussion whatsoever of sending regular forces, only military observers. The Politburo did not meet on October 24, before Brezhnev's letter was sent, nor did it discuss his message after the fact. Gromyko drafted the message for Brezhnev and the two walked and talked with a few colleagues in the corridor.[32] "It was not a considered decision," Israelian explained. "No formal decision was ever made by the Politburo to threaten military intervention. Brezhnev added the threat to put pressure on Nixon to get the fighting stopped. He wanted to put pressure on the United States. He thought it was a clever thing to do."[33]

The threat to consider unilateral action to stabilize the cease-fire was the last in a series of steps taken by the Soviet Union, all with a common political purpose. In the first instance, Brezhnev hoped that joint action with the United States would end the fighting. The threat that the Soviet Union might act alone was added at the last moment to signal to the United States the seriousness of Soviet interests at stake. Brezhnev hoped that if joint action were impossible, the threat that the Soviet Union would consider sending forces would be enough to compel the United States to stop Israel, that the visible preparation of Soviet troops and his warning would succeed in stabilizing the cease-fire and remove the danger to Cairo.

Brezhnev acted in response to four reinforcing considerations: the failure of intensive negotiations with the United States to stop the fighting; the need to safeguard the political position of proponents of détente at home; the reputation of the Soviet Union as a reliable ally; and the multiplicative effect of anger fueled by a sharp sense of betrayal. Counteracting these pressures was a keen appreciation of the risks of any deployment of forces and the desire to avoid a confrontation with the United States.

The first three motives are obvious and easily understood. Brezhnev's decision was also motivated by fury at what he considered to be Kissinger's duplicity. Brezhnev, prone to intensely emotional reactions, suspected—wrongly—that Kissinger had deliberately deceived him and encouraged Israel to violate the cease-fire. Soviet officials, in interviews, referred again and again to Brezhnev's acute sense of betrayal and anger on October 24. Dobrynin described Brezhnev's reaction in vivid detail: "He was very emotional. He felt deceived by Nixon and Kissinger. I was worried about our relations with the United States and worried that Brezhnev's anger with Nixon and Kissinger would lead him to do something rash."[34] Kosygin was also infuriated. At the Politburo meeting on October 25, he charged that "Kissinger visited Moscow, lied to us, went to Tel Aviv, and fraternized with the Israeli people."[35] Israelian recalled that "the fact that the United States refused to cooperate in regulating the Near-Eastern crisis irritated us and made us suspect that Kissinger was acting behind the back of the Soviet Union."[36] Soviet officials felt especially betrayed because they thought that Kissinger had violated the rules of the game that had been mutually agreed upon during the meeting in Moscow.

The pressures acting on Brezhnev could well have led him to decide to send forces to Egypt if Israel did not halt its military offensive and Cairo became directly threatened. The Soviet Union certainly had the capability to move forces quickly to Cairo West Airfield. Soviet General Alexander Ivanovich Vladimirov insists that had the Soviet Union wanted to send paratroops to Egypt, it would have taken very little time; four paratroop divisions were at full readiness and needed only twenty-four-hour notice before they could board transport aircraft for deployment.[37] The Soviet Union did not have the airlift capability for four divisions, but some movement of troops could have begun quickly.[38]

Soviet leaders, however, were sensitive to the risks of escalation and confrontation that could grow out of a deployment of Soviet conventional forces in Egypt. "Of course, it was a situation of the utmost danger," explained Anatoliy Gromyko. "The possibility that the Soviet Union would be involved in military action was real. . . . There was a real possibility of escalation, the consequences of which I cannot envisage."[39] Brezhnev worried about the escalation that could result from any deployment of Soviet troops. His fear of escalation led him to reject any Soviet military involvement in the fighting. As soon as the war began, he repeatedly made his opposition to the dispatch of Soviet troops clear to his colleagues in the Politburo and to President Sadat. It is very likely that when Brezhnev added that last threatening sentence to an otherwise temperate draft message, he was driven by anger and intense emotion. Anxious about the fate of Egypt, despairing of diplomacy, and angry at Kissinger's alleged deceit—yet fearful of the escalatory consequences of unilateral intervention—Brezhnev decided first to propose joint intervention, and then to bargain through bluff. He saw no alternative.[40]

Brezhnev miscalculated badly. His attempt at compellence did not accomplish his immediate or long-term political purposes. The United States misread the message intended and responded with a worldwide alert to signal its own resolve. The Soviet threat failed utterly to elicit the desired response.

The U.S. Resort to Deterrence

The United States responded to the Soviet threat with a worldwide alert of its forces.[41] At 11:41 P.M., about an hour after the meeting began in the White House Situation Room, Admiral Thomas Moorer, the chairman of the Joint Chiefs of Staff, issued orders to all military commands to increase readiness to Defense Condition III (DEFCON III).[42] At 12:20 A.M. on October 25, U.S. intelligence reported that eight Soviet Antonov-22 transport planes were scheduled to fly from Budapest to Egypt within the next few hours and that elements of the East German armed forces had been alerted. In response, the 82nd Airborne Division was ordered to be ready to deploy within four hours. At 12:25 A.M., the aircraft carrier *Franklin Delano Roosevelt* was sent to the eastern Mediterranean and the carrier *John F. Kennedy,* with its task force, was ordered to move at full speed from the Atlantic to the Mediterranean.[43]

Those who participated in the meeting in the White House Situation Room on the night of October 24 were divided in their estimate of Soviet intentions. Some thought the Soviet Union was bluffing; others thought that Moscow would send a limited number of forces to Egypt. Brezhnev's letter and the intelligence data on Soviet military preparations were consistent with both a bluff and a serious intent to deploy forces in the Middle East.

These differences were not important as to the appropriate response chosen by U.S. officials. Those who thought that the Soviet Union might deploy a limited number of forces were determined to deny the Soviet Union political and military opportunity in the Middle East. Those who thought that the Soviet Union was bluffing also accepted the necessity of an alert. Secretary of Defense James Schlesinger, Moorer, and Haig agreed with Kissinger that an alert was the appropriate response to Brezhnev's challenge. Schlesinger argued that even if the probability of Soviet military action were low, the United States must demonstrate that it could act firmly.[44]

The alert served two purposes. If the Soviet Union was indeed intent upon unilateral military action, the alert's immediate objective would be to deter the Soviet deployment. The Nixon administration determined to deny Moscow this opportunity to introduce military forces into the Middle East. Secondarily, the alert was designed to bank resolve and build reputation for future bargaining. If Brezhnev was bluffing, the alert would "educate" the Soviet leadership. It was imperative to demonstrate resolve to convince Brezhnev that the United States could not be coerced by Moscow. Washington wanted to demonstrate resolve firmly, visibly, and quickly. Everyone present at the White House meeting agreed quickly on the necessity of an immediate, highly visible signal that would be noticed rapidly by Soviet leaders and would either "shock" them into abandoning any intention to intervene with military force or would call their bluff.[45]

The worldwide alert was a singularly inappropriate signal on the part of the United States. It was ineffective, potentially dangerous, and ill-considered. It was inherently ineffective because in the context of the Middle East any kind of nuclear threat was disproportionate and not credible. It was potentially dangerous because it moved up the ladder of escalation and increased the risk of confrontation with the Soviet Union. Even more alarming, U.S. leaders made their decision with little attention to the technical and operational requirements of the alert, its risks, or its likely consequences. The alert was chosen in haste, with little consideration either of its capacity to deter Soviet military intervention or of the alternative measures that might have constituted an effective signal with a reduced risk of escalation.

The alert of the 82nd Airborne was also not a carefully crafted signal. William Quandt, then on the staff of the U.S. National Security Council, provides a detailed—and vivid—description of the decision in the White House:

> Later that night, we got a fragment of a message, the tail end of a message, suggesting the imminent arrival of Soviet forces at Cairo West airfield. Kissinger was frantic. He ordered Atherton [the deputy assistant secretary of state for Near Eastern and South Asian affairs] and me to draft a plan to send U.S. troops to the Middle East, immediately, but not to Israel. Atherton and I were bewildered. Where would the forces go? Kissinger replied that he did not know, but that the forces could not go to Israel, but that a plan was to be prepared immediately to deploy forces in the Middle East. This was the only time that Atherton and I were totally confused. We could not conceive of how to meet the request.[46]

After he briefed the president early the next morning, Kissinger recalls, "Nixon was determined to match any Soviet troop buildup in the area."[47] When asked what kind of conventional military action he wanted, Kissinger replied: "We would have put down the 82nd Airborne if the Soviets had sent forces. We never got to that point. We never discussed it. It would have been very dangerous. That's why you get paid, for doing the dangerous jobs."[48]

The possibility of failure of this deterrence received no serious attention, and no contingency plans were in place. There was no discussion of where U.S. troops were to be deployed, nor of the likelihood of combat with Soviet forces. "We had no plan for blocking [Soviet] intervention," confirms Peter Rodman, then special assistant to Kissinger. "We didn't think about it."[49] Thus, instead of considering the consequences and their options should deterrence fail, U.S. leaders merely hoped that deterrence would succeed.

If the Soviet Union had sent forces to Egypt, and the United States had responded with a conventional deployment of its own, even limited encounters between the two forces in the context of a worldwide alert could easily have escalated to a broadening of the conflict. The Soviet Union might have mobilized additional forces in response. Under this not-so-unlikely scenario, the worldwide alert could have worked against the localization and termination of the fighting in the Middle East—the principal objective of both Moscow and Washington.

The Irrelevance and Relevance of Deterrence

"The Soviets subsided," Kissinger claims, "as soon as we showed our teeth."[50] His argument suggests that despite strategic and conventional parity, and despite an acute domestic crisis in Washington (that being the Watergate scandal), the U.S. strategy had persuaded Soviet leaders that Nixon was willing to risk war to block unilateral intervention by Moscow.[51] Soviet leaders purportedly reevaluated the likely costs of intervention, changed their minds, and decided not to send troops to Egypt.

If deterrence is to work, the leaders who are considering military action must change course because they reconsider the likely costs and consequences in the face of the threatened deterrent. Even *before* the United States alerted its forces, however, Brezhnev had no intention of sending Soviet forces to Egypt. As early as October 8, he instructed Ambassador Vinogradov to emphasize Soviet determination not to become involved in the fighting.[52] Again, this time on October 15, during the Politburo meeting, Brezhnev warned Kosygin against misleading Sadat. Although the Soviet government was willing to continue military support to Egypt on a large scale, it would "under no circumstances participate directly in the war."[53] Brezhnev's threat to consider unilateral action was a bluff, issued in frustration at the failure of diplomacy to stop the fighting and in anger at what Brezhnev considered Kissinger's duplicity. Since Brezhnev had no intention of sending forces, deterrence could not have changed his mind. At best, it was irrelevant.

The consequences of the U.S. strategy were not irrelevant. Soviet leaders were genuinely bewildered by the alert; they could not decipher the U.S. "signal." They were also provoked and deeply angered by an action that they could not understand. Shortly after Soviet intelligence picked up signs of the alert, Brezhnev convened the Politburo early on the morning of October 25. The meeting was attended by almost all members, and discussion continued for more than eight hours. General Kulikov began with a briefing on the U.S. alert, including the alert of strategic nuclear forces.

Members of the Politburo had great difficulty interpreting the political intent of the alert. "They could not understand it," Israelian explained. "They asked: 'Are they [the Americans] crazy? The Americans say we threaten them, but how did they get this idea?'"[54] Gromyko was advised by Kornienko, Mikhail Sytenko, who then headed the Department of the Near East, and Israelian that the U.S. reaction was provoked by the last sentence of Brezhnev's letter to Nixon.[55] Brezhnev was incredulous when this explanation was suggested at the Politburo meeting. "Could this be the reason?" he asked. "Could Nixon choose an alert based on this one sentence? But this man Nixon knows that I stopped the airlift as a demonstration of my willingness to cooperate."[56]

Soviet officials were divided in their assessments of the causes and purposes of the alert. Brezhnev thought that Nixon had ordered the alert to demonstrate that he was as courageous as John F. Kennedy—the strong man in a crisis.[57] This interpretation was widely shared by Politburo members. "It seemed to the Politburo," Israelian recalled, "that Nixon's decision was determined mainly by domestic politics. In a situation of growing emotions surrounding Watergate, Nixon had to demonstrate that he was a 'strong president' and that the United States needed him."[58] Many Soviet officials saw the alert as so inconsistent with the ongoing negotiations and the frequent communications between the two capitals that they could find no explanation other than Watergate. The preeminent Soviet expert on U.S. politics, Georgi Arbatov, put it bluntly: "The American alert was designed for home consumption."[59]

However, not all senior officials agreed that the alert was largely a response to Watergate. Kornienko, who was present as an aide to Gromyko at the Politburo meeting, thought that the alert was designed to intimidate the Soviet leadership: "The DEFCON III alert was taken seriously in Moscow. Some of us saw it as an attempt to intimidate us from sending forces to the Middle East. The alert was not dismissed as a response to Watergate. We took it seriously."[60] Dobrynin thought that the alert was intended to intimidate the Soviet Union and to demonstrate resolve for U.S. public opinion.[61]

Irrespective of their conclusions as to the purposes of the alert, Brezhnev and other members of the Politburo were "very emotional, very angry," according to Israelian. "There was no feeling of fear, but of great disappointment and anger."[62] According to Dobrynin, Brezhnev was so emotional because he "felt deceived by Nixon and Kissinger." Dobrynin was concerned "that Brezhnev's anger with Nixon and Kissinger would lead him to do something rash. I was furious, too."[63]

Thus, Politburo members debated the appropriate response to the alert within a highly charged emotional atmosphere. A significant minority supported a military response to the U.S. "provocation." Marshal Andrei Grechko acknowledged that a large-scale mobilization of forces would be very expensive, yet he still recommended the mobilization of 50,000 to 75,000 troops in Ukraine and the northern Caucasus.[64] Dmitri Ustinov, then secretary of the Central Committee in charge of defense production, Andrei Kirilenko, a loyal Brezhnev supporter, K. F. Katushev, responsible for liaison with ruling Communist parties, Yuri Andropov, then head of KGB, the Soviet intelligence agency, and Kosygin all supported the mobilization of some Soviet forces in response to the alert. "We should respond to mobilization," Andropov argued, "by mobilization."[65] Ustinov thought that Soviet forces should be mobilized without public announcement.

Marshal Grechko also urged the Politburo to order the 1,500 Soviet soldiers in Syria to occupy the Golan Heights. "In the past," he exclaimed, "we have never asked anybody if we could send our troops and we can do the same now."[66] His proposal clearly was not a response to the desperate plight of the Egyptian Third Army but a reaction to what he considered a U.S. attempt at intimidation.

Gromyko, Kirilenko, and Kosygin spoke vigorously against the proposal to involve Soviet troops in the fighting. "We shall send two divisions to the Near East," Kosygin argued, "and in response the Americans will send two divisions as well. If we send five divisions, the Americans will send their five. . . . Today nobody can be frightened by anybody. The United States will not start a war and we have no reason to start a war."[67] Kosygin dismissed the U.S. threat as not credible. He did not oppose Soviet involvement in the Middle East because he was intimidated by the United States but rather because of the futility of Soviet intervention.

The discussion grew more heated until the usually silent Brezhnev finally put the question: "Comrades, if we do not react at all, if we do not respond to the American mobilization, what will happen?"[68] Nikolai Podgorny, who formally held the office of president of the Soviet Union, Gromyko, and Boris Ponomarev, who headed the International Department of the Central Committee, agreed that Soviet interests would not suffer if Moscow decided not to respond to the U.S. alert with its own military measures. These officials agreed with the general secretary that the crisis in U.S.-Soviet relations should be resolved by political rather than military measures.

The Politburo then discussed the possibility of sending Gromyko immediately to Washington to confer personally with Nixon. Kosygin recommended that Gromyko express Moscow's bewilderment at the U.S. alert and discuss the possibility of sending Soviet and U.S. observers to monitor observance of the cease-fire. Kosygin's proposal to signal Soviet interest in a cooperative solution in this highly visible manner received no support in the Politburo. In fact, Brezhnev argued that to send a representative to Washington after the United States had alerted its forces would be interpreted as "weakness."[69] He rejected any Soviet attempt at reassurance in the face of the U.S. attempt at deterrence.

In an emotional speech, Brezhnev summarized the Soviet Union's eventual response to the U.S. alert: "The Americans say we threaten them," he said, "but they are lying to us."[70] Thus, he insisted again that the Soviet Union had given the United States no grounds to alert its forces and that a Soviet mobilization in response would accomplish nothing. In strong language, Brezhnev reemphasized his opposition to any preparatory military measures.

The U.S. attempt at deterrence provoked anger, disappointment, and bitterness among Soviet leaders. What U.S. officials regarded as a signal of resolve, Soviet officials interpreted as an attempt to intimidate or a response based on domestic political weakness. Bewildered and angered, a significant group within the Politburo proposed the mobilization of Soviet forces *in response* to the alert. Although Brezhnev opposed a military response, he too could not understand the intent of the alert. Angered by the alert, he rejected a proposal that Gromyko attempt to reassure Nixon personally of Soviet intentions, even though Soviet intentions were benign. Thus, the U.S. strategy had made the confrontation more difficult to resolve. Following the Politburo meeting, Brezhnev wrote to President Nixon that although the Soviet Union had chosen not to respond with military measures, the U.S. action was unprovoked and not conducive to the relaxation of international tensions.[71] Under a different leader, the Politburo might well have chosen differently.

The Failure of Soviet Compellence

The Soviet strategy of threatening unilateral intervention if the fighting did not stop in the Middle East might well have resolved the crisis. In a nutshell, Brezhnev was trying to compel the United States to press Israel to stop the fighting. Once the cease-fire was stabilized and the safety of the Egyptian Third Army was assured, the crisis would most likely have ended. We have already shown how Soviet bargaining provoked escalation by leading the United States to issue a worldwide military alert. The evidence also suggests that the Soviet threat did not resolve the crisis. Like its U.S. counterpart, it was both irrelevant and provocative.

By the time Brezhnev's letter arrived in Washington the fighting had stopped. Ironically, Brezhnev's threat only interrupted the U.S. efforts to compel Israel to allow food and medical supplies to reach the trapped Egyptian Third Army. Kissinger, who had been actively trying to prevent the destruction of the Third Army, stopped pressing Israel immediately after he received Brezhnev's letter on the evening of October 24; he did not resume these efforts until the following morning—after it was apparent that the crisis between the United States and the Soviet Union would be resolved. Kissinger then pressed Israel to permit nonmilitary supplies to reach the Third Army despite the fact that Brezhnev had made no such demand in his letter. By the time the United States finally extracted a commitment from Israel on October 26 to permit a one-time convoy to reach the Third Army, the crisis was over.

The critical period was the thirteen hours from 7:00 P.M. on October 24, when Dobrynin first informed Kissinger of Brezhnev's letter, until 8:00 A.M. the next morning, when President Sadat withdrew his request for intervention by Soviet and U.S. forces. It seemed unlikely to Kissinger that Moscow would send forces without Egyptian consent. During that period, Kissinger met several times with Israel's ambassador to Washington but made no request that Israel break its encirclement of the Third Army. Instead, Israel's leaders received a request from Kissinger for a contingency plan to destroy the Third Army. In the face of the Soviet threat, Kissinger subtly encouraged Israel to consider escalating military action. When asked directly long after the crisis was over, Kissinger confirmed his refusal to be coerced: "The Soviet threat backfired. Only after the Russians caved in, did I turn on the Israelis. After the Soviets threatened, I asked the Israelis to develop an option to defeat the Third Army. Only after I knew that the Russians were caving in, did I press the Israelis really hard on Friday [October 25]."[72]

The United States responded to Soviet strategy by redefining the problem as a test of U.S. resolve and ceased its attempts to compel its ally, Israel.[73] It might be argued that Soviet compellence nevertheless increased U.S. incentives to coerce Israel once the crisis between Moscow and Washington passed. The evidence does not sustain this argument. The United States had tried to compel Israel to observe the cease-fire *before* the Soviet Union issued its threat. Nixon and Kissinger had also decided—again, before the Soviet ultimatum—that they would not permit the destruction of the Egyptian Third Army.[74] Kissinger had also begun his attempt to coerce Israel to permit the resupply of the Third Army before the Soviet Union raised the issue with the United States. And Nixon and Kissinger also worried about a confrontation with Moscow before Brezhnev sent his letter. Thus, the evidence suggests strongly that the United States would have compelled Israel to accept a cease-fire and allow re-supply of the Third Army even in the absence of a Soviet threat because of its over-riding interest in establishing a relationship with Egypt that would endure after the war was over.

The Soviet attempt at compellence was not only unnecessary but also irrelevant, poorly constructed, and counterproductive: Soviet leaders did not have real-time battlefield intelligence and were unaware that the fighting had stopped by the time Brezhnev's letter arrived in Washington; Brezhnev's threat was poorly constructed in that it did not raise the critical issue of the supply of the trapped Third Army; it was counterproductive because it interrupted the U.S. attempt to coerce Israel. Soviet bargaining provoked precisely the responses it had wanted to prevent: an interruption of U.S. efforts to save the Egyptian Third Army and a worldwide alert of U.S. forces that threatened the confrontation that Brezhnev wanted above all to avoid.

The Crisis Is Resolved

When the Soviet Union decided not to respond to the U.S. alert with military measures, the process of escalation stopped. A halt in escalation was necessary but insufficient to resolve the crisis. To settle the crisis, the Soviet Union had to withdraw its threat to consider unilateral military intervention. Brezhnev did so implicitly on October 25 when he accepted Nixon's offer to send U.S. and Soviet observers to monitor the cease-fire. Later that day, the Soviet ambassador to the United Nations supported a resolution in the UN Security Council (Resolution 340) to dispatch a peacekeeping force that, by convention, excluded Soviet and U.S. forces.

"It was not the military threat," according to Anatoliy Gromyko, "but diplomacy that finally found a solution."[75] As Brezhnev was concluding his emotional speech at the Politburo meeting, Konstantin Chernenko, acting informally as secretary to the Politburo, passed to him the text of Nixon's letter (actually drafted by Henry Kissinger). Brezhnev read the long letter aloud to the Politburo, emphasizing what he considered two particularly conciliatory phrases: "I agree with you that our understanding to act jointly for peace is one of the highest value and that we should implement that understanding in this complex situation"; and, "In the spirit of our agreements this is the time not for acting unilaterally, but in harmony and with cool heads."[76] Nixon's proposal provided the Politburo with a face-saving opportunity to end the crisis without confrontation. It was accepted "with relief," and the Politburo ended its meeting.[77]

Several important considerations help to explain Soviet acceptance of a political solution to the crisis. Foremost, Soviet leaders did not consider the stakes in the Middle East to be worth the risk of confrontation and war. When Politburo members began their first meeting after the U.S. alert, the first issue they discussed was whether the Soviet Union was prepared to confront the United States and fight a large-scale war. Despite the differences within the Politburo, the unanimous answer was "no." Kosygin put it bluntly: "It is not reasonable to become involved in a war with the United States because of Egypt and Syria."[78] Andropov, Kirilenko, Ponomarev, Gromyko, Kosygin, and Grechko all made essentially the same point.[79]

The belief that the Soviet relationship with Egypt and Syria was not worth a war with the United States was widespread. "Nobody shared Arab war aims," Israelian said. "Sadat was not Castro. Our relationship with him was not the same."[80] Although the reputation and the interests of the Soviet Union were heavily engaged in Egypt, the Soviet-Egyptian relationship had long been troubled.[81] The Politburo was angered by Egyptian military incompetence, by Sadat's expulsion of Soviet military advisers, and by his failure to heed its advice. Soviet stakes in the region were high but tempered by ideological, military, and personal differences between Arab and Soviet leaders. The Politburo was therefore not prepared to risk a U.S.-Soviet confrontation to save Sadat. Even after he listened to a pessimistic evaluation of Egypt's military situation, Brezhnev said to his colleagues: "We must tell Sadat, 'We were right. We sympathize with you but we can't reverse the results of your military operations.'"[82]

A second consideration was the importance Brezhnev personally attached to good relations with the United States. Brezhnev considered détente the outstanding accomplishment of his foreign policy. Even before the alert, Brezhnev recognized that a deployment of Soviet forces in Egypt would seriously complicate the Soviet relationship with the United States. He therefore strongly preferred a diplomatic solution within the framework that he had negotiated with Kissinger when Kissinger had come to Moscow.

In large part because Brezhnev prided himself on his personal relationship with the U.S. president, he was deeply angered by "Nixon's action." Anger can lead to ill-considered and risky actions because people who are emotionally aroused are less likely to think through the consequences of their choices. In this case, the Soviet Union did not do so because of the impact of crosscutting emotions. Although Brezhnev was angered and disappointed by the U.S. alert, he was also angry with Sadat for consistently ignoring Soviet advice. Anger pulled in opposite directions. These crosscutting emotions moderated Brezhnev's reaction and reduced the impact of his anger at the United States. He was therefore able to temper his response.

One other factor contributed significantly to the resolution of the crisis. There was an important asymmetry in the perceptions of Moscow and Washington as to the actual risks of war. Leaders in Moscow worried about a confrontation between Soviet military forces and those of Israel if Soviet troops were sent to Egypt. They feared that a Soviet-Israeli conflict could easily escalate into a wider engagement that could draw in the United States. Politburo members worried that actions *they* might take might lead inadvertently to war. "The steps we take," Kirilenko urged, "should not lead to war."[83]

Analysts who argue today that the crisis was resolved because the United States manipulated the risk of war miss the fundamental point.[84] Soviet leaders worried about the risk of war as a consequence of *their* military deployment, *before* the U.S. alert. Their evaluation of the risks of war worked in favor of crisis resolution. It served as a powerful incentive to search actively for a political solution and as a brake on a military response to the U.S. alert. However, U.S. leaders did not consider the risk of war and confrontation with Soviet forces to be significant even after their alert. Fortunately, the asymmetrical pattern of the fear of war worked in favor of crisis resolution. Soviet leaders, who worried seriously about escalation, had to make the critical decision about a response to the U.S. alert.

Conclusion

Bargaining is usually ineffective when the two sides maintain radically different understandings of the context. As to the U.S.-Soviet bargaining in 1973, messages were framed in one context and interpreted in another. It is not surprising that the interpretation of critical signals bore no relationship to the intentions of the signal senders. Attempts both to demonstrate resolve and to cooperate failed. Signals had a nearly random, hit-and-miss effect. The crisis, as we have seen, was resolved in spite of the bargaining strategies of both superpowers.

To the extent that bargaining had any impact, it was largely negative because of the way it reinforced Soviet images of the United States as unreliable, unpredictable, and duplicitous—and U.S. images of the Soviet Union as aggressive and treacherous. Ironically, the bargaining process between the two superpowers not only failed to resolve the crisis but damaged the long-term relationship between them. Inappropriate strategies triggered a self-reinforcing cycle of conflict that led to the progressive deterioration of the relationship between the superpowers for the remainder of the decade.

After the 1973 Arab-Israeli war, Brezhnev and the proponents of détente faced a growing barrage of criticism from colleagues who alleged that the United States had tricked the Soviet leadership and used the war as a cover to exclude the Soviet Union from Egypt. Although Kissinger had not engaged in any deliberate deception of the Soviet leadership during the war, he seized the opportunity after the war to initiate a process of negotiation between Egypt and Israel that led to two successive disengagement agreements and culminated ultimately in the Camp David accords in 1978 and the subsequent Egyptian-Israeli peace treaty in 1979. The Soviet Union was almost entirely excluded from this process. Although the United States achieved its strategic objectives in the heartland of the Middle East and successfully moved the two most powerful parties in the region to a peace agreement, flawed bargaining during the crisis of October 1973 marked the beginning of the end of détente between the superpowers. Suspicion and distrust weakened the advocates of détente in both Moscow and Washington and contributed to a "second cold war" between the United States and the Soviet Union that would last for more than a decade.

Notes

1. Henry Kissinger, *Years of Upheaval* (Boston: Little, Brown, 1972), p. 571.

2. Henry Kissinger, interview by author, New York, 19 June 1991.

3. Kissinger, *Years of Upheaval*, p. 573.

4. Ibid.

5. Former member of Prime Minister Meir's staff, interview by author, April 1988.

6. In his book, Kissinger wrote: "It was clear that if we let this go on, a confrontation with the Soviets was inevitable. . . . I told Dinitz [Israel's ambassador to Washington] that the art of foreign policy was to know when to clinch one's victories. There were limits beyond which we could not go, with all our friendship for Israel, and one of them was to make the leader of another superpower look like an idiot. I said to Dinitz that if Sadat asked the Soviets, as he had us, to enforce the cease-fire with their own troops, Israel would have out-smarted itself." Kissinger, *Years of Upheaval*, p. 576.

7. Hanoch Bartov, in his *Dado—Arbaim Ve'Shmoneh Shanim V'Esraim Yom* (Dado—48 Years and Twenty Days), 2 vols. (Tel Aviv: Ma'ariv Book Guild, 1978), vol. 1, p. 592, reports that every five minutes that morning, calls were coming in from the White House warning Israel to stop its offensive. Israel was informed that Kissinger was boiling with rage. This biography of General David Elazar, the chief of staff of the Israeli Defense Forces (IDF) during the war, is based on the private papers of the chief of staff, which are not yet publicly available.

8. Cited by Kissinger, *Years of Upheaval*, p. 579.

9. Ibid.

10. Joseph Sisco, interview by author, Washington, 17 April 1991.

11. Kissinger, *Years of Upheaval*, p. 573.

12. Cited by Kissinger, ibid., p. 583.

13. Galia Golan, "Soviet Decisionmaking in the Yom Kippur War," in Jiri Valenta and William Potter, eds., *Soviet Decisionmaking for National Security* (London: George Allen and Unwin, 1984), pp. 185–217; and Bradford Dismukes and James McConnell, *Soviet Naval Diplomacy* (New York: Pergamon Press, 1979), p. 203.

14. There is some controversy as to how many airborne divisions were moved to the status of ready-for-combat that day. All seven divisions had been on alert since October 11, but some analysts claim that only one airborne division moved to ready-to-move status on 24 October. See Raymond Garthoff, *Détente and Confrontation: American-Soviet Relations from Nixon to Reagan* (Washington, D.C.: Brookings Institution, 1985), pp. 377–378, n. 68. Hart maintains that three of the seven divisions were placed on ready-to-move status on 10 October and the remaining four early on 24 October. See Douglas M. Hart, "Soviet Approaches to Crisis Management: The Military Dimension," *Survival* 26(5) (September–October 1984), pp. 214–222.

15. Hart, "Soviet Approaches to Crisis Management."

16. The Politburo was not told of these military measures. When he was asked at the Politburo meeting on 25 October about Soviet military movements, Marshal Andrei Grechko, responsible for defense, responded that they were routine military maneuvers. Victor Israelian,

interview by author, State College, Pa., 8 January 1992. Evgeny Pyrlin, the deputy director of the Middle East division in the Soviet Foreign Ministry in 1973, confirms that during the October War, "Grechko frequently replied to questions from his Politburo colleagues, 'I just informed Comrade Brezhnev about this,' and all questions became useless. As a rule the Minister of Defense was authorized to order military actions short of the mobilization of reserves and the reinforcement of armored and air divisions. To be frank, Mr. Grechko as the Minister of Defense had wide liberty of action and sometimes didn't inform the political leadership of the details." Evgeny Pyrlin, "Some Observations (Memoirs) About the Arab-Israeli War (1973)," unpublished memorandum commissioned for this project, Moscow, August 1992, p. 5. Andrei Alexandrov-Agentov, a senior aide to Brezhnev in 1973, explained that "Brezhnev liked and trusted Grechko. Very often, Grechko, confident of Brezhnev's trust, authorized measures of military preparedness without Brezhnev's knowledge or approval. He had a free hand." Andrei M. Alexandrov-Agentov, interview by author, Moscow, 19 August 1992. Alexandrov was a career diplomat whom Brezhnev had borrowed from the Ministry of Foreign Affairs when he became chairman of the Presidium of the Supreme Soviet.

17. Victor Israelian, personal communication, 9 March 1992.

18. Victor Israelian, interview by author, State College, Pa., 8 January 1992. In his message to Kissinger on 23 October, Sadat asked the United States to "intervene effectively, even if that necessitates the use of forces, in order to guarantee the full implementation of the cease-fire resolution in accordance with the joint U.S.-USSR agreement." Cited by Kissinger, *Years of Upheaval,* p. 574.

19. Victor Israelian, "The Kremlin: October 1973," unpublished monograph, p. 22.

20. Ibid., p. 23.

21. Ibid., p. 21, and personal communication, 9 March 1992.

22. Israelian, "The Kremlin: October 1973," p. 23.

23. Vadim Zagladin (then deputy director of the International Relations Department of the Central Committee), interview by author, Moscow, 18 May 1989.

24. Cited by Kissinger, *Years of Upheaval,* p. 583.

25. Victor Israelian, interview by author, State College, Pa., 8 January 1992.

26. Vadim Zagladin, interview by author, Moscow, 18 May 1989.

27. Anatoliy Gromyko, interview by author, Moscow, 18 May 1989.

28. General Yuri Yakovlevich Kirshin, interview by author, Moscow, 17 December 1992.

29. Dobrynin, interview by author, Moscow, 17 December 1992.

30. Georgi Kornienko, interview by author, Moscow, 17 December 1991.

31. Victor Israelian, interview by author, State College, Pa., 8 January 1992.

32. Israelian is not certain how this last sentence was inserted. "It is difficult for me to say to whom this idea belonged originally. It is possible that it was born during one of Brezhnev's lobby interviews with his closest colleagues from the Politburo and was immediately put into the message." Israelian, "The Kremlin: October 1973," p. 24.

33. Victor Israelian, interview by author, State College, Pa., 8 January 1992.

34. Anatoliy Dobrynin, interview by author, Moscow, 17 December 1991.

35. Israelian, "The Kremlin: October 1973," p. 27.

36. Ibid., p. 23.

37. General Alexander Ivanovich Vladimirov, interview by author, Moscow, 18 December 1991. William Colby, director of the CIA in 1973, insists that Soviet forces did not need much coordination with Egypt to deploy. "They had a mission there. All they needed was landing times at Cairo West and they could have gotten those at the last moment." William

Colby, telephone interview by author, 11 January 1992. On the other hand, Admiral Nikolai Amelko, deputy chief of the Soviet navy in 1973, argued that the deployment of paratroopers would have required air, logistical, and marine support, which would have required some coordination and time. No such request was made to the Soviet navy in October 1973. Admiral Nikolai N. Amelko, interview by author, Moscow, 18 December 1991.

38. Raymond Garthoff, personal communication, 9 July 1992. Garthoff estimates that it would have taken a considerable length of time to move the full four divisions.

39. Anatoliy Gromyko, interview by author, Moscow, 18 May 1989.

40. Alexander Kislov, Deputy Director of IMEMO, interview by author, Moscow, 18 May 1989. Garthoff, *Détente and Confrontation,* p. 383, concurs with this interpretation of Brezhnev's intentions.

41. Secretary of Defense James Schlesinger and Secretary of State Kissinger made the decision to alert U.S. forces, in consultation with the director of the CIA, William Colby, the chairman of the Joint Chiefs of Staff, Admiral Thomas Moorer, and the president's chief of staff, Alexander Haig, who was with the president in his personal quarters. Present as well in the Situation Room of the White House were the deputy assistant to the president for National Security Affairs, General Brent Scowcroft, and Commander Jonathan T. Howe, the military assistant to the secretary of state at the National Security Council.

42. President Nixon did not participate in the discussions, was not informed of the alert when it was ordered, and only approved the alert retroactively at about 3 A.M. on the morning of 25 October. Overwhelmed by the growing scandal of Watergate, the president was reportedly drunk and exhausted upstairs in his personal quarters in the White House. *Inquiring into the Military Alert Invoked on October 24, 1973,* 93rd Congress, House of Representatives, Report 93-970 (Washington, D.C.: U.S. Government Printing Office, 14 April 1974, 74-09780), p. 3.

43. Barry M. Blechman and Douglas M. Hart, "The Political Utility of Nuclear Weapons: The 1973 Middle East Crisis," *International Security* 7(1) (Summer 1982), pp. 132–156; Garthoff, *Détente and Confrontation,* p. 379; and Kissinger, *Years of Upheaval,* pp. 587–589. At 3:30 A.M., sixty U.S. B-52 bombers were ordered back to the United States from Guam. This had been a long-standing objective of the Pentagon, but the State Department had objected to a visible reduction of the U.S. commitment in Southeast Asia. Under the rubric of the DEFCON III alert, the Pentagon ordered their return.

44. Steven L. Spiegel, *The Other Arab-Israeli Conflict: Making America's Middle East Policy, from Truman to Reagan* (Chicago: University of Chicago Press, 1985), citing interview of Schlesinger, p. 264. William Colby confirmed that "nobody had any problems. Schlesinger and Moorer went along. They had no problems with it." William Colby, telephone interview by author, 11 January 1992.

45. Kissinger, *Years of Upheaval,* p. 584.

46. Interviews conducted by author: William Quandt, Washington, D.C., 7 December 1988; and Alfred (Roy) Atherton, Washington, D.C., 15 March 1990.

47. Kissinger, *Years of Upheaval,* p. 593.

48. Henry Kissinger, interview by author, New York, 19 June 1991.

49. Peter Rodman, interview by author, Washington, D.C., 24 April 1991.

50. Kissinger, *Years of Upheaval,* p. 980.

51. For an explicit version of this argument, see Blechman and Hart, "The Political Utility of Nuclear Weapons," pp. 151–152.

52. Israelian, "The Kremlin: October 1973," pp. 5–6.

53. Ibid., pp. 13–14.

54. Ibid., p. 29.

55. Victor Israelian, interview by author, State College, Pa., 9 January 1992.

56. Ibid.

57. Ibid.

58. Israelian, "The Kremlin: October 1973," p. 26.

59. Georgi Arbatov, interview by author, Moscow, May 19, 1989. Kissinger also had worried about the impact of Watergate but for quite different reasons. At the meeting in the Situation Room of the White House on the night of 24 October, he and his advisers speculated about whether the Soviet Union would have challenged a "functioning" president. His concern about the weakness of the president made Kissinger all the more intent on signaling resolve through a worldwide alert. "We are at a point of maximum weakness," Kissinger said, "but if we knuckle under now we are in real trouble. . . . We will have to contend with the charge in the domestic media that we provoked this. The real charge is that we provoked this by being soft." Kissinger, *Years of Upheaval*, p. 589. It was not only the U.S. media but most of the Soviet leadership that accused Nixon and Kissinger of manipulating domestic politics. The Politburo, however, did not see the domestic crisis in Washington as a weakness to exploit but as a source of American irresponsibility.

60. Georgi Kornienko, interview by author, Moscow, 17 December 1991.

61. Anatoliy Dobrynin, interview by author, Moscow, 17 December 1991.

62. Victor Israelian, interview by author, State College, Pa., 9 January 1992.

63. Anatoliy Dobrynin, interview by author, Moscow, 17 December 1991.

64. The Soviet alert system is designed to allow conventional alert readiness to be raised to high level without alerting any strategic nuclear forces. Joseph J. Kruzel, "Military Alerts and Diplomatic Signals," in Ellen P. Stern, ed., *The Limits of Military Intervention* (Beverly Hills, Calif.: Sage, 1977), pp. 83–89, 98.

65. Israelian, "The Kremlin: October 1973," p. 27.

66. Ibid.

67. Ibid.

68. Ibid., p. 28; and Victor Israelian, interview by author, State College, Pa., 9 January 1992.

69. Israelian, "The Kremlin: October 1973," p. 28. Gromyko also did not want to go to Washington.

70. Ibid., p. 29.

71. Israelian, "The Kremlin: October 1973," p. 28; also cited by Kissinger, *Years of Upheaval*, p. 608.

72. Henry Kissinger, interview by author, New York, 19 June 1991.

73. Garthoff concurs that the alert and the Brezhnev letter that prompted it did not end the crisis or resolve the situation. He argues that the Brezhnev letter did not serve to reinforce U.S. readiness to curb Israel, which was in any case the product of U.S. policy, but slowed it down. See Garthoff, *Détente and Confrontation*, pp. 380 and 383.

74. On 23 October, Nixon and Kissinger had decided to prevent the destruction of the Third Army and Kissinger had so informed Israel. Kissinger, *Years of Upheaval*, pp. 571, 573, and William Quandt, *Decade of Decisions: American Policy Toward the Arab-Israel Conflict* (Berkeley: University of California Press, 1977), p. 194.

75. Anatoliy Gromyko, interview by author, Moscow, 18 May 1989.

76. Israelian, "The Kremlin: October 1973," pp. 29–30.

77. Ibid., p. 30.

78. Ibid., p. 26.

79. Ibid.

80. Victor Israelian, interview by author, State College, Pa., 8 January 1992.

81. Leonid Zamyatin, an official of the Ministry of Foreign Affairs who subsequently headed the TASS news agency, put the relationship in context: "Egyptian-Soviet relations began to deteriorate under Nasser, who was pro-Soviet in his foreign policy but repressive toward Communists at home. We had even lower expectations of Sadat because of our dealings with him when he was in charge of the Aswan Dam project. He was a pain in the neck, always trying to renegotiate contracts. We became more cautious." Leonid Zamyatin, interview by author, Moscow, 16 December 1991.

82. Israelian, "The Kremlin: October 1973," p. 29.

83. Ibid., p. 26.

84. Blechman and Hart, "The Political Utility of Nuclear Weapons," pp. 132–156.

14

The United States and Israel: The Nature of a Special Relationship

Bernard Reich

In a press conference on May 12, 1977, U.S. President Jimmy Carter said, "We have a special relationship with Israel. It's absolutely crucial that no one in our country or around the world ever doubt that our number-one commitment in the Middle East is to protect the right of Israel to exist, to exist permanently, and to exist in peace. It's a special relationship."[1] In February 1993, U.S. Secretary of State Warren Christopher observed that the "relationship between the United States and Israel is a special relationship for special reasons. It is based upon shared interests, shared values, and a shared commitment to democracy, pluralism and respect for the individual." In spring 1994 President Bill Clinton suggested that, in working for peace in the Middle East, a first pillar is the security of Israel. He noted that Israeli Prime Minister Yitzhak Rabin was working for—and taking risks for—peace. The United States would fulfill its "ironclad commitment" to ensure that these risks would not endanger the security of Israel.

This perspective tends to "confirm" the Arab view, in the wake of the 1967 Arab-Israeli war (also known as the Six Day War), that there existed a special and exclusive U.S.-Israeli relationship. But these statements are more than political rhetoric or platitude; they are reflective and representative of hundreds of such statements over time, especially during the period covered by this chapter (1977 to 1994). Nevertheless, there is much that the statements do not say, and though there is a broad-scale commitment on the part of the United States at a very significant level, as in any relationship of this sort there are also areas of discord and questions.

The U.S.-Israeli relationship is not the exclusive one that is often portrayed by Arab spokesmen and others advocating a different Israeli orientation in U.S. policy. Although there was a period of exclusivity favoring Israel following the events of the Six Day War, this lack of a dual relationship began to change after the Arab-Israeli war of 1973 (also known as the Yom Kippur War).[2] By 1977 and the January inauguration of Jimmy Carter into office, there had begun a period in which Arab (especially Egyptian) views were factored into the process and affected U.S. policy. Some of the Arab states (but not yet the Palestinians and the Palestine Liberation Organization [PLO]) became increasingly more important from a foreign policy perspective because they were seen as moving in a general direction toward peace. Thus, there was a change from exclusivity to dual-track diplomacy.

However, the generalized image of a "positive only" U.S.-Israeli relationship ignores the fact that within that linkage there is, has been, and probably will continue to be dissonance on a wide range of issues, both procedural and substantive. As in any relationship of this sort, there is a certain frustration when one actor does not perform in the way that the other would prefer. One actor might be obstinate and problematic, and the decisionmakers involved may carry difficult personalities. Often these views result from efforts to influence those who make policy, indeed even those who will be the chosen policymakers, and to influence the nature and direction of policy. An example: In the spring and summer of 1990 in Israel (with the fall of the national unity government and the efforts by Labor Party leader Shimon Peres to form a government and the ultimate success of Yitzhak Shamir of the Likud Party in doing so), clear U.S. preferences were reflected in the public and private comments of the senior policymakers and decisionmakers in the George Bush administration; the United States was not a disinterested, dispassionate, and uninvolved observer. Although a direct effort to affect the situation cannot be identified from the record, there was a clear view of U.S. preferences. Moreover, the U.S. position probably played a role in the ultimate selection of Labor's Yitzhak Rabin as the new prime minister and the formation of the new government under him. In a similar way, Israeli ambassadors have also made clear, although disowning any efforts at influencing personnel, their views concerning preferred policymakers and policies.

An additional, important political factor in the U.S.-Israeli relationship has been the U.S. Congress. Congress plays a role in the relationship, although it is limited by constitutional and practical factors. It is a crucial actor on such matters as aid, including what (economic and military assistance, loans or grants, and so on), how much, and to whom. Not only is Congress a crucial element in determining what aid Israel gets, it also helps to determine which parties on the Arab side of the equation do not receive aid. Its role goes beyond the formal allocation of aid, with the expression of views on central issues and seemingly unrelated matters often connected to the Israel factor.[3] Congressional concerns about a Jewish state can be traced at least back to 1922, when it unanimously supported the Balfour Declaration (which President Woodrow Wilson had endorsed during his term earlier). The positive perception of public opinion toward Israel reflected in Congress continues to be manifested in substantial levels of economic and military assistance and related policy decisions that favor Israel.

However, the positive elements in the relationship, as well as the overall cordial and congruent nature of the partners' concerns and policies in the region, have not prevented negative elements from manifesting themselves. At the Camp David meeting between President Carter, Anwar Sadat, and Israeli Prime Minister Menachem Begin in September 1978, despite the ultimate agreements, there was discord on many issues. There were elements of discord concerning the Egyptian-Israeli peace treaty; some issues were left for later clarification and resolution. During the subsequent autonomy negotiations, which began in May 1979, agreement was reached as to some issues but not as to the major questions.

During the administrations of Prime Ministers Menachem Begin and Yitzhak Shamir, there were disagreements between the two states on a wide range of issues, including Israel's bombing of the Osirak nuclear reactor in Iraq, its bombing of PLO facilities in Beirut, the Israeli annexation of the Golan Heights, the war in Lebanon of 1982, the Sabra and Shatilla camp massacres, the Jonathan Pollard espionage affair, and Israeli complicity in the Iran-Contra arms-for-hostages deal. There were questions about the *intifada* and Israel's response to it (which also led to image problems for Israel in the United States and the questioning of its methods) as well as Israel's reaction to the Shultz Plan (named for former U.S. Secretary of State George P. Shultz) and assorted efforts in 1988 to deal with these and related questions.

There have been disagreements on the deportation of Palestinians (whether in large numbers or small) and on the building of Israeli settlements: how many, where, what, when. These were particularly acerbic during the tenures of George Bush and Yitzhak Shamir. There was, and is, policy dissonance as to Jerusalem; in fact, the United States retains its embassy in Tel Aviv and does not accept Israel's unilateral declaration of Jerusalem as its capital. And there have been broader policy questions on such matters as the sale of AWACS (airborne warning and control system aircraft) to Saudi Arabia during the administration of Ronald Reagan, the establishment of a dialogue between the United States and the PLO in 1988, and Arab terrorism and the appropriate response to it. During Bush's tenure there were tensions emerging from Israel's role (or, more properly, nonrole) in the Gulf war as well as discord over the subsequent Madrid peace conference.

The framework within which the United States and Israel have interacted with each other has changed over time, and policies perforce have changed to reflect the altered environment. The U.S.-Israeli relationship had its origins during the time that the United States and Soviet Union—the new superpowers—competed for control following World War II. Both superpowers courted Israel in their efforts to incorporate new states into their spheres of influence. Israel was seen as a valuable prize in the newly important, oil-rich Middle East. Nevertheless, within the U.S. government there was substantial disagreement concerning the appropriate policy, and U.S. support for the Jewish state was a presidential decision, often opposed by the senior bureaucrats in the Departments of State and Defense. Today, the U.S.-Israeli relationship operates within the confines of a new world order in which there is no alternative superpower nor U.S.-Soviet competition to curry the favor of states or regional groupings.

A second difference is to be found in the perspectives of a small country confronting a large country (that is, the United States today, the only superpower), which sees the world through a different lens. The United States is a global power with global interests, affected by the residue of the cold war; Israeli interests are more narrow and regional and there are more "life-and-death" issues.

In many respects the relationship can be compared to a ride on a roller coaster, which can be seen as something that will generate amusement and excitement, an overall euphoric sense. During the course of the ride there are a great many abrupt changes of course, extremes of behavior, altering circumstances—there are a great many ups and downs. For riders it can be frightening and tension-filled. When you reach the top, you soon realize you might be going down again and are not quite sure just what lies beyond the hill up ahead. Nevertheless, you are reasonably certain that you will stay on track, but in any event you cannot control the situation in any meaningful way, as others have designed the course and control the speed for you. At ride's end you feel both exhilaration and relief. The U.S.-Israeli relationship is much the same. At the end of the coaster ride, however, it is not always clear that the two riders will disembark at the same place, and there are different perspectives and viewpoints about the ride itself, whether it was really all that much fun and whether a pocketful of additional tickets are worth the price.

The United States and Israel have been linked in a complex and multifaceted special relationship that had its origins prior to the establishment of the Jewish state in 1948 and has focused on continuing U.S. support for the survival, security, and well-being of Israel. But its content has varied over time. During the first decades after Israel's independence the relationship was grounded primarily in humanitarian concerns, in religious and historical links, and in a moral-emotional-political arena. The United States remained very much aloof from Israel in the strategic-military sector. The United States and Israel developed a diplomatic-political relationship that focused on the need to resolve the Arab-Israeli conflict, but though they agreed on the general concept, they often differed on the precise means for achieving that end. Despite a growing positive connection between the two states, especially after the 1967 Six Day War, appreciation of the linkage, especially in the strategic sphere, remained limited.

Relations Between the Carter Administration and Israel

The accession of both Jimmy Carter and Menachem Begin to office in 1977 inaugurated a new period in the relationship, characterized often by increased public tension and recrimination. Egyptian President Anwar Sadat's initiative also reduced the exclusivity of the U.S.-Israeli relationship that had been established after 1967 as a consequence of Soviet policy and the ruptures of relations between some Arab states and the United States.

The Carter and Begin administrations became divided over many issues that directly impacted the health of the U.S.-Israeli relationship. They were in accord in some aspects, however, as on the need to achieve peace and foster the security of Israel. Yet they would often disagree on the methods and mechanisms best suited to achieving those goals, the preferred end results, and the modalities that best served national interests. There were questions regarding the poor personal chemistry between policymakers on either side as well. Senior U.S. and Israeli officials were not always compatible, and this affected the countries' ever-evolving relationship. Mutual dislike and mistrust extended beyond Carter and Begin into the Reagan administration; the United States was unhappy with Begin and his successor, Ariel Sharon, and Israel had strong anxieties about Caspar Weinberger and his policies. There were disagreements concerning the nature of the situation in the region, often focusing on alternative intelligence estimates of the threat to Israel's national security. These differences involved data, analyses, and policy results. The consensus on major issues did not ensure agreement on all aspects or specifics of each problem. As the dialogue increasingly dealt with details rather than broad areas of agreement, there were disturbances in the relationship.

The Carter tenure was filled with episodes of discord between the United States and Israel that generated numerous efforts by each power to influence the policies of the other. Israel's major success was in connection with the October 1, 1977, U.S.-Soviet joint communiqué. Although proclaimed with great fanfare by the Carter administration, Israel was able to secure abandonment of the communiqué within a matter of days by mobilizing Israel's traditional supporters in the U.S. Jewish community and non-Jewish supporters in Congress and elsewhere. It took advantage of strong public sympathy for Israel as well as that which was against reinvolvement of the Soviet Union in the peace process.

The Carter administration had its most noteworthy success in effecting change in the Israeli position at Camp David and in the Egyptian-Israeli peace treaty. The main techniques included high risk/high visibility presidential involvement and Carter's suggestion that Israel could not allow the failure of this president, who might then transfer the blame to Israel in Congress and public opinion. Israel was also influenced by the administration's articulated reassurances for continuing economic and military assistance and by their tangible manifestation in the form of such assistance.

The Reagan Tenure

Ronald Reagan came to office with a very different perception of Israel and its importance. His campaign rhetoric concerning Israel went beyond the customary pledges of friendship, suggesting strong and consistent support for Israel and its perspective regarding the Arab-Israeli conflict. He saw Israel as an important ally and an asset in the struggle against the Soviet Union. He was opposed to dealing with the PLO until that organization dramatically changed its policies by renouncing terrorism, accepting United Nations (UN) Security Council Resolution 242, and acknowledging Israel's right to exist (which it eventually did in 1988). This pro-Israel perspective was retained and reiterated after he took office.

The U.S.-Israeli relationship during the eight years Reagan held office was generally characterized by close positive ties, but there were also specific, divergent interpretations regarding the regional situation, the peace process, and Israel's security needs. Israel bombed an Iraqi nuclear reactor near Baghdad and PLO positions in Beirut during the summer of 1981, and it took action on other issues when it believed its national interest was at stake—even when it understood this would lead to clashes with the United States. The United States strongly opposed the raid on the Iraqi reactor, questioned the Beirut bombings, and postponed the delivery of previously contracted F-16 aircraft to Israel. Other issues emerged, including disputes about settlements in the Occupied Territories and Israel's concern about a perceived pro-Saudi tendency in U.S. policy manifested, in part, by arms supplied to Saudi Arabia, including F-15 enhancements and AWACS. Israeli anxiety was heightened when the Reagan administration suggested that a proposal to resolve the Arab-Israeli conflict put forward by then Crown Prince Fahd of Saudi Arabia (the so-called Fahd Plan) in August 1981, which Israel had rejected, had some merit.

Reagan sought to reassure Israel that the United States remained committed in helping it to retain its military and technological advantages over the Arab states. In fact, Israel was drawn to a Reagan administration proposal of cooperation, and on November 30, 1981, the United States and Israel signed a Memorandum of Understanding on Strategic Cooperation (the MOU) in which the parties recognized the need to enhance strategic cooperation to deter threats to the region from the Soviet Union. For the Begin government it represented an important achievement, suggesting an improved relationship with the United States, and some mitigation of the negative effects of U.S. sales of AWACS and other advanced weapons systems to Saudi Arabia. But this positive aura soon dissipated when Israel decided in December 1981 to alter the status of the Golan Heights by extending the law, jurisdiction, and administration of Israel to that area. The action generated swift negative reactions in Washington, including U.S. support for a UN resolution of condemnation and the suspension of the MOU. Israel was stunned by the extent of the U.S. reaction; the strongly negative response included Begin's castigation of the U.S. ambassador to Israel.

Although Israel's Golan decision exacerbated tensions, the turning point was Israel's 1982 invasion of Lebanon, which called into question the links between the United States and Israel and led to clashes over the nature and extent of Israel's military actions and the U.S. effort to ensure the PLO's evacuation from Beirut. U.S. forces, which had been withdrawn from Beirut following the PLO's evacuation, returned there after the massacres of Palestinians by Lebanese Phalangists at the Shatila and Sabra refugee camps in September 1982, leading to the burdensome involvement of U.S. marines in the turmoil of Lebanon.

The war also precipitated the Reagan "fresh start" initiative of September 1, 1982, which sought to reinvigorate the Arab-Israeli peace process by taking advantage of the opportunities presented by the new situation in Lebanon. Israel, which was not consulted in advance, saw the proposals as detrimental because they departed from the conceptual framework of Camp David and seemed prematurely to determine the outcome of negotiations on several points, including the status of Jerusalem and the futures of the West Bank and Gaza. There were other concerns as well, and these led Israel to reject the initiative. That action, coupled with the refugee camp massacres by the Phalangist militias, resulted in a sharp deterioration in Israel's standing in U.S. public opinion and in further disagreements with the Reagan administration, causing months of rancor. However, by the summer of 1983 the U.S.-Israeli relationship reverted to its earlier positive levels as a consequence of the Kahan Commission Report (which found Israel at fault in the Shatila and Sabra massacres), the failure of Jordan's King Hussein to join the peace process, the increase in Soviet involvement in Syria, the signing of the U.S.-promoted Lebanon-Israel agreement of May 1983, and the Syrian-Soviet opposition to it. The United States and Israel appeared linked by a congruence of policy that included recognition of Israel's strategic anti-Soviet value, their mutual desire for peaceful resolution of the Arab-Israeli conflict, as well as a parallelism concerning Lebanon and the future of that country. This comported well with Reagan's initial perceptions of Israel and presaged a period of positive relations, given tangible expression at the end of November 1983, when President Reagan and Prime Minister Yitzhak Shamir reached agreement on closer strategic cooperation.

Israel and the United States worked together to bring about the May 17, 1983, agreement between Israel and Lebanon that dealt with shaping the Lebanese government in conjunction with Israeli withdrawal and an eventual Israeli-Lebanese peace treaty. (The agreement was never implemented due to Syrian opposition and the opposition of Syrian-supported groups in Lebanon; indeed, Syria, and through it the USSR as perceived in Washington, was excluded from the May 17, 1983, negotiations and resented it.) At the same time, the major issues of discord in the relationship, which centered on the West Bank and Gaza and the Reagan "fresh start" initiative, were not addressed in any meaningful way. There was an air of good feeling that pervaded both the executive and legislative branches of the U.S. government.

Reagan faced other difficult times. The Pollard affair became a prominent issue.[4] Although this intelligence disaster captured headlines in both countries and had some short-term repercussions, it had little tangible or lasting effect on overall relations. Also, U.S. efforts to secure the release of its hostages in Lebanon through arms sales to Iran erupted, in November 1986, into a public scandal that became known as the Iran-Contra affair. This infamous chapter in U.S. history, among other matters, involved active Israeli participation in the planning and execution of some operations of the U.S. National Security Council and demonstrates the high level of strategic cooperation between the two governments during the Reagan administration.

Although interaction ranged over a variety of issues, both countries placed an overarching focus on the peace process throughout Reagan's second term. The concept of an international peace conference became more central during 1987, although little progress was made toward convening such a conference. Israel and the United States agreed on two prerequisites for Soviet participation: the regularization of Soviet Jewish emigration, and the restoration of Soviet ties with Israel broken at the time of the 1967 Six Day War.

The onset of the *intifada* in December 1987 led to public disagreement over the methods employed by Israel to contain the violence and restore law and order. Israel's use of live ammunition provoked protests by the State Department as early as January 1988. Israel's deportation of Palestinian civilians charged with inciting the demonstrations led the United States to vote in favor of a UN resolution calling on Israel to refrain from "such harsh measures [which] are unnecessary to maintain order." Although the State Department minimized the significance of the U.S. vote, describing it as a disagreement among friends that did not affect the broader relationship, this was the first time since 1981 that the United States had voted for a resolution critical of Israel. (In fact, Secretary of State Shultz referred to U.S. support for Israel as "unshakable.") As the demonstrations continued and the United States launched the Shultz initiative to seek an accord, however, tensions continued to grow.

The relationship between the United States and Israel underwent substantial, though incremental, change during the Reagan administration. Ronald Reagan saw Israel as a strategic asset, but there were other issues—a free trade arrangement, intelligence exchanges, and high-level joint groups on political-military and related issues—as well as the more prosaic intercourse of a relationship between two friendly states. The Reagan period marked a time of unprecedented growth in relations. U.S. economic and military assistance reached $3 billion per annum in essentially all-grant aid, and special grants helped Israel to deal with particular economic problems. Strategic cooperation between the United States and Israel reached new levels during this period, and on April 21, 1988 (in the Jewish calendar, the fortieth anniversary of Israel's independence), the two states signed a memorandum of agreement that institutionalized the emerging strategic relationship. Growing links in the military sphere involved joint military exercises, sales and purchases of equipment, training, and related activities. Israel had also gained status as a Major Non-Nato Ally.

With the November 1988 decision of the Palestine National Council (PNC) in Algiers to declare the establishment of a Palestinian state, the policy environment changed dramatically, with repercussions for President George Bush and his administration. This declaration was accompanied by ambiguous statements concerning the peace process, Israel, and terrorism. However, on December 14, 1988, in a press conference in Geneva, PLO leader Yasser Arafat read the script articulating a change in PLO views toward Israel and the Arab-Israeli conflict, renouncing terrorism, recognizing the state of Israel, and accepting UN Resolutions 242 and 338. Arafat thereby met the conditions for beginning a dialogue between the United States and the PLO that had first been enunciated in 1975 by then Secretary of State Henry Kissinger. The same day as the Algiers statement, Secretary of State George Shultz formally announced: "The Palestine Liberation Organization today issued a statement in which it accepted UN Security Council Resolutions 242 and 338, recognized Israel's right to exist in peace and security, and renounced terrorism. As a result, the United States is prepared for a substantive dialogue with PLO representatives." The U.S. ambassador to Tunisia, Robert Pelletreau, was designated as the only authorized channel for that dialogue. This official opening helped the incoming Bush administration to avoid what might have been a difficult issue; at the same time, it moved the process to another level. Skepticism remained and the administration sought to reassure Israel that "those who believe that American policy is about to undergo a basic shift merely because we have begun to talk with the PLO are completely mistaken."

The Bush Tenure

President George Bush took office in January 1989 with no long-range strategic plan or specific policies for the Arab-Israeli issue or the Gulf region of the Middle East. The end of the cold war, the implosion of the Soviet Union, the collapse of the Warsaw Pact, and the emerging new democracies in eastern Europe preoccupied the administration and Congress and entranced the media and public. The Iran-Iraq war had given way to a cease-fire, the departure of Soviet troops altered the hostilities in Afghanistan, and a dialogue with the PLO, established in the last days of the Reagan administration, continued. Within the context of a changing international system the Middle East was not a high national priority.

Much of Bush's first year in office was marked by a coolness on various issues, especially those relating to the peace process. Broad-scale concord, on such matters as the need for peace through direct negotiations, and specific-issue discord, for instance on questions relating to a land-for-peace exchange and related themes, increasingly seemed to be the measure of the dialogue. Nevertheless, substantial U.S. economic and military aid to Israel continued.

During the first year and a half of the Bush administration, Israel and the United States were preoccupied with the peace process and the effort to begin a negotiating process between Israel and the Palestinians. Bush administration frustration with the Shamir government was obvious in its preference for a Peres-led government after a successful vote of no-confidence terminated the tenure of the Israeli government in the spring of 1990 and in its voiced concerns about the prospects for peace after Shamir succeeded in constructing a new government in June 1990. The peace process was moribund when the Iraqis invaded Kuwait in August 1990, attributable, in large measure, to the policies of the Shamir government in Israel (at least in the eyes of the Bush administration).

During the Gulf crisis and the war against Iraq, Israel was relegated to a marginal role. Its position as a strategic asset seemed diminished and there was a widespread view in the Bush administration that Israel was not tactically relevant to potential actions in the Arabian Peninsula and the Persian Gulf. During the crisis Israel did not serve as a staging area for forces nor as a storage depot for military materiel, nor was it utilized for medical emergencies. There was a conscious U.S. effort to build a broad-based international force with an Arab component to oppose Saddam Hussein and to distance Israel from any such activity. Israel was determined not to be used as a tool to break the coalition. From the outset Israel was concerned that it was not part of the coalition. There was no publicly identified role for Israel given U.S.

objectives in the crisis, although the Israelis did endorse the firm and rapid U.S. re-action to Iraq.

The Iraqi scud missile attacks on Israel created a new situation. Responding to the entreaties of President Bush, Israel did not respond with military action against Iraq. Other factors swayed Israel against taking reprisals, including the arrival of U.S. Patriot missile batteries and U.S. cajoling in a crucial telephone conversation between President Bush and Prime Minister Shamir. The visit of Deputy Secretary of State Lawrence Eagleburger to Israel was especially important.

The inauguration of the Arab-Israeli peace process in the aftermath of the Gulf war revived traditional Israeli concerns about the United States as something less than a wholly supportive and reliable ally. This was further complicated by the chemistry (or, actually, the lack thereof) between U.S. and Israeli leaders and by doubts concerning specific Bush administration policies. Differences before the Gulf war were exacer-bated by developments afterward when the United States pressed for movement on an Arab-Israeli peace process even as Israel remained unconvinced that the Arab world was ready to move in that direction. Within several months of the Gulf war cease-fire, the U.S.-Israeli relationship was again characterized by discord and tension, with much of the goodwill just created being dissipated by disagreements over the modali-ties and substance of the peace process and other matters. Tensions developed as the Bush administration appeared to link proposed housing loan guarantees, essential to the settling of Soviet Jews in Israel, to Israel's actions on settlements in the West Bank and Gaza Strip and its responsiveness to the peace process. In testimony before the U.S. House Subcommittee on Foreign Operations of the Appropriations Committee on May 22, 1991, Secretary of State James Baker observed, "I don't think that there is any bigger obstacle to peace than the settlement activity that continues not only un-abated but at an enhanced pace." In the autumn of 1991 tensions became public when Bush asked Congress to postpone consideration of Israel's request for U.S. guarantees of $10 billion in loans. Ultimately the administration placed conditions on the loan guarantees that were impossible for the government of Israel to accept, and the matter was dropped in the spring of 1992 with recriminations by both sides.

The Bush administration clearly favored the Labor Party over Likud (and Yitzhak Rabin or Shimon Peres over Yitzhak Shamir), both in 1990 (during the period of the vote of no-confidence and the formation of a new Israeli government in June) and in the 1992 Knesset elections. Despite numerous denials and claims to the con-trary, the Bush administration and the Shamir government were not harmonious on many of the issues central to peace in the Middle East. The outcome of the June 1992 elections in Israel, with Yitzhak Rabin replacing Shamir as prime minister, was welcomed by the Bush administration as a significant and positive factor that would alter the regional situation, the prospects for progress in the Arab-Israeli peace process, and the nature of the U.S.-Israeli relationship. In late June 1992 Secretary of State Baker called for a quick resumption of Middle East peace talks, reflecting the administration's view that the elections had resulted in the demise of a hard-line Likud government and thereby facilitated the prospects for success in the peace negotiations. They saw the onus now falling upon the Palestinians and other Arabs to make serious compromises and proposals for peace.

At the same time, the overall tenor of U.S.-Israeli relations would improve, and tensions became relieved. During a U.S. visit by Rabin in August 1992, the prime minister and Bush focused on resuming the positive aspects of the U.S.-Israeli relationship. Bush noted that the visit was an important one and "the meetings were also significant for the tone of the discussions. Our time together can best be described as a consultation between close friends and strategic partners." The two leaders announced that they had reached an accord, with the Bush administration supporting loan guarantees for Israel. President Bush noted that "we understand the position [of the Rabin government concerning settlement construction] and all I will say is that I salute this change. We salute what the Prime Minister is trying to do. We understand his position. He understands our position. And obviously, we would not be going forward with this loan guarantee if we did not salute the change."

Bush and Arab-Israeli Peace

U.S. determination to see the peace process through was stressed by Bush in a speech to a joint session of Congress on March 6, 1991: "A comprehensive peace must be grounded in United Nations Security Council Resolutions 242 and 338 and the principle of territory for peace. This must provide for Israel's security and recognition, and at the same time for legitimate Palestinian political rights. Anything else would fail the twin tests of fairness and security."[5] Baker's visits to the Middle East in the spring and early summer of 1991 made it clear that there was no agreement among the concerned parties to convene a conference between the Arab states and Israel that would lead to bilateral negotiations between Israel and the bordering states still at war in Israel. The issues in contention included the venue of a conference (whether in the region or elsewhere), what powers and authority it would have (would it be primarily ceremonial in nature?), under whose auspices it should be conducted (i.e., whether the United Nations would be a factor), which Palestinians and other Arabs could and would attend, and what prior commitments must be made by the participants. There was also discord on both procedural and substantive issues.

Eventually, Baker convened the Madrid peace conference at the end of October 1991. The Madrid conference was attended reluctantly by the parties, who retained substantial concerns about the nature of the conference and from which little could be expected. The conference did not achieve a substantive breakthrough, although it eliminated the procedural barriers to direct bilateral negotiations between Israel and its immediate neighbors when the Israeli and the Syrian, Egyptian, Lebanese, and Jordanian-Palestinian delegations met at an opening public session and an official plenary session and delivered speeches and responses. Bilateral negotiations between Israel and each of the Arab delegations followed.

The Madrid conference was followed by bilateral talks in Washington later in 1991, talks that have continued into 1995 and have directly or indirectly contributed to the September 1993 Israel-PLO Declaration of Principles and the October 1994 Israeli-Jordanian peace teaty. Syria and Lebanon are the remaining Arab participants in Madrid that have not signed an accord with Israel as of December 1995. The first rounds achieved accord on nonsubstantive matters, primarily the time and venue of future meetings. Progress was measured primarily by the continuation of the process rather than by significant achievements on the substantive issues in dispute. The wide gap between the Israeli and Arab positions was not narrowed in these initial encounters, and it could not be bridged by outside actors (such as the United States and the former Soviet Union). The United States adhered to its role as facilitator and sought not to intervene on substantive matters. It was not a party to the bilateral talks and its representatives were not in the room or at the negotiating table, although it did meet separately with the parties and heard their views and perspectives.

In the bilateral negotiations the Israeli-Palestinian and Israeli-Syrian negotiations were the most central and most difficult. In the case of both Jordan and Lebanon the general perception at the time was that agreements would be relatively easy to achieve, although these would have to await the resolution of the Syrian and Palestinian talks. In the case of Syria the central issue was peace and the future of the Golan Heights, with little likelihood of compromise in the short term. In the Israeli-Palestinian discussions the disagreement centered on the Palestinian desire for self-government and the Israeli opposition to that goal. Compromise was elusive, as the positions were mutually exclusive. However, Israeli proposals for elections in the territories and the reality of the situation in the region suggested areas for continued negotiation, ultimately leading to the "Oslo Channel" bilateral negotiations outside of the Madrid process that resulted in the September 1993 signing of the Israel-PLO Declaration of Principles.

A related and parallel process to the Madrid conference included multilateral discussions on several regional issues and an initial organizing conference convened in Moscow in January 1992. The goal was to achieve progress on important regional issues, even without a political solution, that would reinforce the earlier bilateral negotiations. The five permanent members of the UN Security Council and a number of other important powers (including the European Community and Japan) were represented in Moscow. Despite some initial difficulties over the question of Palestinian participation and representation, the talks continued to fortify the basic bilateral process.

Despite the achievements symbolized by the Madrid conference and the subsequent bilateral and multilateral discussions, by the time of the Israeli and U.S. elections in 1992 no substantive breakthrough had occurred and no specific achievement (beyond continuation of the process) had been recorded. Although the administration was pleased with the inauguration of an essentially irreversible process to create peace in the Arab-Israeli conflict, by the end of the Bush administration's tenure no substantive breakthrough with the participant Arab states had occurred. Nevertheless, the Baker team seemed optimistic in the spring of 1992: Although the differences between the parties were still wide, they would eventually narrow and then it would be possible to bridge the gaps. U.S. policy under the Clinton administration has continued to emphasize the U.S. role of facilitator, especially on the Israeli-Syrian and Israeli-Jordanian fronts, with more success with the latter than the former (as shown by the Israeli-Jordanian peace treaty signed in October 1994). But the direction of the process is unmistakably toward cooperation and peace, although many obstacles still exist that could reverse or alter this direction.

A Final Word

Israel's special relationship with the United States—revolving around a broadly conceived ideological factor based on positive perception and sentiment evident in public opinion and official statements and manifest in political and diplomatic support and military and economic assistance—has not been enshrined in a legally binding commitment joining the two in a formal alliance. Despite the extensive links that have developed, the widespread belief in the existence of the commitment, and the assurances contained in various specific agreements, the exact nature and extent of the U.S. commitment to Israel remains imprecise. Israel has no mutual security treaty with the United States, nor is it a member of any alliance system requiring the United States to take up arms automatically on its behalf.

The U.S. commitment to Israel has taken the generalized form of presidential statements (rather than formal documents), which have reaffirmed the U.S. interest in supporting the political independence and territorial integrity of all Middle East states, including Israel. These statements do not, however, commit the United States to specific actions in particular circumstances. The arrangement has been codified in the Sinai II accords of 1975 and the MOU of 1981. Although commitments made in the Egyptian-Israeli peace process and other memoranda are significant, they do not provide a formal and legally binding commitment for U.S. military action.

It has largely been assumed by both parties that the United States would come to Israel's assistance should it be gravely threatened; this perception has become particularly apparent during times of crisis. Despite this perception and the general feeling in Washington (and elsewhere) that the United States would take action if required, there is no assurance that this would be the case. Israeli leaders continue to be interested in military and economic assistance as the primary tangible expression of the U.S. commitment and have been particularly cautious about potential U.S. participation in a conflict, fearing that combat losses might lead to a situation analogous to that in Vietnam. Thus, the exact role of the United States in support of Israel, beyond diplomatic and political action and military and economic assistance, is unclear.

The United States is today an indispensable if not fully dependable ally. It provides Israel, through one form or another, with economic (governmental and private), technical, military, political, diplomatic, and moral support. It is seen as the ultimate resource against potential enemies, it is the source of Israel's sophisticated military hardware, and its interest in lasting peace is central to the Arab-Israeli peace process. Although there is this positive relationship, there is also an Israeli reluctance, bred of history, to abdicate security to another party's judgment and action. Israel will continue to consider its perceptions of threat and security as decisive.

The two states maintain a remarkable degree of parallelism and congruence on broad policy goals. The policy consensus includes the need to prevent war, at both the regional and international levels, the need to resolve the Arab-Israeli conflict, and the need to maintain Israel's existence and security and to help provide for its economic well-being. At the same time, however, there was, is, and will be a divergence of interests that derives from a difference of perspective and overall policy environment. The United States has broader concerns resulting from its global obligations, whereas Israel's perspective is conditioned by its more restricted environment and lesser responsibilities. Israel's horizon is more narrowly defined and essentially limited to the survival of the state and a concern for Jewish communities and individuals that goes beyond the frontiers of the Jewish state.

Despite the generally positive nature of the relationship since 1948, Israelis tend to recall a series of negative episodes as well. They highlight the 1947 arms embargo and the subsequent refusal to provide military equipment or other assistance during the War of Independence and the period that followed; Dulles's aid suspensions and general unfriendliness; U.S. actions in connection with the Sinai War of 1956 and Israel's subsequent withdrawal from the Sinai and the Gaza Strip; and the disappointing lack of action by the United States just prior to the Six Day War in support of its 1957 pledge concerning freedom of passage for Israeli shipping in the Strait of Tiran. In 1967—the year of the Six Day War with Egypt—Israel ultimately decided that the United States would not act unilaterally and that multilateral action would not succeed. Israel determined its need to act alone and estimated that the United States would not object to or seek to prevent its action and, when Israel decided to go to war, it did not consult or inform the United States.

There has also been a divergence on methods and techniques to be employed, as well as discord on specific issues. During the Six Day War there was a clash over Israel's mistaken attack (and causing of casualties) against the U.S. intelligence ship *Liberty.* In May 1968 there was disagreement over Israel's control of the islands of Tiran and Sanafir. They disagreed on the matter of reprisals by Israel in response to Arab *fedayeen* (literally, "self-sacrificers") actions and on the limits placed on the refugees from the West Bank in the wake of the Six Day War. There was major disagreement concerning the value of a great power to resolve the Arab-Israeli conflict, Israel's need for military supplies, and the status of the Occupied Territories and Israel's role with respect to them, including the building of settlements. They have differed over the construction of settlements in the territories and whether they are legal and whether they are in fact obstacles to peace. They have argued over Israel's desire for significant changes in the pre–Six Day War armistice lines as contrasted with the U.S. perspective that there be "insubstantial alterations" or "minor modifications." The two states will continue to hold divergent views on the several elements of the Palestinian issue, particularly the West Bank's future, the rights of the Palestinians, and the potential creation of a Palestinian homeland, entity, or state. These differences became increasingly obvious in the Carter and Reagan administrations.

In many respects the issue of Jerusalem has highlighted the areas of discord. The United States has supported the Partition Plan designation of Jerusalem as a separate entity and has stressed the international character of the city while refusing to recognize unilateral actions by any state affecting its future. The United States refuses to move its embassy to Jerusalem and maintains it in Tel Aviv, thus illustrating the differing perspectives of the two states. (Although both the House and Senate overwhelmingly passed bills in October 1995 to move the embassy to Jerusalem by 1997, President Clinton, thus far, has indicated he would not do so because it might disrupt the peace negotiations.) These perspectives have placed the two states in conflicting positions continuously from 1947 to the present, especially since the Israeli declarations of Jerusalem as the capital of the state and the reunification of the city during the Six Day War. The increase in Israel's dependence on the United States and the areas of policy discord suggest possible reemployment of various forms of pressure utilized previously, including the withholding of economic aid as in the mid-1950s, military aid decisions and delivery slowdowns since 1967 (such as the slow response to Israeli requests during the 1973 war), joining in United Nations censures, moral persuasion, private and open presidential letters, and similar devices.

The general consensus on major issues does not ensure agreement on all aspects or specifics of each problem. As the dialogue has increasingly focused on details, rather than broad areas of agreement, there have been disturbances in the relationship. Israel and the United States understand that this is inevitable but seek to minimize the areas of discord. Strains in the relationship are probably inevitable given the extensive nature of the issues that will be considered in the dialogue. Foreign Minister Yitzhak Shamir described the situation to the Knesset in these terms in September 1982:

> Our relations with the United States are of a special character. Between our two nations there is a deep friendship based on common values and identical interests. At the same time differences between our two countries crop up occasionally chiefly on the subject of our borders and how to defend our security. These differences of opinion are natural; they stem from changing conditions, and they express our independence and our separate needs. . . . Israel is a difficult ally, but a faithful and reliable one. We are certain that what we have in common with the United States is permanent and deep while our disagreements are ephemeral. The permanent will overcome the ephemeral.

In presenting his government to the Knesset in July 1992, Prime Minister Yitzhak Rabin defined the relationship in these terms: "Sharing with us in the making of peace will also be the United States, whose friendship and special closeness we prize. We shall spare no effort to strengthen and improve the special relationship we have with the one power in the world. Of course we shall avail ourselves of its advice, but the decisions will be ours alone, of Israel as a sovereign and independent state." The basic policy guidelines of the government, as approved by the parliament, included: "The government will concentrate efforts to deepen and improve the special relations of friendship which exist between the United States and Israel."

Endurance and Continuity

Changing administrations in Washington, and of governments in Jerusalem, have all affected the nature and content of the links between the United States and Israel within the broad parameters of the enduring special relationship. The patterns of agreement and discord established from the outset have manifested themselves subsequently—broad patterns of concord on the more strategic and existential issues, accompanied by disagreement on the specifics of many of the elements of the Arab-Israeli conflict and on the means to achieve congruent objectives.

At Israel's birth the United States seemed to be a dispassionate, almost uninterested, midwife—its role was essential and unconventional but also unpredictable and hotly debated in U.S. policy circles. Today, fifty years later, some of the policy debate continues, and there are periods of discord in the relationship. Some of this reflects personality and related differences between U.S. and Israeli leaders. But there is little doubt about the overall nature of U.S. support for its small and still embattled ally.

The accession of the Clinton administration to office in 1993 and of the Rabin government in 1992 provided the basis for a continuation of the relationship, but in a more positive mode, with strong and improving personal and country-to-country relations focusing on the Madrid-inaugurated Arab-Israeli peace process. The United States reassured the Israelis that the U.S. commitment to its security would be sustained. And a strong positive personal relationship seemed to develop between the American president and his Israeli prime minister counterpart.

The relationship between Clinton and Rabin continued to grow closer and became more intimate as the peace process, begun at Madrid and amplified by Oslo, continued to make progress. Each achievement seemed to be marked by an added positive glow to both the personal chemistry and the political accord between the two partners. This, of course, was demonstrated and exemplified by the assassination of Rabin in November 1995. Clinton appeared to be personally moved by the death of his peace partner and issued the famous statement "*Shalom, chaver*" (goodbye, friend) that struck close to the heart of their dealings. The substantial size and level of the U.S. delegation to the funeral was essentially unprecedented but reaffirmed the connection between the two states and reflected the close personal ties forged between the two leaders.

The success of Benjamin Netanyahu in his race against Shimon Peres (Rabin's foreign minister and alter ego in the peace process) in the first-ever popular election of the prime minister in Israel in the spring of 1996 illustrated again the unusual nature of the connection. The Clinton administration, seeking continuity in the peace process, clearly preferred that Shimon Peres succeed. Some noted that the Clinton team all but campaigned for Peres (and some of Peres's opponents argued that the U.S. government had actually gotten involved in Israeli domestic affairs). Nevertheless, despite the outcome, the relationship endured and the United States continued to support Israel's security and quest for peace. Even though there was a lack of personal chemistry between Clinton and Netanyahu, many in the Republican-dominated U.S. Congress saw the latter's victory as a positive accomplishment and endorsed his approach.

The period of Netanyahu's tenure in some ways resembled that of Menachem Begin in the relationship between the United States and Israel on the issues of the peace process. The Clinton administration continued to press for progress on the peace process begun at Madrid and expanded in Oslo and by subsequent Israeli accords with the Palestinians and with Jordan. The prime minister of Israel, reflecting a skepticism of the Palestinian position and a deep-seated concern for an arrangement that would ensure Israel's security as well as a personal goal of ensuring the stability of his governing coalition and, hence, his position in office, acted with considerable deliberation and pursued a pace seen by the Clinton administration as far too slow. Clashes of position were reflected in numerous public (and private) conflicts between the two parties. By the middle of 1998 the Clinton administration presented an "ultimatum" to Israel that was ignored and then faded from public view. The two states pursued the peace process and clashed with each other. But, as before, the administration often was not backed by the Congress, which seemed more sympathetic to the Netanyahu approach and position and provided public and private positive reinforcement to the Israeli government.

These episodes and others in the Clinton tenure reflected the themes that marked the Carter-Begin relationship and characterized the broader relationship between the United States and Israel, which centered on endurance and continuity in the quest for peace and Israeli security and on discord concerning the means and procedures (as well as some of the content) of the process to best achieve those ends.

Notes

1. *New York Times,* May 13, 1977.

2. To a great extent this was a consequence of the rupture of diplomatic relations by major Arab states with the United States, and much of what was seen of the region from Washington was viewed through an Israeli prism rather than an Arab perspective, and it was difficult for the Arab states to gain the sympathy and understanding of the American people.

3. An example of the latter is found in the confirmation hearings of Strobe Talbott as deputy secretary of state, when congressional queries and votes tended to focus on what Talbott had written more than a decade earlier on the Arab-Israeli conflict, when he was seen as critical of Israel.

4. Jonathan Jay Pollard, a U.S. Navy intelligence analyst, was arrested in November 1985 and charged with spying. Pollard pleaded guilty in June 1986. Israel denied that its senior officials had knowledge of or had approved any espionage activities against the United States. Shimon Peres apologized and promised a full investigation.

5. The full text is in the *New York Times,* March 7, 1991.

15

The U.S.–PLO Relationship: From Dialogue to the White House Lawn

JoAnn A. DiGeorgio-Lutz

On September 13, 1993, Yasser Arafat, in his capacity as chairman of the Executive Committee of the Palestine Liberation Organization (PLO), stood on the White House lawn to witness the signing of the Declaration of Principles (DOP) and the mutual recognition between Israel and the PLO. Even though the Bill Clinton administration had endeavored to reap some diplomatic profit from the event, the only accolade that the United States could claim was its role as master of ceremonies; Arafat's unprecedented appearance at the White House did not occur as a result of a constructive U.S.-PLO relationship. In fact, Arafat bypassed U.S. diplomacy altogether when he unilaterally took a diplomatic detour through Oslo, Norway, to reach a principled agreement with the Israeli government. This occurred even as Palestinian negotiators participated at the Washington rounds of bilateral talks that began under the Bush administration after the convening of the Madrid conference in October 1991. Arafat's deliberate removal of Washington from the Oslo equation begs the question as to why the PLO leader opted for an alternative strategy despite the implicit recognition of the Palestinian negotiators as PLO arbitrators during the latter stages of the bilateral talks.

In order to answer that question, this chapter examines the precarious nature of the U.S.-PLO relationship from the viewpoint of the PLO. Such an approach deviates from conventional themes that generally emphasize the U.S.-PLO connection from the perspective of U.S. diplomacy, particularly as it relates to the broader Arab-Israeli conflict.[1] Scholarly efforts do not always uncover the myriad dynamics that contribute to the formation of PLO foreign policy, especially toward the United States. Moreover, an understanding of the factors that shape PLO foreign policy helps dispel some of the misperceptions that persist about the organization and provides some insight into the formation of its overall foreign policy behavior.

In laying a foundation, this chapter outlines several characteristics about the over-all nature of PLO foreign policy, followed by a discussion of PLO policy in relation to the United States from the end of the Ronald Reagan presidency in 1988 to Arafat's September 13, 1993, appearance at the White House. Finally, I will offer some concluding remarks about the PLO's current leadership crisis.

Characteristics of PLO Foreign Policy

Much like any state actor, the PLO is subject to a set of factors that influence the formation and direction of its foreign policy. In addition to regional and international dynamics that often necessitate a foreign policy decision, there are three separate political bodies within the PLO that participate in the foreign policy process, bodies that parallel the executive and legislative branches of governments of states. Those bodies are the Palestine National Council (the PNC—the PLO's "parliament-in-exile"), the Executive Committee (which functions as the "supreme executive authority of the PLO"), and the Central Council (originally established by the 7th PNC to serve as an intermediary between the organization's executive structure and the PNC when the latter is not in session). Also contributing to the foreign policy process is the interplay among the PLO's various guerrilla groups, which causes a bureaucratic political effect. In a broad sense, these groups act like political parties that influence foreign policy through their support or rejection of a particular strategy or goal. Bureaucratic politics remained a key element of PLO foreign policy throughout the 1970s and early 1980s, when consensus decisionmaking was the organizational rule and the PLO's constituency was anchored in the diaspora. However, the PLO's adoption of majority-rule decisionmaking in 1984, followed by the voluntary withdrawal of key guerrilla groups from power-sharing positions and the leadership's subsequent turn to the Occupied Territories as the backbone of its legitimacy, led to an erosion of bureaucratic politics as the primary mechanism driving foreign policy. This decline helped pave the way for Arafat to assume a commanding role in the foreign policy process that persists to this day.

This notion—that a constituency shapes foreign policy—is probably more acute for PLO leaders than for most state actors because the PLO does not exercise direct control over people. Thus, the PLO's "constituency" is located in the diaspora and in the Occupied Territories of the West Bank and Gaza. The continued legitimacy of the PLO and its leadership requires that they take into consideration the aspirations and demands of that constituency. Prior to the 1982 Israeli invasion of Lebanon and the subsequent expulsion of the PLO from Beirut, the organization primarily aspired to meet the demands of diaspora Palestinians. After 1982 and the loss of its military presence in Lebanon, however, the PLO redirected its attention toward the West Bank and Gaza as the mainstay of its constituency. Since the *intifada*, and especially since the Gulf war, the leadership of the PLO has increased its focus on the Occupied Territories as the primary determinant of its foreign policy to the exclusion of the diaspora Palestinians, especially those residing in refugee camps. This is partly because of the activities of the Islamic Resistance Movement, or Hamas, which not only rejects the secular-based policies of the PLO but also poses a credible challenge to the continued political viability of the organization and its leadership.

The PLO, like many decisionmaking bodies, evaluates its foreign policy based on the feedback it receives regarding the success or failure of a particular tactic or goal. Furthermore, the presence of a threat or opportunity also serves as a mechanism for gauging the direction of its foreign policy behavior. PLO leadership perceives a threat as any attempt to marginalize the organization's right to act as the legitimate representative of the Palestinian people. Conversely, it views an opportunity as any situation in which it can initiate content and direction of PLO foreign policy and maintain an independent role in the process. Whenever the PLO leadership is able to retain the initiative, it is more likely to pursue pragmatic policies characterized by political accommodation and concessions.

Two additional, general features can be noted about the nature of PLO foreign policy. First, what often appears as a dramatic change in policy is actually the culmination of a series of evolutionary modifications that have occurred over time. For example, a study of PNC resolutions reveals that the PLO gradually modified its use of armed struggle as the exclusive means to achieve strategic objectives.[2] What the organization considered to be the sole means to liberate Palestine in 1968 was changed to a principal means in 1971 and was foremost by 1974, culminating in the renunciation of armed struggle altogether by 1988. Additionally, the same study reveals that the PLO has modified its strategic goals over the years, moving from the goal of total liberation of Palestine in 1968 to acceptance of the Gaza-Jericho First Plan in 1993.[3]

The second feature is the leadership's persistent demand that it retain the initiative over foreign policy based on the organization's authority to act as the sole, legitimate representative of the Palestinian people.[4] Since 1968, the PLO leadership has historically refused to accept a subservient or secondary role by its sustained rejection of any attempt to impose upon the organization externally mandated foreign policy agendas.[5]

Climate of Opportunity

Toward the end of the Reagan presidency an opportunistic political climate emerged that provided the PLO leadership an occasion to launch a more moderate, realistic course of foreign policy. By the 18th PNC (April 1987), the PLO had reunified its previously disaffected bureaucratic groups and reasserted its commitment to United Nations (UN) General Assembly Resolution 38/58, which called for, among other things, an international conference on the Middle East with equal PLO participation.[6]

The PLO gained an additional opportunity shortly after the outbreak of the *intifada* in December 1987. Because the uprising marked the first time that Palestinians had taken matters into their own hands independent of the PLO, the organization's legitimacy faced a potential threat. The leadership of the PLO, however, quickly transformed the *intifada* into an opportunity that allowed it to reassert the organization's leadership role and to direct the course of events in the Occupied Territories.

The international environment was also marked by significant changes. The demise of the cold war was accompanied by the Soviet Union's return to the Middle East as a moderator of peace. By 1988, the reentry of the Soviet Union into the region, coupled with media attention given to the *intifada* and the resulting public outcry in support of the Palestinians, obliged Reagan's secretary of state, George Shultz, to revitalize the Arab-Israeli peace talks. This led to the May 1988 Shultz initiative, which featured the long-standing U.S. goal of a comprehensive settlement to the Arab-Israeli conflict based procedurally on bilateral talks and substantively on UN Security Council Resolutions 242 and 338. Also, according to the Shultz initiative, only the legitimate rather than national rights of the Palestinians would be addressed. Because there would be no direct role for the PLO in the peace process, Palestinian participation would be linked exclusively with that of Jordan.[7]

The U.S. preference for bilateral talks consequent to an international conference that would only serve to launch negotiations stood in contrast to the PLO's predilection for a sustained international forum as a means to achieve a negotiated settlement. Despite these procedural differences, the substantive aims of the United States were not entirely inconsistent with PLO objectives. Since 1983, PNC resolutions indicated that the PLO had gradually narrowed the basis of its rejection of Resolutions 242 and 338. If congruency between the PLO and Washington could be established on a substantive level, then perhaps their respective procedural differences could also be overcome in the future.

Moreover, because the PLO leadership was interested in broadening the organization's foreign policy agenda to include more moderate and less revolutionary behaviors to achieve its political objectives, it was not averse to granting concessions provided it retain the initiative in the formation and direction of that policy. By 1988, moderates within the PLO were contemplating the possibility of openly pursuing a two-state solution to the Israeli-Palestinian conflict as the more attainable and realistic goal. The PLO responded to the Shultz initiative by circulating a position paper authored by an aide to Arafat, Bassam Abu Sharif, to the international media prior to the Algiers Arab Summit conference in early June 1988. In the position paper, Abu Sharif acknowledged that the PLO had already accepted Resolutions 242 and 338. The organization's reluctance to state this "unconditionally," however, had been the failure on the part of the resolutions to address the "national rights of the Palestinian people, including their democratic right to self-expression and their national right to self-determination."[8] With the publication of the Abu Sharif paper, the PLO indirectly signaled to Washington that it might be willing to compromise and recognize the state of Israel in exchange for a direct role in any international peace conference.

Even though these signals did not elicit the response from Washington that the PLO leadership may have hoped for, they did not go unnoticed by the organization's bureaucratic factions and Palestinian constituency in the Occupied Territories. Although both the Democratic Front (DFLP) and the Popular Front for the Liberation of Palestine (PFLP) apparently rejected what appeared to be a unilateral move on the part of Arafat at the expense of the organization's decisionmaking institutions, the Occupied Territories constituency signaled its approval for the chairman's diplomatic offensive and a new foreign policy role for the PLO grounded in pragmatism.[9]

On July 31, 1988, Jordan's King Hussein announced that Jordan was relinquishing legal and administrative ties to the West Bank, which created an opportunity for the PLO leadership in the form of political space. That provided Arafat with ample room to pursue a diplomatic offensive. His thinking was guided by the observation that the effective removal of Jordan from the West Bank political equation meant that any settlement of the West Bank's territorial status would now have to include an active role for the PLO. Capitalizing on the opportunity provided by Jordan, Arafat launched a unilateral campaign to secure international and regional support for a pragmatic two-state territorial solution. Speaking before the European Parliament on September 12, 1988, Arafat indicated the PLO's willingness to negotiate with Israel either on the basis of all relevant UN resolutions or on the isolated basis of UN Resolutions 242 and 338—provided that Israel accept the Palestinian right to self-determination. Arafat also reaffirmed the PLO's commitment to the 1985 Cairo Declaration, in which he condemned terrorism.[10]

The political environment grew more opportunistic as private channels of diplomacy were being explored through Sweden about the possibility of a U.S. Jewish-PLO initiative that could potentially lead to an Israel-PLO dialogue. The Swedish efforts served to activate the initiative developed by PLO and U.S. representatives Mohamed Rabie and William B. Quandt that detailed conditions for a U.S.-PLO dialogue. These events subsequently engaged Secretary of State Shultz and set the stage for the development of the U.S.-PLO dialogue.[11]

The results of the November 1988 U.S. presidential election and the Israeli parliamentary elections (which brought to power a Likud-led coalition without Labor sharing in the premiership), provided additional impetus for the PLO to push forward. Arafat's public sentiment about the PLO's more pragmatic goal of a two-state territorial solution and moderate foreign policy required a measure of official endorsement. That endorsement was made official at the historic 19th PNC (November 1988) in which the PLO explicitly accepted UN General Assembly Resolution 181 and Security Council Resolutions 242 and 338. In addition, the political resolutions adopted at this PNC did not assign any role for armed struggle as a means to achieve Palestinian political objectives, nor was there any reference to the 1968 Palestine National Charter. Instead, the resolutions endorsed by the PNC rejected "terrorism in all its forms," including state terrorism. Even though the language of the resolutions failed to satisfy Shultz, Arafat accommodated the United States at a press conference shortly after the 19th PNC in which he clarified certain ambiguous points. Arafat furthered clarified his position in an address to the UN General Assembly, which met in Geneva on December 13, 1988, following Shultz's refusal to grant the PLO chairman a visa to address the General Assembly in New York. Because the PLO was on the initiating end of its own foreign policy, Arafat was able to finally satisfy Shultz and "renounced" terrorism at a December 14 press conference without significant bureaucratic backlash.

In theory, the PLO had opened the diplomatic door to new foreign policy opportunities when it satisfied Washington's three demands as preconditions for a dialogue. Those demands were: the recognition of Israel's right to exist; acceptance of Resolutions 242 and 338; and the "renouncement" of terrorism. The PLO leadership met those demands in a political climate of opportunity in which the leadership maintained the initiative in the selection of its foreign policy behavior. The PLO's willingness to accommodate Washington paid off when the outgoing Reagan administration announced in December 1988 that the United States was now prepared to commence a "substantive dialogue" with the PLO. This announcement also marked a major shift in U.S. policy toward the PLO.[12]

Although the new dialogue's procedural conditions were limited to contacts with the U.S. ambassador to Tunisia, Robert Pelletreau, the substance of that dialogue would be left for the newly elected Bush administration to define. Subsequently, it would produce little in terms of diplomatic gains for the PLO.

A Change in the Political Climate

During the first round of U.S.-PLO talks, held in Tunis on December 16, 1988, differences surfaced over procedural issues regarding the peace process. The United States insisted on direct, bilateral Arab-Israeli negotiations as part of any peace process. The PLO, however, was not willing to compromise on this point because its preference has always been for an international conference that would include Soviet participation as a means to counter U.S. support for Israel. Moreover, bilateral talks seemed pointless as long as the Israeli government maintained its policy of refusing to negotiate with the PLO. The leadership of the PLO expressed cautious optimism about the status of its newfound relationship with the United States despite the pressures on Arafat from bureaucratic factions, including elements from within his own faction, Fatah, to halt concessionary practices.

The incoming Bush administration heralded the possibility of a successful U.S.-PLO relationship because it represented the first U.S. government that was on speaking terms with all the parties to the conflict. However, the potential for a collapse in the newly established U.S.-PLO relationship also existed. The Bush administration assumed office with the same long-standing convictions and policies regarding the Arab-Israeli conflict that characterized preceding U.S. presidential administrations.[13]

By March 1989, the PLO leadership began to signal the possibility that the dialogue might be headed toward failure. Senior PLO officials expressed their disappointment over the substance of the dialogue that failed to move beyond lectures on terrorism.[14] As a result, several areas of disagreement between the United States and the PLO were left unresolved. Those differences centered around Washington's insistence that the PLO curb the violence of the *intifada*, that the organization cease its military activities in southern Lebanon, and that procedural conditions for the convening of peace talks involve direct bilateral talks. Even though the PLO leadership's assessment of the dialogue remained somewhat sanguine, there was a growing conviction among the leadership that the PLO had granted enough concessions and that "time was running short."[15] Pressures from the PLO's bureaucratic groups in combination with a growing discontent in the Occupied Territories limited Arafat's ability to take unilateral steps to meet Washington's demands.

At a meeting of the PLO's Central Council, the representatives of all the PLO's bureaucratic factions granted Arafat a powerful mandate on April 8, 1989, when they unanimously designated him Palestine's first president. Aside from this show of political support, the bureaucratic factions simultaneously criticized Arafat's unilateral style of leadership, his compromising statements toward the United States, and continued Israeli-Palestinian contacts that threatened to bypass the PLO.[16] The effect of those criticisms temporarily dampened Arafat's ability to act independently.

Regional dynamics constrained Arafat even further as the political environment began to change from opportunistic to threat-driven when Israeli Prime Minister Yitzhak Shamir announced his election plan as part of the Israeli initiative for peace.[17] One of the features of the Shamir Plan called for West Bank and Gaza elections as the means for Palestinians to select representatives to conduct negotiations for a transitional period of Palestinian self-rule. This transitional period would precede future negotiations for a permanent solution for the Occupied Territories that precluded the possibility of a two-state solution. Moreover, the Shamir Plan explicitly stated that the government of Israel would not negotiate with the PLO.

The PLO leadership began to perceive that it was losing the initiative in both the formation and course of its foreign policy. These perceptions proved correct when Egyptian President Husni Mubarak submitted his version of how the Israeli elections should be conducted. When Mubarak's ten points were rejected by the Israeli cabinet, U.S. Secretary of State Baker submitted his "Five-Point Framework" as a preliminary step to bolster Shamir's election plan.[18] Neither Mubarak's ten points nor Baker's five mentioned any role for the PLO.

By 1990 the PLO was compelled to conduct its foreign policy in an international environment that threatened to corner the organization into a subservient role in the peace process. Washington had effectively marginalized the PLO from representing Palestinians in the peace process with its insistence that it extend to Egypt the right to name a Palestinian delegation to conduct talks with the Israelis. Although the United States jeopardized the PLO's right to act as sole legitimate representative of the Palestinian people, the PLO leadership endeavored to maintain this right by offering a compromise solution. The PLO would accept a limitation of its legitimate right to act a sole spokesperson for the Palestinians provided that it be allowed to name its own representatives.

As the United States effectively pushed the PLO into a subservient role, its leadership faced growing internal pressures. In addition to pressure directed at Arafat from the various bureaucratic factions to fall back on a more militant approach,

Palestinians in the Occupied Territories began to signal their growing frustration over the PLO's continued conciliatory policy toward Washington. The PLO leadership could no longer ignore the growing frustration of its West Bank and Gaza constituency. Regional dynamics began to force the organization to respond to the cues and demands it received from the Occupied Territories at the expense of formal contacts with the West.

Alignment with Iraq

Frustration in the Occupied Territories began to mount during the course of the *intifada*. Already into its third year, the uprising had not succeeded in ending Israeli occupation. The Palestinians also began to express their dissatisfaction with the lack of progress in the U.S.-PLO dialogue. There was a growing disillusionment among inhabitants of the Occupied Territories that the PLO policy of continually accommodating U.S. demands had yet to produce any tangible results. The Palestinians in the West Bank and Gaza needed some measure of relief. That relief was temporarily satisfied with the reentry of Iraq into the regional political equation.

A renewed sense of optimism developed among Palestinians in the Occupied Territories during Saddam Hussein's February 1990 visit to Jordan to mark the first anniversary of the Arab Cooperation Council, an economic union forged among Jordan, Iraq, and the PLO. In a speech transmitted over Jordanian television and broadcast throughout the Occupied Territories, Saddam Hussein essentially condemned the West for its unwavering support of Israel and called upon all Arabs to unite in the struggle against the United States. Reacting to Saddam's speech, inhabitants of the West Bank and Gaza Strip began to pin their hopes on Iraq as the new power in the region that could liberate them from the yoke of Israeli occupation.

Political dynamics both inside and outside the Occupied Territories pushed Arafat into taking a nonretractable, hard-line position vis-à-vis the West. Inside the Occupied Territories, increased Israeli settlement activity along with Palestinian concern over the policies of the Likud government (which proved to be more hard-line than the previous Labor-Likud coalition), coupled with the influx of Soviet Jews, fueled both discontent and despair. In Gaza, severe economic pressures in addition to the renewed threat of expulsions when the far-right Moledet Party gained seats in the new Israeli government added to Palestinian despair.[19] The PLO also had to consider the increased activities of Hamas in both Gaza and the West Bank.

In the aftermath of the foiled May 30, 1990, raid on an Israeli beach by members of the Palestine Liberation Front (PLF), Washington pressured Arafat to condemn the PLF leader of the attack, Abu 'Abbas. With a growing belief that renewed violence, or a return to armed struggle, might be the only solution for the Palestinian dilemma, the PLO leadership was faced with a decision: Bow to U.S. pressures to punish Abu 'Abbas as a condition for maintaining a one-sided dialogue or heed the growing discontent in the Occupied Territories over the PLO's continued accommodationist behavior toward the West. In June 1990, when Arafat refused to punish Abu 'Abbas, the United States suspended its eighteen-month dialogue with the PLO.

Following the Iraqi invasion of Kuwait in August 1990, demonstrations in support of Saddam Hussein broke out in the Occupied Territories. One of the driving mechanisms behind the public support of Saddam was the "linkage-issue," in which the Iraqi withdrawal from Kuwait was conditional upon the Israeli withdrawal from the West Bank and Gaza. Hamas was particularly active during this time, distributing leaflets in the territories that called on all Palestinians to take their struggle to Israeli soil and for Baghdad to attack Tel Aviv if the West attacked Iraq.[20] Even though the PLO was attempting to distance itself from its alignment with Iraq, it could not ignore the grassroots support that Palestinians expressed for Saddam without risking its legitimacy in the eyes of its primary constituency. In addition to pro-Iraqi demonstrations, the Palestinians held strikes to protest the U.S. military presence in the Gulf, responding to an event that had transformed itself from a regional dispute into an international conflict.[21]

At the international level, the U.S. veto of a proposed UN resolution calling for an observer force in the Occupied Territories following the Rishon Le Zion killings in Gaza in May 1990 and the inability of the PLO to pressure the UN Security Council to condemn the Haram al-Sharif murders of October 1990 in harsher terms contributed to the PLO's closer alignment with Iraq. The PLO leadership had no other option but to accept the position imposed on it by regional events and its constituency in the Occupied Territories and align with the Iraqi camp during the Gulf war. The PLO paid a heavy price for its decision not to side with the U.S.-led coalition against Saddam Hussein. The effect of that decision left the PLO politically and financially isolated in the postwar environment that promised a new world order in the Middle East.

The Postwar Environment

Following the Gulf war, Bush announced that the United States was prepared to pursue a peaceful settlement of the Arab-Israeli conflict. The PLO, however, found itself without a direct role in the proposed peace conference initiated by the United States. What appeared to be a combined U.S., Arab, and Israeli attempt to bypass the PLO (and Arafat in particular) was met with a measure of resistance by Palestinians. The PLO's main card continued to be the legitimacy and support it received from its constituency in the Occupied Territories.

A renewed but limited opportunity presented itself when the United States announced that a Palestinian delegation would be allowed to attend the peace conference jointly sponsored by the United States and Soviet Union, scheduled to convene at Madrid. The only remaining question was the role that the PLO would exercise in the process. Operating through a Palestinian delegation, the PLO presented Secretary of State Baker with a list of questions when he met with Palestinian representatives Faisal Husseini, Hanan Ashrawi, and Zakariya al-Agha in Jerusalem on July 21, 1991. Among the points that the PLO wanted clarified was the exact role it would be allowed to exercise in the upcoming peace process.[22]

Although no direct role for the PLO was forthcoming, its leadership was willing to operate behind the scenes provided that Washington give its assurance that the peace conference would be based on Resolution 242. The PLO, however, still insisted on its right to appoint Palestinian delegates to the conference. The 20th PNC convened in Algiers in September 1991 and formally endorsed Palestinian participation at the Madrid conference. The PLO's willingness to exercise a limited role in the peace process was partly the result of its weakened position following the Gulf war. PLO thinking was guided by the belief that participation, albeit indirect, could help break the organization's diplomatic isolation. In addition, the collapse of the Soviet Union in August 1991 translated into the loss of a valuable counterweight to U.S. hegemony. In essence, the organization was left without any effective alternatives. On October 13, 1991, the PLO Executive Committee gave its approval for a joint Palestinian-Jordanian delegation.

On October 18, 1991, the United States sent an official invitation to the Palestinian delegation from the Occupied Territories to attend the Madrid conference. Included in the invitation were Washington's three demands for Palestinian participation: no PLO officials; no Palestinians from outside the Occupied Territories; no Palestinians from Jerusalem.[23]

In the absence of an official role for the PLO, Arafat endorsed the attendance of the Palestinian negotiating team. Perceptions among the Palestinian negotiators at the start of the conference rested on the belief that the United States was finally committed to work for a fair and equitable solution to the Israeli-Palestinian conflict. This line of thought rested on the conviction that the demise of the cold war had lessened Israel's strategic importance to the United States. By the end of the first round of bilateral talks, however, the Palestinian negotiators' initial optimism had faded. In a December 1991 press conference held in Jerusalem, the delegates concluded that the continued success of the peace process would require the active participation of the United States. In their view, a stronger U.S. role was needed, especially since Israel demonstrated a lack of commitment to the peace process evidenced by the Jewish state's refusal to negotiate separately with the Palestinian delegation.

Despite the lack of a strong U.S. role and the absence of any tangible gains, the PLO continued to endorse Palestinian participation in the subsequent rounds of the conference. In retrospect, the PLO's approach to this process leading up to the signing of the Declaration of Principles can be divided into two distinct phases: the Shamir phase and the Rabin phase.

The Shamir Phase

The Shamir phase produced a minor PLO policy success in that it marked the first time that Palestinians were officially seated at the negotiating table with the other parties to the conflict. Notwithstanding this public relations success, the terms of Palestinian participation had situated the negotiators at an unfair disadvantage vis-à-vis the other negotiating teams. In terms of this disadvantage, the PLO had no other choice but to accept a restricted delegation in lieu of a visible role because Israel had effectively set the terms.[24]

Also, the initial optimism held by the Palestinian negotiating team at the start of the conference soon gave way to frustration and dwindling public support, especially among the inhabitants of the Occupied Territories. In their assessment of the first round, the Palestinian negotiators expressed the belief that the United States was not exercising an impartial role. Moreover, the talks had failed to yield the momentum that Baker believed would be generated merely by bringing the parties to the negotiating table.[25] (It should be noted, however, that it was never the intention of the United States to impose a solution on the parties to the conflict. Instead, the United States viewed its role in the peace process as a "catalyst" that would merely bring the parties together by ironing out procedural differences rather than concentrate on substantive affairs.)[26]

As the peace rounds progressed, opposition against continued Palestinian participation came from Hamas and the Damascus-based Palestine National Salvation Front (PNSF), which was comprised of various PLO bureaucratic factions. Discontent also existed over Israel's policy of continued settlement activity, the increase in human rights violations, and a growing economic crisis. The United States regained a measure of credibility among the Palestinians when Bush linked the issue of Israel's $10 billion loan guarantee request to a halt in additional settlement building. This small opportunity, however, soon faded as the reality of the talks continued to leave the Palestinians without any concrete gains.

Israel's rejection of the Palestinian proposal for self-rule and the change in the status of the West Bank and Gaza—from occupied lands to disputed lands—necessitated a change in PLO strategy. Part of that centered around discussions regarding possible confederation with Jordan, which triggered an internal debate that threatened to divide the negotiating team. The core of this debate was the issue of whether to achieve Palestinian statehood before or after confederation. In an effort to quell disagreement, Arafat's political adviser, Nabil Sha'th, stated that any plans for confederation automatically presupposed the existence of an independent Palestinian state in accordance with the resolutions adopted by the 19th PNC (1988).[27]

In May 1992, the PLO Central Council endorsed the organization's continued participation in the peace process despite the barrage of criticisms from the bureaucratic factions.[28] Particularly vocal were representatives of the PFLP and Nayef Hawatma's faction of the DFLP, which charged that the PLO's current negotiating strategy had not only sidestepped the issue of the 1948 refugees but also failed to expand the terms of PLO participation to include Palestinians from East Jerusalem at the multilateral rounds. Moreover, the bureaucratic groups accused the PLO leadership of failing to bring to a halt Israel's settlement activities.[29]

The Rabin Phase

The PLO responded to the formation of the new Israeli government in July 1992 under the premiership of Yitzhak Rabin with a mixture of both relief and caution.

The Labor Party's victory at the polls offered some measure of relief from the hard-line policies of the Likud regime. For many Palestinians, however, the memory of Rabin's "iron-fist" policy at the start of the *intifada* provoked caution. Moreover, any optimism the Palestinians might have held at the start of this phase dissolved following Rabin's July 13 inaugural address to the Israeli Knesset, in which he outlined Labor's basic policy.[30] Included in this policy was an offer of Palestinian autonomy along the lines of the Camp David accords without the possibility of statehood. Rabin was also emphatic about the nonnegotiable status of Jerusalem. Additionally, the prime minister alluded to a distinction between security and political settlements when he noted that Israel would continue its settlement activity in areas "along the confrontation lines due to their security importance."

As the peace talks progressed, Arafat came under increasing pressure from the bureaucratic members of the PNSF, including Hamas, to withdraw from the peace process altogether. The PLO leader was further constrained when the United States announced in November 1992 its approval of the $10 billion in loan guarantees to Israel. Israel's expulsion of 417 alleged Hamas supporters in December 1992 granted the PLO an opportunity to temporarily withdraw from the peace process in the face of mounting bureaucratic pressures. Despite the brief moment of internal unity sparked by the deportations, the PLO was unable to prevail and hold out for a total return of the deportees as a condition to its returning to the talks. Aside from the opposition voiced by the bureaucratic groups, members of the PLO's negotiating team, including chief negotiator Haydar Abd al-Shafi, threatened to resign if Arafat did not reject Rabin's initial offer to return 100 deportees.

The change in U.S. presidential administrations (Democrats regained the White House in January 1993 with the election of Bill Clinton) signaled the possibility of a return to a climate of opportunity for the PLO. Clinton's apparent interest in maintaining the peace process along with his pledge to commit the United States to work as a "full partner" portended an opportunity for the PLO to regain the initiative at the negotiating table. However, Clinton's key appointments, as well as his refusal to press Israel to abide by UN Security Council Resolution 799 (which both condemned the deportations of the 417 Islamic activists and called for their immediate return), damaged the credibility of the United States to act as a "fair partner" in the peace process.

Because history affords one an invaluable look at the past, it is understandable now why Arafat insisted on continued Palestinian participation during these rounds of the peace process despite growing pressures to withdraw. At the PLO internal level, the issue of the deportations, rising apathy in the Occupied Territories, the loss of employment, the severe economic crisis that resulted from Israel's closure of the West Bank and Gaza, the increase in human rights violations, and the gains made by Hamas played heavily on Arafat's continued leadership. Externally, bureaucratic opposition to Arafat's unilateral style of leadership, the financial unreliability of Arab regimes, as well as talk of possible Israeli-Syrian rapprochement further constrained the leadership of the PLO from regaining the initiative over its foreign policy. In light of these pressures, Arafat seized upon the opportunity that the newly opened Oslo channel had afforded.

During the Rabin phase Arafat sidestepped Washington and opted for private rather than public channels of diplomacy. The factors that precipitated Arafat's detour through Oslo are not exceedingly complex. They do, however, underscore the PLO's consideration of the Occupied Territories as the primary mechanism guiding the formation of foreign policy along with Arafat's undaunted determination to retain the initiative over the outcome of PLO policy despite mounting opposition to his leadership.

From Public to Private Channels of Diplomacy

As Palestinian negotiators maintained a public diplomatic appearance in Washington, Arafat simultaneously embarked on a private diplomatic gamble by giving the green light to one of his top aides, Abu Alaa, to pursue the back-channel approach through Oslo in search of a separate agreement with the Israelis.[31]

The PLO's foreign policy "success" at Oslo is the result of the opportunities that the closed nature of diplomacy provided. The opportunities afforded by the Oslo channel essentially removed the constraints placed on Arafat's ability to act in a public diplomatic forum. Moreover, the nature of private diplomacy allowed him to position the PLO on the initiating rather than receiving end of foreign policy. In this type of environment, the PLO is more open to compromise and accommodation, evidenced by the stipulations to which Arafat had to agree prior to Israel's final acceptance of the Declaration of Principles.

Critics of Arafat maintain that he negotiated away the rights of diaspora Palestinians, particularly the 1948 refugees' right to return, in deference to the Occupied Territories. In addition, Arafat's agreement to postpone discussion on the status of Jerusalem and his inability to resolve the settlement issue have intensified the opposition to his leadership. The DFLP keenly observed that the PLO under Arafat represents only some, rather than all, Palestinians. However, since the outbreak of the *intifada* and the rise of Hamas as a credible threat, it is not difficult to understand Arafat's isolated preoccupation with the West Bank and Gaza to the detriment of the organization's diaspora constituency.

Conclusion

The Declaration of Principles served for a time to temporize the situation in the Occupied Territories; however, Arafat's leadership remained in jeopardy because of lack of progress in implementing the phases of the accord and a significant upgrading of the standard of living for the Islamist Palestinian group in the Occupied Territories, especially in the Gaza Strip. The Islamist Palestinian group, Hamas, galvanized and led the opposition to Arafat's approach. The challenge to his chairmanship intensified following the additional concessions he provided Israel in Cairo on February 14, 1994, as a means to facilitate the implementation of the Gaza-Jericho First Plan. Arafat's foremost predicament is his need to rebuild internal unity in order to forge a consensus for his incremental approach to solving the Israeli-Palestinian conflict. After the massacre at Hebron on February 24, 1994, Arafat took a more hard-line approach by insisting that the issue of the Israeli settlements be addressed as a precondition for returning to the negotiating table. Although he still retains the initiative for the moment, Arafat is not operating in a climate of political opportunity. Instead, the political environment remains essentially threat-driven.

Although there appears to be some measure of consensus among the PLO's bureaucratic groups and constituencies for the organization's current approach, Arafat's ability to maintain the initiative depends in part on continued progress. However, despite continued progress in negotiations with Israel to implement the Declaration of Principles, such as the September 28, 1995, self-rule accord (which provided for the withdrawal of Israeli troops from the West Bank, therefore extending limited autonomy to the area under the PLO as well as calling for Palestinian elections in January 1996), current dynamics indicate that unless Arafat is able to provide some measure of economic and political relief to the PLO's West Bank and Gaza constituency, the potential still exists for a return to the militant roles that served the organization well in its earlier stages of development—an approach long abandoned by the PLO's more moderate leadership.

As the peace process between Israel and the PLO approaches the end of its fifth year, it is tempting to explain the current deadlock in the talks by reciting the all-too-familiar litany of Israeli transgressions and persistent demands that the PLO/PNA leadership asserts are responsible for keeping the process at a standstill. Moreover, it is equally inviting to lay blame on the unwillingness of the United States to exert more influence on the Likud-led coalition government of Benjamin Netanyahu to implement the second-phase redeployment of troops in the West Bank by withdrawing from at least an additional 13 percent of the area—a compromise figure proposed by the United States. However, notwithstanding such factors as Israeli settlement expansion in the Har Homa area of East Jerusalem, increased housing demolitions, and Palestinian land expropriation alongside the seemingly ineffectual foreign policy of the Clinton administration in the region, the PLO/PNA leadership is more in need of a modification in its own approach to peace rather than waiting for its counterparts to forge change. Specifically, the PLO/PNA leadership needs to reevaluate its outmoded foreign policy behavior that is primarily based on pragmatism. Although this type of behavior served the organization well in the late 1980s and seemingly throughout the early 1990s, as of late, pragmatism has not been able to foster greater Palestinian political support in either Washington, D.C., or Tel Aviv. Moreover, with the untimely assassination of Prime Minister Rabin in November 1995 and the narrow electoral loss of Labor's acting Prime Minister Shimon Peres to a Likud-led government under Prime Minister Netanyahu in May 1996, Arafat essentially lost two negotiating partners who were committed to peace and receptive to this type of policy approach. Additionally, given the complex Palestinian domestic political environment that also shapes the peace process, it is little wonder that Arafat's pragmatic foreign policy has endured up to this point in the absence of an opportunistic political climate in which Arafat can take an initiatory role and advance Palestinian political and economic goals. Instead, it appears that Arafat has taken his policy of pragmatism and dropped it on the doorstep of the Clinton administration in what is apparently a vain hope that the United States will resolve the problem. However, this type of foreign policy behavior is neither pragmatic nor capable of fostering an opportunistic political environment for the PLO leadership. Instead, this approach is subservient and conciliatory because it locates the PLO leadership on the receiving end rather than the initiatory side of the foreign policy process. If the past is prologue, this pattern of behavior is reminiscent of the approach to foreign policy that the organization was forced to adopt following the 1991 Gulf war and the subsequent rounds of the Madrid peace talks. Ultimately, it was the lack of progress during those talks that led Arafat to pursue private rather than public forums of diplomacy in which he initiated accommodation and compromise to reach an agreement with Israel that resulted in the Declaration of Principles.

However, the present environment in which Arafat is attempting to steer the Palestinian people toward statehood is not the same political arena as the 1991 post–Gulf war setting. For one, the current Israeli leadership is neither amenable nor politically able to seek compromise and accommodation with the Palestinians. Netanyahu's version of the peace process seems based on a strategy of delaying as long as possible any further Israeli redeployment in the West Bank. In addition to offering Arafat withdrawal figures that leave the Palestinian president little room for compromise, Netanyahu's latest tactic has been to propose an Israeli referendum on the subject of withdrawal.

Another factor that has changed since the Gulf war is the nature of Palestinian domestic politics. Arafat's penchant for unilateral decisionmaking in private diplomatic forums is not compatible with the openness of a democratic system that, at least electorally, has made its formal appearance in the Occupied Territories. In January 1996, Palestinian voters elected Arafat to the office of the presidency of the PNA along with a mandate for maintaining the peace process with Israel through diplomacy. Even though public opinion in the West Bank and Gaza remains supportive of continued negotiations with Israel over the use of more unconventional forms of participation, there is also a corresponding deterioration of the economic situation among Palestinians that could reverse this trend.[32]

To maintain the status quo of pursuing peace, it appears that Arafat is walking a fine line between pragmatism and conciliation. The distinction between the two is a matter of perception. Whereas the United States cautiously approved the 21st PNC's (April 1996) decision to amend clauses in the Palestine National Charter that questioned the legitimacy of Israel as a state, critics of the decision charge that it was an empty act of conciliation for which the Palestinians received nothing in return. In this current deadlock of the peace process, perceptions, alongside economic and political realities among the PLO/PNA's constituency and disaffected groups, matter considerably. Particularly key are the democratic undercurrents among a growing disaffected constituency that could wave ballots of political accountability at their "elected" leaders should Arafat's pragmatic conciliation fail to produce tangible results. The members of the Palestine Legislative Council (PLC) seem to understand the dynamics of representative democracy more than Arafat. Amid allegations of corruption and lack of progress in the peace process, members of the PLC threatened to call for a vote of no-confidence against Arafat's administration. The PLC decided to postpone this action for a few weeks, pending Arafat's voluntary offer to reshuffle his self-rule cabinet.

Among the PLO/PNA's disaffected groups, the DFLP remains steadfast in its unwillingness to endorse the government created by Oslo and, along with the PFLP, advocates a reformulation of PLO strategy that seemingly does not include compromise. However, the more tenacious threat to Arafat's leadership and the peace process in general remains the suicide bombings and other anti-Israeli militant activities being carried out by Islamic Jihad and Hamas (the bombings carried out by Hamas in Israel in early 1996 are evidence of this fact). Arafat continues to wage an internal war of arrests and detentions against both groups, but this strategy has not been successful in abating the campaign of violence waged by these opponents to the peace process. Arafat's previous attempts to draw Hamas into the decisionmaking structures of the organization have been unsuccessful. His invitation to the Islamic opposition to join the new cabinet he intended to form in the summer of 1998 represents a failed attempt at pragmatism on the domestic front. Arafat's endeavor to co-opt his Islamic opposition through political accommodation came on the heels of Sheikh Yassin's four-month "diplomatic" tour of the Middle East; in addition to seeking medical attention during this trip, Yassin allegedly received huge sums of monetary support for his organization from several governments in the Gulf and elsewhere in the region. Both Islamic Jihad and Hamas have refused Arafat's gesture, citing the continued arrest and detention of their members by the Palestinian police forces as the main reason.

Not to be forgotten in the current mix of Palestinian politics is the role of international actors like the United States and regional Arab governments. Arafat does have access to the White House, which is not powerless to effect change. Regionally, Arafat has approached Mubarak about the possibility of an Arab summit to discuss the stalled peace process. Any measure of success in this area, however, will probably depend on the willingness of the Egyptian president and other Arab leaders to attempt to foster solidarity in the region amid their own domestic problems. So long as Arafat is not willing to modify his current foreign policy approach vis-à-vis the present Israeli leadership, the domestic threats and challenges will probably continue to grow. One possible remaining option might be to simply wait for an electoral change in Israel that would be amenable to peace and open to compromise. However, this option requires time, which seems to be the one element that Arafat does not have in abundance.

Notes

1. See, for example, William B. Quandt, *Decade of Decisions: American Policy Toward the Arab-Israeli Conflict, 1967–1976* (Berkeley: University of California Press, 1977); William B.

Quandt, *Peace Process: American Diplomacy and the Arab-Israeli Conflict Since 1967* (Washington, D.C.: Brookings Institution and University of California Press, 1993); George Lenczowski, *American Presidents and the Middle East* (Durham, N.C.: Duke University Press, 1990); Steven L. Spiegel, *The Other Arab-Israeli Conflict: Making America's Middle East Policy from Truman to Reagan* (Chicago: University of Chicago Press, 1985).

2. See JoAnn A. DiGeorgio-Lutz, "A Role Modification Model: The Foreign Policy of the Palestine Liberation Organization, 1964–1981," Ph.D. diss., University of North Texas, Denton, Tex., 1993.

3. For example, modifications in the PLO's strategic goals include the idea of establishing a secular democratic state following the total liberation of Israel formulated at the 6th PNC (September 1969), the establishment of a national authority at the 12th PNC (1974), the PLO's failure to mention the goal of total liberation at the 14th PNC (1979), possible confederation plans with Jordan at the 16th PNC (1983), acceptance of a two-state solution at the 19th PNC (1988), and the Gaza-Jericho First Plan in 1993, which has not been endorsed by the PNC.

4. This role was formally given to the PLO at the 1974 October Arab Summit at Rabat, which unanimously endorsed the PLO as the rightful spokesperson for all Palestinians. Resolution 2 affirmed "the right of the Palestinian people to establish an independent national authority under the command of the Palestine Liberation Organization, the sole legitimate representative of the Palestinians in any Palestinian territory that is liberated." For the full text, see document 308 in *International Documents on Palestine* (Beirut: Institute for Palestine Studies; and Kuwait: University of Kuwait Press, 1974).

5. The PLO has characteristically refused external attempts to impose strategic as well as tactical behaviors on the organization. Some examples include their rejection of the 1970 U.S.-sponsored Rogers Plan, the United Arab Kingdom Plan initiated by Jordan in 1972, Anwar Sadat's government-in-exile scheme of 1972, and the initial refusal to submit to the U.S. demand to "renounce" terrorism in 1988.

6. See *United Nations Resolutions on Palestine and the Arab-Israeli Conflict*, vol. 3 (Washington, D.C.: Institute for Palestine Studies, 1982–1986).

7. For a lengthy discussion of the Reagan administration and its reactionary policies to international events, see Nasser Aruri, "The United States and Palestine: Reagan's Legacy to Bush," *Journal of Palestine Studies* 18(3):3–22. See also Cheryl A. Rubenberg, "The U.S.-PLO Dialogue: Continuity or Change in American Policy," *Arab Studies Quarterly* 11(4):1–48.

8. For the full text of the paper, see Bassam Abu Sharif, "Prospects of a Palestinian-Israeli Settlement," Algiers, 7 June 1988. Reprinted in *Journal of Palestine Studies* 28(1):272–275. See also *New York Times*, 22 June 1988.

9. *Middle East International*, July 8, 1988.

10. See "A Call for Peace," PLO Chairman Yasser Arafat's speech to the European Parliament, Strasbourg, France, Tuesday, September 13, 1988. Reprinted in *Return* 1(3):34–39.

11. See Mohamed Rabie, "The U.S. Dialogue: The Swedish Connection," *Journal of Palestine Studies* 21(4):54–66.

12. The U.S. pledge not to negotiate or recognize the PLO is spelled out in the "Memorandum of Agreement Between the United States and Israel Regarding the Reconvening of the Geneva Conference," which was signed by U.S. Secretary of State Henry Kissinger and Israeli Deputy Prime Minister and Minister of Foreign Affairs Yigal Allon on 1 September 1975. The text of the memorandum was released by the U.S. Senate Committee on Foreign Relations on 3 October 1975. For the full text, see document 150, p. 267, in *International*

Documents on Palestine, 1975. Although the first two conditions for not recognizing nor negotiating with the PLO were attached to the Sinai II disengagement agreements, the third condition, that is, the renouncement of terrorism, was a stipulation imposed by the Reagan administration.

13. See Muhammad Hallaj, "The PLO's Peace Offensive: False Start or New Beginning?" *Middle East International,* 3 February 1989.

14. *Christian Science Monitor,* March 24, 1989.

15. Ibid.

16. See Lamis Andoni, "The PLO: President Arafat Under Fire," *Middle East International,* 14 April 1989.

17. See "Israeli Government Election Plan," Jerusalem, 14 May 1989, reprinted in *Journal of Palestine Studies* 29(1):145–148.

18. See "Egypt's Ten-Point Response to Israel's Election Plan," Cairo, 2 July 1989, reprinted in *Journal of Palestine Studies* 29(1):144–145. "Secretary of State James Baker's 'Five-Point Framework of an Israeli-Palestinian Dialogue," Washington, D.C., 10 October 1989, reprinted in *Journal of Palestine Studies* 29(1):169–170.

19. For an examination of the conditions in Gaza leading up to the Gulf war, see Sara Roy, "The Political Economy of Despair: Changing Political and Economic Realities in the Gaza Strip," *Journal of Palestine Studies* 20(4):58–69.

20. *Washington Times,* August 14, 1990.

21. *Middle East Times,* September 11, 1990.

22. *Middle East International,* 2 August 1991.

23. *Al-Fajr,* 9 December 1991.

24. See interview with Abdel al-Shafi, *Al-Fajr,* 2 August 1992.

25. For an extended analysis of the first five rounds, see Herbert C. Kelman, "How to Create a Momentum for the Israeli-Palestinian Negotiations," *Journal of Palestine Studies* 22(1):1–38.

26. *New York Times,* October 26, 1991.

27. Foreign Broadcast Information Service, 16 March 1992.

28. See "PLO Central Council, Statement on the Peace Process," Tunis, 10 May 1992 (excerpts), reprinted in *Journal of Palestine Studies* 21(4):149–153.

29. *Middle East International,* 15 May 1992.

30. See "Prime Minister Yitzhak Rabin, Inaugural Address to Thirteenth Knesset," Jerusalem, 13 July 1992, reprinted in *Journal of Palestine Studies* 22(1):146–150.

31. See Mark Perry and Daniel Shapiro, "Navigating the Oslo Channel: Breakthrough in the Peace Talks," *Middle East Insight* 9(6):9–27.

32. CPRS opinion poll, 6–9 March, 10–12 April, 1997, reprinted in *Journal of Palestine Studies* 26 (4):130–131.

16

The Specifics of the Meaning of Peace in the Middle East

Mohamed Sid-Ahmed

It is hard to explain how a "peace" process should have come to occupy the political center stage in the Middle East even though the very concept of peace, when adapted to the specific conditions of the region, has yet to be defined. It should not be defined in terms of what Israel will receive in exchange for evacuating Arab Occupied Territories in accordance with the land-for-peace tradeoff contained in United Nations (UN) Resolution 242: first, that is not a definition; and second, the day that Israel evacuates the Occupied Territories, it will be the way in which the Israeli government defines "peace" that will determine future relations between the parties. All the protagonists must have their say when it comes to defining peace. As long as Israel retains possession of Arab land, it is in a position to dictate what peace means, usually by defining it in terms of its security requirements at the expense of Arab national security.[1]

There are also good reasons to believe that the Israeli government has its own definition of peace. After the Gulf war proved that the Israeli government is not immune from Arab missile attacks, Israeli strategists have become aware that Israel's continued occupation of territory can no longer guarantee its security. True, the damage wrought by the Iraqi scud missiles was limited, but there is no guarantee that Arab or Islamic missiles, which could eventually be fitted with nuclear warheads, will not be used. That is why key Israeli politicians—Shimon Peres, for instance—believe that economic and technological supremacy, in the form of a Middle East market, can be a better and more effective guarantor of Israel's security, even if this entails a pullback from Arab Occupied Territories.

Peres's belief is not shared by other powerful forces in Israel who are strongly opposed to any withdrawal, and, prior to his assassination, Yitzhak Rabin was not ready to alienate them. It would seem that the path of least resistance for the Israeli government would be to limit the definition of peace rather than to actually attain peace; that is, to identify peace in terms of the means rather than the end, in terms of a process rather than its end result. In sum, the attainment of peace entails concessions from Israel that it does not now feel it has to make, and as long as the peace process is kept going, the Arab parties are required to abstain from any meaningful form of resistance. Israel has every interest in maintaining this equation and in letting the Arabs challenge it—if they can!

There are also good reasons to believe that the Bill Clinton administration has its own, undeclared definition of "Middle East peace" as well—as a situation in which the security of Israel and the stability of Gulf oil would be guaranteed without the United States footing the bill. Under this scenario, Saudi Arabia and other Gulf Cooperation Council (GCC) members would eventually assume the costs of maintaining the stability of the region by taking over Washington's financial commitments toward various regional parties, notably Israel, just as those oil-rich countries were made to carry most of the burden of the Gulf war.

The side least prepared to face the challenges of "peace" is, in all likelihood, the Arabs, whose eagerness to restore the Israeli Occupied Territories has overshadowed all other considerations, including the need to come up with a vision of what peace should entail in the specific context of the Middle East.

The Market as a Key to Peace

Thus, there seem to be two rival concepts emerging about what peace in the Middle East should be. Peace, according to then Israeli Foreign Minister Shimon Peres, is to remove all obstructions to a Middle East market, which should be left free, in accordance with the rules of democracy, to regulate interaction between all the regional parties. Though apparently very much in keeping with the "new world order," this argument is ahistorical in that it disassociates the future of the Middle East from its past, that is, from the roots of conflict in the region; it also assumes future relations based on the balance of power that has been and currently is tilted in Israel's favor; as such, such a market will be self-defeating for the very cause of peace. Peace in the Middle East will not be achieved if the basic frame of reference remains Israel's security, that is, to find a solution only to the Jewish problem (more precisely, to the Zionist "solution" of the Jewish problem), irrespective of other critical issues in the region, notably, an ever-growing dissent movement in the name of radical Islam. Peace needs some kind of "historical compromise" between the protagonists.

It seems that the Israeli Labor government used the appeal of market economies in the post-Communist era to update its traditional concept of a Middle East Common Market as the key to peace in the region. Linking the concept of the market to that of democracy, Peres has said that when he bought a Japanese product, for instance, he was in effect casting a vote for Japan. In other words, it is the superior quality of Japanese products that determines their appeal to the customer; this was a vote of confidence for Japan and an expression of the democratic process in practice.

Peres has argued that war and peace between nations is not determined by whether they love or hate each other, pointing out that though the British and the French hate one another and both hate the Germans, a united Europe is possible thanks to mechanisms that regulate integration between these erstwhile enemies, regardless of their feelings toward one another. The implicit meaning of his words is that war or peace in the Middle East will be determined by mechanisms transcending the ill feelings harbored by the Arabs for the Israelis and vice versa, namely, market mechanisms.

Denying that the Jewish people had ever sought to dominate any other people throughout their history, he claimed that all they wanted to do was "buy and sell." In referring to Japan, Peres was obviously drawing a parallel with Israel, implying that, thanks to the superiority of its products and international market connections, Israel could conquer the Middle East market and thus impose its economic hegemony over the region while claiming that its economic performance will not entail political domination.

Moreover, with cutbacks in foreign aid (especially with Republican control of both houses of Congress), further steps toward a Middle East market can be expected, irrespective of progress in the peace process. Knowing that Israel is better placed than Egypt to resist cutbacks in U.S. aid, the pro-Israeli lobby in Washington has proposed a deal to the Egyptian leadership: They would oppose any reduction in U.S. aid, not only to Israel but also to Egypt; in exchange Egypt would intercede with other Arab countries to lift their economic boycott of Israel. The implementation of this deal could well be a first major step toward a Middle East market. This has already been manifestly displayed by the October 1994 Israeli-Jordanian peace treaty and the Casablanca international economic conference (convened in October 1994) in which both Arabs and Israelis participated.

By making future relations in the region a function of market mechanisms and democracy, Peres obviously believes that he is on solid ground. After all, with the collapse of communism and the advent of a "new world order," these have become the values of the age, and the Arabs have no choice but to bow before what is being portrayed as an irresistible wave. It follows that the Arab economic boycott against Israel runs counter to the spirit of the age, all the more so when Arab regimes are not noted as champions of democracy.

In fact, Peres's logic in all this is that the balance of power now prevailing in the Middle East—economic and technological as well as military—is what should determine the future of the region. Indeed, in the postbipolar world, the economic dimension has acquired more importance than ever before. Economic competition has taken precedence over the arms race and global military confrontation and can only thrive in the framework of a market economy. That is not to say that the market should be governed solely by market forces without any checks and controls. Nor does it mean that economic boycotts are necessarily banned. After all, one of the main advocates of the market economy, the United States, has used the weapon of economic boycott against many states (to mention only the most glaring cases in the recent past: Cuba, Nicaragua, Iran, South Africa, and Libya).

Actually, expectations for a breakthrough in the Arab-Israeli dispute are higher outside the Middle East than they are inside the region, if only because most protagonists in the conflict remain skeptical. If the Arab parties have now come to the conclusion that the issue of peace should be taken seriously into consideration, it is out of exhaustion rather than out of a conviction that the conditions for an equitable peace are present; and also, perhaps, because of the emergence of some particularly thorny inter-Arab conflict situations that have been compounded by the growing challenge of radical Islam, which now appear to have acquired more relevance than the conflict with Israel.

At the same time, however, it is reasonable to assume that any Israeli negotiator at this time would seriously consider whether signing a peace agreement that would entail relinquishing an as yet unspecified chunk of occupied Arab territory would be more to Israel's advantage than the status quo. That same negotiator might also question the wisdom of signing a contractual peace accord committing Israel to final borders when more Jewish immigration is expected, not only from the Soviet Union and eastern Europe but eventually from other sources such as South Africa, now that the privileges enjoyed by nonblack, including Jewish, South African communities are expected to cease with the end of apartheid. If peace in the Middle East is in the cards, it is thanks to the new global setting rather than because the parties directly concerned perceive it as a deal that would better respond to their basic aspirations.

Beyond the Bipolar World Order

It has been said that because in the former bipolar world the United States supported Israel while the Soviet Union supported the Arabs, and that because in the new "unipolar" world the United States is the only real sponsor of the peace process, the outcome of the current negotiations is bound to be favorable to Israel alone. This is the viewpoint of the rejectionist front in the Arab and Islamic worlds. It can be argued, however, that the situation cannot be reduced to such a simple deduction.

In the context of the previous bipolar world order and with all parties in the Middle East believing that the peace they aspired to could not be reached in terms of the balance of power as it existed in the region, there was more concern with using any support that could be obtained from a superpower patron to improve a negotiating position rather than actual negotiations. It is no accident that the Madrid conference convened only after the bipolar system had come to an end. Throughout the cold war, Israel was extremely important to the United States from a strategic standpoint. Contrary to what the Arabs believed, Israel's strategic importance derived less from the fact that it was a bulwark on which the United States could rely when it came to a military confrontation with the Soviet Union. Egyptian President Anwar Sadat's efforts to convince Washington that he, as the West's most reliable Arab friend in the Middle East, was better placed than Israel to mobilize the whole region against the Soviet Union in case of war had little credibility in the eyes of U.S. strategists. But now that the cold war has ended, the situation has changed fundamentally. When a war did erupt in the region shortly before the peace process was initiated, it turned out to be not a war with the Soviet Union but an inter-Arab war in the Gulf area, and, in this new context, Israel appeared to be more of a liability than an asset to U.S. strategic interests.

However, the Arabs and not the Israelis hold the most important oil reserves in the world, and oil is a key commodity now that the bipolar world order is being replaced by a multipolar (rather than unipolar) world order based on economic competition and not on military confrontation between developed postindustrial groups of nations. In this competition, whoever is in command of how the main sources of energy are managed and distributed has the upper hand in the new global game. Regions such as the Arab Gulf area, which possesses two-thirds of the world's known oil reserves, are bound to be major players in this game. Moreover, as the Gulf war made abundantly clear, the stability of the Gulf region should not be taken for granted; the Arab-Israeli arena should not become a destabilizing factor. If the United States can no longer support Israel as unconditionally as it once did, it is because the stability of the oil area is acquiring greater importance for U.S. strategic interests as Israel's strategic value as an anti-Soviet bulwark in the Middle East becomes less relevant. As the near military confrontation with Iraq in early 1998 over the amount of access given to UN inspection teams showed, lack of progress on Israeli-Palestinian negotiations undercuts the U.S. position in the Gulf, as the Gulf war allies of the United States in the region were reluctant to support Washington's stance vis-à-vis Iraq at the same time it was seen as being a biased and disengaged broker on the Palestinian issue. In order for the United States to continue to pursue its strategic interests and maintain its position in the Gulf, it must actively seek an equitable resolution of the Arab-Israeli problem—the two arenas are much more interconnected than official Washington realizes.

U.S. Involvement

Clinton's election in 1992 displayed a U.S. preoccupation with domestic problems, especially economic, to the detriment of a sagacious formulation of U.S. foreign policy in general and one toward the Middle East in particular. But despite being more inward-looking than any of the recent Republican administrations, the new administration has opted for the Carter approach, which advocated direct U.S. partnership in the peace talks. This has entailed coming forward with proposals on substantive issues to bring the parties closer together and not, as former U.S. Secretary of State James Baker did, limiting the role of the United States to intervention on procedural matters merely to keep the talks from stalling. This approach has signaled that the United States is not about to disengage itself from the Middle East peace process.

But whatever the form of U.S. involvement in the process, the efforts Washington has furnished so far have not really optimized all available opportunities. The United Nations, for instance, is marginalized and reduced to the status of "observer" despite the fact that the whole process is formally based on UN Security Council

Resolutions 242 and 338 (for the Arab-Israeli conflict as a whole), and on Resolution 425 (as far as Lebanon is concerned). The former secretary-general of the United Nations, Boutros Boutros-Ghali, refused to have anything to do with the Moscow conference, which inaugurated the multilateral talks on the Middle East that piggybacked the Madrid process, because the UN was not properly represented. The European Community (EC) also plays the limited role of "observer." After the dissolution of the Soviet Union, it is obvious that Russian cosponsorship of the peace process is meaningless and that the only relevant sponsor of the whole undertaking is the United States. This means that Washington is alone in deciding how the negotiations are to be conducted.

The Regional Parties

Whatever the reluctance of the regional parties to accept the concessions any peace agreement would entail, they find themselves compelled to consider some form of give-and-take in the name of peace, if only because the rationale that prevailed in the previous bipolar world and that could, at the time, justify resisting involvement in a peace process no longer exists. Other factors also require a negotiated settlement of the conflict, namely:

1. It is impossible to sustain relentless enmity between neighboring states in a world that has become a "global village" with ever-increasing interdependence, interpenetration, and complementarity between states and communities worldwide. The Middle East, including specifically Arab-Israeli relations, cannot indefinitely remain an exception to that rule. The multilateral talks inaugurated in Moscow are significant in this regard. Delegations from some thirty countries, including Israel and many Arab countries, are taking part in the multilaterals, which are addressing a comprehensive range of Middle East issues, including arms control, economic cooperation, the environment, water resources, and the refugee problem. Even before achieving any substantive progress in the field of peace, all Arab parties have come to accept Israel, in principle, as a legitimate regional interlocutor with whom to deliberate over regional problems, even if the actual implementation of solutions to these problems will have to wait until a comprehensive peace is reached.

2. Moreover, it is difficult to make an economic boycott of Israel effective. It could even backfire against its advocates. It is unrealistic to expect third parties, which are in no way involved in the conflict, to seriously apply boycott provisions against Israel at a time when all Arab parties concerned are negotiating with Israel for peace and are trying to convince the international community that they embarked on peace negotiations in good faith. A parallel has been drawn here with Egypt's attempts to convince African countries not to resume diplomatic relations with Israel after Egypt itself had signed a peace treaty with the Jewish state. The Arab boycott of Israel has evolved from being a weapon of resistance to the very idea of peace into a temporary measure to bolster the Arab negotiating position. Its relevance is confined to

putting pressure on Israel to accelerate the peace process, all the more so since
the Jericho-Gaza agreement between Israel and the Palestine Liberation Organization (PLO) in September 1993. This is not the type of argument that
can induce third parties into implementing the boycott consistently.

3. There are also environmental problems, particularly water shortages. Scarcity
of water in the region, compounded by the demographic explosion and a lack
of water-sharing agreements, is causing serious water deficits and heightened
health concerns. The situation is so critical that experts believe water can ultimately become the determining factor in compelling the parties to make
peace.

4. Maintaining stability in the oil-rich Gulf region is of critical importance, not
only for the United States and other industrialized powers but also for many
Arab regimes. In other words, peace in the Arab-Israeli conflict and stability
of the Arab Gulf area have become interdependent factors. At one time it
seemed that Sadat was the only Arab leader willing to subordinate the Arab-
Israeli conflict to inter-Arab tensions and conflicts. Sadat believed that with
Egypt carrying the main burden in the Arab military confrontation with Israel, he was under no obligation to keep the peace process with Israel hostage
to Arab overbidding and militant rhetoric when it was thanks to his October
1973 war that the other Arabs had become rich while Egypt was exposed to
hunger riots. His decision to go to Jerusalem in 1977 was determined more
by his frustration with the behavior of the oil-rich Arab regimes than by a desire to conclude a separate peace with the Jewish state. Today, many of these
regimes, whose very legitimacy stems from their strict adherence to Islam, are
themselves threatened by the upsurge of Islamic fundamentalism combined
with declining oil revenues, growing populations, and budget deficits.

The Upsurge of Islamic "Fundamentalism"

The Islamic upsurge in Arab countries bordering the Mediterranean is a phenomenon that is linked, somehow or other, to the deep sense of frustration felt by wide
sections of Arab society at the way their destinies are being manipulated within the
framework of the "new world order." As they see it, the time has come to apply another frame of reference by which they can preserve their dignity and identity, which
will set them apart from those they perceive as responsible for their manipulation,
namely, the West and Israel. The feeling of the masses that they are not masters of
their own fates has created a "vacuum" that must be filled. If the peace process fails
to offer them any hope, they will inevitably fill it by reasserting their identity
through expressions of protest, including radical Islam. In religious terms, the belligerents perceive their identities as mutually exclusive. For each party, the other is
an object, not a subject of history. No global identity, encompassing all the belligerent parties, can help overcome this state of hostility and antagonism. A "historical
compromise" is very difficult to achieve when the frame of reference becomes meta-
physical (by definition, uncompromising) rather than political.

With the depolarization of the world system, various expressions of identity, hitherto held in check by the acute antagonism between the two world poles, have come to the fore. The rise of political Islam falls into this category, albeit with an extra dimension. It is not only a buoy to which millions are clinging in a sea of uncertainty and confusion; it has also come to be seen as a mobilizing force capable of standing up to what is perceived as Western attempts to find a new "enemy" to replace communism. This feeling is reinforced by statements made by responsible Israelis, including former Israeli head of state Chaim Herzog. In an interview published a few years ago in a Spanish newspaper, he said Israel's future mission will be to protect Western values in the face of Islamic fundamentalism, which has replaced communism as the greatest threat to the region, thereby placing the Judeo-Christian West on a collision course with the Islamic East. He also complained that Israel is not receiving its due reward from the United States for its vital role in serving U.S. global strategy and saving the United States millions of dollars it would have had to pay if Israel did not exist. Herzog reiterated the same arguments in an address delivered last year to the European Community in Holland, when he stated:

> The most destructive force to the peace process in the Middle East is not the Arab-Israeli conflict itself, but the Hamas movement. Because the West does not want to understand this basic change that has occurred in the region, it is always caught by surprise. It is no accident that the West failed to predict all the major events in the region throughout the recent period: the downfall of the Shah, the Soviet invasion of Afghanistan, the rise of Khomeini, the Iraq-Iran war, Saddam's invasion of Kuwait. All this because it does not want to understand that the main enemy has become Islamic fundamentalism.

By deporting some 400 alleged Hamas and Jihad activists early in his tenure, Rabin was acting on Herzog's assumption. More, he was gambling on the acceptance of the assumption by all Arab leaders—including those involved in the peace process, even the PLO—who have come to believe that Islamic fundamentalism, not Israel, represents the main threat to domestic and regional stability. Rabin hoped that this common opposition to radical Islam could lay the groundwork for peace on Israel's terms.

The Gaza-Jericho Agreement

The Gaza-Jericho agreement (also known as the Gaza-Jericho First Plan) was hailed as a turning point in the ultimate resolution of the Israeli-Palestinian conflict. Much was made of the handshake between Yitzhak Rabin and Yasser Arafat on the White House lawn, which was described as the symbol of a solution based on mutual recognition between the parties. Actually, the agreement provided only for PLO recognition of the state of Israel and remained silent on the question of Israel's recognition of an Arab Palestinian state. Under the terms of the agreement, Israel recognizes a Palestinian "entity" enjoying limited administrative self-rule and makes any expansion in the scope of its prerogatives subject to Palestinian good behavior toward Israel in the future.

Mutual recognition assumes a degree of symmetry between the parties. This element is conspicuously lacking in the Gaza-Jericho agreement, which not only allows the Israelis to use the Palestinians for their own ends but also provides a legal framework for the suppression of the *intifada*, the main obstacle to Israel's opening to the Arab world. It is to be questioned whether the structural imbalance and lack of parity that lie at the very heart of the agreement and have led many Arabs to condemn it can be redressed.

After the signature of the 1979 Egyptian-Israeli peace treaty, Syria tried to achieve military parity with Israel on the grounds that this was the only way to restitute the Golan Heights. But its hopes were dashed when the Soviet Union, the only power it could count on to achieve this aim, collapsed. Actually, Syria was already having problems with Moscow even before the collapse, thanks to Mikhail Gorbachev's rapprochement with the West. Can an alternative form of parity be envisaged?

Military parity might be the optimum form of parity, but it is not necessarily the only one. Parity can be subjectively assumed to exist, even in the absence of its objective prerequisites. The *intifada* has been described as the 1973 October War of the Palestinians, in the sense that both events were perceived by the parties concerned as honorable achievements on the strength of which they could enter into negotiations with the enemy without laying themselves open to charges of surrender. The *intifada*, like the October War, wiped out feelings of humiliation and shame and restored confidence in negotiations as an effective instrument that need not lead to the consecration of defeat but could eventually bring about peace based on justice.

Can the identity of parties to a conflict be defined by the parties themselves in terms of subjective criteria, regardless of the validity of these criteria in the eyes of others? Israel attributes the whole of Palestine to Eretz Israel on the basis of the Old Testament, whereas Palestinians lay claim to the same land on the grounds that it was their home for more than twenty centuries. Inevitably, these two mutually exclusive claims collide, with each claimant seeing the other as violating its very identity. The parties cannot hope to establish a stable peace unless they make a serious effort to change their perceptions of each other so that each comes to be seen by the other as potentially complementary, not necessarily inimical, to its own identity.

Obviously the Palestinians cannot change their perception of the Israelis as aggressors as long as they feel they are being used to further Israel's hegemonic ambitions in the region. The feeling of being pawns in a game directed by Israel will only be dissipated if the Palestinians can in turn use Israel to their advantage. Making use of the other must be reciprocal and balanced, a condition that requires minimal parity, albeit subjective parity, between the protagonists. Is this condition fulfilled by the Gaza-Jericho agreement? Or has the agreement instead sanctioned the subordination of Arab Palestine to Israel's ambition of establishing its economic and technological supremacy over the region, a view that has become much more widely held in the Arab world since the Likud Party returned to power with Benjamin Netanyahu as prime minister in 1996? If so, the agreement will need fundamental restructuring in order to become the cornerstone for a just and lasting peace.

Peace as Antithesis

The final shape of peace should be clearly spelled out at this stage of the peace process, if not in full detail, at least as an overall concept. In fact, if the region is to enjoy a stable and durable peace that will not be constantly subject to setbacks, the conceptual framework of this peace must be endowed with characteristics antithetical to those that prevailed throughout the history of the conflict. History and, for that matter, conflict and bipolarity have not come to an end, even if bipolarity no longer assumes the form of a division of the world into two clear-cut military-ideological-geographic blocs (East and West) with some degree of parity between them; rather it has taken the form of a North-South divide with no parity whatsoever between its poles. The talk of a "new world order," based on a common value system, a common economic system, a common market, and no double standards, and where all conflicts can be solved by peaceful means, has been revealed—at least so far—as a myth.

The issue that triggered the conflict initially was that the Jewish problem, which had originated in Europe, was being solved in the Middle East. Jews claim that Arabs victimize them as Europeans had in the past. I argue that this was putting cause and effect on an equal footing. The result was an acute polarization between Jews and Arabs in the Middle East, made still more unyielding by global polarization between the superpowers. But this had come to an end with the demise of the bipolar world order.

It might, indeed, be worth investigating whether the peace process can be guided by the mechanisms now being put in place by the European Community to make any future war between its member states impossible. The project for European unity will be jeopardized if the peoples of Europe come to perceive unity as a mechanism by which Germany will "absorb" the rest of Europe, in a sort of updated version of Adolf Hitler's dream to impose German domination over the continent. This perception is in direct opposition to that upon which the dream of European unity is based: The absorption of Germany into Europe in a manner that will finally and irrevocably put an end to military confrontations. This is very similar to the underlying logic of the project for peace in the Middle East, which entails devising the mechanisms by which Israel can be absorbed into the region rather than impose its hegemony over it. The Rabin and Netanyahu governments had no qualms in putting Israel's security above the principle of land for peace nor in using the security argument to retain at least part of the land while demanding full peace, a peace that would establish a common Middle East market with Israel at its heart. At the same time, the Israeli government discounts justified Arab fears that such a market could represent a threat to Arab security by further deepening economic discrepancies throughout the region. The success of the European Common Market is due to regulatory mechanisms and procedures that prevent any one country from acquiring a status above that of the EC as a whole, a lesson that the Israeli government would do well to remember when it calls for a Middle East common market.

Here the experience of the European Community can serve as a guideline (specifically the measures it is taking and that, no doubt, enjoy Israel's full support) to ensure that the interests of the EC as a whole pass before those of each individual member state, particularly Germany. Actually, the EC has every interest in seeing the model it has put forward to deter any future war in Europe adopted by neighboring regions. It would certainly not want to see the Middle East conflict remain an uncomfortable reminder that certain conflicts are so intractable as to defy all efforts to resolve them and that, even when "solutions" are found, there is always the possibility they will break down, given the difficulty of trying to establish a peace without any losers.

It follows, at least theoretically, that real peace will only be achieved the day the belligerents stop seeing each other as mutually exclusive and begin to consider the possibility of establishing a relationship of complementarity and partnership. But is this realistic? Can Arabs ever become convinced that the presence of Israel in their midst could eventually become an asset rather than a liability? Can Israel become convinced that this would be its only salvation in the long term?

This raises once again the "psychological barrier" argument invoked by Sadat, albeit in a somewhat different setting. No one can deny that the collective Jewish psyche is haunted by the singularities of Jewish history, particularly in Europe. One trait of their specific character is a sort of pathological fear of being exterminated, something due to a long tradition of pogroms culminating in the Holocaust. And though Zionist propaganda has certainly exploited this Holocaust mentality in the Middle East, it is equally certain that the trauma Jews suffered has been instrumental in enabling Israel to sustain a high degree of alertness and a permanent sense of mobilization. Arab insistence on exhibiting inexorable enmity toward Israel has probably reinforced Israeli paranoia and that sense of mobilization, contributing to the strengthening of Israel rather than the opposite.

For Jews, Israel represents a safe haven. The hostility Arabs have demonstrated toward the Jewish state fueled its siege mentality, even after it became militarily superior to all the other states in the region, capable of punishing whoever dared challenge it. It is to be questioned whether Israel's belligerence, which it justifies as necessary for its survival in a hostile environment, can be more effectively moderated through intensifying Arab hostility toward it or rather by defusing this hostility.

But how to dissipate mutual suspicion? How to set in motion a mechanism by which mutual trust will replace enmity? This is no easy task given the unevenness of the protagonists as reflected in the Gaza-Jericho agreement. How can a point of departure based on a superior Israeli bargaining position lead to a point of arrival that would respond to legitimate Palestinian aspirations for self-determination and statehood? The agreement itself contains no guarantee that its implementation will ensure more equality between the two parties rather than greater inequality. A prerequisite for the restitution of Arab land today is mutual confidence. But this is very difficult to come by as long as the parties lack parity and as long as each perceives the other as an aggressor rather than a potential source of mutual benefit. Is there a means of breaking this vicious circle?

It has been said that by signing a peace treaty with Israel, Egypt bypassed the vicious circle without actually breaking it (that is, it went beyond a state of war without having to build a relationship of interdependence with Israel) and that the fact that this arrangement has stood the test of time is proof that a third path is possible. But what has been described as a "cold peace" was the product of the divergent pressures with which Egypt had to contend: not to abandon its treaty with Israel on the one hand and, on the other, to restore its place in the heart of the Arab world. This equation no longer applies in the new regional and global game. Thus, the recipe for consolidating peace is still to be invented.

Notes

1. These and succeeding points were articulated by the author in his debate with then Israeli Foreign Minister Shimon Peres in Cairo in early 1993.

Part Four

The Gulf Crisis and War

17

The United States in the Persian Gulf: From Twin Pillars to Dual Containment

Gary Sick

The United States arrived reluctantly as an active player in the Persian Gulf, but after a quarter-century of resistance, turmoil, and false starts, it emerged as the unquestioned military and political hegemon in the region. In some respects this was merely the story of how the United States slowly reconciled itself to assume the role originated by the British in the nineteenth century. British interests, however, were never identical to U.S. interests, and the underpinnings of U.S. policy by the turn of the century bore little resemblance to the classic British defense of its eastern lines of communication.

The interests of the United States in the Persian Gulf region have been very simple and consistent: first, to ensure access by the industrialized world to the vast oil resources of the region; and second, to prevent any hostile power from acquiring political or military control over those resources. Throughout the cold war, the most immediate threat was the Soviet Union; after the Soviet collapse, Iran and Iraq became the primary targets of U.S. containment efforts.

Other objectives, such as preserving the stability and independence of the Gulf states or containing the threat of Islamic fundamentalism, were derivative concerns and were implicit in the two grand themes of oil and containment. Preoccupation with the security of Israel was a driving factor in U.S. Middle East policy for half a century, and developments in the Arab-Israel arena sporadically influenced U.S. policies in the Persian Gulf (and vice versa). Especially after the end of the cold war, the Israeli factor began to assume much greater importance in the formulation of U.S. policy in the Gulf.

The slow unfolding of U.S. policy contributed to (and occasionally was the victim of) the development of the modern Persian Gulf. This account will focus on a few key turning points, where seemingly unrelated U.S. policy choices eventually resolved themselves into a surprisingly coherent strategic posture.

The Twin Pillar Policy

Prior to World War II, U.S. involvement in the Persian Gulf was minimal. The first sustained encounter with the region was in the nineteenth century, in the days of the great clipper ships.[1] The Persian Gulf and Indian Ocean were regarded as a British preserve, and U.S. political, commercial, and military contact with the region was extremely rare.[2]

The U.S. Middle East Command was established during World War II to oversee the supply route of war materiel to the Soviet Union. Its 40,000 U.S. troops constituted the largest U.S. deployment to the region from that time until Operation Desert Storm in 1991. The small U.S. naval contingent (Middle East Force) that was established in 1947 relied on British hospitality at Jufair on Bahrain Island.

The British announcement in 1968 that it intended to withdraw from its historic position east of Suez came as an unwelcome shock in Washington, which had long relied on the British presence as an essential component of its Soviet containment strategy along the immense arc from the Suez Canal to the Malacca Straits. It also came at the worst possible moment, since U.S. forces were increasingly strained by commitments in Vietnam and Southeast Asia.

The Nixon administration undertook a major review of U.S. Persian Gulf policy when it took office in 1969. This was part of a global effort to redefine U.S. security interests at a time of competing demands on U.S. military forces and a growing reluctance by the American public to support what were seen as potentially costly foreign commitments. The result of this effort was the Nixon Doctrine, which placed primary reliance on security cooperation with regional states as a means of protecting U.S. interests around the world. In the Gulf, it was decided to rely heavily on the two key states of Iran and Saudi Arabia, a strategy that quickly became known as the "Twin Pillar policy."[3]

From the beginning, it was recognized that Iran would be the more substantial of the two "pillars" because of its size, its military capabilities, its physical juxtaposition between the Soviet Union and the Persian Gulf, and the willingness of the shah (unlike the Arab states of the region) to cooperate openly with the United States on security matters. This very special relationship between Washington and Tehran was sealed in May 1972 during the visit to Tehran of President Nixon and his national security adviser, Henry Kissinger.

In two and one-half hours of conversations over two days, a deal was struck in which the United States agreed to increase the numbers of uniformed advisers in Iran and guaranteed the shah access to some of the most sophisticated nonnuclear technology in the U.S. military arsenal. The shah, in return, agreed to accept a key role in protecting Western interests in the Persian Gulf region. All of this was summed up with startling candor at the end of the meetings, when President Nixon looked across the table to the shah and said simply, "Protect me."[4]

This moment was the culmination of several decades of tumultuous political relations between the United States and Iran. In 1953, the Eisenhower administration had carried out a "countercoup" that restored the shah to the throne and ended the political career of nationalist leader Muhammad Mussadiq.[5] By this act, the United States at once lost its political innocence with regard to Iran and guaranteed that it would be held permanently responsible—at least by Iranian popular opinion—for the Iranian ruler's excesses and cruelties. In 1963, a fiery religious leader, Ruhollah Khomeini, led the opposition to a bill that, among other things, extended diplomatic protection to American military advisers. This rebellion, which in retrospect was a rehearsal for the revolution of 1978–1979, led to Khomeini's exile for fourteen years. Although most Americans were scarcely aware of this incident, the Iranian opposition was convinced that the shah was acting on behalf of the United States.

The agreement between President Nixon and the shah in 1972 transformed the previous client relationship. Iran was on the brink of becoming a major power in the oil market and now had free access to the U.S. arsenal of modern weaponry. This was formally acknowledged with Iran becoming the protector of U.S. interests in the region, and the shah increasingly felt emboldened to lecture his great power ally on politics, economics, and strategy. The United States in turn reduced its intelligence coverage of Iran's internal politics and relied on the shah for assistance in putting down the Marxist rebellion in Dhofar, for an assured energy supply at the time of the oil embargo of 1973, and for support in a wide range of political and military operations ranging from the Middle East and Africa to as far away as Vietnam.

This role reversal, however, went almost unnoticed in the Persian Gulf and elsewhere. In Iran, the image of a compliant shah responding to orders dictated in Washington remained vividly implanted in the national psyche. As a consequence, when the revolution exploded in the late 1970s, the United States had the worst of both worlds. It had relinquished much of its independent capacity to assess and influence Iran's internal politics, but it was popularly suspected of orchestrating every move by the shah's regime.

The Twin Pillar policy also involved a tripartite covert action with Israel to destabilize Iraq by supporting a Kurdish rebellion against Baghdad. This plan was adopted in May 1972 during the Nixon-Kissinger visit; it collapsed in 1975 when the shah unilaterally came to an agreement with Saddam Hussein and abandoned the Kurds. It established a precedent for viewing the Persian Gulf as an extension of the Arab-Israel conflict and for U.S.-Israeli cooperation in the region.[6]

The collapse of the shah's regime in February 1979 was the death knell for the U.S. Twin Pillar policy. From the beginning, the policy had been predicated on a close personal relationship with the shah. With his departure and the arrival of a hostile Islamist regime in Tehran, the United States was left strategically naked in the Persian Gulf, with no safety net.

The Carter Doctrine

This blow was compounded in February 1979 by reports of an incipient invasion of North Yemen by its avowedly Marxist neighbor to the south. This event, coming in the wake of the Marxist coup in Afghanistan in April 1978, the conclusion of the Ethiopian-Soviet treaty in November 1978, the fall of the shah, and the assassination of U.S. Ambassador Adolph Dubs in Kabul in February 1979, created the impression that the United States had lost all capacity to influence regional events. That impression was strengthened when Turkey and Pakistan followed Iran in withdrawing from the Central Treaty Organization in March.

Washington responded by dispatching a carrier task force to the Arabian Sea and by rushing emergency military aid to Yemen and the airborne warning and control system, or AWACS, to Saudi Arabia. The United States also undertook a systematic effort to develop a new "strategic framework" for the Persian Gulf. By the end of 1979, the outlines of a strategy had been sketched in, including initial identification of U.S. forces for a rapid deployment force and preliminary discussions with Oman, Kenya, and Somalia about possible use of facilities. Nevertheless, when the U.S. embassy in Tehran was attacked in November, a high-level review of U.S. military capabilities drew the sobering conclusion that U.S. ability to influence events in the region was extremely limited. In late November, when there were serious fears that the U.S. hostages were in danger of being killed, a second aircraft carrier was sent to the area and two additional destroyers were assigned to the Middle East Force.

The Soviet invasion of Afghanistan just before Christmas in 1979 reawakened fears of a Soviet drive to the Persian Gulf and Indian Ocean. The practical effect of the Soviet invasion was to terminate the efforts of the Carter administration to seek mutual accommodation with the Soviet Union, including support for the SALT II treaty. This policy shift was articulated by Carter in his State of the Union address of January 23, 1980, where he stated: "Any attempt by any outside force to gain control of the Persian Gulf region will be regarded as an assault on the vital interests of the United States of America, and such an assault will be repelled by any means necessary, including military force."

This declaration, which quickly came to be known as the Carter Doctrine, bore a remarkable resemblance to the classic statement of British policy by Lord Lansdowne in 1903, when he said the United Kingdom would "regard the establishment of a naval base, or of a fortified port, in the Persian Gulf by any other power as a very grave menace to British interests," an act that would be resisted "with all the means at our disposal."[7] The statement clearly established the United States as the protecting power of the region and effectively completed the transfer of policy responsibility in the Persian Gulf from the British to the Americans.

When Carter made this statement, it reflected U.S. intentions rather than capabilities. By the time the Reagan administration arrived in Washington in January 1981, it would have been accurate to say that the U.S. security structure in the Persian Gulf region was more symbol than reality—at least as measured in purely military capacity.[8] Nevertheless, it was equally apparent that the developments of 1980 marked a major threshold in the evolution of U.S. strategy and a new conviction that this region represented a major strategic zone of U.S. vital interests, demanding both sustained attention at the highest levels of U.S. policymaking and direct U.S. engagement in support of specifically U.S. interests. That was without precedent.

The Reagan administration adopted the Carter Doctrine and over the following seven years succeeded in putting more substantial military power and organization behind its words. The Rapid Deployment Joint Task Force (RDJTF) was reorganized in 1983 as a unified command known as the Central Command, based at MacDill Air Force Base in Tampa, Florida, with earmarked forces totaling some 230,000 military personnel from the four services. Its basic mission reflected the two themes that had wound through U.S. regional policy from the very beginning: "to assure continued access to Persian Gulf oil and to prevent the Soviets from acquiring political-military control directly or through proxies."

The Iran-Iraq War (1980–1988)

Despite the shadow of Soviet military power, all threats to oil supplies and to regional stability came not from Russia and its allies but from political developments within the region. The first of these was the Arab oil boycott at the time of the Arab-Israeli war of 1973, which nearly tripled the price of oil and sent Western economies spinning into a serious recession. The second was the Iranian revolution, and the third was the Iran-Iraq war, which Iraq launched with a massive invasion in September 1980.

The United States asserted its neutrality at the beginning of the war, then later tilted unofficially in favor of Iraq as Iran drove back the Iraqi forces and counterattacked across the border. In 1985–1986, as part of a "strategic opening" to Iran coupled with an abortive effort to free U.S. hostages in Lebanon, the United States and Israel undertook a series of secret contacts and substantial arms transfers to Iran that effectively shifted U.S. policy—at least at the covert level—toward Iran. When the revelation of these arrangements created consternation and threatened U.S. relations with the friendly oil-producing states of the Gulf, the United States reversed field sharply and adopted an openly pro-Iraqi position.[9]

During much of the war, the United States and many other powers adopted a hands-off posture, content to see these two abominable regimes exhaust each other on the battlefield, particularly since the war was having relatively little impact on oil supplies or prices.[10] That nonchalance began to fade in 1985–1986 when Iran began to retaliate for Iraqi air attacks against its shipping in the Gulf by using mines and small armed boats against neutral shipping en route to Kuwait and Saudi Arabia.

In late 1986, Kuwait asked both the United States and the Soviet Union to place Kuwaiti tankers under their flag and provide protection.[11] The Soviet Union agreed to reflag three Kuwaiti tankers, and the United States quickly followed suit by reflagging eleven. The United States moved a substantial number of naval ships into or near the Gulf and began escorting tanker convoys to and from Kuwait.[12] Iran's indiscriminate use of mines led other NATO navies to send minesweepers and other escort ships to the Gulf to protect international shipping.

Although the reflagging decision was seen at the time as a temporary U.S. response to a specific problem, in retrospect it was a fundamental turning point. For the first time since World War II, the United States assumed an operational role in the defense of the Persian Gulf, with all that implied in terms of development of infrastructure, doctrine, coordination with NATO allies, and direct collaboration with the Arab states on the southern littoral. President Reagan's military intervention thus confirmed President Carter's assertion that the Gulf was of vital interest to the United States and that the United States was prepared to use military force in pursuit of that interest. Although the Carter Doctrine addressed the prospective threat from the Soviet Union, its first major implementation involved a regional state, anticipating the massive international coalition that repelled Iraq's occupation of Kuwait in January 1991.

From War to War

United Nations (UN) Security Council Resolution 598 was passed unanimously by the Security Council on July 20, 1987, calling for an immediate cease-fire between Iran and Iraq. This set off a full year of acrimonious debate, punctuated by sporadic missile bombardments of cities and further attacks on oil tankers.[13] A new element in this escalation of the war was the expanded use of chemical weapons by Iraq against civilian targets. Iraq had used poison gas extensively in earlier campaigns, but the targets had been Iranian military forces. On the evening of March 16, 1988, Iraq conducted two bombing raids against the village of Halabjah, which Iranian forces were about to enter. The bombs caught the local Iraqi Kurdish villagers in their homes and in the street, killing at least 2,000 civilians. The UN dispatched an investigating team that confirmed the atrocity. But Iraq was unrepentant. Foreign Minister Tariq 'Aziz wrote to the secretary-general that "in their legitimate, moral, and internationally approved self-defense, our people are determined to use all available abilities and means against the criminal invaders."[14] In fact, in the succeeding months, Iraq used poison gas more frequently and against a wider range of targets, including civilians, than at any previous time in the war. The UN Security Council passed Resolution 612 on May 9, 1988, mandating an immediate end to the use of chemical weapons in the war and holding out the prospect of sanctions against violators, but it had no effect.

During this same period, the Soviet Union announced its intention to withdraw its military forces from Afghanistan by the end of 1988. This resulted in the signing of an accord between Afghanistan and Pakistan on April 14 in Geneva, with the United States and the Soviet Union as co-guarantors.

Throughout this period, political cohesion in Iran was breaking down, and the continued use of mines set off a new round of clashes with U.S. forces.[15] Iraq went on the offensive against Iran's disorganized and disheartened military forces, recapturing the Fao Peninsula in a lightning attack on April 18, then proceeding to push back Iranian forces all along the front. In mid-May, apparently with assistance from Saudi Arabia, Iraq carried out a devastating attack on the Iranian oil transfer site at Larak Island in the southern Gulf, destroying five ships, including the world's largest supertanker.[16] Antiwar sentiment began to appear openly in demonstrations in major Iranian cities. And most disturbing of all for the divided leadership, persuasive evidence began to accumulate that Khomeini was severely ill and virtually incapacitated.

On July 3, a commercial Iranian aircraft was shot down by the USS *Vincennes,* killing all 290 passengers and crew. This terrible accident, coming at the end of a seemingly endless series of defeats, underscored the despair of Iran's position. On July 18, the Iranian foreign minister sent a letter to the UN secretary-general formally accepting Resolution 598. Two days later, Khomeini sent a "message to the nation," read by an announcer, associating himself with the decision, which, he said, was "more deadly than taking poison."[17]

Iraq was taken by surprise and initially resisted accepting a cease-fire, while continuing its mopping up operations. Iraq also continued to demonstrate a contemptuous disregard for the Security Council and for world opinion on the use of chemical weapons. A UN investigative team presented its report to the Security Council on August 1, finding that "chemical weapons continue to be used on an intensive scale" by Iraq. Only hours later, Iraq launched a massive chemical bombing attack on the Iranian town of Oshnoviyeh. However, as international pressure mounted, Saddam Hussein finally agreed to accept a cease-fire on August 6. A UN observer force was rushed to the region, and a cease-fire went into effect on August 20, 1988.

The end of the war provided an opportunity for the Bush administration to reconsider its support for Saddam Hussein in the wake of revelations about Iraq's use of chemical weapons against its own population, the genocidal Anfal campaign against the Kurds, and efforts to develop nuclear and other weapons of mass destruction. The policy of limited cooperation with Iraq, however, remained intact. This policy became an embarrassment after the defeat of Iraq in 1991, when claims were leveled that the U.S. government had chosen to ignore warnings that agricultural credits might have been diverted to the purchase of military equipment. The most sensational charges of criminal responsibility were never substantiated, and the so-called Iraqgate scandal faded after the 1992 U.S. presidential elections. However, documents made available to the Congress and the media did demonstrate persuasively that the Bush administration had pursued a largely uncritical policy toward Iraq during the period between the end of the Iran-Iraq war and the Iraqi invasion of Kuwait.[18]

At a minimum, this policy of tolerance and inattentiveness may have contributed to a false sense of security on the part of Saddam Hussein as he prepared to invade his neighbor to the south. The U.S. ambassador to Baghdad, April Glaspie, was widely criticized for failing to warn Saddam Hussein about the possible consequences of an attack, but any fair-minded review of the record would reveal that she was accurately reflecting the policy of the president and secretary of state during this interwar period.[19]

The Second Gulf War

When Iraqi forces crossed the border into Kuwait at 1 A.M. on the morning of August 2, 1990, they set in motion a series of events that would transform U.S. policy in the Persian Gulf. It marked a turning point in U.S. relations with the Arab states of the Gulf, as pointed out by Shafeeq Ghabra and F. Gregory Gause III elsewhere in this volume. The cooperation between the United States and the Soviet Union on a matter of high strategy and military policy, which would have been unthinkable only a few years earlier, marked the undeniable end of the cold war.[20] The successful creation of a very large international coalition under the auspices of the UN and under the direct leadership of the United States aroused expectations for both the UN and peacekeeping, some of which was expressed in President George Bush's use of the phrase "a new world order" in relation to the Gulf intervention.[21]

The eventual use of missiles by Iraq against Israel underscored the relationship between the Arab-Israel conflict and Gulf policy more clearly than at any time since the oil embargo of 1973. The immediate imposition of a draconian sanctions regime against Iraq, and its continuation over a period of many years, demonstrated both the extent and limitations of collective, nonviolent coercion by the international community. The combined use of air power, lightning ground mobility, and the use of high-tech weapons—many for the first time in combat—in a computerized battlefield environment wrote a new chapter in the conduct of modern warfare and raised some troubling new questions.[22] The media, and especially television, brought these events into the world's living rooms with an intimacy and immediacy that may have been unprecedented in its universality.

Saddam Hussein's forces were ejected from Kuwait with minimal combat casualties.[23] On March 3, U.S. General Norman Schwartzkopf met with an Iraqi military delegation at Safwan airfield in southern Iraq, and the Iraqis quickly agreed to allied terms. Almost immediately, revolts against Saddam Hussein's regime broke out among the Kurds in northern Iraq and among the Shi'a in southern Iraq. Initially President Bush declared that Iraq was violating the terms of the cease-fire by using military helicopters to put down the revolts. He reversed himself almost immediately, however, stating that "using helicopters like this to put down one's own people does not add to the stability of the area. . . . We are not in there trying to impose a solution inside Iraq."[24]

The distinction was critical. Over the following weeks, Iraqi forces brutally suppressed the uprisings and arguably preserved Saddam Hussein in power. The rationale for the change was spelled out two weeks later by White House spokesman Marlin Fitzwater, who noted, "There is no interest in the coalition in further military operations." Arab officials, he said, were telling Washington: "Let Hussein deal with this, then the dust will settle and he's going to have to pay the piper for the war over Kuwait. Or at least that is what we are counting on."[25]

In an interview with David Frost, General Schwartzkopf said he was "suckered" by the Iraqis into agreeing to permit helicopters to fly, ostensibly to move top officials between cities, when they really intended to use helicopter gunships against the rebels.[26] Five years later, also in an interview with David Frost, George Bush commented about Saddam Hussein, "I miscalculated. . . . I thought he'd be gone." With regard to the Safwan meeting, Bush noted, "I think he took us by surprise. . . . We might have handled the flying of helicopters differently. . . . So I think there's room for some ex post facto criticism here."[27]

Whatever the rationale, the U.S. decision to permit Saddam Hussein to use advanced weaponry to suppress the internal revolts after the war made the United States an accessory after the fact to a massacre and ensured, whether inadvertently or not, that Saddam Hussein would retain power in Iraq. When the extent of the repression became known, and as Kurdish refugees began flooding across the border into Turkey, the United States, together with France and Great Britain, established so-called no-fly zones in the north and south. This gesture undoubtedly saved some lives and effectively prevented Saddam Hussein from reestablishing total control over the Kurdish territories. It was, however, much too late to save the many thousands of Iraqis who had spontaneously attacked the symbols of Ba'thist rule in the weeks after the allied victory.

The Clinton Administration and Dual Containment[28]

On May 18, 1993, two months after President Clinton took office, Martin Indyk of the National Security Council staff spelled out the broad outlines of what he called America's "dual containment" policy in the Persian Gulf.[29] Traditionally, the United States had pursued a policy of balancing Iran or Iraq against the other as a means of maintaining a degree of regional stability and to protect the smaller, oil-rich Arab states on the southern side of the Gulf. That was the purpose of the Twin Pillar policy, and it was implicit in subsequent tilts toward Iraq and (briefly) Iran during the Iran-Iraq war. Indyk, however, proclaimed the policy bankrupt and rejected it "because we don't need to rely on one to balance the other." Iraq was boxed in by UN sanctions, Iran was nearly prostrate after the eight-year war with Iraq, and the United States was the predominant power in the Persian Gulf with the "means to counter both the Iraqi and Iranian regimes."[30]

Iraq

The objective of the policy with regard to Iraq was to sustain the coalition that had defeated the armies of Saddam Hussein in Operation Desert Storm and to ensure that Iraq complied with all United Nations resolutions. The United States characterized the existing regime in Iraq as criminal and irredeemable and favored main-

taining the sanctions until Saddam Hussein was gone.[31] This position created difficulties with other members of the UN Security Council, since Article 22 of the enabling Resolution 687 specified that the sanctions would be lifted once Iraq had
eliminated and accounted for all of its weapons of mass destruction.

In the years after the adoption of the policy, the United States reportedly budgeted
approximately $15 million per year for covert actions to destabilize the Saddam Hus-
sein regime and for support of various Iraqi opposition groups.[32] The U.S. Central Intelligence Agency attempted to organize several operations to depose Saddam Hussein,
including a major covert action just before the Clinton administration took office and
at least two others in 1995 and 1996.[33] These operations were unsuccessful.

There was very little debate in the United States about the desirability—even the
necessity—of maintaining strict sanctions against the government of Saddam Hussein. The substantial American consensus in favor of severe sanctions could be attributed in large measure to the Iraqi leader himself. The nature of his attack on
Kuwait, the looting and killing and burning that followed, his ruthless suppression
of dissent, his near-genocidal tactics against his own people, the discovery that he
was much closer to having nuclear and chemical weapons than had been supposed,
his systematic obstruction of UN investigations including physical interference and
mass falsification of documents, and his continued military forays and threats whenever he believed he could get away with it—all of these and more firmly implanted
an image of utter evil and constant threat. That image underscored and reinforced
U.S. insistence on what was the most elaborate network of sanctions ever imposed
on a member state of the UN.

There was, however, considerable sympathy in the United States for the plight of
the people of Iraq, who bore the worst of the brunt of two wars and stringent economic sanctions. This popular concern was no doubt a factor in the U.S. decision
to acquiesce in the limited sale of Iraqi oil under terms negotiated by the UN in
1996.[34] The United States insisted, however, that the misery of the Iraqi people was
directly attributable to Saddam Hussein, who callously used the deprivation of his
own people as a bargaining chip.[35]

In June 1993 and in September 1996, the United States launched cruise missiles
against targets in Iraq. The first case was retaliation for evidence of an Iraqi plot to
assassinate former President George Bush in Kuwait. The second was in retaliation
against Iraqi ground force incursions in northern Iraq in cooperation with the
Kurdish Democratic Party.[36] On several occasions, the United States surged military
forces into the region in response to Iraqi threats or failure to comply with UN Special Commission (UNSCOM) inspections. In February 1998, the United States appeared to be poised for a massive strike against Iraq, when it refused to permit inspection of presidential sites. That crisis was resolved only when the UN
secretary-general, Kofi Annan, went to Baghdad and negotiated a memorandum of
understanding with the Iraqi president.[37]

The bottom line, however, was that the United States, with significant help from a
number of friends, allies, and the UN Security Council, was generally successful in

keeping Saddam Hussein in what Secretary of State Madeline Albright called a "strategic box." By mid-1998, this policy was losing support from the Arab states, which felt that the Iraqi people were being unfairly punished for the misbehavior of their rulers, and from states such as Russia, France, and China that had major political and financial interests in Iraq. The international consensus was preserved, however, primarily because of the unrelenting intransigence and belligerence of the Iraqi leader.

Iran

The other target of dual containment, Iran, posed a very different set of problems. The dual containment policy called for Iran to: (1) cease its support of international terrorism and subversion, (2) end its violent opposition to the Arab-Israel peace talks, and (3) halt efforts to acquire weapons of mass destruction. President Bush had referred to Iran in his Inaugural Address in January 1989, saying that "Goodwill begets goodwill. Good faith can be a spiral that endlessly moves on."[38] There was, however, no talk of goodwill by the Clinton administration. Instead, U.S. officials developed a special vocabulary in which Iran was routinely branded as a "rogue," "terrorist," "outlaw," or "backlash" state. This relentless drumfire of attacks—the mirror image of Iranian depictions of the United States as the "Great Satan"—had its effects in the media, in the Congress, in the public, and in the attitudes of lower-level bureaucrats. With a Democrat in the White House and the Republicans in control of the Congress, a domestic political contest developed over which party could be most vigorous in promoting U.S. policies to deal with Iran.

The debate was galvanized in 1995 when the U.S. oil company Conoco Inc. announced that it had signed a $1 billion contract with Iran to develop the Sirri gas field in the Persian Gulf. Although perfectly legal, the prospect that this deal would breach the wall of containment around Iran generated such a wave of outrage that the company was forced to renounce it. The Congress and the American-Israel Public Affairs Committee (AIPAC) began preparing legislation that would end all trade with Iran and punish any corporations that engaged in investments there. President Clinton, who was preparing for his reelection campaign, quickly preempted this by issuing two executive orders that made it illegal for American oil companies to operate in Iran and established penalties for any U.S. citizen or corporation doing business with Iran.[39] Both decisions were announced by senior administration officials before major Jewish organizations. The U.S. business community, apparently intimidated by the public outcry, remained totally silent.[40]

This process was replayed in presidential election year 1996. The Congress prepared a bill that would impose sanctions on any foreign corporation that invested $40 million or more in the Iranian oil and gas sector. Libya was later added on the floor of the Senate, and the bill became known as the Iran-Libya Sanctions Act (ILSA). Although the bill was certain to create serious problems with America's allies, the Congress saw ILSA as an opportunity to take a public stand against terrorism. The bill passed 415-0 and was signed into law by President Clinton.

In May 1997, Seyyed Mohammed Khatami was elected to a four-year term as president of Iran in a stunning electoral surprise. He conducted a grassroots campaign on the issues of rule of law, civil society, and dialogue among competing ideologies. His campaign struck a resonant chord with the Iranian population, particularly among women and the burgeoning population of young people, many of whom had no memory of the ancien regime. Paired against the well-known speaker of the Majlis (parliament), who represented revolutionary orthodoxy, Khatami attracted the largest number of voters in Iranian history and won a decisive victory with 69 percent of the vote. He carried all of the urban centers in Iran and virtually every province. In August, his reformist cabinet was accepted without exception by the Majlis.

Although Khatami was widely regarded as a candidate of domestic issues, it was his foreign policy moves that attracted the most attention during the first year of his term. In December 1997, Iran played host to the Organization of the Islamic Conference, where it won plaudits for its conciliatory positions and moderation. Iran called for closer cooperation with the UN, an institution it had shunned as a Western tool after the revolution. Iran began a concerted effort to improve its relations with Saudi Arabia and its other Arab neighbors in the Persian Gulf region, with some substantial initial success.

In January 1998, Khatami made an unprecedented "Address to the American People" in the form of an interview on CNN.[41] He praised the achievements of American civilization, went as far as an Iranian politician could go in expressing regret for the hostage crisis, and spelled out very clearly Iran's positions on all of the major issues of concern to the United States:

On terrorism: "Any form of killing of innocent men and women who are not involved in confrontations is terrorism. It must be condemned, and we, in our turn, condemn every form of it in the world."

On the peace process: "We have declared our opposition to the Middle East peace process, because we believe it will not succeed. At the same time, we have clearly said that we don't intend to impose our views on others or to stand in their way."

On weapons of mass destruction: "We are not a nuclear power and do not intend to become one."

Washington responded to the Khatami initiative cautiously but generally positively.[42] The United States toned down its rhetoric and took some small steps to improve relations. But problems remained. Less than sixty days after Khatami took office, the French oil major Total, together with state-owned partners Gazprom of Russia and Petronas of Malaysia, concluded a $2 billion deal to develop an Iranian gas field. These negotiations, which had been underway since Conoco withdrew in 1995, placed Total and its partners in apparent violation of ILSA, which mandated U.S. sanctions against any company investing more than $20 million in the Iranian oil and gas sector.[43]

In May 1998, the United States announced that it would waive the provisions of ILSA on grounds of national security. That decision was due almost entirely to pressure from America's European allies, but it was nevertheless received positively in Tehran.[44] The United States also announced a major redeployment of its Persian Gulf forces, sharply reducing the number of ships and aircraft permanently stationed in the region. This was due primarily to cost factors and personnel pressures, but again it was received positively by Tehran. There was growing awareness among Washington strategists that the initial assumption that the United States could alone confront both Iran and Iraq may have been exaggerated. At a minimum, as the threat from Iran appeared to be declining, the United States could ill afford to deliberately cultivate enemies.

On June 17, 1998, Secretary of State Albright delivered a major speech that responded almost point-by-point to the issues that Khatami had addressed in his interview six months earlier.[45] The speech was notable for its conciliatory tone and for the absence of the rhetoric that had characterized U.S. statements about Iran over the previous five years. The speech offered no specific new policies or initiatives, but it held out the prospect for a new beginning:

> We are ready to explore further ways to build mutual confidence and avoid misunderstandings. The Islamic Republic should consider parallel steps. If such a process can be initiated and sustained in a way that addresses the concerns of both sides, then we in the United States can see the prospect of a very different relationship. As the wall of mistrust comes down, we can develop with the Islamic Republic, when it is ready, a road map leading to normal relations. Obviously, two decades of mistrust cannot be erased overnight. The gap between us remains wide. But it is time to test the possibilities for bridging this gap.[46]

Beyond Dual Containment?

As the twentieth century was drawing to a close, the United States appeared to be exploring cautiously a new security policy for the Persian Gulf that would fall somewhere between the extreme dependence on allies and regional surrogates that had characterized the period before the Iranian revolution and the exuberant unilateralism of the period following the Second Gulf War. Those early signals appeared to reflect the judgment that future access to oil was more likely to be driven by technologies and markets than by politics, that the predations of Saddam Hussein were unlikely to be repeated in the near future, and that the threats emanating from the region could potentially be managed more effectively in a regional context rather than by relying exclusively on the United States as the political and military hegemon. The United States seemed certain to remain the major power in the region, but it was possible to imagine a reduction of U.S. military presence and a concomitant increase of attention to diplomacy and regional security arrangements.

All of those judgments were tentative and could be upset by the kind of surprises that had occurred all too frequently in the Persian Gulf over the previous half-century. Four flash points remained that could—and at some point probably would—interfere with a smooth transition to a more regionally based strategy:

- A breakdown in the Arab-Israel peace process could spill over into the Gulf politically or even militarily, as it had in the past.
- Either the reinvigoration or collapse of Saddam Hussein's regime in Iraq could create a vortex of instability in the heart of the Middle East.
- A new turn of the Iranian revolution could shred the delicate fabric of goodwill that had been created under President Khatami.
- A political or social breakdown in one of the key Arab states of the region could shatter the illusion of contented stability in the Gulf Cooperation Council states.

In any of these cases, the United States would again be called upon to play a central role in the affairs of the region. It would again have to choose—as had happened so many times in the previous fifty years—between an indirect proxy role and some form of military intervention, either independently or as the leader of a coalition.

History provides no reliable guidance. For more than half a century, the United States experimented, often clumsily, with stratagems of all sorts in a variety of circumstances. In the end, as in the cold war, its interests were preserved and it emerged as the dominant power. The challenge of the future would be to blend military power with diplomacy in a region that could no longer be sequestered from the broader issues of the Middle East region and the world economy.

Notes

1. These early contacts led to a treaty with the sultanate of Muscat and Oman in 1833, which is still recalled on occasions of state with Oman.

2. The following comments draw on the author's article "The Evolution of U.S. Strategy Toward the Indian Ocean and Persian Gulf Regions," in Alvin Z. Rubinstein, ed., *The Great Game: Rivalry in the Persian Gulf and South Asia,* Praeger, 1983, pp. 49–80.

3. For a more detailed account of this period, see Michael A. Palmer, *Guardians of the Gulf: The Growth of American Involvement in the Persian Gulf, 1833–1991,* Free Press, 1992.

4. A detailed account of this episode and its implications can be found in Gary Sick, *All Fall Down: America's Tragic Encounter with Iran,* New York: Random House, 1985, pp. 14ff.

5. See the chapters by Mark Gasiorowski and others in this volume.

6. For a more detailed account, see James A. Bill, *The Eagle and the Lion: The Tragedy of American-Iranian Relations,* Yale University Press, 1988, pp. 204–208. Israel had a well-developed strategy, known as the Doctrine of the Periphery, to outflank its hostile Arab neighbors by promoting relations with non-Arab states on the fringes of the conflict. In the case of Iran, this took the form of a very close strategic relationship for more than twenty years.

7. Cited in J. C. Hurewitz, *The Persian Gulf After Iran's Revolution,* Foreign Policy Association Headline Series 244, April 1979, p. 22.

8. Former Secretary of Defense James Schlesinger drew attention to this fact in an article questioning whether the RDJTF was rapid, deployable, or even a force. See "Rapid(?) Deployment(?) Force(?)," *Washington Post,* September 24, 1980.

9. For a detailed examination of this episode, see Theodore Draper, *A Very Thin Line: The Iran-Contra Affair,* New York: Hill and Wang, 1991.

10. The casualty figures for the Iran-Iraq war are often exaggerated. Mohsen Rafiqdust, the former head of the Iranian Revolutionary Guard Force, told Robert Fisk of the *Independent* (June 25, 1995) that 220,000 Iranians were killed and 400,000 wounded during the Iran-Iraq war. That is roughly consistent with Iranian official statements and with independent Western estimates. Iraq has never published any figures on its losses, but Amatzia Baram, a specialist on Iraq at Haifa University, has estimated that 150,000 Iraqis were killed (*Jerusalem Quarterly,* no. 49 [Winter 1989], pp. 85–86). If the standard ratio of two wounded for every man killed is applied, Iraq may have had 300,000 wounded. Thus, an informed estimate of total losses on both sides would equal approximately 370,000 killed and some 700,000 wounded, which is imprecise but plausible. In the case of Iraq, this casualty level is roughly comparable to U.S. losses in the Civil War.

11. See Chapter 18 by Shafeeq Ghabra in this volume.

12. The substantial deployment of U.S. forces to the Gulf was hastened—as was congressional approval—by the Iraqi missile attack on the USS *Stark* on May 17, 1987. Although the buildup was intended to counter Iran, the Iraqi attack galvanized public attention and underlined the threat to shipping in the Gulf.

13. Iraq was much better equipped than Iran, and it fired 3 to 4 missiles to every Iranian missile. The only confirmed use of poison gas was by Iraq—against Iranian troop formations and some civilian sites in Kurdish territory. For a more detailed examination of this armed negotiation, see Gary Sick, "Slouching Toward Settlement: The Internationalization of the Iran-Iraq War, 1987–88," in Nikki Keddie and Mark Gasiorowski, eds., *Neither East Nor West: Iran, the Soviet Union, and the United States,* Yale University Press, 1990, pp. 219–246.

14. Letter to the secretary-general of March 28 (FBIS, March 30, 1988).

15. One mine struck the USS *Samuel B. Roberts* and on April 18, 1988, U.S. forces hit two Iranian oil platforms, Nasr (near Sirri Island) and Salman (in the joint Iran-Oman Lavan field), removing some 50,000 barrels per day from Iran's oil production. In the same action, two Iranian frigates were sunk, another was severely damaged, and four gunboats were damaged or sunk. In 1996, Iran brought a suit against the United States in the International Court of Justice seeking compensation for the loss of the oil platforms on the grounds that the attacks were a violation of international law and contrary to the terms of existing U.S.-Iranian agreements.

16. The bitter dispute between Iran and Saudi Arabia over Iran's participation in the annual hajj deepened the distrust between these two states. Saudi Arabia stepped up its direct support for Iraq, apparently permitting Iraqi aircraft to utilize Saudi airfields during raids on Iranian oil facilities in the southern Gulf. On April 26, 1988, Saudi Arabia broke diplomatic relations with Iran.

17. FBIS, July 21, 1988. On July 25, Khomeini made a six-minute appearance on television from the balcony of his residence. He appeared extremely frail and did not speak.

18. For example, see Murray Waas and Douglas Frantz, "U.S. Gave Data to Iraq Three Months Before Invasion; Persian Gulf: Documents Show Intelligence Sharing with Baghdad Lasted Longer Than Previously Indicated," *Los Angeles Times,* March 10, 1992, p. 1 (one of a series of investigative reports). See also "News Conference, Rep. Jack Brooks (D–TX) Rep. Charles Schumer (D–NY): Special Prosecutor Criminal Dealings with Iraq Prior to Iraqi Invasion of Kuwait," *Federal News Service,* July 9, 1992.

19. A verbatim text of Glaspie's meeting with Saddam Hussein on July 25, 1990, was later released by the Iraqi government and was published by the *New York Times* on September 23,

1990, p. 19. Glaspie, in testimony before the Senate Foreign Relations Committee on March 20, 1991, characterized the transcript as about 80 percent accurate, but with some key passages edited out.

20. See Chapter 22 by Robert O. Freedman and Chapter 23 by Georgiy Mirsky in this volume.

21. Speech by President Bush from the Oval Office, January 16, 1991, two hours after the bombing campaign against Iraqi positions had begun.

22. See, for example, "Needless Deaths in the Gulf War: Civilian Casualties During the Air Campaign and Violations of the Laws of War," *Middle East Watch Report,* Human Rights Watch, New York, November 1991.

23. According to official counts, allied deaths were 146 Americans (35 by friendly fire), 24 British (9 by American fire), 2 Frenchmen, 1 Italian, and 39 among various Arab allies. Baghdad has never given an official count of its casualties, but postwar analyses concluded that Iraq's uniformed losses were far smaller than previously estimated, perhaps as low as 1,500 deaths. Estimates of civilian casualties were uncertain and varied greatly from one observer to another. See John G. Heidenrich, "The Gulf War: How Many Iraqis Died?" *Foreign Policy,* no. 90 (Spring 1993), pp. 108–125. The Associated Press on March 9, 1993 provided an overview of the various estimates.

24. *New York Times,* March 15, 1991, p. 13.

25. Ibid., March 27, 1991, pp. 1, 9.

26. Ibid., March 28, 1991, pp. 1, 18.

27. *Dow Jones News,* January 15, 1996.

28. The following analysis draws extensively on the author's article "Rethinking Dual Containment," *Survival: The IISS Quarterly,* vol. 40, no. 1 (Spring 1998), pp. 5–32.

29. Martin Indyk, "The Clinton Administration's Approach to the Middle East," Keynote Address to the Soref Symposium on "Challenges to U.S. Interests in the Middle East: Obstacles and Opportunities," *Proceedings of the Washington Institute for Near East Policy,* May 18–19, 1993, pp. 1–8. Martin Indyk at the time of this speech had just joined the National Security Council staff. He later became the U.S. ambassador to Israel and then assistant secretary of state for Near East affairs.

30. Indyk, "The Clinton Administration's Approach to the Middle East," p. 4.

31. See, for example, the remarks by Secretary of State Madeline K. Albright at Georgetown University, Washington, D.C., March 26, 1997, as released by the Office of the Spokesman, U.S. Department of State.

32. Elaine Sciolino, "CIA Asks Congress for Money to Rein in Iraq and Iran," *New York Times,* April 12, 1995, p. 1.

33. All of these operations were publicly confirmed after the event by former senior officials of the U.S. government. See Don Oberdorfer, "U.S. Had Covert Plan to Oust Iraq's Saddam, Bush Adviser Asserts; Effort to Remove Leader Came 'Pretty Close,'" *Washington Post,* January 20, 1993, p. 1; and ABC News, "Unfinished Business—the CIA and Saddam Hussein," transcript no. 97062601-j13, June 26, 1997. There have also been detailed reports in the *Los Angeles Times,* the *New York Times,* and other media.

34. Initially, Iraq was permitted to sell up to $2 billion of oil in two 90-day periods after each authorization. The first sales began on December 10, 1995. In 1998, the terms were extended to permit total sales of $4.5 billion—more than the Iraqis were physically capable of producing, given the low price of oil at the time. The sales contracts were monitored closely

by the UN, and the proceeds were allotted to humanitarian relief and repayment of claims from the war and to cover UN expenses in Iraq.

35. United Nations Special Commissioner Rolf Ekeus estimated that Iraq deliberately deprived itself of more than $100 billion in revenues by refusing to cooperate with UN weapons inspections. See the *Washington Post*, "For the Record," January 31, 1997.

36. This attack was particularly controversial since the targets were in the south and unrelated to the ground attack in the north.

37. See "Memorandum of Understanding Between the United Nations and the Republic of Iraq," Associated Press, February 24, 1998.

38. See the text of the Inaugural Address in the *New York Times*, January 21, 1989, p. 10. Iran welcomed this remark and responded by helping to free the U.S. hostages in Lebanon. It is a sore point with Iran that this gesture, in their view, was never reciprocated by the United States.

39. See Executive Order 12957 of March 15, 1995, and Executive Order 12959 of May 6, 1995.

40. For a detailed analysis of the politics associated with the developments of Iranian sanctions, see Laurie Lande, "Second Thoughts," *International Economy*, May–June 1997, pp. 44–49.

41. The transcript of this interview with Iranian President Mohammad Khatami was posted on the CNN web site immediately after it was aired on January 7, 1998. Large portions of the text were published in a number of newspapers the following day.

42. Even before the Khatami election, many senior policy observers and former U.S. officials were calling for changes in the dual containment strategy. These voices included two former national security advisers, a former secretary of defense, three former assistant secretaries of state for Near East affairs, and the former commander of U.S. forces in the Persian Gulf, among others.

43. The trigger level was reduced automatically from $40 million to $20 million on the first anniversary of the legislation in August 1997.

44. The European Union threatened to take the case to the World Trade Organization if the United States imposed sanctions on the French company, on grounds that the U.S. policy was in violation of international trade agreements.

45. Secretary of State Madeline K. Albright, Remarks at 1998 Asia Society Dinner, Waldorf-Astoria Hotel, New York, New York, June 17, 1998, As released by the Office of the Spokesman, June 18, 1998, U.S. Department of State.

46. Ibid.

18

Kuwait and the United States: The Reluctant Ally and U.S. Policy Toward the Gulf

Shafeeq Ghabra

U.S. interest in Kuwait, a small country with a population today of 750,000 Kuwaitis and 1,670,000 non-Kuwaitis, evolved over a long period.[1] In 1990–1991, as a result of the Gulf war, the United States became the most important foreign power in the Gulf region, succeeding Great Britain following its disengagement from the area in the early 1970s. And though the war laid the foundations for a more active U.S. policy in the region, it equally transformed Kuwait's foreign policy objectives and priorities. After the war Kuwait moved from a hesitant and distant relationship with the United States into a relationship of security and cooperation. This chapter traces the development of U.S.-Kuwaiti relations within the context of U.S. policy toward the Gulf and examines the nature of this bilateral relationship, its irritants, and current challenges that confront it.

Early U.S.-Kuwaiti Relations

Shaykh Mubarak, the ruler of Kuwait during the early part of this century, was on a visit to Basra in 1910 when he asked Dr. Binitt, a U.S. missionary with a clinic in Basra, to treat his daughter and come to work in Kuwait. This was the beginning of the American Hospital, a clinic and missionary operation that remained in use until the 1950s.[2] Over the years, the clinic became a symbol of U.S. goodwill, but beyond that, Kuwait remained a British autonomous protectorate. In accordance with an agreement signed with Great Britain in 1899, Kuwait made a commitment not to grant foreigners concessions in the territory of Kuwait without British permission or rent parts of its territory or deal with a foreign power without British approval.[3]

Over a decade later, Shaykh Ahmad al-Jabir, emir of Kuwait from 1920 to 1950, began negotiations with the Anglo-Iranian Oil Company in Kuwait in 1923 for the country's first oil concession. The emir kept delaying a decision, however, because he wanted to bring U.S. companies into the bidding in order to strike the best deal possible. Meanwhile, he, along with the founder of Saudi Arabia, King 'Abd al-'Aziz Al Sa'ud (or Ibn Sa'ud), granted a concession to Major Holmes of Eastern and General Syndicate Ltd. (EGS) to explore the neutral zone, which at the time was a shared territory between Kuwait and Saudi Arabia. The emir was pleased when EGS operations in the Gulf were acquired by the U.S.-based Gulf Oil Corporation in 1927. Shaykh Ahmad was convinced that a better deal could be achieved by negotiating with Gulf Oil and believed that the company's representative "had no political aspirations, being purely commercial as had been proved in Bahrain."[4] He was also disappointed in the "British treatment of Kuwait interests" at the Ojair conference in 1922, when some Kuwaiti territory was given to Ibn Sa'ud.[5]

After years of negotiations, extending from 1928 to 1934, Ahmad managed to convince Anglo-Iranian and Gulf Oil to form the Kuwait Oil Company (KOC). He then signed Kuwait's first oil concession, emerging "as the prime architect of the 1934 agreement and the vast benefits it has brought to Kuwait."[6] According to 'Abd al-Rahman al-Atiqi, Kuwait's minister of oil and finance from 1967 to 1975, although Kuwait was in need of cash, it had intentionally postponed finalizing an oil agreement with the British companies. While the British reached agreements with Bahrain, Iraq, and Iran, Kuwait waited. Ahmad was able to use to his advantage the British desire to limit U.S. involvement in the region.[7] This example provides insight into the way Kuwait's foreign policy emerged. Such a policy sought to balance forces in order to maintain freedom of movement. In this context the U.S. company played such a function.

Until Kuwait's independence in 1961, room was limited for the development of ties with the United States beyond the opening of a consulate, which oversaw the few commercial ties that existed between the two countries. Kuwait, after its independence in 1961, was a typical small country and, therefore, sparked little interest for the United States, especially since U.S. policy in the Gulf was centered primarily around Iran and Saudi Arabia.[8]

Regional Shifts and the Dilemma of a Small State

In its early years of independence, Kuwait's small-state dilemma led to its obsession with maintaining independence from Saudi Arabia, Iraq, and Iran. It did not, however, seek outside commitments from major powers. Instead, Kuwait compensated by seeking the protection of an informal "Arab umbrella." At that time, anti-Western mood was sweeping the region, and independence movements and their effects abounded. A policy of involvement with such powers as the United States or Britain would have been suicidal, so Kuwait safeguarded its independence by becoming involved in Arab affairs and by using its wealth to maintain Arab support.[9] After all, it was the Arabs in general, and Egypt and Saudi Arabia in particular, who prevented Iraq from invading Kuwait in 1961, when Kuwait became independent. That incident reinforced a policy of pan-Arabism and solidarity with Arab causes.

Kuwait's policy overlapped with the populist pan-Arabist trend in the region. This pan-Arabist component, naturally, made Kuwait far more committed to Arab causes and issues, at the top of which sat the Arab-Israeli conflict. The 1967 Arab-Israeli war intensified criticism of U.S. policy in the region, criticism that had been stoked already by the revolutionary rhetoric emanating from Egypt, Iraq, and Syria during the 1950s and early 1960s. Kuwait hoped to safeguard its independence by supporting the broad concept of pan-Arabism and being in the forefront of financial support for development projects in the Arab world.[10] This approach also meant maintaining neutrality in inter-Arab conflicts and differences.

Being a proponent of pan-Arabism, Kuwait became one of the most active Arab states in the Office of the Boycott of the League of Arab States against Israel. When the United States suggested as its ambassador to Kuwait someone who worked as a counselor in Jerusalem, Kuwait refused to accept him.[11] Other factors also served to distance the United States from Kuwait, including the role of the Organization of Petroleum Exporting Countries (OPEC) and its 1971 negotiations with U.S. companies over oil pricing. That year prices were raised by $.29 per barrel, despite President Richard M. Nixon's attempts to prevent the increase. In response, the United States devalued the dollar. The 1973 Arab-Israeli war added to the tensions, leading OPEC to further increase oil prices several-fold. In addition to operating in such Arab groupings, Kuwait also supported policies adopted in the nonaligned movement and in the United Nations (UN) that were typically inimical to U.S. interests.

Kuwait, however, did have vested interests in a cordial relationship with the United States. Kuwait was a non-Communist country, and most of its economic dealings were in Western countries; its huge investments were predominantly in the United States and Europe. Any collapse in the U.S. dollar would, therefore, have ramifications in Kuwait. These economic interests laid the groundwork, despite the 1967 war, for the first official visit by a Kuwaiti emir to the United States, in December 1968. In the Kuwaiti government and among the ruling Sabah family, there had always been those who had worked for better U.S.-Kuwaiti relations. Despite this, however, relations were always clouded by the U.S. position on the Arab-Israeli conflict.[12]

Although foreign investments and business deals were primarily in the West, Kuwaiti politics remained oriented toward the internal and external pan-Arabist and anti-Western currents prevalent in the region. The dual nature of Kuwaiti policy is reflected in the fact that the government had to publicly distance itself from the United States even as it sent most of its students and money to the United States and Western Europe. This constant conflict between local, regional, and international interests continued to characterize U.S.-Kuwaiti relations until August 1990. A similar dilemma, at different levels, affected U.S. relations with the other Arab Gulf states.

Vacuum in the Gulf

Until the early 1970s the British presence in the Gulf was dominant. During the British withdrawal from the Gulf in the late 1960s and early 1970s, it looked as if full independence was imminent in the region. Pumped with self-assurance, Arabs in the Gulf believed that they could protect their resources and the region by themselves. Such confidence was enhanced by OPEC's power after the 1973 Arab-Israeli war.

For the United States, the Gulf's significance increased greatly during the cold war due to the prevalence of oil in the region. A broad U.S. policy of maintaining stability in the Gulf emerged so as to ensure the easy access to and safe transport of oil from the region while keeping the Soviets at bay. After the British withdrew, the United States turned to Iran to fill the vacuum left by their departure. The United States devised the so-called twin pillars policy of sustaining the region's balance through Iranian muscle and Saudi Arabian money.[13]

This policy was guided by the Nixon Doctrine, outlined by the president in his State of the Union address in January 1970. This doctrine reflected the desire of a hesitant superpower to undertake only limited involvement in areas of potential conflict. It was another version of Vietnamization in which Nixon stated that the United States would "rescue" its involvement and presence in other nations' affairs. This policy, a result of U.S. experiences in the Vietnam War, had ramifications in the region to both friend and foe.[14]

The Shah of Iran recognized the reluctance of the United States and took seriously his "mandate" to police the region. He equally wanted no major U.S. role in the area, reflected clearly in a statement he made at a press conference in 1972 rejecting a U.S. naval presence in Bahrain.[15] At the same time, from 1971 to 1979, the shah helped U.S. policy objectives, and he supplied Israel with 50 percent of its oil needs. The Israelis, meanwhile, supported arms shipments to Iran, intending to counterbalance Iraq.[16]

With the 1979 collapse of the shah's government and the Soviet invasion of Afghanistan, the U.S. administration found itself with only Saudi Arabia to rely on. The failure of the twin pillars policy was evident and motivated U.S. policymakers to develop contingency plans for sudden crises in the Gulf.[17] Alert to the dangers that possibly lay ahead in the region, the Carter Doctrine of January 1980 (named for U.S. President Jimmy Carter) replaced the Nixon Doctrine as the U.S. blueprint for the region. According to the Carter Doctrine, which was enunciated in direct response to Soviet actions in Afghanistan, the United States would not tolerate any attempt by any outside force to gain control of the Gulf region. The United States would use all means necessary, including military force, to repel such an attempt.[18]

The Carter Doctrine restated U.S. awareness of the importance of the region's oil supply, especially given the diminishing U.S. share in world production. For example, in 1938 the United States produced 62 percent of the world's oil. Beginning in 1955, 80 percent of all new oil discoveries were in the Middle East. In 1962, the United States began importing 2 million barrels per day and in 1973 had increased that to 5 million barrels per day. Demand continued to rise and discoveries in the United States declined. In Europe, dependency on oil was much higher. In 1962, Europe imported 37 percent of its needs, and in 1972 it imported 60 percent. Japan imported 73 percent of its needs in 1972.[19] During the 1980s it became apparent that Kuwait, Saudi Arabia, the United Arab Emirates (UAE), Iran, and Iraq would be among the few producers of oil in the next century. These countries would also be responsible for most increases in production as well as new reserve discoveries (currently, two-thirds of the world's proven oil reserves are located in the region, including the newly discovered areas in central Asia).

The assassination of Egyptian President Anwar Sadat in October 1981, the bombing of the U.S. Marines barracks in Lebanon in October 1983, and the subsequent U.S. shelling of Lebanese positions and raids on Syrian targets created an overall impression of weakness and a lack of resolve regarding implementation of the Carter Doctrine or any other doctrine for that matter. Even when U.S. administrations wanted to sell arms to Gulf states, they ran into problems with Congress. Two of the results in the 1980s were an inability to push through defense packages to Saudi Arabia and Kuwait; in the end, whatever was sold only came after intense lobbying and serious cuts in the packages.[20]

In the 1980s, any large U.S. military presence in the Gulf was considered dangerous to local rulers. Gulf leaders, fearful of regional and domestic reactions, blocked efforts at U.S. infrastructural buildups in the region. The pre-positioning of weapons and munitions were prohibited except by Oman and Egypt, and in those cases the operations were kept at a minimum. Kuwait stood against the pre-positioning of U.S. equipment and arms in the Gulf, sensing that it would add to the tensions in the region, especially because of the Iran-Iraq war that had begun in 1980.[21]

Kuwaiti Neutrality and the Reflagging of Tankers

When Iraq first invaded Iran in response to internal violence by Shi'a dissidents and in support of the Iraqi quest to gain a hegemonic position in the Gulf, Kuwait and most of the other Gulf states were taken by surprise. Saddam Hussein neither consulted nor informed the Gulf rulers. On the contrary, the Saudis were furious at Saddam for not consulting with them prior to his decision to go to war with Iran. They did not like the fact that Saddam asked for financial help when the war bogged down. None of the Gulf states were sure how the war would proceed. Iraq's quick advance into Iran soon gave way to protracted trench warfare. Very few realized during this early stage that Iran would later pose a serious threat to the security of the entire region.

The fears created by the Iranian counteroffensive against Iraq in 1983 contributed to a reversal from Kuwait's usual policy of neutrality to one in favor of support for Iraq. Support for Baghdad derived from the fact that Iran was a semirevolutionary power, whereas Iraq was a status quo power. As a result, the Gulf states, in addition to Egypt and Jordan, provided Iraq with logistics, money, and weapons. According to Abdullah Bisharah, former secretary-general of the Gulf Cooperation Council (GCC), such support, it was thought, was the only way to contain revolutionary Iran, given that it increasingly threatened the security of Kuwait by supporting clandestine groups that bombed several targets in Kuwait and attempted to assassinate the emir.[22]

When Iran began attacking Kuwaiti oil tankers in 1985, Kuwait realized the need to improve ties with the United States, other Western powers, and the Soviet Union. The need to find a way to stop the war and end Iranian attacks on shipping in the Gulf became a political and security priority. At one point during 1986, Kuwaiti oil production was down to 300 barrels per day, as opposed to 2 million.[23] The war threatened Kuwait's economic lifeline. Reflagging Kuwaiti tankers appeared to be the only way to engage other countries in protecting Kuwaiti shipping. Such operations were not unusual in commercial shipping around the world (as a way to avoid higher taxes).

Under U.S. law, any ship under the U.S. flag is protected by the U.S. Navy. According to Su'ud al-Usaymi, Kuwait's state minister for foreign affairs during that period, the Kuwaiti government decided to make use of this avenue and approached the United States and the Soviet Union during May and June 1986. The U.S. administration under Ronald Reagan declined, however, apologizing on the grounds that the operation was risky and that U.S. laws did not permit such an undertaking. The Soviet government, however, through its ambassador in Kuwait, accepted the proposal within five days of the initial contact, and Kuwait sent a technical delegation to Moscow. As the Kuwaiti delegation negotiated details with the Soviets, the United States reevaluated its previous decision and agreed to the reflagging effort. The Kuwaiti government's leaking of information regarding negotiations in Moscow led to the U.S. change in policy to reflag Kuwaiti tankers in July 1987.[24] Under the arrangement, the U.S. Navy escorted the tankers until they reached Kuwaiti waters.[25]

The reflagging operation was the first step in security cooperation between the United States and Kuwait, although Kuwait tried to keep the reflagging a purely business arrangement that would not affect its neutrality. When the United States asked Kuwait to supply fuel to U.S. vessels protecting tankers, Kuwait, in order to prevent U.S. personnel from docking or coming ashore, provided such fuel through tankers rented from Gulf states; they were given use of a floating dock in Gulf waters. When the United States asked for port facilities, Kuwait refused out of fear that it would create problems with rejectionists in Kuwait and the rest of the Middle East.

Kuwaiti fears were borne out, for example, when Su'ud al-Usaymi met with students at Kuwait University. Many of them were opposed to the reflagging operation. The students rarely mentioned the Soviet reflagging and chose instead to focus on the U.S. role, characterizing it as colonial and imperialist.[26] This feeling among students was affected by the U.S. position on the Arab-Israeli conflict and the overall U.S. Middle East policy. Similar opposition was widespread among Kuwaiti opposition groups and among members of the university faculty. In fact, suspicion of any government policy was normal. Indeed, with the Kuwaiti parliament dissolved since

1986, any governmental policy engaging a foreign power was seen as an attempt to revive old Western colonial designs in the region.

During the reflagging, the Ministry of Oil, headed by 'Ali al-Khalifa al-Sabah, was in favor of more active U.S.-Kuwaiti relations. Cooperation did take place between his ministry and the U.S. Navy. For example, the Kuwaiti petroleum sector funded research on incoming Iranian missiles, leading to the installation of boats with mirrored solar panels in Kuwaiti ports in order to lure the missiles away from their targets.[27] As a result, U.S.-Kuwaiti relations improved and were strengthened during this period. Both sides agreed on the need to end the Iraq-Iran war, the carnage in Lebanon, and terrorism. Between 1985 and 1988, five Kuwaiti airplanes were hijacked by individuals linked to Iran. Bombings in Kuwait against Kuwaiti targets and the U.S. and French embassies all shaped the Kuwaiti government's outlook and brought about improved relations with the United States. During the period of reflagging, U.S. and Kuwaiti delegations exchanged visits. In July 1988, Crown Prince Sa'ad visited Washington (during the visit, Iran accepted a UN-brokered cease-fire with Iraq). In April 1990, U.S. ambassador Nathaniel Howell sent a telegram stating that Kuwait had admitted publicly, for the first time, the presence of a U.S. warship in its port.[28]

Although Kuwaitis saw relations with the United States as improving, the U.S. assessment was quite different. According to a highly knowledgeable and involved U.S. source:

> The reflagging did not improve relations with Kuwait. We had no better relations with Kuwait other than the relations created with the Ministry of Oil. For example, the State Department did not feel we had better relations with the Kuwaiti Foreign Ministry. Even our military office in Kuwait was small and limited in its program. During the reflagging Kuwait would not discuss security issues in the region with the U.S. Kuwait remained as pan-Arab as it could. In the UN the situation continued by which Kuwait condemns the U.S. on a whole range of issues.[29]

From Reserved Cooperation to Dependency

The assumptions and perceptions among both Americans and Kuwaitis regarding their relationship with one another contributed to the lack of any serious cooperation during events leading up to the 1990–1991 Gulf crisis and war. The U.S. lack of preparedness to deal with a major crisis in the Gulf, and its recent history of involvement from Vietnam to Iran to Lebanon, made more serious cooperation unappealing in a region historically inhospitable to foreign intervention. Even when the United States shared intelligence information with Kuwait during the Iran-Iraq war, the Kuwaitis did not always trust its accuracy.

As to Saddam, the United States had overplayed its hand in its efforts to contain Iran during the 1980s; the U.S. shift toward Iraq was, of course, a result of its failed policy vis-à-vis the shah. Saddam became the new guarantor of Gulf security, the pillar of stability,[30] even as his army used chemical weapons against Iraq's Kurdish population. When the U.S. Senate unanimously passed tough sanctions against Iraq, the Reagan administration responded with a lobbying effort against the sanctions and finally rendered them useless.[31]

Despite some negative analyses from specialists on Iraq, reports of the government's internal barbarity, and the potential for confrontation with the United States, Washington continued to turn a blind eye toward Iraq.[32] Once the Iran-Iraq war ended, the United States continued its support of Saddam, including the forwarding of billions of dollars in agricultural loan guarantees and other assistance.[33] The United States was so taken by the demise of communism in Eastern Europe in 1989 that it did not focus on the requirements for security in the Gulf.

However, after the end of the Iran-Iraq war, a group of Kuwaiti officials in the Foreign Ministry began devising future policy. Sensible questions were asked, among them what would Iraq do to keep its 1 million soldiers busy. According to Su'ud al-Usaymi: "No one dared to think, however, that Iraq would under any circumstances attack Kuwait. These thoughts remained unexplored for fear that supporters of Iraq and sympathizers in the Foreign Ministry and in society at-large would view discussions of such as treasonous or anti-Arab."[34]

As a result, once the Gulf crisis erupted in mid-July 1990, neither U.S. nor Kuwaiti officials were sure how to react. Kuwait ran for the Arab umbrella, this time represented by the mediation of King Fahd of Saudi Arabia, President Husni Mubarak of Egypt, Yasser Arafat of the Palestine Liberation Organization (PLO), and King Hussein of Jordan. Arab mediation merely provided a false feeling of security among Kuwaitis and U.S. officials that the crisis would quickly pass.

The entire record leading to U.S. Ambassador to Iraq April Glaspie's fateful audience with Saddam and Assistant Secretary of State John Kelly's announcement that no security arrangements existed between the United States and Kuwait brought to the forefront the difficulties of interpreting messages, signals, and policies in a world full of conflicts and conflicting messages. To use Glaspie's terms, "We foolishly did not realize [Saddam] was stupid."[35] One official in the State Department discussed the situation with his supervisor days before the crisis. "What if Iraq invaded Kuwait? What will we say if it happens, what will we tell our superiors whom we keep telling nothing will happen?" With such thinking, lack of U.S.-Kuwaiti cooperation in such a crisis was not surprising.[36]

When Iraq protested Kuwait's drilling of oil in Kuwait's northern border and, in a letter to the Arab League, protested Kuwaiti oil overproduction, nothing bluntly unusual took place. This was not the first crisis in inter-Arab relations. The love-hate dilemma in those relations has been ever-present since the Arab state system came into being. Crisis had erupted in the past two decades between the two Yemens, Jordan, and Syria, and Egypt and Libya. On the one hand, Arab mediators and Kuwaiti leaders believed that Iraq was pressuring Kuwait in order to gain financial support and a strip of land on the Gulf waters. Kuwait, on the other hand, was willing to compromise on financial issues but not on land. Nevertheless, Kuwait thought that in return for funds to Iraq it could get the Iraqis to agree to demarcate the borders.

This is exactly what Kuwait hoped to achieve in the Jeddah meeting (where Iraq and Kuwait met to resolve the crisis on August 1, 1990). From Kuwait's point of view the amount of support it provided Iraq during the Iran-Iraq war, in the form of much-needed logistical materials and billions of dollars in aid, should have garnered some goodwill in Iraq.

But in Jeddah the Kuwaitis found themselves on the defensive. Any compromise affecting Kuwaiti sovereignty would have made the situation worse, in particular regarding political and military support to Kuwait after the invasion itself. Kuwait hoped for a peaceful end to the crisis yet speculated that a limited Iraqi attack and occupation of a border strip would be employed only as a means of pressure. It also prepared itself for a long political crisis around the issue of demarcation and sovereignty over Bubiyan and Warba Islands, which could provide Iraq with better access to the Gulf but would help it dominate Kuwait, jeopardize its sovereignty, and intimidate Iran. Like many sudden crises in history, this one was lost in the traffic of words and conflicting messages. The actual threat that Iraq posed to Kuwait was lost in a world full of noise.

Consequences of the Invasion

It took an event of the magnitude of the Iraqi invasion for the Kuwaiti government to recognize its security needs and to force the United States to take serious risks to protect its interests in the Gulf. Kuwaitis realized that only U.S. power could change the course of events. Once Iraq invaded Kuwait, U.S. commitment to the Gulf became a commitment to Kuwait's independence. U.S. fear of a power other than a Western power, or one friendly to the West, controlling the region contributed to the U.S. response. Kuwait, in a sense, became a "frontline state."

With the invasion, the U.S.-Kuwaiti relationship entered a new phase. The U.S. government discussed through various channels the Kuwaiti contribution to the effort to liberate the country. The information provided by the resistance and publicity regarding human rights violations in Kuwait were the channels through which the beginnings of such cooperation began. By liberating Kuwait in the context of an international effort, and by supporting UN Security Council Resolutions 773 and 833 regarding Kuwait's boundaries with Iraq, the United States defined its wider security needs in the region.[37]

After liberation the new U.S.-Kuwaiti relationship was evidenced in part by the fact that a major share in the rebuilding of Kuwait went to U.S. companies. U.S. firms were awarded more than $5 billion in contracts by the Kuwaiti government. The U.S. Army Corps of Engineers supervised much of the initial phases of reconstruction, and Bechtel was the major contractor. Reconstruction included reestablishing communications, electricity, and petrochemical facilities and operations. U.S. exports to Kuwait in 1992 totaled some $1.5 billion.[38]

Today, Kuwaiti policies are sensitive to those of the United States, including the dispatching of Kuwaiti soldiers to Somalia, financial support to Bosnia, and the lifting of the secondary boycott of Israel. Kuwait votes with the United States in the UN more than France.[39] As to UN efforts to repeal or retain the resolution regarding Zionism as racism, Kuwait abstained. Furthermore, Kuwait agreed to the establishment of a Voice of America relay station in the country. In addition to such cooperation, there is the common U.S. and Kuwait interest in seeing that Iraq complies with all UN Security Council resolutions. The positive attitude of Kuwait toward issues of democratization, human rights, and political change is also increasingly becoming a model in the Gulf.

On another level, Kuwaiti participation in U.S. programs has risen tremendously since liberation. Delegations from Kuwaiti government ministries have been traveling to the United States for training, especially those in the fields of information, television, internal security, and investigations. Kuwait has also donated land and construction costs for the new U.S. embassy in Kuwait. The May 1994 visit to the United States of a delegation of Kuwaiti members of parliament headed by the speaker of the parliament, Ahmad al-Sa'dun, supports this general trend.

Yet this does not mean Kuwait follows the United States on every issue. For example, Kuwait did not lift the direct embargo on Israel. This is something Kuwait argued is part of an Arab League decision, and it cannot break the consensus on this matter. In addition, Kuwait received aid from Syria, Egypt, and Saudi Arabia, and it is therefore sensitive to the position of those states. Kuwait is aware of its smallness and, as a result, does its best to avoid unnecessary confrontations in the Arab world. This has created, to a certain extent, a Kuwaiti passivity in the multilateral talks on the Arab-Israeli peace process; however, at the same time, Kuwait attended the Doha economic summit in 1997 despite Saudi, Syrian, and Egyptian pressure to boycott the meeting.

On the cultural level, influence is moving essentially only in one direction—from the United States to Kuwait. CNN, NBC, America Plus, videos, movies, the Internet, cafés, schools, department stores, and fast-food restaurants all symbolize the process of Americanization of the younger generation. Kuwaitis realize this is part of the globalization process and, therefore, are not erecting barriers to this cultural interaction, but they must also be wary of losing their own cultural identity as well as making sure this aspect of the relationship is more of a two-way street.

Military Cooperation

On August 2, 1990, Kuwaitis were brought face-to-face with their vulnerability and smallness. The Iraqi invasion was a lesson for Kuwaiti policymakers. The political elite realized that without a reliable security umbrella, Kuwait could not survive in the region. Singapore, Taiwan, and other small states around the world have already moved to protect themselves through security arrangements with major powers. As a result of the Iraqi invasion, Kuwait and the United States entered into a ten-year military defense pact, essentially acknowledging a U.S. security commitment toward Kuwait.[40] In the pact signed in September 1991, the United States did not agree to guarantee Kuwaiti security because that would have required that the arrangement be ratified by the U.S. Senate. After ten years, the parties have the option of renewing the agreement. The agreement points up the significance of U.S. power in maintaining the region's balance and the U.S. role as successor to Great Britain as the Gulf's protector. The agreement does allow the United States to project its power into the region, as it allows the pre-positioning of weapons in Kuwait, the training of Kuwaiti forces, and the conducting of joint maneuvers.[41] The agreement's clauses also provide for arms sales (including sales of F-18s) and cost sharing. (There are no restrictions on the technology that can be sold to Kuwait.) Another part of the agreement details the role of the U.S. presence in Gulf waters. In this context Kuwait provides logistics for a U.S. naval presence, including facilities in Kuwait's port. The size of the pre-positioning operation, in addition to Kuwaiti units, was estimated to be more than sufficient for managing various scenarios of aggression across Kuwait's border. The Kuwaiti government pays for all in-country costs, such as maintenance, fuel, and food.[42] But as a result of the 1994 crisis, Kuwait and the United States agreed to add twenty-four fighter aircraft and to maintain a larger contingent of approximately 1,300 troops, reinforced occasionally by U.S. Marine units.[43]

Kuwait's aim is to create a small elite force as part of its efforts to create a credible military option. This requires establishing brigades that are integrated into a new air force based on the U.S. military doctrine of using mobile forces that utilize a technological edge to deal with a larger invading force. New, more credible officers have been promoted to leadership positions in the Kuwaiti military, and morale is higher today than previously.[44] In comparing Kuwaiti forces to other Gulf forces, U.S. officials working with the Kuwaiti army confirm that a high level of seriousness and commitment is found throughout the Kuwaiti armed forces. The ability to use the technology and coordinate the different weapons has improved dramatically since 1994.[45]

It must be kept in mind that the Kuwaiti military option is based on a potential threat from the Iraqi Republican Guard, in particular its four main tank divisions that could spearhead an Iraqi invasion. The entire plan is to be able to deal technologically and militarily with such an incursion, and much of the parity in this regard has already been established. It is worth noting that Iraq's armed forces have been deteriorating for lack of spare parts since 1991 and that one brigade with technological superiority can repel an attacking division.[46]

In the realm of military cooperation, other Gulf states entered into defense agreements with the United States after the end of the 1991 war: Bahrain did so in July 1992; Qatar signed a cooperation agreement in 1992; Oman agreed to a facility-access agreement prior to 1990; Saudi Arabia also has a set of agreements, mostly limited to air defense. However, the U.S.-Kuwaiti agreement is the most comprehensive. Kuwait also signed defense agreements with Great Britain, France, and Russia, but none of these include pre-positioning arrangements.[47]

Furthermore, Kuwait has enhanced its border by digging a deep, wide trench in the demilitarized zone and erecting an electrical fence along the entire 215 kilometer border. The fence, which is about seven meters wide, is also monitored by nineteen Kuwaiti posts. The aim of such arrangements is to delay an attack and to prevent smuggling.[48]

Problems and Security Dilemmas

Today, dangers still exist in the Gulf as a result of wealth combined with smallness—in contrast to the geographic and population sizes of Iran and Iraq. Kuwait and the other Gulf states, therefore, cannot drop their guard. Iran poses a potential challenge. With 60 million people, Iran is undergoing a military buildup and is expected to have a population of 120 million by the year 2030.[49] The election as president of the relatively moderate Khatami in Iran in 1996 does provide hope that relations with Iran will improve, and more important, that U.S.-Iranian relations may also become less hostile. But in Iraq, Saddam Hussein destroyed the base of a wealthy modernized society. The potential promise of 1970s Iraq ended in catastrophe. The longer the UN sanctions against Iraq and attempts to get rid of Saddam persist, the harder it will become to put Iraq together again. Societies with prolonged periods of dictatorship and war require long periods of transition.

> Any future Iraqi government will find it difficult to accept the financial and territorial penalties incurred under the present regime. More disturbing still for the Gulf states is the thought that any Iraqi government that seemed to acquiesce to the terms might be vulnerable to those in Iraq who are determined to wipe the slate clean and, as Saddam Hussein said when tearing up the 1975 Algiers Accord with Iran, "to restore the lost honor of Greater Iraq."[50]

Recent major cuts in the U.S. military budget raise questions regarding the staying power of the United States in the Gulf. According to one U.S. official, "Today we are cutting back from 570 ships in the navy to 450. We are having cuts in the air force, in bases, in numbers of soldiers. Therefore, with a smaller army, the commitment to make another Desert Storm again is much more limited."[51] According to Daniel Pletka of the research staff in the House Subcommittee on Middle East and North Africa:

> During the Bush administration, Bush had a clear idea of what to do during the [Gulf] crisis. There is no guarantee that in a similar crisis the U.S. administration will react the same way. Look at Clinton in Bosnia, or the administration in Somalia—ten years from now a chance for miscalculation is possible. Saddam was a friend to the U.S.; look what happened. We can make the same mistake with Iraq's new leaders ten years from today. A system friendly to the U.S. in Iraq may make it more convincing for us to side on certain issues with Iraq.[52]

Moreover, U.S. commitments in other regions may be an added burden for future U.S. administrations. For example, the United States had to transfer personnel and ships from the Gulf region to Somalia in January 1993. At the same time, it needed to deal with Iraq regarding the "no-fly" zones. Such scenarios put too much pressure on the United States, so other alternatives must, therefore, be found.[53] The same could be said about the crisis of 1997–1998 that ended with the Kofi Annan deal with Iraq.

These issues may put pressure on the United States to develop multilateral regional security arrangements that possibly include coming to some sort of understanding with states such as Iraq and Iran. A sudden shift in alliances between Syria, Iraq, and Iran may shift the balance in the entire Middle East. In this context, the United States will deal with a new reality in Iraq after the demise of Saddam Hussein. The ability of the United States to deal with Baghdad may be in part motivated by its competition with European countries seeking privileges in Iraq. It may also be motivated by the U.S. need to neutralize Iraq and gain its cooperation on regional and international issues.

According to all U.S. officials interviewed by this author, the thinking after the Gulf war is as follows:

1. Rebuild Kuwait's defense capabilities as the first tier of defense;
2. Use the GCC as the second tier of defense;
3. Use the Damascus Declaration to build a third tier (thereby bringing in Syria and Egypt); and
4. View the United States, Britain, France, and the international community as the last tier.

President Bush had hoped for the establishment of an effective regional security organization. It was thought that the GCC, together with Syria and Egypt, might provide the elements for it. The Damascus Declaration of March 1991 lent the impression that an Arab peace force would be formed.[54] The problem with the declaration was that Kuwait and the other Gulf states feared Syrian-Egyptian intentions over the long term. They also preferred a more direct security arrangement with Washington, believing that the actual decision when the chips are down lies in the hands of the United States. After all, who knows what will happen in Egypt tomorrow, and who can tell and predict future Syrian policy? The Gulf states appreciated Iran's responsible stand during the Gulf crisis, but Iran was antagonized by the Damascus accord and considered it another Gulf attempt to isolate it.[55]

After the failure of an Arab deterrent force to evolve, in October 1991 Oman presented the idea of a Gulf force, but the plan did not receive the attention it deserved at a GCC summit in Kuwait in December 1991. In Washington, there was much sympathy for the Omani call for a 100,000-man army.[56] The United States, ultimately, was disappointed by the lack of cooperation by the GCC states on security issues.

The same reasons for the rejection of the Arab military component of the Damascus Declaration motivated the Gulf states to reject the Omani plan. In the latter case, the states feared dominance by Saudi Arabia and constraints upon individual state decisionmaking. Obsessions with sovereignty and individual autonomy made such a plan unacceptable. The failure of the plan also came at a time when the

Qatari-Saudi territorial dispute and the Qatari-Bahraini territorial dispute had climaxed. Furthermore, Iran took control of three United Arab Emirates islands, thus creating more tension in the Gulf and reminding the states of Iran's presence (and not doing anything to upset Teheran).

The GCC countries, though united in times of crisis, are equally obsessed with sovereignty and territory in times of peace and normalcy. The similarity of their economies and political systems draws them together to repel common dangers; however, it is not enough to unify them. Local nationalism is still a driving force in Gulf politics.[57]

Overall, at both the executive and congressional levels of the U.S. government, there is disappointment with the lack of progress along regional security lines. With Kuwait relying more for its own defense on its arrangements with the United States and with the United States recognizing that no Gulf state possesses the means to challenge Iraq or Iran, the need to present a united GCC to deter Iraq and Iran is of the utmost importance. Such a united front would make the stakes too high for any would-be attacker.[58] In this context, the December 1993 meeting of the GCC heads of state, which resulted in agreements between the GCC countries to build an army of 25,000 men, did not change the situation. The Gulf force is not homogeneous and has no common training or unified military doctrine or command; it is composed of several armies with each taking orders from its own state. On the one hand, this will help with defense in the Gulf, but on the other hand, the United States must still supervise that capability and its development for a long time to come.

Rough Edges

Due to the U.S. role in the liberation and security of Kuwait, Congress is extremely sensitive to any behavior that seems to express a lack of gratitude by Kuwait. The statement in 1992 by Abdul-Aziz Masa'id, former speaker of the Kuwaiti Majlis al-Watani, in which he minimized the U.S. role in the liberation of Kuwait and focused on the role of friendly Arab forces, was seen by U.S. officials as provocative. Furthermore, when the secondary boycott with Israel was not lifted immediately after the war, despite Kuwaiti promises to do so, it elicited an angry reaction from members of Congress until it was lifted in 1993.[59] At the same time that the United States dissects and disapproves of such occurrences, it seeks Kuwaiti support for U.S. policy in the Gulf. It expects Kuwait to politically encourage Arab-Israeli multilateral talks and make progress in matters pertaining to democracy and human rights.[60]

Arms sales are another potential flash point. Some members of Congress object to arms sales as a matter of principle, whereas others object out of concern that the weapons sold could be used against Israel. Congress often raises these issues, and if not satisfied, it can delay or prevent a deal from going through.[61]

On the other hand, these rough edges place an added burden on Kuwait. It forces policymakers to understand the dynamics of the internal U.S. debate and decision-making process. The need to be part of the American debate on the Middle East becomes, therefore, a serious issue. Not unlike Israel, Kuwait feels the pressure of building up its usefulness and importance in the international arena in the eyes of the United States. This may force Kuwait to become sensitive to the priorities of new administrations. It may seek to influence some of these priorities regarding Kuwait, but at the same time, it will have to cooperate with the administration on aspects of U.S. strategy in the region. This delicate policy must be managed creatively without jeopardizing the political independence and regional interests of Kuwait. Examples may include voting behavior in the UN and in international agencies on issues that do not contradict Kuwaiti interests; an increased role and visibility in the multilateral talks, once the peace process gets back on track, with the potential of hosting them in the future; human rights issues in Kuwait and in the region; policy towards Iraq, and so on.

A good example of differing perceptions can be seen in the recent peace process. The tenuous relationship between Kuwait and the PLO due to the PLO's stance during the Gulf crisis and war made Kuwait hesitant on the whole issue. Although the government of Kuwait publicly supported the Oslo Accords, the parliament, with a strong Islamist majority, adopted a negative stand. This prevented Kuwait from making a contribution in the Washington fund-raising meeting in October 1993. But when Kuwait later made a financial contribution of $25 million to the Palestinians, few took notice. Support of the process and financial aid was important for the United States when it needed it in the beginning. Once time elapsed, the United States was less enthusiastic.

There are other examples. Whereas Oman, Bahrain, and Qatar have already hosted the multilaterals, Kuwait has hesitated to make such a decision without Saudi and Syrian consent. Furthermore, the dual containment policy of the Clinton administration, which basically seeks to contain both Iraq and Iran at the same time, is another issue. Kuwait fully supports the U.S. policy of containing Iraq, but it always felt the need to have a dialogue and some kind of a link with Iran. These issues among others seem to adversely affect the relationship between the United States and Kuwait.

The dialogue between the United States and Kuwait is limited. Kuwaiti leaders seldom visit the United States and engage the White House, the Pentagon, and Congress in discussions reflecting needs and perceptions. There seems to be a cultural gap that has to do with the differences in style between American leaders and Kuwaiti leaders.

In fact, the other centers of power in America such as Congress, nongovernmental organizations (NGOs), human rights groups, universities, and the media play a tremendous role. Their position and reactions can tie the hands of the administration or even force it to change course. This aspect is better understood by the Israelis, who know how the system works in the United States. Much dialogue is needed in this direction. Work is also needed in the other direction, that is, through visits to Kuwait by prominent U.S. congressmen, university professors, journalists, and human rights groups.

The recent lecture of Ambassador Larocco on the need for a global Kuwaiti economy that attracts investors, in particular U.S. investors, was a clear message to Kuwait, whose economy seems to have sputtered since the invasion. Larocco called on Kuwait to seek new investments in the context of globalization that can make the American-Kuwaiti relationship justifiable in the eyes of Congress. According to the ambassador, the present amount of U.S. investments in Kuwait does not exceed $300 million, and many of the proposals for investments are lost in the bureaucracy. Recently, however, Kuwait has adopted measures to open up its economy and make it more business friendly.[62]

Conclusion

The Kuwaiti view of U.S. assistance during the Iraqi invasion of Kuwait is overtly positive. This is a fact of public opinion in Kuwait. Kuwaitis therefore feel that they have a special relationship with the United States. The arm's-length relationship that characterized U.S.-Kuwaiti relations prior to the Gulf war is no longer a viable option. U.S. administrations may require different kinds of cooperation from Kuwait. In the relationship between the two parties (a superpower and a small state), Kuwait will sometimes feel pressured on particular issues. Although pressures may put strains on the relationship, Kuwait will always try to resolve matters in the context of friendship and cooperation.

The depth of U.S. commitment in the Gulf was revealed in 1990–1991. In fact, the Gulf is probably one of few regions in the world in which the United States does recognize its vital interests. Since it cannot afford to ignore the region, the United States must find a reliable mechanism for engagement, supervision, and security. This is vital, otherwise the United States will find itself involved in another conflict in the area. Kuwait needs to balance its defensive capabilities. In order to do so, it must rebuild its defense capabilities; it must also develop with the GCC a group defense plan and a contingency plan. This can be done in coordination with the United States and other coalition partners, in an arrangement whereby U.S. involvement can be limited to pre-positioning and naval and air defense.

The recent policy of the United States shows that it is looking for a long-term commitment to the region to prevent instability, political upheavals, adventurism, and chaos that may affect the flow of oil or put substantial oil reserves under the control of hostile governments. At the same time, however, long-term problems such as those with Iraq and Iran, the potential instability in Arab monarchies, arms buildups, economic development and cooperation, human rights, and democratization will continue to pose challenges to the United States in the region. Friendly relations and agreements with the GCC states are important in confronting these challenges and in maintaining the smooth flow of oil at reasonable prices. In this context, U.S. relations with Kuwait are an important part of the vision for a more stable region.

There is no guarantee, however, that the U.S.-Kuwaiti relationship will not be weakened by events and new priorities in the region. If Kuwait outlives its political usefulness in the region, then U.S. interests will dwindle. Regional political realities may in the long run force the United States to compromise with Iraq or other regional powers on issues of interest to Kuwait. This may affect Kuwaiti oil revenues, commerce, and regional standing. In order to counter any deterioration in Kuwaiti-U.S. ties, Kuwait must build its relationship with the United States on a more meaningful level that goes beyond state-to-state relations. It is Kuwait's role, in the midst of its security dilemma, to explain in the American context its goals, its culture, its democratic processes, and its economic vision. The difficult mission for Kuwait is to be better understood in Congress, to build a working relationship with relevant NGOs, human rights groups, and the media, and to create strong links with intellectual circles.

In its history dating back to the 1750s, Kuwaiti society has shown tremendous resiliency. This resiliency has been seen in every major crisis since Mubarak al-Sabah established an alliance with Great Britain in order to protect the country from the Ottomans in 1899.[63] The ability in the past to adapt and to create the proper policies and structures helpful to its survival may be Kuwait's most important asset in facing the challenges that lie ahead.

Notes

1. *Estimated Population, 1997–1998,* Kuwait Ministry of Planning, Central Statistical Office, published in *al-Qabas,* 5 January 1998, p. 2.

2. Abdul Malik Khalaf al-Tammimi, *al-Tabshir fi mantiqat al-Khalij al-'Arabi: Dirasah fi al-Tarikh al-Ijtima'i wa al-Siyasi* (Missionaries in the Arabian Gulf: A Study in Its Political and Social History) (Cyprus: Dar al-Shabab, 1988), pp. 60–61.

3. Jill Crystal, *Kuwait: The Transformation of an Oil State* (Boulder: Westview Press, 1992), pp. 12–13.

4. Archibald H.T. Chisholm, *The First Kuwait Oil Concession Agreement: A Record of Negotiations, 1911–1934* (London: Frank Cass, 1975), p. 14.

5. Ibid., p. 82.

6. Ibid.

7. 'Abd al-Rahman al-Atiqi, interview by author, Kuwait, June 1993. Al-Atiqi served as minister of finance from 1975 to 1981 and is currently a consultant to the emir of Kuwait.

8. Upon independence, Kuwait had a population of approximately 180,000 Kuwaiti citizens and about 250,000 non-Kuwaitis. This estimate is based on the 1965 Kuwaiti census.

9. See the excellent and comprehensive work of 'Abd al-Ridda Assiri, *Al-Kuwayt fi al-siyasah al-duwaliyyah al-mu'asirah* (Kuwait in Contemporary International Politics) (Kuwait: Jamiat al-Kuwayt, n.d.), p. 135.

10. 'Abd al-Rahman al-Atiqi, interview by author, June 1993.

11. It was not until 1990 that an American arriving at Kuwait's airport with an Israeli stamp on his passport was allowed to enter the country.

12. 'Abd al-Rahman al-Atiqi, interview by author, June 1993.

13. Michael A. Palmer, *Guardians of the Gulf: A History of America's Expanding Role in the Persian Gulf, 1833–1992* (New York: Free Press, 1993), p. 89.

14. Ibid., p. 87.

15. Ibid., p. 90.

16. Thomas McNaugher, *Arms and Oil: U.S. Military Strategy and the Persian Gulf* (Washington, D.C.: Brookings Institution, 1985), p. 17.

17. Ibid.

18. Palmer, *Guardians of the Gulf,* p. 106.

19. McNaugher, *Arms and Oil,* pp. 3–4.

20. Palmer, *Guardians of the Gulf,* p. 121.

21. Su'ud al-Usaymi, former minister of justice and former state minister for foreign affairs, interview by author, May 1993.

22. Abdullah Bisharah, former secretary-general of the Gulf Cooperation Council, interview by author, June 1993.

23. Su'ud al-Usaymi, interview by author, May 1993.

24. Ibid.

25. The administration also engaged in the reflagging in order to shore up relations with the Arab states after the Iran-Contra affair revealed that the United States had sold arms to Iran in the hope of engineering the return of U.S. hostages in Lebanon, all of which was contrary to the U.S.-constructed Operation Staunch arms embargo against Iran.

26. Ibid.

27. K, a U.S. official who asked not to be quoted and who was in charge of major aspects of the reflagging operation, interview by author, Washington, D.C., Summer 1993.

28. Ibid.

29. M, a U.S. official involved with U.S.-Kuwaiti relations during the reflagging operation and afterwards, interview by author, Washington, D.C., Summer 1993.

30. Paul A. Gigot, "A Great American Screw-Up: The U.S. and Iraq, 1980–1990," *National Interest* (Winter 1990), p. 4.

31. Ibid., p. 6. The Senate voted 87-0 to impose sanctions on Iraq after the chemical attacks on the Kurds.

32. Ibid.

33. Documents detailing the sales of defense-related items to Iraq were altered by the Bush administration before they were provided to the Government Operations Subcommittee on Commerce, Consumer, and Monetary Affairs. See Carroll J. Doherty, "Panel Democrats Poised to Ask for Probe of Help to Saddam," *Congressional Quarterly,* June 6, 1992, p. 1616, and "Democrats Aim to Reignite Iraqi Aid Controversy," *Congressional Quarterly,* May 23, 1992, pp. 1457–1459. See also Alan Friedman, *Spider's Web: The Secret History of How the White House Illegally Armed Iraq* (New York: Bantam Books, 1993).

34. Su'ud al-Usaymi, interview by author, Summer 1993.

35. Pamela Fessler, "Glaspie Defends Her Actions," *Congressional Quarterly,* March 23, 1991, p. 760.

36. U.S. officials A and B, interviews by author, Summer 1993.

37. The United Nations ruled that the Iraq-Kuwait border be moved 600 meters in Kuwait's favor along a 200-kilometer stretch. See Charles Tripp, "The Gulf States and Iraq," *Survival* 34 (Autumn 1992), p. 54.

38. Corey D. Wright, "United States–Kuwait Business Update," *Business American,* January 25, 1993, p. 13; "To the Victor Go the Rebuilding Contracts," *Business Week,* February 18, 1991.

39. See U.S. Department of State, "Voting Practices in the United Nations 1991," Kuwait Report to Congress Submitted Pursuant to Public Law 101-167, March 31, 1992 (Washington, D.C.: Government Printing Office).

40. This section is based on interviews with U.S. and Kuwaiti officials in Kuwait and Washington, D.C., Summer 1993. Interviewees included members of the State Department, U.S. personnel at the U.S. embassy in Kuwait, and members of the research staff of the U.S. House Foreign Relations Committee and Senate Foreign Relations Committee. Most of those interviewed asked not to be identified.

41. The U.S. troops, numbering some 2,000, were left in Kuwait for a time. In January 1993, joint exercises were again turned into an alert. U.S. troops involved in maneuvers stayed in Kuwait for several months because of a crisis with Iraq over the "no-fly zones." In terms of equipment, the agreement establishes a framework for the pre-positioning of approximately 112 tanks and 1,000 vehicles, in addition to ammunition—enough to equip a brigade of 6,000 soldiers. Initially, there were 200 Americans in Kuwait involved in pre-positioning maintenance.

42. For information on the U.S.-Kuwaiti ten-year defense pact, see Kenneth Katzman, "Kuwait: Current Issues" (CRS Report for Congress), *Congressional Research Service,* June 3, 1993, pp. 1–6.

43. Interviews with American embassy staff and with Kuwaiti military officials, Kuwait, June 1998.

44. "Rebuilding the Kuwaiti Military," *International Defense Review* (26)(1/1993), pp. 157–159.

45. Kuwaiti and U.S. military officials, interviews by author, June 1998.

46. Ibid.

47. Tripp, "Gulf States and Iraq," p. 49.

48. Personal trip to the borders of Iraq and Kuwait by the author, June 18, 1998.

49. Paul Kennedy, *Preparing for the Twenty-First Century* (New York: Random House, 1993), p. 25.

50. Tripp, "Gulf States and Iraq," p. 60.

51. U.S. officials A and B, interviews by author, Summer 1993. On military cuts and reluctant policies in the world, see "Superpower Blues," *International Defense Review* 26 (July 1993), pp. 545–554.

52. Daniel M. Pletka, director of Near East and South Asia Affairs, U.S. Senate Committee on Foreign Relations Minority Staff, interview by author, Washington, D.C., Summer 1993.

53. U.S. official A, interview by author, Summer 1993.

54. Tripp, "Gulf States and Iraq," pp. 44–45.

55. F. Gregory Gause III, *Oil Monarchies: Domestic and Security Challenges in the Arab Gulf States* (New York: Council on Foreign Relations Press, 1994), pp. 33–134.

56. U.S. Officials A and B, Interviews, Washington, D.C., Summer 1993.

57. Gause, *Oil Monarchies*, p. 130.

58. C, a supervisor for activities related to the Gulf in the Clinton administration, interview by author, Summer 1993.

59. Daniel Pletka, interview by author, Washington, D.C., Summer 1993.

60. Michael Van Dusen, Senior Staff Director, House Foreign Affairs Committee, interview by author, Washington, D.C., Summer 1993.

61. Pletka, interview by author, Washington, D.C., Summer 1993.

62. See the text in *al-Rai Amm* (Kuwaiti Daily), May 21, 1998, p. 17.

63. W. Nathanial Howell, "Tragedy, Trauma and Triumph: Reclaiming Integrity and Initiative," *Victimization, Mind, and Human Interaction* 4(3) (August 1993), p. 114.

19

U.S. Input into Iraqi Decisionmaking, 1988–1990

Amatzia Baram

U.S.-Iraqi relations reached their lowest point following the Arab-Israeli Six Day War (June 1967), when the regime of General 'Abd al-Rahman 'Arif severed diplomatic relations in protest of an alleged U.S.-Israeli collusion in the war. Soon afterward, 'Arif considered an improvement in relations, but when the Ba'th regime came to power in July 1968 it reversed the process, and relations with the United States hit rock bottom again. In 1972, Iraq and the Soviet Union signed an Accord of Friendship and Cooperation, but two years later the relationship changed: After the 1973 Yom Kippur War (also known as the Arab-Israeli war of 1973 or the Ramadan War) and oil crisis, Iraq's economic priorities took precedence over ideological concerns, and relations with the West (though not with the United States) improved, at the expense of those with the Soviet Union. U.S.-Iraqi tension eased somewhat as a result of U.S. Secretary of State Henry Kissinger's mediation between the shah of Iran and Saddam Hussein, which led to the March 1975 Iraqi-Iranian agreement. When Saddam cracked down on the Iraqi Communist Party in 1978, and when in December 1979 he criticized the Soviet invasion of Afghanistan, U.S. attention was drawn to the fact that his regime did not behave as a Soviet satellite.

On September 22, 1980, Iraq invaded Iran, planning on a swift and decisive victory in Khuzistan that would encourage the Iranian army to topple the new regime of Ayatollah Khomeini. For the record, the United States criticized the invasion, but its real attitude was very different. There were no illusions in Washington with regard to the nature of the Ba'th regime in Baghdad, but Saddam Hussein attacked a state that had taken Americans hostage and was most hostile to the United States and its allies in the region. As soon as it became clear that the Iraqi army became entrapped in Khuzistan, the United States became concerned that the scales were tipping in favor of Iran. Saddam Hussein, too, once he realized no decisive military victory was forthcoming, turned toward cooperation with both the United States and

313

the USSR. To demonstrate goodwill he promised that the U.S. mission in Iraq was to be treated as an embassy. Bilateral relations improved perceptibly, even though official diplomatic relations were resumed only in November 1984.

The first tangible sign of a thaw in relations was a U.S. Department of State decision in March 1981 to lift a freeze on the sale to Iraq of a handful of planes. A year later the United States removed Iraq from the list of terrorist sponsor states. Once Saddam Hussein banished Abu Nidal from Baghdad, an agricultural program under the auspices of the Commodity Credit Corporation (CCC) was started between the United States and Iraq. In later years, this program became the single most important feature in U.S.-Iraqi relations; indeed, in 1988, U.S. credits for foodstuffs for Iraq were the largest given to any country in the world. U.S. help to Iraq, direct and indirect, also included battlefield intelligence; Operation Staunch, designed to deprive Iran of arms; support in the United Nations (UN) for a resolution calling for a cease-fire; reflagging Kuwaiti tankers; sales of dual-use items; and, according to some, the leaking of military technology.

During the Iran-Iraq war, the U.S. course altered little. Iraq was perceived as the weaker combatant and a useful barrier against Khomeini's expansion and influence in the Gulf; as such it deserved support from the United States. Late in 1983, the State Department urged the U.S. Export-Import Bank (hereinafter Exim) to extend its own credits to Iraq to bolster U.S. exports (other than foodstuffs) and the Iraqi economy, thereby reducing problems for the Iraqi government in light of the increasing deprivation of the general population. A Jordanian-Iraqi pipeline, which was never built and was also vigorously supported by the United States, was to be part of the effort to prevent an Iraqi economic collapse.

Although both economic and political cooperation were growing, relations were still far from ideal due to an unbridgeable chasm in political culture (a chasm even wider in terms of perceived interests). But as long as the war was raging the United States and Iraq clearly differentiated between what was vital and what was desirable and did not allow their differences to disrupt their priorities. There were, however, conflicting views within the U.S. administration with regard to the desirable balance of power between Iraq and Iran and the degree of support for Iraq.

Obstacles in the U.S.-Iraqi relationship included U.S. support of Israel and Iraq's off-and-on support for Palestinian terrorist groups; the issue of human rights (especially the inability of the Ba'th regime to tolerate any dissent and Iraq's use of chemical weapons [CW]); and, lastly, Iraqi stockpiling of weapons of mass destruction. The relative U.S. leniency toward Iraq's development of such weapons during the war stemmed from the perception that the Iraqis were in danger of losing the war and, as it seems, from a lack of intelligence. As demonstrated by declassified documents from 1985–1986, the U.S. administration had very little information on the tremendous Iraqi nuclear and surface-to-surface missile efforts already under way.

U.S. credits to Iraq were yet another potential point of friction. The administration was torn between the Departments of State, Commerce, and Agriculture, on the one hand, and Exim on the other, with the Department of the Treasury and the

Federal Reserve mostly siding with Exim. Whereas Treasury pushed for ever greater credits, the Fed had more and more misgivings. Exim's misgivings were based on an inconsistent financial relationship with the Iraqis and lessons learned from Iraqi treatment of other creditors throughout the 1980s. By 1987, Exim determined that Iraq, in view of its financial difficulties and debt-repayment practices, would cut its debt service rather than its military or civilian imports.

The State Department's assessment of Iraqi financial prospects was far more sanguine, and State strongly disagreed with officials in Defense who tried to prevent sales of dual-purpose technology to Iraq for fear of nuclear and missile technology proliferation. But the worst case of interagency rivalry and cross-purpose action during the war years was the arms-for-hostages deal with Iran in 1985–1986. The Iraqi reaction to the arms deal was very unusual. Although the Iraqi parliament and press—and a few politicians—strongly denounced the deal, President Saddam Hussein and Foreign Minister Tariq 'Aziz were remarkably restrained. Clearly, the Iraqi leadership looked into the abyss and froze in horror: As they saw it, any wrong move could have led to U.S.-Iranian collusion and to their own destruction.

The trilateral arms deal made the Iraqis more aware of the significance of splits within the administration and more suspicious of U.S. intentions. Yet, as disclosed by the Iraqi leadership in later years, until the end of the Iran-Iraq war they were not suspicious that the United States was still arming Iran behind Iraq's back. The public outrage in the United States following the exposure of the Iran-Contra affair, and the administration's subsequent change of course, including the reflagging of Kuwaiti tankers in the second half of 1987, were sufficient to convince the Iraqis that the United States was decisively on their side. This perception started to change again after the cease-fire in the Iran-Iraq war in August 1988.

Much has been said and written about the approach of the George Bush administration toward Iraq in the postwar period. This approach has been considered by many as too lenient, with the result that Saddam was emboldened in his defiance of the United States. For example, Alexander Haig (Secretary of State under President Ronald Reagan) noted in an interview: "The tilt policy Bush had supported during those years brought Saddam to the belief that he would not be challenged in Kuwait . . . and the consequences were a Gulf War and the outcome that the threat of Saddam is still there."[1] Others have pointed out that U.S. diplomacy did not do all it could in the weeks leading up to the Kuwaiti invasion to prevent it. The second contention is easier to substantiate than the first.[2]

In this chapter—based on declassified U.S. documents, public Iraqi sources, and interviews—I shall attempt to demonstrate that the United States, though not doing all it reasonably could to deter Saddam from invading Kuwait (by making clear its objection to some Iraqi policies, i.e., use of CW, proliferation threats, and so on), did enough to alert the Iraqi regime to the fact that in the medium and long terms the two countries were on an unavoidable collision course. It is my contention that by early spring 1990 two things became clear to Saddam and his ruling elite. In the first place, they realized that those in the U.S. administration who supported continued efforts to enhance U.S.-Iraqi cooperation were losing ground. Second, they became fully aware that if they wanted to achieve a number of national Iraqi goals, which they considered crucial to the survival and success of their regime, they were running into progressively tougher U.S. resistance. They were also aware that the two issues were connected: It was precisely Iraq's energetic quest for its cherished national goals that progressively weakened the position of those within the administration who favored a dialogue with and assistance for Iraq. The single most important indication that the United States was changing course was the suspension of the agricultural loan guarantee system, the centerpiece of U.S.-Iraqi economic and political relations.

There is much dispute over whether or not the Iraqi leadership truly believed its own conspiracy theory. It is my intention to show that, although this issue is not unimportant, one should be careful not to overestimate its significance. Either way, the Iraqi regime reached the conclusion that under the existing circumstances U.S. and Iraqi interests were irreconcilable, at least in the medium and long terms. Having realized that time was running out, Saddam decided to change the rules of the game and create new circumstances under which U.S. policy vis-à-vis Iraq could be remolded. The invasion of Kuwait was supposed to create such new circumstances. Long before the U.S. policymakers realized it, Saddam was fully aware it was impossible to cultivate good relations with the United States while achieving his central national goals. Convinced that U.S. reaction would go no further than a limited air attack, he decided to act preemptively.

U.S. Diplomacy After the Iran-Iraq War: A Change of Perspective

During the Iran-Iraq war the administration's pro-Saddam position was based on Iraq's vulnerability and the fact the United States could not afford an Iraqi military defeat. Following the Iraqi victories of April-August 1988 and the cease-fire, both the outlook and the argument were transformed. The United States, it was felt and argued, could not afford a hands-off policy in regard to Iraq because the latter was far too powerful and influential. If left to its own devices, Iraq's capacity to destabilize the whole region was enormous. If, however, the United States continued or even augmented its loan guarantee programs, administration officials argued that it would enable the United States to achieve two goals: To convince Iraq to slow down its nonconventional arms production and to play a constructive role in the Middle East peace process and Gulf security. On the positive side, U.S. policymakers felt that Iraq offered a lucrative market for U.S. foodstuffs and, potentially, technology.[3]

This position appeared in many State Department documents beginning in the fall of 1988, but it did not appear in a major policy document until presidential National Security Directive NSD-26, formulated in the spring of 1989 and signed by President Bush on October 2 that year. The directive stated:

> Normal relations between the U.S. and Iraq would serve our long-term interests and promote stability in both the Gulf and the Middle East. The United States government

should propose economic and political incentives for Iraq to moderate its behavior and to increase our influence with Iraq. . . . [Also], we should pursue and seek to facilitate opportunities for U.S. firms to participate in the reconstruction of the Iraqi economy . . . where they do not conflict with our non-proliferation . . . objectives. . . . The U.S. should consider sales of non-lethal forms of military assistance, e.g., training courses and medical exchanges.[4]

The directive also warned that any of the following would complicate relations and that some would even lead to economic sanctions: renewed use of chemical or biological weapons, any breach by Iraq of International Atomic Energy Agency (IAEA) safeguards in its nuclear program, human rights infringements, Iraqi meddling in the affairs of foreign countries, and noncooperation over the Middle East peace process. But it seems that the directive's main emphasis was on the need to intensify cooperation. Thus, for example, when the president waived a congressional bill in January 1990 that imposed limitations on trade relations with Iraq, the "Waiver" read:

> Iraq is a major military power in the Persian Gulf and increasingly influential in the Arab world. It is also an important supplier of petroleum for the U.S. market. It is in the national interest . . . to maintain existing economic and political incentives . . . to encourage Iraq to moderate its behavior and increase our ability to deal effectively with Iraq. . . . We also wish . . . to facilitate opportunities for U.S. firms to participate in the post-war reconstruction of the Iraqi economy.[5]

Similar arguments against any sanctions aimed at Iraq were brought up by Assistant Secretary of State for Near East and South Asian Affairs John Kelly in his statement to Congress in May 1990.[6] This approach, however, came under increasing criticism as U.S. and Iraqi interests moved further and further apart following the cease-fire in the Gulf.

In March 1988, a few months before the cease-fire, the first major confrontation occurred. The Iraqi army was reported to have used CW against Kurdish civilians in Halabja, causing thousands of casualties. The United States denounced the act,[7] but Iraq was still at war and still looked vulnerable. In June both houses of Congress discussed bills condemning Iraq and calling for sanctions against it, but the bills were not passed.[8] As a sign of the administration's displeasure, in June a State Department official received Jalal Talabani, leader of the Popular Union of Kurdistan (which opposed the Iraqi regime and fought for more autonomy). To protest the official reception, Foreign Minister 'Aziz canceled a scheduled meeting in Washington with Secretary of State George Shultz. A few days later Saddam was too busy to meet Assistant Secretary of State Richard Murphy, who had just arrived in Baghdad with a message from President Reagan.[9] The Iraqi media accused the United States of colluding with Israel and Iran to prevent Iraq from suppressing the Kurdish revolt.[10]

Yet the Iraqi side knew its limits—it still needed U.S. support. To defuse the political tension, in July a senior Iraqi official made it clear that once the cease-fire went into effect (it occurred on August 20, 1988), the U.S. presence in the Gulf would still be sought, at least for the time being, to "keep the Iranians under some check." Iraq also tried to allay U.S. fears for the safety of its allies in the area by insisting that, after the war, Iraq would remain close to Jordan, Egypt, Saudi Arabia, and Kuwait: "Relations with those four countries will be the backbone of our Arab policy," a senior Iraqi official said.[11]

The crisis was over, but not for long. Three weeks after the cease-fire in the Gulf, on September 8, 1988, after apparently being prodded by the press and Congress, the State Department announced that reports of the use of poison gas against the Kurds in northern Iraq had been corroborated. In his meeting a few hours later with Iraqi Minister of State for Foreign Affairs Sa'dun Hammadi, Secretary of State Shultz surprised Hammadi by denouncing Iraq and warned that continued use of CW and abuse of "other human rights" (referring to other aspects of the campaign against the Kurds) would harm U.S.-Iraqi relations. One day later the U.S. Senate passed a bill that imposed widespread economic sanctions on Iraq, and on September 27 the House passed a similar (though weaker) bill. Due to jurisdictional fights over other foreign policy issues and administration objection, neither bill became law, but there was no mistaking congressional feelings toward Iraq.[12]

The State Department, however, had a very different view. Richard Murphy insisted that "we need to move quickly to ensure that our action is seen as anti-chemical weapons, not [as] anti-Iraq or pro-Iran." There is need to get "the CW genie back in the bottle" and to deal with Iraq's human rights violations, but "the U.S.-Iraqi relationship is never-the-less important to our long-term political and economic objectives in the Gulf and beyond." Iraq, Murphy pointed out, had shown signs of moderation in three areas: terrorism, the Palestine issue, and its relations with its conservative Arab neighbors (on all three, though the test-time was very short, this analysis was correct). Murphy also argued that Saddam recognized U.S. instrumentality in facilitating Iraq-Iran peace negotiations (in reality the Iraqis were highly ambivalent about the U.S. role), and in supplying Iraq with modern technology (not surprisingly, this was correct). Thus, Murphy felt that there was a good basis for future cooperation: "We believe that economic sanctions will be useless or counter-productive in terms of our ability to influence the Iraqis. We may want to support . . . action for broader CW purposes, as part of an effort to make an example of the Iraqis, but we should be clear in our minds that this will not produce any results in Baghdad."[13] Murphy also recommended to "continue to speak out on Iraqi human rights abuses, but without gratuitous Iraq-bashing." Finally, Murphy pointed out that although the Iraqis "have curbed their support for Palestinian terrorism," they remained "willing to use international terrorism themselves against their opponents." However, there was no recommendation to place Iraq again on the list of states sponsoring terrorism.[14]

Because U.S. criticism over Iraq's use of CW to suppress the Kurdish revolt was perceived as a threat to one of the regime's core interests, namely, the complete eradication of Kurdish opposition and total control of the north, Baghdad's immediate response was unusually strong. On September 11, 1988, after Iraqi spokesmen angrily denied the "allegations," a mammoth demonstration was organized in front of the U.S. embassy in Baghdad to convey the utmost indignation of the Iraqi people.[15]

A few days later the anti-American campaign was stepped up. Targeting mainly Congress, senior Iraqi officials joined in and the criticism became harsher. Fear of Iraqi victories, argued First Deputy Prime Minister Ramadan, had pushed Congress, or as he called it, "the U.S. Knesset," to try to weaken Iraq by preventing it from "clean[ing] the northern part of its homeland . . . of the traitors." Ramadan went on to say that by saving the Kurdish revolt, Congress wanted to help the Iranians in order to help Israel (which was considered Iran's ally) control the Palestinian uprising in the Occupied Territories. "To remove any delusions . . . and in order to present the true facts," Ramadan suggested, "the American Knesset [should] meet in Israel. . . . [This] would confirm that its policy serves the country in which it meets."[16] *Al-Jumhuriyya* added that the U.S. condemnations were meant to legitimize an Israeli raid on "some Iraqi economic enterprises," apparently chemical missile or nuclear plants, recalling the Israeli raid on Iraq's atomic reactor in June 1981.[17] This fear of a new Israeli raid under a political U.S. umbrella, though in itself unfounded, was all the same a real one.

In a diplomatic gesture designed to diffuse the situation, on October 3, 1988, after a meeting at the UN in New York, the Iraqi foreign minister was reported by a State Department spokesman to have privately assured Secretary of State Shultz that Iraq held the international restrictions on chemical weapons to be applicable "to internal matters, such as dealing with its Kurdish minority, as well as external conflicts."[18]

On the economic level, however, it was business as usual, which sent mixed signals to the Iraqis. Amid all the diplomatic commotion, the Department of Agriculture (USDA) allocated to Iraq $1.05 billion in credits for 1989. By late October 1988 senior U.S. officials and a congressional staff delegation visited Baghdad and were apparently well received.[19] In June 1989 the atmosphere of business as usual was accentuated when Saddam unexpectedly received a large delegation of U.S. businessmen (members of the U.S.-Iraq business forum), and told them: "It is correct that we remember the Irangate scandal [i.e., Iran-Contra]. However, we are not. . . obsessed with the complexes of the past."[20]

Thus, in mid-1989 it seemed that the worst of the crisis in U.S.-Iraqi relations was over. Yet the degree of mutual suspicion was still such that any minor incident, like a declaration by a U.S. official of U.S. concern in regard to the Iraqi missile force, was immediately presented (and possibly perceived) in Baghdad as a sign of U.S.-Israeli collusion against Iraq.[21]

U.S. Credits to Iraq Reexamined

In November 1989, in reaction to the submission of the sanctions bills in Congress, Iraq sounded the first warning against a U.S. decision to apply sanctions. As anticipated by Exim a few years earlier, the Iraqis threatened that if Congress stopped the loan guarantee program, Iraq might no longer repay its debt. And whereas the USDA reacted to these threats by advising "not to unnecessarily anger the Iraqis and trigger a default that could jeopardize the whole CCC program,"[22] Exim was alarmed. Indeed, old fears were rising concerning Iraq's ability and willingness to repay its debts. In two "Country Risk Analyses" issued in January and September 1989, Exim warned that almost all of Iraq's main international creditors were having problems. The Iraqis were repaying Exim and CCC in arrears but only because they were expecting larger loans. Exim reported that "because of their concerns about Iraq's financial behavior, the Fed [the Federal Reserve] and [Department of] Treasury want CCC to scale back" its program. However, by far the most ominous note Exim sounded was in regard to a newly discovered financial scandal, one connected with the Atlanta-based branch of the Italian Banca Nazionale Del Lavoro (BNL).[23]

Immediately upon the start of the investigation of BNL fraud, by the Federal Bureau of Investigation (FBI) and the U.S. Customs Service, Treasury pointed out that both bank and Iraqi officials were suspected of more than arranging unauthorized credit in excess of $2.6 billion; the commodities involved were suspected to include "military-type technology and various controlled chemicals . . . [as well as] illegal export to Iraq of missile-related technology to be used in the Condor II project."[24] Administration worries were not limited to the unauthorized BNL loans. In an interagency meeting in October 1989 the Department of Agriculture, for the first time, expressed deep concern over the future of the CCC program. Because of this, U.S.-Iraqi economic relations came under heavy public fire, and it was felt that it was urgently necessary to investigate three areas: diversion of CCC-guaranteed commodities during transit (for example, food for arms); illegal payments (or "kickbacks") required by Iraq of exporters in order to enter the Iraqi market; and "after-sales services," which required exporters to provide the Iraqis with trucks and other equipment free of charge. Other U.S. government agencies also mentioned that some commodities were double and triple wholesale prices. As the USDA saw it, the investigation could "blow the roof off the CCC."[25]

Indeed, in early October 1989 an Iraqi economic team visiting Washington, D.C., reported to Foreign Minister 'Aziz, himself in the United States at the time, that the United States was ready to release only $488 million in CCC credits, less than half the $1 billion agreed upon for 1990. The foreign minister complained to Secretary of State James Baker that the CCC program was unjustifiably linked to the BNL scandal, "of which Iraq had no part." This, he pointed out, was "a set-back [in bilateral relations], and the government of Iraq is very unhappy." Baker, for his part, explained that the program was not canceled, only suspended pending further investigation. He promised to expedite treatment of the issue and added that the Federal Reserve and Treasury had demanded a thorough investigation of the BNL affair before resumption of the program.[26] By laying the responsibility on the shoulders of other agencies, Baker implied that his department was unhappy with the decision while pleading that his hands were tied. By promising an early resolution of the problem, a promise that it could not deliver, State only enhanced the impression of powerlessness.[27]

As later explained by Acting Secretary of State Lawrence Eagleburger, the State Department was still very interested in continuing the CCC program. U.S. influence in Iraq depended on it, and such influence could help the Middle East peace process, limit missile proliferation, and influence Iraq's behavior in Lebanon.[28] Not surprisingly, the USDA was also unhappy about the suspension, as it noted in a memorandum to the White House. Because Iraq was such an important market for U.S. staples, it pointed out that it was "eager to resolve the new credit to be offered to Iraq quickly." However, in view of the BNL investigation, in addition to the tremendous public sensitivity with regard to cooperation with Iraq, even it had to admit that "a business as usual approach seems unwise."[29]

Worse still, even after a delegation from the USDA visited Baghdad in April and found some of the allegations to be unfounded or easily correctable, the CCC program was not resumed. U.S. Ambassador to Baghdad April Glaspie reported that there was no evidence of diversion of CCC-funded food to other countries (in return for military supplies), high prices were justified, and other aspects could be corrected. "USDA team [is] satisfied that a mutual solution can be reached to meet future program requirements," she wrote.[30]

Glaspie's cable was classified "confidential," and so it could not have been seen by the Iraqis. Yet it is clear that she signaled to the Iraqi side her optimism. Indeed, upon learning that USDA had decided to turn down the second tranche of CCC credits for Iraq on the basis of irregularities, Glaspie disclosed that she had given Iraq hope. In fact, so did the Bob Dole–led delegation of U.S. senators (who had met with Saddam on April 12, 1990) and the investigating delegation from the USDA. Frustrated, Glaspie commented that turning down the CCC credits would send the signal that the administration had decided to join forces with those in Congress who favored sanctions. Canceling the CCC programs, she argued, would be interpreted as purely political and as part of the U.S. conspiracy against Iraq.[31]

In fact, according to a mid-May USDA memorandum, there were two *nonpolitical* problems that justified the suspension: The Iraqis improperly included freight charges in the program and they demanded after-sales services.[32] But there was, of course, the as yet unresolved issue of Iraqi involvement in the BNL fraud, and there were also important *political* reasons. It has to be borne in mind that Glaspie's strong recommendation to continue the CCC program was made only a few weeks after Saddam implied his intent to use CW against Israel. The ambassador assured her superiors (erroneously, as it turned out) that "the Iraqi president, as you know, did not threaten to attack Israel. . . . His threat was . . . if Israel attacks with nuclear weapons, Iraq would use binary chemical weapons."[33] But it seems that Washington knew better (in fact, Saddam and his lieutenants continued to imply the use of chemical weapons in retaliation for a conventional Israeli attack). There were other developments that complicated matters, which were all political and not economic. But then, the CCC program itself was defined as a political tool, no less than an economic one. And so some State Department officials felt that Iraq's political behavior should not have been ignored. Thus, for example, in a letter to the secretary of state in mid-April, U.S. official Robert Kimmitt wrote: "I continue to believe that we should oppose the second tranche [of the CCC] on *political grounds*. . . . If we go forward with CCC and Exim . . . Saddam Hussein will regard that decision as a positive political signal, which will lead him to . . . [continue] his proliferation campaign" (emphasis added).[34]

Iraqi diplomats started to threaten that Iraq would not repay its CCC debt,[35] but the program was not resumed. Even though the official announcement of the suspension was made only as late as May 21, 1990,[36] according to Iraqi sources they had anticipated this shift. Precisely as April Glaspie had predicted, rather than as a reaction to Iraqi excesses, the Iraqi side regarded (or presented) the withholding of the second tranche as a U.S. conspiracy against it. As put by the Iraqi minister of trade to a visiting U.S. member of Congress, it "reflect[ed] unjustified hostility toward Iraq."[37]

Indeed, Iraq's traditional suspicions of U.S. intentions were heightened very soon after the end of the Iraq-Iran war, when the leadership decided that the U.S. position started to shift from support to opposition. In a bizarre meeting between 'Aziz and Baker in Washington, D.C., in October 1989, 'Aziz accused U.S. diplomats of "approaching officials in the Gulf, raising suspicion and fear regarding Iraqi intentions in the region." This, 'Aziz reported, dismayed the Iraqi government because it had been long committed to Gulf stability and to "good relations . . . particularly [with] Saudi Arabia and Kuwait." 'Aziz also complained that the United States demonstrated mistrust when it limited technological exports to Iraq, which were designed solely to develop the economy. He expressed deep concern over the postponement of the second tranche of the CCC credits and over the intention of Congress to legislate economic and political sanctions. Surrealistically, 'Aziz confided to Baker that "some American agencies" were trying to destabilize Iraq. The secretary was greatly surprised and promised to look into it but asked 'Aziz to provide him with more details. 'Aziz promised to do so but never did.[38] In later correspondence, Baker reported to 'Aziz that President Bush asked him to convey to the Iraqis "in the most direct way possible that the U.S. is not involved in any effort to weaken or destabilize Iraq. Having looked into the matter and discussed it with the president I can tell you this with the highest authority. Such an action would be completely contrary to the president's policy, which is to work to strengthen the relationship between the U.S. and Iraq whenever possible."[39]

The Iraqis were not convinced. According to a very knowledgeable insider, the Iraqi leadership felt that Secretary Baker was kept in the dark by the U.S. intelligence community and that the plot was a very real one.[40] The meeting was not all negative: 'Aziz agreed not to subvert U.S. policies over the Arab-Israeli conflict and Lebanon and both parties agreed to expand cooperation.[41] However, in hindsight, in October 1989 it was clear that a time bomb had already started to tick.

The single most important indication that pro-Iraqi elements within the administration were losing ground was the decision to suspend the CCC program. The reason for the Iraqi concern was twofold: The CCC program granted a breathing space of 360 days when it came to repayments for a billion dollars worth of much-needed foodstuffs; and, as Nizar Hamdun, Iraqi ambassador to the United States, explained in October 1989 to the U.S. ambassador in Baghdad, it also helped them to boost Iraq's creditworthiness, as it indicated U.S. confidence.[42] This aspect was of tremendous importance precisely because Iraq's creditworthiness was so low. In late 1989, however, important administration agencies were still working to revive the dying relationship. Thus, in late November, in accordance with NSD-26, the Joint Chiefs of Staff recommended a number of initiatives: exchange of army field manuals and English-language textbooks; visits by the U.S. Central Command staff to the Iraqi armed forces; a series of medical consultative visits to discuss the rehabilitation of wounded personnel; and residency training for Iraqi personnel in a U.S. military medical school. All of these were innocuous issues over which bilateral cooperation could do no harm. However, there were a few other issues that were somewhat more problematic: a training program on aviation safety and security; a mine countermeasure training program for the Iraqi navy; a military officer exchange program; Iraqi officers funded by the Iraqi government to attend U.S. schools at the Staff and War College levels; an Iraqi "briefing team" to visit the United States and discuss with Staff and War Colleges personnel the lessons from the Faw campaign; and aerial reconnaissance training. The Joint Chiefs of Staff agreed with Ambassador Glaspie that "implementation of low-level, non-lethal military assistance would greatly . . . improve dialogue with and access to the senior military leadership and the government of Iraq."[43] Military cooperation with Iraq was still on the agenda as late as January 1990.[44] It is not clear whether the Iraqis were aware of these initiatives; if they were, it must have only increased their frustration because they realized that the administration was unable to deliver limited military cooperation as well.

Turning the Tide: U.S.-Iraqi Relations in Crisis

The next events occurred in early 1990. January and February must have given the Iraqis fits due to the split personality then reflected in the U.S. modus operandi. On January 17 President Bush applied a waiver to a resolution by the House that prohibited any Exim credits and loans to nine countries, including Iraq. The presidential waiver excluded Iraq in the national interest.[45]

Less than one month later the Voice of America (VOA) broadcast an editorial that, as it claimed, was "reflecting the views of the U.S. government." It came in the wake of the monumental changes to Eastern Europe. It analyzed the function of the secret police in the dictatorial regimes of Eastern Europe and predicted the end of police states all over the world, including in Iraq.[46]

Even though Iraq did not figure very prominently in the broadcast (indeed, Iraq's name was added only at the last moment), the timing was very sensitive because the Iraqi leadership was aware of some similarities between its situation and that of deceased Romanian leader Nicolae Ceausescu, namely, a crisis of socioeconomic expectations and tensions between the army and the civilian leadership. It saw in the broadcast "a part of a total and organized plan [to topple the regime]." It asked for clarifications, and Washington officially apologized and informed it that the official responsible was sacked. However, Iraqi sources insist that suspicions did not subside.[47] These were further enhanced by the fact that the second tranche of the CCC credits was not forthcoming.[48] The National Security Council (NSC) and its head, General Brent Scowcroft, were doing their best to push the various government agencies to approve the second tranche, but they failed. This seems to have been transmitted to the Iraqi side.[49]

It also seems that between February and April 1990 the Iraqis concluded they could expect little from the United States in return for good behavior and, more important, that what the United States regarded as good behavior was diametrically opposed to crucial Iraqi interests. Following the VOA broadcast and a few days before an Arab Cooperation Council (ACC) summit in Baghdad, Kelly visited Baghdad and met with Saddam. We have no information as to what Kelly said in that meeting, but the Iraqi president told him that the United States was interested in a state of "no war, no peace" between Iraq and Iran.[50] Saddam's behavior following the meeting was ample proof that, contrary to Kelly's perception, he saw the meeting as the beginning of the end of the era of more-or-less normal U.S.-Iraqi working relations.

In a speech he delivered at the summit of the ACC at the end of the month, Saddam accused the U.S. Navy, then in the Gulf, of trying to fish in troubled waters and implied that it should evacuate the area. Ambassador Glaspie relayed to the Iraqi Foreign Ministry her country's anger. She asked for clarification (which she never received), explaining that the U.S. Navy had been reduced already from fifty vessels in 1988 to six.[51] According to writer Sa'd Bazzaz, as the Iraqi leadership saw it, "in February 1990 the serious planning in the U.S. for an open and forceful action against Iraq . . . started. It became clear that the campaign had begun."[52] This could also be read as Iraqi realization that, conspiracy or not, the United States was determined to prevent Iraqi hegemony in the Gulf. According to 'Aziz, Iraq noticed U.S. displeasure at Saddam's speech at the ACC Amman summit, and in mid-March, after Iraq executed London-based reporter Farzad Bazoft "because he was a spy," all hell broke loose. As Tariq 'Aziz put it, this was when Iraq started to fear a conspiracy.[53]

In his fateful meeting with Ambassador Glaspie just prior to the invasion of Kuwait, Saddam exposed the Iraqi way of thinking during the first half of 1990. According to Glaspie, he explained that there were "some circles in the U.S. government, including in the CIA [Central Intelligence Agency] and the State Department, but emphatically excluding the president and Secretary Baker, who are not friendly towards Iraq-U.S. relations. . . . Some circles are gathering information on who might be Saddam Hussein's successor." These circles, Saddam disclosed, were warning Gulf states against Iraq. These hostile circles were also working to ensure "no [economic] help would go to Iraq [meaning the CCC]." Finally, Saddam mentioned the "USIA [U.S. Information Agency] campaign against himself and the general media assault on Iraq."[54] I was unable to verify the claim that officials were warning the Gulf states, but in his memoirs General Norman Schwarzkopf does mention that a short time before the invasion of Kuwait, he gave orders to test in a war game what he considered to be a realistic scenario "in which the enemy was not the Soviet Union [as before], but Iraq."[55] Tariq 'Aziz, too (not resorting this time to a plot theory), reports that the Iraqi leadership reached the conclusion that Washington was split between supporters and opponents of Iraq, and when such a draw exists, he implied, the pro-Israel lobby "controls the balance."[56] Although the pro-Israel lobby issue was greatly exaggerated (it was unable to prevent extensive cooperation until the BNL fraud was exposed), the splits within the administration and Congress were very real.

By March there were a few more incidents that further soured relations. In the middle of the month Iraq executed reporter Bazoft. At the end of the month the United States and Britain, in a "sting" operation, exposed an Iraqi network to smuggle munitions-list nuclear-related capacitors out of the United States through Britain to Iraq. The administration saw in it a breach of two diplomatic principles: It showed flagrant disregard for U.S. law and it called into question Iraq's willingness to live up to its Non-Proliferation Treaty (NPT) commitments. The embassy in Baghdad was also instructed to deliver a démarche with regard to a conspiracy between an Iraqi diplomat at the UN in New York and an Iraqi expatriate in the United States to arrange for the assassination of another Iraqi expatriate in the United States.[57]

Trying to deflect congressional wrath, Kelly ignored Iraqi intentions, thus issuing a technically correct but incomplete communiqué: "We do not believe that Iraq is close to developing an atomic weapon, nor do we have any indication that Iraq has violated its NPT commitments."[58] Yet the U.S. government was now far more suspicious than it had been in the mid-1980s. In late 1989 there was a widespread presumption on the part of the intelligence community that Iraq was "interested in acquiring a nuclear explosive capability." True, U.S. exports of "dual use commodities for conventional military use" could still be (and were) approved.[59] Yet, as will be shown below, some high-profile attempts were made to prevent exports with nonconventional potential.

According to Baghdad radio and TV broadcasts, on April 1, 1990, Saddam made his thundering threat that, if Israel touches "one square inch of Iraqi soil . . . fire will consume half of Israel."[60] This threat was coupled by placing missile launchers at the H3 military base in western Iraq, facing Israel. According to 'Aziz, in late March, following the nuclear-detonators affair, the atmosphere reminded Iraq of the period leading to the Israeli raid of June 1981, and the Iraqi leadership felt that a "deterrent speech" was in order. This was the sole reason for Saddam's threat. To Iraq's dismay, the United States again took the speech very badly. This was when the Iraqi leadership became convinced that Washington "stopped listening to us" and "made up their minds to hit us."[61] As pointed out above, the Iraqi fear of an Israeli raid was a real one. However, this, too, could be read in a conspiracy-free manner: U.S. anger at the threats against Israel convinced the Iraqis that any attempt to lead an Arab political front against the peace process would meet with U.S. opposition. The State

Department felt that by threatening Israel with a chemical attack Saddam reneged on the Iraqi commitment, given to Shultz a few months earlier, to adhere to the 1925 Geneva Protocol prohibiting the first use of chemical weapons. The embassy in Baghdad was instructed again to deliver a démarche concerning all these issues, including human rights. Embassy officials promised that U.S. criticism of Iraq was not a "green light" to an Israeli attack and suggested that Iraq could ease the tension with Israel "by opening an indirect line of communications." The ambassador was asked, however, to deliver a very strict warning: "Iraq will be on a collision course with the U.S. if it continues to engage in actions that threaten the stability of the region, undermine local arms control efforts and flout U.S. laws."[62] And in another communication: "Without such measures [designed to address the aforementioned U.S. concerns] on your part, what little support that is left in the U.S. for Iraq may further erode."[63]

The State Department also took the opportunity to deliver the same message via the five U.S. senators visiting Baghdad. In their meeting in Mosul on April 12, Republican Senator Bob Dole, who headed the group, personally handed Saddam Hussein an official letter from the delegation warning Iraq that it must stop its nuclear, chemical, and missile "proliferation" as well as "disregard for U.S. law and human rights."[64] The Dole mission was later criticized as appeasing Saddam, as it emphasized the U.S. wish for friendship with Iraq. But Saddam, for his part, could not have ignored the conditions for such friendship, and they were totally unacceptable to him. In fact, Saddam explicitly and forcefully rejected the U.S. nonproliferation policy, saying, "It is the Arabs' right to own whatever weapon their enemy owns . . . If any Arab state would have announced that it had the nuclear bomb, I myself and the Iraqis would have been the first to announce support and respect for this."[65]

What the senators put to him gently, Congress delivered forcefully. Following Saddam's threat against Israel, three bills were discussed on Capitol Hill. One was offered by Senators Daniel K. Inouye (D–Hawaii) and Robert Kasten (R–Wisc.), who proposed a total trade embargo (including a ban on travel) against Iraq. Another proposed bill was sponsored by Congressman Howard L. Berman (D–Calif.). It included, among other items, stricter limitations on exports of dual-use technology, cutting off Exim guarantees, and mandatory U.S. objection to loans to Iraq by international bodies like the International Monetary Fund (IMF). The third proposal was a bill offered by Senator Alfonse D'Amato (R–N.Y.) to cut off all U.S. aid to Iraq until it submitted to an international inspection of its military facilities.[66] An exasperated Senator Tom Lantos (D–Calif.) asked Kelly during testimony: "At what point will the administration recognize that this is not a nice guy?"[67] But views in the embassy in Baghdad and, more important, in the State Department were more optimistic, thus State was still against sanctions. Glaspie reported from Baghdad in late April: "Iraq has modified its behavior and policies in large part because of our diplomatic efforts."[68] John Kelly pointed out in late May to the Senate: "The government of Iraq is signaling that it wants to bring U.S.-Iraq relations back to a more positive level."[69] But Saddam was already light-years away from where the U.S. analysts thought he was. In all probability, the decision to invade Kuwait was made only in late June,[70] but by late May the Iraqi president had clearly chosen a collision course with the United States, Britain, and Israel.

Less than a week after Kelly's upbeat assessment, at the Baghdad Arab League Summit Meeting, Saddam switched yet again. The convening of an extraordinary Arab Summit meeting in Baghdad was in itself a tremendous victory for the aggressive policies adopted by Iraq since the launch of its 'Abid space missile in early December 1989 and an admission of weakness on the part of the pro-Western Arab states. This summit witnessed a major offensive on the part of Iraq and its Arab supporters (chiefly Libya, the Palestine Liberation Organization [PLO], and Jordan) against Israel, Soviet-Jewish immigration, the United States, and, by implication, the Arab moderates. In the summit's concluding resolutions Iraq received support for its "right to take all measures that will guarantee the protection of its national security and . . . the possession of highly-developed scientific and technological means" necessary for its defense. The resolutions added that this had to be done within the framework of international law. Yet the "severe denunciation" of "the scientific and technological embargo" imposed on Iraq by the United States and Britain and of the Western media campaign "against [its] sovereignty and national security" sent a very different message; the Arabs as a collective denounced any attempt to stop Saddam's nuclear, chemical, bacteriological, and missile efforts and even defined these efforts as a positive contribution to "pan-Arab security."[71] Thus, the summit's resolutions should have been interpreted as tacit approval of Saddam's policies. All in all, these resolutions were a shocking demonstration of collective Arab folly. But this was not all.

During the closed sessions Saddam Hussein's other side was exposed when he accused some "Arab Brothers" of flooding the world oil market and bringing down prices. This, he pointed out, had caused Iraq and "the Arab nation" grave economic damages. He threatened that Iraq regarded this as an all-out war against it. He added darkly: "We have reached a point when we can no longer withstand pressure."[72] According to a senior diplomat from the Gulf who attended the summit, Saddam also demanded strong anti-American resolutions, and Egyptian President Husni Mubarak needed all his influence to prevent such resolutions. No one protested the attack on the Gulf Arabs, and the impression left was that of Arab sympathy toward Saddam's demands or, at least, reluctance to confront Iraq. This was further evidence of Iraq's new status, as well as its ability to use it to apply pressure on the Gulf states.

Just before the Baghdad summit the U.S. administration went on record as objecting to any sanctions against Iraq. The State Department's main concerns were that sanctions (especially the Inouye-Kasten bill) "just short of a declaration of war" would damage the peace process, reintroduce Soviet influence, affect the U.S. energy supply (675,000 barrels per day; 8 percent of all imported oil came from Iraq), and damage U.S. exporters of foodstuffs and dual-use technology as other developed countries gladly filled the gap. Conspicuous by its absence is any particular concern about security in or policy toward the Gulf region. More generally, State claimed that the United States had already imposed severe limitations on any exports to Iraq that could be used to produce missiles and chemical and nuclear weapons. State also felt that Congress should not limit the president in his foreign policy.[73] Congressional activity was delayed for a variety of reasons, but State needed to preempt further action. "If our efforts are deemed insufficient," a senior official wrote, "Congress can be expected to enact a host of anti-Iraqi resolutions and amendments in the next session."[74]

Iraqi rage, so explicit at the Baghdad summit, resulted from the U.S. restrictions, some of which had been imposed on Iraq since late 1989. Among them were, in addition to the suspension of the CCC program, curtailing of certain activities by the Department of Commerce to interagency consultation; rescission of the presidential waiver in regard to Exim; the beginning of a concerted international effort to break up Iraq's covert procurement networks; a campaign designed to persuade other countries (e.g., France, USSR, the Federal Republic of Germany, and Japan) to raise nuclear, missile, chemical, and biological warfare concerns directly with Iraq's Arab friends (and themselves to refrain from any exports that could be conducive to such warfare); a ban on nuclear cooperation with Iraq and on exports of technology that could be helpful for Iraq's biological weapons program; and an expansion to fifty of the list of prohibited chemicals (identified as potentially usable in chemical weapons programs), including coordination with other Western powers, including the Australia Group, to deny Iraq chemicals for its weapons industry. Also, since spring 1989, exports of biological cultures were severely curtailed.[75]

These activities were insufficient to stop the Iraqi thirst for nonconventional weapons. Indeed, some dual-purpose technology was still sold and shipped to Iraq well into 1990.[76] However, Saddam's rage displayed at the summit meeting and his remarks to the senators indicate that the U.S. declarations of intent were more than sufficient to alert the Iraqis to the U.S.-led effort. The restrictions were easily monitored, because they were designed to be easily monitored and they signaled that Iraq was, indeed, on a political collision course with the United States. The Iraqis knew that in 1986 the United States managed to "kill" the Condor medium-range ballistic missile program, which they hatched together with Egypt and Argentina, by leaning on the Germans and Italians.[77] The United States could do it again. All the existing evidence in Baghdad pointed in one direction, namely, that when the Ba'th regime worked to achieve national goals, it ran into U.S. opposition; even the sympathetic officials of State and the NSC were unable to prevent U.S. sanctions. Indeed, in terms of U.S. nonproliferation efforts, there was consensus over the aforementioned steps and discord only in relation to some dual-use technology.

Saddam's National Goals

What were Iraq's national goals, so dear to the hearts of Saddam and his close associates and so irreconcilable with long-term U.S. interests? One was the development and use of chemical weapons. However, this was no longer necessary, the Kurdish opposition having been crushed. Far more contentious was the issue of Iraqi ambition in the Gulf. The editor of the government daily newspaper indicated that at the end of the war with Iran, Iraq was bent on wrenching out of the Gulf Arabs "large-scale participation . . . to enable Iraq to re-build itself and to provide [for its citizens] a suitable level of social and economic comfort."[78]

In a number of meetings between Iraqi and Kuwaiti officials during the first half of 1990, Iraqi Minister of State for Foreign Affairs Hammadi demanded that the Gulf states extend to Iraq sufficient support to compensate for past war damages and enable it to rebuild its economy. As implied by the Iraqis, the demand could reach a total of $200–300 billion, a staggering amount even for the Gulf monarchies.[79] Furthermore, according to Bazzaz, the Iraqi leadership felt that there was no way the Gulf zone could "expect stability" unless the Gulf Arabs recognized Iraq's status as the "guardian brother,"[80] meaning the senior member in the GCC.

By the spring of 1990, following a number of diplomatic crises with the United States, it became clear to the Iraqi leadership that under the existing circumstances the United States would never allow Iraq to impose its will on the Gulf Arabs. There was a need, therefore, to break the spell, to create a new reality, and to present the United States with a fait accompli. Under the new circumstances Iraq would be in control of 21 percent of all the oil sold on the world markets, and Saddam hoped that the United States would have no choice but to acquiesce and bargain. This expectation was sounded loud and clear in a meeting Saddam initiated with the U.S. chargé d'affaires, Joseph Wilson, four days after the Kuwait invasion. According to the Iraqi transcript, Saddam offered President Bush a guarantee (what he knew to have been the U.S. chief interest in the Gulf) that oil would flow undisturbed. This was how NSD-26 defined it[81] and how it was repeated in many U.S. diplomatic messages. Saddam's contribution to the U.S. formula was that he would see to it that Gulf oil would be available at a "reasonable price" of $25 per barrel. In return he expected U.S. acceptance of the annexation of Kuwait and Iraq's status as senior U.S. ally in the Gulf.[82]

But Iraq was harboring even greater ambitions. As had become clear since December 1989, Iraq was also bent on achieving Arab leadership. Seen from this perspective Israel was not a threat but rather an asset. At a time when Arab frustration was growing due to a slowdown of the peace talks and the exodus of Soviet Jews to Israel, assuming the mantle of Arab leadership in the political struggle against Israel could secure for Iraq substantial influence in Arab minds after eight years of nonaction from other Arab states. Following Saddam's somewhat inflated promise to burn half of Israel, Arab popular enthusiasm reached amazing levels. The Iraqi president was quick to take advantage of it: Though at first explaining (to the Senate delegation) that what he had meant was only a chemical reprisal for an Israeli nuclear attack, a few days later he and his military commanders continued to imply the use of chemical warheads in retaliation for a conventional attack on *any* Arab country.[83] A confrontational posture vis-à-vis Israel, however, could only lead to tension with the United States. Sheltering terrorists was yet another pan-Arab asset. But here, too, when Saddam hosted again the notorious Abu 'Abbas in the spring of 1990 he was, apparently, reminded by the United States that this could further complicate matters.[84] The Iraqi ambassador's reply to U.S. protests: "Iraq does and will continue to provide access for all Palestinians . . . seeking to liberate Palestine."[85]

Rather than briefly lower his terrorist profile, as he had done in the past, to the consternation of U.S. diplomats Saddam instead restocked his reservoir of terrorists. To Abu 'Abbas, in June 1990, he added Abu Nidal. The United States was aware of terrorist activities planned by these men and a few other Baghdad-based groups. "Iraq should understand clearly," Glaspie was instructed to inform her interlocutors, "the U.S. would respond to any new terrorist acts."[86] The Iraqis were not impressed. A few days after the invasion the State Department reported in an internal document that "there have been increasing signs that he [Saddam] has been rebuilding Iraq's ties to terrorist groups in recent months."[87] Clearly since early 1990, when he decided to break away from his accommodationist policies, Saddam felt that he needed the additional intimidation value and prestige associated with the presence of Palestinian terrorist groups in Baghdad, and he was indifferent to U.S. protests. A month after the invasion the State Department decided to place Iraq again on the list of state sponsors of terrorism.[88]

In June, this listing could still have affected Iraq's economic relations with the United States because it would have effectively ended all the suspended programs and Iraqi oil exports to and technology imports from the United States. But Saddam was already riding high on his way to Arab leadership and financial solvency; once he was in possession of Kuwait and its coveted treasures, a U.S. trade embargo could be easily compensated for by trading with other Western countries. The sponsorship of Palestinian terrorism, however, was irreplaceable under the new circumstances.

Finally, as a result of its ambitions to Gulf and Arab leadership, but also because of what it perceived as a long-term threat from Iran, Iraq was determined to develop an array of nonconventional weapons and missiles. This, too, was anathema to the United States, and U.S. diplomats delivered this message to the Iraqis and their Arab friends loud and clear. Whether the Iraqi ruling elite genuinely saw this as a part of a "U.S.-Zionist conspiracy" or whether the theory was intended only for mass consumption, the United States stood in Iraq's path toward Gulf and Arab hegemony and what it saw as its legitimate national security interests. Baghdad's conclusion was that it was getting very close to the limits of its cooperation with the United States. One thing that guaranteed Saddam success in the domestic arena was his ability to preempt and surprise unsuspecting potential rivals. Saddam had always been the first to break formation and (often literally) stab former allies in the back. The Iraqi leader decided to project these winning tactics to the foreign arena, take the Americans by surprise, and then make them an offer that they could not turn down. U.S. diplomacy was unaware of the full significance of the indications of the changing mood in Baghdad.

On the Eve of the Invasion

In response to Saddam Hussein's implied threat, made in his July 17 speech, to use force against unspecified Arab oil producers who exceeded quotas, and in response to his furious anti-Kuwaiti letter to the Arab League, Kuwait placed its armed forces on alert but stood down by July 20 to make sure Baghdad did not interpret the alert as a provocative move that might call for a military response. By July 20, however, there were already unconfirmed reports of the movement of two divisions of the Iraqi Republican Guards to the Iraq-Kuwait border. (In fact, according to a reliable Iraqi source, troop movements toward the Kuwait border started between July 17 and July 19.)[89] Senior U.S. officials were in touch with their Kuwaiti counterparts, assuring them of their support. The United States also made contact with Iraq to make sure that it was aware of U.S. concern.[90]

At about 9 A.M. (Baghdad time) on July 25, the U.S. intelligence assessment became very ominous. It revealed that three infantry divisions, an armored division, their supporting units, and additional air defense units were in place near the Kuwait border. The Iraqi force was estimated at over 75,000. However, Kuwait and the other Arab monarchies on the Gulf responded with "only minor military activity."[91]

On July 25, U.S. sources already concluded that Saddam had the capability to conquer Kuwait within a few days. But they were at a loss as to his intentions; clearly, they lacked human intelligence from within the ruling circle. In their perplexity, U.S. officials turned to their closest Arab allies, assuming that Saddam's Arab neighbors, due to their proximity and common cultural background, would be either more knowledgeable or intuitively more accurate in their assessments of his intentions. The king of Saudi Arabia and president of Egypt assured Washington that Saddam would not invade, arguing that "the best way to resolve an inter-Arab squabble is for the United States to avoid inflammatory words and actions."[92] Kuwait, for its part, was so scared lest it would provoke Saddam that it refrained from requesting any U.S. military gesture.[93]

On the diplomatic level, following Saddam's July 17 speech, President Bush expressed concern and his administration spoke of reviewing its policy vis-à-vis Iraq.[94] On July 18, the State Department announced U.S. commitments: to ensure the free flow of oil through the Strait of Hormuz; to defend the freedom of navigation in the Gulf; and to support "the individual and collective self-defense of our friends in the Gulf, with whom we have deep and long-standing ties."[95] The first two points had little to do with Kuwait; the third was intentionally vague so as not to commit the United States automatically to direct military involvement.

On July 24, Ambassador Glaspie was instructed to convey to Iraq the U.S. concern over the security of Kuwait and the United Arab Emirates (UAE). "The implications of having oil production and pricing policy . . . enforced by Iraqi guns [are] disturbing," she told Deputy Foreign Minister Nizar Hamdun.[96] At this point it is very likely that this warning only aggravated the situation: U.S. officials were demonstrating extreme annoyance with Saddam but were reluctant to expose their fangs.

On July 25, Ambassador Glaspie was summoned to the Foreign Ministry, only to find herself facing Saddam Hussein in person. Her conversation with Saddam is by now a proverbial example of mutual misunderstanding. The ambassador could not imagine that Saddam would be so ill-informed and rash as to conquer Kuwait City, and she was convinced, at least since April, that Iraq was war-weary and was only concerned with reconstruction.[97] How can one explain the ambassador's optimism at the end of the meeting? It would seem that in addition to an intellectual gestalt ("the Iraqis are tired of war"), which is always difficult to break, there were two more factors. In the first place, she had been effectively isolated from Saddam and his closest circle (his cousins, half brothers, and the command of the Republican Guards). Second, in the rare interview Saddam accorded her, he intentionally sent her a double message. He may have threatened, but he also promised to try negotiations, and he assured her that Iraq was, indeed, tired of war.

As for his own assessment of the U.S. position, Saddam made his view very clear that he did not think the United States was capable of going to war and losing 10,000 people in one battle, as Iraq had done on numerous occasions in its war against Iran. Even though Saddam and his elite recognized that Iraq was not fully prepared for an all-out war, and that it needed "two more years" to get ready (possibly meaning the time necessary in order to build its first nuclear warheads), their calculation was that Iraq was taking relatively little risk with much to gain by an invasion. As reported by Bazzaz, Iraq had a very large army that if not used for economic gains would have become a crippling economic burden; the Iraqi public became addicted to a very high oil income and thus the depressed prices of oil posed a severe danger to the regime; had it not invaded Kuwait, it would have had to conduct an uphill struggle against the overproducers, risking in the meantime major political upheavals inside the country. With a national debt of $70 billion and oil income that covered "only" 50 percent of what was believed needed, and having anyway lost the U.S. agricultural credits (and the abundant source of credit through the Atlanta-based branch of the BNL), the situation seemed desperate enough to dictate an invasion.[98]

The ambassador did warn Saddam that "the U.S. cannot forgive the use of force." But, in reply to his friendly complaints, she also offered sympathy for Iraq's economic plight. Ignoring the inflated defense expenditures, she pointed out that Iraq deserved higher oil income. She also made her famous comment that the United States did not take a position over Arab-Arab disputes. Under different circumstances this was a good way of keeping the United States at a safe distance from inter-Arab bickering, but with four Iraqi divisions on the Kuwait border and more moving in, together with missile and air force units, this comment left Saddam with the feeling that Washington was not fully committed to the defense of Kuwait. Saddam then hinted that, if not satisfied by the Kuwaitis, he would strike a deal with Iran over the Shatt al-'Arab (the confluence of the Tigris and Euphrates Rivers that acts as a border between Iraq and Iran) and crush the Kuwaitis militarily, as he had done to Mulla Mustafa al-Barazani in 1975. Apparently, Glaspie and all those who saw her report were convinced that he was bluffing.

Saddam, for his part, claimed later that Ambassador Glaspie gave him free reign.[99] This claim does not sound credible. In the first place, Saddam had enough indications on both the diplomatic and the military levels that the United States was not indifferent to the fate of its Gulf allies. Second, he must have known that a U.S. ambassador does not make policy. However, the U.S. response to his threatening moves did indicate indecision and reluctance to become fully committed. Thus, for example, in Bush's July 28 cable to Ambassador Glaspie, defined as a "nondocument," the president instructed the ambassador to convey to Saddam his wish to further U.S.-Iraqi friendship; his warning sounded too soft: "We believe that differences are best resolved by peaceful means and not by threats involving military force."[100] Two days before the invasion, Kelly announced that the United States had no defense treaty with a Gulf state and was reluctant to commit the United States to Kuwait's territorial integrity.[101] True, this announcement was made in response to a question by a member of Congress who implied that the United States should not get too involved in the dispute. It is also true that this announcement reflected the legal reality: The United States and Kuwait had no such treaty and, in fact, belabored relations had been somewhat cool for a number of years. But under the circumstances it sent the wrong signal.

The U.S. response was, largely, the result of Saddam's disinformation campaign. Indeed, to blur his intentions Saddam also gave Egyptian President Mubarak a vague promise not to resort to arms. The exact wording of his promise later became a subject of bitter controversy.[102] But whatever the precise wording, it is sufficiently clear that Saddam intentionally sent an equivocal message. In his discussions with both Mubarak and Glaspie, he threatened that if not satisfied he would use force, but he also promised to give negotiations a chance.

How can one explain Saddam's decision to make threats and then blur them? In his meetings with Glaspie and Mubarak he urged them to apply pressure on Kuwait to concede to his demands, and he wanted them to convey his clear threats so as to increase the chances of Kuwaiti capitulation. But Saddam must have known that the chances of that occurring were slight. And so he needed to achieve a two-fold strategic goal: He was determined to avoid a repeat of the ill-fated Kuwaiti initiative of 'Abd al-Karim Qasim in June 1961. Qasim announced his intention to annex Kuwait before issuing the order to prepare an invasion; when he was ready, it was too late—the British were already there. Saddam, whose sense of history is as vivid and relevant to decisionmaking as any strategic consideration, decided to reverse the order of things.[103] To avoid a U.S. preemptive military interference, he needed to send a peaceful message. But then, why threaten at all? Why not attack Kuwait without any warning and thus achieve complete strategic surprise? The answer to this is that Saddam needed to prepare the ground in Iraq and the Arab world in a way that would assure him mass support. Such support in Arab streets could make it difficult for moderate Arab leaders to oppose him. Without Arab support it would have been more difficult (though not impossible) for the United States to go to war.

All this, however, does not explain the Iraqi president's vague threats in his confidential conversation with Ambassador Glaspie. It seems he hoped they would not be clear enough to force the United States to make a decisive countermove. At the same time, however, he needed to gauge the U.S. position, and he left the United States one week to react. He hoped for a feeble reaction. In fact, by sending his mixed message he invited just such a reaction. And when he got what he had asked for, he conveniently ignored the fact that this reaction had to be misleading because it was based on misleading information, which he himself had provided the United States. Finally, Saddam wanted to be able to argue later that he gave the Americans all the necessary warnings and that they chose to stay on the sidelines. This could win him domestic support in the United States. As we have seen, this is precisely what he did: As early as September 1990 Saddam instructed his embassy in Washington to publish a somewhat doctored version of his conversation with Ambassador Glaspie. In it the Iraqi threat and the ambassador's complacency are accentuated beyond what emerges from the ambassador's communications to Washington.

Conclusion

Could the United States have prevented the invasion? There is no clear answer to this question. As we have shown, one week before the invasion the Iraqi president did not think that the United States had the stomach for a major and bloody campaign. This impression was prevalent in the Arab world following the U.S. evacuation of Vietnam and influenced its political thinking. Saddam correctly concluded that in order to drive him out of Kuwait the United States would need huge ground forces. And he did not think that the United States would be ready to expose ground troops to a war of attrition. And Saddam truly believed that this would have to be a war of attrition because he did not understand the significance of the technological gap between the two armies; thus, there is no certainty that the United States could have convinced him to stick to diplomatic means.

The United States clearly did not maximize its leverage on Iraqi policymaking. In the first place, it alarmed the Iraqi leadership by sending it repeated messages that if it did not change policy the two countries were on a collision course. However, U.S. diplomacy did not do all it could reasonably have done to prevent the invasion. To be sure, there were limits to U.S. deterrence: U.S. policymakers had to leave for themselves a degree of freedom so as not to commit themselves to the defense of every square inch of Kuwaiti territory. But they could have found a diplomatic formula that would indicate to the Iraqis more emphatically that they were passing a redline. For example, they could have warned that any use of force would be regarded as a severe infringement on U.S. interests in the Gulf and that in such case the United States would use all necessary means to defend these interests. The United States could also have moved strong naval forces into the Gulf and conducted joint maneuvers with the Kuwaitis. It seems that this was the limit, but still a realistic policy. Such a policy would have forced Saddam to think twice before he gave his army its invasion order. True, such a policy was rendered extremely difficult to implement in view of the Arab perceptions that Saddam was only trying to improve his political bargaining cards. And the Arab friends of the United States were warning against any precipitate action that might have backfired against U.S. interests in the Gulf by feeding into the popular perception of the United States as an aggressive imperialist power taking advantage of the situation to extend its influence in the region; a proactive policy of this kind would also have undermined the legitimacy of the pro-U.S. regimes in the Middle East that would have been inevitably linked to the action. And as long as Kuwait did not ask for joint maneuvers, the United States could only suggest it.

Finally, is it possible that by not reacting swiftly and strongly to what it considered Iraqi excesses (the use of CW; threats against allies of the United States in the Middle East; support for terrorism; development of a nonconventional arsenal), the United States left the Iraqis with the impression of short-term U.S. indecision and thus left open a window of opportunity. Although very possibly true, at present there is not enough evidence to substantiate such a claim.

Notes

This chapter was written during my fellowship at the Woodrow Wilson International Center for Scholars, Washington, D.C., in 1993 and 1994. Data collection was also helped by research grants from the United States Institute of Peace and the Bertha Von Suttner Special Project for the Optimization of Conflict Resolution. I am indebted to all three for their invaluable assistance. My research assistant, Ms. Debbie Lincoln, made a most important contribution to this article, for which I am grateful.

1. Alan Friedman, *Spider's Web: The Secret History of How the White House Illegally Armed Iraq* (New York: Bantam Books, 1993), p. 282.

2. See, for example, Amatzia Baram, "The Iraqi Invasion of Kuwait: Decision-Making in Baghdad," in Amatzia Baram and Barry Rubin, eds., *Iraq's Road to War* (New York: St. Martin's Press, 1994), pp. 19–22.

3. It must also be remembered that the primary attentions of the Bush administration during this period (1989 to pre-August 1990) were devoted to the dramatic events unfolding in Eastern Europe—with the fall of the Berlin Wall and the end of the superpower cold war—as well as events in China that climaxed in the Tiananmen Square massacre in June 1989. This also happened during the Carter administration in its policy neglect of Iran prior to the 1979 Iranian revolution: Its involvement in other events in the region (the 1979 Egyptian-Israeli peace treaty) and in the world (the SALT II negotiations with the USSR and the formal opening of diplomatic relations with China) diverted attention away from the strategic Persian Gulf region.

4. The White House, presidential documents, *Presidential Determination Number 90-7 of January 17, 1990, Application of Export-Import Bank Restrictions in Connection with Iraq*, p. 1.

5. The White House, presidential documents, *Memorandum of Justification for a Waiver of Exim Restrictions with Respect to Iraq*, January 17, 1990.

6. John H. Kelly, Assistant Secretary of State for Near Eastern and South Asian Affairs, *U.S. Relations with Iraq: Statement of Assistant Secretary Kelly Before the Senate Foreign Relations Committee*, May 23, 1990, pp. 2, 5, 10.

7. Richard Murphy, *Statement . . . Before the Sub-committee on Europe and the Middle East, House Foreign Affairs Committee*, October 13, 1988, 100th Cong., 2d sess., p. 17.

8. Pamela Fessler, "Congress' Record on Saddam: Decade of Talk, Not Action," in *Congressional Quarterly*, April 27, 1991, p. 1068; Clyde Mork, *Congress and Iraq, 1990* (Washington, D.C., Congressional Research Service, January 3, 1992), p. 4.

9. *Wall Street Journal*, July 1, 1988. Unnamed Iraqi diplomat in *al-Anba* (Amman), June 30, 1988, *Foreign Broadcast Information Service Daily Report* (hereinafter *FBIS Daily Report*), July 5, 1988, p. 15. See also *FBIS Daily Report*, June 17 and 21, pp. 25 and 19, respectively, on articles in *al-Thawra* (Baghdad) in June threatening the United States with reprisal if such meetings continue.

10. *al-Thawra*, June 13, 1988, pp. 1, 7.

11. *Boston Globe*, July 26, 1988, p. 6.

12. Fessler, "Congress' Record on Saddam," p. 1071.

13. From Richard W. Murphy to Michael Armacost, *Action Memorandum: U.S. Policy Towards Iraq and CW Use*, September 19, 1988, pp. 1–2.

14. Ibid., p. 4. See also U.S. Department of State, Intelligence and Research (hereinafter INR) to the Secretary of State, *Information Memorandum: U.S.-Iraqi Relations: Implication of Passage of Economic Sanctions Bill*, October 18, 1988, p. 1, pointing out that "Iraq is showing signs of adventurism throughout the Middle East" but warning that "the passage of the Sanctions Bill will undermine relations and reduce U.S. influence on a country that . . . [is] one of the most powerful Arab nations."

15. See, for example, *Mid East Markets* (London), September 19, 1988, pp. 12–14; *Middle East Economic Survey* (Cyprus), September 19, October 3, 1988; *Middle East Economic Digest* (London) (hereinafter *MEED*), September 23, 1988, p. 18; *Washington Post*, September 9, 1988.

16. Deputy Prime Minister Taha Yasin Ramadan in *al-Thawra*, September 15, *FBIS Daily Report*, September 21, 1988, p. 16. See also Culture and Information Minister Jasim in *Jerusalem Post*, September 11, 1988. The accusations of collusion with Iran were fanned, no doubt, by some conciliatory words that Iran's Majlis Speaker Hasimi Rafsanjani directed toward the United States in late 1988. See, for example, *Iran News Agency* from Tehran, November 25, 1988, *FBIS Daily Report*, September 21, 1988, p. 32.

17. *al-Jumhuriyya* (Baghdad), September 19, 1988, *FBIS Daily Report*, September 22, 1988, p. 15. See also *Iraqi News Agency* (hereinafter INA) from Baghdad, October 24, 1988, *FBIS Daily Report*, October 26, 1988, p. 21; *al-Jumhuriyya*, September 16, 1988, *FBIS Daily Report*, September 20, 1988, p. 21; and see allegations, following U.S.-Syrian discussions on the presidency of Lebanon, that the United States was conniving with Syria to support Iran against Iraq in the Geneva negotiations, *al-Thawra*, October 19, 1988, *FBIS Daily Report*, September 20, 1988, p. 22. For an accusation of U.S.-Israeli collusion against Iraq's missile program designed to deprive Iraq of advanced technology, see INA, April 20, 1989, *FBIS Daily Report*, April 21, 1989, p. 15.

18. *Washington Post*, October 4, 1988. The Iraqis admitted the use of chemical weapons during the war, including in Halabja in March 1988, but they never admitted the use of poison gas after the cease-fire. See an interview with Vice President Taha Muhyi al-Din Ma'ruf in Paris, *Le Monde*, November 10, 1988, in *FBIS Daily Report*, November 10, 1988, p. 24.

19. INA and *Voice of the Masses* from Baghdad, October 29, 30, and 31, 1988, *FBIS Daily Report*, October 31, 1988, p. 30.

20. Baghdad Radio, June 7, 1989, in *FBIS Daily Report*, June 8, 1989, p. 25. See also Fu'ad Matar, *al-Tadamun* (Amman), July 10, 1989, *FBIS Daily Report*, July 26, 1989, pp. 19–22.

21. See an angry Iraqi attack following expressions of such concern by Assistant Secretary of Defense Richard Armitage ("The Arab nation . . . realizes well that Washington has only been in a hostile Zionist trench"), *al-Thawra*, April 21, *FBIS Daily Report*, April 25, 1989, p. 29.

22. U.S. Department of State, *Memorandum for the Secretary: CCC Credit for Iraq,* October 11, 1989, reproduced in U.S. House of Representatives, Committee on Banking, Finance, and Urban Affairs, *The [BNL] Scandal and . . . the [CCC] Program,* 102d Cong., 2d sess., May 21, 1992 (Washington, D.C.), part 1, p. 290 (hereinafter *The BNL Scandal and the CCC Program*).

23. *Alert Report—Iraqi Payments Situation Further Deteriorates,* Export-Import Bank of the U.S.A., Country Risk Analysis Division, January 23, 1989; Exim, *Iraq Country Review Update,* September [?] 1989.

24. Letter from U.S. Department of the Treasury, U.S. Customs Service, Atlanta, Georgia, to Robert L. Barr Jr., U.S. Attorney, Northern District of Georgia, Sept. 21, 1989. Following the exposure of an Iraqi network that tried to smuggle nuclear triggers from the United States, administration officials expressed fears that the BNL funds were also used to procure such triggers. Thomas C. Baxter to Mr. Corrigan, *Office Memorandum: Lavoro,* April 5, 1990.

25. *Memorandum of Conversation: USDA Comments on Investigations of Iraq and the BNL Scandal,* October 13, 1989, p. 2; Letter from Robert Barr, U.S. Attorney, et al., U.S. Department of Justice, to S. Kelly, Federal Reserve Bank, Atlanta, Georgia, January 9, 1990; and see also U.S. Department of State, *Memorandum for the Secretary,* October 11, 1989, also in *The BNL Scandal and the CCC Program,* part 1, p. 290.

26. Cable from the U.S. Secretary of State to the Embassy, Baghdad, *Secretary's October 6 Meeting with Iraqi Foreign Minister Tariq 'Aziz,* October 13, 1989.

27. For U.S. Department of State displeasure at the need to suspend the second tranche of the Commodity Credit Corporation (CCC) program, see, for example, U.S. Department of State, Action Memorandum for the Secretary, *The Iraqi CCC Program,* October 26, 1989; and Glaspie assuring 'Aziz of Baker's hope that the issue "can be resolved quickly," in Letter from Embassy, Baghdad, to Secretary of State, *Tariq 'Aziz's Reply to Secretary's Letter,* October 24, 1989.

28. Letter from Lawrence Eagleburger to John Robson, Deputy Secretary of the Treasury, November 8, 1989, reproduced in *The BNL Scandal and the CCC Program,* part 2, p. 299.

29. Letter from Alan Charles Raul, Office of the General Counsel, Department of Agriculture (USDA), to Stephen I. Danzansky, Deputy Assistant to the President and Director, Office of Cabinet Affairs, The White House, including *Paper, USDA Position on Iraq,* October 30, 1989, reproduced in *The BNL Scandal and the CCC Program,* part 2, p. 239.

30. Cable from Embassy, Baghdad, to Secretary of State, *USDA Team Meetings with GOI Ministry of Trade,* April 22, 1990.

31. From an interview with a senior administration official, Washington, D.C., June 1994.

32. USDA, from Richard T. Crowder, Under Secretary for International Affairs and Commodity Programs et al., *Memorandum for Richard T. McCormack, Under Secretary of State et al., Report of Administrative Review of Iraq GSM Program,* May 16, 1990.

33. Cable from Am[erican Embassy], Baghdad, [signed Glaspie], to Sec. State, Subject: *Hamilton Sub-Committee,* April 25, 1990.

34. [Under Secretary of State for Political Affairs] Robert Kimmitt to the Secretary, *Note: DC Meeting on Iraq,* April 17, 1990.

35. Cable from Am[erican] Embassy, Baghdad, to Sec. of State, *Iraq Minister of Trade/Finance Discusses USDA GSM Credit Guarantee Program,* July 9, 1990. In fact, apparently to avoid suspicion that they were planning a U turn in their relations with the United States, the Iraqis continued to pay their debt. The last monthly payment of $150 million was deposited on August 1, 1990. Interview with a U.S. Department of Agriculture official, Washington, D.C., April 22, 1994.

36. USDA, Press Secretary, Office of the Secretary, *News: Administrative Review of Iraq GSM-102 Program,* May 21, 1990.

37. Glaspie, American Embassy, Baghdad, to the Sec. of State, *Public Iraqi Gestures Toward the USG,* July 3, 1990.

38. USDA, *Secretary's October 6th Meeting with . . . 'Aziz,* October 13, 1989. After the Kuwait crisis 'Aziz complained that following the Iraqi-Iranian cease-fire U.S. officials started warning the Gulf states that Iraq was dangerous; they started levelling "false accusations" against Iraq of using poison gas against its Kurds; and the CIA started to plot to topple the regime and assassinate Saddam Hussein. 'Aziz to Viorst, *The New Yorker,* June 24, 1991, pp. 64–67; 'Aziz to *Milliyet* (Istanbul), May 30 1991, in *FBIS Daily Report,* June 4, 1991, pp. 13–14; Sa'd Bazzaz, editor of the government daily *al-Jumhuriyya, Harb Talidu Ukhra* [War and the One After] (Amman, 1992–1993), pp. 151–152.

39. From Secretary of State to Embassy, Baghdad, *Message from the Secretary to Tariq 'Aziz,* Oct. 21, 1989.

40. Bazzaz, War and the One After, p. 152.

41. From Secretary of State to American Embassy, Baghdad, *Tension in US-Iraqi Relations: Demarche,* April 12, 1990.

42. Interview with a senior U.S. State Department official who dealt for a few years with Iraq during the second half of the 1980s, Washington, D.C., June 28, 1994.

43. Joint Staff, Information Service Center, USCINCCENT Macdill, to Joint Chiefs of Staff, Washington, D.C., *Proposed U.S.-Iraqi Military Initiatives,* November 29, 1989 (in reply to suggestions from American Embassy in Baghdad from June 19, 1989).

44. From Joint Staff, Washington, D.C., to USCINCCENT Macdill. *Proposed U.S.-Iraqi Military Initiatives,* January 3, 1990.

45. The White House, presidential documents, *Memorandum of Justification for a Waiver of Exim Restrictions with Respect to Iraq,* January 17, 1990.

46. *Voice of America,* Washington, D.C., transcript of a broadcast, February 15, 1990.

47. Bazzaz, War and the One After, p. 159.

48. Saddam, in his conversation with April Glaspie on July 25, 1990, *New York Times,* July 13, 1991.

49. See report of a conversation between National Security Advisor Brent Scowcroft and Iraqi Ambassador Nizar Hamdun, from the National Advisory Council to Robert Kimmitt, *National Advisory Council Meeting on Iraq CCC Program,* March 5, 1990.

50. See report of conversation from Tariq 'Aziz to Milton Viorst, in *New Yorker,* June 24, 1991, pp. 64–67.

51. Interview with a senior U.S. diplomat, Washington, D.C., June 28, 1994. See also from Secretary of State to American Embassy, Baghdad, *Tension in US-Iraqi Relations: Demarche,* April 12, 1990.

52. Bazzaz, War and the One After, pp. 159–160.

53. 'Aziz to Viorst, *New Yorker,* June 24, 1991, pp. 64–67.

54. *New York Times,* July 13, 1991. See also an Iraqi threat in early July that they would not be "passive" in the face of "an anti-Iraqi campaign by . . . certain elements in the U.S. government." The main reason for the Iraqi anger was the discontinuation of the CCC program "reflect[ing] unjustified hostility towards Iraq." Cable from Glaspie, American Embassy in Baghdad, to Secretary of State, *Public Iraqi Gesture Toward the U.S. Government,* July 3, 1990.

55. General H. Norman Schwarzkopf, *It Doesn't Take a Hero* (New York: Bantam Books, 1992), p. 289.

56. 'Aziz to Viorst, *New Yorker,* June 24, 1991, pp. 64–67.

57. Interview with a senior U.S. official, Washington, D.C., 1994.

58. John H. Kelly, *U.S. Relations with Iraq: Statement of Assistant Secretary Kelly Before the Senate Foreign Relations Committee,* May 23, 1990, p. 6.

59. U.S. Department of State, Bureau of Oceans and International Environmental and Scientific Affairs, *Memorandum: SNEC [Subgroup on Nuclear Export Control] Cases of Interest,* November 21, 1989.

60. *Baghdad Radio and TV,* April 2, 1990.

61. 'Aziz to Viorst, *New Yorker,* June 24, 1991, pp. 64–67.

62. Secretary of State to American Embassy, Baghdad, *Tension in US-Iraqi Relations: Demarche,* April 12, 1990.

63. Secretary of State to Embassy, Baghdad, *Chemical Weapons,* April [exact date unmarked], 1990.

64. A. Jock Covey to Robert Kimmitt, *Briefing Memorandum: NSC Deputies Committee Meeting on Iraq, April 16, 1990 White House Situation Room,* April 16, 1990, p. 5. Interview with a senior U.S. Department of State official, June 28, 1994; and Merrill W. Ruck, Rear Admiral, United States Navy, Assistant Deputy Director, Politico-Military Affairs J-5, and the Joint Staff, *Memorandum for the Record: PCC on Iraq,* April 13, 1990.

65. See the Iraqi version of the meeting, emphasizing Saddam's defiance and the conciliatory aspects of the senators' message. *al-Thawra,* April 17, 1990.

66. Fessler, "Congress' Record on Saddam," p. 1075.

67. Ibid.

68. Glaspie Cable, *Hamilton Subcommittee,* April 25, 1990.

69. John H. Kelly, *U.S. Relations with Iraq: Statement of Assistant Secretary Kelly Before the Senate Foreign Relations Committee,* May 23, 1990, p. 6.

70. Bazzaz, War and the One After, p. 23.

71. INA in Arabic, May 30, 1990, 12:50 P.M.

72. The speech was made on May 30, 1990, but it was broadcast only after the Iraqi-Kuwaiti dispute came out in the open on July 18, 1990. See Baghdad Radio, July 18, in *FBIS,* July 19, 1990, p. 21.

73. See, for example, Kelly's statement before the Senate Foreign Relations Committee, *U.S. Relations with Iraq,* May 23, 1990.

74. A. Jock Covey to Robert Kimmitt, *Briefing Memorandum: NSC Deputies Committee Meeting on Iraq, April 16, 1990,* p. 2.

75. Ibid., pp. 1ff; J. G. Mullins to W. S. Broomfield, [exact date not marked] April 1990; Kelly's statement before the Senate Foreign Relations Committee, *U.S. Relations with Iraq,* May 23, 1990; Memo from Richard Clarke to the Acting Secretary [of State Lawrence Eagleburger], *Action Memorandum, Export of Manufacturing Oven to Iraq,* July 18, 1990; Richard Murphy, *Statement . . . Before the Subcommittee on Europe and the Middle East, House Foreign Affairs Committee,* October 13, 1988, p. 18.

76. Interview with a former U.S. Department of Defense official, Washington, D.C., July 21, 1994.

77. Ibid.

78. Bazzaz, War and the One After, pp. 24, 36.

79. Bazzaz, War and the One After, pp. 39–45. Tariq 'Aziz, speaking on Baghdad Radio, July 18, 1990, in *FBIS-Near East,* July 18, 1990, p. 23.

80. Bazzaz, War and the One After, pp. 24, 36.

81. Tom Gallagher, CDR, U.S. Navy, J-5, MEAF, X-49336 (Joint Staff), *Position Paper: Heightened Tension Between Iraq-Kuwait-UAE,* prepared for [Under Secretary of Defense for Policy Paul] Wolfowitz, July 25, 1990.

82. For the Iraqi version of this conversation, see *Meeting Between President Saddam Husayn and American Charge d'Affaires Wilson on 6 August, 1990,* newsletter, Iraqi Embassy, Washington, D.C. (September 1990).

83. For the first version, see Saddam's meeting with the Dole delegation, *al-Thawra,* April 17, 1990. For the "Arab" version, see, for example, General Muzahim Sa'b Hasan, Air Force Commander, Radio Monte Carlo, April 22, *FBIS Daily Report,* April 23, 1990, p. 13; Saddam, in a speech to a rally, Baghdad Radio, June 18, 1990, *FBIS-NES,* June 19, 1990, p. 21.

84. Glaspie Cable, *Hamilton Subcommittee,* April 25, 1990.

85. From Sec[retary of] State to Am[erican]Embassy, Baghdad, *Demarche on Abu 'Abbas,* June 20, 1990. See also from NEA and Secretary of State to American Embassy, Baghdad, *Congressional Questions for the Record,* June 21, 1990; from Secretary of State, to American Embassy, Baghdad, *Demarche on Abu 'Abbas,* June 23, 1990.

86. From Sec[retary of] State to Embassy in Baghdad et al., *Iraq and Terrorism,* June 27, 1990.

87. From Maurice D. Busby to Robert M. Kimmitt, *Information Memorandum: The Terrorist Threat from Iraq,* August 7, 1990.

88. From Katherine Shirley and John Kelly, to the Acting Secretary, *Action Memorandum: Returning Iraq to the Terrorism List,* September 1, 1990.

89. Bazzaz, War and the One After, p. 24.

90. Colonel Gary W. Nelson, USA J-5 MEAF, *Information Paper: Iraqi Threats to Kuwait,* July 20, 1990.

91. From SSODIA/JSI-6, to SSOAU and others, *item #00407725,* July 25, 1990, 02:05.

92. Elaine Sciolino, *New York Times,* September 23, 1990, p. 18; Bob Woodward, *The Commanders* (New York: Simon and Schuster, 1991), pp. 213–215.

93. Interview with a Gulf Arab diplomat, Washington, D.C., June 15, 1994.

94. See report of the U.S. press in *HaAretz,* July 19, 1990.

95. See U.S. Department of State cables to U.S. embassies in the Middle East as reproduced in *New York Times,* March 21, 1990.

96. *Washington Post,* October 21, 1992, quoting parts of the cable.

97. Glaspie Cable, *Hamilton Subcommittee,* April 25, 1990.

98. Bazzaz, War and the One After, pp. 23–38.

99. Saddam Hussein's interview with *Hurriyet,* February 10, 1992, in *FBIS,* February 13, 1992, pp. 22–23.

100. *New York Times,* April 5, 1992; *Washington Post,* October 21, 1992.

101. *New York Times,* September 23, 1990, p. 18.

102. See Amatzia Baram, "The Iraqi Invasion of Kuwait: Decision-making in Baghdad," in Amatzia Baram and Barry Rubin, eds., *Iraq's Road to War* (New York: St. Martin's Press, 1994), p. 18.

103. Bazzaz, War and the One After, p. 26. See also a detailed report of the reasons why Qasim failed, by the commander of Qasim's force assigned to storm Kuwait, Major General (retired) Khalil Sa'id, *al-Thawra,* August 21, 1992.

20

From "Over the Horizon" to "Into the Backyard": The U.S.-Saudi Relationship and the Gulf War

F. Gregory Gause III

Operations Desert Shield and Desert Storm represent a turning point in the close but complicated relationship between the Kingdom of Saudi Arabia and the United States. Although the Saudis had relied on U.S. security guarantees as an essential element of their defense policy since the 1940s, they had, at least since the 1960s, preferred to play down the military aspect of U.S.-Saudi relations to their own public and to regional audiences in the larger Arab and Muslim worlds. And though the rulers of the kingdom did call on U.S. military assistance in times of crisis previous to the Iraqi invasion of Kuwait, that assistance was largely limited to air and naval forces. Never before had U.S. ground troops in such numbers been stationed in the kingdom. Never before was the Saudi regime confronted with such a stark choice in terms of declaring its ultimate reliance on the United States for its security.

This chapter sets out the essential dilemma faced by the Saudis in the security realm, explaining why the regime must rely on outside power protectors when faced with a direct threat from larger regional neighbors, despite the problems such a choice poses. It then briefly reviews the history of the U.S.-Saudi security relationship, highlighting the tensions Riyadh has experienced in trying to maintain its defense links to Washington while asserting, for domestic and regional audiences, its independence from the United States. The background of the Saudi decision to invite U.S. and other forces into the kingdom after Saddam Hussein's invasion of Kuwait is then discussed, along with developments in the U.S.-Saudi relationship since the war and the potential consequences of those developments for the regime.[1]

The Saudi Defense Dilemma

The defense policy dilemma faced by the Saudi regime is the direct product of the country's oil wealth and the political strategy the regime has chosen for using that wealth. Oil makes the kingdom important to the rest of the world, but oil wealth also increases its vulnerability in a number of important ways. Most obviously, it makes Saudi Arabia a potential target for larger ambitious neighbors, as the Iraqi invasion of Kuwait clearly demonstrated. On a deeper and less obvious level, the characteristics that oil wealth has brought to domestic politics exacerbate Saudi security problems. The Saudi regime's ability to mobilize its population for defense is limited by the ethos of the particular type of rentier state the kingdom has become. Demands by the state upon citizens, like military service, are avoided because such demands could bring forth pressures for citizens to have a say in state policy. The Saudi population, small relative to potentially threatening neighbors, already complicates defense planning. Inability to utilize fully the human resources that exist compounds those complications.

A strategy of self-reliance for defense and security is both inadequate and politically troublesome for Saudi Arabia. The inadequacy of self-reliance is to some extent a simple matter of numbers. According to the 1992 census, the Saudi population was 16.9 million, of which 12.3 million were citizens.[2] Since that time, the citizen population has probably increased by about 1 million. Iran's population is over 65 million. But numbers are not the whole story. The Saudi population is, by these statistics, not that much smaller than Iraq's. The combined population of the members of the Gulf Cooperation Council (GCC) is very close to that of Iraq. Despite the demographics, no one in 1990 suggested that the Saudis by themselves or with their GCC allies could confront the Iraqi invasion of Kuwait.

It is the political context of the states that renders a policy of self-reliance even less feasible than the numbers suggest. The mobilization of citizen manpower into the armed forces would require obligatory military service, a very real demand of the state upon its citizens (one the United States, for example, has now chosen to avoid). A ruthless and efficient authoritarian state like Iraq or Syria can extract a large proportion of its manpower from society for military purposes. States animated by revolutionary fervor, like Iran in the 1980s, or by democratic ties of loyalty between citizen and state, like Israel (for its Jewish citizens), can call upon the population for military service and receive enthusiastic answers. Saudi Arabia (and the other Gulf monarchies) lack these kinds of mobilization abilities.

This is attributable to the type of rentier state the Saudis have chosen to build with their oil money. The Saudi "social contract" as it has developed since the early 1970s, if not before, rests upon the provision of benefits *to* citizens, not the extraction of resources (taxes and service) *from* them. Instituting a national service requirement would upset that implicit deal between state and society. In the West, the need to mobilize citizen armies contributed to pressures for popular participation in government. The ruling families in the Gulf want to avoid exacerbating the already growing demands in their societies for greater participation. Moreover, from the perspective of rulers who remember the prevalence of Arab military coups in the 1950s and 1960s, including in the armed forces people whose loyalties to the regime are questionable would decrease rather than increase security.

Military recruitment strategies in the kingdom reflect these social realities. There is no military draft in Saudi Arabia; military service is voluntary. Discussions in official Saudi circles immediately after the Gulf war about doubling the size of the armed forces, which would probably entail some kind of draft or obligatory service, appear to have been shelved.[3] Military service is not among the top professions in the country in terms of social status. With economic opportunities relatively plentiful for better-educated, young, male citizens, the incentives to join the military are limited.

Moreover, there are official and unofficial barriers to military recruitment of some groups within the kingdom. Saudi Shi'a (who make up approximately 10 percent of the Saudi citizen population) rarely join the military and even more rarely advance in the officer corps, a result of government discouragement and social custom within the community.[4] There are persistent reports, unconfirmed and unconfirmable officially, that those who do not hail from Najd (Central Arabia) cannot advance in the military hierarchy and are barred from certain sensitive positions (like that of fighter pilot). Needless to say, one-half of Saudi Arabia's human resources—female citizens—are not available for military service. Taken together, these factors mean that the kingdom cannot and will not mobilize human resources for military purposes with the same efficiency as larger neighbors. Demographic, social, and political constraints combine to rule out a policy of self-reliance in security matters.

A simple comparison of Saudi Arabia to other regional powers as to the size of armed forces relative to population points out the barriers to military mobilization. In 1990 the Saudi armed forces, including active-duty National Guard forces, totaled 111,500. Iraq, with less than double the Saudi citizen population, had a military establishment at least five times as large in 1990. Syria, with roughly the same population (only 2 million greater) had a standing armed force of over 400,000 in 1991. Jordan, with less than one-half of the Saudi citizen population, had an active force of 101,000 in 1991, nearly the same size as the Saudi forces. Israel, also with less than one-half of the Saudi citizen population, had a standing force of 141,000 and a reserve force of over 500,000 in 1991.[5]

The political and demographic barriers to full utilization of the military manpower resources in the kingdom, combined with the number of potential military threats in the region, dictate that the Saudis seek outside allies. It is logical, in such a situation, that a small state should seek the most powerful ally it can in order to deter potential enemies—and win a fight, if necessary. Thus, the U.S.-Saudi security relationship makes much sense for Riyadh. But because the nature of the security threats facing the Saudi regime are not limited to military invasion by a larger neighbor, the relationship with the United States becomes more complicated.

The lack of firm, institutionalized political links between the Saudi regime and its society opens up a new set of threats in the foreign policy sphere. It is not just military attack that the Saudi regime worries about. It also fears *political* intervention originating from abroad, based on the powerful transnational ideological platforms of pan-Arabism and Islam, aimed at stirring up its own domestic populations against it. A succession of ambitious regional figures have used propaganda and subversion, as well as military pressure, against the kingdom: Gamal 'Abd al-Nasser of Egypt in the 1950s and 1960s, Ayatollah Khomeini in the 1980s, and Saddam Hussein in 1990–1991. None of these challengers succeeded in bringing down the Saudi regime, but they all left their mark on the minds of rulers. The irony is that, having built substantial bureaucratic and coercive infrastructures, the Saudi regime is less susceptible today to this kind of foreign ideological pressure than it may have been in the past. Citizens' interests are much more focused on domestic agendas rather than on glorious but impractical transnational agendas. But it is difficult for the rulers to appreciate this change when little, if any, citizen input into the foreign policy decisionmaking process is tolerated.

Close ties with the United States open up the Saudi regime to attacks by regional enemies. Charges that the rulers have forfeited the country's independence in exchange for U.S. protection have been staples of Arab propaganda since the 1950s. Such charges are aimed at encouraging the Saudi population to oppose the regime and shake its stability domestically. As will be discussed later, the U.S. connection in the military sphere is disquieting to at least some part of the Saudi public, so these kinds of charges are seen by the Saudi rulers as having at least some potential to create domestic problems for them. This is the Saudi dilemma when it comes to relations with the United States—military security rationales require the U.S. link; domestic security imperatives require that the link be as unobtrusive as possible. Walking this tightrope has not been an easy task for the Saudis.

The Background to the U.S.-Saudi Security Relationship

U.S. interests in Saudi Arabia begin in 1933, with the granting by King 'Abd al-'Aziz of an oil concession to Standard Oil of California (SOCAL). Although SOCAL gave the king better terms than he could expect from British Petroleum, then awash with oil from Iran and Iraq, there was also a strategic element in the Saudi decision to grant the concession to a U.S. company. Britain was the patron of the Hashemite regimes in Jordan and Iraq, rivals of the Al Sa'ud whom 'Abd al-'Aziz had ejected from Hijaz less than a decade previously. Britain was also the protecting power of the smaller Gulf and South Arabian states and directly ruled Aden. With the exception of Yemen, Saudi Arabia was surrounded in the 1930s by British power. And though 'Abd al-'Aziz was careful to maintain friendly relations with London (risking civil war in the late 1920s to stop raids by his "fanatical" Wahhabi followers, the Ikhwan, into Iraq and Transjordan), he also sought the support of other outside powers to balance British influence, thus his desire for some political connection to the United States is understandable.

Washington was hesitant at the beginning to respond to Saudi political overtures. It was not until World War II that U.S. policymakers began to perceive strategic interests in the Gulf area. Even then, the region was viewed largely as a British preserve in the global division of labor between Washington and London. In 1942 and 1943, the United States supplied lend-lease financial aid to the kingdom, whose two main sources of revenue—oil production and pilgrimage traffic—had been severely curtailed by the war; it did so not directly but through Great Britain. It was only in 1944 that U.S. aid began to go directly to Riyadh, in exchange for the rights to use the large air base at Dhahran. The historic meeting of King 'Abd al-'Aziz and President Franklin Roosevelt on the latter's yacht in the Great Bitter Lake of the Suez Canal in 1945 was the first direct contact between leaders of the two countries.

Despite this new channel, the United States continued in the late 1940s to resist Saudi requests for a direct military alliance, which the Saudis wanted to counter the British-backed Hashemites. Although the United States sent numerous messages to Riyadh supporting the independence and the territorial integrity of the kingdom, a formal alliance was ruled out. The most the United States was willing to offer in terms of a military relationship was the supply of some equipment and the dispatch of a training mission in 1951, in exchange for a five-year extension of the Dhahran base rights.[6]

Even though the United States was hesitant to make a formal alliance commitment to Saudi security at this time, Washington was hardly indifferent to the kingdom. The importance of oil as a strategic commodity was underlined by the World War II experience, and U.S. economic and military planners began to see the Gulf as a centrally important area in overall U.S. strategy. Although the ambitious plans of Harold Ickes to, in effect, nationalize U.S. oil interests in the kingdom during the war fell afoul of congressional and oil company opposition, Washington sought to cement its economic relationship with Riyadh after the war by encouraging the U.S. oil consortium that formed the Arabian-American Oil Company (ARAMCO) to provide more financial support to the Saudi regime. By granting the oil companies the right to deduct from their U.S. taxes the increased share of oil revenues they paid to the Saudis, Washington in effect subsidized the Saudi regime, allowing the oil companies to pay 50 percent of their oil revenues from the kingdom to Riyadh without affecting their bottom line. The "50-50" deal, originally implemented in Venezuela, was applied to Saudi Arabia in 1950.[7]

The 1950s began to see a reversal of the pattern of Saudi desire for a close U.S. security relationship and U.S. reticence to give formal defense commitments. U.S. military supplies to the kingdom during the 1950s were substantial (though not in comparison to what would come later)—well over 100 tanks of various types and thirty-seven aircraft.[8] King Sa'ud was the first Arab leader to be received in the White House after the announcement of the 1957 Eisenhower Doctrine, which was named for U.S. President Dwight D. Eisenhower and aimed at containing communism in the Middle East.[9] However, the costs to Saudi Arabia in terms of regional and domestic politics of the close relationship with the United States became more apparent as the 1960s approached. The fall of monarchical regimes in Egypt and Iraq, in part because of domestic reactions to their close associations with Britain and British bases in those countries, brought home to the Saudis that an outside power link was not an unmitigated blessing. The pressures that built up around the rise of Gamal 'Abd al-Nasser and his brand of Arab nationalism in regional politics made association with Western powers a domestic and regional liability.

Thus, the dilemma for the Saudi leadership became acute. Just at the time when the U.S. link became important for military security, its political ramifications became very negative. The Saudi regime walked the tightrope. Military purchases from the United States were in essence halted from 1958 to the mid-1960s, as identification with the United States became more dangerous and the regular army came to be seen as a threat to the domestic security of the regime. The lease on the U.S. air base at Dhahran was allowed to run out without renewal in 1962 (its military usefulness to the United States for cold war purposes much diminished with the advent of intercontinental and sea-launched ballistic missiles). However, when Egyptian air units in Yemen began to attack areas across the Saudi-Yemeni border in 1962, the Saudis requested that U.S. fighter planes stationed at Dhahran fly demonstrative sorties over Saudi cities as a warning to Cairo.[10] In 1965 the U.S. military supply relationship with Saudi Arabia was renewed with the supply of Hawk antiaircraft systems.

Events in the late 1960s combined to increase U.S. military interest in Saudi Arabia and to lessen Saudi fears of the domestic and regional consequences of their U.S. tie. The announcement of British intent to withdraw from relationships with the smaller Gulf monarchies increased the U.S. strategic interest in the Gulf. Still mired in Vietnam, the United States had no intention of taking on new defense commitments in any formal way in the Gulf, but U.S. strategy was aimed at encouraging Iran, and to a lesser extent Saudi Arabia, to build up military forces (with U.S. weaponry) and act as regional proxies for U.S. interests. With increasing oil revenues in the early 1970s (before the price shock of 1973), Saudi Arabia's weapons purchases from the United States increased from $15.8 million in 1970 to $312.4 million in 1972.[11] With Egypt's defeat in the 1967 Arab-Israeli war and the concomitant decline in importance of Nasserist pan-Arabism in the region, the political risks of association with the United States went down. Yet, this is exactly the time that Saudi Arabia asserted its independence from the United States, in a most public and risky manner—the oil embargo and oil price increases of 1973–1974. In the minds of many Saudis, risking confrontation with the United States over Arab-Israeli issues at that time was their country's finest hour.

This brief period of confrontation with the United States quickly ended. The fourfold increase in oil prices made Saudi Arabia that much more central to U.S. policymakers and made the United States that much more important to Saudi Arabia economically, both as a consumer of oil and as a location for Saudi investments. The new oil wealth deepened the Saudi linkages to the United States. In the military sphere Riyadh directed the vast majority of its arms spending toward the United States. U.S. training missions instructed Saudi forces in the new weaponry. The U.S.

Army Corps of Engineers undertook enormous building projects in the kingdom. As Saudi Arabia was now a more valuable prize, its need for an outside protector increased. In January 1979, as the Iranian revolution was unfolding, the Saudis requested a display of military support from the United States, which complied by sending a squadron of F-15s to the kingdom (though it was publicly announced that the planes would not be armed in order not to irritate the new Iranian government).[12] In October 1980, at the outbreak of the Iran-Iraq war, U.S. AWACS (airborne warning and control system) aircraft were dispatched to the kingdom to strengthen its air defenses. Finally, with Iranian attacks on Saudi and Kuwaiti shipping growing in the 1980s, U.S. naval forces were sent to the Gulf in 1987 to protect that shipping. Though the original request came from Kuwait, the U.S. forces also escorted shipping bound for Saudi Arabia.

In the financial sphere Saudi petrodollars were recycled through U.S. (and British) banks, the Saudi government became a major purchaser of U.S. Treasury bonds, and Saudi private wealth found investment opportunities in the United States. At an April 1993 meeting in Washington on U.S.-Gulf business links, sponsored by the U.S. Department of Commerce, the GCC, and the American-Gulf Chamber of Commerce, it was reported that direct Gulf investment in the United States totaled $407 billion as of the beginning of 1992.[13] As oil prices were (and still are) denominated in U.S. dollars, the real return to Saudi Arabia of its oil sales depended on the strength of the U.S. currency. The sinews binding the United States and the Saudi regime became stronger and more ramified as a result of the oil price increases of the 1970s.

Yet the dilemma for Saudi policymakers of the domestic and regional consequences of a close relationship, at least publicly, with the United States remained. Whereas Arab nationalist pressures might have declined in the region, the Islamic political resurgence, represented in part by the Iranian revolution, was equally hostile to a U.S. military presence in the kingdom and equally able to address Saudi citizens over the head of their government. The Saudis would not support the Camp David accords, despite heavy U.S. pressure to do so. When Reagan administration officials came calling in Riyadh, at the beginning of 1981, to encourage Saudi Arabia to sign up for Secretary of State Alexander Haig's "strategic consensus" policy for the Middle East, with its emphasis on U.S. military access to regional bases, the Saudis politely refused. The GCC, of which Saudi Arabia is the largest and most important member, in its first summit meeting in May 1981 declared member states' desire "for keeping the entire region free of international conflicts, particularly the presence of military fleets and foreign bases."[14] Even as the U.S. Navy was escorting Saudi shipping in the Gulf in 1987–1988, the Saudis were very concerned to emphasize that U.S. forces had no basing rights in the kingdom. For the Saudis, a U.S. presence "over the horizon," close enough to come to the kingdom's aid but far away enough to avoid the political problems associated with the U.S. connection, was the ideal situation.

This dilemma of needing the United States in the security sphere but fearing the domestic and regional consequences of public identification with the United States forms the backdrop to the Saudi decision to invite U.S. and other foreign forces into the kingdom in early August 1990.

The U.S.-Saudi Relationship and the Gulf War

The Saudi decision to invite hundreds of thousands of U.S. troops, as well as other foreign units, to the kingdom was a major change in the nature of the U.S.-Saudi relationship. It can only be understood in light of the existing relationship between Saudi Arabia and Iraq. Riyadh had supported the Iraqi war effort against Iran politically and financially. Since the end of that war in 1988 the Saudis had been unable to resume their preferred geopolitical position of rough equidistance between the two larger Gulf powers. Ideological differences with Iran remained a serious stumbling block. Although there was certainly no love in Riyadh for Saddam Hussein, there was a continuing belief that a strong Iraq was necessary to balance Iranian ambitions.

Thus, Saudi Arabia's initial response when Iraq began to raise demands against Kuwait in the summer of 1990 was to seek a negotiated settlement that would give the Iraqis some tangible gains. The Saudis were noticeably silent when Baghdad threatened Kuwait on the issue of Kuwaiti oil production, in some measure because they themselves wanted to see Kuwait abide by its OPEC production quota (OPEC being the Organization of Petroleum Exporting Countries). At the OPEC meeting of July 25–27, 1990, Kuwait agreed to cut its production to the quota level. When Iraq continued to pressure Kuwait, the Saudis and Egyptian President Husni Mubarak joined in a mediation effort in late July that resulted in the Kuwaiti-Iraqi meeting of August 1 in the Saudi city of Jeddah, just one day before the invasion.

Circumstantial evidence indicates that although there was no detailed Saudi-Egyptian plan put forward to the parties at Jeddah, the thrust behind their mediation effort was to extract some concessions from Kuwait to mollify Saddam. Egyptian President Husni Mubarak revealed after the invasion that he had told the Kuwaitis that they should make an offer including border modifications and financial aid to Iraq.[15] Saudi decisionmakers have not been as revealing about their stance in those days, but there are indications that Riyadh had about the same idea. The Saudis had pressured Kuwait before the invasion to reduce their oil production to their OPEC quota, as Saddam had demanded.[16] Crown Prince Hassan of Jordan told an interviewer that on August 2, King Fahd had asked King Hussein of Jordan to get the Iraqis "to withdraw to the disputed area" on the border, not completely out of Kuwait.[17] Yemeni President 'Ali 'Abdallah Salih said that on August 5 King Fahd had told him that Kuwait had been mistaken in its hard-line policy toward Iraq.[18]

Comments by Saudi Defense Minister Prince Sultan ibn 'Abd al-'Aziz in late October 1990 also give some hint as to the Saudi stand. Prince Sultan, after assuring that Saudi Arabia would not accept any solution short of unconditional Iraqi withdrawal from Kuwait and the return of the Kuwaiti government, referred to the general Saudi position on how to settle inter-Arab problems. He said that "any Arab who has a right vis-à-vis his brother Arab must assert it, but not by means of using force. This is an undesirable thing." He indicated that Saudi Arabia "is among those who call for Arab national security, including brotherly concessions from Arab to Arab, whether such a right is established or more doubtful." He went on to say that "it is not a bad thing for any Arab country to give a brother Arab country land, or money, or access to the sea."[19] The Western press saw Sultan's remarks as a signal of Saudi willingness to compromise with Iraq.[20] However, given that the quote came directly after Sultan's direct refusal to accept anything but an unconditional Iraqi withdrawal from Kuwait, it might be more accurate to interpret his remarks as an indication of what Saudi policy was *before* the invasion, defending Saudi efforts at avoiding this crisis and indirectly criticizing the Kuwaitis for refusal to compromise.

The Saudis' sense of shock and betrayal at the Iraqi invasion reflected not only the unprecedented nature of the action, but also the feeling that Saddam had reneged on a tentative agreement that the Saudis had constructed for his benefit.[21] Their perception of Saddam's ultimate intentions must have been colored by this very specific sense that the Iraqi leader could not be trusted to keep his commitments. Little else can explain the relatively quick decision by the Saudis to abandon their historical position regarding U.S. ground forces. Although much has been made of the two-day delay in taking this decision, and of the hints of differences of opinion within the Saudi royal family over it, more striking is the ease with which the Saudis reversed their past aversion to an open U.S. military presence in the kingdom and the lack of substantial opposition within the ruling elite to that policy. Even if some members of the royal family were unhappy with the decision, they did not make a public or even a quasi-public issue out of their feelings. The religious establishment, which might also have been expected to oppose the deployment of U.S. troops, officially approved the policy line in a *fatwa* (religious judgment) by Shaykh 'Abdallah bin 'Abd al-'Aziz bin Baz, now the Grand Mufti of the kingdom.[22]

Once they accepted the U.S. military presence, the Saudis were in effect committed to the U.S. strategy of confrontation with Saddam. Between mid-August 1990 and late February 1991 Saudi Arabia took a back seat to U.S. political and military leaders in the crisis. During this period the regime used its propaganda organs, diplomatic weight, and financial clout to garner support within the Arab and Muslim worlds for its policy. Although attracting considerable political and some military support from other governments in the region, the regime's efforts to persuade Arab and Muslim public opinions of the legitimacy of the decision met with much less success.

As the crisis proceeded, and particularly in the postcrisis period, some of the old reservations about a high-profile U.S. military presence in the kingdom began to resurface. In late November 1990 King Fahd, in a speech to the country, denied that Saudi Arabia had made any agreements for the permanent stationing of foreign forces in the kingdom.[23] In a statement to the press immediately after the Gulf war, Saudi Defense Minister Prince Sultan referred to a commitment on the part of the United States to withdraw its forces from the kingdom once their mission was completed.[24] In September 1991, during one of the U.S. confrontations with Iraq over application of the United Nations (UN) resolutions, Prince Sultan expressed misgivings about the very public way in which the United States was using Saudi Arabia as a military staging area against Iraq and urged Washington to spread its deployments out to Kuwait and even to capture an airfield in Iraq itself to use as a base.[25] During subsequent U.S.-Iraqi confrontations in October 1994 and September 1996, Sultan reiterated his reluctance to allow the United States to use Saudi facilities to stage attacks on Iraq.[26] Saudi Arabia, unlike the smaller Gulf monarchies, has not negotiated a formal defense agreement with the United States in the wake of the war.[27]

The continuing worry in the Saudi regime about limiting to the greatest extent possible the public profile of its U.S. military connection stems from fears about the domestic consequences of that connection. It is within Islamic political currents in the kingdom that disquiet about the role of the United States is greatest. During the crisis there were some indications of discontent within religious circles about the U.S. military presence, but manifestations of that discontent were limited.[28] After the Gulf war indications of unease from Islamic political circles over the new relationship between the kingdom and the United States emerged more clearly. In the spring of 1991 over 400 religious officials and political activists addressed a petition to King Fahd regarding changes they wanted to see in the kingdom's policies. Although the bulk of the petition dealt with domestic issues, the signers also called on the government to avoid alliances that run counter to Islamic legitimacy and to acquire arms from a variety of sources, including the building of a domestic arms industry.[29] Both of these statements could be read as a warning about overreliance on the United States.

The clearest indication of opposition to the direction of U.S.-Saudi relations came in a detailed, forty-six page Memorandum of Advice directed to the king in the summer of 1992 and signed by over 100 Islamic political activists. The bulk of the memorandum, like the shorter petition mentioned above, dealt with domestic affairs. It did, however, in much clearer terms than the other petition, challenge the foreign policy lines set down by the kingdom in the wake of the Gulf war. It called for an end to the practice of giving loans and gifts to what it termed "un-Islamic" regimes like "Ba'thist Syria and secular Egypt," pointing to the folly of funding Saddam's Iraq during its war with Iran. It said that the Gulf crisis pointed out the "lack of correspondence between the enormous military budgets and the number and capabilities of the forces" and called for expanding the army to 500,000 men (an increase of at least 400 percent), obligatory military training, the diversification of foreign arms sources, and the building of a domestic arms industry. The signers criticized the government for not supporting Islamic movements but rather providing aid to states that "wage war" against such movements, like Algeria, and called for a strengthening of relations with all Islamic tendencies, be they states, political movements, or individuals.

The signers of the memorandum were very leery of the close relations the government had with Western regimes, "which lead the assault against Islam," and particularly in "following the United States of America in most policies, relations and decisions, like the rushing into the peace process with the Jews." It urged the government to "avoid any kind of alliance or cooperation which serves imperialist goals" and to "cancel all military treaties and conventions which impinge on the sovereignty of the state and its independence in administering and arming its military." The memorandum was particularly scathing regarding the kingdom's reliance on arms supplies from the United States, a country that "gives us what it wants, denies us what it does not want us to have, exploits us in times of trouble, and bargains with us during times of calamity."[30]

In November 1995, a bomb destroyed the Riyadh office of the American training mission working with the Saudi National Guard. Five Americans and two Indian employees of the mission were killed. Four Saudis were arrested for the bombing and confessed on television to being members of the Islamic opposition. They were executed in May 1996.[31] Less than one month later, in June 1996, a car bomb exploded in front of an apartment building housing U.S. Air Force personnel in Dhahran (in Saudi Arabia's Eastern Province). Nineteen Americans died and nearly 400 Americans, Saudis, and others were wounded. As of summer 1998, there have been no convictions either in Saudi Arabia or the United States of the perpetrators of the Dhahran bombing. The American personnel, most of whom were involved in maintaining air reconnaissance of the "no-fly zone" in southern Iraq, were subsequently moved from Dhahran to an isolated desert airbase south of Riyadh.[32]

These indications of domestic opposition to a high-profile U.S. role in Saudi security plans, as well as the current indications that the regime wants to avoid inflaming that opposition, should not obscure the fact that the U.S.-Saudi security relationship since Desert Storm has been extremely close. Between August 1990 and the end of 1992 Saudi Arabia placed weapons orders worth more than $25 billion with U.S. arms manufacturers.[33] The centrality of Saudi arms purchases for U.S. suppliers was made clear in the January 1994 agreement between Riyadh and five of the largest U.S. military contractors, allowing the Saudis to stretch out payments for many of those weapons.[34] Falling oil prices and the depletion of financial reserves during Desert Storm have placed new fiscal constraints on the Saudi government, but it remains the most important foreign customer for U.S. weapons manufacturers. As of 1997, more than five years after the Gulf war, approximately 5,000 U.S. military personnel and anywhere from 100 to 200 U.S. warplanes are stationed in Saudi Arabia at any one time, along with an extensive naval force in and around the Persian Gulf.[35] Military consultations between the two countries continue at the highest levels. The continuing economic importance of the kingdom for the United States was underlined by the Saudi decision in February 1994 to buy $6 billion in commercial aircraft from U.S. rather than European companies. President Bill Clinton personally lobbied Saudi leaders, including King Fahd, on the issue.[36]

Conclusion

Even after the experience of the Gulf war, the dilemma that characterizes Saudi relations with the United States remains. The need for a U.S. security link is clear. Much of the reluctance to acknowledge that need before the Saudi public and the region has disappeared. Yet the Saudi leadership continues to feel at least somewhat constrained by important elements of domestic public opinion in codifying that relationship in an open military alliance or in formally and publicly permitting U.S.

military bases in the kingdom. This tension in U.S.-Saudi relations predates Desert Storm and continues despite that extraordinary phase in the history of security ties between Washington and Riyadh. It is a permanent part of the relationship.

Notes

1. Much of the material in this chapter is culled from previous work the author has done on security and political issues in the Gulf area. See F. Gregory Gause III, *Oil Monarchies: Domestic and Security Challenges in the Arab Gulf States* (New York: Council on Foreign Relations Press, 1994); idem, "Saudi Arabia: Desert Storm and After," in Robert O. Freedman, ed., *The Middle East After Iraq's Invasion of Kuwait* (Gainesville: University Press of Florida, 1993); and idem, "Gulf Regional Politics: Revolution, War, and Rivalry," in W. Howard Wriggins, ed., *Dynamics of Regional Politics: Four Systems on the Indian Ocean Rim* (New York: Columbia University Press, 1992).

2. Results of the Saudi census were reported in *New York Times,* December 18, 1992, p. A8. The demographic analysis firm of Birks Sinclair and Associates, publisher of the *Gulf Market Report* with long experience in the region, estimated the 1992 Saudi population to be 12.3 million, of whom 8.1 million were citizens. The Birks Sinclair estimate was cited by Roger Hardy, *Arabia After the Storm: Internal Stability of the Gulf Arab States* (London: Middle East Programme Report, Royal Institute for International Affairs, 1992).

3. See *New York Times,* October 13, 1991, pp. 1, 18; October 25, 1991, p. A9, for references to the Saudi proposals. Since that time there have been no moves to expand the size of the Saudi military.

4. Leaders of the Saudi Shi'a community addressed a petition to King Fahd in 1991. In it they complained of a "quarantine" against the entrance of Saudi Shi'a into the armed forces. Practically identical versions of this petition can be found in *Makka News,* no. 7 (April 6, 1991), and in *Arabia Monitor* 1(6) (July 1992). The former is published by the Organization of the Islamic Revolution in the Arabian Peninsula, an Iranian-supported exile group with a U.S. post office box in Bowling Green, Kentucky. The latter is a monthly newsletter published in Washington by the International Committee for Human Rights in the Gulf and Arabian Peninsula. Both have apparently stopped publication as a result of an agreement between the Saudi government and Saudi Shi'a activists in late 1993. *Washington Post,* October 16, 1993, p. A15; *New York Times,* October 29, 1993, p. A11.

5. Figures taken from International Institute for Strategic Studies, *The Military Balance, 1990–91* and *The Military Balance, 1991–92* (London: Brassey's for the International Institute for Strategic Studies, 1990, 1991).

6. Nadav Safran, *Saudi Arabia: The Ceaseless Quest for Security* (Cambridge: Harvard University Press, 1985), pp. 58–69.

7. For an account both of Ickes's plans and the 50-50 deal, see Daniel Yergin, *The Prize* (New York: Simon and Schuster, 1991), chs. 20–22.

8. Safran, *Saudi Arabia,* pp. 103–104.

9. King Sa'ud of course had his own agenda, aimed at strengthening the Saudi position in the region, in backing the Eisenhower Doctrine. Those ambitions themselves led to some strains in the U.S.-Saudi relationship. See David W. Lesch, *Syria and the United States: Eisenhower's Cold War in the Middle East* (Boulder: Westview Press, 1992), pp. 127–189, and David W. Lesch, "The Saudi Role in the 1957 American-Syrian Crisis," *Middle East Policy* 1(3) (1992).

10. Safran, *Saudi Arabia*, pp. 92–96.

11. U.S. Congress, House of Representatives, Committee on Foreign Affairs, Subcommittee on Near East, *New Perspectives on the Persian Gulf*, 93rd Congress, 1st Session (Washington, D.C.: Government Printing Office), p. 47.

12. Safran, *Saudi Arabia*, p. 301.

13. *al-Hayat*, April 23, 1993, p. 12.

14. R. K. Ramazani, ed., *The Gulf Cooperation Council: Record and Analysis* (Charlottesville: University Press of Virginia, 1988), doc. 9, p. 28.

15. *New York Times*, November 8, 1990, p. 14.

16. *New York Times*, July 18, 1990, pp. D1, D5; July 25, 1990, p. 8; July 27, 1990, p. 2.

17. *New York Times*, September 21, 1990, p. 1.

18. *New York Times*, October 26, 1990, p. 11.

19. *al-Hayat*, October 22, 1991, pp. 1, 7.

20. *New York Times*, October 23, 1990, p. 1; October 27, 1990, p. 4.

21. In a speech to Saudis in early January 1991, King Fahd emphasized the sense of personal betrayal he felt when he heard that Saddam had invaded Kuwait. *New York Times*, January 7, 1991, p. 10.

22. The full text of the *fatwa* can be found in *al-Sharq al-'Awsat*, August 21, 1990, p. 4.

23. *al-Sharq al-'Awsat*, November 28, 1990, p. 3.

24. *al-Hayat*, March 14, 1991, p. 1.

25. *New York Times*, September 30, 1991, p. A5.

26. Charles Aldinger, "Saudis Declined to Base U.S. Arms," Reuters (on-line), November 4, 1994; "Saudi Against Hosting U.S. Raids on Iraq," Reuters (on-line), September 11, 1996.

27. Personal interview with a ranking Saudi official, Jeddah, October 1992. See also *New York Times*, October 13, 1991, pp. 1, 18; October 25, 1991, p. A9.

28. See remarks by Dr. Safar al-Hawali, dean of Islamic Studies at 'Umm al-Qura University in Mecca, published by the *New York Times*, November 24, 1990, p. 21. See also *New York Times*, December 25, 1990, p. 6.

29. The author obtained a copy of the "Islamist" petition from sources in Saudi Arabia. English-language versions of this petition can be found in *Foreign Broadcast Information Service*—Near East and South Asia (hereinafter *FBIS*/NESA), May 23, 1991, p. 21 (translation of a version published in the Cairo newspaper *al-Sha'b*); *Makka News*, no. 8, June 16, 1991; and Middle East Watch, "Empty Reforms: Saudi Arabia's New Basic Laws," pp. 61–62.

30. The author obtained copies of the Memorandum of Advice in Saudi Arabia. All translations are mine. One of the copies was dated Muharram 1413, which corresponds to July 1992, indicating that it was in circulation before the fall of 1992, when Western news organizations reported on it (*New York Times*, October 8, 1992, p. A6).

31. For an interesting discussion on the background of one of those executed, see Ethan Bronner, "In Bomber's Life, Glimpse of Saudi Dissent," *Boston Globe*, July 7, 1996.

32. John C. Roper, "U.S. Saudi Arabia Agree on Troop Move," *United Press International* (on-line), July 31, 1996.

33. Arms Control Association, "U.S. Arms Transfers to the Middle East Since the Invasion of Kuwait—Fact Sheet," October 8, 1992 (Washington, D.C.: the Association).

34. *New York Times*, February 1, 1994, p. A6.

35. International Institute for Strategic Studies, *The Military Balance 1997/98* (Oxford University Press, 1997), pp. 26, 140.

36. *New York Times*, February 17, 1994, p. 1.

21

The Invasion of Kuwait and the Gulf War: Dilemmas Facing the Israeli-Iraqi-U.S. Relationship

Yair Evron

The objective of this chapter is to describe and analyze Israeli policy during the Gulf crisis and war. Although much of the essay is devoted to Israeli policy toward Iraq, there will be a special discussion of the U.S.-Israeli relationship during that period and how it affected Israeli policy preferences.

Israel's geostrategic position and its conflict with the Arab world raise several policy issues. Yet since its establishment Israel has assigned the greatest importance to its relationship with the United States. Policymakers have differed at times about foreign policy orientations (for example, the importance attached during part of the 1950s to a French orientation), but there has been a constant consensus among them that the connection with the United States is critical. Although the two countries have differed sharply at times about certain policy issues, both sides have strived to avoid a major falling out.

Over the years two sets of variables have affected U.S. policy toward Israel. First, ideological, moral, and emotional attachments combined with the influence of the pro-Israeli lobby to create a basic moral commitment to the security and very existence of Israel. Second, Israel was perceived as a strong regional military power that could serve as an ally during periods of regional crisis. Although the first set of variables has been effective throughout the existence of Israel, the second emerged only in the 1960s, became more salient during the late 1960s and early 1970s, and reached its culmination during the early 1980s. Thus, both "soft factors" and "hard" realpolitik considerations contributed to the creation of a "special relationship" with Israel.[1] Clearly, the relative weight of these different factors has varied with time.

The Israeli-Iraqi Deterrence Relationship

The eight-year war between Iraq and Iran well served Israeli strategic interests. The "eastern front" concept, a focus of much discussion and expectation during part of the 1970s, became a complete mirage with Syria isolated and the peace with Egypt holding firm. Consequently, Israel's relative military situation greatly benefited. However, with the end of the Iran-Iraq war in 1988 and with Saddam Hussein shifting his attention and ambitions to the Arab parts of the Middle East, Israel again faced threats from the east.

To be sure, during 1988 and 1989, Saddam cooperated with Egypt and other Arab countries in establishing a central moderate bloc in the Arab world. Moreover, even from the mid-1980s, Iraq—involved as it was in the exhausting war with Iran and seeking whatever support it could get from Egypt—made diplomatic noises in support of the peace process with Israel. In response, some in Israel favored signaling Iraq of Israel's readiness to pursue a process of accommodation. Indeed, Israel sent a tacit signal in that direction when it let it be known it would not obstruct plans to lay an Iraqi pipeline through Jordan up to Aqaba. At the same time, however, Israeli decisionmakers remained very suspicious of Iraqi intentions and assumed that once Iraq was freed from the war it might join an anti-Israeli coalition.[2]

By 1990, Saddam began to seek a new position of influence in the region and to this end used the old Arab means of placing himself at the head of a "rejectionist" front, that is, in opposition to the 1979 Egyptian-Israeli peace treaty and to the approach calling for peaceful settlement of the Arab-Israel conflict. This quickly brought Iraq into deep discord with Egypt.[3] Thus, as had happened before, inter-Arab competition spilled over into the Arab-Israeli conflict, or, more accurately, the Arab-Israeli conflict was used as an instrument in the context of inter-Arab competition. However, as we shall discuss later, by the late 1980s the attitude of many Arab elites toward Israel had already changed, thus proving Saddam Hussein's strategy ineffective.

To be sure, Saddam's new stance did not immediately bring about a major division in the Arab world. For some time, the leaderships of Egypt and the Gulf states belonging to the central bloc tried to downplay these differences. But Saddam's stance quickly evolved into a real threat to this emerging bloc. Indeed, the extent of Saddam's ambition to alter the balance of power within the Arab world to his own advantage was reflected by Syrian reactions. Always sensitive to changes in power relationships within the Arab state system and fearful of Iraqi ambitions, by late 1988 Syria had already begun to move toward reconciliation with Egypt. When Iraq invaded Kuwait, the possibility of a change in the Arab balance of power was such that Egypt, with Syrian cooperation, led the way to the formation of the anti-Iraqi Arab coalition, which was ready to join the United States in constituting the international war coalition.[4]

Already in 1988–1989, fears persisted in Israel that the eastern front concept might become a reality. Of particular concern to Israel were the various developments and activities in Iraq with respect to the buildup of nuclear and other weapons of mass destruction and of surface-to-surface missiles (SSMs, better known as scuds) with ranges that reached into Israel. These Israeli concerns combined with Iraqi suspicions about Israel's counteractivities to bring about what might be called a "deterrence dialogue" between the two states.[5]

During 1989–1990, two factors led to the Iraqi initiation of that dialogue: First, the decision to use threats against Israel as part of the above-mentioned overall Iraqi strategy against the Egyptian-led "peace" bloc in the Arab world; and second, Iraqi fears that Israel was planning to attack the Iraqi nuclear infrastructure. Iraq's reactions to that perceived threat were multifaceted, consisting of appeals to the international community to pressure Israel into placing its own nuclear facilities under international controls, as well as threats to Israel that any attack on Iraqi "industrial" facilities would be met by harsh Iraqi retaliation. In addition, the Iraqis devoted a good deal of resources and energy to the development and quick deployment of military assets that could have substantiated their deterrent threats against Israel, including the deployment in western Iraq of SSMs capable of reaching Israel. Finally, Iraq constantly referred to its chemical weapons capability, emphasizing that it was capable of delivering this as well to Israel.

Israel, as mentioned, became increasingly concerned about the Iraqi buildup of weapons of mass destruction. It was primarily concerned about the nuclear effort and during 1989–1990 communicated its apprehensions to the United States and other Western powers. Indeed, by that time Western intelligence services had become equally concerned about Iraqi activities and decided to take measures against them. This, coupled with Israel's continued public reports about the Iraqi activity, led, as mentioned earlier, to the Iraqi threats to retaliate against Israel if the latter was to attack Iraqi facilities.

Moreover, by April 1990, Saddam had intensified the Iraqi deterrent campaign against Israel and, at least rhetorically, assumed an even more bellicose posture when he threatened to "burn half of Israel" (presumably referring to use of Iraq's chemical weapons capability).[6] This extreme locution caused a shift in Israeli and international perceptions of Iraqi intentions. Until that point the Israeli assessment of the Iraqi leadership tended to be cautious and tentative. On the one hand Iraqi military capabilities were seen as a potential danger to Israel, but on the other the Iraqi leadership was perceived as rational and not necessarily harboring any military intent against Israel. The April speech was still interpreted as primarily a deterrent threat—but with the added nuance of a more aggressive intent.

Israel actually had no intentions of attacking the Iraqi nuclear facilities and sought to reassure Iraq in this regard by sending messages to Baghdad through Washington and Cairo. Indeed, Saddam, for his part, sought to reassure Washington about his own intentions, stressing that his speech was meant to serve only as a deterrent. However, probably as part of his campaign to emerge as the leader of the Arab world, on June 18, 1990, Saddam extended his deterrence posture against Israel by stating that Iraq would retaliate against Israel not only if it attacked Iraq, but also if it attacked any Arab territory "from Mauritania to Syria." This general threat could have covered many contingencies and, if seriously intended, could have led to a direct confrontation between Israel and Iraq if there was any clash between Israeli forces and any Arab force or community. Although it seemed inconceivable that Saddam indeed meant what he said, the enhanced threat deepened Israeli concerns.

During the Kuwaiti crisis, Iraqi threats to strike at Israel continued. They specified an Israeli attack on Iraq as the cause for a counterattack on Israel. However, the nature of the response was kept ambiguous: Usually, chemical weapons were not mentioned but occasionally they were referred to. Moreover, the use of the latter was sometimes referred to as a response to any form of Israeli attack, whereas other statements invoked that threat only as a response to an Israeli attack with nonconventional weapons. As the crisis unfolded, Iraqi strategy moved from deterrence to coercive threats. For example, Iraq warned that if the international embargo continued, it would attack Israel. But more often, Iraq warned that if the United States initiated war against it, it would retaliate against Israel as well. As the outbreak of war drew closer, Iraqi threats intensified. For example, after the failure of the Geneva meeting between U.S. Secretary of State James Baker and Iraqi Foreign Minister Tariq 'Aziz on January 7, 1991, 'Aziz declared explicitly that if war broke out Iraq would certainly strike at Israel.[7]

The Iraqi threats were credible precisely because they reflected a wider political strategy. Iraq's intention was to undermine the international coalition; therefore it sought to provoke Israel into military retaliation, hoping that this would impel the Arab states to opt out of the coalition. Without their political backing, the war against Iraq would cease. In addition, successful missile attacks on Israel would bolster Saddam Hussein's prestige in the Arab world and inflame popular sentiment. The Iraqi signals, therefore, ceased to serve a deterrence strategy and became a valid indication of Iraqi intentions.

Throughout that period, Israel insisted that it was not involved in the crisis and would not intervene in it. At the same time, it adopted a strong deterrence posture against Iraqi strikes at Israel, warning Iraq that Israeli retaliation would be extreme. However, the nature and scope of the retaliation were not specified, nor was there any indication of the proportion between provocation and retaliation. Indeed, the ambiguity surrounding the nature of the possible Israeli retaliation led many observers to assume that it might involve the use of nuclear weapons,[8] although Israeli spokesmen never made any explicit reference to this. The Israeli intention was probably to keep Saddam Hussein guessing and increase his uncertainty. The ambiguity also allowed Israel freedom of choice in the event deterrence failed. It could then decide whether to retaliate or not and in which way, according to its assessment of gains versus costs at the time.

As it happened, the Israeli deterrent threats did not deter Iraq from launching a series of SSM strikes at Israel. The main reason for Israel's forbearance reflected the very Iraqi rationale for launching these strikes; it was feared that retaliation by Israel might undermine the campaign that the coalition forces were conducting against Iraq. This campaign promised to bring about the destruction of the Iraqi military machine, thus eliminating one of the most powerful hostile Arab armies, one that might have joined a war coalition against Israel in the event Iraq survived the crisis without a military confrontation.

It was clear from the outset that the interests of Israel and of some of the Arab parties in the coalition coincided or even partially overlapped. All were afraid of the growing power of Iraq under Saddam and of his brute ambitions. Egypt, for its part, was also concerned that Iraq was trying to lead an Arab coalition seeking to undermine Egyptian centrality in the Arab state system and propounding an alternative to Egypt's policy on the resolution of the Arab-Israeli conflict. Syria, as always in the past, was more concerned about Iraqi power than about its own fortunes in the context of the Arab-Israeli conflict. Finally, both the Arab parties of the coalition and Israel espoused a U.S. orientation (Syria had adopted one following the Soviet empire's disintegration and the USSR retreat from a central position in the Middle East).

U.S.-Israeli Relations Before and During the War

The strong anti-Soviet stance of the Reagan administration (until the second half of the 1980s) reinforced the closeness that had characterized U.S.-Israeli relations since the 1960s. The end of the cold war, which roughly coincided with the last years of the Reagan administration and the beginning of the Bush administration, seemed to raise doubts about the depth of the special relationship. Interestingly enough, these doubts were voiced primarily by Israeli observers and analysts, who tended to argue that with the passing of the great global conflict U.S. interest in the special relationship with Israel would disappear, as the new structure of the international system had its own dynamism (and hence, objectively, the nature of U.S.-Israeli relations would change).

This analysis, however, seemed to overlook the input of Israeli policy into U.S. policy formulation. Israeli policy had much more to do with U.S. formulation of its policy vis-à-vis Israel than the change in the structure of the international system. The disagreements between the Israeli government under Likud leadership on the one hand and the U.S. policy planners on the other deepened during the second half of the 1980s. With the decline in Soviet power in the Middle East and the emergence of the United States as the predominant external power in the region, the superpower's need to stabilize this region has increased as well. A paradox emerged: During the era of competitive bipolarity U.S. and Soviet interests were in profound competition in the region, and this made the resolution of conflicts there (primarily the Arab-Israeli one) more difficult. Yet, at the same time, the two superpowers did cooperate in preempting major crises and even more so in terminating regional wars—all this when there was the danger that such crises might escalate into a direct superpower confrontation. Thus, the competition made peace less likely but, at the same time, preempted unlimited regional wars and added a certain measure of stabilizing deterrence to the regional strategic situation.

Yet when competitive bipolarity ended and the United States became the predominant power, the potential for conflict resolution or at least management increased, even as the element of stabilization, in the event of war, through joint superpower crisis management disappeared. The need, therefore, for managing the various conflicts through political means became more salient. In addition, the decline of Soviet influence prompted some of its former Arab allies to seek a political accommodation with the United States. This willingness, supported as it was by leading U.S. allies such as Egypt and the Gulf states (primarily Saudi Arabia), created an opportunity for the United States to further fortify its position in the Middle East. However, these positive developments left one major issue outstanding: The need for a substantive political process designed to manage the Arab-Israeli conflict. The basic notion of the parameters for such management has always been available in Washington, that is, "territory for peace." But precisely such a plan ran sharply counter to the Israeli government under Likud.

From 1984, Labor and Likud cooperated in national coalition governments, but the Likud component was sufficiently strong to block any peace initiative based on the territory-for-peace approach. Indeed, one major effort initiated by then Foreign Minister Shimon Peres in 1987, the "London Agreement" (which in fact amounted to the initiation of a peace process between Israel and Jordan but formally and structurally accorded with the idea of an international conference), was clearly rejected by then Prime Minister Yitzhak Shamir. Gradually, the special relationship between the United States and Israel, augmented by the perception of Israel as a strategic asset, was increasingly strained by the pair's disagreements concerning the peace process.

Here it should be emphasized that the analysis mentioned above, according to which the U.S. commitment to Israel as well as the special relationship between the two countries was largely an outcome of cold war bipolarity, never fully reflected the multifaceted U.S. approach to Israel. I shall return to this point later. In any case, U.S. policy on the peace process and its ability to exert pressure on Israel within that context were colored, during the Bush administration, by the Gulf crisis and war, to which we now turn.

Initially, Israeli analysts were convinced that Iraq was too exhausted following its long war with Iran to turn its energy westward and challenge the Egyptian approach to the conflict and promote a militant alternative. Israeli decisionmakers were thus convinced that Iraq did not present an immediate threat. On the contrary, some analysts maintained during the Iran-Iraq war that Iran posed a much graver threat to Israel than Iraq. Only from 1989–1990, as mentioned earlier, did Israeli analysts become increasingly concerned about Iraqi intentions. However, on the eve of the Kuwaiti crisis Israeli analysts, similar to U.S. ones (as well as Egyptian, Saudi, and Kuwaiti), reckoned that Iraq was not about to invade Kuwait.

But the invasion, naturally, changed all that. Israeli analysts now began to take the Iraqi overall military threat very seriously. Iraq's ability to move large military formations over long distances and the precision with which its forces undertook the actual invasion further impressed the danger upon Israel. The destruction of the Iraqi military machine became a major strategic interest for Israel. Initially, Israeli decisionmakers and the Israeli media doubted U.S. readiness to mount a quick military reaction to the invasion. The decisiveness with which the administration did react, however, quickly changed that perception. While backing U.S. policy, Israel insisted that the crisis itself was unrelated to it. Once the war started, the possibility that Israeli retaliation against Iraq might weaken the coalition was sufficient to dictate a policy of uncharacteristic self-restraint.

Thus, when the United States turned to Israel (following the first Iraqi SSM strikes) and both begged and demanded Israeli forbearance, this was met with understanding in Jerusalem. When attacks continued, however, the pressure within Israel to retaliate increased, and indeed a strong lobby in the military insisted that this course be taken. Nevertheless, it appears that both the political leadership and the highest military command realized early on that Israeli strategic interests would not be served by any retaliation. In addition, the United States used a "carrot" by offering Israel several inducements so that the urge to retaliate, so deeply rooted in the Israeli psyche, would not come to the fore.

Already during the war several Israeli observers began to realize that decisive U.S. action would considerably enhance its political and strategic position in the Middle East. The outcome would be—so the argument ran—that in the aftermath of the war, the United States would be in a much stronger position to apply pressure on both Israel and the Arab states to reach a political compromise. Such a realization was held primarily by some of the "realist doves" (other, more radical Israeli left-wingers, driven by outdated anti-American feelings, opposed the war altogether). On the "right" side of the political spectrum, it was initially expected that the United States would prove itself a paper tiger and at the last moment duck war. This perception was also rooted in an overall anti-American approach, based on the argument that the U.S. could not be relied upon. The correlate to this, of course, was that Israel should not heed U.S. preferences regarding the territories. Once the war broke out and their analysis proved wrong, the right-wingers were initially delighted at the destruction of Iraqi military capabilities, but eventually some of them began to realize that following the war the United States might take a stronger stance toward Israel. However, the main leadership of Likud gave full backing to the U.S. effort.[9]

Indeed, once the war was over, with the United States enjoying a reinforced position in the Middle East, Washington began energetically to launch a new peace plan. This time, however, two elements in the Arab world were perceived in a very new light in the United States. On the one hand, the full-fledged backing that the Palestine Liberation Organization (PLO) had given Saddam created total distrust in Washington, even among officials who had previously been interested in making overtures toward the PLO. On the other hand, the participation of Syria in the coalition contributed to the emergence of a strong U.S. inclination to try and bring about peace between Damascus and Jerusalem on the basis of the territory-for-peace approach.

The predominant position that the United States acquired in the Middle East was based on its credibility as a power ready to back its commitments through use of force. In a region characterized by the widespread use of force (or threat thereof) for the achievement of political objectives, such a U.S. posture was perceived as essential to the active pursuit of a peace process between Arabs and Israelis. Indeed, this posture laid the groundwork for developments that led to the Madrid peace conference of late 1991.

The enhanced domestic prestige the administration gained from the war also allowed Washington to disregard both the Likud government and the pro-Israeli lobby in the United States on a central outstanding issue between the two countries: the loan guarantees.[10] Here, indeed, the administration was ready to create a real crisis with Israel. Thus, following the Gulf war, the United States was ready to apply greater pressure to both Israelis and Arabs in order to facilitate a process leading to the resolution of the conflict.

U.S.-Israeli-Jordanian Relations

One of the most paradoxical developments that occurred during the war involved the relationships among the United States, Jordan, Iraq, and Israel. This requires a brief look backwards. Beginning in the 1930s (some developments having taken place even in the 1920s), there gradually emerged an accommodative relationship between the Zionist leadership and then Israel, on the one hand, and the Hashemite rulers in Transjordan and then Jordan on the other. This was based on the mutual realization of a set of shared or at least coincidental interests between these two entities. This relationship had its ups and downs, but from the 1950s on Israeli governments not only grasped these shared interests but also perceived Jordan as an important strategic asset in the sense that it served as a buffer zone between Israel and the more militarily powerful Iraq (and, to a lesser extent, Syria).[11] It was only in 1981 that an Israeli government first began to alter this basic perception. In the second Likud government (1981–1984), several leading decisionmakers began to voice the view of "Jordan is Palestine," meaning that the Palestinian problem must be resolved in a Jordanian framework with the correlate that the West Bank could then be annexed into Israel. A direct implication of that approach was the undermining of the Hashemite regime. Although the de facto Israeli-Jordanian cooperation in some dimensions of day-to-day security continued even then, this attitude surely created serious concern in Jordan. Indeed, the Israeli invasion of Lebanon in 1982 and some of its unstated objectives further aggravated that concern.

The return of Labor to the national coalition government had a reassuring effect. But the rejection of the London peace plan of 1987, the collapse of the coalition government in 1990, and the return to a government of Likud and the extreme right-wing parties rekindled Jordan's apprehensions. Presumably this concern about Israeli intentions toward Jordan, combined with other considerations, helped in strengthening the Jordanian-Iraqi relationship. The thing that began to concern Israel was the growing military cooperation between Iraq and Jordan during 1990, including visits by Iraqi military missions. During the crisis and the war itself, there was some concern that Iraqi forces might be deployed in Jordan, thus posing a direct threat to Israel and violating a long-standing Israeli casus belli. A very grave strategic situation might then have affected Israeli-Jordanian relations.

However, the saliency of constant geostrategic variables in the Middle East manifested itself yet again. The tremendous importance for Israel of an independent Jordan under the Hashemite leadership as a buffer zone, and the basic Jordanian interest in maintaining its independence from all its Arab neighbors (including Iraq), combined to bring about de facto strategic cooperation between the two countries during the war.[12] Indeed, it was the Israeli definition of an Arab military intervention in Jordan as a casus belli that helped Jordan in persuading Iraq not to send military forces to Jordan during the war. Thus, Israeli deterrence helped Jordan in keeping some distance from Baghdad in the best interests of both Israel and Jordan. This complicated game helped to re-create the tacit alliance between Israel and Jordan in regard to two basic issues: military stability along the Israeli-Jordanian border and the preemption of foreign Arab military intervention in Jordan. Indeed, the cognitive impact on the Likud leaders was quite significant. At long last, the same Likud decisionmakers that worked to undermine the Israeli-Jordanian tacit cooperative relationship suddenly realized the tremendous strategic importance of Jordan as a buffer country for Israel. This changed perception served as the background for Israeli-Jordanian high-level contacts during the war, all of which came to fruition with the October 1994 Israeli-Jordanian peace treaty.

Although Israeli-Jordanian relations improved during the war itself, U.S.-Jordanian relations deteriorated as a result of the pro-Iraqi posture Jordan undertook during the crisis. It took several years and the patient work of Jordanian diplomacy to reestablish close relations with Washington.

U.S.-Israeli Relations Immediately Following the War

The rise to power of Labor in the summer of 1992 helped to relieve some of the strains that had begun to appear between the United States and Israel as the Madrid process moved too slowly (to a large extent because of Israeli procrastination, especially since the Netanyahu election). The readiness of Labor to adopt a clear agenda of land for peace eliminated a major bone of contention between the two governments. From then on, no conflict appeared to create tensions between the different sets of factors—"soft" and "hard"—that contributed in the past to the intimate relationship between Washington and Jerusalem. Thus, the end of the cold war did not threaten that relationship. The "soft" variables continued to influence U.S. policy, possibly more so under the Bill Clinton administration. Then again, though the Soviet threat disappeared, the emergence of several regional anti–status quo powers as well as radical fundamentalism, both of which are perceived in Washington as endangering U.S. interests, gave a new rationale for U.S.-Israeli strategic interests. Indeed, one might argue that this or similar regional strategic considerations will continue to contribute to the strategic cooperation between the two countries.

Then again, a U.S. involvement in the implementation of a future peace agreement between Israel and Syria would probably further strengthen this strategic cooperation. This involvement might comprise the deployment of U.S. forces on the Golan as well as a strong formal commitment to operate against any party that violates the agreement (the only candidate being Syria, if it opted to do so and especially if it violated the military aspects of the agreement, such as the demilitarization of the Golan).

Finally, in due time and following the signing of peace treaties between Israel and all its neighbors, one could envisage the emergence of a regional alliance (formal or informal) comprising some of the regional powers, including Israel, with the participation of the United States. This would add yet another dimension to the ongoing relationship between the two countries.

Notes

1. See Chapter 14 in this volume, by Bernard Reich, on the subject of the U.S.-Israeli "special relationship."

2. For a presentation of the different Israeli approaches to Iraq and to the Iraq-Iran war up to the mid-1980s, see Joseph Alpher, "Israel and the Iran-Iraq War," in Ephraim Karsh, ed., *The Iran-Iraq War: Impact and Implications* (London: Macmillan, 1988).

3. See Tareq Y. Ismael, *International Relations of the Contemporary Middle East* (Syracuse, N.Y.: Syracuse University Press, 1986); Roland Dannreuther, *The Gulf Conflict: A Political and Strategic Analysis,* Adelphi Paper No. 264 (London: International Institute for Strategic Studies, Winter 1991–1992). A useful collection of Saddam Hussein's speeches, including his speech at the Arab Cooperation Council (ACC) conference on February 24, 1990, when the division between Iraq and Egypt began to emerge, can be found in Ofra Bengio, *Saddam Speaks on the Gulf Crisis* (Tel Aviv: Dayan Center, Tel Aviv University, 1992).

4. On the origins and development of the Gulf crisis, see, inter alia, Bruce Maddy Weitzman, "The Inter-Arab System and the Gulf War," *Occasional Papers Series* 2(1) (Atlanta: Carter Center, Emory University, 1992); Dannreuther, *The Gulf Conflict,* p. 25; Lawrence Freedman and Ephraim Karsh, *The Gulf War* (Princeton: Princeton University Press, 1993); Walid al-Khalidi, "The Gulf Crisis: Origins and Consequences," *Journal of Palestine Studies* 20(2) (Winter 1991).

5. For an extended discussion of this deterrence dialogue, see Yair Evron, *Israel's Nuclear Dilemma* (Ithaca: Cornell University Press, 1994).

6. See text of the speech in Bengio, *Saddam Speaks.*

7. See IHT, January 8, 1991.

8. See, for example, *Economist,* September 20, 1990.

9. For reservations about the possibility that peaceful negotiations involving the need for territorial compromise and U.S. pressure in that direction will follow the end of the war, see Prime Minister Shamir's comment made in late February 1991: "Some will try to use political means to deprive Israel of what they did not succeed in taking from us by force. . . . We will not flinch, we will not run away, we'll have to summon all our wisdom and guile. . . . We must overcome the Iraqi monster, and overcome the political negotiations confronting us . . . [and then] we can breathe freely." For an analysis suggesting that Shamir was hoping that Is-

raeli restraint during the war might provide Israel with a better bargaining card during the political negotiations that presumably would follow the war, see Joseph Alpher, "The Arab-Israel Peace Process Before and After the Gulf Crisis," in Shlomo Gazit, ed., *The Middle East Military Balance, 1990–1991* (Tel Aviv: Jaffee Center for Strategic Studies, Tel Aviv University, 1992).

10. The extensive Soviet Jewish immigration to Israel beginning in 1989, which brought a half-million new immigrants over the following five years, created the need for significant capital transfers to Israel. Israel asked the United States for loan guarantees to the tune of $10 billion spread over five years. These guarantees would have allowed Israel somewhat lower interest rates and other convenient terms.

11. On the early phase of Israeli-Jordanian relations, see, inter alia, Dan Shuftan, *Optia Yardenit: Israel, Yarden Vehaplestinaim* [Jordanian Option: Israel, Jordan, and the Palestinians] (Tel Aviv: Hakibutz Hameuchad, 1986) [in Hebrew]; Avi Shlain, *Collusion Across the Jordan* (Oxford: Oxford University Press, 1988).

12. On the change in Likud's perception of Jordan's usefulness for Israel's security following the Gulf crisis, see, inter alia, Joseph Alpher, "The Arab-Israel Peace Process Before and After the Gulf Crisis," in Gazit, *The Middle East Military Balance, 1990–1991*.

22

The Soviet Union, the Gulf War, and Its Aftermath: A Case Study in Limited Superpower Cooperation

Robert O. Freedman

Under the leadership of President Mikhail Gorbachev, the Soviet Union withdrew from most areas of the Third World—using the United Nations (UN) as a cover for the withdrawals whenever possible—and reestablished détente with the United States; in the Middle East not only did Moscow not retreat during the Gorbachev era, it became much more politically active. This desire to play a major role in the Middle East, despite increasingly severe internal problems throughout the Soviet Union, was reflected in Moscow's rapprochement with erstwhile enemies Egypt and Israel, its deepening relations with Iran, and major improvements in relations with the conservative shaykhdoms of the Persian Gulf. It was also reflected in Moscow's behavior both during the period of Iraq's occupation of Kuwait and the postwar, U.S.-led Arab-Israeli peace process. Indeed, even as the Soviet Union was collapsing around him following the abortive coup of August 19–21, 1991, Gorbachev sought to utilize the Middle East peace process as a device for rebuilding his personal prestige and demonstrating that the Soviet Union was still a major factor in world affairs.

Moscow and the Invasion of Kuwait

The Iraqi invasion of Kuwait on August 2, 1990, took Moscow by surprise despite explicit provisions requiring Baghdad to advise it of such an action in the 1972 Soviet-Iraqi Treaty of Friendship and Cooperation.[1] The invasion posed a number of problems for Moscow. On the one hand, it was a clear-cut case of aggression and a major violation of the new world order, which Gorbachev said he was trying to create to solve problems politically and not by force. In addition, once the United States committed itself to Saudi Arabia's defense and began to build up its military forces in the desert kingdom, Moscow faced the choice of whether or not to actively support the United States. Such support would preserve the momentum of super-power cooperation, and Moscow would continue to benefit from its improved relationship with the United States, especially in the areas of strategic arms agreements and economic cooperation. A second consideration involved the politics of the Arab world. Egypt and Syria had denounced the Iraqi invasion and had pledged support to Saudi Arabia, as had the other members of the Gulf Cooperation Council (GCC). Jordan, newly unified Yemen, the Sudan, and Yasser Arafat (leader of the Palestine Liberation Organization [PLO]) sided with Iraqi President Saddam Hussein; the North African states adopted a more neutral position (except for Morocco, which backed Saudi Arabia). Here the question for Moscow was whether or not to continue Gorbachev's policy of improving ties with the conservative Arab regimes, many of whom had money that could be loaned to the USSR (Kuwait had already done so).[2] In the process, by backing the new Saudi-Syrian-Egyptian axis, which seemed likely to dominate the Arab world if Iraq was defeated, Moscow could prevent the United States from becoming the sole superpower guarantor of the region.

A related consideration for Moscow was the status of Kuwait itself. Moscow had established diplomatic relations with Kuwait in 1964 and, until 1985, it was the only Gulf shaykhdom to have diplomatic relations with Moscow, from which it also bought military equipment. Moscow held out Kuwait as the model of a small Gulf state that enjoyed good relations with both superpowers and urged other Gulf shaykhdoms that were members of the GCC to follow the Kuwaiti example of looking to both superpowers for support in a region in which they might be threatened by more powerful neighbors.[3] Oman and the United Arab Emirates (UAE) had followed Kuwait's example in 1985, as did Qatar in 1988. Thus, if Moscow did not actively oppose Iraq's annexation of Kuwait, it risked the loss of its ties to the Gulf states; conversely, an activist Soviet policy aimed at getting Iraq out of Kuwait might well be rewarded by a Saudi Arabian decision to reestablish diplomatic relations with the USSR, long a major Soviet goal.

Although issues of U.S.-Soviet and Soviet-GCC relations were important considerations among Soviet decisionmakers, Iraq was not without its supporters in the USSR. The 1972 Soviet-Iraqi treaty was still operative. Iraq paid hard currency—an increasingly scarce commodity in the USSR—for its arms purchases, and Moscow had some 7,830 civilian advisers working in such areas as oil exploration, oil drilling, grain elevator construction, and hydroelectric projects, as well as military advisers in Iraq.[4] Those advisers not only earned hard currency but could also be considered agents of Soviet influence in Iraq. Between 200 and 1,000 of the 7,830 Soviet advisers were what Moscow called "military specialists";[5] given Soviet cutbacks around the world, Iraq was one of the few places remaining where Soviet military specialists could serve under relatively good conditions, and the Soviet military would be loathe to cut off this relationship.[6] Finally, for the "old thinkers" in the USSR—and these grew more influential in the August 1990–February 1991 period as Gorbachev increasingly turned to the right and abandoned his liberal positions (a development that reached its apogee with the resignation of Foreign Minister Eduard Shevardnadze in December 1990, warning of a coming dictatorship)—Saddam Hussein was "standing up to the imperialists who wanted to dominate Middle East oil, and who were building a major military position near the southern border of the USSR, just as Moscow was pulling out of East Europe, thus decisively altering the balance of power against the USSR." Included in this group were hard-liners such as the Soyuz faction of the Supreme Soviet, senior army officers, and Communist Party officials.[7]

In addition, from the point of view of Moscow's Middle East position, some Soviet commentators argued that Iraq might emerge from the confrontation with enhanced prestige in the Arab world due to the linkage of its invasion of Kuwait to the Palestinian cause. This was another reason, they argued, for not actively opposing Iraq.[8] Besides these three major considerations, there were three additional factors that permeated Soviet thinking as to the Iraqi invasion. The first is what might be termed "Afghan syndrome." Shared by both liberals and hard-liners, this was an aversion to sending any Soviet soldiers abroad to fight, lest they get caught up in a quagmire like Afghanistan. (The Afghan syndrome is in many ways similar to the Vietnam syndrome that affected U.S. policy for many years; in fact the latter was instrumental in Congress's thwarting of Henry Kissinger's efforts to support the forces of Jonas Savimbi against the Soviet and Cuban-backed Popular Movement for the Liberation of Angola in 1976.) A second consideration was the economic crisis that had begun to pervade the USSR. Given Moscow's increasingly serious economic problems, with a shortage of food and goods in Soviet stores, there was little inclination to expend Soviet resources on a major commitment of Soviet troops to an anti-Iraqi war. Finally, there was the Muslim issue. Although Muslims stood on both sides of the Iraqi-Kuwaiti conflict, Soviet government officials and academics feared a very negative impact on the increasingly restive Muslims of Soviet central Asia and Azerbaijan if Soviet soldiers were seen killing Muslims in Iraq.[9]

Given these problems, Gorbachev adopted what might be termed a "minimax" strategy: He did the minimum necessary to satisfy the United States, the oil-rich GCC states, and Syria and Egypt—all of whom were actively supporting the allied coalition—while striving to maintain maximum influence in Iraq, something that would not have been possible if Moscow was part of the military coalition confronting Saddam Hussein. Thus, the USSR supported all twelve UN resolutions condemning Iraq in the prewar period while cooperating with the United States at the UN once war broke out. To be sure, whenever votes came up at the UN Security Council involving the use of force against Iraq, Moscow sought to delay them so as to give Iraq "one more chance"; when the final resolution authorizing the use of "all necessary means" to free Kuwait was passed at the end of November 1990, Moscow obtained a forty-five-day "goodwill pause" to enable diplomacy to have additional time, thereby giving Gorbachev yet another opportunity to claim he was trying to save Arab lives. In addition, Gorbachev twice sent his Middle East adviser, Yevgeny Primakov, to Baghdad to lobby Saddam Hussein into working out a solution to the diplomatic impasse. Moscow also refused to commit any of its forces to the coalition, even a symbolic hospital ship, despite the urging of the United States and then refused to share information it had on the Iraqi military—after first agreeing to do so. Although this policy may have been aimed at maintaining Moscow's military neutrality and influence in Iraq once war broke out, it did raise questions about Moscow's cooperation in the anti-Iraqi effort, as did Gorbachev's decision to keep Soviet military and economic advisers in Iraq following the invasion of Kuwait, although this move appears to have backfired as the Soviet specialists became de facto hostages.

Moscow's behavior during the actual war was similar to its prewar behavior, although its rhetoric took on a more anti-American tone. At first Gorbachev stressed a diplomatic solution and sought to end the war as soon as possible. Then he complained about the U.S. escalation of force, which he said went beyond UN resolutions; he again sent Primakov to Baghdad and then tried to mediate between the United States and Iraq on terms for a settlement, seeking to "plea-bargain" for Saddam Hussein. Had the war been prolonged, with numerous U.S. casualties, the U.S. government might have viewed Gorbachev's mediation efforts as a valuable mechanism for extracting U.S. troops from the war. As it was, however, Iraq proved to be so weakened by the allied bombing, and the ground war turned out to be so short, that Gorbachev's efforts at mediation, especially Moscow's positive portrayal of the first Iraqi peace plan that was full of unacceptable linkages, proved counterproductive. The United States perceived the Soviet efforts as undesirable meddling rather than positive assistance, although President George Bush was careful to display only the highest, face-saving respect for Gorbachev so as to maintain at least minimal U.S.-Soviet cooperation.[10]

In sum, U.S.-Soviet cooperation during the crisis was, at best, limited. Although a far better situation than during the 1973 Arab-Israeli war, when a direct superpower military confrontation nearly occurred (the two superpowers were actively aiding the opposite sides of the conflict), the Iraqi crisis revealed that Moscow was too closely following its own perceived national interests to become a genuine partner for the United States.

In looking at the effect of this Soviet behavior on its position in the Middle East, the answer would appear to be mixed. On the one hand, Moscow was able to exploit the crisis to gain diplomatic relations with Saudi Arabia and Bahrain, as well as $3 billion of economic aid from the GCC. Second, given its military neutrality and its efforts at mediating the conflict, Moscow may in the future be able to reestablish its economic and political position in Iraq, especially if Saddam Hussein remains in power.[11] Yet the poor performances displayed by Soviet weaponry and training exercises during the conflict—despite the predictions of high-ranking Soviet officers—and the stringent limits set by the cease-fire agreement on Iraq's military capability, together with its debts and reparations payment obligations, may in the future limit Iraq's interest in and ability to pay for Soviet arms.

Another positive consequence of the war for Moscow was a further improvement of relations with Iran; both states were closely coordinated during the war, maintaining neutrality while trying to mediate the conflict. Moscow and Tehran shared the goal of getting U.S. forces out of the Gulf as soon as possible, and this appeared to be a foreshadowing of their future cooperation.

Although there were certain gains for Moscow as a result of the war, there were losses as well. The overwhelming military victory of the United States, while Moscow stayed on the diplomatic sidelines, underscored the fact that the United States was the world's number-one great power; Moscow was being marginalized despite its diplomatic activities. In addition, the United States became the major outside influence in the new Arab axis (Egypt, Syria, and Saudi Arabia), which emerged as the dominant force in Arab diplomacy at war's end. Moscow had to be concerned by this development because of the possibility that these key states of the Arab world, whose armies the United States had actively supported while Moscow only did so with rhetoric, might remain in the U.S. sphere of influence for a considerable period of time. Given the fact that the Middle East is the only Third World region in which Moscow maintained an active interest during the Gorbachev era, this outcome would not be a positive one for the Soviet Union; as soon as the war ended, Moscow, despite its internal problems, set about to improve its position in the region.

Moscow and the Post–Gulf War Situation from the Cease-Fire to the Abortive Coup

The Arab-Israeli Peace Process

When the Gulf war came to an end, Moscow had one central concern in the Middle East: that the United States, because of its military victory over Iraq in cooperation with Saudi Arabia, Egypt, and Syria, would dominate the region politically. The primary problem for Moscow was the possibility that the United States would follow through on its wartime planning and establish a major base system in the Persian Gulf region with both troops and planes to augment the large naval presence it had maintained in the region for more than a decade.

A second problem for Moscow lay in the U.S. effort to bring about an Arab-Israeli settlement. Although Moscow had long sought such a settlement (and had even warmed relations with Israel during the Gorbachev era in an effort bring such a settlement about), Gorbachev seemed concerned. Given the weakening of the PLO's diplomatic position due to Arafat's support of Saddam Hussein and the possible efforts by King Hussein of Jordan to get back into the good graces of the United States after bitter clashes during the war, the United States might orchestrate an arrangement: A delegation of West Bank and Gaza Palestinians, together with King Hussein, might negotiate a peace settlement with Israel, thereby freezing out not only the PLO from the process but also the Soviet Union.

Since Moscow was beset by increasingly severe economic problems during the postwar period and now was openly asking the United States and Western Europe for massive economic aid, it obviously could not directly oppose U.S. efforts in the Middle East. Nonetheless, it could quietly reinforce parties in the Middle East opposed to postwar U.S. hegemony; leading that list was Syria.

For its part, Syria had emerged from the Gulf war with an improved economic and political position. More than $2 billion in economic aid from the GCC states had at least partially enabled Syrian President Hafiz al-Asad to stabilize the Syrian economy while making it possible for him to purchase twenty-four scud missiles from North Korea[12] (and, quite possibly, M-9 missiles from China). In addition, Syria was playing a mainstream role in Arab politics for the first time in many years, a development that enhanced its political prestige both in the Arab world and in the West, where Syria's role as an ally in the conflict with Iraq was greatly appreciated. Moreover, Syria seized the opportunity to oust Iraqi-supported General Michel Aoun, who commanded the Lebanese army and opposed the Syrian presence in Lebanon, from power and reinforce the position of the pro-Syrian Lebanese government. Finally, al-Asad's main Arab rival, Saddam Hussein, had suffered a crushing defeat in the war; al-Asad may have hoped, particularly in the early part of the war's aftermath, that Saddam would be ousted from power and replaced by a more pro-Syrian regime.

Syria was not the only country to greatly improve its position as a result of the war; so too had that of its main enemy, Israel. By not retaliating against Iraqi scud missile attacks, and thus helping to preserve the coalition against Iraq, Israel had gained great goodwill in the United States and western Europe. (Much of it, however, soon dissipated because of the Shamir government's aggressive construction of settlements in the Occupied Territories.) Israel also obtained economic and military assistance, including antichemical warfare equipment from Germany and the Patriot antimissile system from the United States. Since Syria's main deterrent (or means of attack) against Israel was chemical-tipped missiles, it could not be too happy about this development or the fact that Israel could now concentrate its forces against Syria given that almost all of Iraq's offensive power was eliminated by the allied attack.

As Syria began to engage in postwar diplomacy, al-Asad sought to strengthen his diplomatic position vis-à-vis both the United States and Israel by holding out an olive branch to the now weakened PLO and again coordinating his policy with King Hussein. Thus, he released hundreds of Arafat's followers from jail on the eve of Secretary of State James Baker's visit to Damascus in mid-March 1991, an action that elicited this comment from Arafat: "This positive initiative will help end the strain between us and our brothers in Syria."[13] Two weeks later, he hosted King Hussein, the first visit to Damascus of the Jordanian monarch in more than a year.[14] Next he met Egyptian President Husni Mubarak in Cairo, and the two Arab leaders came out with a plan for an international conference to resolve the Arab-Israeli conflict, with a major role for the five permanent members of the UN Security Council;[15] he also met with Iranian President Hashimi Rafsanjani to coordinate policy. With his diplomatic position now stronger, al-Asad sent his foreign minister, Faruq al-Shar'a, to Moscow for talks with Gorbachev, in which both the Persian Gulf situation and the Arab-Israeli conflict were discussed. During the meeting, Gorbachev praised al-Asad and "expressed his belief that Syria's initiative-taking policy can do a great deal both to restore Arab unity and to resolve the Arab-Israeli conflict—in a spirit of realism and with an eye to the various interests that come together there." Gorbachev also promised to develop relations of "friendly cooperation" with Syria "in all areas, including the defense sphere—with due consideration, of course, for the new international situation and capabilities that are limited by the current state of the Soviet economy."[16] Although Moscow was clearly expressing the limits of its willingness to offer Syria military aid (indeed, Moscow's unwillingness to give advanced surface-to-surface missiles to Syria may have been the reason al-Asad turned to North Korea and China for such weapons), nonetheless, a diplomatic link to Moscow was useful to al-Asad as he moved ahead in the diplomatic negotiations with Israel and the United States over the peace process.

His next move stemmed from an offer by the Syrian-backed Palestine National Salvation Front for a reconciliation with Arafat;[17] that was followed up in late May, when a high-ranking PLO delegation of Arafat supporters went to Damascus to negotiate a modus vivendi with al-Asad.[18] At the same time, Syria signed a treaty with Lebanon, consolidating its influence in that country. As Syria's diplomatic position strengthened, al-Asad took a hard-line position over the ground rules for talks with Israel in a ten-hour meeting with Baker during his visit to Damascus on April 23, 1991. In particular, Syria called for any peace conference to have a permanent structure to which parties could go back for help in breaking deadlocks, for a "significant role" for the UN in the talks, and for Israel to make an advance commitment to abide by UN resolutions on land for peace.[19] Since Israel was taking an almost diametrically opposed position (only a symbolic, one-day "regional" peace conference that would lead to direct talks between Israel and its Arab neighbors, no role for the UN, and no advanced commitment on land for peace), Baker's shuttle diplomacy soon reached an impasse.

At this point, Baker, who had been in Moscow in mid-March, returned to the Soviet Union, this time meeting Soviet Foreign Minister Alexander Bessmertnykh in the Soviet Caucasus. He received a commitment from Bessmertnykh to cosponsor the Middle East peace conference—something Moscow had long wanted.[20] Bessmertnykh also told Baker he would visit the Middle East in May, and Baker may have hoped Bessmertnykh would use Moscow's influence with Syria to get al-Asad to moderate his position on the modalities for holding a peace conference. And though Moscow was ever mindful of its need for economic assistance from the United States, Gorbachev did not appear to share the U.S. interest in pressuring al-Asad. Moscow itself had long wanted an active and "effective" international conference to work out an Arab-Israeli peace conference,[21] and the one-shot "ceremonial" conference proposed by Israel did not meet Soviet needs. An extensive international peace conference, cosponsored by the Soviet Union, would give Moscow the opportunity to demonstrate its continued significance in the Middle East and in the larger world order as well. In addition, under Gorbachev Moscow had seen the UN as an effective tool for both covering the retreat of the USSR from Third World conflict areas, such as Angola and Cambodia, and for limiting unilateral U.S. actions, as in the Gulf war. Consequently, a major role for the UN in an Arab-Israeli settlement was very much in the Soviet interest.[22] Thus, on two issues—an active international conference and a UN role in the conference—Soviet and Syrian interests coincided, and there was no indication of any Soviet pressure on Syria during Bess-mertnykh's visits to Damascus during his mid-May visit to the Middle East. Indeed, according to the Syrian foreign minister, Faruq al-Shar'a, the USSR and Syria had identical viewpoints on the peace process, "especially regarding the structure of the international peace conference, the participation of the United Nations and the European Community, and the continuity of the conference."[23] Whether or not the Syrian foreign minister was accurate in portraying the Soviet position (Bessmert-nykh himself was very reserved in his comments on these issues), Syria's position clearly toughened—as Baker was to find out when he visited Damascus in mid-May (several days after the Bessmertnykh visit) and after meeting with the Soviet foreign minister in Cairo.[24] The failure of Baker's Damascus visit may well have prompted the unplanned return of Bessmertnykh to the Syrian capital as the Soviet foreign minister sought to demonstrate to the United States that Moscow was doing every-thing possible to facilitate the peace process.

On balance, the Bessmertnykh visit to the Middle East seemed primarily aimed at "showing the flag," fact-finding, and improving Moscow's bilateral relations with the countries visited—Syria, Jordan, Israel (with whom full diplomatic relations were not restored, perhaps to reassure the Arabs in the face of Israeli West Bank set-tlement-building), Egypt, Saudi Arabia, and also Switzerland, where Bessmertnykh met Arafat (and thereby aided the Palestinian leader's postwar political rehabilita-tion). A columnist in *Izvestia* summed up the Bessmertnykh visit in these words:

> Baker's fourth tour of the region this year and Bessmertnykh's first were marked by col-laboration between the two powers. This was shown not only by the consultations be-tween the two ministers in Kislovosk and Cairo, but also by the fact that it was the United States which advocated that the USSR be cochairman of the peace conference. . . . The United States realizes that despite the victory for U.S. weaponry, it will not be able to carry the burden in isolation without Soviet participation. After all, even given the fact that our power has been weakened by domestic strife, the Arabs continue to see us as a counterweight to the U.S.-Israeli alliance.[25]

Two months after the Bessmertnykh visit, however, Syria suddenly accepted the U.S. terms for the conference, al-Asad saying that the U.S. plan was "an acceptable basis for achieving a comprehensive solution and a peace process in the region, es-pecially since these proposals are based on UN Resolutions 242 and 338 which apply to all fronts and secure legitimate Palestinian rights."[26] Since the United States had acceded to Israeli wishes about having essentially symbolic roles for the UN and European Community at the conference, the Syrian president appeared to have de-cided that the future interests of his country—in the short term at least—lay in fol-lowing the U.S. lead, and he had on these two points. Nonetheless, Syrian television quoted al-Asad as saying that he highly valued "President Bush's pledge that the United States and the USSR will be a catalyst for peace and that they will have a spe-cial responsibility to make the conference succeed in its objectives as defined by the relevant UN resolutions."[27]

Once al-Asad had decided to attend the conference, Moscow both praised the Syrian leader's decision and urged the Palestinians to follow his example.[28] Given the Soviet Union's clearly reduced influence not only in Syria but in the region as a whole, Gorbachev clearly could not push the Syrian leader to hold out for a major UN role—much as he might have wanted to. Instead, Gorbachev capitalized on the joint U.S.-Soviet sponsorship of the conference; in an interview on the rapidly evolving Middle East situation, a Soviet Foreign Ministry official emphasized Moscow's role as a joint sponsor of the conference.[29] The Soviet Union continued this theme in late July as Bush journeyed to Moscow for a summit meeting with Gorbachev. On July 31, the two world leaders jointly announced plans to issue formal invitations to a Middle East peace conference in October:[30]

> While recognizing that peace cannot be imposed and that it can only result from direct negotiations between the parties, the United States and the Soviet Union pledge to do their utmost to promote and sustain the peace-making process. To that end, the United States and the Soviet Union, acting as cosponsors, will work to convene in October a peace conference designed to launch bilateral and multilateral negotiations. Invitation to the conference will be issued at least ten days before the conference is to convene. In the interim, Secretary Baker and Foreign Minister Bessmertnykh will continue to work with the parties to prepare for the conference.[31]

At the same time, Soviet Foreign Minister Bessmertnykh announced the USSR was ready to establish full diplomatic relations with Israel if the Jewish state attended the Middle East peace conference.[32]

Moscow's renewed role in the Middle East peace process was played up by the Soviet media, as an Arabic language radio broadcast on August 2 noted:

> For the first time the U.S. side has referred to a just and durable Middle East peace— this is Soviet terminology—the essence of which is that peace in the region can only be established when it is just. Also important is the fact that the Gorbachev-Bush statement was issued in Moscow. *Our commentator believes that this refutes allegations in the Arab world that the Soviet Union plays a weak role in the Middle East settlement. Once again, it was stressed that a durable peace in the region is impossible without the Soviet Union's participation.* (emphasis added)[33]

Seventeen days later, Gorbachev was temporarily overthrown in a coup that ultimately led to the collapse of the Soviet Union. However, before examining the impact of the coup on Soviet policy toward the Middle East, we will analyze Soviet policy toward the Persian Gulf from the end of the Gulf war until the abortive coup.

Soviet Policy Toward the Persian Gulf

Once the Gulf war ended, a major military victory for the United States and its allies, Moscow urged that the nations of the Persian Gulf region (including Iran) take primary responsibility for their own security, that the UN play an important role in the process, and that foreign forces be no larger than they had been on August 1,

1990—the day before the Iraqi invasion of Kuwait.[34] Consequently, Moscow was heartened when the GCC states, meeting with Syria and Egypt in Damascus in early March 1991, announced their reliance on Syria and Egypt to be the "nucleus for an Arab force which would guarantee the security and peace of Arab countries in the Gulf region"[35] and also promised Egypt and Syria billions in economic aid. Given Syria's role in the alignment, as well as the Gulf states' call for improved relations with Iran (Saudi Arabia and Iran restored diplomatic relations with one another in mid-March), Moscow may have hoped that with Iran actively opposing a major U.S. military presence in the Gulf, the United States could be prevented from establishing military hegemony in the region. Unfortunately for Moscow, however, a rift between Saudi Arabia, on the one hand, and Egypt and Syria on the other led to the pullout of the forces of the non-Gulf states,[36] and the GCC nations remained highly suspicious of Iran. Consequently, it appeared as if the United States might play a major military role in the region after all. Despite the statement of Saudi General Prince Khaled ibn Sultan (who had commanded the Arab and Islamic forces in the coalition) that he did not think Saudi Arabia would need or want a larger U.S. military presence than it had before the war,[37] Moscow was clearly concerned as U.S. Secretary of Defense Richard Cheney toured the Gulf in early May 1991 seeking to expand the U.S. military presence in the region.[38] Indeed, over the summer, in addition to arranging further arms sales to Arab allies, the United States continued to negotiate military arrangements; in early September, shortly after the abortive coup in Moscow, a military agreement was signed with Kuwait.[39] One month later, the United States signed a military agreement with Bahrain.[40]

The continuing concern over Iraq, whose leader survived the war (and massacred Iraqi Shi'a and Kurds who had engaged in a postwar uprising), and fear of the potential threat from Iran were the main causes for the agreements negotiated by the Gulf states with the United States as well as for the continued security discussions between the United States and Saudi Arabia. Moscow, though supporting the U.S. efforts to achieve a stringent cease-fire resolution, continued to protect the Saddam Hussein regime. Although the massacres were widely reported in the Soviet press,[41] Moscow not only opposed any trial of Saddam[42] but also strongly cautioned the UN against any intervention on behalf of the Kurds that might infringe on Iraq's sovereignty.[43] Although this attitude may have reflected Soviet concern over possible future UN intervention on behalf of increasingly restive Soviet national minorities, like the Lithuanians, it also seemed aimed at protecting Saddam. Thus, whereas such Soviet liberals as Georgiy Mirsky openly called for the termination of the Soviet-Iraqi treaty on the grounds of Saddam's genocide,[44] Gorbachev's Middle East adviser, Yevgeny Primakov, said he believed Saddam "has sufficient potential to give us hope for a positive development of relations with him."[45] Although U.S. humanitarian efforts on behalf of the Kurds were praised, Moscow also displayed concern they would provide a pretext for U.S. forces to remain in northern Iraq. Consequently, Moscow warmly supported the beginning of negotiations between Saddam and Kurdish leaders, hoping this would expedite the departure of U.S. troops.[46]

When it was revealed that Iraq was hiding nuclear weapons research material, however, Moscow took a tougher line toward its erstwhile ally.[47] Having already joined with the United States (and the other members of the UN Security Council) on July 17 in a resolution compelling Iraq to pay the full costs of destroying its chemical and biological weapons, ballistic missiles, and nuclear material and requiring that all states report to the Security Council the steps they had taken to ensure their citizens and corporations did not supply Iraq with military material or the technology and machinery to produce it,[48] a Soviet Foreign Ministry official, in an Interfax interview on July 2, 1991 (Interfax is a news agency in Moscow), pointedly stated: "Should Baghdad's suspected involvement in nuclear weapons development be confirmed, the USSR would proceed not from the interests of the early re-establishment of its cooperation with Iraq, but rather from the will of the international community which is urging Baghdad to create all the necessary conditions for a peaceful settlement in the Gulf."[49]

Nonetheless, the United States began to hint that a military strike to destroy Iraq's nuclear installations was being considered after Iraqi soldiers, on June 28, fired over the heads of UN inspectors who were filming the hasty withdrawal of equipment from an Iraqi military base.[50] This prompted the Soviet ambassador to the UN, Yuri Vorontsov, who had cooperated closely with the UN representative from the United States on Iraqi issues, to caution against the use of force: "Neither the United States nor anyone else has said one word within the walls of the United Nations about a resort to military options. We are talking strictly in terms of diplomatic solutions." However, the same Soviet UN ambassador did issue a strong warning to Iraq: "This is a very serious matter and the letter we received today [from Iraq] is not a satisfactory answer to all the questions in this business. Until these things are cleared up, there is no chance that the Security Council will address such questions as relieving the economic sanctions against Iraq. Iraq must understand that it is in its interest to resolve this."[51]

As U.S. pressure on Iraq mounted, the right-wing Soviet newspaper, *Krasnaya Zvezda*, which had supported Iraq during the Gulf war, warned:[52] "We have had enough of military operations. Common sense should prevail on both sides. The world can quite well do without a second round of 'Desert Storm.'" In a similar vein, Soviet Foreign Ministry spokesman Vitaly Churkin, speaking on CNN, cautioned against the use of force, warning that it would have "negative consequences . . . larger than maybe the intended goal of those actions."[53] The Soviet Foreign Ministry was, however, willing to endorse another strong UN condemnation of Iraq, and on August 15 it joined the United States and other members of the Security Council in condemning Iraq's "serious violation of its obligation" to cooperate fully with the International Atomic Energy Agency (IAEA) and the special UN commission established to oversee demolition of its weapons of mass destruction. The resolution also demanded that Iraq "provide full, final and complete disclosure . . . of all aspects of its programs to develop weapons of mass destruction and ballistic missiles with a range greater than 93 miles" and "cease immediately any attempt to conceal" research work on nuclear, chemical, biological, or ballistic missile programs and give UN inspectors complete access to all parts of the country. Iraq was also warned not to interfere with overflights by surveillance planes or helicopters and to provide Iraqi facilities to assist the inspections.[54]

In sum, even as Moscow sought to retain influence in Iraq (especially in the immediate aftermath of the war) by protecting Saddam's regime, once Iraqi nuclear ambitions became clear in the two months before the coup Soviet criticism of Iraq mounted in large part because of Moscow's concern over its own vulnerability to nuclear proliferation; nevertheless Moscow continued urging the United States not to use military force a second time against Iraq. Consequently, when news of the coup reached Iraq, Saddam Hussein was overjoyed, and Iraq issued a statement praising the new Soviet government: "It is natural for us to welcome this change, as do the countries that were hurt by the policies of the former regime. . . . We hope that this change will contribute toward restoring the correct international balance to prevent hegemony and aggression. . . . Iraq will positively respond to every initiative of friendship from the Soviet Union to its new age."[55]

Unfortunately for Saddam, the coup proved abortive and Gorbachev, upon his return to Moscow, condemned Saddam, and Soviet-Iraqi relations sharply deteriorated as the USSR began to cooperate even more closely with the United States in its Middle East policies.

Soviet Policy Toward the Middle East from the Collapse of the Coup to the Collapse of the USSR

In the aftermath of the abortive coup, major changes took place in the USSR. The individual republics, led by Russia under Boris Yeltsin, became increasingly assertive, the Baltic states were given permission to leave the USSR, and Gorbachev found himself in a far weaker political position. The Soviet leader, over the next few months, strived to arrange a new union agreement that would preserve his position as the country's leader, but he was to run into increasing opposition from both Yeltsin and the leader of Ukraine, Leonid Kravchuk. Under the circumstances, Gorbachev had little time for foreign policy initiatives other than to request more economic aid from the West and to draw closer to the United States in order to exploit President Bush's warm personal regard for him. However, the conservatives who had blocked his policies had been removed from power as a result of the failed coup. Thus, Gorbachev moved to closely align Soviet policy with the United States all over the world, especially in the Middle East, although some of the "old thinkers" in the Soviet foreign policy establishment, such as Primakov, continued to strive for a more independent Soviet position.

Perhaps the most important change in Soviet policy was toward Israel. In the two-year period before the coup Soviet-Israeli relations had developed extensively in the cultural, economic, and political spheres, and Moscow had decided to allow free emigration of Soviet Jews to Israel[56] (300,000 had arrived between October 1989 and

August 1991). However, there were still three main problems affecting bilateral relations: Moscow's unwillingness to join the United States in repudiating the UN General Assembly "Zionism is racism" resolution; Moscow's unwillingness, despite urging by the United States and Israel, to allow direct flights of emigrants from Soviet cities to Israel; and, most important of all, Moscow's reluctance to establish full diplomatic relations with Israel. In the two-month period following the coup, Moscow fulfilled all three Israeli expectations.

Speaking at the UN on September 25, 1991, new Soviet Foreign Minister Boris Pankin (Bessmertnykh had been replaced for not opposing the abortive coup) stated: "The philosophy of new international solidarity signifies, as confirmed in practice, the de-ideologizing of the UN. Our organization has been renewed and it is imperative that once and for all it rejects the legacy of the 'Ice Age' in which Zionism was compared with racism in an odious resolution."[57] Three weeks later, Aeroflot signed an agreement with Israeli's quasi-governmental Jewish Agency and Israel's El Al Airlines to establish direct immigrant flights from Moscow and St. Petersburg to Tel Aviv.[58]

Although neither move was popular in Arab circles or among Soviet conservatives (*Pravda* complained on October 10 that "the Arab Foreign Ministers now have to rebuff not only the United States but also the USSR on [the Zionism is racism resolution] in the UN"),[59] the most controversial issue was the reestablishment of full diplomatic relations between the USSR and Israel. Liberal circles in the USSR had long been campaigning for it, whereas conservatives strongly opposed the move. On October 15, *Pravda* asserted, in an article highly critical of Israel, that "on territorial questions, the United States is much closer to the aggressor than to its victims."[60] By contrast, an editorial in *Izvestia,* reflecting the liberal point of view, noted on September 25:

> After M. S. Gorbachev, swayed by his ambitious advisers, tried unsuccessfully to snatch the initiative in ending the war in the Persian Gulf, the invitation extended to the USSR to take part in an Arab-Jewish reconciliation looked more like an act of kindness on the part of the White House rather than a calculation. U.S. Secretary of State Baker's series of tours of the countries of the region wove the fabric of the peace process. Former USSR Foreign Minister Bessmertnykh, literally following in the footsteps of his U.S. colleagues, saw for himself that they were able to manage very well without us and therefore sensibly did not bother to launch any initiatives. . . .
>
> We will not end up in the absurd role of a dummy cochairman (of the peace talks) if we remain honest and fair, and that means we cannot go to the conference retaining full diplomatic relations with despotic Iraq while refusing to restore such relations with the democratic state of Israel.[61]

Given the cross-pressures, Gorbachev delayed the reestablishment of full diplomatic relations with Israel—Israel's price for agreeing to Moscow's cochairmanship of the peace talks—until literally the last minute. Nonetheless, after two rounds of talks between Pankin and Israeli Foreign Minister David Levy in Jerusalem, on October 18 Moscow agreed to reestablish full diplomatic relations. Immediately thereafter,

Pankin and Baker, in a joint statement issued in Jerusalem, invited Israel, the Arab states, and the Palestinians to attend the Middle East peace conference that was to convene in Madrid less than two weeks later, on October 30, 1991.[62] It should be noted that at the time of Gorbachev's decision to resume full diplomatic relations, former Israeli Prime Minister Shimon Peres, together with a large delegation of Israeli businessmen, was in Moscow to discuss expanded trade relations; an *Izvestia* article on October 14 noted that there were already 200 Soviet-Israeli joint ventures at work, and the "impressive group of representatives from the Association of Israeli Industrialists represented 1,100 Israeli enterprises that provided 80 percent of Israeli industrial production."[63] A TASS news agency report of the Gorbachev-Peres meeting stated that Peres "has close links with business circles in his country that are interested in expanding cooperation with the Soviet Union"; another TASS report of Gorbachev's earlier meeting with Shoshana Cardin, director of the National Conference on Soviet Jewry, in which the issue of diplomatic relations with Israel had been raised, noted that the organization "enjoys wide support of state figures and business circles,"[64] marking a 180-degree turn in Soviet thinking. It would thus appear that Soviet media reports dealing with the decision to resume diplomatic relations with Israel were aimed, at least in part, at convincing otherwise reluctant Soviets that the resumption of diplomatic relations with Israel would serve to aid the USSR's increasingly faltering economy and satisfy the United States, which had long called for the reestablishment of full diplomatic relations between Israel and the USSR.

A second area of U.S.-Soviet cooperation came in regard to Afghanistan; the Soviet invasion in 1979 had destroyed détente between the superpowers. Although Moscow had pulled its troops out of the country by February 1989, the United States had wanted Moscow to cease sending arms to the Najibullah regime as well, and Baker had negotiated this issue with both Shevardnadze and Bessmertnykh. On September 13 the two countries reached an agreement to stop supplying arms to the rival groups in Afghanistan beginning on January 1, 1992, and not to increase the supply of arms until then.[65] Given the sensitivity of the Soviet prisoner-of-war (POW) issue to Moscow, Baker also promised to help resolve the issue of Soviet POWs. The two countries also urged other states "to follow the United States and USSR in limiting their assistance to Afghanistan to 'humanitarian assistance only'" and stated, "We expect that our joint steps will facilitate launching an intra-Afghan negotiating process and should lead to a pause followed by a complete cessation of hostilities." The joint statement also noted that both the United States and USSR wanted an independent and nonaligned Afghanistan and pledged to support a "free electoral process that is not subject to manipulation or interference by anyone." The two countries also requested that the United Nations, "with the support of the concerned governments, including those of Islamic countries, work with the Afghans to convene a credible and impartial transition mechanism."[66] Although in signing the arms cut-off agreement with the United States Gorbachev may have hoped to end the problem of Soviet military involvement in Afghanistan once and for all while improving U.S.-Soviet relations, given the heavy involvement of Iran, Saudi Arabia, and Pakistan in supplying arms to the rival Mujahadeen factions it remained to be seen if the joint U.S.-Soviet arms cutoff would affect the level of fighting, much less lead to elections and the formation of a truly "independent and nonaligned" Afghanistan. Nonetheless, Moscow later praised Iran for its willingness to cut off arms shipments to the Shi'a Mujahadeen it supported, and *Krasnaya Zvezda* reported on September 24 that UN Secretary-General Javier Perez de Cuellar had persuaded both Iran and Saudi Arabia to cease arming the Afghan guerrillas.[67] Pakistan, however, remained the major problem in terms of arms supplies, and many in Moscow continued to see Pakistan's goal as an Afghan-Pakistani federation so as to create a more powerful state with which to confront Pakistan's longtime rival, India.[68]

A third area of U.S.-Soviet cooperation in the Middle East in the postcoup period—albeit a much more limited one—was arms control. Although Moscow and Washington had long discussed the problem of the proliferation of nuclear weapons to the Middle East, it was not until July 1991 that, at the United Nations, they agreed, together with the other permanent members of the UN Security Council, to support a "zone free of weapons of mass destruction in the Middle East."[69] It was not until mid-October, however, that a specific agreement on controlling arms sales to the Middle East was reached. The guidelines, agreed to in a London meeting by the five permanent Security Council members, stipulated that they would "avoid arms sales that would aggravate an existing conflict, increase tension or destabilize a region, break international embargoes, encourage terrorism, or be used other than for legitimate defense." They also agreed to avoid exports that would "seriously undermine the recipient state's economy" and to inform each other about Middle East sales of tanks, armored combat vehicles, artillery, military aircraft and helicopters, naval vessels, and certain missile systems.[70] However, given the drop in oil production, arms sales were the major source of hard currency for Moscow, and any limit on its ability to sell weapons (even a limit as small as this one) posed a real problem. Indeed, prior to the agreement, in an interview with an Abu Dhabi newspaper, a Soviet weapons official had noted that "in the absence of an agreement with the United States banning arms sales to the Middle East, Soviet arms exports to the region will be continued, and all the advanced weapons that are still in good shape were up for sale." He noted, however, that the USSR remained bound by all UN resolutions, especially those banning the sale of military hardware to the Iraqi regime.[71] An *Izvestia* correspondent, however, also writing before the limited UN agreement, urged that the UN work out a register of arms shipments and sales and that developed states agree to stop the shipments of the high-tech weapons upon which they had a monopoly.[72] Following the agreement, in a burst of optimism, Soviet Foreign Minister Pankin stated that the USSR favored gradual cuts in arms supplies to the Middle East and, if the forthcoming Madrid conference produced positive results, these supplies might discontinue.[73] In any case, though Gorbachev may have been willing to sign such an agreement to placate the United States, the USSR was to disintegrate soon after the agreement was signed. It remains to be seen whether the successor states, all of whom are starved for hard currency, will agree even to the limited check on their arms sales stipulated by the October 18 agreement.

The Arab-Israeli peace process represented the fourth major area of postcoup co-operation. Following the coup and the beginning of the disintegration of the USSR (the Baltic states were to gain independence in early September), cosponsoring such a major world event as an Arab-Israeli peace conference was of particular importance to Gorbachev, both for his own prestige and for his argument that keeping the union together enabled the country to play an important role in world affairs. Conse-quently, Gorbachev dispatched a number of missions to the Middle East from early September until the convening of the Madrid peace conference on October 30, in what appeared to be Moscow's most serious effort to date to help bring about an Arab-Israeli settlement.

However, the first, led by Middle East adviser Yevgeny Primakov, had a number of other goals as well. The leaders of the countries he visited—Egypt, Saudi Arabia, the United Arab Emirates, Kuwait, Iran, and Turkey—had all supported Gorbachev during the coup; Primakov was sent both to give them Gorbachev's personal thanks for their support and to assure them Gorbachev was now firmly in control. A sec-ond goal was to discuss bilateral relations between the USSR and each country vis-ited. Perhaps most important of all, however, Primakov actively sought their finan-cial aid for the faltering Soviet economy, and the special envoy had a number of Soviet economic specialists among his delegation to facilitate this task.[74] In Abu Dhabi, the UAE capital, Primakov announced that the Soviet Union "has a new idea for building relations with Arab states, which is based on developing and deepening economic links."[75] Upon returning from his trip, Primakov stated that "in a num-ber of countries we were given serious financial support, credits for purchasing food and consumer goods."[76] He also noted that all the countries he visited wanted to de-velop economic relations with the USSR because of its large market, the opportu-nities resulting from the conversion of the Soviet military industry, and the USSR's scientific production potential.[77]

Primakov also used the trip to make a number of political statements on Soviet policy, such as the one in Turkey in which he stated that the USSR was against any new intervention by the allied forces in Iraq but that Iraq had to strictly comply with UN Security Council resolutions.[78] In evaluating his trip Primakov stated that all of the countries he visited "clearly did not want the disintegration of the USSR" and saw the need to preserve its united economic and strategic area. He also pointedly noted, "The leaders I have met want a USSR presence in the Near and Middle East because this would preserve the balance of power. Nobody wants some power to maintain a monopoly position there."[79]

Whereas Primakov was upbeat about the political achievements of his visit, a *Krasnaya Zvezda* correspondent cynically noted that the chief aim of Primakov's trip was "to persuade rich Arab Shaykhs to help us with 'live' money." The correspon-dent went on to state that "if we are able to give the Americans assistance in the Near East, maybe we will accelerate the receipt of aid from the U.S. and the West."[80]

Some of this assistance was to be provided during a visit to Arafat in Tunis, undertaken by Soviet Deputy Foreign Minister Alexander Belogonov on the eve of the Palestine National Council (PNC) debate in late September over whether or not to participate in the peace conference given Israel's conditions. Soviet-PLO relations were rather sensitive at this time because a number of PLO figures, including the high-ranking leader Farouk Kaddoumi, had supported the coup; once the coup had failed Arafat sent a telegram of support to Gorbachev. The PLO ambassador to Moscow, Mabil Amr, when asked by *Komsomalskaya Pravda* on September 7 about the Palestinian reaction to the coup, replied: "I will be frank and say that the statements of these Palestinian figures were too hasty and shocked Y. Arafat to some extent." He noted, however, that "such remarks cannot adversely influence the development of relations between our states, especially as the official PLO viewpoint set out by the President of Palestine was totally different."[81]

Belogonov had no fewer than three meetings with Arafat, holding discussions that he termed "frank and businesslike." Also, possibly in an effort to repair the Soviet-PLO breach and rebuild Soviet influence in the PLO, he gave Arafat a message of gratitude from Gorbachev for his support.[82] The Soviet deputy foreign minister was at least partially successful in his efforts to act as a peace-process facilitator between the United States and the PLO, as Arafat allowed Palestinian spokeswoman Hanan Ashrawi to meet Baker in Amman on September 20;[83] a week later the PNC voted to attend the Middle East peace talks. It would be incorrect to attribute too much influence to the Soviet mediation effort, however, since the PLO, which had supported Saddam Hussein during the Gulf war, had little choice about entering the peace talks, even under Israeli conditions, lest it lose further prestige in the Arab world at a time when the *intifada* was waning and Egypt and Saudi Arabia were also pressing Arafat hard for a positive response to the talks. Nonetheless, Moscow hailed the PNC decision[84] and in the period leading up to the peace conference kept in close contact with the PLO, as two high-ranking members of the organization, Abu Mazin and Yasser Abd Rabboo, journeyed to Moscow for a meeting with Pankin on October 10.

A third major trip to the Middle East was undertaken by Pankin himself in mid-October, as the Soviet foreign minister traveled to Israel, Egypt, Syria, and Jordan and then met Arafat in Paris. Although the most important aspect of his trip was the agreement to resume full diplomatic relations with Israel (and thereby ensure the convening of the Middle East peace conference in Madrid), Pankin also noted he had "very friendly and sincere" conversations with al-Asad[85] and useful talks with King Hussein and Arafat as well. Like Primakov, he claimed that none of the leaders he visited wanted the Soviet Union "to retire from the political arena." "All understand perfectly well that our troubles and all our problems are problems of maturing. The Union of Sovereign States [Gorbachev's new name for the USSR] remains and will continue to be a great power. The world needs it."

Gorbachev was also to undertake a Middle East–related trip, although it was to the Madrid conference, not to the region itself. The Soviet leader apparently had two more goals during his visit. The first was to again meet President Bush and, hopefully, obtain more U.S. aid to help the Soviet economy. The second was to demonstrate to his domestic opponents, above all Yeltsin, whose power was increasing, that as a world leader he still commanded respect, and that for the country to play a major world role it had to remain intact. Nonetheless, testifying to the growing independence of the Soviet republics, Gorbachev had to take along, as part of his delegation, Vladimir Lukin, the chairman of the Russian Parliament's Foreign Affairs Committee, and the foreign minister of the Republic of Tajikistan. When asked whether Gorbachev could speak for the Soviet Union, Lukin replied, "of course, but the question is, what is the Soviet Union?"[86]

If Gorbachev had hoped that Bush would offer him additional economic assistance during their preconference meeting, he was to be disappointed, although the U.S. president was lavish in his praise for the Soviet leader: There was "no difference, certainly from my standpoint, in the respect level for President Gorbachev."[87] Bush also used the opportunity to thank Gorbachev "for the very constructive role that the Soviet Union has played in the actions leading up to this conference. We're grateful to him for that."[88]

Rhetoric aside, it was clear that the United States totally dominated the peace conference. A "senior European diplomat" told *New York Times* correspondent Thomas Friedman that, when he asked a Soviet official supposedly working on seating arrangements, the Soviet official just shrugged and said "you have to ask the Americans. We don't know anything. The Americans are handling everything."[89] Similarly, an Arab delegate to the talks noted, "Let's face the facts. The United States is running the show. The Soviet Union cannot even feed its people and asks the world for food."[90]

Ironically, this was precisely what Gorbachev was to do during his address to the peace conference. After praising U.S.-Soviet cooperation for making the conference possible and urging the delegates not to miss the opportunity for peace, Gorbachev appealed to the world community to aid the Soviet Union because "what is happening in the Soviet Union has a larger bearing than any regional conflict on the vital interests of the greater part of today's world."[91]

Less than two months after the opening of the Madrid peace conference the Soviet Union collapsed, replaced by the Commonwealth of Independent States; Gorbachev lost his job. During this period not only did the republics of the former Soviet Union become independent but a major transformation of Middle East politics took place—the outcome of which is far from being decided. Not only was the Soviet Union no longer a unified entity influencing the states of the Middle East, but the states of the region, particularly Turkey, Iran, Saudi Arabia, Pakistan, and even Israel, were now engaged in a competition for influence in the Muslim republics of the former Soviet state. Moreover, there was growing concern that Soviet nuclear scientists, and possibly nuclear weapons, could slip into the Middle East. In any case, the Madrid conference, which revealed to the world the weakness of the Soviet Union's position in the world, is a useful point of departure for analyzing the decline of Soviet influence in the Middle East since the Gulf war.

Conclusion

The Gulf war, which took place just as the Soviet Union was facing increasingly severe economic and political crises, was a major turning point in the erosion of the Soviet position in the Middle East. The brevity of the war, coupled with Gorbachev's unwillingness to actively support the U.S.-led coalition, marginalized the Soviet role in the region at the close of the war. Following the war, Gorbachev initially sought to shore up the Soviet position and prevent the United States from dominating both the Gulf and the Arab-Israeli peace process by adopting positions that were supportive of U.S. aims on the surface (after all Moscow now needed more and more Western assistance) yet subtly reinforced anti-American forces in the region. In the Gulf, Moscow both supported Iran's call for self-security and continued to protect Saddam's regime against further U.S. military intervention. In the Arab-Israeli peace process, Moscow first gave tacit support to the hard-line position of Hafiz al-Asad, but when al-Asad, in mid-July, opted for the U.S. peace plan, Moscow quickly sought to make the best of the situation by emphasizing the fact that the U.S. peace initiative called for joint U.S.-Soviet sponsorship of the peace conference. Following the abortive coup, with the removal of a number of hard-liners from the Soviet leadership, Gorbachev, now in a desperate political situation, moved to shore up his position by even more closely cooperating with the United States, whose leader, George Bush, held him in far greater respect than did Soviet countrymen. Thus, he removed the last obstacles in the Soviet-Israeli relationship by agreeing to join the United States in denouncing the UN General Assembly resolution equating Zionism with racism, agreed to allow direct flights of emigrants between the USSR and Israel, and established full diplomatic relations with the Jewish state. He also signed an agreement with the United States cutting off arms to Afghanistan and agreed, albeit in a limited way, to curtail arms shipments to the Middle East. Finally, he aided, though only marginally, the convening of the Madrid peace conference in the expectation that he could use the occasion to elicit more economic aid from the West and also demonstrate domestically that he was still a major actor on the world scene.

Unfortunately for Gorbachev, all of his efforts to use Middle East events to shore up his domestic political position proved futile, and less than two months after the Madrid peace conference the Soviet Union fell apart.

Epilogue

In the immediate aftermath of the Soviet Union's collapse, Russian President Boris Yeltsin adopted an anti-Iraq policy, not only voicing support for the sanctions against Iraq but also dispatching two warships to help enforce the anti-Iraqi embargo in the Persian Gulf. Foreign Minister Andrei Kozyrev made a visit to the GCC states at the end of April 1992 in an effort to obtain financial support from the oil-rich kingdoms. He succeeded in getting a promise from Oman for $500 million for the development of Russia's oil and gas industry and $100 million for the modernization of its oil fields.[92] While fending off criticism of Russian arms sales to Iran, Kozyrev sought to promote Russian arms sales to the GCC states. (This was also the goal of Defense Minister Pavel Grachev, who visited the United Arab Emirates in January 1993 and headed a Russian delegation to the International Weapons Fair in Abu Dhabi in February.)

Although this pro-GCC, anti-Iraqi policy was followed by Yeltsin throughout 1992, the Russian leader soon ran into strong criticism. On the far right of the Russian political spectrum was Vladimir Zhirinovsky, who attacked Yeltsin for selling out Iraq, a Russian ally, and called for the unilateral lifting of sanctions on Iraq. More moderate, centrist Russians also questioned the wisdom of Russia's close cooperation with the United States on the embargo, given Iraq's $7 billion debt to Russia and its potential as a future market. On the other side were those who asserted that a unilateral lifting of the embargo would not only seriously damage U.S.-Russian relations (and jeopardize billions of dollars of aid from NATO states) but would also alienate the oil-rich states of the GCC, which Moscow had cultivated since the days of Gorbachev. In addition, they argued, by aiding the GCC states and avoiding any rapprochement with Iraq, Moscow could offer the GCC states an alternative to the protection of the United States and other NATO states.

By January 1993, political pressure from the center and right of the Russian political spectrum began to have its effect on Yeltsin, a politician who has always tacked with the political wind. At that time, Yeltsin began to attack the renewed U.S. bombing of Iraq (although the Russian Foreign Ministry, under the then very pro-U.S. Andrei Kozyrev, initially supported the bombing). In addition, Yeltsin began to authorize visits to Iraq by Russian government ministers, and Iraqi ministers began to visit Moscow. In February 1993, Yeltsin sent Igor Melichov, the deputy director of the Middle East Department of the Russian Foreign Ministry, to Iraq. While Melichov reportedly said the goal of his visit was to "strengthen and promote Russian-Iraqi ties," his superior in the Foreign Ministry, Viktor Posuvaliuk, claimed Melichov's comments were taken out of context and were falsely interpreted by foreign journalists.[93] But Posuvaliuk also stated that Russia could not ignore "the potential for Russian-Iraqi cooperation." The moderate Russian newspaper *Nezavisimaya Gazeta* condemned the Melichov visit as stupid because it worked against Russia's goal of the stabilization of the moderate Arab states in the Gulf.[94] Yeltsin, however, persisted in his policy of maintaining low-level contact with Iraq and in some ways moved to embrace the old minimax policy of Gorbachev. These low-level contacts were, however, insufficient for Yeltsin's opponents. In April 1993, the former deputy defense minister of the USSR, General Achalov, a conservative Supreme Soviet deputy, and Duma speaker Ruslan Khasbulatov's chief of staff journeyed to Iraq with a group of right-wing parliamentarians. In Iraq, Achalov said the Russian people and the former USSR had never betrayed Iraq but that the Soviet and Russian leaderships had.[95] *Izvestia,* on April 8, 1993, responding to Achalov's visit, stated that Iraq would continue to be a place of pilgrimage for the Russian opposition as long as Saddam Hussein remained in power.[96]

In June 1993, following the abortive Iraqi attempt to assassinate former President George Bush, who was visiting Kuwait, the United States again bombed Iraq. Russian Foreign Minister Kozyrev supported the U.S. attack (which Washington had told Moscow of in advance), noting: "We cannot consider hunting presidents, even former ones, to be normal. Tolerating this would be tantamount to endorsing a policy of state terrorism."[97]

Yeltsin's parliamentary opponents denounced the attack on Iraq, and the Supreme Soviet lodged an official protest. Vice President Alexander Rutskoi, an opponent of Yeltsin, condemned Kozryev for his approval of the U.S. attack, asserting that such support meant "ignoring Russia's own national interests."[98] Meanwhile, Yeltsin upgraded Russia's diplomatic contacts with Iraq, dispatching an economic delegation, headed by Oleg Davydov, the minister of external economic relations, to Baghdad in August.[99]

When the crisis between parliament and Yeltsin escalated into a full-scale confrontation in late September 1993, there were rumors in Moscow that Saddam Hussein was bankrolling Yeltsin's opponents.[100] Nonetheless, Yeltsin's victory meant the temporary defeat of his pro-Iraqi opponents, led by Khasbulatov. This may have accelerated negotiations between Moscow and Kuwait on a defense cooperation agreement, which was signed during a visit by Kuwaiti Defense Minister Ali Sabah al-Salim al-Sabah to Moscow in late November 1993. According to *Kommersant*, the treaty called for Russia to aid Kuwait in the "elimination of the threat to sovereignty, security and territorial integrity and repelling aggression."[101]

The treaty was a clear rebuff to Iraq, which still refused to recognize Kuwait's independence or the newly demarcated Iraqi-Kuwait border, and to Iraq's supporters in Moscow, as were the joint naval maneuvers conducted by Kuwait and Russia in the Gulf in late December 1993. Indeed, *Pravda*, the primary voice of the Russian right-wing nationalists, noted angrily on January 11, 1994, that because of the naval maneuvers, "the door to cooperation with Iraq—a rich and influential state with which we used to be linked by very close ties—has thereby essentially been slammed shut."[102] Reinforcing what appeared to be a thrust of building up ties to the GCC states, Vice Premier Aleksander Shokhin visited the United Arab Emirates in late November 1993. In the UAE, he stated that his visit was taking place within the context of the Russian foreign policy aimed at creating prerequisites for boosting Russian exports. He also noted that Russian foreign policy was becoming more pragmatic. "While ensuring the country's political goals, its main orientation is the solution of Russia's economic problems. Such a policy is more reliable and serves both economic and political purposes."[103]

Having concluded the treaty with Kuwait (thus satisfying the GCC states) and having emphasized the importance of economic goals in Russian foreign policy, Yeltsin made a gesture toward Iraq, thereby continuing his neo-minimax policy. By the spring of 1994 Russian diplomats began to argue that since Saddam Hussein had begun to comply with UN demands on surveillance of its nuclear weapons capability, some gesture acknowledging his changed behavior should be made. One such

Russian gesture was an invitation to Iraqi Deputy Prime Minister Tariq 'Aziz to visit Moscow in July 1994. Russian Deputy Foreign Minister Boris Kolokov, in an *Izvestia* interview, stated that 'Aziz had been told by Moscow that Russia opposed lifting sanctions until Baghdad recognized Kuwait's independence, agreed to the demarcation of their mutual border, and tried to ascertain the fate of missing Kuwaiti soldiers and civilians. If Iraq did these things, Kolokov indicated, Moscow would vote to lift the sanctions. If they were lifted, Moscow would even resume arms sales to Iraq, thus edging out Western states that would otherwise gain the economic benefit at Russia's expense.[104] Any such supply of arms to Iraq, of course, would damage Russian-GCC relations because the GCC states would now see Russia arming both their major enemies, Iran *and* Iraq.[105] Needless to say, such action by Russia would also severely harm Russian-American relations, which by fall of 1994 had become strained over a number of issues, including Bosnia, the expansion of NATO, and Russian arms sales to Iran.

In October 1994, however, Russian policy toward Iraq suffered a major embarrassment. At that time, Saddam Hussein again moved his army toward Kuwait, an action that precipitated a major U.S. reaction. President Clinton moved U.S. troops to Kuwait and warned Saddam not to invade. Yeltsin sought to exploit the situation by sending Kozyrev to Baghdad, where he claimed to have gotten Saddam Hussein's promise to pull back his troops and recognize Kuwait's border and sovereignty—in return for a gradual lifting of the sanctions. Not only was this deal rebuffed by the United States and Britain, it became a moot point because Iraq's parliament did not meet to recognize Kuwait and the Iraqi-Kuwait border. The end result of the crisis was a further strengthening of relations between the United States and the GCC states and a major embarrassment for Russia. The situation was not alleviated to any major degree when Kozyrev returned to Iraq in November and belatedly extracted the desired promises from the Iraqi parliament.

Despite this embarrassment, Moscow continued to pursue its policy of improving relations with Iraq. At the end of January 1995, an Iraqi parliamentary delegation visited Russia and was received by Prime Minister Chernomyrdin. Deputy Foreign Minister Posuvaliuk warned in February that unless the UN Security Council responded to Iraq's positive steps, the situation in the region would further deteriorate.[106] In August 1995 the Russian deputy foreign minister, who was also the country's highest ranking Middle East specialist, asserted that Russia was "doing more work than others to normalize Kuwait's relations with Iraq." (Kozyrev visited Kuwait on August 2, the fifth anniversary of the Iraqi invasion, to offer Kuwait reassurance.) He also noted that Iraq's "disarmament file is close to being closed and work on the biological file is preceding in the same direction."[107]

Much to Russia's discomfort, however, the temporary defection of Saddam Hussein's son-in-law, Hussein Kamil, to Jordan led to Iraq's disclosure of hidden weapons information. Perhaps seeking to make the best of the situation, a Russian foreign ministry spokesman said, "It is unimportant what considerations Iraq took into consideration in deciding to lift the previous veil of secrecy on military programs. In the end, not motives but the result plays a more important role." The spokesman went on to say that Moscow hoped that the reaction of Washington and of other Russian partners in the UN Security Council "will be adequate to Baghdad's new demonstration of readiness to fulfill the U.N. resolutions."[108] Neither the United States nor the GCC was persuaded by the Russian logic, however, and the sanctions remained in effect.

While Russia was seeking to get the Security Council to lift the sanctions against Iraq, Saddam Hussein continued to dangle the prospects of major economic deals for Russia's hard-pressed economy. In late April 1995, Yuri Shafranik, Russia's energy minister, visited Iraq and offered to resume work on mothballed oil projects from the Soviet era. At the same time, Vagit Alekperov, the enterprising president of Lukoil, stated that his company wanted to develop Iraqi oil. As a result of the Shafranik visit, an agreement was signed providing Russia with drilling rights to two major oil fields in southern Iraq, as well as rights elsewhere in the country, although they were not to become operative until sanctions were lifted.[109] Meanwhile the Russian Duma, controlled by right-wing forces, voted overwhelmingly on April 21, 1995, to lift the sanctions against Iraq and set forth three goals for Russian policy: (1) to pressure the UN Security Council to repeal the embargo, (2) to collect Iraq's debt if the embargo were to be partially lifted, and (3) to support Russian business investment in Iraq and large-scale cooperation with that country.[110]

The victory of right-wing and Communist forces in the Duma elections of December 1995 was good news for Russian-Iraqi relations. In January 1996, Yevgeny Primakov, an old friend of Saddam Hussein, replaced Andrei Kozyrev as foreign minister. Primakov stated that Russia would continue to observe the sanctions against Iraq and would not lift them unilaterally, but the advent of Primakov may have convinced Saddam Hussein to begin to bargain in earnest with the UN for an oil-for-food agreement, an action he took one week after Primakov's appointment.[111]

By the time Primakov became Russia's foreign minister, it was clear that Yeltsin had three major interests in developing Russia's relationship with Iraq. The first, through international diplomatic activity, was to demonstrate both to the world and to a hostile Duma that Russia was still an important factor in the world, despite its weakened condition and was both willing and able to oppose the United States. Indeed, as Andrei Piontkowski of the Center for Strategic Studies in Moscow stated during the October–November 1997 Iraqi crisis: "For 30 years we were a superpower equal to the United States. Now the political elite is in a difficult period, feeling diminished, and compensates at least by standing up to the U.S. on minor issues."[112] The second interest Yeltsin's Russia has in Iraq is in regaining the $7 billion dollars that Iraq owes to Russia, something that cannot be achieved until sanctions against Iraq are lifted. The third interest in Iraq is in acquiring contracts for Russian factories and oil and gas companies, although the actual activities of these companies cannot begin until sanctions are lifted.

To spur the Russians to greater efforts to lift the sanctions, Saddam Hussein increased his ties to the influential Russian oil company Lukoil, which was granted part of a multibillion dollar deal to develop Iraq's West Kurna oil field. The deal, reminiscent of the oil concessions when Iraq was a colony of Britain, enabled Lukoil to keep 75 percent of the profit and also freed the company from paying Iraqi taxes.[113] Given the nature of this "sweetheart deal," Lukoil has become a major factor in the "Iraqi lobby in Moscow," pushing for the lifting of sanctions. In addition, even with sanctions in place, Russia had become the major purchaser of Iraqi oil under the UN-approved oil-for-food agreement and committed itself to purchasing 36.7 million barrels in 1997.[114]

Given these interests, Primakov's behavior in both the October–November 1997 and January–February 1998 Iraqi crises is perfectly understandable. Following the expulsion of U.S. weapons inspectors and the departure of the other inspectors, Primakov, with dramatic flair, called U.S. Secretary of State Madeline Albright back from her visit to India, met with her and other members of the UN Security Council at 2 A.M. in Geneva, Switzerland, on November 20, and with the help of France, which also has major economic interests in Iraq and has opposed the U.S. use of force, got their agreement to a deal whereby all the weapons inspectors, including the Americans, were allowed to return to Iraq in return for a vague promise to work for the lifting of sanctions. For the moment at least, Primakov and Yeltsin could bask in international acclaim for averting a U.S. attack on Iraq. As Aleksei Pushkov, a correspondent for _Nezavisimaya Gazeta_, noted, "The denouement—perhaps a temporary one—of the latest crisis involving Iraq that was achieved by Primakov demonstrated the ability that Russia still has in world affairs, even in its current very weakened state."[115] Moscow's efforts to defuse the crisis indeed did prove short-lived, as in January 1998 Saddam began backtracking on the agreement reached with Primakov by prohibiting inspections of his "palaces" and other sites where chemical and bacteriological weapons activities were suspected. As the United States and Britain massed military forces in the Persian Gulf and an attack on Iraq appeared imminent, Primakov again scurried to solve the crisis, although this time the Russian diplomatic effort was far more disjointed than it had been in November. First, with deputy foreign minister Viktor Posuvaliuk in Baghdad, the Russian foreign ministry claimed it had reached a satisfactory agreement on inspection of the palaces, only to have that agreement immediately repudiated by Baghdad. Then, perhaps to regain the initiative for Moscow, Yeltsin himself seemed to take over leadership of the Russian diplomatic effort, threatening a world war if the United States bombed Iraq and pledging that Russia "would not allow" such an attack under any circumstances.[116] Then, he asserted UN Secretary-General Kofi Annan would go to Iraq, before Annan agreed to do so. Although Annan was ultimately to go to Baghdad and negotiate an agreement satisfactory to both the United States and Iraq, it is clear that unlike the November 1997 crisis, this time Russia had ceded the diplomatic initiative to the UN secretary-general. To be sure, Moscow benefited by the fact that Yeltsin's bluff was not called and by the Security Council's decision to allow Iraq to sell more oil, which may enable Russia to get an early start in refurbishing Iraq's oil fields. Nonetheless, with all its diplomatic activity, Russia was very far from getting the sanctions lifted. In addition, should Saddam Hussein backtrack on his agreement with Annan and should subsequent Russian diplomatic efforts fail to prevent a U.S. attack, Primakov's limited diplomatic achievements—which in any case were made possible by an American willingness to make every diplomatic effort possible before an attack was made—may well pale into insignificance.

Notes

1. See the interview with Yevgeny Primakov, *Time,* March 4, 1991, p. 42.

2. In May 1990, Kuwait had agreed to give Moscow a two-stage $1 billion loan. See *Izvestia,* citing the Kuwaiti ambassador to the USSR, December 24, 1990.

3. Cf. Robert O. Freedman, *Moscow and the Middle East: Soviet Policy Since the Invasion of Afghanistan* (Cambridge: Cambridge University Press, 1991).

4. Interview with Konstantin Katushev, Soviet Minister of Foreign Economic Relations, *Sovietskaya Rossiya,* August 26, 1990 (Foreign Broadcast Information Service [hereinafter *FBIS*] August 27, 1990, p. 27).

5. Most Soviet officials, including Gorbachev, cited the lower figure. In an *Izvestia* interview of August 16, 1990, Lt. General V. Nikityuk, first deputy chief of the Main Directorate of the Soviet Armed Forces General Staff, differentiated between "specialists," who "give assistance in mastering and operating military hardware supplied under contract," and "advisers," who "are called upon to resolve questions of building the armed forces" (*FBIS,* August 20, 1990, pp. 17–19). Interviews by the author with Soviet scholars and government officials in Moscow and Washington, however, elicited the higher figure. One of the points made by Nikityuk in the interview was that as a result of the work of the Soviet military advisers, the USSR had obtained "considerable amounts of foreign currency."

6. Confidential interview, Moscow, October 1990. Such service enabled Soviet specialists to accumulate hard currency for the purchase of cars, VCRs, and other commodities difficult to obtain in the USSR.

7. *Krasnaya Zvezda, Sovietskaya Rossiya,* and *Pravda* were the fora for their position. By contrast, *Moscow News* and *Komsomalskaya Pravda* reflected liberal viewpoints, calling for the USSR to help the international community punish Saddam Hussein. *Izvestia,* the government newspaper, took a midpoint in this debate, but many of its commentators, especially Alexander Bovin, supported the liberal position. For an analysis of the debate in the Supreme Soviet on Soviet intentions in the conflict, see Suzanne Crow, "Legislative Considerations and the Gulf Crisis," Radio Liberty Report, vol. 2, no. 50, 1990, pp. 2–3.

8. Cf. *Pravda,* August 17, 1990.

9. Confidential interviews by the author, Moscow, October 1990.

10. For a detailed examination of Soviet policy during the war, see Robert O. Freedman, "Moscow and the Gulf War," *Problems of Communism,* July–August 1991, pp. 1–17.

11. Indeed, by the early spring of 1994, as an example of its attempt to improve its position with Iraq, Russia, together with France and China, had been pressuring the United States and Great Britain within the UN Security Council to end the embargo placed upon Iraq following the Gulf war. It might have been successful if not for Saddam's ill-timed and heavy-handed moving of Iraqi troops toward the Kuwaiti border in October 1994, thereby precipitating a crisis that called for the introduction of U.S. troops and reinforced the U.S.-British position within the Security Council to maintain the embargo. (When the crisis erupted Moscow attempted to diplomatically intervene in a way that would have benefited Iraq.)

12. See report by Thomas Friedman, *New York Times,* March 15, 1991.

13. Cited in report by Thomas Friedman, *New York Times,* March 14, 1991.

14. Cited in report by Sarah Gach, *Washington Times,* March 26, 1991.

15. Cited in report by Youssef Ibrahim, *New York Times,* April 2, 1991.

16. TASS report, *Pravda,* April 5, 1991 (translated in *Current Digest of the Soviet Press,* vol. 43, no. 14, p. 23).

17. Cited in report by Alan Cowell, *New York Times,* April 9, 1991.

18. For an evaluation of the motives of al-Asad and Arafat in renewing their cooperation, see Lanus Andeni, "The PLO and Syria: A Tricky Relationship," *Middle East International,* no. 401 (May 31, 1991), pp. 11–12. See also the comments by a PLO delegate to the Damascus meeting, Yasser Abd-Raboo, who said the PLO, Jordan, and Syria have identical views on the role of the peace conference in the Middle East (Tunis Radio, May 29, 1991; *FBIS,* May 30, 1991, p. 3).

19. Cited in report by Thomas Friedman, *New York Times,* April 24, 1991.

20. Cited in report by John Goshko, *Washington Post,* April 26, 1991.

21. See Robert O. Freedman, *Soviet Policy Toward Israel Under Gorbachev* (New York: Praeger, 1991).

22. See the interview by Bessmertnykh on the eve of his trip to the Middle East, in *Neues Deutschland,* April 29, 1991 (*FBIS,* May 1, 1991, p. 13).

23. Damascus Domestic Service, May 9, 1991 (*FBIS,* May 9, 1991, p. 27).

24. For a report of Baker's unsuccessful visit, in which Syria reportedly rejected Baker's compromise plan for a UN observer, see the report by Thomas Friedman, *New York Times,* May 13, 1991.

25. Article by V. Skosyrev, *Izvestia,* May 16, 1991 (*FBIS,* May 16, 1991, pp. 24–25).

26. Cited in report by Thomas Friedman, *New York Times,* July 15, 1991.

27. Ibid. See also the article by Caryle Murphy, *Washington Post,* August 20, 1991.

28. Cf. Radio Moscow report, in Arabic, July 15, 1991 (*FBIS,* July 17, 1991, p. 19), Interfax interview with Soviet Foreign Ministry official, July 24, 1991 (*FBIS,* July 25, 1991, p. 18), and USSR Vice President Gennady Yanaev's comments to a visiting Palestine National Council delegation as reported by TASS, July 24, 1991 (*FBIS,* July 26, 1991, p. 18).

29. Cf. Interfax, July 24, 1991 (*FBIS,* July 25, 1991, p. 17).

30. Cited in a report by Ann Devoy and Michael Dobbs, *Washington Post,* August 1, 1991.

31. Cited in *Jerusalem Post,* August 1, 1991.

32. Cited in a report by David Hoffman, *Washington Post,* August 1, 1991. See also report by Walter Ruby, *Jerusalem Post,* August 1, 1991.

33. Cited in report by Serge Schmemann, *New York Times,* August 2, 1991.

34. *FBIS,* August 5, 1991, p. 17.

35. *Izvestia,* March 20, 1991. For the official Soviet plan for Gulf security, see TASS, March 16, 1991 (*FBIS,* March 18, 1991, pp. 14–16).

36. Cited in a report by Caryle Murphy, *Washington Post,* May 11, 1991.

37. For a report on the background for this development, see ibid.

38. Cited in report by Judith Miller, *New York Times,* April 29, 1991.

39. See Chapter 18, by Shafeeq Ghabra, for details.

40. *Washington Post,* October 28, 1991.

41. TASS, April 5, 1991 (*FBIS,* April 8, 1991, pp. 16–17).

42. Soviet Foreign Ministry spokesman Yury Gremitskikh, as cited by TASS, April 18, 1991 (*FBIS,* April 19, 1991, p. 2).

43. Cf. comments by Foreign Minister Bessmertnykh, in a letter to the UN Secretary-General as cited by TASS, April 10, 1991 (*FBIS*, April 11, 1991, p. 2).

44. *Izvestia*, April 24, 1991.

45. "Paris, Europe Number One," in French, April 28, 1991 (*FBIS*, April 30, 1991, p. 10).

46. Ministry of Foreign Affairs chief spokesman Vitaly Churkin, as cited by TASS, April 29, 1991 (*FBIS*, April 30, 1991, p. 3).

47. Cited in report by R. Jeffrey Smith and Trevor Rowe, *Washington Post*, June 27, 1991.

48. Cited in report by Paul Lewis, *New York Times*, June 18, 1991.

49. *FBIS*, July 3, 1991, p. 19.

50. Cited in report by Jon Goshko, *Washington Post*, July 6, 1991.

51. Cited in ibid.

52. *Krasnaya Zvezda*, July 19, 1991, p. 30.

53. Cited in report by Gary Lee, *Washington Post*, July 29, 1991.

54. Cited in report by John Goshko, *Washington Post*, August 16, 1991.

55. Cited in report by Caryle Murphy, *Washington Post*, August 20, 1991.

56. Cf. Freedman, *Soviet Policy Toward Israel Under Gorbachev.*

57. Interfax, September 30, 1991 (*FBIS*, October 2, 1991, p. 19), and *New York Times*, September 25, 1991.

58. *Izvestia*, October 15, 1991 (*FBIS*, October 16, 1991, p. 21).

59. *Pravda*, October 10, 1991 (*FBIS*, October 11, 1991, p. 8).

60. *Pravda*, October 15, 1991 (*FBIS*, October 18, 1991, p. 13).

61. *Izvestia*, September 25, 1991 (*FBIS*, October 2, 1991, p. 19).

62. TASS, October 18, 1991 (*FBIS*, October 21, 1991, p. 22). See also the article by Thomas Friedman, *New York Times*, October 19, 1991, and the article by Jackson Diehl, *Washington Post*, October 19, 1991. (At a news conference following the announcement of the restoration of full diplomatic relations, Pankin said, "In the past, the Soviet Union tended to sort of side with the Palestinians and the Arab states, while the United States sided with Israel, and this did not bring any tangible fruit. The new approach is certainly not to have any protégés.")

63. *Izvestia*, October 14, 1991 (*FBIS*, October 18, 1991, p. 12).

64. TASS, October 2, 1991 (*FBIS*, October 3, 1991, p. 4).

65. Interfax, September 13, 1991 (*FBIS*, September 14, 1991, p. 21). See also the report by David Hoffman, *Washington Post*, September 14, 1991.

66. Cited in report by Thomas Friedman, *New York Times*, September 14, 1991.

67. *Krasnaya Zvezda*, September 24, 1991 (*FBIS*, September 24, 1991, p. 13).

68. *Izvestia*, September 18, 1991 (*FBIS*, September 24, 1991, p. 14).

69. Cited in report by Sharon Waxman, *Washington Post*, July 10, 1991.

70. Cited in *Washington Times*, October 19, 1991.

71. *Al-Ittihad al-Usbu'i* (Abu Dhabi), September 19, 1991 (*FBIS*, September 23, 1991, p. 13).

72. *Izvestia*, September 23, 1991 (*FBIS*, September 25, 1991 pp. 8–9).

73. TASS, October 22, 1991 (*FBIS*, October 23, 1991, p. 8).

74. Cf. TASS, in English, September 14, 1991 (*FBIS*, September 16, 1991, p. 15). See also Robert M. Danin, "Moscow and the Middle East Peace Conference After the Coup," *Middle East Insight*, vol. 8, no. 2 (September–October, 1991), pp. 4–8.

75. *Pravda*, September 16, 1991 (*FBIS*, September 17, 1991, p. 12).

76. TASS, September 21, 1991 (*FBIS*, September 23, 1991, pp. 10–11).

77. TASS, September 20, 1991 (*FBIS*, September 23, 1991, p. 11).

78. Moscow Radio World Service, September 21, 1991 (*FBIS*, September 23, 1991, p. 10).

79. TASS, September 20, 1991 (*FBIS*, September 23, 1991, p. 11).

80. *Krasnaya Zvezda,* September 26, 1991 (*FBIS,* October 8, 1991, pp. 14–15).

81. *Komsomalskaya Pravda,* September 7, 1991 (*FBIS,* September 10, 1991, p. 9).

82. TASS, September 20, 1991 (*FBIS,* September 23, 1991, pp. 11–12).

83. Cited in report by David Hoffman, *Washington Post,* September 21, 1991.

84. Cf. comments of a Soviet Foreign Ministry official to TASS, October 2, 1991 (*FBIS,* October 3, 1991, p. 8).

85. TASS, October 20, 1991 (*FBIS,* October 21, 1991, pp. 23–24).

86. Cited in report by Fred Hiatt, *Washington Post,* October 29, 1991.

87. Cited in report by John Yang and Fred Hiatt, *Washington Post,* October 10, 1991.

88. Cited in report by Andrew Rosenthal, *New York Times,* October 30, 1991.

89. Cited in report by Thomas Friedman, *New York Times,* October 30, 1991.

90. Associated Press report, *Baltimore Sun,* October 31, 1991.

91. TASS, October 30, 1991 (*FBIS,* October 30, 1991, p. 13).

92. *Izvestia,* May 5, 1992 (*CDSP* 44, no. 18 [1992]:15).

93. *Izvestia,* February 10, 1993 as cited in *Commonwealth of Independent States and the Middle East,* Hebrew University of Jerusalem (hereafter *CIS/ME,* vol. 18, no. 2 (February 1993):17–19.

94. Ibid., 19.

95. *CIS/ME* 18, no. 4 (April 1993):39.

96. See also the commentary in *Nezavisimaya Gazeta,* April 16, 1993 (*CDSP* 45, no. 15 [1993]:22).

97. *Izvestia,* June 29, 1993 (*CDSP* 45, no. 26 [1993]:13).

98. Interfax, June 28, 1993, cited in *CIS/ME* 18, no. 6 (1993):28.

99. *Sevodnya,* August 13, 1993 (*CIS/ME* 18, no. 8 [1993]:3).

100. *Komsomalskaya Pravda,* October 26, 1993 (*CIS/ME* 18, no. 10 [1993]:31).

101. *Kommersant,* December 1, 1993 (*FBIS;FSU,* December 2, 1993, 11).

102. *Pravda,* January 11, 1994 (*FBIS;FSU,* January 12, 1994, 25).

103. Itar/Tass, November 29, 1993 (*FBIS;FSU,* November 29, 1993, 18).

104. *Izvestia,* August 9, 1994 (*CDSP* 46, no. 32 [1994]:18).

105. See "Uneasy Eyes on Iraq and Iran," *Middle East* (London), January 1994, p. 7.

106. Interfax, February 2, 1995, cited in *CIS/ME* 20, nos. 2–3 [1995]:37.

107. *Krasnaya Zvezda,* August 3, 1995 (*FBIS:FSU,* August 4, 1995, 9).

108. Interfax, August 24, 1995 (*FBIS:FSU,* August 25, 1995, 13).

109. *CIS/ME* 20, nos. 4–5 [1995]:45.

110. Ibid., 46.

111. See the report by Robert Corzine, "Saddam Casts Shadow over Oil Market," *Financial Times,* January 26, 1996.

112. Cited in Charles Trueheart and David Hoffman, "France and Russia Differ from U.S. in Agendas on Iraq," *Washington Post,* November 13, 1997.

113. Cited in Alexander Tutushkin, "Russia's Oil Companies Stake Out Iraqi Oil Fields," *Kommersant Daily,* March 26, 1997 (translated in *CDSP,* vol. 49, no. 12 [1997]:19).

114. Cited in Daniel Pearl, "Saddam's Deals Undermine U.S. Position," *Wall Street Journal,* October 26, 1997.

115. *Nezavisimaya Gazeta,* November 28, 1997 (translated in *CDSP,* vol. 49, no. 48 [1997]:11.

116. Cited in David Hoffman, "Yeltsin Warns U.S. Again on Using Force," *Washington Post,* February 6, 1998.

Part Five

Retrospective and Reassessment

23

The Soviet Perception of the U.S. Threat

Georgiy Mirsky

Throughout history, the official Soviet mentality was chronically one of a besieged fortress. "Capitalistic encirclement" was the key word, the implacable struggle of the two world systems was an axiom, the famous expression *kto kovo* (who will beat whom) both motto and leitmotif. And the imperialist monsters biding their time to attack and destroy the first country of the victorious proletariat changed names: First it was Britain and France, then Nazi Germany and Japan, then the United States. But the essence of the external imperialist threat remained the same, the mortal danger was always there, and the options facing the beleaguered Soviet people never varied: Tough it out or perish.

Soviet citizens always felt they were unique, in more than one way. Even those who knew that life in the West was incomparably better and that the party propaganda praising the advantages of socialism was a huge fraud still believed that, given half a chance, the United States and its allies would attempt to crush the Soviet Union. Why? Because everybody was convinced that the Soviet Union—our country—was the biggest pain in the neck for world capitalism, the source of constant anger, fear, and irritation. By and large people did not question the necessity to maintain our armaments on the same level as the United States or to have allies and military footholds in diverse areas to counteract the U.S. encirclement policy. This was why Moscow's activist policy in the Middle East never met with disapproval, inasmuch as it was regarded as a counterbalance to dangerous U.S. expansion in that sensitive region. Discontent and irritation emerged later when one Arab-Israeli war after another demonstrated the incapacity of Soviet clients to effectively use the weaponry they had received from the USSR.

At this point, a question may be asked: Was it really so important for Kremlin rulers to take into account public opinion, considering the totalitarian nature of the regime? Certainly, political actions used to be taken without anybody in the Kremlin even thinking about the possible reaction of the people. Anything was certain to be approved. However, a protracted pattern of political activity, as distinct from a single action, in a specific area had better be popular and easy to swallow by the masses. The point is that, unlike during Stalin's rule, successor Kremlin regimes were based not so much on the *feuhrerprinzip* (principle of a single leader) as on the principle of collective leadership. It was an oligarchy ruling by consensus that was not confined solely to the Politburo but had to exist in lower party echelons as well. Signals that the "apparatchik aristocracy," the party, and management bosses were constantly sending to the very top might be vague, but still they could give a clue as to the prevailing opinion on specific issues inside the dominant class as a whole. And this opinion largely reflected views and beliefs of much broader sections of the population, even of the masses, it may be said. For, contrary to the concepts of some Sovietologists, the Soviet state, inhuman and antihuman as it was, could still be called the "people's state" in the sense that there was a close affinity between ideas, views, and cultural and social tastes of the rulers and the ruled. Soviet propagandists were not far from the truth when they claimed that they were representatives of the people who were in charge in the Soviet Union. Sure, they were exploiting and humiliating the people, depriving them of human rights and liberties, condemning them to a miserable and beastly life. However, all of this was being done not on behalf of some closed and privileged strata, as had been the case in prerevolutionary Russia, but on behalf of those sons of peasants and workers who had made it to the top. Thus, the Soviet elite was never socially and culturally alienated or even differentiated from the bulk of the population. The big shots and the masses basically shared the same mentality.

This helps to explain why it was important for any long-term political strategy to meet with the approval, if not the actual backing, of the people. Popular tastes, traditions, and prejudices, in their turn, could be used by policymakers for the rationalization of their line. The Middle East was a perfect example of convergence of popular beliefs—crude and false but mostly genuine—and the Kremlin's realpolitik. A widespread apprehension of U.S. aggressive designs coupled with anti-Semitism (since the U.S. ally, partner, and "vanguard striking force" in the Middle East happened to be a Jewish state, distasteful almost by definition to quite a few Russians, Ukrainians, and others) helped to ensure solid popular backing for an activist and militant anti-American line of Soviet policy in the Middle East. In practice, of course, it was translated into a strategic alliance with left-wing Arab regimes against the U.S.-Israel axis.

What were the motives of the Soviet leadership in the confrontation with the United States in the Middle East? Here, too, we must take as a starting point the overall Soviet concept of the global struggle between socialism and capitalism.

Some Western authors seemed to have overestimated the degree of the ideological component of Soviet foreign policy. They believed that ideology was paramount in determining the Kremlin's actions. Others, on the contrary, tended to focus almost exclusively on geopolitics. In fact it was a combination of both. There is no doubt that such people as Nikita Khrushchev, Leonid Brezhnev, Andrei Gromyko, Mikhail Suslov, and the rest sincerely believed in the inherent superiority of socialism and its ultimate victory over capitalism on the global scale; but at the same time they could not but realize that it was highly improbable for them to actually see the great triumph of Marxism-Leninism in their lifetimes. It was necessary for them to create conditions for this triumph, that is, to strengthen by all means the forces of world socialism and to weaken the imperialist enemy. To achieve this, it was imperative for the Kremlin leaders to change the global balance of forces, foremost in the political and military spheres, since they already lost faith in socialism's ability to achieve greater productivity of labor (in accordance with Lenin's concept). It was, of course, Lenin who predicted that it would be precisely in the sphere of productivity that socialism would eventually prove superior to capitalism. As early as the 1960s it was already impossible to seriously believe in such an eventuality given the obvious and growing gap between the economies of the two world systems. Thus, stress had to be placed on the undermining and sapping of the imperialist forces in the noneconomic sphere since the economy increasingly looked like the Achilles' heel of socialism. The adversary had to be defeated on a different battlefield, and it was clear that it was first in the sphere of military power and second in the ability to appeal to anticolonial, anti-Western sentiments of Third World nations that socialism could really have an edge over capitalism.

As to the first factor—military power—the Kremlin had to be very cautious about using it, especially after the Cuban missile crisis demonstrated the limits of brinkmanship. A world war was tacitly acknowledged to be suicidal, although the top military brass was reluctant to admit it. The awesome military might of the Soviet Union was to be used in three dimensions: First, as a reminder to Western Europe that tens of thousands of Soviet tanks were ready to roll in should the imperialists try to stage a counterrevolution in the socialist camp; second, as a counterbalance to U.S. sea power (this was why so much emphasis was laid on the expansion of the Soviet Navy); third, as a means of arming Soviet allies in the Third World.

The second factor—spreading Soviet influence in the Third World—was more promising, and the prospects seemed bright indeed of transforming the national liberation movement into a strategic ally against the West. Broadly speaking, this was the picture: To strike a military blow at the citadel of world capitalism was too dangerous due to the inevitable nuclear disaster it would entail; internal contradictions of capitalism were growing but the results were too slow in coming; the situation in Europe was frozen, forces on both sides engaged in trench warfare with no prospect of a breakthrough in either direction; the developing countries seething with discontent and driven by the dynamics of anticolonial inertia presented an excellent opportunity of undermining the imperialist system from within rather than engaging it in a frontal clash.

Finally, it must be said that if this kind of global thinking existed in the minds of the top leaders, this was not the case with the people down the road, with those who were planning and implementing the actual policy. For them, it was a given: The cold war was on, the United States was the enemy, everything had to be done to weaken it. It was a zero-sum game not necessarily motivated by ideological hatred and intransigence. The Communist commitment of the diplomats and the scholars in think tanks was actually skin-deep, as evidenced by the subsequent transformation of many of those people in the post–Mikhail Gorbachev era: They have quietly forgotten their Marxism and perfectly adapted to the new situation.

The Soviet Union and the Middle East in the Eras of Khrushchev and Brezhnev

If, during the Khrushchev and Brezhnev eras (1953 to 1982), you asked any young Soviet diplomat just out of the Institute of International Relations (MGIMO) about the significance of the Middle East for the USSR, he would answer matter-of-factly: Too vital to yield even an inch to the Americans. If you had pressed him for specifications, he would have mentioned the geostrategic dimension first, oil second, and the necessity to back our allies, the Arab anti-imperialist forces, third.

Upon a closer look, however, all three dimensions would prove to be not so terribly vital to the interests of the Soviet Union. From the geopolitical and strategic point of view, nobody in his right mind could imagine U.S. tanks rolling across the Arab deserts to the Caucasus in a new world war. In the "IBM era" the value of any piece of territory was greatly reduced anyway. As to oil, the USSR had plenty of it to begin with; any attempt to deprive the U.S. allies of Middle East oil would have been extremely dangerous since it was clear that the West would not hesitate to protect its access to that commodity with military force. The only thing left, therefore, was the USSR's strategic alliance with the left-wing Arab regimes.

This alliance was born under Nikita Khrushchev, who, in 1955, struck the famous arms deal with Egyptian President Gamal 'Abd al-Nasser. At the time, Khrushchev overruled the objections of the Soviet ambassador to Egypt, who was dismayed by the very idea of dealing with such a patently non-Communist and politically doubtful character as Nasser. Khrushchev was not inhibited by Marxist dogmatic puritanism. He regarded Nasser and his like as valuable partners in the anti-imperialist struggle. It was a bold and imaginative pattern; fabulous opportunities seemed to be in the offing.

From then on, the new alliance rapidly gained momentum. It expanded to involve Syria, Iraq, and Algeria, and, later, the Palestine Liberation Organization (PLO) and South Yemen. For a brief moment it seemed that Sudan, too, joined the "progressive camp"; Libya always was an embarrassing partner, but Mu'ammar al-Qaddafi's anti-imperialism appeared on balance to be more important than his bizarre theories, which were clearly incompatible not only with Marxism but also with the "revolutionary-democratic ideology" shared by Nasserists and Ba'thists. Typical of our attitude toward Qaddafi was a curious fact: Sometime in the 1970s, after one of his particularly vicious anti-Communist outbursts, it was decided to publish a reply to Qaddafi—not in *Pravda*, of course, but in the *Literary Gazette*, and a high-ranking official in the Central Committee's International Department was entrusted with this job. At the last moment, however, the article, which sounded very lucid and convincing to me, was taken out of the newspaper; apparently somebody higher up in the hierarchy decided that it was not worthwhile annoying the erratic colonel.

Pertaining to ideology, two observations might not be out of place. First, Khrushchev's new course of aligning Moscow with Nasser-type leadership was, of course, a purely pragmatic matter devoid of any ideological overtones. But in a socialist state it had to be rationalized and explained in terms of Marxist theory. This is when academic scholars, myself included, were called upon to work out a plausible theory aimed at proving in a convincing manner exactly why it was not only possible but necessary and highly helpful for the Great Cause to establish an alliance with such people as Nasser. The concept we elaborated was that of "Revolutionary Democracy," a non-Marxist, nonproletarian set of ideas and politics founded first on anticolonialism and second on the alleged impossibility of resolving the urgent problems of the developing countries on the basis of capitalism. The idea was that, although anti-imperialist nationalists were not ready to acknowledge and adopt Marxism's eternal truth, the logic of life would sooner or later teach them that only by following the socialist path could they hope to overcome their countries' backwardness and dependence on imperialism. Thus, the anticolonial, anti-imperialist revolution would inevitably grow into a social one, directed against both foreign and domestic oppressors. The national liberation movement would be transformed into a national-democratic revolution with a clear anticapitalist content and, later, into a popular-democratic revolution of a distinct socialist orientation.

The key terms in this concept were "noncapitalist development" and "socialist orientation." It was assumed that someday Nasser and his ilk would realize the futility of their hopes to modernize their countries and to build an industrial society within the framework of the world capitalist system with the help of the domestic bourgeoisie. Then, socialism would come naturally to them as the only way out of the horrible mess left behind by the imperialist exploiters.

Moreover, these theoretical constructions had very little to do with a genuine desire to build a happy socialist society in the dirt-poor and miserably backward Third World countries. I am not referring now to beliefs and motivations of the scholars who were busy writing memos, papers, and monographs on the issue: To the contrary, actual policymakers were indifferent to the results of "noncapitalist development" in Asia and Africa. What mattered, for them, was the involvement of the states ruled by the "revolutionary democrats" into a worldwide anti-Western coalition. Ideology for them was secondary; it was just instrumental in bringing about decisive change in the correlation of world forces. The Third World leaders who proclaimed their allegiance to socialism, even if only of a homemade and not Marxist variety, were ipso facto committed to the Soviet Union and the socialist community in the international arena. Just how successful they were in regard to the socialist transformation of their states was largely irrelevant. The main thing was to get into the "soft underbelly" of the capitalist system—Asia, Africa, and Latin America—so as to eventually besiege imperialism in its citadel. The more Third World countries proclaimed socialism as their goal, and thus became hostage to Soviet political support, arms deliveries, and so on, the better. Each of these countries could, from that moment on, be regarded as a loss to the United States and its allies: It was a zero-sum game. The propaganda aspect was important, too. Certainly what mattered for Brezhnev was being able to say in his report at the next party congress: "Comrades, the period under review has demonstrated once more that ideas of socialism are on the march throughout the globe; more countries now stand under the banner of socialism."

In regard to practical politics in the Middle East, the Kremlin's strategy aimed at ensuring a position of strength for the Arab allies in their confrontation with Israel, which was viewed as America's stooge. Disappointment and bitterness set in each time the Arab forces were defeated by Israel; over and over again, an escalation in arms deliveries followed. The more the USSR became committed to the protection of its Arab allies, the more it had to up the ante or else prepare to lose face.

At the same time, there is no evidence that Moscow ever wanted to escalate the Arab-Israeli confrontation to the point of large-scale war. First, Soviet leaders feared that Arab armies would be soundly beaten; second, they were apprehensive about the war spilling over into a U.S.-Soviet armed conflict signaling the outbreak of a nuclear world war. I happened to witness twice the worry and upset of high-ranking Soviet officials as Israeli forces seemed on the verge of closing in on Cairo and Damascus in 1967 and 1973. The PLO, too, was to be supported only inasmuch as it represented a nuisance in harassing Israel, but it was never regarded as a liberation army built up to recapture Palestine or even a part of it.

The official Soviet position, of course, was in accordance with UN Resolution 242. In the International Department of the Soviet Communist Party Central Committee, which was the place where policy guidelines were usually outlined (this also occurred in various academic institutions), debates took place from time to time over goals in the Middle East. The main issue was whether it would serve our interests if Resolution 242 was implemented and a Palestinian entity created. Opinions differed sharply, some people feeling that the Arabs would no longer need our military backing and that Moscow would lose its leverage.

Gorbachev, Perestroika, and New Political Thinking

At first, Gorbachev's foreign policy course was quite traditional, which is not surprising given his background as a career Soviet apparatchik. Even when he embarked on a course of far-reaching domestic reforms, the habitually tough anti-imperialist line showed no signs of slackening. The perestroika leaders, breaking new ground at home, were anxious to cover their flank in the forum of foreign policy. They felt they could not advance on two fronts simultaneously and they were afraid of being perceived as soft on imperialism. So Gorbachev and Shevardnadze preferred to be seen as strong and tough vis-à-vis the West; accordingly, Soviet Middle East policy remained for a time basically unchanged.[1]

Things began to move with the advent of the "new political thinking," particularly when "de-ideologization" of foreign policy was announced. This entailed a decline of ideological priorities and "socialist" commitments abroad. I remember speaking at a conference convened by Shevardnadze in 1987, with all of the Soviet ambassadors abroad participating. When I professed my disillusionment with the practical results of the "socialist orientation" in the Third World, it was a shock to many. However, a group of our ambassadors in the African states approached me after my talk and hastened to thank me for my outspokenness. "At last, somebody has told the truth," they said. "We knew all along that this socialist orientation was a fraud and a failure but, of course, in our official reports things just had to look quite different."

Inevitably, reappraisal of our long-standing line in the Middle East was due to come. More and more, scholars and journalists began questioning the very foundations of our policy in the Arab-Israeli conflict. Doubts were expressed as to the wisdom of our 1967 decision to break off diplomatic relations with Israel. A new approach was shaping up with regard to the Camp David accords.

It is well known that opposition to Camp David and bitter denunciation of Egyptian President Anwar Sadat's political line were the cornerstones of Soviet policy in the Middle East in the 1980s.[2] Much later, in the days of perestroika, I ventured an opinion that it was high time Egypt was readmitted into the family of Arab states. Immediately, a prominent party official with an Arabist background retorted: "Well, and how about the slogan, 'Bury Camp David?'" In spite of the utter absurdity of this position, the official stand on Camp David remained steadfast during the first perestroika years. But this, too, began to change as glasnost gained strength.

Some authors, Western as well as Russian, seemed to underestimate the role of the ideological factor and, correspondingly, of glasnost in the demise of Communist rule. As the ideological barriers were crumbling, suddenly it became possible to question the Soviet past as a whole. When Gorbachev finally, albeit reluctantly, gave the green light to de-Stalinization, little did he think that very soon it would turn into de-Leninization and de-bolshevization. Then, an end to the cold war and to the confrontation era was announced. Almost overnight, the United States ceased to be an enemy; the very word "imperialism" disappeared from the newspapers. The party apparatus suddenly realized that the bottom line was not there any more, the cornerstone fell out, the raison d'être of the system's having vanished. This partly explains why the resistance to the overthrow of the Communist regime in the aftermath of the August coup was so feeble: The heart was no longer there; the ideological commitment was gone.

Even before the final collapse, there was a sea change in foreign policy. Anti-imperialism as a guideline disappeared; promoting socialism worldwide became a futile task. Diplomatic relations with Israel had to be restored. De-ideologization meant that our relations with the Arab world were no longer dictated by the commitment to leftist Arab regimes and the need to deny the United States the dominant role in the area. Since the United States was not an enemy any more, why bother about Israel as an enemy foothold?

When the Gulf crisis erupted with the Iraqi invasion of Kuwait, the Soviet Union for the first time sided with the United States in a confrontation with a Third World country—and a socialist-oriented country at that. Some took it very hard. When I spoke at the Academy of the Warsaw Treaty Organization in Moscow at the height of the crisis, I bluntly told my audience that, in my opinion, Saddam Hussein was a gangster and a butcher. There was an uproar, angry exclamations, and some colonels even walked out. These were the kind of people who arrived by the hundreds to attend the recent reception at the Iraqi Embassy in Moscow to celebrate the 1958 Iraqi revolution. For them, Saddam is a hero, an anti-American, anti-Jewish, anti-democratic, tough, no-nonsense leader. In short, he is their kind of man.

Faced by strong opposition to his allegedly pro-U.S. policy, Gorbachev tried, for the last time, to play a relatively autonomous role.[3] Middle East adviser Yevgeny Primakov was sent to Baghdad to lobby for a compromise solution. Had he succeeded, it would have been a serious boost to Gorbachev's prestige. First it would have placated the Russian "patriots" unhappy with what they perceived as Gorbachev's subservience to Bush. Second, it could have assuaged the Arabs, who by that time were mad at Gorbachev over the issue of Jewish immigration to Israel. Soviet ambassadors in Arab capitals were reporting to the Kremlin that Soviet prestige in the Arab world was at an all-time low. Arabs felt that Gorbachev (much loved by Bush) could, if he wished, have persuaded the U.S. president to channel the bulk of the Soviet Jews to the United States rather than to Israel. If Gorbachev was not even trying to do this, it could only mean that he did not care about Arabs at all.

Gorbachev, of course, knew that he could not do any such thing. The only way to restore, if only partially, Soviet prestige in the Arab world was to save Iraq from imminent disaster. But Primakov's mission was doomed from the beginning. Later Primakov told me that, given three more days, he would have persuaded Tariq 'Aziz and thus Saddam Hussein to make concessions that would have prevented the U.S. ground offensive. The question arises: Just who did Primakov think he was that the U.S. president would give him three days when everything was already decided and D-Day had already been fixed?

At the subsequent Madrid conference the Soviet Union tried to posture as an independent actor, but nobody took it seriously; the USSR was no longer a superpower. Paradoxically, it was Bush who tried to place the Soviet Union on a superpower basis for the last time. In fact, his "new world order" envisaged a situation in which both superpowers were to continue playing a dominant role in world affairs, but in cooperation and not in confrontation. Gorbachev would undoubtedly have gone along with that, but it was too late. The hands on the clock were nearing midnight.

Post-Communist Russia and the Middle East

Currently Moscow has little foreign policy to speak of. The main trend is to maintain good relations with the West, although the rising tide of Russian nationalism can already be seen as threatening the seemingly well-established pattern. Anti-Western and anti-American backlash in particular is evident in Russian public opinion.

In the foreseeable future, only the Middle East offers Russia the chance to play a role in world affairs. Europe is lost to Russian influence, cut off as it is by Poland and Ukraine both geographically and politically. Even if it were not so, the united Germany effectively prevents Russia from playing any major role in European affairs. The Balkans are a powder keg. In the Far East and Southeast Asia more powerful players are flexing their muscles: Japan, China, the United States. Tropical Africa and Latin America are largely irrelevant to Moscow at this point. The only region left is the Middle East.

In that region Russia has commitments, political and military investments, allies, and leverage of sorts. As a successor state to the Soviet Union, Russia is cochair, along with the United States, of the Geneva Conference. Like the United States, Russia can now wield some influence, although to a far lesser degree, in both the Arab world and in Israel. Russian diplomats can sit at international conferences on the Middle East, pretending to be on equal footing with the United States. Thus, Russia can be perceived (by the Russians themselves, of course, and in Russian public opinion) as not having been pushed out of the picture altogether in world affairs.

Perception is what matters, not substance. As former U.S. Speaker of the House Tip O'Neill once said, all politics is local. For any government in Moscow, it is vital to be seen by the people as not neglecting Russian national interests abroad, as pursuing an independent foreign policy worthy of a great power. The Russians like to think of their country as a great power, no longer as a superpower. An honorable role in the Middle East will be good for their self-esteem. And it is in the Middle East alone that Russia has a tradition of diplomatic success. The Middle East is where its foreign policy future lies.

Notes

1. Information for this point was obtained in conversations the author conducted with Alexander Yakovlev, a top adviser for Gorbachev.

2. Probably the best scholarly expression of Soviet anger and frustration is Yevgeny Primakov's book on Sadat, entitled *Story of Betrayal.*

3. For more on Gorbachev's role during the Gulf crisis and war, see Chapter 22 by Robert O. Freedman in this volume.

24

The U.S.-GCC Relationship: Is It a Glass Leaking or a Glass Filling?

John Duke Anthony

The Middle East regional grouping with which the United States has developed its most extensive and multifaceted relationship is the Gulf Cooperation Council (GCC), composed of Bahrain, Kuwait, Oman, Qatar, Saudi Arabia, and the United Arab Emirates (UAE). The GCC region's prodigious oil reserves, to be sure, have long figured prominently in any public discussion of the area.[1] However, the nature of U.S. involvement in the GCC countries in reality is much more diverse and complex than a focus on their energy resources alone would suggest. Although the United States has recently twice deployed armed forces to the region, most Americans still seem unaware of U.S. interests there other than oil.

The GCC countries have played, and are likely to continue to play, a major role in regional and world affairs. Despite broad agreement on this factual premise, there are few scholarly assessments of what the U.S. gains and does not gain from its relationships with the GCC countries. This chapter provides such an assessment, albeit mainly from only one side of the equation: what the GCC (as a nonsupranational organization) and its members do and do not contribute to their relationships with the United States.[2] The U.S.-GCC relationship is approached in terms of negatives and positives, or, metaphorically, from the idea that the relationship is a glass that is leaking and a glass that is filling. The "leaking," or negativist, thesis is presented first. We will look at five stated U.S. interests: strategic, economic, political, commercial, and defense.

The Glass Is Leaking: The Negativist Assessment

U.S. Strategic Interests

Both negativists and positivists agree that the United States, for at least a half-century, has had several *strategic* interests related to the Gulf. The four most important have been: to prevent the Strait of Hormuz and hydrocarbon resources in the region from falling under the control of a power hostile to the United States; to ensure access for the United States and its allies to the region's energy reserves on manageable terms; to preserve the sovereignty, independence, and territorial integrity of all the Gulf states, since local conflicts could invite intervention by a hostile power and/or interfere with the region's production and transportation of oil; and to foster support for U.S. efforts to achieve a just, lasting, and comprehensive settlement of the Arab-Israeli conflict.

The negativist argument (that is, the argument of those who view negatively the extent to which GCC states have contributed to the achievement of these goals) goes as follows: Reaching back to the 1950s—before any of the other GCC members were independent—Saudi Arabia, the largest, most populous, and most powerful GCC country, refused to join forces with Western efforts to create and sustain regional defense systems, such as the Baghdad Pact and the successor Central Treaty Organization, despite the fact that Riyadh was avowedly anti-Communist and opposed to Soviet encroachment in the region. Further, even after being directly threatened by Iran in the 1980s and then Iraq in the early 1990s, the GCC governments have not been able to develop effective defense cooperation arrangements to deter neighbors. Nor has the group made much progress in working out the terms for ongoing regional defense coordination with other major Arab countries, such as Egypt and Syria.

Likewise, despite the existence of bilateral defense cooperation agreements between the United States and all of the GCC countries (except Saudi Arabia), the GCC states have not been able to reach *formal collective* agreements with the United States on deployment of forces, pre-positioning of weapons and related materiel, *multilateral* military exercises, and other measures that, the negativists insist, would help maximize deterrence and defense capabilities.

Moreover, even several years after being physically threatened and attacked by Iran and Iraq, the GCC remains unable to adopt and follow a unified policy toward Tehran and Baghdad. To be sure, of the six GCC members, Kuwait and Saudi Arabia remain the most opposed to normalization of relations with Baghdad in the absence of complete compliance with all United Nations (UN) Security Council resolutions resulting from Iraq's 1990–1991 invasion and occupation of Kuwait. By contrast, other GCC member states, though insisting that Iraq implement the resolutions, have followed a somewhat different course. They retain ties with Iraqi President Saddam Hussein's government and periodically call for finding ways to ease the effect of the sanctions on the Iraqi populace. In addition, there have been, and remain, differences among the GCC members over how best to deal with Iran. Thus, the entire Gulf region has been, is, and is likely to remain, an unpredictable if not unstable area. So goes the main negativist argument.

Other negativist concerns include the expense entailed in ensuring protection of U.S. access to the region's oil, which is likely to remain a heavy drain on scarce U.S. military and financial resources. In this regard, many are quick to recall that in 1967 Kuwait and Saudi Arabia (and in 1973 these two GCC states plus Qatar and the UAE), used their oil as a political weapon against the United States. "Not only that," say the negativists, "these countries also cooperated with other OPEC [the Organization of Petroleum Exporting Countries] members in rapidly raising the price of their oil to consumers, setting off worldwide economic dislocations."[3]

Given the foregoing background, negativists ask: "What assurance can there be that, if the United States continues to rely heavily upon imports of Gulf oil, the GCC's governments, perhaps under less friendly regimes than are now in power, might not do the same thing again?" Such considerations offer a persuasive rationale for diversifying U.S. oil imports away from all the Gulf producers, that is, not just the GCC countries but Iran and Iraq as well. It is not a reach to then argue (as the negativists do) that such considerations constitute a compelling reason to work toward the ultimate reduction of U.S. dependence on imported oil entirely.

Along these lines, negativists argue GCC states have not contributed as much as they could to political stability and development within their region. The support by some GCC states for a breakaway movement in southern Yemen in 1994 is cited as an example. Such support merely prolonged the civil war there and raised questions about the ability of GCC countries to develop a consistent and supportive policy toward Yemen. GCC member states, even among themselves, have been unable to resolve border disputes to the extent that individual countries have boycotted ministerial-level GCC meetings. Even worse, Bahrain and Qatar and Saudi Arabia and Qatar have engaged in armed clashes.

Lastly, in terms of the major U.S. strategic interests noted, negativists complain that the GCC countries persist in enforcing their primary economic boycott of Israel. On such questions as the future status of Jerusalem, the Israeli settlements on expropriated Palestinian land in the Occupied Territories, and other highly controversial issues in the Middle East peace process, the negativists believe that the attitudes and viewpoints of most GCC countries' leaders are at odds with many in the United States. They also fault the GCC members for not pressing Syria and Lebanon to reach a peace agreement with Israel and for having manifested, until recent times, less than an overwhelming endorsement of what the United States has done to date to move the parties toward a just, durable, and comprehensive settlement of the Arab-Israeli conflict.

U.S. Economic Interests: GCC Shortcomings

In faulting GCC countries for their impact on U.S. economic interests, the negativists highlight several areas of concern (in addition to the Arab oil embargo already noted). For them, almost all GCC states continue to suffer record annual budget deficits caused by oil prices depressed since 1983, lowered return on some foreign investments, and the tremendous expense of paying for Operations Desert Shield and Desert Storm. As to Kuwait, there are the added costs of reconstruction of its war-ravaged economy, environment, and infrastructure. Another concern, as expressed by one observer, is "the high percentage of GCC states' GNP [gross national product] that is spent on security, defense, public enterprises, subsidies, and public welfare benefits, not to mention funds consumed by waste, conspicuous consumption, and the support of large ruling families."[4]

To continue, a consequence of such economic shortcomings is that the United States can no longer look to the GCC countries for help with the U.S. budget deficit through the purchase of U.S. Treasury notes. Neither can the United States any longer count on GCC countries to invest in U.S. securities and real estate or make sizable contributions to international banks and development funds.

Notwithstanding the GCC countries' past actions, yet another negativist concern is that in the mid-1990s GCC governments have reduced considerably the level of direct bilateral foreign economic assistance. Negativists maintain that continued deficit financing by the GCC states could bring them into competition with the U.S. government and U.S. business for loans in international money markets. Further, the long-term economic viability of the GCC states is questionable. They ask: How could it be otherwise given their dependence upon a single, depletable natural resource? In addition, technological trends—for example, development of an electric-powered automobile or utilities fueled by nuclear fusion—may result in these countries becoming less important to the United States in the next century.

According to negativists, GCC economic prospects are clouded further by three other phenomena: Agricultural production is expensive, heavily subsidized, and relies largely on rapidly depleting, nonrenewable groundwater resources; small populations whose level of training for work in high-tech industries is limited, and women and certain minorities—for example, Shi'a Muslims—sometimes have difficulty finding employment in the areas of national security and defense; and the consequent dependence on large numbers of foreign workers, many of whom are not encouraged or allowed to emigrate to GCC countries for the purpose of becoming citizens or otherwise developing a long-term stake in the societies of GCC states.

Lastly, the GCC's efforts at promoting economic integration and rationalization among its members have not gone very far. The reason, in large part, is twofold: These states still compete more than cooperate in developing infrastructures, utilities, and hydrocarbon-based industries; and the volume and value of their trade with each other, in comparison with their economic partners further afield, remains very small.

To continue, as in most other regional efforts to establish customs unions and a common market, GCC visionaries and leaders alike are frequently stymied. Scarcely a day passes when the enthusiasm of even the most proactive and optimistic among them is subdued when confronted with the many regionwide realities of reluctance rooted in conservative and parochial interests. In short, the negativist viewpoint holds that in the GCC region, as elsewhere, economic nationalism remains far more deeply entrenched and vibrant than the will to endorse, let alone implement, notions of supranational authority or shared sovereignty.

U.S. Political Interests: GCC Weaknesses

A substantial number of U.S. negativists find considerable fault with the domestic political systems of GCC countries. The force of domestic political opinion has frequently made it difficult for GCC leaders to pursue pan-GCC foreign policy objectives toward the United States openly and effectively. All GCC-state economic strategists and planners, for example, want to increase the extent of trade, investment, and technological cooperation with the Western world in general and with the United States in particular. Yet, they and their fellow GCC citizens are keen to avoid granting the U.S. corporate sector the maximum advantages possible or proceeding on a "business-as-usual" basis until the United States has exercised the maximum leadership and influence possible in bringing about a satisfactory end to the Arab-Israeli conflict. Some go further, saying that the United States must work harder at diminishing the inconsistency in its application of various moral principles and international legal norms on matters of importance to Arabs and Muslims.[5]

These kinds of political difficulties aside, the U.S. and GCC governments have unofficially fenced off from their bilateral discourse significant areas of difference and disagreement over their respective internal political systems. Indeed, each would regard any negative commentary by the other as an unacceptable intrusion into internal affairs and would react accordingly. And though the U.S. and GCC governments have declared their respective domestic political systems "off limits" to the other, this restraint does not extend to foreign policies.

In this regard, many negativists maintain that the GCC countries have insufficiently taken into consideration U.S. political interests in inter-Arab and inter-Islamic councils. For example, notwithstanding the extraordinary role of several GCC countries in hosting Israelis involved in the multilateral dimensions of the Arab-Israeli peace talks, negativists cite the GCC-state inability or unwillingness to take a leading role in *formally recognizing* Israel *by name* through peace treaties or normalized relations with the Jewish state to the maximum extent possible, without regard to a settlement of the Arab-Israeli conflict.

Many negativists also fault other aspects of the GCC countries' foreign policies: for example, the support that some citizens give to radical elements in Middle East, African, and Asian countries; reluctance to stand with the United States and Israel on certain UN resolutions, such as the one rescinding the 1975 UN General Assembly's "Zionism-is-racism" resolution, and other U.S. positions protective or exonerative of Israel; and unwillingness to enter into serious discussions about regional nonproliferation of nuclear weapons until or unless the United States insists that Israel, a nuclear state within their midst, be held accountable to the same criteria, that is, that it be required to become a signatory to the nuclear Non-Proliferation Treaty (NPT), which all the GCC countries have signed but Israel has not.

On balance, however, U.S. criticisms of the political component of GCC countries' foreign policies, positions, actions, and attitudes vis-à-vis international issues have never been as great as those that U.S. officials direct toward other Arab countries. Indeed, as shown below, the benefits that the United States derives from GCC countries' foreign policies in general far outweigh the negative.

U.S. Commercial Interests: GCC Disadvantages

Negativists and positivists agree that U.S. commercial interests have steadily increased in the GCC since the mid-1970s. They also agree that these encompass a growing U.S. need to export U.S. goods and services to GCC countries, in part to pay for increasing U.S. imports of oil and petrochemicals from these producers.

The negativists, however, claim that GCC governments have made it unnecessarily difficult for Americans to trade, invest, and engage in mutually profitable joint ventures. They charge that if the United States is the trading partner of choice for GCC countries, then GCC member states could not be more self-defeating in pursuing that choice.

Some of the points of contention consistently articulated by the negativists are: prohibitions in most GCC countries on foreign ownership of real estate and on outright ownership of companies; prohibition on equity participation in petroleum, electricity, and communications companies; lack of effective dispute resolution mechanisms based on Western norms; the improving but still insufficiently effective enforcement of laws against copyright, trademark, and patent violations; the absence of a common external tariff or a customs union; difficult entry and residency procedures; the limitation of capital markets; the very beginnings of privatization of state-owned industries and services; the high percentage of GNP spent on security, defense, and other nonproductive sectors of their societies; and the uncertain situation regarding long-term water resources, seen by the lack of a single river or a perennially flowing stream in the entire GCC region. Additional complaints include a legal and bureaucratic system that appears to give unfair advantage to GCC host country nationals over foreign partners and employees; stringent labeling or quality standards that often keep out U.S. products while admitting those from Europe or Japan; and the uncertain extent to which the GCC countries are truly committed to interstate competition in light of various member-country de facto limitations on cross-border banking, trade, and labor movement.

The GCC countries are increasingly aware that many potential U.S. investors have jaded, pessimistic, and, in many cases, erroneous views regarding the prospects for mutually beneficial trade, investment, and joint ventures. In response, virtually all GCC countries have mounted campaigns to counter this less than positive image. To date, however, for many U.S. business leaders, the gap between the problems and the potential remains substantial.

U.S. Defense Interests: GCC Limitations

One of the most frequently heard negativist criticisms is GCC inability thus far to develop greater self-reliance in the area of military preparedness. Many critics focus on the absence of a more effective pan-GCC system of deterrence and defense against threats to the member countries from within their own neighborhood. The negativists, in particular, fault GCC countries for the following: an unwillingness to consider granting the United States one or more military bases from which it could be in a position to defend these countries more effectively from threat or attack; reluctance to accommodate U.S. logistical and operational needs to the extent some U.S. military planners would like, given the constraints on U.S. forces in terms of size and the distances from which they would have to be deployed, especially since most U.S. military planners believe that a future armed conflict in the GCC region will likely be quite different from the last one, in which the Iraqi invader, in effect, allowed the United States and the allied coalition six months to mobilize and deploy; and unwillingness, notwithstanding the need for some semblance of geopolitical balance among great power supporters, to agree on a more unified approach to procurement that would enhance the effectiveness of military equipment and defense systems via specifications standardization and interoperability.

Additional shortcomings cited are lukewarm commitment to building a pan-GCC force in sufficient size and strength to enhance the credibility of collective defense capabilities and combined national force structures; reluctance to adopt a unified command and control structure and a system for mobilization and deployment familiar to Western forces that would be required to come to their defense; continuation of border disputes that tend to vitiate political trust and confidence among member countries; and failure thus far to create fully professional armed forces with promotions and assignments based solely on merit and experience (placing aside the concern for ensuring loyalty and enhancing political-military capabilities).[6]

For these and other reasons, there are few who regard the GCC and its member countries in positive terms. Finally, the negativists declare that the GCC and its member countries cannot: hold their own in the strategic context; ensure unhindered U.S. and other foreign access to the region's energy resources; manifest the critics' desired kinds of political commitment befitting an ally or partner; muster the will to extend the benefits of a level playing field for U.S. commercial interests; and bear a greater financial or soldierly share of the burden of defending the region. They therefore conclude that the GCC collectively and its member countries, either singly or jointly, should not be taken seriously in any U.S. plan for protecting and enhancing U.S. interests in the region.

The Glass Is Filling: The Positivist Assessment

U.S. Strategic Interests

The positivist school of thought stands in marked contrast to the negativist school discussed above. It argues that the GCC and its member countries have made numerous important contributions to global strategic interests in general and to U.S. and other Western strategic interests in particular; this is likely to continue to be the case until far into the future. In fact, the positivists contend GCC countries have consistently brought a far greater number of assets to the strategic equation than negativists are willing to acknowledge.

With respect to strategic issues in general, positivists do not deny the degree to which the GCC member countries are weak, vulnerable, and exposed to the threat of stronger powers bent on subverting their independence, threatening the region's vital maritime arteries, and sabotaging energy production facilities. They would concede it is the failure of GCC governments to resolve intra-GCC disputes that impinges negatively on prospects for more rapid progress in defense cooperation. In fact, they concede such failures invite the interference, in support of one of the disputants, of a power hostile to GCC and/or U.S. interests.

At the same time, however, positivists point out GCC countries have and will continue to take steps to compensate for these shortcomings. In this regard, the words of a former high-ranking GCC official are instructive: "We are under no illusion as to our lack of effective power to dissuade our adversaries. The lack of such power has forced us to adopt a strategy, however, that, on balance, is almost as effective. That is, not having the requisite credible power of our own, we have had no choice but to *borrow* it from our friends."[7] He continues:

> We're well aware that the means may not have pleased everyone. However, the end result has been, and continues to be, compatible with our strategic interests and those of our friends. At the end of the day, with two important exceptions—the eruptions of the Iran-Iraq war in 1980 and the Kuwait crisis in 1990—this strategy, on the whole, has been successful. Given the circumstances in which we are placed, it has been *our* strategy every bit as much as our friends may like to claim that it is their strategy.[8]

In this light, the positivists fault the negativists for overlooking or disregarding the fact that a significant number of the strategic constants and more than a few of the variables vis-à-vis the GCC region are not in U.S. hands, or any other country's for that matter. For example, the globally vital Strait of Hormuz (which the United States and other nations seek to keep open) straddles sea lanes that pass into, through, and out of waters that are not within the sovereign reach of the United States but are in the riparian GCC countries. Their cooperation is more than desirable: It is absolutely critical for success in any U.S. or other allied country's efforts to protect and, if necessary, defend these waterways.

The same is true of the oil fields located in GCC states, as well as their gas-gathering systems, desalination plants, refineries and transportation fleets, harbors and airports, pipelines, military bases and supply depots, armed forces academies, and defense procurement agencies. Without exception, actual day-to-day control of virtually every one of these strategic networks and assets is under the sovereign, administrative, financial, logistical, and operational control of the GCC countries themselves.

The positivists also point out that Saudi Arabia, often supported by Kuwait, played an important role in rallying the world's broad and critically located Muslim populations against Soviet expansion, an answer to the negativist attack on the duo's failure to join Western-sponsored defense pacts against the Soviet Union.

This strategic role extended into the long southern frontier of the USSR, most prominently into the leadership and tangible assistance that Saudi Arabia and other

GCC countries provided against the Soviet invasion and occupation of Afghanistan; across the northern half of Africa, where Moscow repeatedly sought footholds in the last several decades; into those parts of Southeast Asia where Communist influence was blunted in the last quarter-century—Indonesia, Malaysia, and the Philippines. The positivists thus argue that the net effect of protecting nearly one billion inhabitants of the Islamic world was as crucial as blocking Soviet expansion into Western Europe.

The GCC's past contributions have been in broad accord with U.S. global strategic interests. As to current and future U.S. strategic needs, the GCC countries' role vis-à-vis several issues is even more significant. For example, the positivists point out that within U.S. planning circles, a broad consensus exists on GCC countries' central link to U.S. strategic imperatives for arriving at 2020 C.E. with its superpower status and the concomitant benefits intact. In short, these states are viewed as essential to the U.S. ability to defend itself and its interests abroad against any and all would-be adversaries and—the other half of the equation—to steadily improve its standard of living.

The positivists contend they are on solid ground. It is a tenet among strategic planners that, for the foreseeable future, the United States has no option but to ensure that it remain financially, industrially, and technologically strong. Economic, and especially financial, strength across the board is, of course, central to the prospects for success. To be sure, the 1992 presidential mantra was "It's the economy, stupid!" However, the crafters of such catchy clichés missed the more important point: Far more fundamental, though much less appreciated and far less discussed, is *energy*. Indeed, it is both raw and refined energy—as opposed to the more ill-defined and disputed concept of "economics"—that is undeniably essential to all three of the strategy's key components. Finally, at the root of the energy factor is the GCC region, if only because it contains and controls more than half of the world's hydrocarbon energy resources—the key to the strategy's prospects.

On matters pertaining to the strategic calculus of interests vis-à-vis the GCC countries, the positive outweighs the negative. Indeed, among the world's 193 nation-states heavily dependent upon oil and gas for economic growth and development, one country—the United States—dwarfs all others in terms of its privileged and strategic position vis-à-vis the owners of these prodigious energy supplies. The United States is the world's single largest importer and consumer of the GCC region's finite, depleting hydrocarbon resources and is more engaged than any other in the production, refining, and marketing of the GCC countries' energy supplies.

U.S. Economic Interests: GCC Contributions

U.S. and other national economic interests in the GCC region are herein defined as, first and foremost, assured *access* to GCC countries' energy resources without regard to price or levels of production. Throughout this century, it has been overwhelmingly Western oil companies (mostly U.S.) that have not only enjoyed such access but also occupied the most envied and lucrative positions in the development of the GCC states' oil and gas reserves.[9]

Despite these powerful U.S. economic advantages, GCC countries played roles in the 1967 and 1973 Arab oil embargoes, inexcusable in negativist eyes. (The negativists also hark back to the frequent and sharp OPEC price hikes of the 1970s, which many still tend to confuse with the oil embargo.) In so doing, they express fear that OPEC (i.e., the GCC and other Arab oil-producing countries) might once again take advantage of a world energy shortage to manipulate oil prices for political or economic ends.

In response, positivists point out that the first of these very damaging blows to U.S. and other Western interests occurred more than a quarter century ago; the last took place more than two decades ago. Both preceded the GCC's founding. The positivists thus argue against clinging to the past.

Recent realities include GCC countries' roles and reactions regarding: Israel's air attack in the summer of 1981 on the Osirak nuclear reactor at Tuwaitha, near Baghdad; the 1982 Israeli invasion and occupation of Lebanon; the Iran-Contra affair; and Israel's efforts to forcibly repress the Palestinian *intifada* (uprising). The positivists stress that the GCC countries *did not* proclaim another oil embargo against the United States or other Western countries in spite of continuing strong U.S. support for Israel and assorted anti-Arab and anti-Muslim provocations.

The positivists further point out GCC actions in the aftermath of the August 1990 Iraqi invasion of Kuwait and the UN resolution barring purchases of either Kuwaiti or Iraqi oil as long as Iraq occupied Kuwait. Their actions resulted in a positive global effect: Decisiveness and boldness achieved not only the GCC countries' own economic goals but also those of allies and partners, including the United States. The specifics are worth recalling, because they enabled the United States, other members of the allied coalition, and the GCC members themselves to achieve common strategic and economic objectives.

The GCC countries met with one another, and the four GCC members of OPEC—Kuwait, Qatar, Saudi Arabia, and the UAE—called for an emergency meeting of OPEC to obtain, through consultation and consensus, the necessary support to legitimize increased oil production to compensate for the UN embargo. In calling for the meeting, the GCC members risked the further alienation of fellow OPEC members—Iraq, Libya, and other Arab countries—who only days earlier had voted against a resolution in the Arab League, sponsored by the GCC governments, calling for the mobilization and deployment of Arab forces in the GCC countries' defense.

Despite being outnumbered and militarily outgunned by their opponents, the GCC members of OPEC succeeded in obtaining authorization to raise production levels commensurate with the embargo-induced shortfall, thereby bringing demand for oil back into balance with supply and ensuring a steady flow of oil in adequate amounts at manageable prices. In effect, by moving quickly to compensate for the deficit in oil production, the GCC countries had a profound and very salutary influence on the manner in which the world was able to respond to the energy dimension of the conflict.

The positivists will not downplay the overall positive role that the GCC oil-producing countries have played, and continue to play, inside OPEC. They note that the GCC members of OPEC have repeatedly exercised a restraining influence within OPEC councils and have been a consistently moderate force within OPEC for two decades, working to keep prices in tandem with, or lower than, rates of inflation. Indeed, from 1987 to 1990, several GCC oil-producing countries helped keep oil prices down by exceeding OPEC-assigned production quotas.

The positivists will not view GCC countries exclusively in terms of energy. Rather they recognize the benefits the United States derives from an economic relationship with the GCC countries extend beyond oil. In fact, the GCC countries have provided substantial investment capital to both the public and private sectors of the United States and other industrial economies for most of the past twenty years.

Such investment, the positivists note, has played a significant role in the overall well-being of millions of Americans, contributed to U.S. corporate vitality, indirectly augmented federal and state tax revenues, constituted employment for several million Americans, and provided funds that enable research and development and lower overall production and per unit costs for the defense, civil aviation, telecommunications, and power-generating industries—all of which are fundamental components of U.S. strategic objectives. No remotely comparable contribution can be attributed to any, let alone six, of the more than 120 other countries that together with the GCC states make up the developing world. Moreover, for most of the GCC's existence, it has been second only to Japan as the single greatest underwriter of the U.S. national deficit. A corollary benefit of the billions invested in U.S. Treasury securities is the low and stable U.S. interest rate.

GCC countries remain key to continued international support for the U.S. dollar, in which the GCC countries' oil and gas exports are denominated. Such support, day in and day out, even when the dollar has been weak, has given the United States a privileged and much envied advantage over all other oil-importing countries. The positivists highlight the fact that this support has been, and continues to be, essential to the ongoing stability of the dollar in monetary transactions and to the strength of the U.S. financial system worldwide.

In addition, U.S. strategic, economic, political, commercial, and military interests have all benefited from GCC countries' developmental assistance to the world's poorer nations. As a percentage of their gross national products and their incomes per capita, GCC member states have long ranked second to none in philanthropy to the world's less fortunate peoples, as grants, concessional assistance, and in-kind aid to more than eighty developing countries for the past quarter-century attests.

To be sure, since 1991, continued low oil prices, the costs of Desert Shield/Desert Storm, and Kuwaiti reconstruction, among other things, have resulted in major cutbacks in the GCC countries' foreign aid. Also, some former aid recipients, notably Jordan and Yemen, were dropped for political reasons. However, the GCC states' charitable and international development agencies have continued to operate, with beneficial results for such economically needy and strategically important countries as Egypt and Syria as well as for numerous institutions serving the humanitarian and developmental needs of the Palestinians under Israeli occupation.

One of the GCC's greatest contributions to the economic side of the U.S.-GCC equation has been, and continues to be, the sharing of the financial burden. For example, the GCC countries defrayed U.S. and allied costs during Desert Shield/ Desert Storm; by any standard, this was a major contribution to the reversal of Iraq's aggression, the liberation of Kuwait, and the defense of the GCC countries. Indeed, with the possible exception of the NATO alliance and the Organization of American States, no other regional grouping of countries was as well positioned as the GCC states to cover most of the costs associated with defense in the Iran-Iraq war, in the 1990–1991 Kuwait crisis, and in the October 1994 renewal of Iraq's threat to Kuwait. Had the GCC countries been unable to contribute in this way, the international coalition of forces may not have been as forthcoming or as large.

Certainly, in debating the extent to which the United States should become involved in reversing Iraq's aggression against Kuwait in 1990, negativists were quick to complain that the United States had no business mounting an operation so massive and of such uncertain duration in the absence of guarantees that Americans would not bear the costs alone. The need to deal with the U.S. national debt, the perennial U.S. budgetary deficit, the hope of many for a "peace dividend" for the pending troop reductions in Europe—these and other causes and campaigns were backed by powerful U.S. domestic interest groups that weighed into the debate, mainly on the negative side, about whether the United States was right to respond in the way and to the extent that it did.

In rebuttal, the positivists argue that their opposing arguments in favor of the massive U.S. mobilization and deployment have been vindicated. One should not lose sight or make light of what the GCC countries contributed during the crisis. From this perspective, had the international coalition not been able to deal quickly and effectively with this unfolding monetary dynamic of the crisis in its earliest days, there is little doubt that Iraq would have calculated differently and probably acted much more adventurously than it did following its invasion of Kuwait. In meeting this challenge, GCC countries and their supporters therefore demonstrated that the *financial* component of mounting a credible deterrence and defense can be as important as the *military* component. The GCC countries' cooperation on oil supplies and policies during the Kuwait crisis was thus a major factor in bringing the conflict to an end.

In addition to providing free fuel, water, utilities, and other provisions for aircraft, ships, and land-based vehicles, GCC countries contributed billions in cash to cover other costs incurred in responding to these conflicts and crises, including deployment costs themselves, weapons and equipment maintenance, and aircraft leasing. They also spared no effort, along with the United States, in persuading Japan as well as Germany and other European Community countries to assume a significant part of the expenses incurred by countries as a result of the UN-mandated embargo. In so doing, Egypt, Jordan, Turkey, and Yemen—the four hardest hit by the enforcement of the sanctions—plus Bangladesh, eastern Europe, India, Morocco, and the Philippines, had their plights eased to a greater degree than would otherwise have been the case.

Lastly, the positivists emphasize the important and very costly logistical and operational decisions that the GCC countries and their allies took to deny Iraq any economic benefits from its actions. Pursuant to the UN-sanctioned embargo, Saudi Arabia shut two pipelines that had previously carried Iraqi oil through the kingdom to export terminals on the Red Sea. Turkey, which sided with the GCC countries throughout the crisis and beyond, also closed two pipelines that had carried Iraqi oil to a terminal on the Mediterranean. Ships carrying Iraqi oil were denied entry to any GCC countries' ports. The multinational naval forces, powered by free GCC countries' fuel, followed up on these decisive actions and effectively prevented tankers from delivering Iraqi or Kuwaiti oil or oil products.

The positivists, returning to their initial economic premise, rest their case by asking: What might have happened had the GCC countries not acted to limit the impact of the Kuwaiti crisis on world access to petroleum supplies, important as such access is, not only to the level of petroleum prices but to world economic and political stability?

U.S. Political Interests: GCC Strengths

The domestic political structures, systems, and dynamics of GCC countries and the United States—components that all sides agree ought to be immune from interference—are but half of any equation that seeks to evaluate the political component of the U.S.-GCC relationship. The other half, which both parties agree is more "legitimately debatable," is external and rooted in the other aspects of foreign policy.

Except for most of the history of the Israeli-Palestinian conflict and the plight of the Muslims in Bosnia-Herzegovina, Chechnya, and elsewhere, the GCC countries' foreign policies have more often than not paralleled or complemented U.S. and other Western objectives. Moreover, the nature and orientation of international relations since the establishment of the GCC have been moderate, conventional, and predictable, as well as broadly compatible with most of the categories of the U.S. and other Western interests examined here.

The positivists believe that examples of the GCC's moderate, moderating, and, at times, even mediating behavior abound. As evidence they point to the outcomes of GCC summit meetings and summits and meetings of the League of Arab States, the Organization of the Islamic Conference (OIC), OPEC, and the UN, which are the four most important international organizations in which GCC countries' foreign policies are manifested. In support of this view, they advance some interesting arguments.

First, regarding the Israeli-Palestinian conflict, the GCC's and the GCC countries' contributions to a peaceful settlement have been far greater and come over a far longer period of time than is generally known. For example, at pan-Arab summits in Fez, Morocco, in 1982, in Algiers in 1988, and in Casablanca in 1989, the GCC countries had a significant impact on Arab League deliberations on how best to end the Israeli-Palestinian conflict. The GCC countries' proactive and forceful support of a peaceful settlement ultimately contributed to the PLO's recognition of Israel, its renunciation of terrorism, and its acceptance of a two-state solution (i.e., assisting in the strategic shift in PLO policy away from armed confrontation to a political and diplomatic resolution).

The Madrid conference in October 1991, at which GCC countries were represented, launched the most sustained Arab-Israeli and Israeli-Palestinian peace talks to date. Subsequently, GCC representatives have been first and foremost among all other nondisputant Arab parties in signaling support for the peace process. With minimal fanfare and in keeping with their traditional political values of moderation, balance, and low-key style, GCC representatives have participated throughout the peace process on issues of arms control, water, the environment, regional economic development, and refugees.

Moreover, the GCC itself, with the approval of its members, has been instrumental in arranging in the Arabian Peninsula and Gulf states region—in Bahrain, Oman, and Qatar—the first-ever official meetings of Israeli delegations with delegations from GCC countries and other Arab states. In the fall of 1994, all six GCC governments not only announced their formal rescission of the secondary and tertiary categories of the Arab League's fifty-year-old economic boycott of U.S. and other foreign firms that do business with Israel, but also participated with Israelis in a major international business conference in Casablanca shortly afterwards. In addition, three GCC countries—Kuwait, Saudi Arabia, and the UAE—have surpassed all Arab, Middle East, Islamic, and other developing nations in the amount of economic assistance pledged in support of the Palestinian Authority, the principal Palestinian governmental body engaged in the transfer of Israeli colonial domination and control to Palestinian self-rule.

Second, in the interplay of subregional political dynamics at the eastern edge of the Mediterranean, the GCC countries have been similarly effective as a moderating and mediating force on more than the question of Palestine. For example, they have been consistently supportive of the 1989 Saudi Arabia–mediated Taif Accord to amend the Lebanese constitution. They and many others, including the United States, reason that in no other way will Lebanon's legitimate government be able to consolidate its authority. They also worked diligently with the international community to facilitate the successful release of hostages (their own and others, including Americans), in Lebanon.

Regarding Syria, the GCC states have been more proactive than all others in pursuing policies of "constructive engagement" with the Damascus regime. Within days of the liberation of Kuwait in March 1991, the six GCC foreign ministers, together with their counterparts from Egypt and Syria, convened in Damascus to begin forging what they insisted would be the basis for a new Arab order. To be sure, many negativists have dismissed the resulting agreement, the Damascus Declaration, as being inconsequential, mainly because its envisioned cooperation in matters pertaining to defense has yet to come to fruition. However, the declaration is mainly concerned with matters of a political nature, especially those that, in the absence of consensus, could become contentious and, if unresolved, might lead to intraregional acrimony and tensions or armed confrontation.

In pursuit of these components of the Damascus Declaration (and subsequent declarations) pertaining to issues of economic reform, development, and enhanced regional trade and investment, the eight foreign ministers continue to meet regularly on a twice-yearly basis. In the process, the GCC countries have helped to forge a significant degree of political balance among key friends and allies within the League of Arab States. At the same time, they have added important geostrategic and geopolitical depth and balance to their relationships with Iran and Iraq.[10]

Third, further afield, in 1987 the GCC's heads of state and foreign ministers worked harder than any other Arab leaders to bring about a rapprochement between Algeria and Morocco, at odds with one another for thirteen years over the former Spanish ("western") Sahara territory. The rapprochement and growing North African admiration for the GCC countries' achievements in economic and political cooperation paved the way for the establishment of the Arab Maghreb Union—a grouping of Algeria, Libya, Mauritania, Morocco, and Tunisia.

Fourth, with regard to Egypt—the most populous Arab country, a major center of Arab and Islamic culture, and one of the region's strongest military powers—the positivists argue that the constructive political roles that the GCC and its member countries have played have been no less significant. In the aftermath of the Camp David accords between Egypt and Israel, which caused Egypt's expulsion from the Arab League and OIC, the GCC countries were among the leading forces for politically reintegrating Egypt into the Arab world, resuscitating Egypt's regional position and prestige, and paving the way for its readmission. Here, again, much broader international interests than those of the GCC and the United States were served.

Fifth, in the Gulf itself, the GCC countries have contributed directly to strategic objectives with regard to enhancing regional security. For example, providing continuous logistical, operational, and financial support for the 1987–1988 Gulf ship protection scheme (the "reflagging") helped to bring about the 1988 ceasefire in the Iran-Iraq war and to ensure freedom of navigation in the region.

Overlooked by many in the process was a pan-Arab political and diplomatic milestone: This security action, which the GCC countries persuaded Arab colleagues to accept at the 1987 pan-Arab summit in Jordan, represented the first Arab consensus in history in support of a U.S. or any other foreign military presence in the region. Subsequently, this consensus has been extended and enhanced through the five bilateral defense cooperation agreements, noted earlier, that individual GCC states have signed with the United States.

U.S. Commercial Interests: GCC Advantages

The positivists acknowledge that most if not all of the limitations and shortcomings noted by the negativists, addressed earlier in the section on U.S. commercial interests in the GCC region, are valid. However, they point out the premier position of the United States among all the world's countries as the trading partner of choice for most of the GCC countries. Even where the United States is not in first place, as in the case of Oman and the UAE, it frequently occupies a spot among the top five trading partners.

Moreover, although the United States has experienced overseas trade deficits overall in recent years, trade with the GCC countries has frequently yielded a surplus. In the mid-1990s, U.S. annual exports in commercial goods and services to the GCC region averaged $25 billion and imports approximately $13 billion. Such exports supported more than 650,000 U.S. jobs and were the primary source of livelihood for nearly 2.4 million Americans. Annual U.S. defense sales to the GCC countries constituted additional billions of dollars in income to the U.S. defense industry and were the source of primary, high-paying jobs for tens of thousands of Americans.

In addition, the positivists point out that the more than 700 U.S.-affiliated companies that operate in the GCC states employ 16,000 Americans and are the direct means of support for more than 50,000 U.S. dependents in the GCC region. In all of this, perspective is important: The value of U.S. private sector investments in the GCC economies represents half the world's investment in the GCC.

These investments, the positivists emphasize, pay more than dividends: They are critical to the economic growth and standard of living in the United States. Again, context is essential: The number of U.S.-GCC countries' joint ventures exceeds by far those of any other country. The positivists suggest that one should not lose sight of the fact that, cumulatively, all of these demonstrably positive features of the commercial dimension of the U.S.-GCC members' relationship have made, and continue to make, their mark on a much broader U.S. national interest; U.S. trade with the GCC states helps substantially to reduce the overall U.S. trade deficit.

The positivists also point out that since the GCC countries promote free-market economies and are strong proponents of private ownership and since their merchants have long manifested a commercial acumen that is the envy of many, U.S. companies have a competitive edge in the GCC states' markets. As thousands of GCC citizens are graduates of U.S. institutions of higher education, there is also a broad-based preference for U.S. technology, standards, and management techniques.

In support of their argument, the positivists emphasize that the array of incentives and benefits for U.S. and other foreign firms to do business in the GCC remains extensive. They include: free, or heavily subsidized, fuel, utilities, and water; extensive financial assistance; full repatriation of profits; extended tax holidays; tariff exemptions for capital imports; no personal taxation; free land use in specialized industrial zones; offshore banking arrangements; and free trade zones.

It is increasingly apparent to U.S. corporate leaders that the GCC is becoming, in effect, one market instead of six. Initially, many were unimpressed by the limited size of the GCC market in terms of consumer goods and services. Subsequently, however, fewer and fewer deny the reality that the GCC region is rapidly becoming a hub for trade, services, and investment opportunities in the eastern Mediterranean, the Indian subcontinent, East Africa, the Caucasus, and central Asia—a megamarket that embraces more than one billion people.

U.S. Defense Interests: GCC Strengths

The positivists are quick to note that the GCC countries have done what no other Arab nations have ever done: They have forged the series of Defense Cooperation Agreements with the United States, Great Britain, France, and Russia to ensure that they are never again exposed to a threat from anyone without adequate mechanisms capable of deterring any threat and mounting an effective defense if deterrence should fail.

Negotiated over a three-year period in the aftermath of the 1990–1991 Kuwait crisis and war, the agreements have in common commitments by the respective GCC countries to: pre-position vital military equipment to be used in defending the GCC signatory to the agreement; conduct regular exercises and maneuvers with the non-GCC country partner to the agreement; and extend such other assistance as mutually may be agreed upon by the parties.

The positivists are unabashed protagonists when it comes to defending the value of the new U.S.-GCC defense arrangements for the region. They argue forcefully that the contribution these agreements make—to the GCC countries, to the United States, the other great powers, and, most of all, to expansionist-minded leaders in the region—cannot be overestimated.[11] To be sure, the agreements fall short of being formal basing arrangements and are considerably less than formal treaty commitments. Even so, they constitute a clear signal, particularly to Baghdad and Tehran, of an unambiguous U.S. and allied coalition determination to support the GCC member countries' defense.[12] They further signal the GCC countries' determination to do whatever necessary to uphold their inalienable right to self-preservation. They do more than draw lines in the sand; they demarcate no-trespassing points in the sky and sea as well.[13]

To the surprise of even many of the positivists, these agreements have worked more quickly and effectively than anticipated. Joint exercises have increased to an all-time high, military training programs have expanded at an unprecedented rate, and U.S.-GCC states' military cooperation at practically every level has intensified to a degree that, ten years ago, virtually no one imagined would be possible.[14]

Two dramatic manifestations of the value of these agreements have already occurred, once when Iraqi troops moved toward Kuwait in October 1994 and again in reaction to a possible similar threat to Kuwait and Saudi Arabia in August 1995. The rapid integration of the brigade-sized pre-positioned equipment in Kuwait and other defense materiel stored elsewhere in the GCC region was decisive in ending these episodes.[15]

If these and similar agreements succeed in ushering in an era of regional peace and stability in the Gulf, the positivists recognize the GCC countries brought to the table essential military, financial, logistical, technological, and infrastructural assets.

The low-key, behind-the-scenes contributions of the GCC itself, as a forum within which regional perceptions and priorities can gain consensus and other forms of support, will also be seen as critical.

Even without allowing the United States a formal military base in the region, GCC countries' contributions to member and allied defense requirements are considerable. They are, by any standard, immense. Moreover, the GCC states, in concert with the United States, followed by Great Britain and France, helped line up additional support in the UN Security Council, Europe, and the rest of the international community to pressure Iran to accept UN Security Council Resolution 598—adopted by the Security Council on July 20, 1987, it was the first unanimously adopted UN peacekeeping resolution since the Korean War—thereby accommodating collective pressure to bring about a cease-fire in the Iran-Iraq war, one of this century's longest interstate conflicts.

Throughout the Iran-Iraq war and Desert Storm, the GCC countries' assistance to armed forces of friendly foreign powers and their quiet cooperation with the coalition were critical. Saudi Arabia used its AWACS (airborne warning and control systems aircraft) to monitor and help protect the reflagged tankers, flew its F-15 aircraft to provide protection for Saudi and U.S. AWACS, and, within its territorial waters, worked to clear mines to protect vessels from all over the world. Such assistance and cooperation protected the interests not only of the kingdom, but also of more than 100 countries with individuals, investments, and interests in the region that were threatened.

There are other, lesser-known facts. For example, when the USS *Stark* was attacked by Iraq in May 1987, Bahrain's navy rescued U.S. sailors who would have otherwise drowned. Further afield, at the southernmost end of the Gulf, Oman allowed emergency landings of U.S. aircraft on its territory, thereby saving the lives of thirty-seven U.S. pilots. In the face of Iranian threats to its security, the UAE (home to thousands of Iranian nationals) also allowed U.S. naval vessels to repair in UAE shipyards.

Looking to the future, the GCC and its member countries are attempting to construct a credible regional defense structure based on deterrence that acknowledges that responsibility for the security of member countries—as opposed to the main shipping lanes, which lie in international waters and, hence, are an international responsibility—resides with the countries themselves. The GCC's modest, 10,000-man joint force is stationed at Hafr al-Batin, a settlement near the Saudi-Kuwaiti border. The force is in the process of being expanded to 25,000. The negativists are correct, however, in arguing that such a force is unlikely to be an adequate deterrent to a menacing power. They are equally correct in noting that these agreements essentially obligate the United States to intervene on behalf of the GCC states against external threats (especially given President Bill Clinton's emphasis on "dual containment" of Iraq and Iran that, by default and/or design, strategically attaches the United States to the GCC countries).

The positivists concede the point. They counter, however, that the mere existence and readiness of the joint force telegraphs an important message to Baghdad,

Tehran, and all others in the international community, namely, that an attack on any one of the GCC countries will be considered as an attack upon all. As such, the force symbolically gives credibility to the GCC countries' commitment to collective security. Moreover, the fact that the force not only exists but is being strengthened and expanded is likely to facilitate the highly political task of reestablishing another allied coalition in support of the GCC countries' right to self-defense.

The GCC states' demographic, industrial, and technological constraints notwithstanding, since 1983, all six countries have participated in joint military exercises and bilateral maneuvers. Recognizing the constraints of their limited populations for building and sustaining large land forces, the six members have focused on augmenting and improving the credibility of their air forces and achieving a more effectively coordinated air defense network.

Few negativists seem to appreciate the major geopolitical and political-military roles the GCC played with other Arab and Islamic nations in the effort to free Kuwait. Indeed, in addition to turning to the United States and European powers for help, the GCC countries' leaders also successfully enlisted Egypt and Syria, thereby broadening the base of the allied coalition, demonstrating that other key Arab states opposed Iraq's aggression, and making the Desert Storm operation more palatable to the international community.

Lastly, the GCC military leaders acknowledged the crucial necessity of enhancing the coalition's capabilities for rapidly deploying to the area. As the United States is farthest away from the GCC region, the challenge of being rapidly deployable is formidable. Effective military strategy requires that much of the equipment, vehicles, ammunition, and related military hardware be in place before intervention.[16] In the final analysis, one truism in this regard continues to dwarf all others: Defense equipment and systems not in place have never deterred anyone.

Conclusion

This chapter has sought to evaluate the U.S.-GCC relationship in terms of its overall value to U.S. stated strategic, economic, political, commercial, and defense interests. Negativists and positivists differ widely in their assessments of the GCC and the U.S.-GCC relationship. The conclusion is obvious: The GCC and its members, like other regional organizations and their members, can be likened to a glass that is leaking *and* a glass that is filling.

However, there are disagreements in assessment, perception, and interpretation, as well as differences in interests and frameworks of analysis. Thus, a net assessment of the GCC, at least in terms of U.S. interests, does not differ fundamentally from one of NATO, the Organization on Security and Cooperation in Europe, the Organization of American States, the Organization of African Unity, and the Association of Southeast Asian Nations.

Analytical differences and disagreements are not uncommon; they are more the rule than the exception, as there are individual biases and preoccupations among analysts. An additional explanation is that it frequently reflects the different ways that analysts deal with the complex and changing realities within which members of regional organizations live—not only in terms of their immediate environment but also in terms of their relationships with other countries, including the United States. One need only consider failures in the former Yugoslavia, Cuba, Haiti, Rwanda, Somalia, and the international drug trade to appreciate that, among regional organizations, the GCC and its member countries are not alone in their imperfections and limitations.

As the 1990s draw to a close, it is clear that the GCC countries have done more than most Arab and Islamic countries to help bring about a peaceful resolution of the Arab-Israeli conflict. The maxim "It takes two to tango" can be applied in the sense that the Israeli government led by Prime Minister Netanyahu was more interested in Arab surrender than in an Israeli-Arab peace that could endure. The failure to move the peace process forward to a successful conclusion lay in the capitals of Israel and the United States, not in the GCC region.

The GCC's counsel in military matters may not always have been welcomed, but only the most hawkish take issue with the more generalized view that the GCC countries' refusal to countenance yet another bombing of Baghdad in 1998 was wise. Their recommendations of caution and restraint, coupled with their strong support for the mission of the UN secretary-general, helped spare the United States, and possibly the GCC states themselves, a potential disaster.

Regarding Iran, the United States can only welcome the moves toward détente and potential rapprochement between the GCC countries and Iran. Mired for twenty years in its own myopic vision of Iran's position and role in the region as the GCC countries' largest neighbor, Washington stands only to benefit from the GCC countries' efforts to engage Tehran in expanding their joint cooperation on matters of mutual interest and concern. The dictum "Better to engage than enrage" is applicable.

As for Iraq, in the run-up to the new millennium, the GCC countries remained opposed to lifting the sanctions on Iraq in the absence of Baghdad's failure to comply fully with the most important UN Security Council resolutions enacted against it in the aftermath of the 1990–1991 Kuwait crisis. These included the resolutions pertaining to compensation, return of the vast amount of stolen equipment, documents, and national artifacts, and, most important, the return or full accounting for the Kuwaitis and other nationals seized and held hostage by Iraq since the end of Iraq's aggression.

Many Americans and others think these matters are of little significance. They fail to see their relevance in the larger balance-of-power considerations and strategic calculus of Gulf defense and stability. The GCC countries, however, view these matters differently. Their leaders point out that in an American context, the number of Kuwaiti and other citizens missing and unaccounted for in Iraq, nearly a decade after the end of the war, is equivalent to 250,000 Americans being missing and unaccounted for in Canada or Mexico or 1 million British or French citizens being missing and unaccounted for in a neighboring country. These are but a few of the more slippery stepping stones that lie in the path of the GCC countries' march toward the next century.

In conclusion, from the practical perspective of the U.S. national interest, the GCC glass is more half full and filling than half empty and leaking. The strategic and economic strengths are simply undeniable. The combination of geological realities, energy economics, and the exercise of national sovereignty—always a potentially volatile mixture—is likely to ensure the GCC countries' importance in regional and global affairs for quite some time to come. They have an abundant supply of vital energy; they lie astride a crossroads between Europe, Asia, and Africa; and they are critical not only to the Western alliance but to much of the rest of the world as well.

Notes

1. See, for example, John Duke Anthony, "Energy: The Gulf Region's Engine of Development," in *Wall Street Journal*, special supplement on Saudi Arabia, July 28, 1989, p. 1.

2. The sources for this essay are predominantly firsthand observations by the author, who has been invited to attend, as an observer, each of the GCC's Heads of State Summits since the organization's inception in 1981. They are supplemented by information and insight obtained in the course of conducting more than 200 interviews with the GCC secretariat and officials from GCC member countries and private-sector leaders; the author has also participated in a number of background briefings, interviews, and other sessions with U.S. officials responsible for pursuing U.S. goals in and among the GCC countries. A condition insisted upon by virtually all of these officials, Arab as well as those of the United States, is that they not be quoted or otherwise mentioned as a source by name.

3. Author's interview with a retired career U.S. Foreign Service officer, who was posted for a total of eight years to U.S. embassies in three GCC countries during the period examined in this chapter, Washington, D.C., December 1994.

4. Ibid.

5. See Robert G. Lawrence, *U.S. Policy in Southwest Asia: A Failure in Perspective,* National Security Essay, Series 84-1 (Washington, D.C.: National Defense University Press, 1984). Former Undersecretary of State George W. Ball has written that during 1970 to 1991 in the United Nations (UN) Security Council, the United States "cast 69 vetoes, of which 39 were devoted to avoiding even mild censure of Israel. In practically all cases where it has used its veto to protect Israel, America has acted alone. Even such friendly nations as Great Britain and France have refused to join in our Israeli-inspired vetoes, and have either voted for the relevant resolution or abstained." George W. Ball and Douglas B. Ball, *The Passionate Attachment: America's Involvement with Israel, 1947 to the Present* (New York: W. W. Norton, 1992), p. 307.

6. For an account of different schools of thought within the GCC countries on these matters, see John Duke Anthony, *The Dynamics of GCC Summitry Since the Kuwait Crisis* (Washington, D.C.: U.S.-GCC Corporate Cooperation Committee, Occasional Papers Series, No. 2, 1993), pp. 2–9.

7. Author's interview with Abdalla Y. Bishara, GCC Secretary-General (1981–1992), Kuwait, September 1987.

8. Ibid.

9. See Joseph C. Story, *U.S.-Arab Relations: The Economic Dimension* (Washington, D.C.: Middle East Policy Association and the National Council on U.S.-Arab Relations, 1985).

10. See the official Arabic text and English translation in *Damascus Declaration for Coordination and Cooperation Among the Arab States,* Secretariat General, "Coordination and Cooperation Among the Arab States," Secretariat General, Cooperation Council for the Arab States of the Gulf (Riyadh: GCC), Articles One and Two (1) A-C, pp. 5–9. See also John Duke Anthony, "Betwixt War and Peace: The 12th GCC Heads of State Summit," in *Middle East Insight* 8(6) (July–October, 1992), pp. 54–61.

11. See U.S. Secretary of Defense William Perry, "U.S. Security Policy in the Gulf," remarks to the Middle East Policy Council, Washington, D.C., December 7, 1994. For an early analysis of a system of deterrence backed by credible defense capabilities (that is, among the United States, GCC, and allies), see John Duke Anthony, et al., *A Postwar Gulf Defense System* (Washington, D.C.: Coalition for Postwar U.S. Policy in the Middle East, 1991).

12. See John Duke Anthony, "After the Gulf War: The GCC and the World," in Ibrahim Ibrahim, ed., *The Gulf Crisis: Background and Consequences* (Washington, D.C.: Center for Contemporary Arab Studies, Georgetown University, 1992), pp. 121–140; see also John Duke Anthony, "If Our Friends Are Weak, So Are We," in *President's Report* 8(1) (Winter–Spring 1993) (Washington, D.C.: National Council on U.S.-Arab Relations), pp. 1–3, and 16.

13. Ibid.

14. Author's interviews in October 1994 with U.S. armed forces commanders whose units responded to the threat; see also, Perry, "U.S. Security Policy in the Gulf."

15. Author's interviews in October 1994 with U.S. armed forces commanders whose units responded to the threat.

16. Ibid.

25

New U.S. Policies for a New Middle East?

William Quandt

The dominant picture that emerges from an examination of U.S. policy in the Middle East is of Washington stumbling from one mistake, one missed opportunity, one erroneous calculation to another. It is easy to recall things that went wrong, things that should have gone better.

Everyone has their own best example of a particular tragedy that might have been avoided. Policy toward Iran certainly stands out as one of the major errors of U.S. diplomacy in the past twenty or thirty years. In human terms, one can look at Lebanon and wonder what might have been done to spare that fragile and admirable democratic experiment from the fate that befell it in the 1970s and 1980s. One can also ask what might have been done to prevent the two oil shocks of the 1970s that certainly affected the entire world, poor countries more so than rich ones; all of it cost many billions of dollars in lost income and stalled development.

Although it is easy to see these flaws, U.S. policy in the Middle East in the past forty to fifty years has been remarkably successful *in terms of the standard definition of U.S. national interests*. Although this is something of a contrary view, I think it reasonably accurate within the framework of stated U.S. objectives in the Middle East.

The normal definition of U.S. interests in the Middle East, and probably a narrow definition in the minds of many, has consisted of essentially three points. One was to ensure that the Soviet Union, our global rival and adversary, did not succeed in extending hegemony into the Middle East. Given what we now know, that may never have been a likely prospect, but after World War II, with U.S.-Soviet competition for influence in Iran and Turkey and the establishment of the Kremlin's domination in Eastern Europe, there was a real concern that Soviet power would extend quickly into the Middle East and perhaps be very difficult to curtail. For the entire post–World War II period until 1990, the problem of how to deal with the Soviet Union was number one on the list of Middle East policymakers in Washington.

The second issue was oil. There were times when access to oil was taken for granted, but everyone understood that the Gulf region was the single largest source of oil in the world; indeed it comprises two-thirds of the globe's proven oil reserves. We simply could not ignore the strategic significance of that fact.

Third was the special relationship between the United States and Israel. The relationship has not always been a comfortable one, but every president since Harry S. Truman has felt a special commitment to Israel's security and well-being that has not been matched by a comparable commitment to any other single state in the region.

If one takes these three points as the definition of Washington's major interests in the region—containing the Soviet Union, oil, and Israel's security—we can then determine how successful U.S. policy has been. Compared to our policy in Southeast Asia for example, U.S. policy has been a relative success, certainly in terms of costs, both human and economic. Calculating the human costs to the United States of pursuing our policies, with all the mistakes made over this entire forty-five-year period, it is estimated that at most some five hundred Americans lost their lives. In Southeast Asia, the number exceeded fifty thousand. This is not meant to minimize those losses, only to put them in perspective.

In economic terms, the cost of pursuing U.S. policies in the Middle East is not so easy to calculate. For implementing Middle East policy between 1945 and 1990, Congress authorized, just in terms of budget outlays, about $150 billion to $200 billion (in current dollars), which, of course, seems a huge amount of money. This works out to somewhat more than $3 billion per year over this entire period. These numbers are inexact at best, but compared to the costs of supporting the North Atlantic Treaty Organization (NATO) or financing the war in Vietnam, the expense for U.S. policy in the Middle East has been quite low. It has cost, by and large, a little more than one-half of today's annual defense budget, spread over forty-five years.

In general, the human and economic costs for the United States in pursuing its Middle East policies have been tolerable, and the basic objectives have been successfully achieved. It is probably no exaggeration to say that if the United States had not had access to Middle East oil at low prices in the 1950s and early 1960s, the rebuilding of Europe and Japan along democratic lines as a bulwark against Soviet expansion would have been infinitely more complicated. In a way, then, the Middle East did fit into the grand strategy of the United States during this era.

In pursuit of these three main interests the United States relied on a whole series of policy instruments: economic and military assistance, arms sales, covert interventions, military presence, diplomacy—particularly in the Arab-Israeli peace process since 1967—and occasionally the direct use of U.S. military forces, as in Lebanon in 1958 and 1982 and the war against Iraq in 1990–1991. During the cold war era, the U.S. public seemed willing to support these policies, by and large. There were occasional debates and protests but never anything like the massive alienation from official policy that occurred as the costs of our involvement in Southeast Asia grew in the 1960s and 1970s. For the most part, Democrats and Republicans, year after year, were prepared to support the main thrust of U.S. policy in pursuit of these three key interests.

The Gulf crisis and war of 1990–1991 looks very much like the end of an era in U.S. foreign policy—a kind of watershed. It occurred just at the end of the cold war when the United States was fully mobilized following the intense military buildup under the Ronald Reagan administration in the 1980s. Oil was seen to be at risk. Washington's military strategy promised success with relatively few U.S. casualties. The United States had Arab allies on its side to fight against another Arab regime, and it had other countries willing to help foot the bill. That is what made it possible to mobilize the 500,000 U.S. troops, to fight the war efficiently and successfully, and to sustain public support. But note, this was not the beginning of a new burst of enthusiasm for redrawing the map of the Middle East. Pax Americana was not in the back of anybody's mind in official Washington after settling accounts with Saddam Hussein in Kuwait. Instead, it looks very much as if the Gulf intervention was the last act in a play according to the old rules of how the United States would engage with the Middle East before new realities had taken hold.

The new realities that will inform the conduct of U.S. foreign policy in coming years include the following. First, there is clearly a reduced sense of involvement with the rest of the world on the part of most Americans, their representatives in Congress, and their president. Foreign policy is simply no longer a high-priority issue, perhaps because the U.S. public is no longer obsessed by the threat of nuclear war and global rivalry with the Soviet Union. But it is still striking to look at the results of an early 1990s public opinion poll in which Americans were asked to list the issues they thought were important and to see that a mere 1 percent of Americans mentioned any issue whatsoever involving foreign policy. This does not necessarily mean the United States is headed toward isolationism. But this is certainly a period of retrenchment and therefore very selective involvement in foreign policy engagements abroad.

In addition, for economic reasons there will be less spending on foreign aid. Therefore, some of the normal instruments of policy will be less available for future decisionmakers as they consider how to deal with the Middle East. It may be true that one can make a very impressive case that large amounts of money should be mobilized on behalf of a particular country in order to prevent some disaster, but it is not going to be easy in the current mood to persuade Americans, even though the Middle East continues to receive the lion's share of the economic aid that is available.

The third element of the new reality is that the United States no longer has a grand organizing theme to its foreign policy. Containment, for all its limitations and oversimplifications, gave a certain thrust to U.S. foreign policy during the cold war. With the end of the cold war, Washington is not sure which issues deserve priority. Are humanitarian crises around the world enough to prompt U.S. intervention? If so, why did the United States refrain from intervening in Rwanda, when Tutsis were being slaughtered by Hutus? Unfortunately, there is no longer a measure that indicates what is important and what is not—at least no easily available one. As a result, there is a somewhat ad hoc quality to decisionmaking.

When it comes to the Middle East, this leaves U.S. foreign policy with four policy themes, one of which is sound, one of which is badly flawed, one of which is widely seen in the region as hypocritical, and one of which is now primarily rhetoric. The first is an old but continuing one—the importance of promoting Arab-Israeli peace in the region. One can argue endlessly over whether the United States has played this role well or whether tactics at any given time or in any given administration have been suitable. But the effort to try to bring about a historic reconciliation between Israel and its Arab neighbors has been a worthy one, and there has been success. Insofar as there is some intellectual content to U.S. foreign policy in the Middle East today, it largely revolves around this topic. Middle East specialists in the U.S. government know more about the intricacies of Arab-Israeli negotiations than any other single issue. Some of them know a great deal by now. They have spent years on the issues involved in the negotiations between Israel and the Arabs. There are problems of bias and selective perception, but there is a strong desire in Washington, in official circles, for this negotiation, this peacemaking process, to succeed.

This desire for a successful conclusion to the Arab-Israeli negotiations, however, has not been accompanied during the Clinton era by a serious strategy for attaining that goal. The Oslo accords of September 1993, which raised hopes in many quarters, were achieved largely without American involvement. Some concluded that an active American mediation role was no longer needed, except on the Syrian front, where the top leaders were still not on speaking terms. Instead of pressing the parties to move quickly toward agreements, the Clinton administration adopted the role of "facilitator," leaving it to the parties to set the pace. Rabin's assassination in November 1995 dealt a fatal blow to this strategy, especially when he was replaced by hard-line Likud leader Benjamin Netanyahu. From mid-1996 onward, the peace process has been at a virtual stall, and the Clinton administration, despite some efforts, has been unable to break the deadlock on fundamentals.

Without a viable strategy of peacemaking between Israel and its Arab neighbors, the United States will find it increasingly difficult to maintain the good working relations that it has with most countries of the region. Moderate Arab leaders will be weakened, and their successors may well be less inclined toward peace and cooperation with the United States. The Palestinians, who have come close to accepting the idea of a mini-Palestinian state in the West Bank and Gaza, are going to find that they will have to settle instead for tiny enclaves within the West Bank, totally surrounded by Israeli forces—in short, Bantustans rather than a real state of their own. Instead of being the cornerstone of a comprehensive Arab-Israeli peace, such an outcome will insure that tensions remain high in the Arab-Israeli arena for years to come. But few in Washington, least of all the Republican-dominated Congress, seem very worried at such a prospect.

The second Middle East policy theme, which is not fully developed and on the whole not well considered, has been the so-called dual-containment idea propounded by the Clinton administration. Dual containment, as discussed elsewhere in this book, abandons the traditional balance-of-power approach of the United States in the Persian Gulf area (which viewed Iran and then Iraq as a U.S. surrogate and as a counterweight to the other) and outlines in ambiguous terms a policy of containing *both* Iran and Iraq. For a while it seemed as if dual containment would have a short lifetime. The concept, however, continued to guide U.S. policy into the late 1990s.

It is hard to see how, over the long term, a policy of dual containment will be a viable approach to the complexities of the Gulf region. It is simply inconceivable that the United States can continue to advocate a policy of no serious engagement with a country as large and important as Iran. By 1998, the policy of unquestioned hostility toward Iran was being reconsidered but still had a strong constituency among some in Congress. The key event that forced Americans to rethink the policy of dual containment was the remarkable election in May 1997 of Mohammed Khatami, with over 70 percent of the vote. Khatami was not well known to Americans but presented himself as a moderate and, indeed, some aspects of life in Iran began to show signs of liberalization after his election. Whether Iran's foreign policy would also change remained to be seen, but by mid-1998, the Clinton administration was showing signs of readiness for a better official relationship with Teheran. This would doubtless take time and would be preceded by an increase in unofficial contacts, but the perception of Iran as little more than a state that supports terrorism and preaches hatred of the West was in abeyance in Washington.

Concerning Iraq, although one can understand the lack of any desire to deal with Saddam Hussein, Washington still needs a longer-term vision of what its policy should be toward that country, especially with regard to the post-Saddam period when it arrives. Meanwhile, there is the humanitarian issue of how to avoid undue hardship for the Iraqi population, while keeping pressure on Saddam Hussein to comply with UN resolutions. By early 1998, a formula had been agreed upon, with support of the United States, to allow Iraq to increase its oil exports and to use the revenue to purchase food and medicine. At some point, however, a judgment will have to be made on whether Iraq has essentially complied with the UN resolutions and whether sanctions should be lifted, at least conditionally. Since Saddam is so widely distrusted, and with good reason, it will take very convincing evidence for most Americans to support a policy of removing all sanctions on Iraq as long as Saddam is in power. Once he is gone from the scene, however, there is no strategic reason not to be much more forthcoming in relations with Baghdad. And that message should be clear to the Iraqi people and their future leaders now.

The third theme in American policy targets the spread of weapons of mass destruction in the region. To a large degree, the war against Iraq in 1991 was fought with this concern in mind, and much of the hostility toward Iran has also been motivated by a concern that Iran is seeking a nuclear option. But here is where the hypocrisy comes in. The United States has been perfectly prepared to look the other way as countries such as Israel have developed nuclear weapons, and Egypt, Syria, and others have long had chemical capabilities. Missiles able to deliver mass destruction weapons exist in a number of countries, including Saudi Arabia, Israel, and Egypt, but only those in Iran and Iraq are singled out for comment. Any effort to encourage the development of a zone free of weapons of mass destruction runs into the problem of Israel's undeclared nuclear capability. Since the testing of nuclear weapons by India and Pakistan in 1998, American policy on nonproliferation has been subject to a serious challenge. At some point, rethinking policy on this sensitive and important topic will be required in Washington, and the underlying hypocrisy of the American stance will have to be recognized. It is not that all regimes with mass-destruction weapons pose identical threats to regional peace; but there is no chance of developing a credible policy for dealing with the real problems if one seems to be looking the other way when one's friends acquire weapons that in other hands are seen as intolerable.

The fourth theme, which has not been fully elaborated by any means, is that the time has come for the United States to place more emphasis on democratization and economic reform in the region. Many of the countries in the Middle East are in need of fundamental economic and political reforms, but one has the very strong impression that, so far, the application of this theme to the Middle East is halfhearted at best and tends not to go beyond encouraging privatization of state-owned industries. That is certainly not a satisfactory way of translating serious political concepts into policies that might have significance to Middle Easterners who, in fact, do want to see economic change, who do want to see more responsible and accountable governments, and who are fed up with the corruption of their own leaders. But there is always the dilemma of imposing one's own views, which may ultimately produce a negative backlash, versus promoting ideas and practices that may produce stable, reliable, and prosperous friends for the United States. The issue of how best to support reformist regimes may not be so easy to avoid in the future. Many of the leaders with whom the United States has had cordial relations—King Fahd, King Hussein, King Hassan, Husni Mubarak, and even Yasir Arafat and Hafiz al-Asad, are getting on in years, and succession will soon take place to a new generation of leaders. This will be the moment when we will see if the United States is inclined to go beyond rhetoric and provide actual support and encouragement for democratization. It is simply not a viable stance to argue that the Middle East is an exception to the trend toward democracy because of some alleged incompatibility of Islam and democracy. Indonesia, the largest Muslim state, has shown that opposition to a dictator who has clung to power too long can take the form of demands for more democracy. The same may be expected in many parts of the Middle East in years ahead. In Indonesia, the United States finally encouraged Suharto to step down. Similar moments will doubtless confront future American presidents in the Middle East. Clinging to the old order while professing a belief in democracy will not serve American interests.

As well as the United States has protected its basic interests during the past fifty years, it has often done so by dealing with illegitimate regimes, a situation that still exists today and that is increasingly worrisome. The United States actually has quite good relations with almost every government in the region, except for Iran, Iraq, Sudan, and Libya. But at the more popular level—among *both* Islamists and nationalists—there is a deep antipathy for U.S. policies. In the future, threats to U.S.

influence will be difficult to deal with because they will be less clear-cut. The fragility of the regimes in the region is a reality over which the United States has very little influence. It is tremendously difficult to resuscitate a regime that has lost its fundamental legitimacy. The United States, for example, probably could not have done a great deal to prevent the Iranian revolution by the time it reached a critical mass.

In the future, the United States, despite its perception as the only remaining global power, cannot hope to impose a design of its own on the Middle East. There is a certain inevitability that Middle Easterners will view the United States with suspicion simply because it is the most powerful country in the world—quite apart from its policies. No country that feels weak and vulnerable will feel comfortable dealing with a much more powerful country. So there is now built into the structure of diplomacy one strike against the United States: On the one hand, everyone is awed by U.S. power, but on the other, they distrust it. This suggests that the Middle East will remain a troubled area and that the United States will face many obstacles in its efforts to protect its traditional interests, a challenge made more serious by the erosion of serious interest in foreign policy in many circles in the United States.

26

Islamist Perceptions of U.S. Policy in the Middle East

Yvonne Yazbeck Haddad

The umbrella ideology of Islamism is casting an increasingly large shadow as Islamist groups strive to create a unified ethos in order to enhance their own sense of empowerment in facing repressive regimes and what they view as Western and Zionist hegemonic policies in the Muslim world. Designed as an alternative to liberal humanism and socialism, as well as to fundamentalist secularism and Marxism, Islamism has left itself vulnerable to attacks from various quarters, including the regimes of some Arab countries, secularists, Zionists, humanists, socialists, and feminists.[1] During the past fifteen years, the U.S. press as well as some people in the U.S. academy and government have created a consummate stereotype, commonly identified as "Islamic fundamentalism" or "Islamic extremism."[2] Individuals and groups who fall into this category tend more and more to be demonized by those who oppose or fear them, rendering them unworthy of being taken seriously in their criticism of U.S. policies.[3] Thus, Islamism as an "-ism" increasingly provides a handy means of objectification for those who seek to undermine its legitimacy.

Currently, a profound sense of victimization on the part of Islamists has led to the development of a parallel stereotype: The alliance between Israel and the United States, which is generally depicted as "the crusader-Zionist conspiracy," the Western demon bent on the eradication of Islam.[4] This perception has its roots in the worldview of the Muslim Brotherhood, "the mother of all Islamist movements" in Egypt. Hasan al-Banna, who founded the Muslim Brotherhood in 1928, identified a comprehensive venue of operations for his organization in order to realize his futuristic vision of a vibrant Muslim nation (the *umma*). The focus was to be on the development of a new Muslim human being brought about through moral and spiritual rearmament, a new society actualized through economic development and social justice, and a new vibrant nation free of foreign domination. He perceived the Muslim nation to be in mortal danger as a consequence of the abolition of the office of the caliphate (the generally acknowledged leader of the Islamist community dating to the initial successor of the Prophet Muhammad) in 1924 by Mustafa Kemal Ataturk in Turkey. The caliph had provided a sense of Islamic unity maintained by commitment to Islamic values in societies governed by Islamic law. From his vantage point, foreign interests, at the time mainly British, appeared to work diligently to divide the Muslim world into nation-states to facilitate their subjugation and to insist on implementing the Balfour Declaration of 1917, which had promised a national homeland for European Jews in Palestine. For al-Banna, the Balfour Declaration was not only a means of maintaining colonial interests in the area but was a continuation of European crusader designs on the holy lands.

Many different views and perspectives are represented under the rubric of Islamism. It is currently popular in Western scholarship to distinguish between the mainline Muslim Brotherhood on one side and al-Jama'at al-Islamiyya, Islamic groups such as al-Takfir wa al-Hijra, al-Jihad, and al-Qutbiyyun in Egypt, Hamas of Palestine, and Hizbullah of Lebanon on the other. The Islamic groups are generally referred to as militants, extremists, or terrorists, whereas the Brotherhood and its affiliates in other Arab countries such as the Islamic Action Front of Jordan and Jam'iyyat al-Islah of Kuwait are perceived as more moderate and willing to participate in the democratic process.

Ahmad Kamal Abu al-Magd, a former cabinet member during the Anwar Sadat regime in Egypt, distinguishes between five groups seeking Islamization. The first call themselves the *Salafiyyun* and are noted for their inflexible adherence to the classical teachings of Islam, leaving little room for modern reinterpretation.[5] The second group is the Sufis, who emphasize the spiritual dimension of Islam and focus their efforts exclusively on seeking a spiritual revival. The third group carries the banner of Islam but is in total rebellion against the prevailing Muslim condition. Attempting to move beyond Islam, they are nonetheless eager to hang on to Islamic slogans. The fourth group consists of several movements adamant in their demand for the reinstitution of Islamic law *(shari'a)* as the constitution of the state. For them, the control of political power is the most effective way to work for Islam. The fifth group that al-Magd identifies is composed of the moderate majority who believe in the use of reason in applying the teachings of Islam as a guide for life.[6]

Although all Islamists appear to agree on an agenda of bringing about the kinds of changes that provide empowerment and well-being for Muslim society, they differ on the means of actualizing change and on issues of political and religious pluralism in an Islamic state. Meanwhile, there is general agreement among Islamists and secularists that U.S. foreign policy in the Middle East has been skewed in favor of Israel since the 1967 Arab-Israeli war (also known as the Six Day War, or June War). This perception has left an indelible mark on Islamist identity and its worldview. This chapter will analyze these perceptions and the Islamist response. It is based on Islamist literature, which is polemical and generally hostile as to Israel and U.S. foreign policy as well as the Palestinian self-rule question. Illustrations used in this chapter are taken mainly from Islamist journals, newspapers, and other publications and are supplemented with interviews I conducted with Islamists in Jordan, Egypt, Kuwait, Tunisia, and the United States.

Islamism: A Reaction to Disempowerment

Islamism is not a reactionary movement; it does not want to replicate the Islamic community of the Prophet Muhammad in the seventh century. Rather, it seeks control of the present and future of Muslim destiny.[7] From its inception it has been reactive, responding to direct and imagined challenges posed by internal conditions as well as its violent encounter, during the last two centuries, with a dominant West, which has insisted that the only universal values worth adhering to are those developed in the West during the Renaissance and the scientific revolution that is evident in rational, liberal, or Marxist thought. Its ideologues operate with a heightened sense of awareness of the importance of monitoring events in the world, particularly those that affect their lives, and responding to them. They see themselves as manning a defensive operation, the responsibility of which is to safeguard society from total disintegration.[8]

Islamism was initially a reaction to the internal sense of decay in Muslim society. A central theme in most Islamist literature is a response to the deep awareness of the backwardness of Muslims, a critical assessment of what went wrong historically, and an effort to rectify the situation in order to bring about a vibrant future. Revival is seen by its advocates as a crucial means of infusing life into a community that is bogged down in centuries-old ideas and traditions that have led to the ossification of Islamic society, restricting its ability to adapt to the fast-changing reality of the modern world. The revivalists produced a literature that portrayed Islam as a forward-looking, creative, and open ideology receptive to movement and change. They sought to remove the shackles of Islamic society, freeing it from the constraints of the values and interpretations of the past. Their goal was to initiate involvement in the unfolding history of the world, taking control of the lives of their constituency and participating in shaping the future. Unity of the community was seen as an essential component of this venture.

The challenge of modernity to the prevailing Islamic system arrived already formulated and fully developed, in an alien environment where a different set of issues was being addressed. Westernizers, both indigenous and foreign, perceived European models as prefabricated systems that were transferable and ready for borrowing and implementation because they have worked in the West; hence they advocated liberalism, secularism, and socialism. Since the 1967 Arab-Israeli war there has been a growing perception that imported, Western, ready-made models of development and modernization, touted as instant solutions for domestic and foreign problems, have failed to bring about the results hoped for by advocates. More important, they are perceived to have failed even in the West itself.

Islamism is a reaction to the denial of the right to self-determination. The lack of democratic institutions and the absence of governments that operate under the law and for the well being of the people in the region are increasingly identified as major causes of backwardness. Islamist leader Tawfiq Muhammad al-Shawi of Egypt, for example, identifies such specifics as the following: the lack of freedom of determination (the right to choose the ruler) on the part of the polity and the lack of accountability on the part of the ruler; the fact that the *shari'a* has been replaced in most countries by laws legislated by governments; the separation of the law from government, that is, the replacing of an independent jurisprudence by a European model in which "law is the will of the state"; and the loss of a comprehensive unity, a byproduct of Western efforts to divide and conquer.[9]

Islamism is a reaction against disempowerment and what is seen as the irrelevance of the nation-states created in the region as a result of the Sykes-Picot Agreement constructed during World War I, through which the British and the French artificially divided much of the Middle East into spheres of influence that were later sanctioned via postwar agreements into the mandate system comprised of state units that had hitherto not existed. There is general consensus in Islamist literature that the dominant world order that has prevailed since the nation-states in the area were carved out has not allowed for the inclusion of Arabs as full citizens of the world. Arab nations and peoples have continued to be subservient to foreign domination, which Islamists describe as a continuing predatory relationship.[10] Their diagnosis is based on the belief that the core problem is the failure of these nation-states to adhere to the sources of strength in Islam itself that brought about the great and powerful Islamic civilization of the medieval world. In many cases, the analysis goes on to show that the ideology that is supposed to bring about the revival of Muslim society and its potency in the world, although cast in Islamic idiom, continues to rely on Western standards and values as necessary for that revival.

Islamism is also a reaction to a profound feeling on the part of Muslims that they have been victimized over the centuries at the hands of Western Christians. The litany of perceived outrages includes European treatment of Muslims during the crusades. They cite the fact that Eastern Christians, Jews, and Muslims in Jerusalem were massacred by the Western invaders during the First Crusade whereas Salah al-Din (Saladin) treated the crusaders magnanimously by giving them assurance of safe passage after he led the Muslim recapture of the city eighty-eight years later in 1187. It includes the *reconquista* in Spain during which a ruthless de-Islamization policy gave Muslims the options of conversion, expulsion, or execution. It includes the colonialist movements of the nineteenth and twentieth centuries, along with the activities of Christian missionaries. It also includes the reality that in the Soviet Union Muslims living under Communist hegemony were not allowed to practice their faith or study the tenets of their religion. And it includes the perception that for five decades Zionism has been one more element of the long and continuous effort supported by Christians to eradicate Islam and Muslims from the holy places. Bosnia and Kosovo are seen as the current manifestations of European efforts to eradicate the indigenous European Muslim population.[11]

Along these lines, Islamists perceive Christian missionary activity as having been designed to separate Muslims from Islam. These efforts are believed to have been inspired by the long history of Christian fanaticism against Islam, culminating in the commissioning of missionaries to march under the banner of Christ into Muslim countries in order to convert them. The legacy of missionary sermons and speeches (now translated into Arabic) provides a rich illustration of the accuracy of this perception. For example, it has been noted that although there had been concern over the Jewish danger, the Bolshevik menace, and the yellow peril, Islam posed the greater danger since it is capable of expanding and forming the only wall against imperialist interests.[12]

Islamism is a reaction to the demonization of Islam. Muslims are offended and angered at the way in which Islam has been defamed in inflammatory political statements, such as former U.S. Vice President Dan Quayle's comparison of Islamic fundamentalism to Nazism and communism,[13] and statements supporting Zionist interests in popular novels, such as Leon Uris's *The Hajj*.[14] Islamists are very aware that since the late 1970s there has been a dramatic increase in the number of articles in the U.S. press dedicated to Muslim-bashing. These tend to depict Muslims as irrational and vengeful and motivated by religious zeal and fanaticism that arise out of an innate hatred of the West, its Judeo-Christian heritage, and its secularist values. For Muslims, among the most infuriating statements was the 1990 Jefferson Lecture on "Islamic fundamentalism" by prominent Arab historian Bernard Lewis,[15] which generated a heated response from many sources. Islamists observe that Lewis identified historical and cultural differences as the causes of Muslim anger, completely ignoring the specific policies and actions of Western nations that foster the perception among Muslims that, as long as the lives of Westerners are not at stake, fairness does not matter. One Muslim author wrote: "His twenty-six-page address was remarkable for the absence of the word 'Israel.' Nor was any mention made of the United States support of the Zionist state, which inflames Muslim passions worldwide. Any U.S. diplomat who has served in a Muslim country or taken even a cursory glance at Muslim media can verify this feeling."[16] Such distorted presentations of Islam are seen by Muslims as conscious efforts at revisionist history, inspired by contempt for Islam or motivated by political considerations in an attempt to maintain unwavering U.S. support for the state of Israel. They tend to validate for Islamists their perceptions that the West has a double standard by which it measures events in the area.

Islamism is increasingly a reaction to what is perceived as Western and Zionist fears of Islam. Although the theme of the "threat of Islam" may have been manufactured for Western political reasons,[17] it provides a useful tool in recruiting young Muslims into the fold. The "mighty" West and Israel that have humiliated and subjugated Muslim nations claim that they fear nothing but Islam. If the oppressors know what is the source of strength, they ask, when will the Muslims awake?[18]

Islamism is a reaction to Zionism. Israel's 1967 preemptive strike, which resulted in a devastating defeat of Jordan, Egypt, and Syria, is generally referred to as *'udwan,* or aggression. Its policies are perceived as Judaizing and aimed at disempowering, dispossessing, and displacing the Palestinians in an effort to destroy their identity. What is perceived as its persistent rejection of United Nations (UN) resolutions and violation of the Geneva Convention have fostered, nursed, and inflamed the Islamic response. It is enhanced by what is seen to be U.S. intervention at the United Nations in support of these policies, which has made the international community ineffective in implementing resolutions that would uphold justice.[19] Israeli justifications for the confiscation of property as its divine right and Western silence regarding these activities elicited a response from Abdullah Kannun, a noted North African author and a member of the Higher Council of Islamic Research of al-Azhar, that is typical among Islamists. Advocating the Islamization of the conflict, he affirmed that although the Arabs are the protectors of Palestine the land belongs to all Muslims. Muslims must therefore be aware of the connection between Zionism and the kind of Christian religious zealotry that had been experienced earlier by the Muslims during the crusades: "The Palestinian issue is an Islamic, not only an Arab issue. Zionism is the stepdaughter of imperialism *(rabibat al-isti'mar)*. Imperialism is the hidden image of the Crusades undertaken by Western Christians against the Muslims of the East."[20]

On another level Islamism can be said to be a kind of mirror image of Zionism. It may be seen as an attempt to emulate what is perceived as a winning Israeli formula in which religious zeal, divine justification, scriptural proof-texting, and victimization are employed to mobilize Jewish as well as Euro-American Christian support for the state. For some Muslim observers, the essence of the issue is that the state of Israel is a Jewish state. "Zionism is therefore the means of the Jewish religion to realize itself, a means of the Jewish people to create their unity in confrontation with all others in the region," says Kamil al-Baqir, a leading Islamist.[21] The question thus remains: Why is it acceptable for Jews to have a Jewish state and not for Muslims to form an Islamic state? Islamist leader Abdullah Kannun notes that the "educated civilized West is not ashamed to boast of its Christianity to explain Zionism in its religious context and to support it by quotations from the Bible, but the ignorant, underdeveloped East is ashamed to call for an Islamic revenge."[22]

Islamism and the "Double Standard"

Islamism is a reaction to what is perceived as the double standard *(al-izdiwajiyya)* that is used by the West in its foreign policy in the Middle East. For example, in demonizing the Islamists, Westerners claim that there is no room for religion in the modern nation-state.[23] Islamists consider this not only to be hypocritical in light of Western support for Israel and enduring and prominent symbols of religiosity in the West, but in a very profound way the proof of the double standard. Hence they believe that the West is not against religion per se but against Islam. "Pakistan and Israel," says one writer, "are two countries created solely on the basis of religion and faith. But you may read in the Western press that Pakistan is backward and reactionary because it has emerged in the name of religion. Nothing whatsoever of this nature is said about Israel."[24]

There is a growing perception among Islamists that Jews and Christians, driven by religious fanaticism, triumphalism, and imperialism, have been engaged in a "thousand-year war" with Muslims, which the latter are losing because they are not driven "by a parallel religious sentiment in order to repel this fanatic aggression."[25] Major events in the area have contributed to this perception, such as the civil war in Lebanon, which has cast an aura of suspicion on the allegiance of Arab Christians and the efficacy of Arab nationalism, the success of the Iranian revolution, which validated for the faithful the Qur'anic teaching that God will give victory to those who believe, and Operations Desert Shield and Desert Storm, which were widely perceived as a vindication of the projected Islamist worldview that blamed "the problem of Israel" on Western bigotry and religious fanaticism and were seen as a continuation of the crusader-Zionist efforts to destroy Islam.[26]

Muslims have been intrigued by the fact that Israel and its supporters boast that it is the only democracy in the area. They note that it functions as a democracy "for Jews" while denying religious minorities—both Christian and Muslim—equal access to resources such as water,[27] housing,[28] health, education,[29] jobs, and the ability to purchase land. Some go so far as to argue that Israel's actions have been devoid of any compassion or human values.[30] The executive secretary of Islamic Jihad in Palestine, Dr. Fathi Shikaki, said in an interview: "I would ask them how they could talk about justice, democracy, and human rights while a methodical process of genocide has been taking place for decades against the Palestinian people."[31]

Muslims are very aware of the double standard that comes into play when the U.S. press, members of the academy, and some government officials label Muslims as extremists. They see that the charge of extremism is arbitrary depending on the interest of the accuser. According to Islamist leader 'Abd al-Baqi Khalifa, for example:

> Extremism is ascribed to violent events according to the interests of those who are making the judgement. For example, the war in Afghanistan prior to the Mujahideen was presented by the Soviet media as a war of evil people against the Russians who had come to Afghanistan to develop it and restore security to the area and prevent American domination over it. In the American and Western media it was depicted as a war of liberation undertaken by the Afghan people against an invading army.[32]

Khalifa further notes that the international press is under the influence of the decisionmakers and acts as their mouthpiece providing epithets for those they seek to criticize. Thus, "the warriors of Abkhazia are separatists, the southerners in Sudan are [liberationists], the demonstrators in Moscow are criminals and in Peking are freedom lovers, the Kurds in Iraq are victims, in Turkey, they are professional criminals. These are the contradictory depictions that have made the word 'extremist' predominantly a kind of political curse word rather than a name for anyone in particular."[33]

Islamists perceive that there is a pronounced discrepancy between professed U.S. values and U.S. actions; that justice, self-determination, and human rights appear to be victims of national interest; that in the last analysis "might makes right"; and that Muslims are rendered weak *(mustadhfun)* by the empowerment of Israel. Aware of the enormity of the Holocaust and of European-Christian guilt for the sins of Nazism and anti-Semitism, they still question why Western society found a way to expiate those sins at the cost of Palestinian-Christian and Muslim lives. They note that the Ecumenical Council convened by the Pope asked Christians to stop cursing Jews in the Catholic Church and that the World Council of Churches absolved the Jews from the historical events that led to the crucifixion of Jesus Christ. Yet, they ask, why is this the fault of the Muslims? Why, they ask, should the Arabs of Palestine pay the price for this error by the church with their homeland, their dignity, their present, and their future?[34] "When various churches compete to please Israel and flatter the Jews, does this point to anything but that the religious leaders have sold their conscience to Satan . . . ? The Arabs [of Palestine] are threatened by general extinction, their homes are blown up, their villages eradicated from existence, and still [their efforts at] self defense are considered a crime and an insurrection. . . . This dreadful tribulation is bound to awaken sleeping Islam."[35]

Islamists and the Gulf War

To Islamists, Western hypocrisy and duplicity was manifest in the Gulf war. The real motive was never to defend international law, enforcement of which varies from case to case and depends on whether the aggressor is a Western country or a Third World country. The objective of that campaign was to "control the oil resources, protect Israel, and achieve U.S. hegemony over the West [Europe] itself."[36]

Operations Desert Shield and Desert Storm tapped into a reservoir of Islamist distrust of Western policies in the Middle East that have long been depicted as hypocritical, duplicitous, and racist. Even as the U.S. administration in 1991 insisted that there was no linkage between Kuwait and Palestine, Muslims throughout the world saw indisputable parallels between the two that fostered the already strong perception of the double standard of Western dealings in which the United States violated the very values it professed. These parallels include issues relating to boundaries, the use of weapons, and rewards for aggression. Desert Storm/Desert Shield was perceived by Islamists as a link in the chain of Christian oppression of Muslims. Islamists initially condemned the Iraqi aggression against Kuwait. However, when the United States assumed the leadership in redressing the aggression and did not allow for a negotiated settlement, the majority saw U.S. intervention as a continuation of colonial policies designed to rob Arabs and Muslims of their wealth, to foster the dismemberment of the Muslim peoples by maintaining their divisions into nation-states, and to destroy Arab power in order to maintain Israel's supremacy in the area.

Islamists ask why Iraq's aggression was immediately redressed while that of Israel has been relegated to diplomacy and negotiations that have been protracted over thirty years. They heard the George Bush administration affirm there could be no room for negotiation or delay in regard to the Iraqi invasion of Kuwait. They ask why Saddam Hussein had to implement the UN resolutions immediately and completely, given that Israel has been allowed to circumvent all UN resolutions except the one recognizing it as a state, with which it has only partially complied, since the resolution also stipulates the existence of a Palestinian state and the repatriation or compensation of the refugees. The following statement typifies the Arab feeling toward what is perceived to be a double standard:

> Everybody in congress stated accurately that Iraq stood in violation of the United Nations Charter and United Nations resolutions. But no one congressman or congresswoman mentioned the potential relevance of the fact that in the 23 years before Iraq started violating the United Nations Charter, Israel had been violating it every month and every week and every day. No one mentioned the 42 United Nations Resolutions on the subject. So while they were invoking the legitimacy of the United Nations, none in congress had enough honor, enough self respect, enough integrity even to acknowledge that there was another country besides Iraq in the Middle East which at that moment stood in violation of the United Nations Charter.[37]

Islamists heard President Bush and Secretary of State James Baker affirm repeatedly that aggression should not be rewarded—yet they recall that when Israel invaded Lebanon in 1982 the United States gave it the green light. They remember that 20,000 Lebanese and Palestinians were killed and over 30,000 wounded during the invasion and that Israel also used U.S. chemical weapons of mass destruction (napalm, phosphorus, and fragmentation bombs) against civilian targets. When the United Nations passed a resolution to apply sanctions on Israel, the United States vetoed the measure. Soon after, the U.S. Congress voted $1.5 billion as a gift to Israel to compensate for the cost of the war. Islamists also remember that in October 1990, during Operation Desert Shield, Israeli troops "massacred" seventeen Muslims at the Aqsa mosque. The fact that Congress soon afterwards authorized a $700 million grant to Israel is seen by Islamists as a reward for the taking of Muslim life.

The Bush administration accused Saddam Hussein of not respecting the international boundaries set by Britain. Islamists have questioned why, after nearly half a century, the United States has not restricted Israel to the boundaries delineated for it by the United Nations and why it has been allowed to continue occupying territories designated for Palestinian residence as well as parts of Syria and Lebanon.

The Bush administration justified the military operation against Iraq by depicting Iraq's invasion of Kuwait as a violation of Kuwait's right to self-determination. Islamists ask why the United States acquiesces in Israeli occupation and annexation of Palestinian territory and refuses to recognize the Palestinian right to self-determination. In denying that Iraq occupied Kuwait to liberate Palestine, Secretary Baker said, "No one should enslave a people in order to liberate another." Islamists agree but fail to understand why U.S. policymakers permit Israel to "enslave" the Christians and Muslims of Palestine in order to liberate the Jews.

Another example for Muslims of the U.S. double standard is the tragic situation in Bosnia. This hesitation by the American administration to intervene was seen by

Islamists as living proof of the contradiction in Western conduct. Noting that the Western conscience in general had been sympathetic to the plight of Bosnian Muslims, they found it strange that "Western policymakers have not bothered to translate the sympathy of their nations into action, and all they do is maneuver so as to contain the trends in Western public opinion. . . . Instead of acting to save Bosnian Muslims from Serbian concentration camps, the West has been content with guaranteeing the passage of food and humanitarian aid as if to feed the Muslims before being slaughtered."[38]

Muslims see a discrepancy in the way that Americans respond to human tragedies, which seem to be determined by the religious affiliation of the victims as Jewish or as Muslim. "Both the Holocaust and the slaughter of Bosnian Muslims are emotional issues; yet what makes questioning the extent of the Holocaust off limits and criticism of Bosnian Muslims, who are undergoing a similar campaign of extermination by the Serbs, acceptable? Muslims are no less sensitive to the mass executions of their European brethren than are Jews in America of their European counterparts."[39]

For many, the double standard in the policy toward Bosnia provides yet more proof of Western perfidy, one more example of Western outrages committed against Muslims and people of the Third World.

> The West's collusion and connivance, which has so far enabled the Serbs to seize more than 70 percent of Bosnia before occupying it completely, serves to obliterate five centuries of Islamic civilizational presence in Europe. It will only bring back to the minds of Muslims the repetitive image of the Westerners and their conduct when they occupy other people's countries: physical liquidation, usurpation of land, obliteration of cultural and civilizational remains, and enslavement of those who remain alive, stripping them of their cultural identity. The tragedy in Bosnia is that of Andalusia, that of Palestine, that of the Red Indians in America, and that of the black peoples in Africa.[40]

Islamists and the "New World Order"

In 1992, Munir Shafiq, a Christian with Marxist sympathies who converted to Islamism in the seventies, wrote an Islamist analysis of U.S. policy in the Middle East as it appeared to be unfolding as a consequence of the declared "new world order." His assessment is typical of the genre of Islamist literature on the subject. Shafiq warned about several important changes in U.S. policy that became possible after the success of Operation Desert Storm, noting that these changes were reminiscent of earlier colonial intervention in the region. Desert Storm left parts of the Arab world under "American military occupation," he said, a hearkening to the post–World War I period, when Muslims fought each other for the spoils promised by the British only to find themselves sectored and chopped up. Shafiq called the U.S.-Soviet-Zionist decision to open Soviet Jewish immigration to Palestine the establishment of "Israel II," since the number of immigrants could reach 3 million, doubling the Jewish population of Israel. He said:

Thus while there was jubilation at the end of the Cold War, a [new] war has been declared on the Arabs and the Muslims through this frightening emigration which can be seen as Balfour Declaration II, or Israel II. No one, no matter what good intentions he may harbor towards the United States of America, can but see this immigration of millions except as an aggressive act against Palestine, the Arabs and the Muslims similar to that of the Balfour Declaration.[41]

He noted that the U.S. policy of disarmament, disempowerment, and dismemberment of Iraq and the ensuing policy of economic strangulation have left that nation in a position worse than that which obtained during the colonial hegemony after World War I: "Anyone who connects these sanctions to what happened in Kuwait makes a grave error." He insisted that the sanctions imposed on Iraq after the war supported the primary U.S. goal of maintaining the strategic military superiority of Israel over all Arab countries combined. The Arabs are to be restricted to arms that can maintain their regimes and suppress their own people, but not any "arms with teeth." The purpose is to maintain an Iraq that is paralyzed internally with no central authority and no possibility of extending its authority within its borders for some time to come.

Shafiq named this division of Iraq into three contending regions "Sykes-Picot II," a reincarnation of Sykes-Picot I, the operation that is seen as originally carving up and dismembering the Islamic body. These inequitable divisions are seen as maintaining Western interests through the maldistribution of wealth and resources in the region. Regardless of the success of its divide-and-conquer policy, he said, the West has not been satisfied with the developments in the area during the last four decades. Nasserism, Palestinian resistance, and the rise of Iraq threatened Western interests, hence the new policies affirming the Zionist plan for hegemonic dominance of the area. Shafiq argued that in order to achieve the Israeli strategic vision of the Balkanization of the Arab world, the policy has been to "seek to divide the region according to religious affiliation, ethnic origin, nationalist identity, regional and sectarian interests, in essence, the recasting of the area as a mosaic of minorities."[42] It will also seek to impede any scientific or technological progress in Arab and Muslim nations.

He went on to say that U.S. interest in promoting an Arab-Israeli peace is an effort to recast the configuration of the area. It seeks to sacralize Israel as part of the Middle East regardless of Arab and Islamic interests, Arab and Islamic security, or dreams of an Arab and Islamic common market or economic integration. In order to achieve this, the United States has resorted to nineteenth-century colonial policies of utilizing military force under the guise of international legitimacy.[43] The new strategic role for Israel in the region, Shafiq said, is different in some aspects from that which obtained during the cold war. Its overwhelming superiority in arms will be maintained as a reserve and combat-ready force to be called upon in time of need. If peace with the Arabs is achieved there will be no need to keep its forces deployed at the borders in constant readiness. Its new role calls for a greater political, diplomatic, and economic participation throughout the Arab world, which is to be dismembered in order for Israel to partake of water resources, the marketplace, and development projects.[44]

Islamists and the Zionist Lobby

The Islamist literature depicts the West as dominated by the Zionist lobby. This image has had several mutations as Zionist influence is perceived to have gained control of the inner circles of policymakers who determine the destiny of the region. Interviews I conducted with Islamists in Egypt in 1985 made clear that they resented the double standard with which they were treated. One leader talked about the "evenhanded" policy, which was then the buzzword used by the administration to describe the habit of the West "to stroke Israel with the palm of their hand and whack us with the back." That same year, the joke in Jordan was, Why doesn't Israel want to become the 51st state of the United States? The answer: It would then have to be satisfied with being represented by two senators whereas now it has one hundred.

In interviews I conducted in 1989, the image of Zionist control of the U.S. government became even more dominant. One Islamist depicted the United States as a colony of Israel (a view that is shared by Arab secularists). He compared the state of affairs in the United States with the former British rule over Egypt, noting that there were three specific areas in which British power manifested itself. In the first place, Egyptians were not allowed to have an independent foreign policy but had to defer to Britain for direction. In the second place, there were foreign British residents in Cairo who made sure that Egyptian policy was in accord with the interests of Britain. In the third place, Egyptian tax revenues were sent to Britain to sustain its power. He drew the parallels by concluding, "What you have in the United States is a government that is unable to formulate an independent foreign policy without first asking how will Israel react. Secondly, the Congress is accountable to the Israeli lobby, which functions as a foreign agent placing the welfare of Israel above that of the United States. In the third place, the lobby assures the flow of billions of U.S. tax dollars to Israel."

Unwavering support for the state of Israel in the U.S. Congress was taken for granted by Islamists. Members of Congress were seen as fearful of losing their jobs if they questioned unqualified support for Israel. By being thus silenced, Islamists saw Congress as sanctioning acts of violence by Israel as well as supporting Israeli policies, through routine funding, of "dehumanizing" the Palestinian people. This did great damage to U.S. credibility. One Egyptian Islamist referred to the "Hostages on the Hill" in reference to the U.S. Congress. The image has not improved. The influence of the Zionist lobby is perceived as being unprecedented in U.S. history. With the ascendancy in the Bill Clinton administration of Martin Indyk, a former Zionist lobbyist who is perceived as supporting Likud policies, to the National Security Council in charge of U.S. policy in the region, some Islamists refer to the "Israeli-occupied White House."[45]

U.S. Foreign Policy and the Clinton Administration

For Islamists, the Clinton administration assumed authority at a critical time in history. Due to the collapse of the Soviet empire, the U.S. administration not only has been able to implement its policies unimpeded by considerations of balance of power, it has also chosen to shed its cooperative arrangements with old "allies," such as Pakistan and the Afghan Resistance Movement, and to rearrange its priorities. The Arab and Islamic worlds find themselves weak and divided in the wake of Desert Storm. Not only is there apprehension on the part of Islamists concerning the new world order as it is being shaped, they feel victimized by increasing demonization that targets them as the potential enemy.

The Clinton administration has not initiated anything that would allay these fears. The prevailing perception is that the Arabs continue to provide the convenient target for proving U.S. virility, hence the unleashing of "Tomahawk diplomacy" against Baghdad (a reference to U.S. Tomahawk cruise missiles). Although many among the Islamists would have welcomed the killing of Saddam Hussein, the targeting of an industrial complex has confirmed for the Islamists their suspicion that the United States seeks to maintain Israeli scientific and technological superiority while denying the Arabs any such opportunity.

Despite their struggle for empowerment during this century, Islamists feel, it has been determined that Arabs should be maintained in weakness, mediocrity, and subservience. For many in the Islamist movement, the actions of the Clinton administration and its pronouncements to date have confirmed the perception of many Muslims that it is Tel Aviv that dictates policy in the area. Clinton's statements in response to terrorist activities make clear the United States condemns violent radicalism and extremism in any form yet praise Islam as a religion and emphasize that there is no inevitable "clash of civilizations" between the West and the Islamic world. These comments are welcomed in the Islamic world, but most Muslims still remain unconvinced and essentially respond by saying that actions speak louder than words.

An address by Martin Indyk (currently assistant secretary of state for the Near East and North Africa) on May 18, 1993, has raised further concern about the future of the region. Indyk outlined a Manichaean vision, one where the world is portrayed as a potential nightmare should the nationalists or Islamists realize their dream and form a united front. The alternative vision that the administration promotes is one of harmony and bliss in which Israel would attain its "normalization" in the region. He stated:

> In other words, the "vision thing" was very clear to this President before he came into office. He understands that the Middle East is finely balanced between two alternative futures: one in which extremists, cloaked in religious or nationalist garb, would hold sway across the region, wielding weapons of mass destruction loaded into ballistic missiles; and the other future in which Israel, its Arab neighbors and the Palestinians would achieve an historic reconciliation that would pave the way for peaceful coexistence, regional economic development, arms control agreements and growing democratization throughout the Middle East.[46]

In his address, Indyk dismissed the Islamists as a set of "troublemakers." He declared them the byproduct of "decades of neglect and dashed hopes for political participation and social justice that have nurtured some violent movements cloaked in religious garb that have begun to challenge governments across the Arab world with the potential of destabilizing the region."[47] His remedy is to create a market economy and provide some vision of democracy. Unfortunately, his emphasis on the "vision" rather than the reality, coupled with the U.S. record of support for autocratic regimes and silent approval of the subversion of democratic elections in the Occupied Territories, in Algeria, and in Egypt, has most Islamists apprehensive at the prospect.

Indyk stated that the United States is not an impartial arbiter of the peace process; rather he affirmed that "the President and the Secretary of State made it clear that our approach in the negotiations will involve working with Israel, not against it. We are committed to deepening our strategic partnership with Israel in the pursuit of peace and security."[48] This affirmation did not bode well for permanent peace in the area and in fact probably assured further growth of the Islamist movement. Furthermore, it served to undermine the very regimes (Egypt and the Gulf nations) the United States wishes to support. Those regimes are put in the position of seeming to collude in the empowerment of Israel at the expense of the Arab population.

In his speech to the Jordanian parliament in 1994, President Clinton appeared to be reiterating Indyk's vision of a Manichaean worldview. He portrayed the Middle East as "an arena of struggle between the forces of tyranny and freedom, terror and security, bigotry and tolerance, isolation and openness." In the process, he spelled out for Islamists the choices between good and evil in the area, with the good being assured when they associate with Israel. Meanwhile, administration policy appears to depict Islam in a similar fashion: At one end of the spectrum is Islam, represented by the faith that is confined to personal belief and ritual practices, on the other are extremist groups that insist on the political dimension of Islam and therefore are dubbed violent and terrorist. Although this policy affirms a respect for the religion of Islam, it is a disemboweled Islam that has no input into human, social, economic, and political values, which some Islamists have dubbed "American Islam." Meanwhile, the Clinton administration has made several unprecedented gestures to the American Muslim community to demonstrate their inclusion in the American mosaic. The president sent greetings to Muslim leaders in the United States on the occasion of the Islamic holiday. He also included Islam in his directive that employees can display religious objects of their particular faith at their workstations. The First Lady invited Muslim representatives to the White House for an *iftar* (breaking the Ramadan fast) dinner, to the consternation of some in the Zionist lobby.

Such gestures, however, have not changed the Islamist perception that the current administration associates international terrorism with Muslims. The Clinton administration's promoting and signing of the Anti-Terrorism Act of 1996 after the Oklahoma City bombing, which sanctioned the profiling of Arabs and Muslims (not in the image of Timothy McVeigh) at airports as potential terrorists, is seen as proof of such perceptions:

The West attempts to tie international terrorism with Islam, while the historical record is studded with the crimes of the West which confirm that all forms of extremism and terror were invented in the West which spread them in the world through the Mafia, Nazism, Neo-Nazism, racial discrimination, abduction of heads of state and ambassadors, stalking the leaders of national liberation movements, assassination of innocent civilians, attacking peaceful cities with nuclear bombs, using internationally banned weapons, poisoning water sources and food supplies, blockading civilian populations and denying them the simples of their rights to life.[49]

Several generations of Arabs have been socialized to believe that Palestine is an Arab issue. Each generation has been provided with a "proof" of the injustice perpetrated against the Palestinian people so as to cement this perception. "The question of Palestine was not the only Arab issue; rather, it was their central issue." The Arabs have also had the burden of dealing with the issues of division and unity, of economic retardation and development, of resources and dependency, and of their perception of their civilization.[50] Since 1967, the issue of Palestine has been adopted increasingly as part of the Islamic agenda. It seems all too clear that an unjust peace that thwarts all hopes will only intensify the anger at what is seen as long-standing injustice and will fuel the flames of Islamist reaction.

After the 1967 Arab-Israeli war, one American administration after another has invited the Arabs to trust American even-handedness and come to the peace table and reap the benefits. And they have come. Over fifteen Arab nations established some sort of relations with Israel after the signing of the Oslo agreement. The consequences are perceived to be the increased arrogance on the part of the Israeli government. Many in the area feel that the Islamists were vindicated, that Israel does not want peace but pacification and the legalization of its acquisition of the rest of the land of the Palestinians with the indigenous population relegated to isolated Bantustans, while Yasser Arafat, the president of the Palestinian entity, is seen as the enforcer for Israeli security interests. As one Islamist put it, "The Peace Process turned out to be the process by which Israel acquires Palestinian land piece by piece by piece."

Increasingly, people in the area believe that the peace process is based on a flawed idea that the United States is an impartial mediator. Speeches by President Clinton and Vice President Gore at the occasion of the fiftieth anniversary of the declaration of the state of Israel make evident that America is not impartial "but act[s] in support of Israel and its act of aggression to confiscate land, deport its occupants and eradicate what is left of the Muslim population of Palestine."[51] Or as a June 1988 statement signed by twenty-six Kuwaiti organizations put it: "Fifty years have passed and Israel's record of aggression grows larger, and with it grows the condemnation of the international organizations which are incapacitated by the American veto which stands at the ready to support the oppressor against the oppressed."[52]

Western commentators point to the fact that various Arab governments appear to have wearied of the Palestinian leadership and the Palestinian cause. The Gulf war precipitated an exodus of Palestinians from yet another Arab country, Kuwait. That, however, does not translate into Muslim abandonment of the issue of Palestine and Jerusalem. For Islamists, the danger facing the Muslims is not "the Palestine problem" as much as the "problem of Israel." For Muslims, Palestine is a cause. It represents the demand for the right of a people to self-determination, democracy, and freedom. It is also the demand that the West recognize that an Arab person is equal to a European person or, as some Palestinians put it, that a European Jew is not better than a Palestinian Christian or Muslim and has no superior right to rob, destroy, expel, kidnap, or kill without consequences. Palestine is a demand for the end of the colonial era, an end to the era of "Christian arrogance"[53] and "Jewish insolence,"[54] a demand that the superior international Islamic law prevail, which would guarantee justice and freedom to Muslims and to religious minorities who dwell among them.

Islamists believe that American foreign policy has targeted them as worthy victims for annihilation. They hope that one day the West will wake up to the tragedy it has perpetrated. Those in the West may yet apologize for the destruction of Palestine, they may even offer restitution, but will they ever be able to correct the wrong that they have done? As Rashid Qabbani, the mufti of Lebanon put it:

> The West has been brilliant in the crime of ridding itself of the Jewish problem and dumping it into the heart of the Arab world by supporting the Zionist entity and [establishing] Israel in Palestine in 1948. After WWII Western nations began seeking forgiveness from Israel for what Nazism had done to the Jews. Will the Western conscious[ness] awake one day to seek forgiveness for the crime which they committed by establishing Israel in Palestine and by evicting the Palestinian people from their homes and land? Will the West seek forgiveness for the suppression, terrorizing and humiliation that Israel has been meting out for fifty years to the oppressed Palestinian people and for the loss of their land at the hand of the West? Should it occur, of what value will Western apology be? For it is the West that daily provides Israel with the weapons of mass destruction, prepared for the annihilation of the Palestinians and the Arabs.[55]

Notes

1. For example: "The black intellectual trend has lately been able to make Islam a synonym to terrorism and darkness through the media which is controlled by the 'Muslim' states. He who prays five times a day is an iniquitous terrorist . . . she who wears a hijab is an iniquitous terrorist; he who reads the Qur'an is an iniquitous terrorist, and he who refuses usury, drinking, Eastern dancing, social dancing and mixing of men and women is an iniquitous terrorist; he who advocates the study of Islamic history and Islamic religion is an iniquitous terrorist; he who calls for an Islamic economic, cultural, political unity is an iniquitous terrorist. . . . Anyone who belongs to Islam is bloody and reactionary who must be destroyed. What would satisfy them is for the Muslims to abandon Islam and follow others in religion, thought, way of life and conduct . . . only then would it be proper to call them enlightened." Hilmi Muhammad al-Qa'ud, "Al-Fikr al-Aswad . . . wa al-Fitan al-Thaqafiyya," al-Mujtama' 24(1081) (December 28, 1993), p. 56.

2. In an interview, Dr. Fathi Shikaki, secretary-general of the Islamic Jihad Movement in Palestine, protested the designation of terrorist. See Omar Maxwell, "No Peace Until Pales-

tine Is Free," *Inquiry* 1(6) (January 1993), p. 21: "I do not know how the Palestinian is described as a terrorist when his scream is a response to his pain and suffering while defending his land against Jewish Russian soldiers, who had never (and neither their fore-fathers) set foot in any inch of Palestine. The West's attempt to homogenize our countries is the source of all terrorism and chaos. We are calling for peace based on justice, rights and dignity. We must be dealt with as equals and as carriers of a great civilization. Only then will peace prevail in our region and the whole world."

3. An example: "In recent days, the West has started to triumphantly declare that in today's world, Arabs do not matter. For them Muslims also do not matter and they would like to keep it that way. The media and Western political and propaganda machines are assiduously asserting that Islam is incompatible with civilization. Their main points are that Islam lacks democracy, is devoid of compassion and has no rights for women. In doing so they have splendid examples, or in fact props; Saudi Arabia is rendering the best service. It is allegedly run according to the Quran, so there is no democracy and no rights." Abdurrahman Abdullah, "The Final Battle for the Soul of Afghanistan," *Inquiry* 1(3) (June 1992), p. 19.

4. See, for example, Muhammad 'Amara, "al-Ta'addudiyya: al-Ru'ya al-Islamiyya . . . wa al-Tahaddiyat al-Gharbiyya," [Proceedings of the Conference on Political, Sectarian and Ethnic Pluralism in the Arab World] (Herndon, Va.: IIIT, 1993), pp. 1–34.

5. For a sampling of Salafi literature, see 'Abd al-Rahman 'Abd al-Khaliq, *al-'Usul al-'Ilmiyya li al-Da'wa al-Salafiyya* (Kuwait, 1402H); 'Umar Sulayman al-Ashqar, *Ma'alim al-Shakhsiyya al-Islamiyya* (Kuwait, 1984). For a criticism of Salafi thought, see Muhammad Fathi 'Uthman, *al-Salafiyya fi al-Mujtama'at al-Mu'asira* (Cairo, 1982).

6. Ahmad Kamal Abu al-Magd, *Kitab al-Qawmiyya al-'Arabiyya wa al-Islam* (Beirut, 1980), pp. 32–33. For a different categorization, see Khurshid Ahmad, "Islam and the New World Order," *Middle East Affairs* 1(3) (Spring/Summer, 1993), pp. 10–11.

7. See Yvonne Yazbeck Haddad, "The Authority of the Past: Current Paradigms for an Islamic Future," in Toby Siebers, ed., *The Authority of the Past* (Ann Arbor: University of Michigan Institute for the Humanities, 1993). For Islamist discussions on the future, see Ahmad Kamal Abu al-Magd, "Al-Muslimun Da'wa li-Iqtiham al-Mustaqbal," *al-'Arabi* 292 (March 1983); Fu'ad Muhammad Fakhr al-Din, *Mustaqbal al-Muslimin* (Cairo, 1976); 'Abd al-'Aziz Kamil, *al-Islam wa al-Mustaqbal* (Cairo, 1976); 'Abd al-Halim 'Uways, *al-Muslimun fi Ma'rakat al-Baqa'* (Cairo, 1979); Sayyid Qutb, *Islam: The Religion of the Future* (Chicago: Kazi Publications, 1977).

8. Muhammad al-Ghazali, *Ma'rakat al-Mushaf fi al-'Alam al-Islami* (Cairo, 1964); Muhammad al-Hasani, *al-Islam al-Mumtahan* (Cairo, n.d.); Muhammad Farag, *Al-Islam fi Mu'tarak al-Sira' al-Fikri al-Hadith* (Cairo, 1962); Muhammad al-Ghazali, *Kifah Din* (Cairo, n.d.); Muhammad Jalal Kishk, *al-Ghazu al-Fikri* (Cairo, 1975); 'Abd al-Sattar Fathallah Sa'id, *al-Ghazu al-Fikri wa al-Tayyarat al-Mu'adiya li al-Islam* (Cairo, 1977).

9. Tawfiq Mahmud al-Shawi, "Istratijiyya 'Ilmiyya li al-Tayyar al-Islami," *al-Mujtama'* 24(1081) (December 28, 1993), p. 22.

10. Abdullah, "The Final Battle," p. 19.

11. One author described the minarets of Yugoslavia in the following words: "This remains a living testimony to the glorious and often forgotten Islamic heritage of the last remnants of Europe's indigenous Muslim population, a people, a society, a civilization possibly on the verge of extinction. This is not a fate different from the fate experienced by the indigenous Muslims of Sicily, Italy, Spain, Portugal, Hungary, Malta, etc. many centuries earlier." Saffet Catovic, "Europe's Islamic Heritage in Jeopardy," *Inquiry* 1(6) (January 1993), p. 28.

12. See Ziyad Muhammad 'Ali, '_Ida al-Yahud li al-Haraka al-Islamiyya_ (Amman, 1982), p. 21.

13. Graduation speech at the U.S. Naval Academy, Annapolis, Maryland, May 30, 1990.

14. "We Muslims are very distressed at the growing number of attacks of the Western Jewish American media against Islam. . . . We are prone to think that the Jewish and Zionist groups with all their great influence in the West and America have determined to turn the West against Islam and to push Christianity and Islam into a violent confrontation that will destroy both and keep the Zionists as winners." Ghannushi, in an interview appearing in _al-Majalla_ 24(1081) (December 28, 1993), p. 28.

15. See Bernard Lewis, "The Roots of Muslim Rage," _Atlantic Monthly_ 226(3) (September, 20, 1990). An editorial by Charles Krauthammer appearing in the _National Review_ reiterates the same ideas, as does "The New Crescent of Crisis: The Global Intifada," _Washington Post,_ February 16, 1990. Cf. Daniel Pipes, "The Muslims Are Coming, the Muslims Are Coming," _National Review,_ November 19, 1990, pp. 28–31.

16. Mowahid H. Shah, "A New Cold War Within Islam?" _Christian Science Monitor,_ July 30, 1990, p. 19.

17. In an interview with the first secretary of the U.S. embassy in Qatar, Yusuf al-Qaradawi is reported to have said: "It is not in America's interest to be an enemy of Islam, the Islamic forces and the Islamic movements that are balanced and moderate. However, there are individuals and powers who have an interest in maintaining that Islam is something to fear and revile. They envision for American policy makers and to those in power that Islam is a frightening demon which represents what they call the green threat which they must be cautious of after the passing away of the red Communist threat. This in reality is a myth. For Islam, especially that represented by the moderate groups which we advocate, is not a danger to anyone." _al-Mujtama'_ 24(1081) (December 28, 1993), p. 31.

18. David Ben Gurion, the first prime minister of Israel, is reported to have said, "We fear nothing but Islam"; Yitzhak Rabin reportedly declared, "The religion of Islam is our only enemy"; and Shimon Peres warned, "We will not feel secure until Islam puts away its sword." 'Ali, '_Ida,_ pp. 45–46.

19. 'Abd al-Hamid al-Sayeh, _Madha Ba'd Ihraq al-Masjid al-Aqsa?_ (Cairo, 1970), pp. 23, 178ff.

20. Abdullah Kannun, "Al-Muslimun wa Mushkilat Filastin" in _Kitab al-Mu'tamar al-Rabi' li-Majma' al-Buhuth al-Islamiyya,_ pp. 36, 38.

21. Kamel Baqir, "Jawhar al-Qadiyya al-Filastiniyya," [The Essence of the Palestinian Issue], in _Kitab al-Mu'tamar al-Rabi'_ [Book of the Fourth Conference], p. 136.

22. Abdullah Kannun, "Makanat Bayt al-Maqdis fi al-Islam," in _Kitab al-Mu'tamar al-Rabi' li-Majma' al-Buhuth al-Islamiyya,_ vol. 2, p. 39.

23. "And it was the West, champion of the separation of Church and State, cradle of secularism, that helped in the creation of this state founded on the idea of the return to the Promised Land. The intrusion of religion into politics didn't bother European socialists, nor American technocrats. Neither did it bother the atheists of Moscow who were the first to recognize the State of Israel." Habib Boulares, _Islam: The Fear and the Hope,_ p. 25 as quoted in _Inquiry_ 1(3) (June 1992), p. 42.

24. Muhammad M. al-Fahham, "The Restoration of Jerusalem," in _The Fifth Conference of the Academy of Islamic Research_ (Cairo: Government Printing Office, 1971), p. 53.

25. Muhammad al-Ghazali, _Qadhaif al-Haqq_ (Kuwait, 1984), p. 109.

26. Yvonne Yazbeck Haddad, "Operation Desert Shield/Desert Storm: The Islamist Perspective," in Phyllis Bennis and Michel Moushabeck, eds., *Beyond the Storm* (New York: Olive Branch Press, 1991), pp. 248–260.

27. See Konstantin Obradovik, ed., *The Inalienable Rights of the Palestinian People* (London: Outline Books, 1985), pp. 292–301.

28. See Obradovic, *The Inalienable,* pp. 245–291.

29. Munir Farah, "Impact on Education," in Naseer A. Aruri, ed., *Occupation: Israel Over Palestine* (Belmont, Mass.: AAUG, 1983) 295–318; and Naseer Aruri, "Universities Under Occupation," in the same volume, pp. 319–336.

30. See, for example, Hasan Khalid, "Kalimat al-Wufud" (Statement of the Delegates), *Kitab al-Mu'tamar al-Rabi': al-Muslimun wa al-'Udwan al-Israili,* vol. 2, (Cairo, 1968), p. 29.

31. Omar Maxwell, "No Peace Until Palestine Is Free," *Inquiry* 1(6) (January 1993), p. 22.

32. Abd al-Baqi Khalifa, "al-Tatarruf: Mafahimuh . . . Asbabuh . . . Nata'ijuh . . . 'Ilajuh," *al-Mujtama'* 24(1076) (November 23, 1993).

33. Ibid.

34. al-Ghazali, *Qadhaif,* p. 223.

35. Ibid., p. 225.

36. Rachid Ghannouchi, "Islam and the West: Realities and Prospects," *Inquiry* 2(7) (March/April 1993), p. 45.

37. "The Great Betrayal," *Al-Mashriq* (January-February 1991), p. 9.

38. Ghannouchi, "Islam and the West," p. 46.

39. Ahmad Abul Jobain, *Islam Under Siege: Radical Islamic Terrorism or Political Islam?* Occasional Papers Series No. 1 (Annondale, Va.: United Association for Studies and Research, June 1993).

40. Ghannouchi, "Islam and the West," p. 46.

41. Munir Shafiq, "al-Istratijiyya al-Amerikiyya wa-Athar al-Nizam al-'Alami al-Jadid 'Ala al-'Alam al-'Arabi," *Qira'at Siyasiyya* 2(1) (Winter 1992), p. 10.

42. Ibid., p. 22.

43. Ibid., p. 19.

44. Ibid., p. 23.

45. "This is a surrender to the Jews who have assumed the power in the United States, so that the White House and those in it have become an instrument in the hand of the Jews." Unsigned editorial, "al-Wilayat al-Muttahida Taraf Munhaz Yad'am Isra'il wa-Atma'aha," *al-Majalla* 29(1299) (December 5, 1998), p. 9.

46. Martin Indyk, "Address to the Soref Symposium, The Washington Institute, May 18, 1993," p. 3.

47. Ibid., p. 8.

48. Ibid., p. 17.

49. Zaghlul al-Najjar, "Kayf Yara al-Muslimun al-Ghaarb? . . . wa-madha Yakshha al-Gharb min al-Islam? Surat al-Gharb Tarikhiyan wa-Nafsiyan 'Ind al-Muslimin, *al-Mujtama'* 29(1302) (February 6, 1998), p. 52.

50. Salim al-Hoss, "Qadiyyat al-'Arab Ba'd al-Salam," *al-Majalla* 727 (January 16–21, 1994), p. 38.

51. Unsigned editorial, "al-Wilayat al-Muttahida Taraf Munhaz Yad'am Isra'il wa-Atma'aha," *al-Majalla* 29(1299) (May 12, 1998), p. 9.

52. "Bayan Min Jam'iyyat al-Naf al-'Am bi-Munasabat Murur Khamsin 'Aman 'Ala Ightisab Filastin," *al-Mujtama'* 29(1302) (February 6, 1998), p. 14.

53. See, for example, the repeated references to crusader arrogance in Fathi Bakhkhush, "Daqqat Sa'at al-Jihad: al-Umma fi Khatar" [The Hour of Jihad Has Struck: The Nation Is in Danger] *Risalat al-Jihad* 9(93) (November 1990). He condemns the U.S.-led coalition of Desert Storm: "The Crusaders have come this time with a military campaign under the leadership of oppressive America, arrogant with its devastating power" (p. 58). He also writes that the Islamic nationalist rejection of U.S. policies in the region has enraged "oppressive American Crusaderism" because it perceives it as a "threat to its contending power and its [ability] to impose its arrogance on the world" (p. 59). He also calls the forces gathered for Desert Storm "the greatest terrorist Crusader force in history," which can only be resisted by a religious response. "If one of the characteristics of this age is that American arrogance has reached the highest peak, a parallel characteristic is the ability of armed believing nations to mire this arrogance in the dust" (p. 61).

54. Yitzhak Shamir is quoted as having boasted in a radio broadcast that "he is proud of the terrorist record of the Stern Gang including the assassination of Swedish Count Bernadotte on a United Nations Peace Mission in 1948, the assassination of Lord Moyen, the British Minister of State for Middle East Affairs, and the massacre of Deir Yasin." See "Kalla al-Sihyuniyya Haraka 'Unsuriyya" [No, Zionism Is a Racist Movement] *Risalat al-Jihad* 10(103) (October 1991), p. 6. Cf.: "The Israeli enemy backed by the forces of imperialism, never ceases to disclose his real designs which are no less than wresting more Arab territories, and thereby impudently paying no heed to the legitimate rights of the Palestinian people." Abdul-Aziz Kamel, "The Opening Address," *The Sixth Conference of the Academy of Islamic Research* (Cairo: al-Azhar, 1971), p. 17. Abba Eban, former Israeli Ambassador to the United Nations, was reported to have said, "If the General Assembly were to vote by 121 votes to 1 in favor of Israel returning to the Armistice lines . . . Israel would refuse to comply with that decision." *New York Times,* June 19, 1967.

Several recent examples are cited by Fahmi al-Huwaidi, the popular Egyptian journalist, including the following: "The most recent example of 'good intent' comes from Morocco during the middle of January when the Moroccan government handed Israel the remains of Jews who drowned when their boat overturned while attempting to flee to Israel in the fifties. Israel's response to this gesture was insolent and in bad taste. It marked the event by placing a cornerstone for the erection of a monument to commemorate the victims in Maaleh Edumim, the large settlement established between Jerusalem and Jericho in the West Bank and which the Palestinians seek to have removed." Fahmi al-Huwaidi, "Bayn Bolard wa al-Shaykh Ahmad Yasin: Jawasisuhum Lahum Thaman wa-Munadiluna bila Thaman!" *al-Majalla* 729 (January 30–February 5, 1994), p. 34.

55. Rashid Qabbani, "al-Gharb Yamuddu Isra'il bi-kul Aslihat al-Damar al Shamil," *al-Mujtama'* 29(1299) (May 12–18, 1998), p. 25.

Postscript:
Americans and the Muslim World—
First Encounters

Robert J. Allison

Before the geographic area we now call the Middle East was called the Middle East, before the British colonies on the North American mainland became the United States, and before petroleum powered the world's economy, Americans and Muslims had a strange and profound encounter. This encounter was part of the long afterglow of the Crusades, as when English mercenary John Smith, fighting for the Austrians against the Ottoman Turks, was captured in Transylvania. Smith killed his Muslim captor and escaped, returning by way of Russia to England, which he left again, this time to sail west and found the colony of Jamestown. In 1645, as novelist and naval historian James Fenimore Cooper tells us, a ship built in Cambridge, Massachusetts, fought an Algerian ship in the Atlantic, in what Cooper called the first American naval battle. In the 1680s, New Yorkers raised money to redeem sailors captured in North Africa, and in 1700, an American sailor returned to Boston from captivity in Algiers. The Puritan clergy used his story of captivity and resistance to Islam to bolster the faith of their flocks.

Eighteenth-century American and European literature made the Muslim world a counterpoint to the idea of individual autonomy, the central feature of the emerging American ideology. Political writers, such as John Trenchard and Thomas Gordon in England, the authors of *Cato's Letters*, and Charles Secondat Montesquieu in France, author of the *Persian Letters* and *Spirit of the Laws*, used Muslim states such as Morocco, Turkey, and Algiers as examples of how not to construct political societies. The American colonists who rebelled against England in 1776 and then set to forming their own political society had not only read these books, but they had incorporated them into their way of thinking. In the Barbary states of North Africa, and in the Ottoman Empire, at least as it was presented to them by European writers, Americans saw an example of the kind of political society they did not want to create.

Travelers and other observers saw signs of decay in Muslim societies, and Americans were determined to avoid the causes and thus prevent the symptoms. The most influential book on the subject was the Abbé Volney's *The Ruins, or a Survey of the Revolution of Empires* (1792), a meditative reflection drawn from his travels in Egypt and Syria. *The Ruins* speculated on how the great Mesopotamian civilization came to collapse, and Volney found the answer in political intolerance fed by religious fanaticism. President Thomas Jefferson found Volney's *Ruins* so important that he undertook to translate it, enlisting the help of American diplomat and poet Joel Barlow.

This ideological picture of the Muslim world was colored by the experiences of American sailors held captive in Algiers, Tripoli, and Morocco. Between 1785 and 1815, a dozen American ships were captured by the North African states, who held the sailors hostage. This captivity forced American leaders to grapple with a variety of problems: What was the responsibility of the U.S. government to its citizens? Should the United States pay ransom for citizens held captive? Should the United States pay tribute to foreign powers in order to protect its citizens? Different American leaders had different responses to these questions. John Adams calculated that paying tribute to Algiers would be less expensive than fighting a war, that Americans were the most reluctant people on earth to pay the kind of taxes that would be required to build a navy, and since Britain and France paid tribute to Algiers, there was no harm in the Americans emulating their example. Thomas Jefferson, on the other hand, believed it would be essential to American liberty to fight Algiers and Tripoli, not only to protect American citizens but to demonstrate to England and France that the Americans were a different sort of people, who would not engage in the kind of corrupt diplomacy of Europe. Jefferson's assertion of America's "difference" won the day, and one of his administration's first acts in 1801 was to send an American fleet to the Mediterranean to blockade Tripoli. The pope praised the American navy for subduing Tripoli, accomplishing what the Christian nations of Europe had been unable, or unwilling, to do.

The captivity of American sailors in Algiers raised another issue, directly related to the idea that Americans were less corrupt and more noble than Europeans and that the Americans had created a political society whose virtue would endure forever. The Americans who wrote about their captivity in Algiers called the experience slavery. The irony of Americans being held as "slaves" in Africa was lost on very few. Benjamin Franklin's last published work was a parody of a Georgia congressman's defense of African slavery in America, putting the Georgian's words in the mouth of a Muslim official justifying the enslavement of Christians in Algiers. Royall Tyler, author of the first American play, wrote a novel entitled *The Algerine Captive*, connecting American captivity in Algiers to American complicity in the African slave trade.[1]

American misunderstanding of the Muslim world rested on a profound ignorance of the Islamic religion, Muslim society, and the wild misinterpretations of the prophet Muhammad, who was known to eighteenth-century European and American writers as "Mahomet." Puritan minister Cotton Mather contrasted the liberty with which Europeans and Americans could reason with the tyranny of Muslim society. Heaven shone on "*our Parts of the Earth*" in allowing "Improvements of our *modern Philosophy*," while no follower of the "thick-skull'd Prophet" was permitted to question the scientific truths revealed to Muhammad.[2]

We do not know where Mather learned about Muhammad, but the only English-language biography of Muhammad had been written in 1697 by Anglican clergyman Humphrey Prideaux. Prideaux's interest in Muhammad was only coincidental to his real purpose, which was to expose the folly of religious indifference. Prideaux had planned to write a major work on Constantinople's fall to the Muslims in 1453. But his growing alarm at the state of English society, the "giddy humour" with which too many young people embraced "fashion and vogue" rather than religion, and the ease with which men and women criticized the church, alarmed Prideaux, and he wrote his book on Muhammad as a sober warning. Mecca had been a prosperous trading town, the people had been more attentive to their commercial interests than to their spiritual needs, they had allowed the faith of their fathers to degenerate, and Muhammad had exploited their religious laxity to impose his own religious and political agenda. The Muhammad emerging from Prideaux's work, and from the other English-language tracts on Islam, was an ambitious man. His ambition found a religious outlet, and the Meccan merchants' religious indifference allowed him to secure his religious tyranny.[3]

Prideaux's "Mahomet" was a warning sign in the young American republic of the 1790s. Many Americans welcomed the French revolution that enshrined liberty and reason in the place of monarchy and tradition. But others worried about the consequences, and in France's revolution, they saw an anarchy that would ultimately be replaced by a tyrant. Vice President John Adams reached back into French history, writing a series of essays warning about the consequences of anarchy and disorder. In England, Edmund Burke warned in *Reflections on the Revolution in France* that liberty would be the victim of equality. Thomas Paine responded to Burke with his *Vindication of the Rights of Man*, which seemed, on its arrival in America, to be as much an answer to Adams as to Burke. Secretary of State Thomas Jefferson had an advance copy of Paine's pamphlet and sent it to the printer with a note praising Paine's attack on "the political heresies" that had lately sprung up, confident that "our citizens would rally again round the standard of common sense." Paine's book was printed in America with Jefferson's endorsement on the cover. American readers took Jefferson's jab at "political heresies" as a reference to Vice President Adams. In response to this perceived attack on Adams, his son, John Quincy, writing under the name Publicola, compared Jefferson to "the Arabian prophet" who called on "all true believers in the Islam of democracy to draw their swords," and paraphrasing the Muslim creed "There is no God but Allah, and Muhammad is his Prophet," the younger Adams had Jefferson and his zealous supporters shouting, "There is but one Goddess of Liberty, and Common Sense is her prophet."[4]

The situation seemed similar to that of seventh-century Mecca. Jefferson was a well-born, respectable man like Prideaux's Muhammad, but by countenancing the free thought of Thomas Paine and others, he would ultimately destroy the liberty he pretended to defend. In 1795, a Philadelphia publisher specializing in religious works published the first American edition of Prideaux's *Life of Mahomet*, and

Prideaux's preface, warning of the dangers of infidelity and religious indifference, seemed especially pertinent in the new nation.

But this was not the only possible reading of Prideaux's *Mahomet*. The Adams administration, which took office in 1797, tried to quell the political storm by imposing a sedition act, making it a crime to criticize or bring ridicule upon the president. One of the fifteen victims of the act was Vermont Congressman Mathew Lyon, who was sent to federal prison for suggesting that President Adams appointed men to office for their political loyalty rather than their accomplishments and that the president was fond of pomp and parade. (Lyon was reelected to Congress while in prison.) Having seen how far criticizing the president directly would take him, Lyon's son James, a printer, launched an indirect criticism. While his father was in jail, James Lyon published the second American edition of Prideaux's *Life of Mahomet*, this one without the preface warning of infidelity. Without this preface, the book takes on a different cast, and the Mahomet is a religious zealot who will tolerate no opposition and forbids "all manner of disputing about his religion," just as Adams and the Federalists had forbidden political disputes. Prideaux's conclusion could not have been more eloquently phrased for Lyon's purpose: "And certainly there could not be a wiser way devised for upholding of so absurd an imposture than by thus silencing, under so severe a penalty, all manner of opposition and disputes concerning it."[5] If Lyon had said this, his prison term would have been extended.

A second biography of Muhammad appeared in America in 1802, with the descriptive title *The Life of Mahomet; or, the History of that Imposture which was begun, carried on, and finally established by him in Arabia: and which has Subjugated a Larger Portion of the Globe, than the Religion of Jesus has yet set at Liberty*. The anonymous author found Islam to be "deeply affecting to a Philanthropic heart," as it degraded men and women "to the rank of brutes by the consummate artifice and wickedness" that had been created by one man, the prophet Muhammad. Islam had so depraved its adherents that this author thought they could be saved only by Christian conquest to free them from "that system of blasphemy and iniquity by which they are at present enslaved." Missionaries and teachers would be helpless against the rulers who used "carnal weapons" on their subjects and respected no argument but force.[6]

Muslim societies were more than distant symbols. In 1785 and 1793, Algiers captured a dozen American ships and held over one hundred American sailors captive. In this crisis, Susanna Rowson, an English actress living in America, wrote a play, *Slaves in Algiers, or, a Struggle for Freedom*. Loosely basing it on Cervantes's *Il Cautivo*, Mrs. Rowson added a tangled family dynamic to make her story current with an American audience. Although the Western characters Constant, Augustus, Olivia, and Rebecca are essential to the plot, the story centers on Fetnah, who has been sold into the dey's harem by her father, the merchant Ben Hassan, who began his career as a London rag merchant and had betrayed everything in his quest for wealth—he had left England for Algiers, had converted from Judaism to Islam, and finally had sold his daughter to the dey because he and Fetnah's mother "loved gold better than they did their child."[7]

Ben Hassan will do anything for money; Fetnah, though the Dey's "chosen favorite," laments her imprisonment in the splendid palace. "I like them very well," she says of the luxury surrounding her, "but I don't like to be confined." She asks, is "the poor bird that is confined in a cage [because it is a favourite with its enslaver] consoled for the loss of freedom? No! tho' its prison is of golden wire, its food delicious, and it is overwhelmed with caresses, its little heart still pants for liberty: gladly would it seek the fields of air, and even perched upon a naked bough, exulting, carrol forth its song, nor once regret the splendid house of bondage."

Fortunately for Fetnah, at this moment Rebecca arrives in Algiers "from that land where virtue in either sex is the only mark of superiority. . . . She was an American." Rebecca, also consigned to the dey's seraglio, assures Fetnah that "woman was never formed to be the abject slave of man" and stirs Fetnah's natural love of liberty. Fetnah declares, "I feel that I was born free, and while I have life, I will struggle to remain so." Fetnah accepts the struggle, and the virtuous Americans even convince the dey to accept it, telling him to "sink the name of subject in the endearing epithet of fellow-citizen," and he agrees to "reject all power but such as my united friends shall think me incapable of abusing." The Americans tell the dey to prove by his conduct "how much you value the welfare of your fellow creatures," as they return to the land "where liberty has established her court," hoping for the day when "Freedom" will "spread her benign influence" through every nation.[8]

The Americans in Susanna Rowson's play are great teachers, teaching the Dey how to be a better ruler and teaching the people of Algiers to be good citizens. The American war against Tripoli (1801–1805) gave the Americans more opportunities to teach the lesson of American prowess and virtue. From the first naval engagement in August 1801 until the peace treaty was signed in June 1805, Americans regarded the war as a constant lesson in their own distinctive national character. President Jefferson was determined to cut the American military budget, to chastise Tripoli, and to do both as a lesson to European nations on proper modes of international conduct. Jefferson's decision to blockade Tripoli rather than launch a direct attack and to blockade using the smallest possible force led to disaster, as the *Philadelphia*, the second-largest ship in the American fleet, ran aground off Tripoli in October 1803. But the navy turned this disaster into a triumph, as Lieutenant Stephen Decatur and a small crew disguised themselves and a captured Tripolitan vessel and sailed into Tripoli harbor in February 1804, destroying the *Philadelphia* without losing a man. Americans saw Decatur's deed as evidence of their own prowess and courage. The naval bombardment of Tripoli in August 1804 gave further proof of American courage, and when Tripoli and the United States signed the treaty on board the USS *Constitution* (the first time a Barbary state signed a treaty on an enemy warship), it confirmed for Americans their new place in the world.[9]

Barely a year after the war began, a play conveying this message was performed on the New York stage. No copies survive of *The Tripolitan Prize, or, American Tars on an English Shore*. We know it only from a caustic review by Washington Irving. The American tars reach the English shore after being chased by a Tripolitan ship—

it seems a violent storm in the Mediterranean sent both ships to the English channel, where they fight it out. Improbable as this may have been, it allowed the Americans to win their battle against Tripoli within sight of England, and on the stage, crowds of Englishmen and women watched the American victory. Irving noted with sarcastic disgust that the American audience, particularly those in the galleries, spent the entire play "hallooing and huzzaing" the American captain and his crew on stage. The captain bellowed at one point, "What! an American Tar desert his duty!" and the American audience responded "Impossible! American tars forever! True blue will never stain!!" The battle, Irving wrote, was "conducted with proper decency and decorum," after which "the Tripolitan very politely gave in—as it would be indecent to conquer in the face of an American audience."[10]

We do not have such rich records of the audience response to other literature written in response to the Tripolitan war. But these cultural effusions—plays, poetry, novels, and paintings—all convey the same themes the audience celebrated in *The Tripolitan Prize* and *Slaves in Algiers.* Joseph Hanson's 1806 poem, *The Musselmen Humbled, or a Heroic Poem in Celebration of the Bravery Displayed by the American Tars, in the Contest with Tripoli,* said that the Americans had won the war against Tripoli as they were armed with "the formidable powers of justice and freedom," which gave them "that invincible courage, which terrified and overcame the plundering vassals of the tyrannical bashaw." Hanson asked, "[W]hat can be effected by the slaves of tyrants? who fight for plunder and despotic masters: who defend no laws, but such as are oppressive; and protect no pow'r, but that which disrespects 'em."[11]

An 1812 play by Bostonian James Ellison, *The American Captive, or Siege of Tripoli,* saw this same reason for the American victory. In the play, Abdel Mahadi had seized power in Tripoli from his older brother, Ali ben Mahadi, whom he said was too weak to rule. Ali was "too mild to reign," he had "courted peace, and peace attain'd created heavy taxes!" Instead of peace, Ali should have "courted the crimson hand of war." Abdel, on the other hand, will use "*plunder*" to preserve his power and save his subjects from "that damn'd abyss, to which my brother's mild and milky reign had doom'd them." Plunder alone "can prop our sinking realm" and save it from the "misery and want" brought by peace. Ali's daughter, Immorina, and her fiancé lament this triumph of "*ambition*" over "*virtue*," taking solace that while "*crime* may for a season triumph," only "*virtue*" can secure "a monarch's bliss, his count[r]y's welfare, and his subject's love."[12]

As in Rowson's *Slaves in Algiers,* this debate on internal affairs is enriched by the arrival of American captives. In this play, one of Abdel's cruisers has captured an American ship. The arrival of Americans causes great excitement in Tripoli, as one Tripolitan woman asks Immorina, "Do you know what *Americans* are?" Immorina answers, "*Men,* are they not, like other men?" "Pshaw," the old woman says, the Americans are "*Indians!* Yes indeed, *Indians!*" They would scalp any man or woman they caught, "and I'm sure this proves them not to be *men.*" Immorina corrects her. The Indians, she says, are the natives of America but only "inhabit the western regions of that vast country, and are savage, and barbarous, like our wild Arabs." On the other hand, "those whom we denominate Americans" are like the Europeans in "customs and manners," are civilized, polished, enterprizing, brave, and hospitable.[13]

The civilized, polished, enterprising, brave, and hospitable Americans are represented in this play by Captain Anderson, the captured master of the ship. Anderson and Abdel form a striking contrast of American and Tripolitan power. In their first meeting, Abdel is decked out in a "sumptuous Turkish habit," his turban decorated with a large diamond crescent, his jeweled sash barely hiding the dagger on his hip. Abdel asks Anderson if his father is a noble. Anderson replies, "If to be the son of him who served his country, in the time of peril, be that which you call noble, I am of the most noble extraction, but if, from pamper'd lords and vicious princes, alone descend the gift, then I am not." Anderson's father bore "the proudest title man can have"—he was "An honest man."[14]

Anderson contrasts not only with the corrupt and gaudy Abdel but also with other American characters in the play. Jack Binnacle, one of Anderson's crew, wonders why the United States does not simply "blow Algiers, Tunis, and Tripoli up, and put an end to these nests of pirates?" Anderson applauds Binnacle's spirit and pledges to "fight till my heart-strings snap" rather than "be tributary to any nation," but he wants a permanent solution. Simply destroying the coastal cities would allow marauders like Abdel to move into the interior. Anderson wants to reform Tripoli so tyrants like Abdel cannot flourish. Anderson's plan, carried out with the help of Princess Immorina and the Jew Ishmael, is to escape from Tripoli, secure support from the navy for the deposed Ali, who will return to power and end the depraved power of Abdel once and for all.[15]

To the tune of "Washington's March," Anderson and Ali return to Tripoli, and Anderson prays "to be granted that heroic courage, that energy of soul, which so distinguish'd the father of my country, the matchless hero of the western world." Anderson kills the despotic Abdel, declaring that "*A slave* has power to strike a *tyrant* dead." Although Immorina tells Anderson that he now ranks "among the Prophets," the American is more interested in being placed alongside Washington.[16]

As in Susanna Rowson's *Slaves in Algiers,* and *The Tripolitan Prize,* Anderson in *The American Captive* teaches the Muslim tyrant a lesson. A contemporary American songwriter promised that if any despot dared insult the American flag, "We'll send them Decatur to teach them 'Good Manners.'"[17]

And yet some American writers questioned the ability of their country to teach moral lessons to others. In the spring of 1787, while her father, the American minister to France, toured the southern part of that country, sixteen-year-old Martha Jefferson wrote to keep him informed of events in the world. Germany, Russia, and Venice, she reported, were at war against Turkey, and the plague had struck in Spain. She only briefly mentioned these world events, but then she found a story that captured her interest. "A virginia ship comming to spain," she wrote, "met with a [Algerian] corser of the same strength. They fought and the battle lasted an hour and a quarter. The Americans gained and boarded the corser where they found chains that had been prepared for them. They took them and made use of them for the algeri-

ans themselves." Martha saw the irony in this turn of events. But instead of relish-
ing the American victory, she saw only compounded tragedy. "They returned to virginia from whence they are to go back to algers to change the prisoners to which if
the algerians will not consent the poor creatures will be sold as slaves." The Algerians had wanted to enslave the Americans, a fact that might have justified their own
enslavement. But not to Martha Jefferson, who asked her father, "Good god have we
not enough? I wish with all my soul that the poor negroes were all freed. It greives
my heart when I think that these our fellow creatures should be treated so terribly
as they are by many of our countrymen."[18]

The capture of American sailors, who were put to work in Algiers or Tripoli,
touched Americans' consciences. The plight of these "slaves" in Algiers and Tripoli
stirred Americans to raise money for their redemption. The Americans could boast
that they had created a society different from the tyrannies of the Old World, but
the captivity of Americans in North Africa reminded them that this was not the case.
In Ellison's *The American Captive*, Jack Binnacle, a captive sailor, tells Hassan the
overseer about America. "It's a charming place, Mr. Overseer; no *slavery* there! All
freeborn sons!" Hassan answers, "No Slavery, hey? Go where the Senegal winds its
course, and ask the wretched mothers for their husbands and their sons! What will
be their answer? *Doom'd to slavery, and in thy boasted country, too!*"[19]

A New England newspaper ran an item in 1794 headed "Profession versus Practice," a satire on fugitive slave ads, and an attack on "ranting southern demagogues,"
like Thomas Jefferson, who preached "*universal equality*" while practicing "*piratical
barbarity.*" The ad promised a reward for the return of an "American slave" to his master, "Ibrahim Ali Bey" of Algiers. It described the slave as an "ungrateful Villain" and
"incorrigible infidel," who refused to renounce "his Christian errors" and had escaped
with a "borrowed" manumission certificate. Freed slaves, the ad warned, were lending
their freedom papers to other slaves, who used this "new invented species of *robbery*"
to escape. How odd, the ad concluded, that these Christians would think this sharing
was "*meritorious*. What strange, absurd ideas the Christians must have of *merit*."[20]

The true story of a free black man helping an enslaved African escape appeared in
several New England papers in 1795 and was paired with the story of an American
captive redeemed from Algiers. Cato Mungo, reportedly an African prince, was returned by benevolent friends to Ouidah, in West Africa, and George Burnham, an
American captain from New York, was ransomed by friends in 1794. Cato Mungo
and George Burnham's stories were paired under the heading "Curses of Slavery,"
and the pairing made Burnham's suffering seem slight. Cato Mungo gave a "long
and melancholy account of the treatment of the poor Africans in that land of cru-
elty" and suggested that Africans take "some measures" to redeem "such of our
brethren as it would be in our power to restore to their families and connections."
He repeated in horror that "several of the Royal family of this kingdom" were now
"doing drudgery in the kitchens of the *United States!!!*"[21]

Cato Mungo had been helped to escape by Mawyaw, a free black man living in
Connecticut, where slavery was still legal. Although slaves in Connecticut were

treated more decently than were slaves in other states, they were still slaves. Mawyaw had helped Cato Mungo escape to Massachusetts, where slavery had been abolished in 1783. Connecticut's legislature had recently rejected an emancipation plan, Mawyaw reported, allowing "self-interest" to check its benevolence. Although the state was giving away millions of dollars' worth of public lands, "their souls were not large enough" to free African slaves. The legislators "did not think themselves justifiable in taking away the property of individuals," Mawyaw reported. He was not surprised: He noted that Americans "could not find in themselves generosity enough" to redeem their countrymen "now in slavery in the kingdom of Algiers." Americans were in no position to assert their moral superiority to the Algerians.

Benjamin Franklin's last published essay carried this same theme. Franklin, as president of Pennsylvania's antislavery society, had signed a petition to Congress in 1790 calling for an end to the slave trade. Franklin may have expected this to be his last public act. But a Georgia congressman, James Jackson, took to the floor of the House to denounce Franklin for suggesting that slavery was morally wrong. Jackson blasted Franklin and the Quakers, who had also submitted an antislavery petition, for being overzealous moral meddlers whose ignorant and misguided efforts at reform would undermine both the American economy and the well-being of the slaves. Slavery, Jackson said, was justified by religion, economics, politics, and history. The Georgians who enslaved Africans lifted their slaves out of barbarism and taught them the Christian virtues. If the slaves were freed, Jackson said, it would ruin Georgia's economy, since no one would work in the rice fields and these blacks would not work unless they were forced to do so. And what would happen to the freed people? They would not stay and work, and if they moved to the frontier, the Indians would kill them. Georgia's keeping of slaves was the benevolent option, as it taught slaves Christianity and allowed them to cultivate Georgia's rice.

Franklin read Jackson's speech in the *Federal Gazette* in March 1790. Franklin knew he had to reply. No American political leader had ever publicly said that slavery was a good thing: All had been committed to its extinction. Jackson's speech marked a change. Franklin knew he had to respond. Franklin had written his first newspaper essay more than seventy years earlier, had later tangled with Cotton Mather and the British ministry in print, and knew how to devastate an adversary. He wrote his response to Jackson under the name "Historicus" and said he liked Jackson's speech very much. It reminded him of something he had read many years before, a speech given by the dey of Algiers.

Sidi Mehemet Ibrahim, the dey of Algiers, had given a speech similar to Jackson's in 1687. Franklin said he had read it in a book called *Martin's Account of his Consulship.*[22] The dey was provoked by a group of religious zealots, the Erika, or "Purists," who had petitioned Sidi Mehemet to abolish Christian slavery and piracy, which the Erika said were unjust and against the teachings of the Qur'an. Franklin then quoted Sidi Mehemet's speech, which turned out to be James Jackson's speech, with Erika substituted for Quakers and Christian slaves substituted for Africans.

James Jackson's argument justifying the slavery of Africans in America also justified the enslavement of Americans in Africa.

Algiers should not give up enslaving Christians, Sidi Mehemet warned, as it would ruin the nation's economy merely to gratify "the whims of a whimsical sect." He asked, "If we forbear to make slaves" of Christians, "who in this hot climate are to cultivate our lands? Must we not then be our own slaves?" As for the freed slaves, Sidi Mehemet and Jackson both feared they would not easily make the transformation to freedom. If the Christians stayed, they could not be considered the equals of Muslims. They would not "embrace our holy religion; they will not adopt our manners; our people will not pollute themselves by intermarrying with them."

They would become "beggars in our streets" and would pillage Algerian property. They would not work unless they were forced to do so, and if sent to the frontiers, they were too ignorant to establish a "good government" and would be massacred by wild Arabs. They were not to blame for their ignorance or weakness—these were traits they brought with them from their backward homelands, where most peasants, Spanish, Portuguese, French, and Italian, were treated as slaves. The Algerians had improved their lives by allowing them to work "where the sun of Islamism gives forth its light." Sending the freed people home would be denying them this benefit; it would send them "out of light into darkness."

After listening to Sidi Mehemet's arguments, the leaders of Algiers decided, according to Historicus, that to go on record as saying that slavery violated moral law was "at best *problematical*." Algiers would hold on to slavery, and so, in 1790, would the United States. Franklin had made up the Erika, Sidi Mehemet, and *Martin's Account of his Consulship*. But unfortunately, he had not made up James Jackson. The similarities between Jackson's real speech and Sidi Mehemet's fictional one showed that "men's interests and intellects operate and are operated on with surprising similarity in all countries and climates, whenever they are under similar circumstances."

Franklin knew this better than most of his countrymen. They thought they had seen in the Muslim world all that they hoped to avoid in the new world: political and religious tyranny, subjugation of women, and craven self-interest. They also believed that they had created a political system that would prevent these evils, or at least hold them in check. Americans had developed an image of themselves and their society by looking at the Muslim world, holding an image of people and places that helped them, they thought, construct their own nation and identity. But Franklin told them their image of themselves was wrong, only partly because they carried in their heads a hopelessly distorted picture of Muslim history and society.

Notes

1. For more on these themes, see Robert J. Allison, *The Crescent Obscured: The United States and the Muslim World, 1776–1820* (New York: Oxford University Press, 1995); Ray Watkins Irwin, *The Diplomatic Relations of the United States with the Barbary Powers, 1776–1816* (Chapel Hill: University of North Carolina Press, 1931); and James Field, *America and the*

Mediterranean World, 1776–1882 (Princeton: Princeton University Press, 1969). On the general perceptions of Islam in the West, see Norman Daniel, *Islam and the West: The Making of an Image* (Oxford: Oneworld, 1993).

2. Cotton Mather, "The Christian Philosopher" [1721] reprinted in *Cotton Mather* (n.p.).

3. Humphrey Prideaux, *The History of the Life of the Great Imposter Mahomet* (Philadelphia: Stewart and Cochran, 1796), 2–3.

4. Merrill D. Peterson, *Thomas Jefferson and the New Nation: A Biography* (New York: Oxford University Press, 1970), 438, 440.

5. Humphrey Prideaux, *The True Nature of Imposture, Fully Displayed in the Life of Mahomet* (Fairhaven, Vt.: James Lyon, 1798), 76–77.

6. *The Life of Mahomet; or, the History of that Imposture which was Begun Carried on, and Finally Established by Him in Arabia; and Which has Subjugated a Larger Potion of the Globe, than the Religion of Jesus has Yet Set at Liberty. To Which is Added, an Account of Egypt* (Worcester, Mass.: n.p., 1802), 83–84, 85.

7. Susanna Haswell Rowson, *Slaves in Algiers, or a Struggle for Freedom* (Philadelphia: n.p., 1794), 5.

8. Ibid., 9–10, 65–68, 71, 72.

9. For a striking example of this, see the song written by Francis Scott Key honoring the heroes of Tripoli, which in verse and cadence became the foundation of the "Star-Spangled Banner," which he wrote a few years later during the War of 1812 against England. Allison, 204–206.

10. Irving's review from the New York *Morning Chronicle*, quoted in William Dunlap, *History of the American Theatre* (New York: J. and J. Harper, 1832), 301–302.

11. Joseph Hanson, *The Musselmen Humbled; or a Heroic Poem in Celebration of the Bravery Displayed by the American Tars, in the Contest with Tripoli* (New York: n.p., 1806), 3, 7–9.

12. James Ellison, *The American Captive, or Siege of Tripoli* (Boston: n.p., 1812), 9, 12, 35.

13. Ibid., 24–25.

14. Ibid., 20–21.

15. Ibid., 18–19, 37–38.

16. Ibid., 34, 51.

17. New York *Evening Post,* 15 March 1806.

18. Martha Jefferson to Thomas Jefferson, Paris, 3 May 1787. *Papers of Thomas Jefferson,* Julian Boyd et al., eds. (Princeton University Press, 1950–), 11:334.

19. Ellison, *American Captive,* 37–38.

20. "Profession vs. Practice," Boston *Federal Orrery,* 24 November 1794; Boston *Mercury,* 25 November 1794; Newburyport *Morning Star,* 26 November 1794.

21. "Curses of Slavery," *Rural Magazine, or Vermont Repository* (March 1795), 118–124. Cato Mungo's story was reprinted in Salem *Gazette,* 13 January 1795; Boston *Federal Orrery,* 29 January 1795; Portsmouth *Oracle of the Day,* 31 January 1795. For African Muslims enslaved in America, see Allan D. Austin, *African Muslims in Ante-Bellum America* (New York: Routledge, 1996).

22. Benjamin Franklin, "On the Slave Trade," *The Works of Benjamin Franklin,* Jared Sparks, ed. (London: Benjamin Franklin Stevens, 1882), 2:517–521.

About the Editor
and Contributors

Erika Alin is assistant professor of political science at Hamline College in St. Paul, Minnesota. Her publications include *The United States and the 1958 Lebanon Crisis: American Intervention in the Middle East* (1995).

Robert J. Allison teaches American history and intercultural contact at Suffolk University in Boston. He is the author of *The Crescent Obscured: The United States and the Muslim World, 1776–1815* (1995.)

John Duke Anthony is president and CEO of the National Council on U.S.-Arab Relations in Washington, D.C., which he founded in 1983. He is the author of numerous books and articles, most notably *Arab States of the Lower Gulf: People, Politics, Petroleum* (1975).

Amatzia Baram is senior lecturer in the Department of Middle Eastern History and deputy director of the Jewish-Arab and Middle East Research Centers at the University of Haifa. Among his publications are *Culture, History, and Ideology in the Formation of Ba'thist Iraq, 1968–1989* (1991) and *Iraq's Road to War* (coeditor, 1994).

JoAnn A. DiGeorgio-Lutz is assistant professor of political science at the University of North Texas. A specialist on the PLO, she has published articles in *Mediterranean Quarterly* and *International Studies Quarterly*.

Yair Evron is professor of political science at Tel Aviv University. His publications include *War and Intervention in Lebanon: The Israeli-Syrian Deterrence Dialogue*.

Sir Sam Falle is a retired British diplomat. He served in Iran from 1949 to 1952, in Lebanon from 1952 to 1955, on the Middle East oil desk in London from 1955 to 1957, and in Iraq from 1957 to 1961. He was ambassador to Kuwait from 1969 to 1970, and he has also been ambassador to Sweden and high commissioner to Singapore and Nigeria. His remarkable autobiography is entitled *My Lucky Life, in War, Revolution, Peace and Diplomacy* (1996).

Robert O. Freedman is the Peggy Meyerhoff Pearlstone Professor of Political Science and acting president of the Baltimore Hebrew University. He has written a number of books and articles on the Middle East, among them *Moscow and the Middle East* (1991) and *Israel Under Rabin* (editor, 1995).

Mark Gasiorowski is associate professor of political science at Louisiana State University. He has published many articles on Iranian politics; he is the author of *U.S. Foreign Policy and the Shah: Building a Client State in Iran* (1991) and *Neither East nor West* (coeditor, 1990).

F. Gregory Gause III is assistant professor of government at the University of Vermont. Among his publications are *Oil Monarchies: Domestic and Security Challenges in the Arab Gulf States* (1994) and *Saudi-Yemeni Relations: Domestic Structures and Foreign Influence* (1990).

James Gelvin is assistant professor of history at the University of California–Los Angeles. His articles have appeared in a variety of publications, including the *Journal of Interdisciplinary History* and the *International Journal of Middle East Studies*.

Fawaz A. Gerges is visiting fellow at the Center of International Studies at the Woodrow Wilson School of Public and International Affairs at Princeton University and is a faculty member at Sarah Lawrence College. His publications include *The Superpowers and the Middle East: Regional and International Politics, 1955–1967* (1994).

Shafeeq Ghabra is professor of political science at Kuwait University. He has published many works, including *Palestinians in Kuwait: The Family and the Politics of Survival* (1987). In September 1998, he assumed the position of director of the Kuwait Information Office in Washington, D.C., on leave from Kuwait University.

Yvonne Yazbeck Haddad is professor of history at Georgetown University. She has published numerous books and articles on Islam, including *Contemporary Islam and the Challenge of History* (1982) and *The Islamic Impact* (1984).

Peter Hahn is associate professor of history at Ohio State University and recipient of the Stuart L. Bernath Lecture Prize from the Society for Historians of American Foreign Relations. He has published a number of articles and is author of *The United States, Great Britain, and Egypt, 1945–1956: Strategy and Diplomacy in the Early Cold War* (1991).

Paul W.T. Kingston is assistant professor of political science at the University of Toronto, Scarborough College. A specialist on Middle East development policy during the immediate post–World War II period, he is author of *Debating Development: Britain and the Politics of Modernization in the Middle East, 1945–1958* (1996).

David W. Lesch is associate professor of Middle East history at Trinity University in San Antonio, Texas. His articles have appeared in a variety of publications, and he is author of *Syria and the United States: Eisenhower's Cold War in the Middle East* (1992).

Georgiy Mirsky is a distinguished scholar at the Institute of World Economy and International Relations in Moscow. He is the author of numerous books and articles in Russian and English, and he has been an adviser to Soviet and Russian leaders.

Malik Mufti is assistant professor of political science at Tufts University. He is author of *Sovereign Creations: Pan-Arabism and Political Order in Syria and Iraq* (1996), as well as articles on Turkey and Jordan in the *Middle East Journal* and *Comparative Political Studies*.

Richard B. Parker served in the U.S. Foreign Service from 1951 to 1979, including in the U.S. embassy in Jordan in the mid-1950s, on the State Department's Jordan-Iraq desk in the mid- to late 1950s, and as ambassador to Algeria, Lebanon, and Morocco. He has published numerous articles and four books, the latest of which is *The Politics of Miscalculation in the Middle East* (1993).

William Quandt is the Harry F. Byrd Professor of Government and Foreign Affairs at the University of Virginia. He served as a staff member on the National Security Council from 1972 to 1974 and from 1977 to 1979 and was actively involved in the negotiations that led to the Camp David accords and the Egyptian-Israeli peace treaty. Among his many books are *Peace Process: American Diplomacy and the Arab-Israeli Conflict Since 1967* (1993) and *Camp David: Peacemaking and Politics* (1986).

Bernard Reich is professor of political science and international affairs at George Washington University. He has published numerous articles and books, including *The United States and Israel: Influence in the Special Relationship* (1984) and *Securing the Covenant: United States–Israel Relations After the Cold War* (1995).

Robert B. Satloff is executive director of the Washington Institute for Near East Policy. Among his publications are *The Politics of Change in the Middle East* (editor, 1993) and *From Abdullah to Hussein: Jordan in Transition* (1995).

Sussan Siavoshi is associate professor of political science at Trinity University in San Antonio. She is the author of several works on Iran, including *Liberal Nationalism in Iran: The Failure of a Movement* (1990).

Gary Sick is the executive director of the Gulf/2000 project at Columbia University, a research and documentation program. He was the principal White House aide for Iran on the National Security Council staff at the time of the Iranian revolution and hostage crisis and is the author of two books on U.S. Persian Gulf policy.

Mohamed Sid-Ahmed is one of the leading commentators and writers on Middle East affairs in the Arab world. Currently a columnist for *al-Ahram* and *al-Ahaly* in Egypt, he is the author of a number of publications, including *After the Guns Fell Silent* (1975) and *Egypt After the Treaty* (1979).

Janice Gross Stein is Harrowston Professor of Conflict Management at the University of Toronto. She has published a number of articles and books on Middle East affairs and international relations, including *We All Lost the Cold War* (1984) and *Peace-Making in the Middle East: Problems and Prospects* (1985).

Index